J. Kresslern

Inside
Smalltalk

Volume I

Wilf R. LaLonde

School of Computer Science
Carleton University

John R. Pugh

School of Computer Science
Carleton University

PRENTICE HALL
Englewood Cliffs, New Jersey 07632

Library of Congress Cataloging-in-Publication Data

LaLonde, Wilf R.
   Inside Smalltalk / Wilf LaLonde, John R. Pugh.
      p.   cm.
   ISBN 0-13-468414-1 (v. 1)
   1. Smalltalk (Computer program language) 2. Object-oriented
programming. 3. Smalltalk-80 (Computer system)   I. Pugh, John R.,
1950-   . II. Title.
QA76.73.S59L35   1990
005.13'3--dc20   90-6785
                                                          CIP

Editorial/production supervision: Christina Burghard
Cover design: Wanda Lubelska
Manufacturing buyer: Lori Bulwin

 © 1990 by Prentice-Hall, Inc.
A Division of Simon & Schuster
Englewood Cliffs, New Jersey 07632

Printed in the United States of America
10 9 8 7 6 5 4 3 2

ISBN 0-13-468414-1

Prentice-Hall International (UK) Limited, *London*
Prentice-Hall of Australia Pty. Limited, *Sydney*
Prentice-Hall Canada Inc., *Toronto*
Prentice-Hall Hispanoamericana, S.A., *Mexico*
Prentice-Hall of India Private Limited, *New Delhi*
Prentice-Hall of Japan, Inc., *Tokyo*
Simon & Schuster Asia Pte. Ltd., *Singapore*
Editora Prentice-Hall do Brasil, Ltda., *Rio de Janeiro*

Table of Contents

Preface

INTRODUCTION

In the seventies, structured programming revolutionized the way programmers constructed software systems. Today, many are predicting that the object-oriented programming paradigm will be the second major revolution in software engineering and that object-oriented systems will become the predominant programming tools of the nineties. In the two volumes of **Inside Smalltalk**, we take an in-depth look at the Smalltalk-80 environment — the programming system that most consistently adheres to the object-oriented paradigm and that has served both as a model for object-oriented extensions to existing languages and as the basis for a new generation of languages supporting inheritance. It can be argued that Smalltalk has had more impact on software development in the last decade than any other programming language. Smalltalk fosters the notions of *programming in the large* and *programming by extension* rather than by *re-invention*. Smalltalk provided the foundation for window-based graphical user interfaces, for the development of truly reusable class libraries, and for the introduction of on-line tools such as code browsers. Our objective in **Inside Smalltalk** is to provide a comprehensive survey of the Smalltalk environment, the language, and the library. A secondary goal is to show how interactive graphical applications can be constructed using object-oriented programming techniques and the unique Smalltalk programming environment. Moreover, we show how Smalltalk's underlying philosophy of reusing and extending existing code permits the development of such applications with high productivity.

Programming in Smalltalk is different from programming in other languages such as Pascal, C, or Ada because of the major influence played by the object-oriented programming paradigm, the large class library, and the interactive programming environment. Developing programs in Smalltalk requires familiarity with all three of these components and the learning curve for programmers is therefore longer than for more traditional languages. Although there is no substitute for programming with the Smalltalk system itself, our objective is to reduce this learning curve by providing a comprehensive description of the Smalltalk language, the class library and programming environment and by illustrating the use of object-oriented programming techniques to develop interactive graphical applications. The need for a Smalltalk guru to be close at hand when learning the system will then be minimized. In addition, **Inside Smalltalk** will be a valuable reference to accomplished Smalltalk programmers whenever they venture into uncharted territory in the class library.

Be forewarned that it will take you considerably longer to become an accomplished Smalltalk programmer than an accomplished Pascal programmer. However, the return on your investment will be an ability to develop interactive graphical applications with all the features of modern user interfaces; e.g., windows, menus, mouse interaction. Indeed, a major emphasis of the second volume is to describe the Smalltalk features that make this possible; namely, the model-view-controller paradigm for constructing user interfaces and the graphical and window classes in the library. At the time of this writing, and despite the fact that it is this material that gives Smalltalk much of its appeal, no in-depth presentation of the graphical and user interface classes was available in any other text.

Although the Smalltalk language is itself quite small, the Smalltalk system is large. Initially this limited its use to expensive, powerful workstations. However, efficient implementations of Smalltalk are now readily accessible to large numbers of users on the current generation of personal computers bringing the power of Smalltalk to the classroom and a mass audience.

ORGANIZATION OF THE BOOK

Inside Smalltalk consists of two volumes with the first volume divided into 4 major sections. The second volume concentrates on the window and user interface classes and describes how Smalltalk may be used to develop applications involving WIMP-based (Windows, Icons, Menu, and Pointer) user interfaces.

VOLUME ONE

The first section of Volume One introduces the fundamentals of object-oriented programming and Smalltalk, the second describes the Smalltalk programming environment, and the final two sections divide the class library into basic classes (objects, magnitudes, and collections), and graphical classes. A common thread throughout the latter two sections is to describe a set of related classes from the class library, to explain some of the rationale behind design decisions taken by the designers, and then to show how new classes may be added to extend the existing classes in some useful way. In addition, Chapter 10 is devoted entirely to extended case studies describing the implementation of graphics-based applications. Problem sets are included at the end of each chapter; these range from simple exercises, to extensions of examples presented in the text, and finally to major projects.

Fundamentals

In this section, we introduce the reader to the fundamental concepts of object-oriented programming. Using a language independent approach, Chapter 1 characterizes object-oriented programming as programming with objects, programming by simulation, computation via message passing and programming in the presence of polymorphism, inheritance, and a large class library.

Chapter 2 describes how these fundamental notions manifest themselves in Smalltalk. Smalltalk is a language somewhat smaller in size than Pascal and based on a surprisingly small set of concepts; namely objects, messages, classes, subclassing, and inheritance. Our approach is to introduce these new concepts by relating them to their counterparts in traditional programming paradigms and programming languages. In particular, programming in Smalltalk is introduced by contrasting Smalltalk code with its Pascal equivalent.

The Programming Environment

Developing Smalltalk programs is characterized by a total integration of tools and an absence of modes. Editors, file managers, compilers, debuggers, and print utilities are all included within the Smalltalk environment. Chapters 3, 4, and 5 provide an introduction to the integrated collection of powerful and sophisticated tools that together form the Smalltalk programming environment. Chapter 3 provides an introduction to basic features of the user interface, in particular, windows and menu interaction and how to enter, edit, and evaluate Smalltalk code. Chapter 4 describes the central role played by browsers in the programming process both for navigating the class library and for editing and compiling additions to this library. Chapter 5 describes the use of inspectors to investigate the internal state of objects and the use of notifiers and debuggers to view and modify the state of a suspended computations.

Basic Classes

In this section, we describe the basic classes — those classes that form the core of the class library. Chapter 6 introduces the default behavior for operations such as copying, printing and comparing that are supported by class Object — the ultimate superclass of all classes. Chapter 7 describes the Magnitude classes including the numeric, character, date and time classes. Chapter 8 describes the Collection and Stream classes that are as fundamental to Smalltalk as lists are to Lisp. To provide a better understanding of the numerous and closely related collection classes, we consider the classes from a logical perspective partitioning them into four major logical groups.

Graphics

In this section, the classes supporting the interactive creation and manipulation of graphical images are surveyed and their use illustrated through three case studies. Chapter 9 explains the use of forms and the bitblt operations that serve as a base for the Smalltalk graphical model. Interaction with the mouse and keyboard is addressed together with a description of simple graphical interaction techniques. The chapter concludes with a review of the path or trajectory classes (arcs, circles, curves, lines, linear fits, and splines) and the use of pens.

Chapter 10 presents three extended graphical examples: film loops, a magnifying glass, and a simple video game. Film loops are never ending movies and show how simple animation sequences can be developed. Techniques for obtaining flicker-free displays and for storage of graphical forms on disk are also introduced. The latter facility illustrates the use of object mutation — the ability for one object to mutate into another. The magnifying glass application allows a user to move a magnifier over the display while magnifying the image under the magnifying glass. This application illustrates advanced graphical programming techniques and, in particular, describes how circular rather than rectangular forms may be manipulated. Finally, the video game illustrates the evolutionary approach that characterizes the design and development of Smalltalk applications. The design decisions that took place during the development of the game are described in detail along with the use of notions such as reusability, specialization, and generalization that differentiate object-oriented design from traditional design methodologies.

VOLUME TWO

Windows

In Volume Two, we describe the Smalltalk classes that provide (1) the familiar overlapping windows, pop-up menus, and mouse interaction facility that characterize the Smalltalk user interface and (2) the model-view-controller framework for the construction of user interfaces. Chapter 1 provides an introduction to the model-view-controller paradigm, dependency maintenance, the distinction between process management and window management, and the window transformation protocol. Chapter 2 provides an overview of the existing window classes and provides a detailed description of the basic views and controllers that support the window classes described in subsequent chapters. Extensive examples are provided to show how views and controllers can be created and used. Chapters 3 through 7 describe menu, switch, text, form (graphics), and pop-up windows respectively. Each of these chapters describes the differences between the standard classes and pluggable classes and shows (1) how users can use the existing classes, (2) how they may be modified to provide extensions, and (3) how new classes based on the existing ones can be created for special applications. Finally, Chapter 8 provides an extended example to illustrate the construction of a large-scale window application. It deals with the construction of a window maker — an editor that helps users create user interfaces. In the process, a design for a library of switch forms and a library editor is developed. The existing window classes are extended to support the window maker application and more than a dozen subwindows are designed to support the window maker editor.

WHO SHOULD READ THIS BOOK?

Smalltalk provides a new programming paradigm and the two volumes are therefore aimed at readers who are receptive to new ways of thinking about problem solving and new programming language concepts. We expect that most readers will have some programming experience in a procedural language. Programmers familiar with Pascal, C, Ada, or Fortran will find the language easy to learn and will be pleasantly surprised at the extensive set of support tools in the environment.

To gain full benefit from the book, readers should have access to a Smalltalk system and be prepared to adopt an exploratory hands-on approach to programming and problem-solving. **Inside Smalltalk** is for the professional programmer and serious student who wish to use the Smalltalk system as a powerful, efficient prototyping and development environment. The book can be effectively used in undergraduate and graduate courses in object-oriented programming or software engineering where Smalltalk will be a language of instruction. The book will be particularly valuable for students carrying out extensive thesis and project work in Smalltalk.

SMALLTALK DIALECTS

Two releases of Smalltalk-80 have been licensed by the Xerox Corporation. These are known as Smalltalk-80 Version 1 and Smalltalk-80 Version 2 respectively. Version 2 includes several features, notably support for multiple inheritance, not supported by Version 1. ParcPlace Systems[1] now has exclusive worldwide ownership of the Smalltalk-80 system. The Smalltalk language[2] is available under royalty-free license from ParcPlace. Smalltalk-80 Version 2 is now accepted as the standard Smalltalk-80 system and it is this dialect of Smalltalk that is described in this book. Indeed, whenever we use the term Smalltalk in this text we are referring to Smalltalk-80. Smalltalk-80 for Sun, Macintosh, Apollo, DEC, Hewlett Packard, and 80386 MS-DOS systems is available from ParcPlace Systems. Smalltalk-80 code is almost entirely portable across different host platforms. The Smalltalk-80 system is now marketed by ParcPlace Systems under the name Objectworks for Smalltalk-80.

Digitalk[3] markets Smalltalk/V, a dialect of Smalltalk for Macintosh and IBM PC computers. Excluding the user interface classes, there is a great deal of commonality between the Smalltalk V and Smalltalk-80 class libraries. Similarly, the range of programming tools is similar, although there are distinct differences in the structure and functionality of specific tools such as the browser, in the method of interaction with the environment and in the degree of integration with the specific platform

ACKNOWLEDGMENTS

First and foremost, we would like to acknowledge the great contribution made to the software community by the group of researchers at the Xerox Palo Alto Research Center (PARC) who were responsible for the development of the Smalltalk system. In particular, we single out Alan Kay, Adele Goldberg, and Dan Ingalls, who in 1987 received formal recognition of their work with the 1987 ACM Software Systems Award. In recognition for the development of a software system that has had a lasting influence, that has reflected contributions to new and still evolving concepts, and that has resulted in commercial

---

[1] ParcPlace Systems, 1550 Plymouth Street, Mountain View, CA 94043.
[2] Goldberg, A. and Robson, D., *Smalltalk-80: The Language and its Implementation* (Reading, Mass.: Addison-Wesley, 1983).
[3] Digitalk, Inc. 9841 Airport Road Bvld. Los Angeles, CA 90045.

acceptance, the Xerox PARC group received the award for seminal contributions to object-oriented programming languages and related programming techniques. Smalltalk was cited as having provided the foundation for explorations in new software methodologies, graphical user interface designs, and forms of on-line assistance to the software development process. Our thanks also to ParcPlace Systems for continuing to develop and market the Smalltalk-80 system.

We also thank Dave Thomas, who many years ago foresaw the potential of object-oriented programming and motivated us to become involved in research in the area. To the many students at Carleton University in Ottawa and to others who attended our object-oriented programming and Smalltalk workshops, our sincere thanks for being such willing guinea pigs for much of the material that now appears in this book. Our thanks also to the reviewers and, in particular, Richard Bernat of the University of Texas at Austin and Bharot Jayaraman of the University of North Carolina at Chapel Hill, for their helpful comments. To Marcia Horton, Christina Burghard, and their colleagues at Prentice Hall, for their support and patience in the development of the book. Finally, on a more personal note, we thank our respective wives, Marla Doughty and Christine Pugh, for their support and understanding, and our children, Brannon, Robin, Chloé, and Gareth, who have yet to understand why their "daddies" were too often unavailable.

1

Object-Oriented Programming

1.1 INTRODUCTION

In terms of its influence on the programming community, object-oriented programming (OOP) is predicted to be to the nineties what structured programming was to the seventies. But what is it that makes a system or programming language object-oriented? What exactly is meant by the term object-oriented? In this chapter we try to answer these and related questions. We will introduce object-oriented concepts in a language independent manner. However, because terminology in the field has not been standardized and since we will be describing Smalltalk in the rest of this book, we will use the terminology adopted by Smalltalk.

1.2 OOP IS PROGRAMMING BY SIMULATION

Object-oriented programming is most easily described as **programming by simulation**. The programming metaphor is based on personifying the physical or conceptual objects from some real-world domain into objects in the program domain; e.g., objects are clients in a business, foods in a produce store, or parts in a factory. We try to reincarnate objects from the problem domain into our computer models, giving the objects in our program the same characteristics and capabilities as their real-world counterparts. This process is often referred to as **anthropomorphic programming** or **programming by personification**.

The power of simulation as a programming metaphor can be seen from the success of the window-based user interfaces now common in personal workstations. The Apple Macintosh™, for example, uses a *desktop* metaphor in which icons representing such common office objects as documents, folders, and even trash cans appear on the desk. Interactively, a user can open documents, copy them, store a document with other documents in a folder, or place a document in the trash can. Operations on the desktop objects mimic the way their real-world counterparts are manipulated. When implementation domain objects have a direct mapping to problem domain objects, the resulting software is far easier to understand and use.

Consider the following problem specification for a simple video game.[1] A typical display for the game is shown in Fig. 1.1. The objective of the game is to remove all the bricks from the wall. When the ball strikes a brick, the brick disappears. The ball can be redirected using the paddle, which the player can move to the left or right using the mouse. The ball bounces off the sides, bricks, and paddle in a conventional fashion. A player is provided with at most three balls (one at a time) to remove the bricks. A ball is lost if it passes below the paddle; i.e., if the player misses it! Demolishing the bricks with the allotted three balls is a win — failure to do so is a loss.

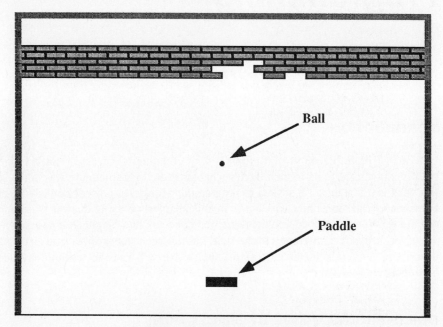

Figure 1.1 Simple video game.

An object-oriented solution to this problem would simulate the objects in the real video game. Software objects would be constructed to represent the paddle, the sides, the ball, the bricks in the wall, and so on. Furthermore, operations on these objects would represent problem-domain tasks such as moving the ball and the paddle, determining if the paddle has struck the ball or whether the ball is lost, removing bricks from the wall, and so on.

---

[1]Problem taken from D. H. Bell et al., *Software Engineering — A Programming Approach* (Englewood Cliffs, New Jersey: Prentice-Hall International, 1987).

1.3 TRADITIONAL VERSUS OBJECT-ORIENTED PROGRAMMING

Object-oriented programming is fundamentally different from traditional procedural or algorithmic approaches. Object-oriented programming describes a system in terms of the objects involved. Traditional programming approaches, on the other hand, describe systems in terms of their functionality. We will use the video game example to illustrate the differences between the traditional and object-oriented approaches.

1.3.1 A Traditional Approach

The classical top-down stepwise refinement approach to problem solving involves refining a problem solution into greater levels of detail based on functional decomposition. Taking a functional approach, we might first describe the solution to our video game in terms of the abstract statement:

Video Game

The next step in the solution might be to decompose this statement into the following:

WHILE Someone wants to play DO
    Set Initial Game Display
    Play a Single Game
ENDWHILE

The design could now be refined further by taking some of the abstract functions in the current solution such as **Set Initial Game Display** and **Play a Single Game** and decomposing them in a similar fashion.

Set Initial Game Display
    Draw Wall
    Draw Sides
    Initialize Paddle

Play a Single Game
    Set Score to 0
    Set Balls Left to 3
    WHILE Balls Left > 0 DO
        Play a Ball
        Decrement Balls Left
    ENDWHILE

The next step might be to refine the **Play a Ball** module.

Play a Ball
    Enter new Ball into Game
    WHILE Ball is in Play DO
        Check Ball Position
        Update Score & Display
        Move Ball
        Move Paddle
    ENDWHILE
    Remove Ball from Game

We are refining the solution to the problem algorithmically in a step-by-step manner, with each step in the process describing a solution to the problem at a certain level of abstraction. Systems refined in this way are most easily described using a diagram (see Fig. 1.2) where major modules are hierarchically organized and where each module represents a function or subproblem in the solution. A design produced using a functional decomposition approach fits very nicely with the procedural approach to programming encouraged by early languages such as Fortran, Pascal, or Cobol, where the subroutine, procedure, or subprogram is the predominant mechanism for structuring code. There is a direct mapping between functional modules in the design and procedures in the code.

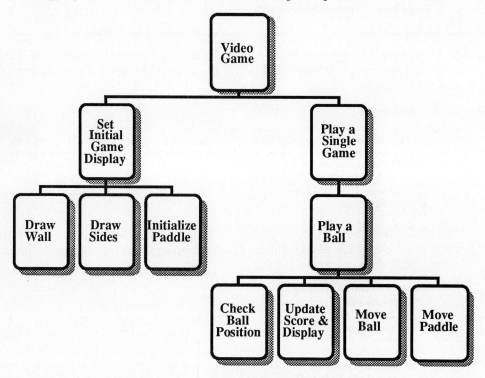

Figure 1.2 Functional decomposition of the video game.

1.3.2 An Object-Oriented Approach

If we take an object-oriented approach to this problem, our first concern is to try to identify not the functions but the objects that will be involved in the computation. The easiest objects to identify are those with real-world counterparts. In the case of our video game example, this leads us to think of objects such as the **bricks**, the **wall**, the **sides**, the **paddle**, the **ball**, and the **video game** itself, as shown in Fig. 1.3.

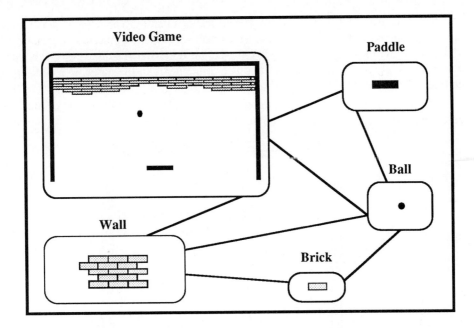

Figure 1.3 Object-oriented decomposition of the video game.

Once the objects have been identified, the next task is to identify their characteristics and the interrelationships between them. For example, the paddle and the ball are clearly interrelated. When the paddle strikes the ball, the ball will change direction. Similarly there is a relationship between the wall and the ball. Component or *part-of* relationships can also be identified. This kind of relationship exists between individual bricks and the wall. The wall is made up of bricks. In this way, we can establish how the game objects interact with each other to achieve a simulation of the video game.

1.3.3 Objects Encapsulate State and Operations

Objects are characterized by their state and the operations that can be performed on that state. Generally, objects have components and the state of an object is therefore characterized by the state of its components. For example, a ball might consist of a radius and a position. A paddle, side, or brick might be described by position, width, and height. Similarly the state of a video game might consist of a ball, a paddle, a wall of bricks, and a set of sides (see Fig. 1.4).

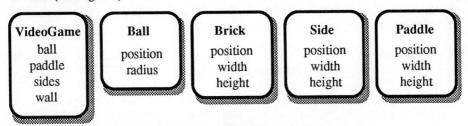

Figure 1.4 Objects are characterized by their state.

Each kind of object supports a set of operations that may be applied to the object to modify or interrogate its state. For example, a ball responds to requests to report or modify its position. Similarly, a ball can be asked whether it is located behind the game paddle or whether it is colliding with any of the other components in the game. We could perform similar analyses on the other objects in the video game.

Conceptually, we can characterize objects such as the ball in our example as an encapsulation of both state and operations (behavior), as shown in Fig. 1.5.

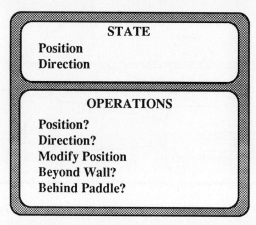

Figure 1.5 Conceptual view of a ball.

By encapsulation, we mean the ability to conceptually group together in an object both the state of the object and the allowable operations on that state. For another example, consider a stack that encapsulates both a representation, perhaps an array or a list, and the operations push, pop, isEmpty, etc., which may be applied to the stack to modify or interrogate its state.

1.3.4 Objects Communicate via Message-Passing

An object-oriented system can be described as a set of objects communicating with each other to achieve some result. Each object can be thought of as a small virtual computer with its own state (or memory) and its own set of operations (or instruction set). Computation is achieved by sending **messages** to objects. When an object receives a message it determines whether is has an appropriate operation, script, or **method** to allow it to respond to the message. The definition of the method describes how the object will react upon receiving the message. In object-oriented terminology, we refer to the collection of operations that define the behavior of an object as the **protocol** supported by the object.

Method	A synonym for operation. Invoked when a message is received by an object.
Protocol	The set of messages to which an object responds.

Rather than calling a procedure to carry out an operation, we speak of sending a **message** to an object. The object receiving the message is referred to as the **receiver**. Thus, we speak of sending the **are you behind the paddle** message to a ball (see Fig. 1.6). Ignoring terminology, the effect of sending a message to an object can be equated to a traditional function call, with the object receiving the message acting as an argument to the function. The result of sending a message to an object is to invoke the appropriate **method**, which then returns an object as a result. In the case of the **are you behind the paddle** message, the result returned would be either the object true or the object false.

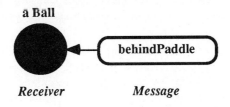

Figure 1.6 Message-passing.

More generally, messages consist of a **selector** that uniquely identifies the operation required of the receiver, and a set of zero or more **arguments**. For example, to modify the position of a ball in the video game, we must supply the new position for the ball as part of the message (see Fig. 1.7).

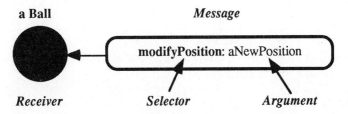

Figure 1.7 Message components.

In contexts such as distributed computing, message-passing often implies concurrency. In object-oriented programming, this is generally not the case. Message-passing is synchronous; i.e., a standard function call/return mechanism is used. A second message cannot be sent until the result of sending a first message has been returned; i.e., the sender of a message is blocked until a response is received.

1.4 OOP IS PROGRAMMING WITH ABSTRACT DATA TYPES

The object-oriented approach to programming has much in common with the notion of programming with **abstract data types**. In fact, object-oriented programming can be thought of as subsuming this style of programming and extending it with two additional programming notions — polymorphism and inheritance.

Objects (and abstract data types) adhere to an important fundamental principle for structuring software systems — **information hiding**. The idea behind information hiding is that users of an object need not have access to either the representation or the implementation of the operations. It is useful to think of objects as providing two views of themselves: one to potential users or clients of the object and another to implementors of the object. Users of the object may modify its state but only indirectly by invoking the operations supported by the object. The major advantage of this approach is that it allows an implementor to modify the implementation of an object in a manner that is transparent to users. Users or clients of the object do not have to be notified of the change. This separation of the object's user interface from its implementation is essential for the production of maintainable and reusable software.

Consider the example of a stack. The user's view of a stack is an advertised message protocol that allows a user to create and modify stacks (see Fig. 1.8). The user has no knowledge of, and cannot directly access, the representation of the stack. The state of the stack can only be modified indirectly through the supported operations. The implementor's view includes knowledge of the representation used for the stack and the detailed code used to implement each message (see Fig. 1.9). If an implementor decides to change the representation of the stack from an array to a list and modifies the implementation of the operations accordingly, the user would be unaware that such a change had taken place. Any code that made use of the old version of the stack would work equally well with the new version.

```
                        Stack

     push: anObject
           "Push anObject onto the stack."
     pop
           "Pop an element off the stack."
     top
           "Return the top element of the stack."
     isEmpty
           "Is the stack empty?"
     ...
```

Figure 1.8 User's view of a stack.

The notion of using a data type without detailed knowledge of its representation is a familiar one. Traditional programming languages all provide support for a set of basic data types; e.g., integers, reals, characters, arrays. Each data type supports a set of well-known operations; e.g., the arithmetic operations for integers. Users do not need to know whether

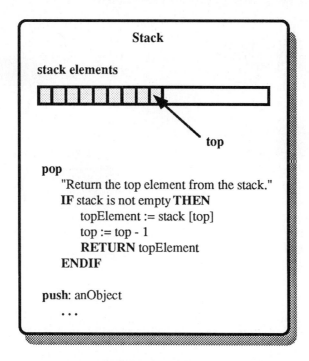

Figure 1.9 Implementor's view of a stack.

integers are represented using a sign-magnitude or two's-complement representation. An object can now be defined as follows:

Object   An abstraction from the problem domain with private state and characterized by the message protocol that it supports.

Earlier, we drew attention to the correspondence between the functional decomposition approach to programming and the procedural languages such as Pascal, Fortran, and Cobol. In a similar way, the encapsulation and information hiding required by the data abstraction approach are provided by the modules and packages of the next generation of languages like Modula 2 and Ada.

1.5 OOP IS PROGRAMMING VIA CLASSIFICATION

Real-world systems depend on our ability to classify and categorize. Elephants, tigers, polar bears, horses, and cows are all mammals (see Fig. 1.10); lead, silver, and platinum are metals; savings, checking, and term deposits are types of bank accounts; and so on. Through classification, we are able to associate characteristics common to all members of a class. All mammals are vertebrates (have backbones), are warm-blooded, and have hair on their bodies; all metals have atomic weights; and all bank accounts have balances.

Figure 1.10 Object classification — animals.

In OOP, the **class** is the abstraction that captures the attributes and operations common to a set of objects. A class describes the representation and message protocol followed by each of the members, or in OOP terminology, the **instances**, of the class. Every object is an instance of some class.

Class	A description of a set of objects with similar characteristics, attributes, and behaviors. A synonym for type.
Instance	An individual object that is both described by and a member of a particular class.

Consider the example of savings accounts in a bank. The private state associated with each account might consist of at least an account number and a balance. The representation of the object can be thought of as a Pascal record — a collection of heterogeneous components or fields. The fields of an object are referred to as **instance variables** since they will be present in every instance and they are changeable (variable). All savings accounts therefore have two instance variables: account number and balance.

Instance Variable	A component part or field of an object.

Operations on savings accounts might include withdrawals (**withdraw**: anAmount), deposits (**deposit**: anAmount), and queries about the balance (**queryBalance**).

Logically, an object is an indivisible encapsulation of state and operations. However, since all instances of a class support the same set of operations, the methods or operations can be physically associated with the class. Only the state or private information relating to a specific object resides in the instance. Consider instances of the class **SavingsAccount**. Each instance has its own account number and balance. However, the operations for making deposits, withdrawals, and balance queries can be shared by all instances and stored in the class. When a message is sent to an instance, the system searches for the operation in the class of the instance. Fig. 1.11 illustrates the shared operations associated with class **SavingsAccount** and three instances each maintaining its own private state.

This physical view of classes and instances leads us to the following alternative definitions:

Class   A repository for methods that can be executed by all instances belonging to that class.

Instance   A repository for data that describes the state of an individual member of a class.

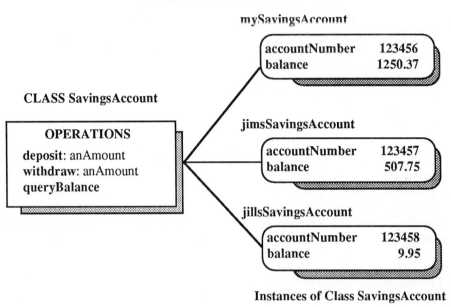

Figure 1.11 Classes versus instances.

1.6 OOP IS PROGRAMMING WITH POLYMORPHISM

One of the most important characteristics of object-oriented programming is that the interpretation of a message is in the hands of the receiver; i.e., the same message can be interpreted in different ways by different receivers. Operations exhibiting this property are said to be **polymorphic**. Messages can be thought of as late-bound procedure calls, where the actual method or procedure to be invoked is not determined until the message is actually sent to a specific receiver.

Consider the following message expression:

anObject **at**: 1 **put**: 'first'

It is not possible to determine what effect this code will have until the class of object bound to the variable anObject is known. If anObject is an array, the effect is to make string 'first' be the first element of the array. However, if anObject is a dictionary, the effect is to either add a new association to the dictionary with key 1 and value 'first' or, if the key 1 previously existed within the dictionary, to modify the value associated with the key 1. Yet another interpretation would arise if anObject was a search tree.

One of the major advantages of polymorphism is that it allows the overloading of names. Hence, the same name can be used throughout a system to denote a commonly used and well-understood operation. As we shall see later, many common message selectors in Smalltalk such as **new**, =, **do:**, and **copy** are redefined as many as twenty times. This consistency in operation naming across class boundaries helps significantly reduce the name space in large systems.

1.6.1 Static Versus Dynamic Binding

As a further example of the desirability of polymorphism, consider an application where various kinds of geometric figures such as rectangles, triangles, squares, and circles are to be displayed and manipulated. To capture the figure abstraction in a type definition in a traditional language such as Pascal, we could define a variant record with a tag field that discriminates between the different possible figure types. We could then implement a display operation on the variant record type. To decompose the implementation into well-designed components, we could provide one figure-specific procedure for each discriminant. In that case, the display procedure would have to use some sort of case logic (see Fig. 1.12) to determine the type of figure involved in order to call the correct figure-specific procedure. Because the association between each figure-specific procedure and the type of parameter required is known at compile-time, the coupling between the two is known as **static binding**.

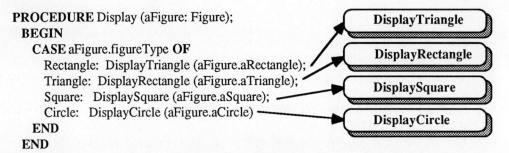

```
PROCEDURE Display (aFigure: Figure);
  BEGIN
    CASE aFigure.figureType OF
      Rectangle: DisplayTriangle (aFigure.aRectangle);
      Triangle: DisplayRectangle (aFigure.aTriangle);
      Square:   DisplaySquare (aFigure.aSquare);
      Circle:   DisplayCircle (aFigure.aCircle)
    END
  END
```

Figure 1.12 Static binding.

In a similar fashion, we could define operations to move a given figure or compute its area. These procedures would share the same case logic as the Display operation above.

In an object-oriented language, we must again implement a **display** method for each of the triangle, rectangle, square, and circle figures. However, the same name is used in each case. Consequently, it is no longer the programmer's responsibility to determine the correct method to invoke. A programmer can send the message **display** to any figure; e.g., by executing 'aFigure **display**'. Based on the type of aFigure, the correct **display** method will be located and executed by the system. Clearly, the correspondence between the operation **display** and its parameter *aFigure* is determined at execution-time rather than at compile-time. This run-time coupling is known as **dynamic binding** (see Fig. 1.13).

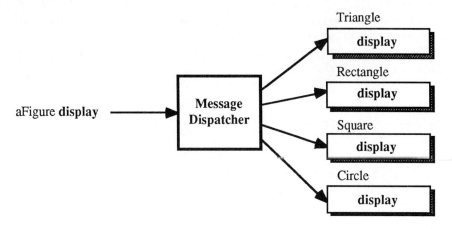

Figure 1.13 Dynamic binding.

This polymorphic solution is more adaptable to change and reuse. Consider extending our figure example to allow another object type, say Pentagon. In both solutions, we would provide pentagons with all of the operations supported by the other figures. However, in the traditional solution, we must also modify all operations on figures since they all contain case logic similar to that in Fig. 1.13. In every situation, a new case must be added. In a large system, this kind of activity is extremely error-prone. Chances are that we will fail to make one or more of the necessary changes. In an object-oriented system, the changes required are localized — we simply implement the necessary operations on pentagons without changing anything else.

1.7 OOP IS PROGRAMMING WITH INHERITANCE

We often think of objects as **specializations** of other objects. Precious metals are specializations of metals, sports cars are specializations of cars, romance novels are specializations of books, and so on. All precious metals are metals but not all metals are precious metals. Similarly, all sports cars are cars and all romance novels are books, but the reverse is not true. Extending this notion, we can view one class of objects as a subclass of another. Taking the argument still further, we can create hierarchies of classes based on

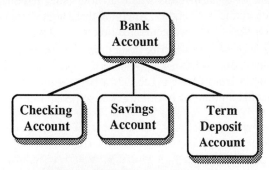

Figure 1.14 Bank Account hierarchy.

logical 'is-a' relationships. In Fig. 1.14, checking accounts, savings accounts, and term deposit accounts are all bank accounts. Similarly, in Fig. 1.15, quadrilaterals and triangles are polygons, and squares and rectangles are special kinds of quadrilaterals. Furthermore, a square is a special kind of rectangle.

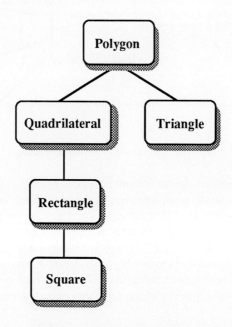

Figure 1.15 Polygon hierarchy.

1.7.1 Specialization and Generalization

What does it mean to say that one class is a subclass of another? Intuitively, we mean that the subclass has all the characteristics of the more general class but extends it in some way. Precious metals have all the characteristics of metals but, in addition, they can be distinguished from some metals on the basis of monetary value. Similarly, quadrilaterals are specializations of polygons with four sides. Polygons can have any number of sides. Squares are specializations of quadrilaterals where all four sides have equal length, and adjacent sides are perpendicular to one another. Applying these arguments in reverse, we can describe the superclass of a class as being a generalization of the class.

One of the best ways to describe something new to someone else is to describe it in terms of something that is similar; i.e., by describing how it differs from something known. Quoting an example from Cox,[2] a zebra is a horse with stripes! This concise definition conveys a substantial amount of information to someone familiar with horses but not with zebras.

[2]B. Cox, *Object-Oriented Programming: An Evolutionary Approach* (Reading, Mass.: Addison-Wesley, 1986).

Object-oriented programming languages embody these notions of specialization and differential description. Classes are hierarchically organized in subclassing relationships. When one class is a subclass of another, it is said to assume or **inherit** the representation and behavior of its superclass. Because of the sharing achieved through inheritance, the new class has to describe only how it is different from the superclass. Logically, a brevity of expression is achieved. Physically, this permits a sharing of operations — an operation provided in one class is applicable to each and every subclass.

Subclass	A class that inherits methods and representation from an existing class.
Superclass	A class from which another class inherits representation and methods.

To get a better feel for these ideas, consider the simple hierarchy of bank account classes shown in Fig. 1.16. To keep the description manageable, we have reduced the problem to bare essentials. Assume that all bank accounts, whether checking, savings, or term deposits, have an account number and a balance and that, in addition, term deposit accounts have a term associated with them. Class **BankAccount**, therefore, has two instance variables, **accountNumber** and **balance**, and all three subclasses inherit this representation so that all instances have at least these two fields. Subclass **CheckingAccount** adds no additional instance variables; neither does subclass **SavingsAccount**. Class **TermDeposit-Account**, however, introduces an additional instance variable **term**, giving term deposits a total of three instance variables. In general, subclasses can add new instance variables but they can never remove them. The same applies for methods. Subclasses can add methods with the same names as methods provided in a superclass but they cannot eliminate methods. Fig. 1.16 illustrates the class hierarchy and the state of one instance for each of the three subclasses.

All types of bank accounts support operations to query the balance of an account. If an operation has identical implementations in each subclass, we can implement the operation once only in the common superclass **BankAccount** and have the three subclasses inherit the operation. Other operations, such as querying the term of an account, will have to be specific to class **TermDepositAccount**. In some situations, a common operation that we might wish to implement once in a superclass may have to be duplicated in the subclasses if its implementation depends on the particular type of account. For example, it might be the case that the operations for deposits and withdrawals can be shared by savings and checking accounts but that a different implementation of these operations is required for term deposit accounts. Fig. 1.17 illustrates a specific design for the placement of operations within the bank account class hierarchy. Operations should be placed as high in the hierarchy as possible so that they may be shared by as many subclasses as possible.

Object-oriented languages like Smalltalk support large reusable class libraries. The Smalltalk class library, for example, is organized in a single hierarchy with the most general class **Object** at the root. Class **Object** contains operations that can be inherited by all objects; e.g., a default print operation that prints the receiver's class name. In all, Smalltalk contains in excess of 250 classes with over 2,000 methods. The extensive class library fosters the notion of **programming by reuse** rather than **by reinvention**.

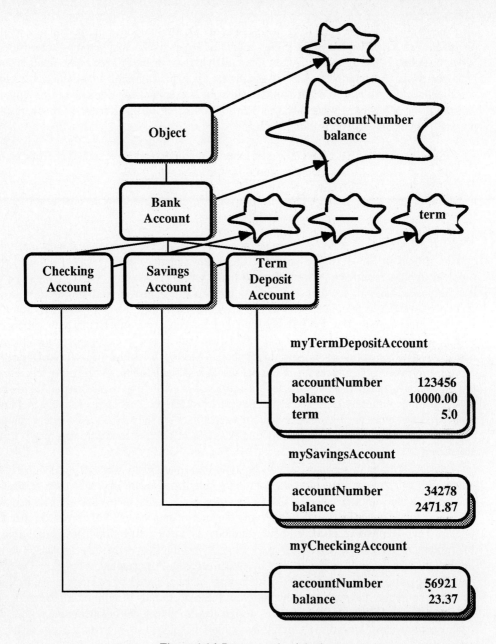

Figure 1.16 Representation inheritance.

When a message is sent to an object, the system first looks for a method with the same selector name in the class of the object. If found, the method is executed; otherwise, the search is continued in the superclass, and the above process is repeated. Ultimately, a method will be found and executed or the top of the hierarchy will be reached (class **Object**, for example, has no superclass). The latter situation is an error since it indicates the use of a message for which there is no corresponding method. In this case, an error notification is generated. To illustrate this search process, consider the following example. Fig. 1.17 should be used to determine (and verify) which method is actually executed.

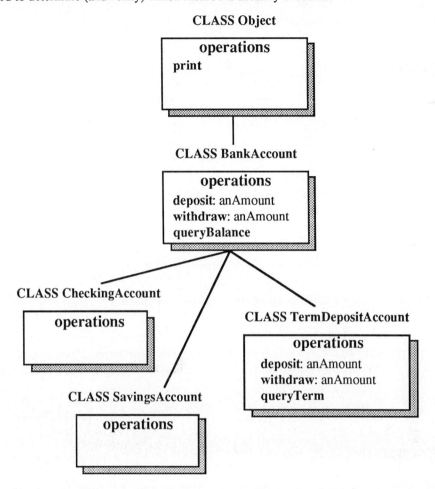

Figure 1.17 Operation inheritance.

Message Sent	Which Method Is Executed
aTermDepositAccount **queryTerm**	use method in class **TermDepositAccount**
aCheckingAccount **queryBalance**	use inherited method in class **BankAccount**
aSavingsAccount **queryTerm**	error - no method in superclass chain
aSavingsAccount **print**	use inherited method in class **Object**

In summary, a new class may differentiate itself from its superclass in a number of ways. In particular, the new class may

- support additional operations other than those inherited.
- support new implementations of operations that could otherwise be inherited.

- override existing operations supported by the superclass but inappropriate for the new class by adding an operation that signals an error.
- contain only a restricted subset of the instances of the original class.
- add additional state.

1.8 SUMMARY

Object-oriented programming can be characterized as:

- **Programming with objects.** Objects have state and can answer questions about themselves. Objects are data types. They encapsulate the state or representation of an object together with operations on that state and support the principle of *information hiding*.
- **Programming by simulation.** Applications are designed and implemented as a simulation or animation. Objects model entities in the real world. This style of programming is often referred to as *programming by personification* or *anthropomorphic programming*.
- **Computation by message-passing.** Scripts (or methods) define how an object will respond to a given message.
- **Programming in the presence of polymorphism.** Messages may be interpreted in different ways by different receivers.
- **Programming in the presence of inheritance.** Code sharing is achieved through the inheritance of representation and behavior from one class of object to another. New classes are defined as specializations of existing classes.
- **Programming in the presence of a reusable class library.** New applications are constructed from an existing library of parts.

1.9 GLOSSARY

selected terminology

abstract data types The style of programming that separates the external interface (the user's viewpoint) from the representation and implementation details (the implementor's viewpoint).

anthropomorphic programming The programming metaphor that embodies the objects with intelligence to decide how to react to requests on their own.

class A description of a set of objects with similar characteristics and attributes.

dynamic binding A requirement that the operation intended by a specific name can be determined from the name of the operations and the type of parameters at run-time (as opposed to compile-time).

information hiding The notion that a data type's representation and implementation need not by known by users of a data type.

inheritance A mechanism that allows one class of objects to share the methods and representation of another class of objects.

instance An individual object described by a particular class.

instance variables Variables found in all instances of a class; components of an object.

message A request sent to an object to carry out some task.

message pattern A method selector together with names for any arguments required by the selector.

message protocol The messages to which an object can respond.

method A description of how an operation on an object is to be computed.

object A component of the Smalltalk system represented by some private data and a set of methods (operations).

polymorphism The ability to take on several meanings. Messages are polymorphic in the sense that the actual method invoked is determined by the type of the receiver.

programming by personification A synonym for anthropomorphic programming.

programming by reinvention The undesirable notion that programming can be done by unknowingly duplicating the functionality of existing code.

programming by reuse The notion that operations in a class can be used by a subclass without reprogramming or modifying the existing classes.

programming by simulation The programming metaphor that is based on personifying the physical or conceptual objects from some real-world domain into objects in the program domain; e.g., objects are clients in a business, foods in a produce store, or parts in a factory.

selector The component of a message that uniquely specifies the operation requested; e.g., **at:put:** is the selector in "anArray **at:** 1 **put:** 'hi'".

specialization The notion that one kind of object is a special case of another; e.g., precious metals are a specialization of metals, sports cars a specialization of cars, and romance novels a specialization of books.

static binding A requirement that the operation intended by a specific name can be determined from the name of the operations and the type of parameters at compile-time (as opposed to run-time).

subclass A class that inherits methods and representation from another class.

superclass A class from which another class inherits representation and methods.

2

Smalltalk Fundamentals

2.1 INTRODUCTION

Programming in Smalltalk is different from programming in traditional languages such as Pascal, Fortran, or Ada. A major difference is that the language is object-oriented rather than procedure-oriented and is based on concepts such as objects and messages rather than procedures and functions. Although these concepts are new to many programmers, they are often overshadowed by a more visible difference. Smalltalk is much more than a programming language — it is a complete program development environment. It integrates in a consistent manner such features as an editor, a compiler, a debugger, a spelling checker, print utilities, a window system, and a source code manager. Such features are traditionally associated with an operating system rather than a programming language. Smalltalk eliminates the sharp boundary between application and operating system by modelling everything as an object.

Becoming a productive Smalltalk programmer requires much more than a familiarity with the language. You must become adept at using the development tools provided by the Smalltalk programming environment and, perhaps most important of all, become familiar with the extensive library of existing classes (or data types) supplied with the Smalltalk system. Be forewarned that it takes considerably longer to become an accomplished Smalltalk programmer than an accomplished Pascal programmer. Interactive experimentation and on-line familiarization are essential. Smalltalk encourages an exploratory approach to programming. The payoff, however, is well worth the extra effort. You will be able to develop interactive graphical applications with all the features of modern user interfaces (e.g., windows, menus, mouse interaction) at low cost. Smalltalk applications can be developed with high productivity because of Smalltalk's underlying philosophy of reusing and extending existing code rather than reinventing code.

Programming in Smalltalk therefore requires at least a knowledge of the following:

- the fundamental language concepts; namely objects, messages, classes, and inheritance,
- the syntax and semantics of Smalltalk,
- how to interact with the Smalltalk programming environment to build new Smalltalk applications (Smalltalk is an interactive language that favors a **learn by doing** or exploratory approach to programming), and
- the fundamental system classes, such as the numeric, collection, graphical and user interface classes. Designing new Smalltalk applications requires a knowledge of the existing capability of the Smalltalk system. Programming in Smalltalk is often termed **programming by extension**. New applications are constructed by extending the existing Smalltalk class library.

In this chapter, we consider the first two requirements. An introduction to the Smalltalk programming environment is given in Chapters 3 through 5. Chapters 6 through 10 describe the numeric, collection, and graphical classes respectively.

We assume that the reader is a programmer with some experience in a traditional language such as Pascal and is familiar with fundamental programming language concepts. Wherever possible in this chapter we will contrast Smalltalk code with its Pascal equivalent. In addition to the obvious benefit of drawing comparisons between Pascal and Smalltalk, we adopt this approach to speed up the discussion by relating Smalltalk concepts to those that the reader is already familiar with.

Smalltalk is a language somewhat smaller in size than Pascal and is based on a surprisingly small set of concepts; namely **objects**, **messages**, **classes**, **subclassing**, and **inheritance**. The sparse number of primitive concepts and the consistent manner in which they are used make Smalltalk a language that is relatively easy to learn. The biggest problem for beginning Smalltalk programmers is not learning the syntax and semantics of the language but becoming familiar with the substantial Smalltalk system library and the interactive programming environment. Familiarity with the language does not translate to familiarity with the system.

For ease of reference, whenever we introduce a major Smalltalk concept we will provide a short definition. A glossary of major Smalltalk terms is included at the end of this chapter.

2.2 OBJECTS IN SMALLTALK

As we mentioned earlier, everything in Smalltalk is an object. System components (such as the compiler and the debugger), primitive data elements (such as integers, booleans, and characters), and graphic elements (such as rectangular areas, drawing pens, and bitmaps) are all objects. As we shall see later in this chapter, even control structures are implemented by passing messages to objects.

2.2.1 What Is a Smalltalk Object?

Method   A synonym for operation. Invoked when a message is received by an object.

Object   A component of the Smalltalk system represented by some private data and a set of methods or operations.

Conceptually, an object can be thought of as a virtual computer with a memory and a primitive instruction or operation set. An object has memory — private data or state that is kept within the object. An object is also capable of computation. It can respond to any of a predefined set of messages. This message set is referred to as the **message protocol** supported by the object. When an object receives a message, it must first decide whether it "understands" the message, and if so what its response should be. If an object can respond to a message directly, a method or function corresponding to the message is selected and evaluated. The result of evaluating the method is returned to the sender of the message as the result.

Message protocol   The set of messages to which an object can respond.

As a more concrete example of a Smalltalk object, suppose we have an object, say aPoint, that represents a position on the Smalltalk display screen. The state of aPoint will contain at least two components: first, an object representing the xCoordinate of the position of the object on the screen and, second, the yCoordinate. In Pascal terms, we might think of aPoint as a record with two fields: xCoordinate and yCoordinate.

What message protocol might be supported by the object aPoint? Assume that aPoint allows a sender to query its x and y coordinates by supporting the protocol **x** and **y**. For example, sending the **x** message to aPoint using the Smalltalk expression

aPoint x

would return an object representing its x coordinate. For the sake of discussion, assume that aPoint also supports the protocol **distanceFrom**: anotherPoint. The effect of sending the message **distanceFrom**: to aPoint using a Smalltalk expression of the form

aPoint distanceFrom: anotherPoint

is to return the distance between aPoint and anotherPoint.

2.2.2 Information Hiding: Internal and External Views of an Object

Objects in Smalltalk encapsulate both procedures and data. They support the well-accepted software engineering concept of **information hiding**. To control the complexity of large programs, we must partition programs into modules. Moreover, we should hide as much information as possible within a module and minimize the interface presented to users.

It is useful to think of a Smalltalk object providing two different views of itself: one for users of the object and another for implementors of the object. We will call these views the external and internal views respectively. The **internal view** describes the representation of the object and the algorithms that implement the methods (or operations). The **external view** is the view of the object as seen by other objects.

The external view, or what we can do with an object, is described by its message protocol — the set of messages to which the object responds. To a user, the internal view of an object is private. It is owned by the object and may not be manipulated by other objects unless the object specifically provides a protocol for doing so. For example, the external view of **aPoint** is shown in Fig. 2.1. If **aPoint** did not support a protocol for accessing its x and y coordinates, it would be impossible for any other object to gain access to this information. The only way to ask an object to perform any computation is by sending it a message.

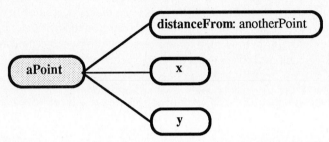

Figure 2.1 The external view or message protocol supported by aPoint.

Contrast this approach with that of Pascal, which provides almost no support for information hiding. If we wanted to access or modify the contents of the **xCoordinate** field of **aPoint**, we could do so easily using an expression of the form

aPoint.xCoordinate

Moreover, in Pascal, we have no way of preventing a programmer from directly accessing the representation of **aPoint** in this way. The opposite is true in Smalltalk. Unless the programmer provides specific accessing methods as part of the message protocol for the object, it is impossible to access the internal structure of the object.

The separation between the internal and external views of an object is fundamental to the programming philosophy embodied in Smalltalk. To use an object, it is necessary to understand only its protocol or external view. The fundamental advantage of this approach is that, provided the message protocol or external view is not changed, the internal view may be changed without impacting users of the object. Similar facilities for information hiding are provided by the module facility in Modula 2 and the package in Ada.

2.2.3 Literal Objects

Certain types of objects can be described literally in Smalltalk. For example, literals are used to describe **numbers**, **symbols**, **characters**, **strings**, and **arrays**. We will not dwell on syntactic issues in the examples that follow. Each of these classes of objects will be discussed more fully in later chapters. For the moment, we will let the examples speak for themselves.

Smalltalk	Pascal	Commentary
34	34	The integer **34**.
-17.62	-17.62	The floating point number **-17.62**.
1.56e-3	1.56E-3	The floating point number **.00156** written in exponential form.
'a string'	'a string'	A string of characters.
#solutions	no equivalent	A symbol with the name **solutions**. Each symbol is unique — two symbols with the same name cannot co-exist.
$c	'c'	The character lowercase c.
#(-25 'a string' $c)	no equivalent	An array of three objects. Unlike Pascal, objects within an array do not have to be homogeneous. Individual objects within an array can be referenced using integer indices from 1 to the size of the array.

2.3 SENDING MESSAGES

Message expressions in Smalltalk describe who is to receive the message, which operation is being selected, and any arguments necessary to carry out the requested operation. The components of the message are called the **receiver**, the **selector**, and the **arguments** respectively. For instance, in the Smalltalk expression

$$1 + 5$$

the integer **1** is the receiver of the message, + is the selector that uniquely identifies which operation is to be selected, and **5** is the argument necessary to carry out the operation. More important than the new terminology involved here is the manner in which this expression is evaluated. As illustrated in Fig. 2.2, expressions in Smalltalk and Pascal are evaluated in fundamentally different ways.

In a Pascal-like language, we might describe the evaluation in the following way. The addition operator is applied to the two integer operands 1 and 5, returning the result 6. From an object-oriented viewpoint, it should be viewed differently. The message + **5** is being sent to the integer object **1**. Integer objects know how to respond to this message and the integer object **6** is returned as a result. Notice the change of emphasis. It is the **receiver** of the message (the integer object **1**) that determines how the expression is evaluated. In a Pascal-like language it is the addition **operation** that is dominant.

Smalltalk supports three primitive types of messages, known as **unary**, **binary** and **keyword** messages.

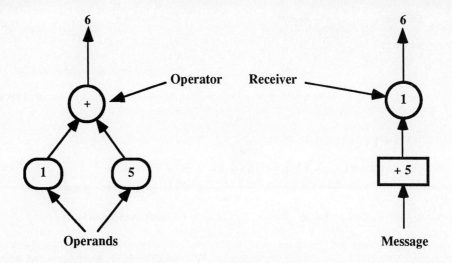

Figure 2.2 Traditional versus Smalltalk expression evaluation.

2.3.1 Unary Messages

Unary messages have no arguments, only a receiver and a selector. They are equivalent to Pascal functions with a single argument. Examples follow.

Smalltalk	Pascal	Commentary
5 **factorial**	factorial (5)	The message consisting of the selector **factorial** is sent to the integer **5**. The integer object **120** is returned as the result.
16.79 **rounded**	round (16.79)	The message consisting of the selector **rounded** is sent to the float **16.79**. The integer object **17** is returned as the result.
$a **asInteger**	ord ('a')	The message consisting of the selector **asInteger** is sent to the character **a**. The integer object representing the ordinal value of the character is returned as the result.
'abcdef' **size**	size ('abcdef')	The message consisting of the selector **size** is sent to the string **'abcdef'**. The integer object **6** representing the length of the string is returned as the result.

Pascal style unary operations are not available in the traditional syntax. The following example shows a unary minus operation.

Smalltalk	Pascal	Commentary
3 **negated**	-3	The message consisting of the selector **negated** is sent to the integer **3**. The integer object **-3** is returned as the result.
no equivalent	+3	

2.3.2 Binary Messages

In addition to the receiver, binary messages have a single argument. They are equivalent to Pascal binary operations. The selectors for binary messages are special single or double characters. Single character selectors include common arithmetic and comparison operators such as +, -, *, /, <, >, and =. Double character selectors include such operators as ~= (not equal), <= (less than or equal), and // (integer division). Examples of binary messages follow.

Smalltalk	Pascal	Commentary
55 + 100	55 + 100	The message **+ 100** is sent to the integer **55**. The selector is **+** and the argument is **100**. The result is to return the integer **155**.
'abc' ~= 'def'	'abc' <> 'def'	The message **~= 'def'** is sent to the string **'abc'**. The selector is **~=** and the argument is the string **'def'**. The receiver and the argument strings are compared for inequality. The boolean object **true** is returned.

2.3.3 Keyword Messages

Keyword messages are messages containing one or more keywords, with each keyword having a single argument associated with it. The names of keywords always end in a colon (:). The colon is part of the name — it is not a special terminator. Keyword messages are equivalent to Pascal functions with two or more arguments. Examples follow.

Smalltalk	Pascal	Commentary
28 **gcd**: 12	gcd (28, 12)	The message **gcd: 12** is sent to the integer **28**. The selector is **gcd:** and the argument is the integer **12**. The result returned is the greatest common divisor of the receiver **28** and the argument **12**, that is, the integer object **4**.
#(4 3 2 1) **at**: 4	no equivalent	The message **at: 4** is sent to the array containing **(4 3 2 1)**. The selector is **at:** and the argument is the integer **4**. The result returned is the integer object **1**, the object associated with the index (or subscript) **4** in the array.

5 **between:** 3 **and:** 12 between (5, 3, 12)	The message **between:** 3 **and:** 12 is sent to the integer **5**. The selector is **between:and:** and the arguments are the integers **3** and **12** respectively. The result returned is the object **true** since 5 lies in the range 3 to 12 inclusive.

The selector in a keyword message is formed by concatenating together all of the keywords in the message; e.g., **between:and:**. The same keywords may appear in different message selectors, providing the concatenation of the keywords forms a unique selector.

2.3.4 Evaluation of Message Expressions

The receiver or argument of a message expression may itself be a message expression. This gives rise to complex message expressions and the need for an evaluation order. For example, the following message expression contains unary, binary, and keyword messages.

4 factorial gcd: 4 * 6

Many languages, Pascal included, base the evaluation of expressions on priorities assigned to different operators. For instance, multiplication (*) is usually assigned a higher priority than addition (+). Smalltalk's evaluation rules, however, are based on the type of messages (unary, binary, and keyword) involved in the expression. In order of application, the evaluation order is as follows:

1. **Parenthesized** expressions
2. **Unary** expressions (evaluated from left to right)
3. **Binary** expressions (evaluated from left to right)
4. **Keyword** expressions

Note: all binary operators have the same priority level.

Fully parenthesizing a message expression removes all ambiguity about the evaluation order. Each of the following examples is shown with its fully parenthesized form to illustrate the order of evaluation.

Expression	Fully Parenthesized Expression
2 **factorial negated**	(2 **factorial**) **negated**
3 + 4 * 6 + 3	((3 + 4) * 6) + 3
15 **gcd:** 32 // 3	15 **gcd:** (32 // 3)
2 **factorial** + 4	(2 **factorial**) + 4
5 **between:** 1 **and:** 3 **squared** + 4	5 **between:** 1 **and:** ((3 **squared**) + 4)
4 **factorial gcd:** 4 * 6	(4 **factorial**) **gcd:** (4 * 6)

2.3.5 Cascaded Messages

Cascaded messages are a concise way of specifying that multiple messages be sent to the same receiver. A **cascaded message** consists of a series of message expressions separated by semicolons (;), where the first message expression specifies the common receiver. For example, imagine we wanted to modify the first three elements of an array anArray. The message **at:** index **put:** aValue modifies an element of an array. We could send the same message to anArray three times

anArray at: 1 put: 3. anArray at: 2 put: 8. anArray at: 3 put: 5

or alternatively use the cascaded message expression

anArray at: 1 put: 3; at: 2 put: 8; at: 3 put: 5

No receiver is specified for the second and third **at:put:** message — implicitly the receiver is the same as the message preceding the first semicolon. The result of evaluating a cascaded expression is the result of sending the last message in the cascade. In this case, since **at:put:** returns the modified value, the result returned would be 5. To return the modified array as a result, the message **yourself** could be added to the cascade.

anArray at: 1 put: 3; at: 2 put: 8; at: 3 put: 5; yourself

When a **yourself** message is received by any object, the object (or receiver) is returned.

2.3.6 Dynamic Binding and Message Overloading

The same message can be interpreted in different ways by different objects. For example, consider the following examples.

5 + 100

(200 @ 200) + 100

Both examples use the message + **100** but the receiving objects react to the message in very different ways. In the first example, the receiver is the integer **5** and the selector + is interpreted as indicating integer addition. In the second, the receiver is the point with x and y coordinates equal to 200 (the binary selector @ when sent to an integer creates an initialized instance of the Smalltalk class Point). In this expression, the selector + is interpreted as indicating addition defined on points. The point with x and y coordinates equal to 300 is returned.

As we discussed earlier, it is the receiver of the message that determines how the message is to be interpreted. This means that the same message sent to different objects will produce different results. For example, we could use the generic selector **printString** to generate printed representations of points, rectangles, and so on. Consider

aPoint **printString**	Prints a point in the form x@y; e.g., 100@200.
aRectangle **printString**	Prints a rectangle in the form "originPoint corner: cornerPoint"; e.g., 100@100 corner: 200@200.

The actual print method invoked by an expression such as anObject **printString** is determined by the type of the object receiving the message. If the receiver is a point, then the method for printing points is selected. The decision about which print method to evaluate in response to a **printString** message is delayed until run-time and is based on the type of the receiver. This is called **dynamic binding**. Some messages in Smalltalk have as many as twenty different implementations for different types of objects.[1]

When the same selector is accepted by different classes of object, we say, in programming language terminology, that the selector is overloaded. Alternatively, if we equate message expressions to function calls in Pascal, we can view messages as functions that are generic in their first argument.

Smalltalk	*Pascal*
receiver **selector**	selector (receiver)
receiver **selector**: first	selector: (receiver, first)
receiver **selector**: first **with**: second	selector:with: (receiver, first, second)[2]

2.3.7 Variables and Assignment

Variable names in Smalltalk are simple identifiers consisting of a sequence of letters and digits beginning with a letter. Although they have the same syntax as their Pascal counterparts, variables in Smalltalk are vastly different. All variables in Smalltalk are object pointers or pointer variables in the Pascal sense. For example, in Pascal if we have a variable named **x** and an assignment statement of the form

$$x := \text{'a String'}$$

we refer to the value of **x** as the string **'a String'** or to **x** as containing the value **'a String'**. In Smalltalk, a similar assignment would take the form:

$$x \leftarrow \text{'a String'}$$

and we would say that the variable **x** is bound to (or points to) the object 'a String' (see Fig. 2.3).

In Pascal, the equivalent would be described by the expression

$$x\uparrow := \text{'a String'}$$

In Smalltalk, variable names are used to refer to the object pointed to by the variable. Assignment expressions are used to change the object to which a variable is bound or points to. Consider the following:

Smalltalk	*Pascal*	*Commentary*
x ← y	x := y	The variable **x** is bound to the same object that is bound to the variable **y**.

---

[1] Actually, there is only one **printString** method in class Object. Method **printString** invokes method **printOn:**, and it is this method that is reimplemented by subclasses to override the default print behavior found in the **printOn:** method in class Object.

[2] Of course, in Pascal, the colons would not be legitimate characters in the function name.

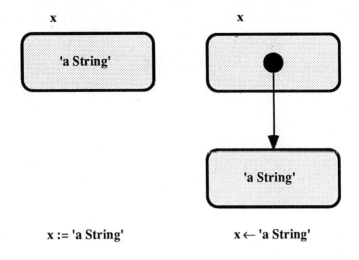

x := 'a String'   x ← 'a String'

Figure 2.3 Pascal versus Smalltalk assignments.

Note that there is a subtle but important difference between the Smalltalk and Pascal versions in the previous example. An assignment such as x := y in a language such as Pascal involves making a copy of the contents of y and placing it into the space occupied by x. In Smalltalk no copying takes place, x is simply bound to the same object as y (see Section 6.2.2 for an in-depth discussion of this subject). Consider the following examples:

Smalltalk	Pascal	Commentary
x ← x + 1	x := x + 1	The message **+ 1** is sent to the object bound to variable **x**. Variable **x** is then bound to the object returned by evaluating the message expression **x+1**.
table **at:** index **put:** 3	table [index] := 3	The element of the array **table** at position **index** is bound to the integer object **3**. The argument to the keyword **put:**, the object **3**, is returned as result.
x ← 3. x ← $3	no equivalent	The first assignment expression binds **x** to the integer object **3**. The second then rebinds **x** to the character object **$3**. Notice that the period (.) is used as a statement separator in exactly the same way as the semicolon (;) in Pascal. It can also terminate the last sentence if we wish to add it.

The last example illustrates another important difference between Smalltalk variables and Pascal variables. The type of a Pascal variable must be predeclared at compile-time — no type is provided when a Smalltalk variable is declared. For instance, a Pascal variable declared as type integer cannot subsequently take on a character value. For that reason, Pascal is known as a **strongly typed** language. Smalltalk variables, on the other hand, are not typed. Smalltalk objects are typed but not the variables that refer to them. A Smalltalk variable can be bound to any object of any type. The declaration syntax and the scoping rules pertaining to Smalltalk variables are discussed in a later section.

2.3.8 Allocation and Deallocation of Objects

Another major difference between Pascal and Smalltalk is the method of dynamically allocating and deallocating objects. In Pascal, it is necessary to explicitly deallocate objects when they are no longer needed — in Smalltalk this process is handled automatically. The example below illustrates the dynamic allocation of an array of size 10 to a variable **aTable**. In the Pascal case, the array element type must be specified. In both Pascal and Smalltalk, the allocation process is carried out in a similar fashion. Pascal has a **new** function while Smalltalk sends a **new:** message to the class **Array**. However, in Pascal, if we wish to reclaim the space pointed to by variable **aTable**, we must explicitly ask that it be deallocated using the **dispose** function. Moreover, it is the programmer's responsibility to ensure that this space can be safely reclaimed; i.e., to ensure that no other references to the deallocated objects exist. In Smalltalk, this task is handled automatically by a **garbage collector**[3] that periodically reclaims all objects that are no longer referenced.

Smalltalk	*Pascal*
	TYPE
	table = **ARRAY** [1..10] **OF** integer;
	pointerToTable = ↑table;
I aTable I	**VAR**
	aTable: pointerToTable;
aTable ← Array **new:** 10.	new (aTable);
	...
	dispose (aTable)
	...

2.4 CONTROL STRUCTURES WITH MESSAGE-PASSING

Unlike Pascal, no additional syntactic structures need to be added to the language to describe control structures. Control structures are implemented in terms of objects and message passing. In particular, Smalltalk control structures involve a class of object known as a **block**. For the moment, a block can be thought of, at least syntactically, as an analog of the Pascal **begin ... end** construct; i.e., simply a way of grouping together a set of statements. A block literal consists of a sequence of expressions separated by periods and delimited by square brackets; e.g.,

$$[x \leftarrow 3. \ y \leftarrow 4]$$

---

[3]The garbage collectors implemented in current versions of Smalltalk-80 are, unlike early garbage collectors, extremely efficient, consuming only 2-3 per cent of available CPU time.

The result returned when a block is evaluated is the object returned by the evaluation of the last expression in the block.The empty block [] returns the special object **nil** when evaluated.

Fig. 2.4 contains a summary of the control structures in Smalltalk along with their Pascal equivalents.

Smalltalk	Pascal

Assignment

variable ← expression

variable := expression

Conditional Selection

boolean expression
    ifTrue: [
        true block]
    ifFalse: [
        false Block]

IF boolean expression **THEN**
    statement
ELSE
    statement

boolean expression
    ifTrue: [
        true block]

IF boolean expression **THEN**
    statement

boolean expression
    ifFalse: [
        false block]

IF NOT boolean expression **THEN**
    statement

Conditional Repetition

[boolean expression] **whileTrue:** [
    loop body]

WHILE boolean expression **DO**
    statement

[boolean expression] **whileFalse:** [
    loop body]

WHILE not boolean expression **DO**
    statement

Fixed Length Repetition (integers only)

initial value **to:** final value **do:**
    [loop control variable |
        loop body]

FOR loop control variable **:=**
    initial value **TO** final value **DO**
        statement

repeat value **timesRepeat:** [
    loop body]

FOR loop control variable **:=**
    1 **TO** repeat value **DO**
        statement

Figure 2.4 Smalltalk control structures.

2.4.1 Conditional Selection

Control structures for conditional selection are expressed using blocks as shown in the following. In each case the Pascal equivalent is given. As in Pascal, Smalltalk allows statements to be freely formatted by the programmer. Statements should be laid out in a manner that visually enhances the logical structure of the code using indentation as appropriate.

Smalltalk

```
number1 < number2
    ifTrue: [
        maximum ← number2.
        minimum ← number1]
    ifFalse: [
        maximum ← number1.
        minimum ← number2]
```

Pascal

```
IF number1 < number2 THEN
BEGIN
    maximum := number2;
    minimum := number1
END
ELSE
    BEGIN
        maximum := number1;
        minimum := number2
    END
```

The Smalltalk version of the if-then-else statement should be interpreted as follows:

1. The message **< number2** is sent to the object referenced by **number1**. All numbers respond to the selector **<** (less than) by returning one of the boolean objects, **true** or **false**, depending on the argument passed in the message.

2. If **number1 < number2** returns **true**, the message **ifTrue:** [...] **ifFalse:** [...] will be sent to the boolean object **true**; otherwise it will be sent to **false**.

   The constant **true** responds to a message with selector **ifTrue:ifFalse:** by evaluating the expressions in the argument associated with the **ifTrue:** keyword; i.e., the block, [**maximum ← number2. minimum ← number1**].

   Similarly, **false** responds to a message with selector **ifTrue:ifFalse:** by evaluating the expressions in the argument associated with the **ifFalse:** keyword; i.e., the block, [**maximum ← number1. minimum ← number2**].

3. The object returned by the conditional selection is the value of the evaluated block. In this example, the object bound to **minimum** will be returned since an assignment expression of the form **minimum ← number?** is the last statement in both the **ifTrue:** and **ifFalse:** blocks.

The boolean objects **true** and **false** also accept the single keyword messages **ifTrue:** and **ifFalse:**. The following are examples of their use.

Smalltalk

```
salesAmount < 100
    ifTrue: [discount ← 0.15]

number >= 0
    ifFalse: [number ← number negated]
```

Pascal

```
IF salesAmount < 100 THEN
    discount := 0.15

IF NOT (number >= 0) THEN
    number := -number
```

The literal **true** responds to an **ifTrue:** message by returning the value of the block argument; **false** responds to the same message by returning the special object **nil**.

Conversely, **true** responds to an **ifFalse:** message by returning **nil**, and **false** responds to the same message by returning the value of the block argument. Note that the arguments to message selectors **ifTrue:ifFalse:**, **ifTrue:**, and **ifFalse:** must be blocks even if the block contains only a single message expression or is empty.

Since conditional selection is implemented in terms of message expressions, a conditional selection can itself be embedded within a message expression. For instance, the last example could have been written as follows:

number ← number >= 0 **ifFalse**: [number **negated**] **ifTrue**: [number]

2.4.2 Conditional Repetition

Smalltalk provides a conditional repetition form equivalent to the Pascal **while ... do** statement. It is again based on blocks and makes use of the fact that blocks are bonafide objects and thus can support their own message protocol. Consider the following program fragments to compute the sum of the first 100 integers:

Smalltalk

```
sum ← 0.
number ← 1.
[number <= 100] whileTrue: [
        sum ← sum + number.
        number ← number + 1].
sum
```

Pascal

```
sum := 0;
number := 1;
WHILE number <= 100 DO
    BEGIN
        sum := sum + number;
        number := number + 1
    END
```

The Smalltalk version of the while ... do statement should be interpreted as follows:

1. The message **whileTrue:** [...] is sent to the block [**number < 100**].

2. In response to the **whileTrue:** message, the receiver, the block [**number < 100**], evaluates itself.

3. If evaluating the block returns the object **true**, the **whileTrue:** argument block is evaluated and the **whileTrue:** message is again sent to the block [**number < 100**], and steps 1, 2, and 3 are repeated.

    If evaluating the block returns the object **false**, the **whileTrue:** argument block is not evaluated again and the **whileTrue:** message returns the special object **nil** as the result.

Note that the result returned by a **whileTrue:** message will always be **nil**. To return the required result when the fragment of Smalltalk code is evaluated, we evaluate the variable **sum** on exit from the while loop.

The effect of sending a **whileTrue:** message to a block is to repeatedly evaluate the block argument while the block receiving the message evaluates to true. This provides a conditional structure that repeats zero or more times.

A **whileFalse:** message is also understood by blocks. Its semantics are similar to the **whileTrue:** semantics but are reversed; i.e., the effect of sending a **whileFalse:** message to a block is to repeatedly evaluate the block argument, while the block receiving the message evaluates to false rather than true. The result returned by **whileFalse:** is always the special object **nil.** The previous example could be rewritten to use **whileFalse:** instead of **whileTrue:** as follows:

Smalltalk	*Pascal*
| ```
sum ← 0.
number ← 1.
[number > 100] whileFalse: [
      sum ← sum + number.
      number ← number + 1].
sum
``` | ```
sum := 0;
number := 1;
WHILE NOT (number > 100) DO
   BEGIN
         sum := sum + number;
         number := number + 1
   END
``` |

2.4.3 Fixed-Length Repetition

Deterministic looping over integers is provided by the **to: finalValue do: aBlock** message defined on integers. The **do:** keyword argument is a single argument block. Block arguments are declared at the head of a block and delimited from the expressions in the block by a bar (I). Each block argument name is syntactically preceded by a colon ":". The previous example for computing the sum of the first 100 integers could be recoded as follows:

Smalltalk	*Pascal*
| ```
sum ← 0.
1 to: 100 do: [:index |
      sum ← sum + index].
sum
``` | ```
sum := 0;
FOR index := 1 TO 100 DO
   BEGIN
         sum := sum + index
   END
``` |

The **to: finalValue do: aBlock** message on integers evaluates the single argument block **aBlock** for each integer in the interval given by the value of the receiver up to and including **finalValue.** The argument to the block takes on successive values in that interval on each evaluation of the block. In the example above, the block is evaluated for each value of the block argument, **index**, which takes on the successive values in the interval 1 to 100 inclusive.

Smalltalk	*Pascal*
| ```
sum ← 0.
1 to: 100 by: 2 do: [:index |
      sum ← sum + index].
sum
``` | ```
sum := 0; index:=1;
WHILE index < 100 DO
   BEGIN
         sum := sum + index;
         index := index + 2
   END
``` |

The **to: finalValue by: stepValue do: aBlock** message defined on integers is a variation of the **to:do:** message that specifies the amount by which the block argument is to be incremented on each evaluation. For positive step values, the repeated evaluation terminates when the loop index is greater than the **finalValue**. This is illustrated above. For negative steps, the loop terminates when it is less than **finalValue**.

As we will see later, it is a simple matter to add new methods to integers to support additional control structures. For example, we might wish to add a **downTo**: finalValue **do**: aBlock, where the block argument is decremented by 1, instead of incremented, on each evaluation of the block.

An even simpler form of deterministic loop is provided by the **timesRepeat**: aBlock protocol that evaluates a zero-argument block a fixed number of times. The number of evaluations is specified by the receiver, an integer. For example, the expression

5 timesRepeat: [...]

would evaluate the block five times.

The Pascal **for** statement allows fixed length iteration where the index variable of the loop may be of any ordinal type. For example, given the following type **color**,

TYPE color = (red, green, yellow, blue)

we could construct a **for** statement to iterate over subranges of the values of the type; e.g.,

FOR hue:= red TO blue DO BEGIN ... END

The Smalltalk equivalent is the **do**: construct that applies to many more classes of object. For example, we can write

```
(1 to: 10) do: [:loopIndex | ... code ... ]
#(red green blue) do: [:loopIndex | ... code ... ]
#(5 'hi' 1.5) do: [:loopIndex | ... code ... ]
aSet do: [:loopIndex | ... code ... ]
anOrderedCollection do: [:loopIndex | ... code ... ]
```

In Smalltalk, control structures are implemented by passing messages to objects. Consequently, we can implement the **do**: for each different class of object that we would like to iterate over. This is a great advantage because control structures can be constructed not only to iterate over simple ranges of integers, but also to traverse such data structures as arrays, lists, trees, bank accounts, or circuit elements.

2.4.4 An Example: Testing for Primes

To illustrate the equivalent of Pascal's nested control structures in Smalltalk and to discuss a larger example, we will consider the development of a Smalltalk fragment to test whether or not a given integer is prime. For our purposes, a number is defined as **prime** if it is positive and evenly divisible by itself and 1. The algorithm used initially rejects all even numbers greater than 2. For odd numbers greater than 3, the integer is divided by a series of odd trial divisors, until either the number divides evenly into one of the trial divisors in which case it is not prime, or alternatively until the divisor becomes larger than the square root of the number, in which case the number is prime. Pascal and Smalltalk versions of code to solve this problem are shown below.

Pascal

```
FUNCTION isPrime (candidate: integer): boolean;
    VAR divisor: integer; prime: boolean;
    BEGIN
        prime := true;
        IF candidate <= 0 THEN
            prime := false
        ELSE IF candidate > 3 THEN
            IF candidate MOD 2 = 0 THEN
                prime := false
            ELSE
                BEGIN
                    divisor := 3;
                    WHILE ((divisor * divisor) <= candidate) AND prime DO
                        IF candidate MOD divisor = 0 THEN
                            prime := false
                        ELSE
                            divisor := divisor + 2
                END;
            isPrime := prime
    END;
```

Smalltalk

isPrime
```
    | candidate divisor |
    candidate ← self.
    candidate <= 0 ifTrue: [↑false].
    (candidate >= 1 & (candidate <= 3)) ifTrue: [↑true].
    (candidate \\ 2) = 0 ifTrue: [↑false].
    divisor ← 3.
    [divisor * divisor <= candidate] whileTrue: [
        (candidate \\ divisor) = 0
            ifTrue: [↑false]
            ifFalse: [divisor ← divisor + 2]].
    ↑true
```

Several explanatory comments are required to understand the Smalltalk code. But first note that the Smalltalk code is more concise than the Pascal code — primarily because of Pascal's inability to terminate evaluation of a function before the end. In Smalltalk, an expression preceded by an up arrow (↑) is termed a **return expression**. A **return expression** indicates that the result of evaluating the expression following the up arrow is the result to be returned and evaluation of the code is to terminate.

Two unfamiliar binary selectors are introduced: & and \\. Selector & denotes the **and** operation — its result is true if both the receiver and argument are true. Selector \\ defined on integers returns the integer remainder when the receiver is divided by the argument.

As in Pascal, variables must be declared before they can be used. But as explained earlier, variables are untyped — hence no type declaration is necessary. The form

| candidate divisor |

declares **candidate** and **divisor** to be **temporary variables.** These variables exist only while the code fragment is being evaluated. All temporary variables are initially bound to the special object **nil**.

In Smalltalk, the receiver of the **isPrime** message is called **self**. Explicitly assigning **self** to a local variable, as we did via assignment **candidate** ← **self**, is actually superfluous because **self** can be referenced anywhere in the method. However, it serves to make the Pascal and Smalltalk versions easier to compare.

2.4.5 User-Defined Control Structures

No analog of the Pascal **repeat ... until** or **case** statements is provided in the Smalltalk system. However, since control structures are implemented by sending messages to objects, it is possible for the programmer to add new control structures to the system. We will show examples of how this may be done in later chapters. To whet your appetite, we will introduce a few examples of advanced control structures that may be created in Smalltalk. However, we will not yet discuss the details of their implementation.

Very often we want to apply a function to each element of a data structure such as an array, a list, or a tree. For example, it is traditional to sum the elements of an array by extracting successive elements and adding them to a running sum. Alternatively, we might want to print out the values stored in a binary tree by traversing the nodes of the tree in some specified order such as post-order.

Each of these tasks require us to successively generate elements from a data type and apply a function to each generated element. Such control forms are often called **generators**. Lisp programmers will recognize them as **mapping functions**. The **do: aBlock** message, when sent to an array receiver, successively supplies the objects in the array as the argument to the single argument block provided after keyword **do:**. For example, the code

```
sum ← 0.
table do: [:element | sum ← sum + element]
```

sums the elements in array **table**. As each object from the array is generated, it is bound to the block argument **element** and the message expression **sum ← sum + element** is evaluated.

Many other useful variations of this form are possible. We will give just one further example. Rather than simply applying a function to each object of an array, we often want to select only those objects that satisfy some constraint. Perhaps we want to collect into a new array only the nonzero elements of an existing array. This requires us to generate each element from the original array, test whether the element is zero or not, and, if it is nonzero, add it to the new array. The expression

```
#(0 3 0 4 2 0 0) select: [:element | element ~= 0]
```

would perform this task and return the array **#(3 4 2)** as the result; i.e., it collects the nonzero elements into an object of the same class as the receiver. A final example is

```
#(1 2 3 4 5) collect: [:element | element squared]
```

which returns **#(1 4 9 16 25)**.

2.5 CLASSES

The **class** is the fundamental abstraction mechanism in Smalltalk. It groups together objects with similar characteristics. Classes allow the programmer to abstract out the common attributes and behaviors of a set of objects. A **class** describes the common protocol followed by each object in the set; individual objects following that description are termed **instances**. One class description serves to describe all instances of that class, and every object in the Smalltalk system is an instance of some class.

Class	A description of a set of objects with similar characteristics and attributes.
Instance	An individual object described by a particular class.

In previous sections, we have been exposed to some of the basic Smalltalk system classes: integers, characters, strings, booleans, blocks, arrays, and so on. We have seen examples of instances of each of these classes: **3** is an instance of class **Integer**, **'hello'** is an instance of class **String**, [x ← **4 factorial**] is an instance of class **Block**. We have also examined some of the protocol that instances of these classes follow. For example, the class **Integer** supports the following protocol: **factorial, +, -, *, /, to:do:, to:by:do:, gcd:**, and so on. The class **Array** supports the protocol **at:** and **at:put:**. In later chapters, we will examine the complete protocol supported by each of these classes.

Up to this point, we have seen how messages can be sent to instances of predefined classes. The Smalltalk environment provides an enormously rich set of such classes, but the essence of programming in Smalltalk is identifying, creating, and manipulating new classes of objects. To illustrate the description of classes and the creation of instances, we will define a new class **Complex** to perform calculations in complex arithmetic. Note: Class names in Smalltalk must begin with an uppercase letter.

2.5.1 Designing a New Class

The first step in designing a new class is to develop a specification for the class; i.e., to define the message protocol or **outside view** of the new class. The specification should provide all the information required by users of the class but *only* that information. No information superfluous to the needs of users should be provided. The specification of the class should be completed *before* any implementation issues are considered. Developing the specification consists of the following three steps:

1. Listing the names of the operations required.
2. Fleshing out the operations by describing the parameters in detail.
3. Specifying the semantics of each operation informally.

We will assume, for brevity's sake, that we only wish to create, add, and multiply complex numbers and also access and modify their real and imaginary parts.

2.5.2 Class Protocol versus Instance Protocol

The message protocol for a class is described in two parts: the **class protocol** and the **instance protocol**.

Class Protocol   A description of the protocol understood by a class.

Instance Protocol   A description of the protocol understood by instances of a class.

The **class protocol** describes messages that are sent to the class rather than to the instances. Typically, the class protocol contains protocol for creating and initializing new instances of a class. Classes can be thought of as factories for creating instances. For example, it is the responsibility of class **Complex** to create new instances of the class. The expression

Complex newWithReal: 1.0 andImaginary: 3.5

sends the message **newWithReal:** 1.0 **andImaginary:** 3.5 to the class **Complex**. The intent is to return a new instance of class **Complex** with real and imaginary components initialized to 1.0 and 3.5 respectively. For class **Complex**, the class protocol might be specified as follows:

instance creation

newWithReal: realPart **andImaginary:** imaginaryPart
>   Returns an instance of class **Complex** with real part **realPart** and imaginary part **imaginaryPart**.

Method categories are used in Smalltalk to group together methods that provide similar functionality. For example, the class method **newWithReal:andImaginary:** would be placed in a category with the name *instance creation*. Category names have no semantic significance — they are used externally for documentation purposes. Internally, category names are used by the programming environment to group related methods.

The **instance protocol** is the message protocol supported by instances of the class; i.e., messages that may be sent to any instance of the class. For example, the message protocol for adding two complex numbers is part of the instance protocol. In the expression

complex1 + complex2

the receiver of the message + **complex2** is the instance **complex1**. A subset of the instance protocol for the class **Complex** might be the following:

accessing

realPart
>   Returns the real component of the receiver.

imaginaryPart
>   Returns the imaginary component of the receiver.

realPart: realValue

Sets the real component of the receiver to **realValue**. Returns the modified receiver.

imaginaryPart: imaginaryValue

Sets the imaginary component of the receiver to **imaginaryValue**. Returns the modified receiver.

arithmetic

+ aComplex

Returns a complex number equal to the sum of the receiver and the argument **aComplex**.

* aComplex

Returns a complex number equal to the product of the receiver and the argument **aComplex**.

If the instance and class protocols for **Complex** are sufficiently complete, we should be able to write code that manipulates complex numbers, despite the fact that we have yet to consider how to represent complex numbers or how to implement any of the operations. For example, the following message expressions would create two complex numbers and then compute two more, one equal to the sum of the originals and the other equal to their product. It is a good practice to try "programming" with a new class as soon as its protocol has been specified. More often than not, this process reveals deficiencies in the protocol. Clearly, it is better to discover such problems at the specification stage rather than after the class has been implemented.

```
| complex1 complex2 complexSum complexProduct |
complex1 ← Complex newWithReal: 2.5 andImaginary: 3.1.
complex2 ← Complex newWithReal: -1.0 andImaginary: 0.5.
complexSum ← complex1 + complex2.
complexProduct ← complex1 * complex2
```

2.5.3 Implementing a Class Description

The **inside view** of a Smalltalk class description, the implementation viewpoint, can be made more concrete by performing the following two steps:

1. Deciding on a suitable representation for instances of the class.
2. Selecting and implementing efficient algorithms for the methods or operations.

When describing the representation, we must distinguish between **instance variables** and **class variables**. **Instance variables** are variables denoting the private data or state of an individual instance of a class. **Class variables**, on the other hand, are variables shared by all the instances of a class.

Suppose we have two instances of class **Complex**, referenced by variables **complex1** and **complex2**. What distinguishes them from one another? They both follow the same instance message protocol and thus can share a single copy of the method associated with each message. Instance methods, therefore, can be stored in the class description. However, **complex1** and **complex2** must have their own private data — in particular, their individual real and imaginary parts. We speak of the real and imaginary parts as **instance variables** of the class **Complex**. That is, each instance of a class will have its own **instance variables**. For example, if we send the message **realPart** to both **complex1** and **complex2** as in

complex1 **realPart**
complex2 **realPart**

we expect to obtain possibly different results because the method implementing the **realPart** message will extract independent values for the respective real components of **complex1** and **complex2**.

Some variables can be shared by all the instances of a specific class. Such variables are called **class variables**. For example, **Pi** is a class variable representing the mathematical quantity π in class **Float**. Similarly, class **Date** contains class variables such as **WeekDayNames** — an array of symbols representing the days of the week (**Monday**, **Tuesday**, ...), **MonthNames** — an array representing the months of the year (**January**, **February**, ...), and **DaysInMonth** — an array containing the number of days in each month (**31, 28, 31,** ...).

2.5.4 Describing a Class

Smalltalk class descriptions consist of the following seven components:

class name	A name that can be used to reference the class.
superclass name	The name of the superclass (the role of superclasses will be discussed later in this chapter).
class variables	Variables shared by all instances of the class.
instance variables	Variables found in all instances of the class.
pool dictionaries	The names of lists of shared variables that are to be accessible to the class and its instances (described in more detail later). Unlike class variables, the pools can be referenced by other unrelated classes.
class methods	Operations that are understood by the class.
instance methods	Operations that are understood by instances of the class.

Returning to our example, the class name is **Complex**, the superclass is class **Object**, and there are no class variables or pool dictionaries. In general, the choice of superclass is often critical to the implementation of a class, since it specifies what representation and methods may be inherited automatically from other classes. For the moment, we will ignore this issue and simply specify that the superclass of **Complex** is class **Object**. All Smalltalk classes, except **Object** itself, are ultimately subclasses of class **Object**.

Complex numbers can be represented in at least two ways — two independent floating point numbers or an array of two such numbers. As long as the choice does not impact the performance of the class, it doesn't matter which representation we choose — the external view presented to users of the class **Complex** is independent of the choice of representation.

We will choose two numbers to represent the real and imaginary parts respectively. Hence, each complex number has two instance variables, **realPart** and **imaginaryPart**.

The full description of class **Complex** is shown in Fig. 2.5. Programming in Smalltalk is carried out within an interactive program development environment. It is not normal, therefore, to add new classes to the system by compiling a file containing the complete class description.[4] New classes are added to the Smalltalk system incrementally using a tool known as a Browser. The class definition is first entered and compiled into the system followed by the method definitions. Each method is compiled incrementally into the existing system and can immediately be tested. The system provides a template to guide the addition of new classes and methods. This process will be described in detail in succeeding chapters. For the time being, we will present the entire listing of the class definition.

Class Complex

class name	Complex
superclass name	Object
instance variable names	realPart imaginaryPart

class methods

instance creation

```
newWithReal: realValue andImaginary: imaginaryValue
    "Returns an initialized instance of class Complex ."
    | aComplex |
    aComplex ← Complex new.
    aComplex realPart: realValue; imaginaryPart: imaginaryValue.
    ↑aComplex
```

examples

```
example
    | complex1 complex2 |
    complex1 ← Complex newWithReal: 2.5 andImaginary: 3.1.
    complex2 ← Complex newWithReal: -1.0 andImaginary: 0.5.
    ↑complex1 * complex2.

    "Complex example"
```

instance methods

accessing

```
realPart
    "Returns the real component of the receiver."
    ↑realPart
```

```
imaginaryPart
    "Returns the imaginary component of the receiver."
    ↑imaginaryPart
```

---

[4]This is often done, however, to add externally created classes to the system; for example, for porting code across machines — this operation is referred to as "filing in" a class definition.

realPart: realValue
>"Modifies the real component of the receiver to realValue."
>realPart ← realValue

imaginaryPart: imaginaryValue
>"Modifies the imaginary component of the receiver to imaginaryValue."
>imaginaryPart ← imaginaryValue

arithmetic

+ aComplex
>"Returns an instance of class Complex equal to the sum of the receiver and the argument aComplex."
>| realPartSum imaginaryPartSum |
>realPartSum ← realPart + aComplex **realPart**.
>imaginaryPartSum ← imaginaryPart + aComplex **imaginaryPart**.
>↑Complex **newWithReal**: realPartSum **andImaginary**: imaginaryPartSum

* aComplex
>"Returns an instance of class Complex equal to the product of the receiver and the argument aComplex."
>| realPartProduct imaginaryPartProduct |
>realPartProduct ← (realPart * aComplex **realPart**) -
>   (imaginaryPart * aComplex **imaginaryPart**).
>imaginaryPartProduct ← (realPart * aComplex **imaginaryPart**) +
>   (imaginaryPart * aComplex **realPart**).
>↑Complex **newWithReal**: realPartProduct **andImaginary**: imaginaryPartProduct

Figure 2.5 Class Complex.

2.5.5 Describing Methods

Whenever a message is sent in Smalltalk, a method with a message pattern matching the message is searched for in the class of the receiver. If such a method is found, it is evaluated. Otherwise, the search continues in the superclass. Failure to find a matching method results in an error message. All methods in Smalltalk have the following form:

message pattern
>"A comment stating the purpose of the method"
>| temporary variables |
>method body

The message pattern consists of the message selector, together with names for any arguments required. It is common practice to include a comment describing the purpose of the method immediately following the message pattern. Comments in Smalltalk are delimited by double quotes ("). Comments may also be included within the body of the method. Temporary variables may be declared for use during the evaluation of the method. They are declared by placing their names between vertical bars (|) following the method comment. The body of the method is a sequence of expressions separated by periods. By convention, the message pattern is typed at the left margin while all other lines are indented by at least one tab to increase the clarity of the code. We will boldface all message selectors to increase the readability of the code, but note that this is our convention — message selectors are not boldfaced within the Smalltalk system itself.

Every method must return an object as a result. The default result is the receiver of the message. Alternatively, a return expression (an expression preceded by up arrow symbol ↑) can be used to return a specific result. Evaluating a return expression terminates the evaluation of the method.

Consider the instance method for addition: **+ aComplex**:

```
+ aComplex
    "Returns an instance of class Complex equal to the sum of the receiver and the
    argument aComplex."
    | realPartSum imaginaryPartSum |
    realPartSum ← realPart + aComplex realPart.
    imaginaryPartSum ← imaginaryPart + aComplex imaginaryPart.
    ↑Complex newWithReal: realPartSum andImaginary: imaginaryPartSum
```

This method will be invoked whenever an expression of the following form is evaluated.

```
complexSum ← complex1 + complex2.
```

This method has one argument, a complex number **aComplex**, and two temporary variables, **realPartSum** and **imaginaryPartSum**. The method returns a complex number equal to the sum of the receiver and the argument. The first two expressions compute the real and imaginary components of the sum. The final expression sends the message **newWithReal:andImaginary**: to the class **Complex** to create the required instance representing the sum. Note that in the expression

```
realPartSum ← realPart + aComplex realPart
```

the first occurrence of **realPart** refers to the instance variable **realPart** of the receiver — **complex1** in our example. A method has direct access to the instance variables of the receiver but not to those of any other instance. To retrieve the real component of **complex2**, we must send a **realPart** message to the argument **aComplex**.

2.5.6 Variables and Scope

As with traditional languages, it is important to understand what variables may be referenced within a method and the lifetime of these variables; i.e., what scoping mechanisms the language provides for controlling access to variables, and how and when space is allocated and deallocated. Smalltalk provides two basic types of variables: **private variables** and **shared variables**. **Private variables** are accessible only to a single object, while **shared variables** may be shared by several objects. Private variables begin with a lowercase letter, while shared variables begin with an uppercase letter.

Private Variables

Private variables include both **instance variables** and **temporary variables** (see Fig. 2.6). The **instance variables** of an object are the parts or components of the object — they are directly accessible only by that object. Instance variables come in two varieties: **named instance variables**, referenced by name, and **indexed instance variables**, referenced by an integer index.

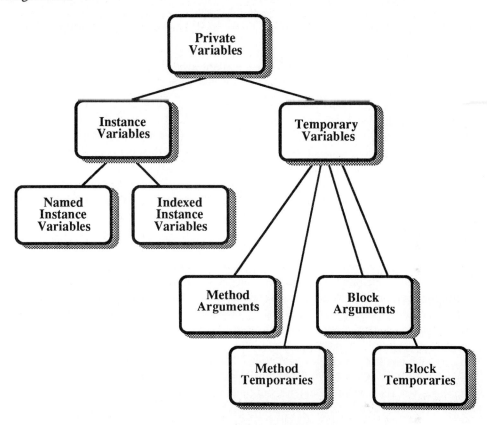

Figure 2.6 Private variables.

The **named instance variables** of the receiver of a message may be referenced in any instance method of the class of the receiver or its subclasses. Since it is impossible to directly refer to the named instance variables of a object other than "self", access to the named instance variables of other objects must be obtained by sending messages to the appropriate object. It is a common mistake to attempt to refer to instance variables within a class method — only instances have access to instance variables.[5]

Indexed instance variables are unnamed instance variables of the instances of a class. They can only be accessed by sending a message to the instance with an index specifying which (indexed) instance variable is desired. For example, the system classes **Array** and **String** have indexed instance variables. Each instance of a class with indexable instance variables can have a different number of instance variables. The number is specified when the

---

[5]Actually, classes can have instance variables too but these instance variables are local to the class and inaccessible from the instances. This is a little known feature of Smalltalk that is rarely (if ever) used.

object is created by sending a **new: size** message to the class. Individual instance variables can be referenced using **at:** and **at:put:** messages. Consider the following examples:

table ← Array **new:** 20	Returns an instance of class Array of size 20; i.e., an array with 20 indexable instance variables.
table **at:** 3 **put:** 'abcde'	The third instance variable of **table** is to reference the string object **'abcde'**.
(table **at:** 3) **at:** 2	The expression **table at: 3** returns the object **'abcde'**. This object is a string that itself has indexed instance variables — it receives the message **at: 2** and the character **$b** is returned.

Classes that have indexed instance variables may also have named instance variables. For example, class **Set** has a **size** instance variable to refer to the number of objects in a set in addition to indexed instance variables that refer to the members of the set. Most system and user classes have only named instance variables.

Temporary variables include **method arguments, method temporaries, block arguments**, and **block temporaries** (see Fig. 2.7). Method temporaries must be explicitly declared below the message pattern; method arguments and block arguments are implicitly declared — the context indicates that they are variables; block temporaries must be explicitly declared after the block arguments (they are not permitted prior to version 2.4). The scope of **method arguments** and **method temporaries** is limited to the method in which they are defined. The scope of **block arguments** depends on the version of the system being used. Prior to version 2.4, block arguments were unrestricted and accessible from outside the block in the containing method; e.g., distinct blocks with the same block argument name were actually referencing the same block argument and it could actually be explicitly declared as a method temporary. In version 2.4 and later, block arguments (and block temporaries) are local to the block in which they are defined. Nested blocks can refer to outer block arguments and temporaries only if they are not locally redefined. Method and block temporaries can be changed via assignment statements but method and block arguments may not be assigned into. Additional details are provided in chapter 6.

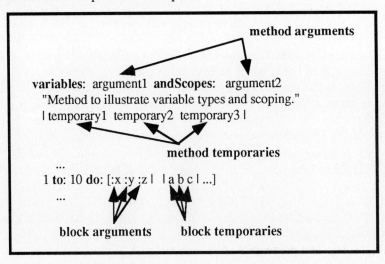

Figure 2.7 Variable types in method definitions.

Shared Variables

Shared variables include **global variables**, **class variables** and **pool variables** (see Fig. 2.8). They differ in the degree of sharing they each support.

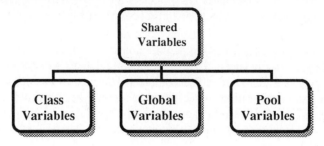

Figure 2.8 Shared variables.

Global variables	Shared by all objects.
Class variables	Shared by all instances of a class. They may be referenced within any class or instance method of the class (or its subclasses — see the next section).
Pool variables	Shared by a defined subset of the classes in the system. **Pool variables** are stored in dictionaries known as **pool dictionaries**. The variables in a pool dictionary can be made accessible to any class by declaring the name of the pool dictionary in the pool dictionary list of the class definition.

Class variables are most often used to allow constants to be accessed by all instances of a class (and its subclasses). For example, class **Float** has a class variable **Pi**, whose value is the mathematical constant π, and the class **Date** has array constants **MonthNames** and **WeekDayNames** that contain the names of the months of the year and the days of the week respectively.

Global variables are stored in a special instance of class **Dictionary** named **Smalltalk**. Dictionaries are collections of associations between names (or keys) and values. Several global variables are predefined in Smalltalk. For example, **Display** is a special instance of the graphical class **Form** that refers to the current display screen, and **Transcript** is a special instance of the class **TextCollector** that allows text to be displayed in a screen window known as the System Transcript window.

To add new variables to the global dictionary **Smalltalk**, an **at:put:** expression is used to enter the variable name as a key in the dictionary and to associate an initial value with the name.

Smalltalk **at:** #ANewGlobal **put:** nil   Adds the name **ANewGlobal** and its initial value **nil** to the global variable dictionary **Smalltalk**.

Note that the global variable must be specified as a symbol rather than a string to ensure that only one global can exist with that name; i.e., the prefix # is significant.

Pools are collections of variables whose scope is a defined subset of the classes in the system. **Pool variables** are stored in **pool dictionaries** — collections of name/value associations. **Smalltalk**, the dictionary of global variables, is a pool dictionary that is globally accessible. The class variables of a class are also stored in a pool dictionary that is accessible to the class, its subclasses, and instances of the same.

Pool dictionaries can be defined and made accessible to particular classes by declaring the name of the pool dictionary in the pool dictionary list of a class description. This allows the sharing of variables between classes that are not related via class/subclass relationships. Sharing of variables is more normally accomplished through an inheritance mechanism based on class/subclass relationships — see the next section. For example, the pool dictionary **TextConstants** includes variable names such as **Tab**, **Cr**, ..., allowing unprintable ASCII characters to be referenced by name. This dictionary is shared by many of the classes that manipulate characters and text.

Programmers may create new pool dictionaries by declaring the name of the pool dictionary as a global variable and associating a dictionary with the global. Variables may then be added to the dictionary using **at:put:**. More specifically, the steps are the following:

Smalltalk **at**: #ANewPoolDictionary **put**: Dictionary **new**
> Creates a new global variable named ANewPoolDictionary that references an empty dictionary.

ANewPoolDictionary **at**: #ANewPoolVariable **put**: nil
> Creates and adds a new pool variable **ANewPoolVariable** to the pool dictionary **ANewPoolDictionary**.

Smalltalk adopts the following stylistic conventions with respect to variable names. Shared variables are always capitalized — private variables are not. Multi-word private variables are written with each word except the first capitalized, with no spaces between the words. Recall that the class name for complex numbers was written **Complex**, while the selector for creating instances of class Complex was **newWithReal:andImaginary:**. Selectors and keywords within selectors start in lowercase.

2.5.7 The Pseudo-Variable self

Suppose we added the **isPrime** method developed earlier in the chapter to the integer instance protocol. The actual mechanics for doing this will be discussed in the section dealing with the Smalltalk browser. Integers could then be tested using messages of the form

> 7 **isPrime**
> 256 **isPrime**

To allow reference to the particular receiver in use when a method is evaluated, Smalltalk provides the pseudo-variable **self**. As with all pseudo-variables, **self** cannot be changed by assignment within a method and is bound to the receiver by the system when evaluation of the method commences. If the **isPrime** instance method had been invoked with an expression such as **7 isPrime**, then **self** would refer to the instance 7.

isPrime
```
    "Tests whether the receiver is a prime or not."
    | divisor |
    self <= 0 ifTrue: [↑false].
    (self >= 1 & self <= 3) ifTrue: [↑true].
    (self \\ 2) = 0 ifTrue: [↑false].
    divisor ← 3.
    [divisor * divisor <= self] whileTrue: [
        (self \\ divisor) = 0
                ifTrue: [↑false]
                ifFalse: [divisor ← divisor + 2]].
    ↑true
```

2.5.8 Methods Can Be Recursive

The pseudo-variable **self** provides us with the means to refer to the receiver of a message within a method. This implies that we can send further messages to the receiver (or more commonly a new receiver based on the original) from within the method and consequently invoke the same method recursively.

The following example illustrates a recursive definition of the **factorial** method defined on integers.

factorial
```
    "Returns the factorial of the receiver."
    self = 0
        ifTrue: [↑1]
        ifFalse: [↑self * (self - 1) factorial]
```

Evaluation of the expression 4 **factorial** is executed by sending the multiply message to self, in this case 4, with the result of evaluating the expression (self - 1) **factorial**, in this case the result of evaluating the expression 3 **factorial**. Recursion in object-oriented systems commonly follows the pattern of sending the same message to successive receivers, each of which is closer to some simple receiver for which the result of sending the message is known. In the preceding example, the receivers of the factorial message are 4, 3, 2, 1, and 0. The result of sending the factorial message to 0 is known to be 1.

2.6 INHERITANCE

When a class A is defined as a subclass of another class B, it is convenient if the subclass B can use the methods defined in A. The mechanism that permits the methods in A to be used by B is known as inheritance. **Inheritance** permits representation and methods to be shared by distinct but related classes of objects. It was developed because designers typically define new classes by saying "The new class is just like this existing class except ...." In Smalltalk, a new class is described by stating how it is different from some existing class. This gives rise to a style of programming known as **differential programming** or inheritance programming. It dramatically reduces the amount of code required in large systems, is a powerful organizational tool, and facilitates program modification, extension, and maintenance.

Inheritance in Smalltalk is based on the notion of **subclassing**; i.e., defining one class as a subclass of another. The classes in the Smalltalk system are arranged in a single inheritance hierarchy with the most general class **Object** at the top. A class may have any number of subclasses, but each class has a single **superclass**. The ability to inherit from only a single superclass is restrictive, but since the Smalltalk class library is implemented in this manner, we will ignore the possibility of multiple superclasses or **multiple inheritance** for the the moment.[6]

Fig. 2.9 illustrates a small subset of the hierarchy under class **Object** and, in particular, describes the subclassing relationships between the numeric classes in Smalltalk. In Smalltalk terminology, **Number** is the superclass of classes **Float, Integer**, and **Fraction**. These classes are themselves subclasses of class **Number**. Classes **Float, Integer**, and **Fraction** can be thought of as specializations of class **Number**, while classes **LargeNegativeInteger, LargePositiveInteger**, and **SmallInteger** can be thought of as specializations of **Integer**. Subclasses such as **Float, Integer**, and **Fraction** follow the protocol for their superclass **Number** but also introduce protocol relevant only to themselves. For example, integers respond to the message **factorial** while floats and fractions do not.

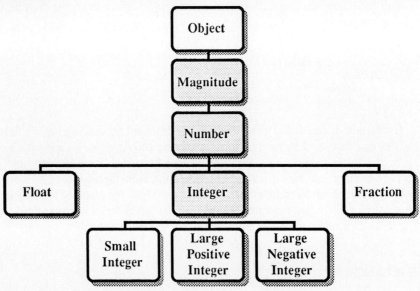

Figure 2.9 Numeric class hierarchy.

A class that is a subclass of another automatically inherits or shares the representation and protocol of that class. In addition, the subclass may also

- support additional capability by adding new methods,
- augment the representation by adding additional class and instance variables, and
- override methods that would otherwise be inherited by providing its own version.

---

[6]Multiple inheritance is not used within the standard Smalltalk system release. Non-primitive support for the concept is provided in Smalltalk-80 version 2 releases but not in version 1.

Note that a subclass automatically inherits the representation of its superclass. Unlike method inheritance, this cannot be overridden.

2.6.1 Method Inheritance

To understand how methods are inherited, we need to examine the method lookup mechanism. When a message is sent, the methods in the class of the receiver are first searched to find a method that has a message pattern matching the selector of the message. If the search is successful, that method is evaluated. If no match is found, the search is continued in the superclass of the receiver, and if no match is found at that point, the search again continues up the inheritance or superclass chain. The first method found in the inheritance chain is always used. If no matching method exists, the search will ultimately reach class **Object** (the root of the tree), and if no method is found there, an appropriate error message will be generated.

2.6.2 An Example: Constrained Pens

To illustrate subclassing and inheritance, we will implement a specialization of the system class **Pen** called **ConstrainedPen**. A subset of the protocol for class **Pen** is shown in Fig. 2.10.

Class Pen

class name	Pen
superclass	BitBlt
instance variables	frame location direction penDown
class variables	SinArray
comment	My instances can scribble on the screen, drawing and printing at any angle. Since I am a BitBlt, scribbling can be done with different source forms.

class methods

instance creation

new
    Return an initialized instance of class Pen.

class initialization

initialize
    Initialize the class Pen.

instance methods

initialization

defaultNib: widthInteger
    Nib is the tip of a pen. This is an easy way to set up a default pen where the source form is set to a black square whose sides are widthInteger long.

accessing

direction
>   Answer the receiver's current direction; 0 is towards the top of the screen.

frame
>   Answer the rectangle in which the receiver can draw.

frame: aRectangle
>   Set the rectangle in which the receiver can draw.

location
>   Answer where the receiver is currently located.

moving

down
>   Set the state of the receiver's pen to down (drawing).

go: distance
>   Move the pen in its current direction a number of bits equal to the argument, distance. If the pen is down, a line will be drawn using the receiver's source form as the shape of the drawing brush. Otherwise, nothing is drawn.

goto: aPoint
>   Move the receiver to position aPoint. If the pen is down, a line will be drawn from the current position to the new one using the receiver's source form as the shape of the drawing brush. The receiver's set direction does not change.

home
>   Place the receiver at the center of its frame.

north
>   Set the receiver's direction to facing the top of the display screen.

place: aPoint
>   Set the receiver at position aPoint. No lines are drawn.

turn: degrees
>   Change the direction of the receiver by an amount equal to the argument, degrees.

up
>   Set the state of the receiver's pen to up as opposed to down (no drawing); i.e., off the drawing frame. This is different from north which causes the pen to point upward.

Figure 2.10 Class Pen.

Pens are the Smalltalk equivalent of turtles in Logo. A pen is an object that can draw within a specified rectangular frame (or window) on the Smalltalk display. Class **Pen** includes protocol to change the position of the pen on the screen, change the direction (in degrees) it is facing, and set the state of the pen. If the pen is moved when the state of the pen is down (as opposed to up), the pen draws on the display. The default drawing nib of the pen is a single pixel. Nibs of other shapes, patterns, and sizes can be specified.

To illustrate programming with pens, consider the following example method. Note that the Smalltalk screen coordinate system has its origin at the top left corner. The x-axis increases to the right of the screen while the y-axis increases down the screen.

example
"Draw an equilateral triangle with sides of length 200."
| crayon |
"Creates a new instance of class Pen with a black nib that is 2 pixels wide and 2 pixels high. The initial direction of the pen is north, the drawing frame is the entire display screen, the initial location of the pen is at the center of the screen, and the state of the pen is down."
crayon ← Pen **new defaultNib**: 2. "get a pen with a medium size nib"
crayon **up**. "stop drawing"
crayon **goto**: 350@250. "move to start point"
crayon **down**. "start drawing"
"Draw an equilateral triangle with sides 200 units long."
3 **timesRepeat**: [crayon **go**: 200; **turn**: 120]

The specialized class **ConstrainedPen** is to be restricted so that instances can only move, and hence draw, in the horizontal and vertical directions. This new class of object might be useful if we were drawing flowcharts or constructing diagrams. To share code that already exists in class **Pen**, class **ConstrainedPen** should be a subclass of **Pen**.

ConstrainedPen automatically inherits the representation of all classes in the inheritance chain (see Fig. 2.11). The inheritance chain consists of classes **Pen**, **BitBlt**, and **Object**. The instance variables for **Pen** are **frame**, a rectangular area into which the pen is constrained to draw; **location**, a point representing the current position of the pen; **direction**, a float representing the direction the pen is pointing; and **penDown**, a boolean describing the state of the pen. In addition, class variable **SinArray**, a table of sin values, is also inherited by **ConstrainedPen**. **Pen** is a subclass of class **BitBlt** — an extremely general class providing fundamental operations for displaying and modifying text and graphics. **Pen** is a subclass of **BitBlt**, so that it can inherit the operations for drawing lines on the display with different *nib styles* and also the operations to perform automatic clipping to the frame of the pen. The instance variables for class **BitBlt** will be inherited by class **ConstrainedPen**, but we will not need to access them directly. We will inherit operations that manipulate them from class **Pen**. No additional instance variables are required for class **ConstrainedPen**.

It is instructive to consider which methods can be inherited without modification by **ConstrainedPen**. Since instances of class **Pen** have the same representation as instances of **ConstrainedPen**, we can inherit the class method **new** for creating instances. Similarly, the instance methods that access or modify the state of a pen; i.e., **direction, frame, frame: aRectangle, location, up, down, home, north**, and **defaultNib: widthInteger** can also be inherited.

The methods involving movement of the pen need more careful consideration. There are three possible options for each method.

- Inherit the method from a superclass.
- Implement a modified form of the method.
- The method is not appropriate for the class — make it an error to use it.

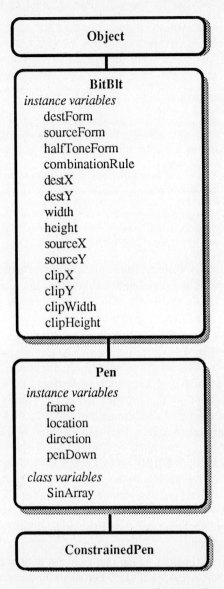

Figure 2.11 Representation inheritance for class ConstrainedPen.

The instance methods **goto: aPoint** and **place: aPoint** in class **Pen** allow movement to random points. The first is clearly inappropriate for the class **ConstrainedPen** because it can result in something being drawn. The second, however, is legitimate because no drawing results. Therefore, we must ensure that method **goto:** is not inherited. This can be achieved by taking advantage of the error handling protocol supported by class **Object**. We re-implement the method in class **ConstrainedPen** (see Fig. 2.12) to generate an error message; i.e., the body of the method becomes

self shouldNotImplement

This message will eventually, through the inheritance chain, be found in class **Object**. The result will be a standard error report that "although this message is appropriate for the superclass of the receiver, it is not appropriate for the class of the receiver."

Now, consider method **turn: degrees** for rotating the pen direction. It must be modified to constrain drawing in the vertical or horizontal directions. Since the pen can only move in these two directions, we could augment the instance protocol of **ConstrainedPen** with methods **south**, **west**, and **east** to allow the pen direction to be changed. Method **north** can be inherited. We might also want to introduce special variations of **turn:** such as **turnLeft** and **turnRight**. Indeed, it might be more appropriate to add these to **Pen** rather than to **ConstrainedPen** since it is a useful generalization, but we won't pursue that here. What to do with the method **turn:** is still unresolved. We cannot allow instances of **ConstrainedPen** to inherit the **turn:** method from class **Pen**. We could override the inheritance mechanism using **self shouldNotImplement**, as described above. Alternatively, we could introduce a modified **turn:** message that constrains its argument to a multiple of 90 degrees. For the sake of illustration, we will choose the latter option. An obvious way of implementing the modified **turn:** method is to truncate the argument **degrees** to a multiple of 90 and invoke the **turn:** method in class **Pen**. However, we need some way of referring to the **turn:** method in the superclass. If we use the expression

self **turn**: degrees

the effect will be to invoke the **turn:** method in **ConstrainedPen** recursively. Smalltalk provides the pseudo-variable **super** to allow references to methods higher up in the inheritance chain.

2.6.3 The Pseudo-Variable super

Pseudo-variable **super** provides access to methods in the superclass chain even if the method has been redefined in the class. Like **self**, **super** refers to the receiver of the method. However, when **super** is used, the search begins in the superclass of the class containing the method definition. Be careful — this is not always the same thing as starting the search in the superclass of the receiver.

The modified **turn:** message for ConstrainedPens making use of **super** is shown below.

```
turn: degrees
    "The direction of the receiver is turned clockwise through an amount equal to the
    argument degrees. The argument is automatically truncated to a multiple of 90
    degrees."
    super turn: (degrees roundTo: 90)
```

Now, consider method **go: distance**. At first sight, we might think that it can be inherited directly from class **Pen** because a pen's direction is constrained to horizontal or vertical movement. However, examination of the method reveals that it invokes the message **goto:**. The **goto:** message will be sent to the receiver of the **go:** message, a **ConstrainedPen**. But this message was previously overridden for constrained pens to make it an error. This example illustrates the fact that problems can arise with the inheritance of a method if the inherited method itself invokes methods that have been overridden in the subclass. To achieve the desired effect, we must re-implement **go:** in ConstrainedPen as a clone of the **go:** in Pen, but with the **self goto:** reference replaced by **super goto:**.

go: distance
> "Move the receiver in its current direction a number of bits equal to the argument, distance. If the pen is down, a line will be drawn using the receiver's source form as the shape of the drawing brush. Otherwise, nothing is drawn."

| angle newDirection |
angle ← direction **degreesToRadians**.
newDirection ← angle **cos** @ angle **sin**.
super **goto:** newDirection * distance + location

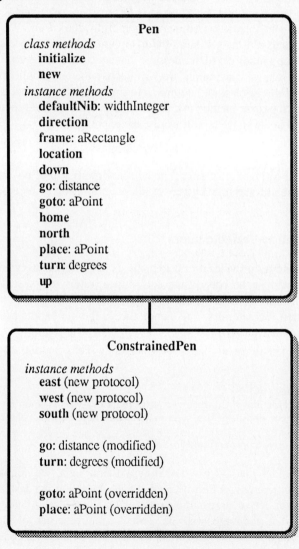

Figure 2.12 Hierarchical inheritance of methods.

Fig. 2.12 summarizes the final method inheritance hierarchy for classes **Pen** and **ConstrainedPen**. Note that other changes are possible. For example, we might wish to introduce a **direction:** method to permit absolute settings of the direction. Methods **east**, **west**, and **south** could then be implemented using this new operation. We might also want to add additional turn operations like **turnLeft**, **turnRight**, and **turnBack**. Method **turnLeft**, for example, could simply consist of the code "self **turn:** -90". Using "self" instead of "super" would ensure that future changes (if any) to **turn:** in **ConstrainedPen** would be reflected in the new methods. Of course, many of these operations also make sense for standard pens. This suggests that some of the methods in **ConstrainedPen** ought to be migrated up into class **Pen**. When the classes affected are both user defined, this is a natural improvement to make. When system classes are affected, more deliberation is needed. Unless the change is fundamental and important, it is generally safer to leave library classes alone since they might change from release to release. The full definition of class **ConstrainedPen** is shown in Fig. 2.13.

Class ConstrainedPen

class name	ConstrainedPen
superclass	Pen

class methods

examples

example
"Illustrates the use of constrained pens."
| quill |
quill ← ConstrainedPen **new.**
quill **home; place:** 300@300; **down.**
4 **timesRepeat:** [quill **go:** 100; **turnLeft**]

"ConstrainedPen **example**"

instance methods

moving

goto: aPoint
"This message is not appropriate for this object."
self **shouldNotImplement**

go: distance
"Move the receiver in its current direction a number of bits equal to the argument, distance. If the pen is down, a line will be drawn using the receiver's source form as the shape of the drawing brush. Otherwise, nothing is drawn."

| angle newDirection |
angle ← direction **degreesToRadians.** newDirection ← angle **cos** @ angle **sin.**
super **goto:** newDirection * distance + location

south
"The direction of the receiver is set to face the bottom of the screen."
direction ← 90

east
"The direction of the receiver is set to face the right of the screen."
direction ← 0

west
"The direction of the receiver is set to face the left of the screen."
direction ← 180

turn: degrees
"The direction of the receiver is turned clockwise through an amount equal to the argument degrees. The argument is constrained to a multiple of 90 degrees by rounding."
super **turn:** (degrees **roundTo:** 90)

turnLeft
"The direction of the receiver is turned to the left 90 degrees."
super **turn:** -90

turnRight
"The direction of the receiver is turned to the right 90 degrees."
super **turn:** 90

Figure 2.13 Class ConstrainedPen.

2.6.4 Abstract Classes

The shaded classes **Magnitude, Number,** and **Integer** (see Fig. 2.9) are termed **abstract classes.**

> **Abstract class**   A class that specifies protocol but is unable to implement it fully because its subclasses may have different representations.

Because an abstract class does not fully implement its protocol, no instances of abstract classes may be created. The role of an abstract class is to specify the protocol common to all of its subclasses, with the subclass providing the implementation where no common implementation can be provided in the abstract class itself.

Class **Magnitude** is an abstract class used to describe objects that can be compared along a linear dimension. The subclasses of **Magnitude** are classes **Character, Date, Number,** and **Time.** The common protocol specified by the class **Magnitude** reflects the fact that all instances of each of the subclasses can be compared with one another using the relational operators. For example, we can ask a number if it is greater than another or we can ask a date if it is less than another, and so on. The instance protocol for magnitudes includes (among others) the operations

```
aMagnitude  <    anotherMagnitude
aMagnitude  <=   anotherMagnitude
aMagnitude  >    anotherMagnitude
aMagnitude  >=   anotherMagnitude
```

Since the representations for instances of the subclasses **Character, Date, Number** and **Time** are clearly different, each subclass provides its own implementation for operations that are dependent on the representation. Operations that reference their representation directly are primitive operations — if the representation were changed, they would require modification. The implementation of primitive operations must be the responsibility of the subclasses.

For messages where it is the responsibility of a subclass to provide the implementation, an abstract class implements the method by generating an error message. The **subclassResponsibility** protocol supported by class **Object** can be used to generate a message indicating that a subclass should have overridden the implementation of this method. This is useful when a new subclass is added and the programmer forgets to implement the entire protocol specified by the abstract superclass. Methods in the abstract class that must be re-implemented by subclasses should have the body

self **subclassResponsibility**

Non-primitive operations can be implemented in terms of other primitive and/or non-primitive operations and therefore can be implemented once in the abstract class. For example, in the case of magnitudes, only the primitive < operation is implemented by the subclasses. Operations such as > and <= are non-primitive because they can be implemented in terms of <. They only need to be implemented once in the abstract class, as shown below.

comparing

< aMagnitude
    "Answer whether the receiver is less than the argument."

    ↑self **subclassResponsibility**

<= aMagnitude
    "Answer whether the receiver is less than or equal to the argument."

    ↑(self > aMagnitude) **not**

> aMagnitude
    "Answer whether the receiver is greater than the argument."

    ↑aMagnitude < self

>= aMagnitude
    "Answer whether the receiver is greater than or equal to the argument."

    ↑(self < aMagnitude) **not**

Abstract classes have an important role to play in Smalltalk and in object-oriented programming. As we have seen, they allow the protocol common to a collection of classes to be identified quickly. By browsing the abstract superclasses, for example, it is easy to determine what operations are common to all types of numbers, to all types of integers, and so on. Another benefit is that they can be used to maximize the sharing of code through inheritance. Consider the "Bricks" video game that was described at the beginning of Chapter 1. An initial class hierarchy for the game is shown in Fig. 2.14.

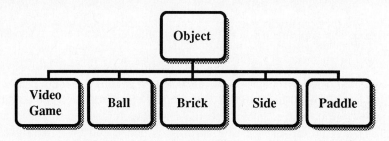

Figure 2.14 Initial video game class hierarchy.

The problem with this class hierarchy is that it is impossible to specify a protocol common to all game elements. A new class hierarchy incorporating two abstract classes is shown in Fig. 2.15. The **VideoGameComponent** abstract class ties together the game parts and allows subclasses to share a common representation and common operations. The **MovingGameComponent** abstract class allows a distinction to be made between dynamic and static game objects and allows the move operations to be shared by both the **Ball** and **Paddle** classes. Container classes for the bricks — **Wall** and for the left, top, and right sides — **Sides**, are also introduced.

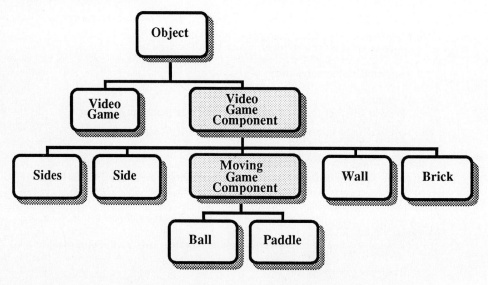

Figure 2.15 Class hierarchy with abstract classes.

2.7 SUMMARY

In this chapter, we have described how the fundamental concepts of object-oriented languages — objects, messages, classes, and inheritance, manifest themselves in Smalltalk. In particular, we have discussed

- the use of literals to describe numbers, symbols, characters, strings, and arrays,
- the use of variables and the assignment operation in Smalltalk,

- the construction of message expressions using unary, keyword, and binary messages,
- the concepts of dynamic binding and overloading,
- storage allocation and garbage collection,
- control structures via message-passing,
- class versus instance protocols,
- named versus indexed instance variables,
- private versus shared variables,
- the pseudo-variables **self** and **super**,
- subclassing,
- representation and method inheritance, and
- the use of abstract classes.

2.8 EXERCISES

Unless you are familiar with the Smalltalk user interface, we suggest that, for the moment, the following exercises be completed as paper exercises only.

1. Translate the following Pascal expressions into Smalltalk (assume all Pascal variables are of type Integer).

   a. units := number **mod** 10
   b. hundreds := number **div** 100
   c. tens := (number **mod** 100) **div** 10
   d. number := (hundreds * 100) + (tens * 10) + units

   The binary selector // is the equivalent of the Pascal **div** operator. Selector \\ is the equivalent of **mod**.

2. Translate the following Pascal fragments into Smalltalk (assume all Pascal variables are of type Integer).

   a. **IF** value > 5 **AND** value < 10
      THEN
          acceptable := true

   b. **IF** value > 5 **AND** value < 10
      THEN
          acceptable := true
      ELSE
          acceptable := false

   c. **FOR** i := 1 **TO** rows **DO**
          FOR j := 1 **TO** columns **DO**
              table [i, j] := i + j

   d. {Compute the smallest power of 2 greater than a specified bound}

      value := 2;
      power := 1;
      WHILE value <= bound **DO**
          BEGIN
              value := value * 2;
              power :=power + 1
      END

3. Add a method **asLetterGrade** to class **Integer** that returns a character representing the letter grade corresponding to an examination mark in the range 0 to 100. Use the following table of mark-letter grade values:

<= 50	F
51-60	D
61-70	C
71-80	B
> 80	A

4. Add a method **isPalindromic** to class **String** to determine whether or not a string is a palindrome. A palindrome reads the same backwards and forwards; e.g., message expression

'madam' isPalindromic should return **true**. (The message expression **string size** returns the size of **string**.)

5. Add a method **fibonacci: n** to class **Integer** that returns the nth number in the Fibonacci series. The Fibonacci series begins with 0 and 1 and each subsequent number in the series is the sum of the previous two numbers. Implement the method both nonrecursively and recursively.

    Implement a new method that returns the nth number in any Fibonacci series. By any fibonacci series, we mean a series that starts with any two arbitrary successive integers; e.g., 23, 24, 47, 71, ...

6. Add a method **asEnglish** to class **Integer** that returns a string representing the English form of the number. For example, the expression **139 asEnglish** returns the string **'one hundred and thirty nine'** as a result. To make the task simpler, you may wish to restrict the integer receiving

the message to values in the range 0 to 999. (The expression **String new: size** creates an instance of class String of the specified size; **aString copyFrom: startIndex to: endIndex** extracts a substring. Choose a reasonable maximum size for the string. The binary selector **,** (comma) is the string concatenation operator. For example, the expression **'abc', 'def'** returns **'abcdef'**).

7. Add methods to class **Pen** described in this chapter to draw geometric designs such as spirals and dragon curves.

8. Complete the definition of class **Complex** given in this chapter. What additional operations are required? Show how they would be implemented.

9. If Smalltalk is consistent with the object metaphor, a class should be an object and hence an instance of some class. Investigate whether or not this is so.

2.9 GLOSSARY

selected terminology

abstract class A class that specifies protocol but is unable to implement it fully because its subclasses may have different representations.

binary messages Messages with one argument. Binary messages selectors are special single characters (<) or double characters (<=).

block An object representing a sequence of Smalltalk expressions.

cascaded messages Multiple messages sent to the same receiver. Indicated syntactically by a semicolon; e.g., aReceiver **message1; message2; againWith: 0**.

class A description of a set of objects with similar characteristics and attributes.

class protocol The messages understood by a class.

class variables Variables shared by a class (and all subclasses) and their instances.

external view The view of an object required by a user (as opposed to an implementor); the object's interface; the object's protocol.

global variables Variables shared by all classes and their instances.

indexed instance variables Instance variables that are referenced by an integer index (unlike named instance variables); components of an indexable object; e.g., anArray referenced via anArray **at: 1**, anArray **at: 1 put: 2**.

information hiding The notion that we should hide as much information as possible (both representation and implementation details) from a user by minimizing the interface presented to the users.

inheritance A mechanism that allows a class of objects to share the methods and representation of another class of objects.

instance An individual object described by a particular class

instance protocol The messages understood by instances of a class.

instance variables Variables found in all instances of a class; components of an object.

internal view The view of an object seen by an implementor; the object's representation and implementation.

keyword messages Messages with one or more arguments. Each argument is preceded by a keyword; e.g., aReceiver **at:** 1 **put:** 20.

message A request sent to an object to carry out some task.

message pattern A method selector together with the names of the arguments required by the selector.

message protocol The messages that objects respond to.

method An operation; the code implementing an object's operation.

named instance variables Instance variables that may be referenced by name (unlike indexed instance variables).

object A component of the Smalltalk system consisting of private data and a set of methods (operations).

pool variables Variables shared by a specified set of classes (and their subclasses) and their instances.

private variables Variables accessible only to a single object. Examples are instance and temporary variables.

programming by extension Programming new applications by extending the existing Smalltalk class library.

pseudo-variable A variable whose value may not be changed. Examples are *self* and *super*.

return expression An expression preceded by an up arrow ($\uparrow$) indicating that the value of the expression is to be returned as the result of a method.

selector The component of a message that uniquely specifies the operation requested; e.g., **at:put:**.

self A predefined pseudo-variable that refers to the receiver of a message.

shared variables Variables accessible to a group of classes and their instances. Examples are class variables, pool variables, and global variables.

subclass A class that inherits methods and representation from an existing class.

super A pseudo-variable that refers to the receiver of a message but additionally provides access to a method defined higher up in the hierarchy. When super is used, method lookup begins in the superclass of the class in which the method containing *super* is defined.

superclass A class from which another class inherits representation and methods.

temporary variable A variable whose lifetime is limited by the task for which it was created. Method arguments, method temporaries, and block arguments are examples of temporary variables.

unary messages Messages with no arguments — only a receiver and a selector.

3

An Introduction to the Smalltalk User Interface

3.1 INTRODUCTION

In the next three chapters, we provide an introduction to the Smalltalk-80 programming environment — an integrated collection of powerful and sophisticated programming tools. These tools subsume many of the roles normally provided by the operating system in more traditional environments. The Orange book[1] by Goldberg, which is over 500 pages long, is solely dedicated to describing the Smalltalk environment. Rather than provide a comprehensive guide to this environment, our aim in these initial chapters is to describe those features that are needed to develop simple Smalltalk applications. In particular, we describe how to build, debug, and edit Smalltalk programs by explaining how to

- enter and exit from the Smalltalk system,
- manipulate Smalltalk menus and windows,
- enter and evaluate fragments of Smalltalk code,
- use browsers to navigate through the Smalltalk class library,
- extend the system with new methods and classes,
- file Smalltalk source files in and out, and
- use notifiers and inspectors to perform simple debugging tasks.

---

[1] A. Goldberg, *Smalltalk-80: The Interactive Programming Environment* (Reading, Mass.: Addison-Wesley, 1984).

3.1.1 Smalltalk Provides an Integrated Programming Environment

Developing programs in Smalltalk is different from the traditional approaches typically used to develop programs in languages such as Pascal or C. There are two major differences: the absence of modes and the interactive, incremental style of application development.

When developing Pascal programs, programmers typically use a set of largely independent tools: an editor for program construction and modification, a compiler for compilation of program modules, a linker for linking component modules together, and possibly, a run-time debugger for debugging. Together, these tools form an environment for developing Pascal programs. Because the tools are independent, program development can be described as **modal**. At any particular time, the system is in a particular mode; e.g., edit mode or compile mode. To change modes, programmers must leave the current tool, return to the operating system level, and invoke the new tool. More advanced systems permit mode changes from within a tool, eliminating the need to exit to the operating system.

On the other hand, developing Smalltalk programs is characterized by a total integration of tools and an absence of modes. Editors, file managers, compilers, debuggers, and print utilities are all included **within** the Smalltalk environment. All tools are available at all times. The Smalltalk programmer carries on a series of activities or conversations with individual tools. These activities can be interleaved. Activities or conversations can be interrupted and resumed at any time without loss of context or information. Switching from one activity or conversation to another is as simple as clicking a mouse button.

The second major difference between Smalltalk and languages such as Pascal and C is that program development is *interactive* and *incremental*. By incremental, we mean that Smalltalk applications are developed by piece-meal additions or changes to the Smalltalk system. The Smalltalk system contains an extensive on-line library of classes. Moreover, the source is written almost entirely in Smalltalk. More important, this source can be viewed and modified by the programmer. When building an application, the programmer automatically inherits the capabilities of this library of reusable code. Programming is by extension — the programmer modifies and/or extends the capabilities of the existing classes and adds new classes that inherit from existing classes. Programming is totally interactive. New or modified source code can be recompiled and tested in a matter of seconds. Sequences of such modifications result in working prototypes and eventually elaborate designs that can be polished and turned into finished applications. This style of program development could be described as programming by iterative enhancement.

3.1.2 Try It Yourself

With access to a Smalltalk system, these chapters can be used as a hands-on tutorial about the Smalltalk environment. The material in each chapter is designed to be completed in a single interactive session. As is the case with learning any new system, you will undoubtedly make mistakes. Don't worry. Any changes you make to your Smalltalk system are **not** permanent. Indeed, we encourage you to experiment freely and to explore the system beyond the introductory view we provide in these chapters. For readers without access to a Smalltalk system, screen dumps are provided at each significant step in the discussion.

3.1.3 Not All Smalltalks Are Exactly Alike

You may notice that your Smalltalk system is different in small ways from the Smalltalk environment described in the Orange and Blue[2] books and in this book. Your menus, for example, may have slightly different entries than those illustrated. Don't worry, the basic functionality described in this chapter will certainly be present in your system. The implementor may have modified or added additional capability to your Smalltalk system.

3.1.4 Not All Computers Are Alike

A Smalltalk implementation requires that the host computer have a keyboard, a black and white bit-mapped display (see Fig. 2.1), and a pointing device. Unfortunately, there are no standard keyboards, displays, or pointing devices. Keyboards differ in the layout of their keys and in the number of function keys available. Display screens have different resolutions and may or may not support color. Mice, joysticks, graphics tablets, and even keyboards can all be used as pointing devices. Even mice come in one-, two-, or three-buttoned varieties.

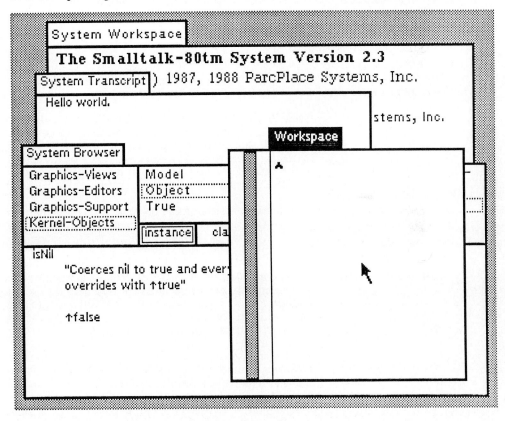

Figure 3.1 Typical Smalltalk display.

---

[2]A. Goldberg and D. Robson, *Smalltalk-80: The Language and Its Implementation* (Reading, Mass.: Addison-Wesley, 1984).

This lack of a standard hardware configuration will not concern us unduly. In this chapter, we are more concerned with the small number of functions and tasks we need to perform than the particular screen resolution or type of pointing device that is available. For example, selecting an object from the screen can be achieved in many ways, but all selections involve two basic activities: pointing at the object we want to select and confirming the selection. In Smalltalk and most other systems, pointing is achieved by moving a graphical cursor on the display screen. In one system, this might be achieved by attaching the movement of the cursor to the movement of a mouse or joystick. In another, the cursor might be controlled using special keyboard function keys to incrementally move the cursor up, down, right, and left. Confirming the selection might be done by depressing a mouse button or, alternatively, a keyboard function key.

Consult the documentation provided with your system to find out how to achieve each of the tasks we describe in this chapter. Most of the chapter is independent of hardware considerations. Since a mouse is by far the most commonly available pointing device on systems supporting Smalltalk, we will describe activities in terms of mouse interactions. Readers who are familiar with mouse-based interactive systems may wish to skip the next section.

3.1.5 Pointing Device Mechanics

Two fundamental interaction sequences, **selection** and **extended selection**, are carried out with the pointing device when interacting with the Smalltalk system.

Selection	Used to indicate a position on the Smalltalk display screen; e.g., to indicate where text, when typed from the keyboard, should be inserted. Two activities are involved in making a selection: (1) moving the cursor on the screen to the desired position, and (2) confirming the position you have selected to the Smalltalk system.
	With a mouse, selection can be achieved by moving it to position the cursor at the desired point, and confirmation can be achieved by single clicking (briefly pressing and releasing) a mouse button.
Extended Selection	A two part selection process that delimits a region of the screen; e.g., to select a section of text, we need to select both the start and end points of the text. Similarly, to size and position a rectangle on the screen, we need to select two opposite corners of the rectangle.
	With a mouse, extended selection is achieved in the following manner. Position the cursor with the mouse to indicate a start position, depress (but do not release) a mouse button to begin the selection, drag (move with the mouse button still depressed) the mouse to a final position, and finally release the button to confirm the final selection. Visual feedback is always provided during the dragging operation. For example, when selecting text, the currently selected text is complemented (white characters on a black background) on the display.

We will see many further examples of **selection** and **extended selection**. Find out, by consulting your system documentation, how selection and extended selection operations can be performed in your Smalltalk system. You may find that extended selection operations can be performed in more than one way.

3.2 GETTING STARTED

3.2.1 Activating Smalltalk

Consult your system documentation for specific instructions on creating and activating your Smalltalk system.

Activate your Smalltalk system.

Once activated, the display screen will be similar to that shown in Fig. 3.1. Smalltalk is now ready for use.

A typical Smalltalk display has several windows displayed over a dark background. Each window consists of a framed rectangular area with a small title or label in its top left-hand corner. Windows may overlap each other and can be simplistically thought of as overlapping pieces of paper resting on a desktop. Strictly speaking, Smalltalk uses the term **view** for window. We will use the more familiar window terminology. Fig. 3.2 shows four of the most common types of windows: **Workspace**, **System Workspace**, **System Browser** and **System Transcript** windows. The most common uses for each of these windows are the following:

Workspace	A window used as a scratchpad area where fragments of Smalltalk code can be entered, stored, edited, and evaluated.
System Workspace	A special workspace window that acts as a repository for Smalltalk expressions (or expression templates) for performing common Smalltalk tasks. These expressions can be easily selected, modified, and evaluated by the programmer. The System Workspace window avoids the need to remember and retype often used expressions.
System Browser	A window in which most programming activities are carried out. The Smalltalk class library can be viewed, existing classes modified, and new classes added.
System Transcript	A window primarily used by the Smalltalk system and by programmers as a notice board on which to display error information or messages describing the progress of a Smalltalk activity.

A unique feature of the Smalltalk environment is the ability to work on a series of tasks in parallel and to move back and forth between these tasks without loss of context or information. Each task (or conversation) is carried out within its own window. Though many windows (tasks) may be visible on the desktop at any time, only one window (task) is active at any given moment. This window, known as the **active window**, will have its label tag highlighted (inverted). For example, in Fig. 3.1, the **Workspace** window is active.

3.2.2 Changing the Active Window

To change the active window, perform a **selection** operation with the mouse. Move the cursor into the window to be activated and confirm the selection; i.e., click the red mouse button — see the next section for a discussion of mouse button terminology. The activated window will be brought to the "top" of the desktop and have its label inverted. In Fig. 3.2, the **System Browser** window has been made active. This technique can be used to interrupt one conversation, commence another, interrupt it, restart the original and so on. The saving and restoring of the state of each conversation is handled automatically by the Smalltalk system.

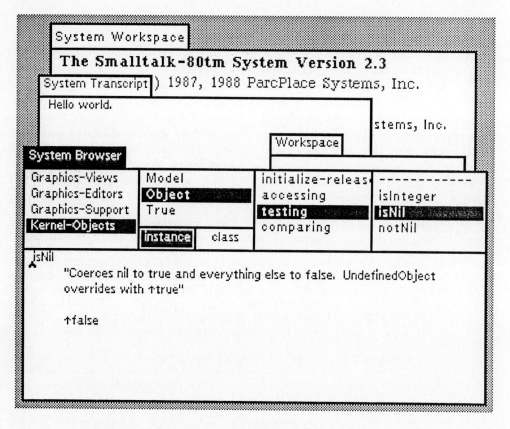

Figure 3.2 Display after the System Browser window is activated.

Repeatedly change the active window from one window to another.

Make all windows inactive by selecting an area of the display where no window resides. Now, move the cursor into any window. When all windows are inactive simply moving the cursor into a window activates that window automatically.

3.2.3 The "Ideal" Smalltalk Mouse

Smalltalk systems distinguish three types of mouse interaction and traditionally describe these activities by associating each with a different colored button on an "ideal" three-buttoned mouse (see Fig. 3.3). The ideal Smalltalk mouse has three buttons colored red, yellow, and blue. Sometimes these buttons are referred to as the left, middle, and right buttons respectively. The notion of red, yellow, and blue buttons is taken from the Orange book by Goldberg. We use the terms because they are part of the terminology used by Smalltalk programmers. Indeed, the terms are even used within the Smalltalk source code itself.

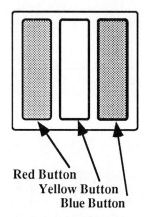

Red Button
Yellow Button
Blue Button

Figure 3.3 "Ideal" three-buttoned colored Smalltalk mouse.

The most common activities associated with each button are the following:

red or left button
Selecting information; e.g., selecting a piece of text, selecting a menu item, or selecting a new active window.

yellow or middle button
Activating a menu to invoke an action concerning the **contents of a window**; e.g., carrying out an editing operation on text within the window.

blue or right button
Activating a menu to invoke an action concerning **the manipulation of the window** itself; e.g., moving or closing a window.

With a three-buttoned mouse, a single button can be associated with each type of interaction. Of course, most Smalltalk systems do not have mice with three buttons, never mind colored buttons! However, the three types of interaction can be obtained very simply using any available pointing device. For example, both ParcPlace Systems™ and Apple Smalltalk (see Fig. 3.4) use the following scheme for use with a single button Macintosh mouse. The red button is obtained using the single mouse button, while the yellow and blue buttons are obtained by depressing the Option and Command keys respectively along with the single mouse button. On a two-buttoned mouse the following scheme is often used. The left and right buttons are used to obtain the red and blue buttons respectively, while both buttons are depressed to obtain the yellow button.

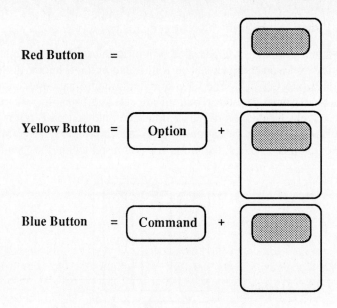

Red Button =

Yellow Button = Option +

Blue Button = Command +

Figure 3.4 Simulating a three-buttoned mouse.

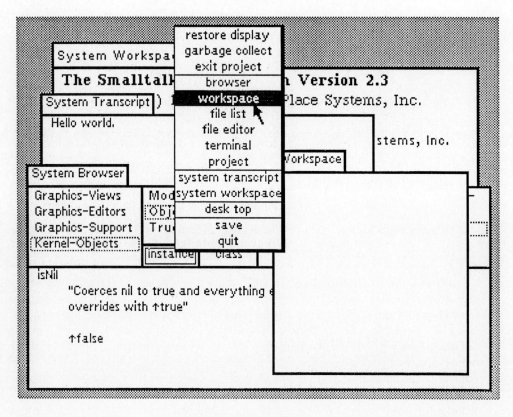

Figure 3.5 System Menu.

3.2.4 Using Pop-Up Menus

Many Smalltalk activities are initiated by making choices from on-screen menus. These menus are known as **pop-up menus** since they are not permanent fixtures on the screen but "pop up" when you activate them. Three of the most common menus — the System, Yellow and Blue Button menus — are described below.

System Menu Allows the programmer to choose one of several **global** system actions such as quitting Smalltalk, opening new windows, saving (or taking a snapshot of) the current state of the Smalltalk system, and restoring (or redrawing) the display (see Fig. 3.5). This menu is activated by moving the cursor into an area outside of any window (i.e., in any area with the background pattern) and pressing the **yellow** button.

Note that the items found in these menus and the order in which they are found may differ from one Smalltalk system to another. For example, the entry 'desk accessories' is not found on most systems — on a Macintosh computer, it provides access to system desk accessories. The result of selecting each of the entries in the system menu will be discussed in later sections.

Yellow Button Menu Allows the programmer to choose one of several actions to be performed on the **contents of the active window**. This menu is activated by depressing the **yellow button** when the cursor is within the window. The menu choices depend on the type of window. For text windows, it will typically include text editing operations such as cut, copy, and paste, and commands to evaluate Smalltalk code (see Fig. 3.6). To refer to the yellow button menu of a particular window, we will simply use the name of the window; i.e., the expression Workspace Menu implies the yellow button menu of the Workspace Window.

Blue Button Menu Allows the programmer to choose one of several actions to be performed on the **active window** — an action that is independent of the kind of window; e.g., moving, framing, collapsing, and closing the window (see Fig. 3.7). This menu is obtained by depressing the **blue button** when the cursor is within the active window. We will use expressions such as the Workspace Window Menu to refer to the blue button menu of a particular window.

To summarize, the system menu is used to perform system operations such as leaving Smalltalk or creating new instances of common Smalltalk windows; the yellow button menu is used for operations on the contents of the window such as editing text in the window; and the blue button menu is used for operations such as closing or resizing that apply to the window itself.

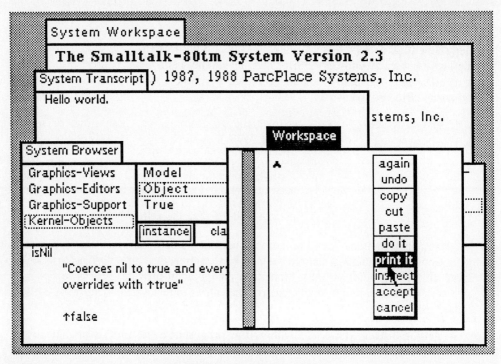

Figure 3.6 Yellow Button Menu.

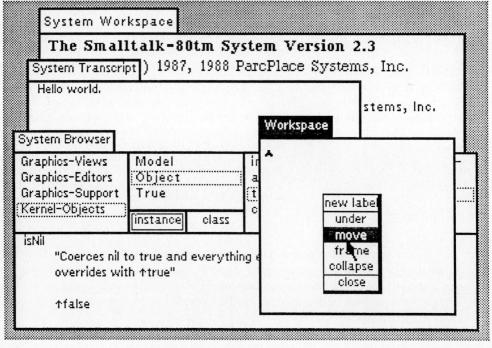

Figure 3.7 Blue Button Menu.

3.2.5 Making a Menu Selection

Choices are made from pop-up menus using an extended selection process. The first selection (depressing the mouse button) activates the requested menu, and the second or confirming selection (releasing the mouse button) chooses from the list of menu choices. Moving the graphics cursor through the menu choices (with the mouse button still depressed) highlights each choice in turn. For example, **move** is the highlighted choice in the **blue button menu** shown in Fig. 3.7. The second selection confirms the current menu selection as the menu choice selected. To exit from the menu without making a menu selection, move the cursor outside the menu and confirm (release the mouse button).

> *Gain some experience activating each of the three standard menus. Activate the System menu and exit without selecting any of the menu choices. Do the same for the yellow and blue button menus for **each** of the windows open on the display.*

3.2.6 Restoring the Display

You may have noticed earlier when moving from one window to another that Smalltalk does not always redraw windows that are deactivated. The **restore display** option in the System Menu is used to update the display. Smalltalk then successively redraws each of the windows on the display, including those that may be partially or even totally obscured.

> *Activate the System Menu and choose "restore display" (see Fig. 3.5).*

3.3 MANIPULATING WINDOWS

Smalltalk programmers never have quite the desktop space they would like for their Smalltalk windows. Some systems such as the Tektronix Smalltalk have a neat solution. What is seen on the display is the contents of a viewport onto a larger logical display window. Using a joystick or the mouse and some hardware support, we can quickly pan or change the viewport to view a different portion of the logical display. For the majority of us that do not have this kind of capability, we must pay more attention to the organization of the windows on the display. Fortunately, the Smalltalk environment makes it simple to create new windows and to close, collapse, reframe, and move existing windows.

3.3.1 Creating New Windows

New windows are most often created from the **System Menu** (see Fig. 3.5). Various types of window can be opened using the **project, file list, file editor, system transcript, browser, system workspace**, and **workspace** menu choices. For the moment, we will consider only **Workspace windows**. A **Workspace window** is an initially empty window in which text can be entered, edited, stored, and evaluated. It is generally used as a scratchpad or temporary work area.

> *Activate the System Menu and choose Workspace.*

Notice that the system cursor has changed shape to look like the top left corner of a rectangle (see Fig. 3.8). We are being asked to frame the area on the screen that the workspace window is to occupy. An extended selection is used. Move the corner cursor to the position where the upper left-hand corner of the window is to be located. Confirm the selection (depress and hold down the red button). The cursor now changes shape, it looks like the bottom right-hand corner of a rectangle. Drag the corner cursor until it is positioned where the bottom right corner of the window is to be located. Note that as you drag the corner, the outline of the window is displayed to provide visual feedback. Confirm the selection by releasing the red button. A window will appear in the designated frame. Some Smalltalk systems flash the selected rectangle rather than display the outline.

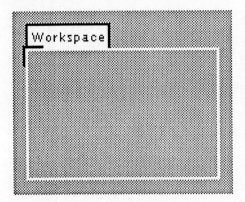

Select the left-hand corner of the window frame

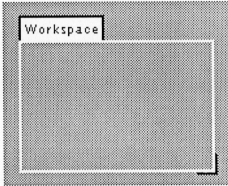

Drag the corner cursor to its desired position

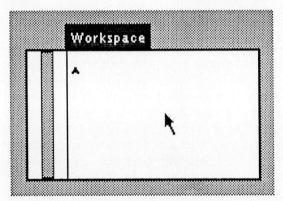

Figure 3.8 Framing a Smalltalk window.

Frame a new Workspace window. Remember — the first selection anchors the top left-hand corner and the second anchors the bottom right.

3.3.2 Manipulating Windows

Existing windows are manipulated from the blue button menu. This menu is seen when the blue button is held down while the cursor is within the boundary of the active window or when the red button is depressed while the cursor is in the label tab of the window. The most commonly used menu choices are **move**, **frame**, **collapse**, **close**, and **under**.

move
: To relocate a window on the display. A **selection** operation is required to specify the new origin or top left corner of the window.

    When **move** is selected, the window disappears except for its label tab. The label tab becomes the system cursor and can be dragged around the screen by moving the mouse. Move the label to the desired position and confirm the selection (click the red button) to anchor the label. The window is then redrawn in its original size at this location. In some Smalltalk systems, the outline of the window rather than the label tab may be moved around with the cursor to determine the new window location.

frame
: To relocate and resize a window. As with opening a new window from the system menu, an **extended selection** operation is required to specify the top left and bottom right corners of the window frame.

collapse
: To collapse a window so that only its label tab remains on the screen. The label tab may be placed at any desired location on the screen. A window that has been collapsed may be subsequently reopened and its contents restored by selecting **frame** from the blue button menu. In some Smalltalk systems, a collapsed window may be reopened by simply clicking on the label tab.

    When **collapse** is selected, the window disappears except for its label. The label becomes the system cursor and can be dragged around the screen by moving the mouse. Move the label to the desired position and confirm the selection (click the red button) to anchor the label.

close
: To remove a window from the screen completely. Closing removes all record of the workspace window from the system. The window cannot be subsequently restored. For that reason, if changes have been made to the contents of a window, a **confirmer menu** will appear on the screen when **close** is selected. The confirmer requests confirmation that the window should be closed.

Confirmer Windows

Confirmer menus are used within Smalltalk whenever a 'yes' or 'no' type of answer to a question is required. In the example shown in Fig. 3.9, the confirmer informs the programmer that the contents of the window that is about to be closed have not been saved; i.e., the contents will be lost if the window is closed. The confirmer menu gives the programmer the opportunity to cancel the close request by selecting 'no' (clicking the red button within the 'no' menu entry) from the menu. Selecting 'yes' (clicking the red button within the 'yes' menu entry) closes the window.

under
: Sometimes a window may be totally obscured by another window — **under** may be used to select the window under the active window beneath the cursor. You must have some idea where the obscured window lies. The obscured window will be made visible and will become the active window.

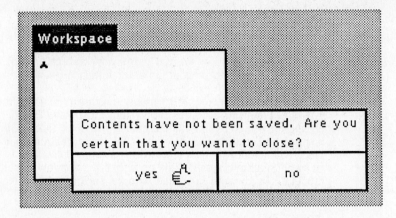

Figure 3.9 A Confirmer window generated when closing a Workspace window.

Become familiar with the Window Menu menu selections: move, frame, collapse, close, and under. Experiment with a Workspace window.

Try opening a workspace, typing some text into the window, and then trying to close it. Is it possible to leave the confirmer window without responding to the question asked?

3.3.3 Relabelling Windows

The string in the label tab of a window may be changed by selecting **new label** (sometimes **label**) in the blue button menu.

new label To relabel a window. When this menu item is selected, a prompter window appears requesting the new label for the window (see Fig. 3.10). The prompter initially contains the existing label. Typing in the new label followed by a carriage return relabels the window.

It is sometimes useful to have different workspaces contain different information; e.g., different sets of test cases to be tried out during the development of an application. To be able to easily distinguish between the workspaces, it is convenient to be able to relabel them.

Prompter Windows

A **prompter window** is a "fill in the blank" type of window where the user is expected to supply some requested information in response to a prompt. Text can be typed into the prompter window and edited using the standard Smalltalk editing commands. Text can be implicitly accepted by typing a **carriage return** or, alternatively, explicitly accepted by selecting **accept** from the **prompter yellow button** menu.

Once a response is accepted, the prompter window disappears from the display. Some kind of response must be given to the prompter. Moving the cursor outside the prompter window causes the prompter to flash to indicate that a response must be given before any other task can be undertaken. To cancel the request that generated the prompter, delete all text from the prompter and select **accept**; i.e., return a null string as the response.

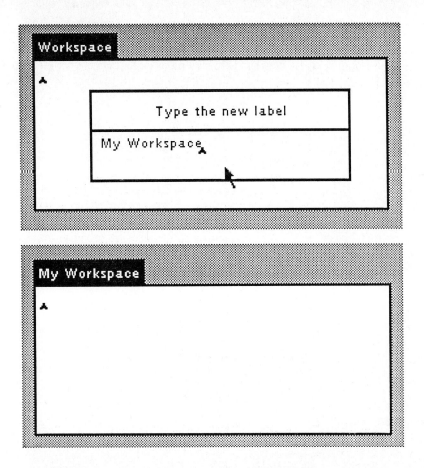

Figure 3.10 A Prompter window generated when relabelling a window.

3.3.4 Scrolling Through Windows

It is often impossible to display all of the contents of a text document within a window on the display. Consequently, only a portion of the contents of a document may be visible at any one time. The portion of a text that is visible may be changed by moving or scrolling the text up and down through the window. In this way, we can systematically view all of the text. All windows in which text can be entered and edited, for example **Workspace, System Workspace,** and **System Transcript** windows, are scrollable.

Smalltalk uses **scroll bars** to control the portion of a text document that is visible in a window. The **scroll bar** is an area to the left of the active text window. Fig. 3.11 shows the scroll bar to the left of a Workspace window. Scroll bars are only visible when the cursor is inside an active scrollable window.

Within the scroll bar is a gray scroll bar marker that provides visual cues about the text being displayed. More specifically, the length of the marker indicates what proportion of the document is visible within the window, and the position of the marker indicates which part of the document is being displayed. For example, in Fig. 3.11, the scroll bar marker is at the top of the scroll bar, indicating that the initial part of the text document is being displayed. The height of the scroll bar marker is only a fraction of the height of the scroll bar, indicating that the text document is several times larger than the portion displayed in the window.

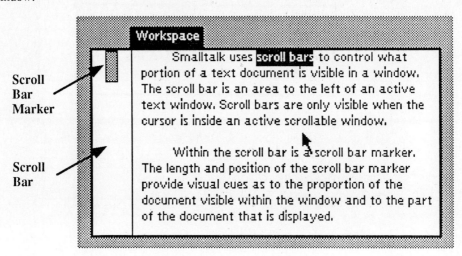

Figure 3.11 Organization of scrollable windows.

In Fig. 3.12, the height of the scroll bar marker is equal to the height of the scroll bar, indicating that the visible text is all of the text document — as would be the case when the text was initially entered.

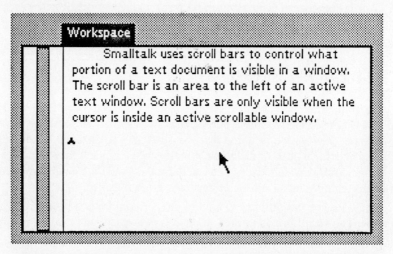

Figure 3.12 Height of scroll bar marker indicates that document is completely visible within the window.

Finally, in Fig. 3.13, the position of the scroll bar is at the bottom of the scroll bar region, indicating that the visible portion of the text is at the end of the text document. The height of the scroll bar as compared to the height of the scroll bar region indicates that the visible text is only a small portion of the complete document.

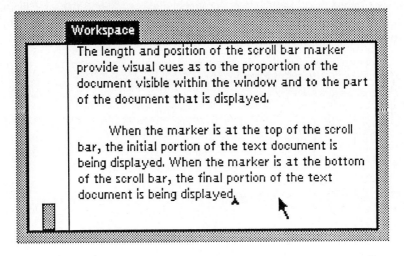

Figure 3.13 Position of scroll bar marker indicates displayed text is at the end of the document.

Scrolling Operations

There are three possible scrolling operations. Text may either be scrolled up or down one or more lines at a time or, alternatively, a specific section of the document can be selected. If the cursor is moved to the vicinity of the scroll bar, three different cursor shapes can be obtained. When the cursor is just to the right of the scroll bar marker, an upward-pointing half arrow is seen. Moving the cursor further to the left, a horizontal-pointing arrow is obtained. Finally, when the cursor is to the left of the scroll bar marker, a downward-pointing half arrow is seen.

Scrolling Forwards and Backwards

Scrolling text forwards and backwards is achieved with a simple **selection** using the respective up and down half arrow cursors. The cursor is moved into the area necessary to acquire the up or down arrow shaped cursor and then the selection is confirmed (by clicking the red button). The text will scroll up or down as requested. The amount scrolled is controlled by the vertical position of the cursor within the scroll bar region when the selection is made. The line of text nearest the cursor becomes the top line in the window if scrolling forwards or the bottom line if scrolling backwards. When scrolling forwards, larger scroll increments are obtained by selecting scrolling with the cursor toward the bottom of the scroll bar region. Note that experience is needed to familiarize yourself with scrolling. The most obvious problem at the beginning is that the scrolling direction is usually the opposite of that expected.

In Fig. 3.14, the up arrow cursor is being displayed. Selecting in this situation will scroll the text in the window such that the line nearest the cursor will become the top line in the updated window — in this case, the line beginning "Within the scroll bar...." Note that the text is scrolled toward the end of the file by the up arrow cursor. This is counter intuitive.

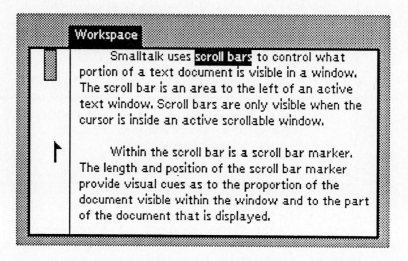

Figure 3.14 Scrolling forwards through a document.

In Fig. 3.15, the down arrow cursor is being displayed. Selecting in this situation will scroll the text in the window such that the line nearest the cursor will become the bottom line in the updated window — in this case, the line beginning with "document visible within ...". Text is scrolled toward the beginning of the file by the down arrow cursor.

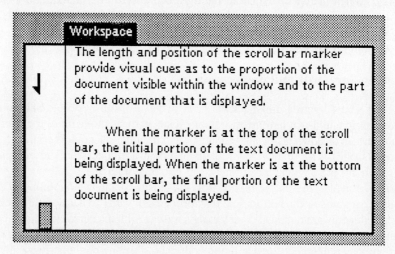

Figure 3.15 Scrolling backwards through a document.

Jumping to a Specific Section of a Document

Two techniques are provided for moving quickly to an absolute position within a text document using the horizontal cursor. The first involves positioning the horizontal arrow cursor at a height within the scroll bar that reflects the portion of the text document you wish to view and selecting with the red button. For example, in Fig. 3.16, the horizontal cursor is positioned approximately in the middle of the scroll bar. Selecting at this point will display text from the middle of the document into the window.

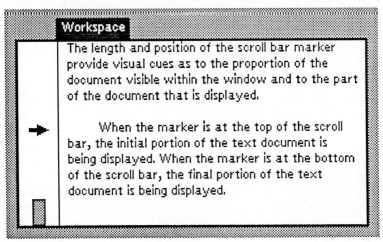

Figure 3.16 Jumping to a specified position within a document.

Alternatively, the scroll bar marker can be dragged to a desired position within the scroll bar. This is achieved using the horizontal arrow cursor and an extended selection. First, the horizontal cursor is obtained and moved within the scroll bar. When the red button is held down and moved up and down within the scroll bar, the scroll bar marker moves with the cursor. The scroll bar marker can now be dragged to the desired position within the scroll bar region. Notice that the scroll bar marker now moves up and down as the horizontal cursor is moved up and down. As it is dragged, the text displayed in the window changes. The scroll bar marker is dragged until the desired text is displayed within the window. Releasing the red button confirms the selection.

Gain some experience scrolling through text documents. Activate the System Workspace window. Move through the text using all three types of scrolling operations.

3.4 EDITING TEXT

Text editing operations can be applied to any window in which text may be entered and evaluated. This includes Workspace, System Workspace, and System Transcript windows. To illustrate the Smalltalk text manipulation facilities, we will enter and edit some text in a workspace window.

3.4.1 Inserting Text

Activate an empty Workspace window (open a new window if necessary). Notice the caret (^) or text insertion point in the top left-hand corner of the window.

Text can be inserted into a document simply by typing from the keyboard. Characters will be entered into the document at the position immediately following the caret.

Type in a series of sentences. Notice that the caret (^) or text insertion point is always positioned after the last character inserted.

(If nothing appears on the screen when you type, the cursor has wandered out of the Workspace window. Move it back into the window and the text you have typed will appear.)

Notice how the caret always follows the last character typed. To insert text between existing characters, move the text insertion point to the desired position using the cursor and perform a **selection** operation (by clicking the red button). Notice that the insertion point can be placed between characters. Once again, text typed from the keyboard will be inserted after the text insertion point. Note that the **carriage return**, **tab**, and **delete** keys all function as expected when inserting text. Many Smalltalk systems support the use of different text styles (e.g., boldface, italic, and so on) and multiple typefaces (e.g., Helvetica, Times Roman, and so on) in multiple character sizes. Consult your documentation for more details.

Type several lines of text into the workspace. Now, try inserting new text between existing words, inserting a new line of text between existing lines, and inserting text at the beginning and end of a line.

3.4.2 Selecting Text

A number of editing operations, for example replace and delete, require the following steps for execution:

- Select the text to be edited.
- Apply the editing operation to the selected text.

Text to which the operation is to be applied must first be selected using an **extended selection** operation. Each selection identifies one boundary of the selected text. It does not matter whether we select the start point first and then select the endpoint or vice versa. After the initial selection has been made (by depressing the red button), dragging the cursor (moving the cursor with the red button depressed) highlights the text between the initial selection point and the current position of the cursor. When the desired text is highlighted, confirm the selection (by releasing the red button) to anchor the endpoint of the selected text. The selected text remains highlighted after the selection is complete.

A selection may span as many lines as required in either direction from the first selection point. If one of the endpoints of the text to be selected is not within the visible part of the document, drag the cursor outside the window (above or below) to scroll the document. Scrolling stops when the cursor is moved back within the window.

More specialized methods for text selection are also available. These provide fast methods for selecting words, the text between pairs of delimiter characters, or all the text in a document. All of these selections involve double clicking the red button without moving the cursor (clicking twice in succession).

select a word	Double click the red button with the cursor at the beginning of, in the middle of, or at the end of a word.
select all the text in the document	Double click the red button with the cursor at the beginning or the end of the text in the document.
select the text between a pair of delimiters	Double click the red button with the cursor just after the left delimiter or just before the right delimiter. Valid delimiter pairs are parentheses (...), square brackets [...], single quotes '...', and double quotes "...".
select the text just typed in	Press the Escape key to select the text typed since the last mouse click.

Type in a number of lines of text into the workspace.

Practice making text selections. Try all possibilities: forward selections, backward selections, single word, multi-word, multi-line, text between delimiters, all the text in a document, and so on.

3.4.3 Replacing Text

To replace text, select (highlight) the text to be replaced (see Fig. 3.17a) and then simply type the replacement text. The selected text is replaced by the replacement text (see Fig. 3.17b). Text typed from the keyboard always replaces currently selected text. Insertions can be thought of as replace operations where the text to be replaced is the empty string.

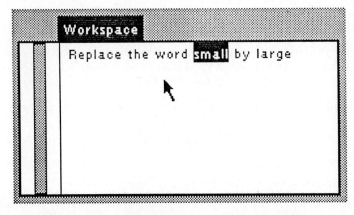

Figure 3.17a Replacing text — select text to replace.

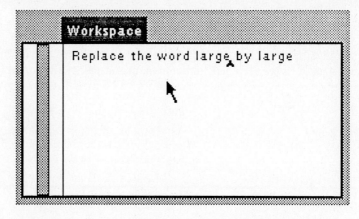

Figure 3.17b Replacing text — enter replacement text 'large'.

3.4.4 Deleting Text

To delete a section of text, select the text to be deleted (see Fig. 3.18a) and use the **delete** key to perform the deletion (see Fig. 3.18b). The **backspace** key is also often used to perform deletions. Note, however, that in some Smalltalk systems **backspace** deletes the selected text and also deletes the character immediately before the selected text. In other systems **backspace** and **delete** are synonymous.

Gain experience with the replace and delete operations.

3.4.5 Cut, Copy, and Paste

Cut, **copy**, and **paste** are primitive editing commands that can be applied to text that has been previously selected. They are available in the **yellow button menu** of the active window's text pane.

cut	Deletes the currently selected text.
copy	Makes a copy of (or remembers) the currently selected text.
paste	Pastes a copy of the text from the most recent **cut** or **copy** operation so that it replaces the selected text in the active window. If there is no selected text to replace, the text is inserted following the current insertion point. Paste operations may be repeated to paste the same text into a document more than once.

Copying text from one place to another requires a copy (to copy the text) followed by a paste (to paste a copy of the text at the new position). Text may be moved from one window to another by performing a cut in one window, selecting the new window, and performing a paste operation.

Practice using the cut, copy, and paste operations.

Select a section of text from the Workspace window and copy it into the System Transcript window.

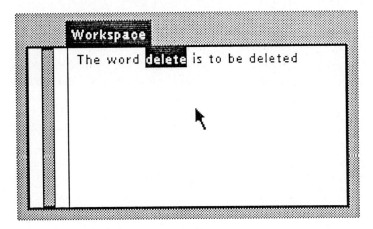

Figure 3.18a Deleting text — select text to delete.

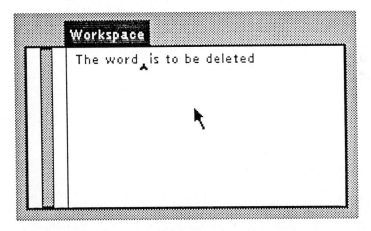

Figure 3.18b Deleting selected text — hit the delete key.

3.4.6 Again and Undo

Again and **undo** are two more editing operations that can be activated from the **yellow button menu** of a window's text pane. Operation **undo** is useful for recovering from editing mistakes. It reverses the effect of the last edit operation. Operation **again** is useful when the same edit operation must be repeated many times over; e.g., replacing all occurrences of one string by another or finding all occurrences of a string.

undo	Reverses the effects of the last edit command. For example, **undo** can be used after a **cut** to paste back the deleted text or after a **paste** to delete the pasted text and restore the original text (if any).
again	Repeats the last **replace**, **copy**, or **cut** operation. Operation **again** can be used after a **replace** to repeat the replace operation on the next occurrence of the text that was changed. Selecting **again** with the **shift** key depressed replaces **all** occurrences of the text with the replacement text. Operation **again** can be used after a **cut** or **copy** operation to find and select the next occurrence of the text that was cut or copied.

*Practice using the undo and again operations. In particular, investigate the effect
of each command after a replace, cut, copy, and paste operation.*

The **again** facility is an example of a "watch what I do and then repeat it" feature. To
replace one string by another, there is no need to involve the system in a dialog that provides
the input string and the replacement string. It is simply a matter of making the change on
the first occurrence. If other occurrences also need replacing, the **again** operation can be used
to repeat it — either one step at a time, to have the opportunity to **undo** a candidate
replacement, or all at once (by depressing the shift key).

Many Smalltalk systems allow keyboard control sequences to be used as well as menu
selections to activate the **cut, copy, paste, undo,** and **again** operations. Consult your
documentation.

3.5 EVALUATING SMALLTALK EXPRESSIONS

Smalltalk is an interactive system — expressions can be typed in, selected, and immediately
evaluated in any text window. Smalltalk expressions are evaluated using the **do it** and **print
it** commands from the **yellow button menu** of the active window.

3.5.1 Evaluating Code in a Workspace Window

To evaluate a Smalltalk expression, type it into a Workspace window, select it for
evaluation (using the normal method for selecting text), and evaluate it by selecting either
the **do it** or **print it** commands.

do it   Evaluates the selected expression (or sequence of expressions).

print it   Evaluates the selected expression (or sequence of expressions) and
prints a representation of the object returned by the evaluation. The
result returned is highlighted.

*Clear the Workspace window (select everything and use cut). Now type in the
following expression:*

32 + 17 * 2

Select the expression and choose 'print it' from the Workspace menu.

The expected result, 98, is printed (see Fig. 3.19). Note how the result remains
highlighted so that it is already selected to be deleted if required. What happens if we try **do
it** instead of **print it**?

Delete the result (98) of the previous evaluation.
*Reselect the expression: 32 + 17 * 2*
Choose 'do it' from the Workspace menu.

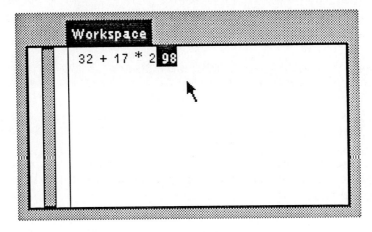

Figure 3.19 Evaluation of expression '32 + 17 * 2'.

This time no result is printed. The expression was evaluated but the resulting object was thrown away. Operation **do it** is most useful in cases where an expression is evaluated for its side-effect rather than its result. For example, a side-effect of evaluating an expression might be a graphical operation such as drawing a spiral on the display screen with a Smalltalk pen.

Experiment. Type in other expressions for evaluation. Suggestions include

> 5 **factorial**.
>
> 50 **factorial**.
>
> Date **dateAndTimeNow**.
>
> Pen **new mandala**: 30 **diameter**: 360.
>
> Transcript **show**: 'this text will be written in the Transcript window'; **cr**.
>
> Rectangle **fromUser**.

Note that if you select more than one expression for evaluation at the same time, only the result of evaluating the last expression will be printed.

3.5.2 Evaluating Existing Smalltalk Code

The selection and evaluation of Smalltalk code is not restricted to workspace windows. These operations can be performed from any text window. The **System Workspace** window (see Fig. 3.20), for example, contains a set of commonly used Smalltalk expressions for accessing files, system maintenance, and querying the system. By providing these in the workspace, users can quickly select and evaluate them without having to type or remember the rarely used messages.

3.5.3 Compilation Errors

When an expression is selected for evaluation, it is first compiled and then executed. The compiler detects any syntactic errors in the expression. Visual feedback is provided when such errors occur by inserting an error message at the point in the expression where the error was discovered.

Type in the following Smalltalk code and evaluate it.

```
| sum |
sum ← 0.
1 to: 100 do: [:i | sum ← sum + i].
sum
```

Now, make a deliberate error — remove the period following sum ← 0 and evaluate the code again. Note how the error message is placed at the source of the error (see Fig. 3.20) and remains highlighted so that it can be removed easily.

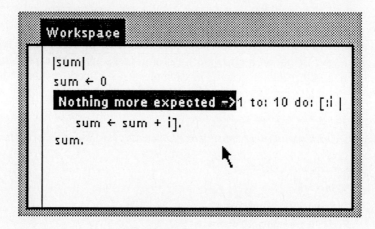

Figure 3.20 Syntax errors.

The message '**nothing more expected** →' indicates that the expression **sum ← 0** was complete and that **1 to: ...** is not a valid continuation of that expression.

For some errors, Smalltalk can help in correcting the error.

Correct the original error.
Now make the following deliberate error:
    Remove the declaration of the temporary variable | sum |
Reevaluate the code.

The first occurrence of **sum** is highlighted to indicate where the undeclared variable error was discovered, and a menu is displayed (as shown in Fig. 3.21). The menu contains possible corrective actions that can be invoked. The first four entries offer the choice of defining **sum** as a **temp** (temporary variable), **class var** (class variable), **global** (global variable), or **undeclared**. In our case, the correct action would be to select **temp** and let the evaluation continue. Invoking **correct it** invokes the Smalltalk **spelling corrector**. Assuming that you have misspelled **sum**, the spelling corrector searches through the system for names that bear a resemblance to **sum**, displays them in a menu, and allows the programmer to select an alternative spelling.

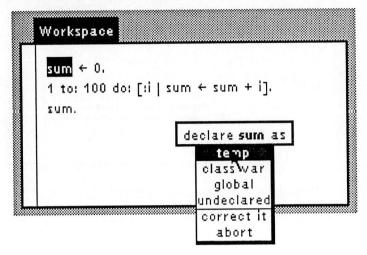

Figure 3.21 Undeclared variable menu.

Make other deliberate errors; e.g.,

1. *Remove the closing] bracket.*
2. *Replace 'sum' by 'sam' in 'sum ← 0.' (Then try invoking the spelling corrector to change it back.)*

3.6 QUITTING FROM SMALLTALK

Activate the System Menu and choose Quit.

A menu will appear offering 3 choices (see Fig. 3.22).

Save, then quit	Takes a snapshot of the current state of the Smalltalk system and then quits. This snapshot or Smalltalk image can subsequently be reloaded to continue the Smalltalk session.
Quit, without saving	Quits from the Smalltalk system without saving any of the modifications made to the system during this Smalltalk session.
Continue	Cancels the quit operation and continues the Smalltalk session.

Choose **Quit, without saving** to exit the system and avoid saving the changes you made; i.e., to discard all modifications made to the Smalltalk system during your session.

Choose 'Quit, without saving' from the Quit menu.

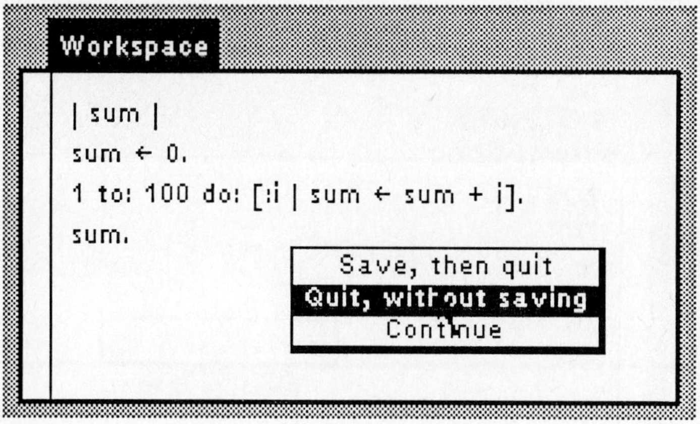

Figure 3.22 Quit menu.

3.7 SUMMARY

This chapter has provided a first introduction to the Smalltalk user interface. In particular, we have discussed the following:

- the 'ideal' Smalltalk three-buttoned mouse,
- the use of pop-up menus,
- common system, yellow, and blue menu entries,
- window manipulation commands such as open, close, frame, and so on,
- prompter and confirmer windows,
- text editing commands,
- commands for expression evaluation, and
- how to exit from Smalltalk.

3.8 EXERCISES

Some of the exercises that follow involve the evaluation of Smalltalk code. When a semantic error is discovered during the evaluation of Smalltalk code, execution halts and a notifier window is displayed. The notifier displays a message describing the cause of the error. If you are not familiar with the use of notifiers and debuggers to debug Smalltalk code, we suggest that, until these topics are fully covered in Chapter 5, you simply close the notifier window (select close from the blue button menu) and debug your code manually.

1. Type in the Smalltalk code fragments generated from exercises 1-4 of Chapter 2 and execute them.

2. Change the layout of the windows on the display by resizing and moving all visible windows.

3. Move the contents of the system workspace into the system transcript. Can the transcript hold it all?

4. Create several small workspaces inside of (or on top of) a larger one. Then activate the larger workspace. Can you make the smaller workspaces visible again?

5. While a piece of code is executing in one window, can you activate a second window? Try evaluating 120 factorial.

6. What do the yellow button menu commands **accept** and **cancel** do in a Workspace window? Try typing in some text to a workspace, selecting **accept**, typing in some additional text, and finally selecting **cancel**.

7. The **delete** key (sometimes, the **backspace** key) is used to delete a text selection. What happens if delete is used without selecting text?

8. What happens if "**do it**" or "**print it**" are selected when no text selection has been made?

9. Smalltalk systems provide alternative "control key" sequences for performing tasks such as editing, underlining, changing fonts, and changing emphasis, and also provide short cuts to avoid typing often used symbols. For example, on the Macintosh, both ParcPlace™ and Apple Smalltalk support the standard keyboard equivalents Ctrl x, Ctrl c, Ctrl v, and Ctrl z for cut, copy, paste, and undo respectively.

Determine the effect of the control key sequences Ctrl t and Ctrl f in your Smalltalk system. Do the same for the following list. In each case, a section of text should be selected within a text window before typing the control key sequence.

Ctrl 0, Ctrl 1, Ctrl 2, ... Ctrl 9,

Ctrl -, Ctrl b, Ctrl w,

Ctrl Shift -, Ctrl Shift b,

Ctrl [, Ctrl (, Ctrl <, Ctrl ", Ctrl '

3.9 GLOSSARY

pointing device operations

selection A fundamental interaction sequence used for many tasks within the Smalltalk environment; e.g., to indicate the point at which text, when typed from the keyboard, should be inserted, or to change the active window. Two activities are involved in making a selection: first, moving the cursor on the screen to the desired position, and second, confirming the position by clicking the red button.

extended selection A two part selection process used, for example, to select the start and end points of a text selection, the top left and bottom right-hand corners of a frame for a window, or to activate and choose a selection from a pop-up menu.

mouse interaction terminology

single clicking The process of pressing and then immediately releasing a mouse button.

double clicking The process of pressing and then immediately releasing a mouse button twice in quick succession.

dragging The process of moving the mouse with the mouse button depressed. Used to perform an extended selection operation where a two part selection process is required.

menus

System Menu Allows the programmer to choose one of several **global** system actions such as quitting Smalltalk, opening new windows, saving (or taking a snapshot of) the current state of the Smalltalk system, and restoring (or redrawing) the display.

Blue Button Menu A pop-up menu that allows the programmer to choose one of several actions to manipulate the selected window. These include moving, framing, collapsing, and closing the window.

Yellow Button Menu A pop-up menu that allows the programmer to choose one of several actions to be performed on the contents of the selected window. The menu choices depend on the type of window. For text windows, it typically includes text editing operations such as cut, copy, and paste, and commands to evaluate Smalltalk code.

mouse buttons

red button Mouse button used to select information.

yellow button Mouse button used to activate a menu for editing the contents of a window. The cursor must be within the boundaries of the desired window when the button is depressed.

blue button Mouse button used to activate a menu for manipulating the window itself. The cursor must be within the boundaries of the desired window when the button is depressed.

Smalltalk windows

Workspace Workspace windows used as scratchpad areas where fragments of Smalltalk code can be entered, stored, edited, and evaluated.

System Workspace A Workspace window that acts as a repository for Smalltalk expressions (or expression templates) that perform common Smalltalk tasks. Prevents the programmer from having to remember and retype often used expressions.

System Browser A window for carrying programming activities like viewing the Smalltalk class library, modifying existing classes and methods, and adding new classes.

System Transcript A window primarily used by the Smalltalk system and by programmers as a notice board to display error information or print messages describing the progress of a Smalltalk activity.

Confirmer A window used to request a 'yes' or 'no' type of answer to some question. Confirmers are most often used to ask the user to confirm whether or not a request for some undoable action should be carried out.

Prompter A window that requires a "fill in the blank" response from a user — used to extract textual information in response to a user command.

blue button operations (window menu)

new label Command used to change the name in the window's label tab. A prompter appears to query the user about the new name.

under Command used to select a window that is under the active window and the cursor. The obscured window is made visible and also becomes the active window.

move Command used to relocate a window on the screen. A **selection** operation is required to specify the new location of the window. The window is not resized by this operation.

frame Command used to relocate and resize a window. As with opening a new window from the system menu, an **extended selection** operation is required to specify the top left and bottom right corners of the window frame. Thus the window is both resized and repositioned.

collapse Command used to collapse a window so that only its label remains on the screen. The label may be placed at any desired location on the screen. A window that has been collapsed may be subsequently reopened by selecting **frame** from the window menu.

close Command used to remove a window from the screen permanently. All record of the workspace window is lost from the system. The window cannot be subsequently restored.

text editing terminology

text insertion point The point (indicated by a caret) within an active text window where text will be inserted either by a paste operation or by typing characters on the keyboard.

text selection The process of selecting a region of text for subsequent manipulation. Carried out using an extended selection operation.

yellow button text editing commands

again An editing operation that repeats the last **replace**, **copy**, or **cut** operation. Can be used after a **replace** to repeat the operation on the next occurrence of the replaced text. With the **shift** key depressed, **all** occurrences are replaced. Can be used after a **cut** or **copy** operation to find and select the next occurrence of the text that was cut or copied.

undo An editing operation that reverses the effects of the last edit command. For example, **undo** can be used after a **cut** to paste back the deleted text or after a **paste** to delete the pasted text and restore the original text (if any).

copy Makes a copy of (or remembers) the currently selected text.

cut Deletes the currently selected text.

paste Pastes a copy of the text from the most recent **cut** or **copy** operation so that it replaces the selected text in the active window. If there is no selected text to replace, the text is inserted following the current insertion point. Paste operations may be repeated to paste the same text into a document more than once.

yellow button evaluation commands

do it Evaluates the currently selected text without displaying the result.

print it Evaluates the currently selected text and displays the result.

4

Programming with Browsers

4.1 INTRODUCTION

Browsers (alternatively **browser windows** or **browse windows** — see Fig. 4.1) are without a doubt the most important and most used software development tools in the Smalltalk programmer's arsenal. Browsers are an integral part of the programming activity; they are used to navigate through the Smalltalk class library, to view and modify existing classes and methods, and to add new classes and methods.

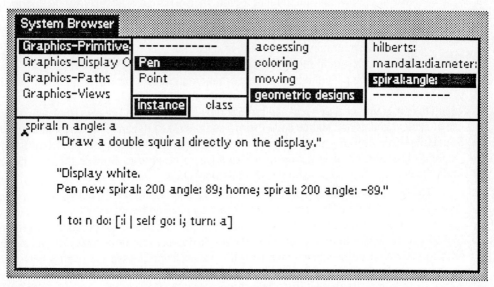

Figure 4.1 System Browser window.

The central role played by browsers in the programming process is more easily appreciated by understanding how program development in Smalltalk is different from that in languages such as Pascal and C. Programming in Smalltalk is programming in the presence of a large reusable class library. Building an application in Smalltalk can be thought of as extending this base library — a process termed **programming by extension**. Through the mechanism of inheritance, new classes are created by describing how they differ from some existing class of object — a process often termed **differential programming**.

This view of programming as extending the existing class library makes it essential that tools be provided to navigate through the class library, and that the addition of new classes and methods be carried out in such a way that the new functionality can be immediately exercised within the context of the whole Smalltalk system. Adding a new method to an existing class, for example, is achieved by simply incrementally compiling the definition of the new method into the system. In languages such as Pascal and C, it is necessary to recompile any changed program components and then link together every component part of the program. For large programs consisting of many hundreds of components, this is a slow process, especially if it must be repeated after every small change to a program.

Many of the activities we normally associate with program development are carried out using browsers in Smalltalk. Code is edited, listed, formatted, compiled, and tested using browsers. In particular, browsers are used for four distinct purposes:

- Viewing the source code for existing classes and methods.

- Modifying existing methods and classes.

- Adding new methods and classes to the library.

- Extracting valuable cross reference information from the library; e.g., extracting a list of classes that implement a particular message or displaying the hierarchical relationships between classes.

Apart from a small number of primitive operations, all of the source code for the class library may be viewed (and modified) by the programmer — Smalltalk is an open system. With several thousand methods and over a hundred classes, browsers help the Smalltalk programmer overcome the problem of information overload. They provide a tool through which the programmer may view and modify the Smalltalk class library. They supersede the use of static manuals and source code listings and provide a dynamically updated view of the Smalltalk system at any moment in time. Because a Smalltalk application builds on the existing class library, it is far more informative to be able to browse through the class library than to study a paper listing of an individual class.

The most commonly used browser, the **System Browser** (see Fig. 4.1), provides access to the entire Smalltalk class library. More specialized browsers, which provide access to only a subset of the library, may also be created. Experienced Smalltalk programmers typically have several browsers open on the display at any one time. One browser might be used to view an existing library method while another one is used to create a new method that is a variation or extension. Multiple browsers make it possible to conveniently view and/or modify different parts of the class library simply by switching from one browser to another.

4.2 SYSTEM BROWSERS

System Browser windows are created by selecting **browser** from the **system menu**. A System Browser window is divided into five scrollable panes (or subwindows) and two switch panes labelled **class** and **instance** (see Fig. 4.2). The top four panes are termed **list panes**, while the bottom pane is a **text pane**. **List panes** contain fixed lists of menu selectors. Each item in the list is selectable but cannot be edited directly. **List panes** are scrollable. To view all the available items within a list pane, it may be necessary to scroll through the contents of the list pane. Text within a **text pane** may be scrolled, selected, edited, and evaluated. The standard window operations are available through the blue button menu; i.e., browsers can be closed, collapsed, moved, and framed.

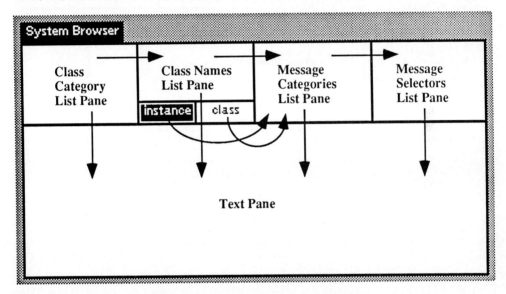

Figure 4.2 Structure of a System Browser.

In multi-pane windows, only one pane, known as the **active pane**, is active at any time. Panes within an active browser are activated simply by moving the cursor into the pane. Each **list** and **text pane** has a menu, accessible through the yellow button, that contains operations to be applied within the context of currently selected items in the list panes. Fig. 4.3 shows typical yellow button menus associated with each of the browser panes. The actual entries in these menus will differ from system to system and will also change depending on the selections made within the list panes of the browser at the time the menu is activated.

To enable programmers to move around in the library quickly and easily, the library is indexed. Related classes are grouped together into class categories, and related methods within individual classes are grouped into message categories. The four list panes, therefore, provide four levels of indexing into the class library. From left to right these panes are termed the **class categories pane, class names pane, message categories pane,** and **message selectors pane** respectively (see Fig. 4.2). In addition, to determine whether class messages

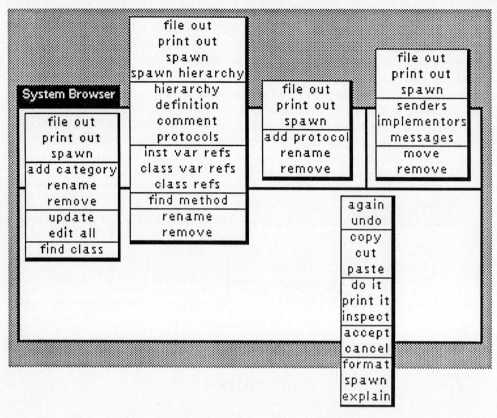

Figure 4.3 System Browser — Yellow Button Menus.

or instance messages are displayed in the **message categories** and **message selectors** panes, either **class** or **instance** is selected from the **instance-class** switch panes. These act as on-off switches — selecting class deselects instance and vice versa. Selections are made from the list pane and instance-class switches using the red button. When a browser window is deactivated or collapsed, the current selections from the menus are remembered and restored when the browser is reactivated or framed at some later stage.

4.3 VIEWING EXISTING CLASSES

A system browser provides access to all the relevant information concerning classes within the class library. For example, we can display the following information:

- The definition of a class to determine its instance and class variables.
- The class hierarchy local to a given class to determine its relationship with related classes.
- The class and instance protocol supported by a class.
- The source code for any method.

Information relating to a class is displayed in the text pane of the browser by selecting entries from the list panes and from the various pane menus. What is displayed in a list pane of a browser is related to the selections previously made in neighboring list panes (to the left). The arrows in Fig. 4.2 indicate the dependencies between the panes of the browser. Selecting a particular class category, for example, displays the classes within that category in the class names pane. Selecting a particular class displays a list of message categories in the message categories pane. The list will be either a list of instance message categories or a list of class message categories, depending on the state of the class-instance switches below the class names pane. Next, selecting a particular message category displays the selectors of the methods in that category in the message selectors pane. Finally, selecting a message selector causes the code for that method to be displayed in the text pane at the bottom. Other kinds of information may also be displayed in the text pane; e.g., the definition of a class. We will discuss this in more detail in following sections.

The yellow button menu entries are also dependent on the selections made in the list panes. The menu entries for each list pane in Fig. 4.4 are those displayed when an item from that pane is selected. Fewer or different entries may be displayed if an item is not selected in a pane. Menus in your system may differ slightly from those shown.

In Fig. 4.4, the class category **Graphics-Primitives** is selected. The class names displayed in the class names pane are therefore the classes in this category. The class **Pen** is selected and this, together with the fact that the **instance** menu item is selected, determines that the message categories for instances of class **Pen** will be displayed in the message categories pane. The message category **geometric designs** is selected, indicating that the message selectors for instance methods in the category **geometric designs** in the class **Pen** are displayed in the message selectors pane. Finally, the selector **spiral:angle:** is selected, causing the Smalltalk code for this method to be displayed in the text pane.

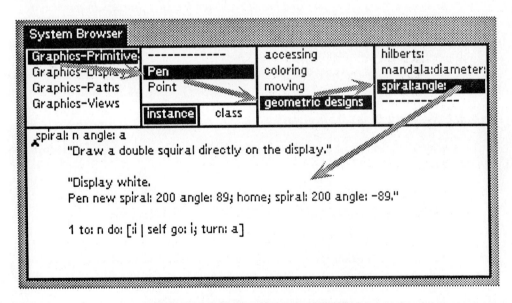

Figure 4.4 Browser Pane dependencies.

4.3.1 Finding a Class

Although classes are organized in a hierarchy, they are displayed in a different manner in a browser. For example, classes associated with graphics primitives are collected together under the category **Graphics-Primitives** independent of their inheritance structure. From the point of view of a user, classes are categorized into sets of functionally related classes.

Even so, finding a class within the system can be frustrating for the beginning Smalltalk programmer. It is not likely that you will know the category of the class you are looking for — considerable time can be spent searching through the class categories. A fast way of finding the category for a class is to send the class a **category** message. For example, evaluating the expression

Pen category

in a workspace returns the category **Graphics-Primitives**. This class category can be easily found by scrolling the class category pane since the pane is sorted alphabetically.

Alternatively, some Smalltalk systems have a **find class** entry in the yellow button menu of the class categories pane. Selecting this menu entry invokes a prompter that asks for the name of the class to be located. When the class name is entered, the required class category is automatically selected in the browser. Additionally, operation **find class** is useful when the spelling or the exact name of a class is unknown. Typing a pattern string using the character '*' as a wild card character brings up a menu of classes matching the pattern. For example, in Fig. 4.5, the pattern P* is entered in the find class prompter. As shown in Fig. 4.6, a menu of class names beginning with the letter P will be displayed. Selecting one causes the browser to position itself at that class.

> *Activate a System Browser and browse through the class library. In particular, look for each of the following classes: Date, Integer, Spline, Quadrangle, Bag, and Character. If there is no find class facility, you will need to interrogate the system to find the category of each class.*
>
> *If there is a find class facility, look for classes that end in "View", "Controller", or "Collection".*

4.3.2 Viewing Class Definitions

To display the definition of a class in the text pane of a browser, proceed with the following four steps:

- Select the class category from the class categories pane.
- Select the class from the class names pane.
- Set the instance-class switches to **instance**.
- Select **definition** from the yellow button menu of the class names pane.

Fig. 4.7 shows the definition of class **Pen**. The definition displays the class name, the name of the superclass, instance variables, class variables, pool dictionaries, and the class category. Note that selecting **definition** when the **instance-class** switches are set to **class** displays the definition of the metaclass[1] for **Pen**; i.e., the definition of the class for which class **Pen** is an instance.

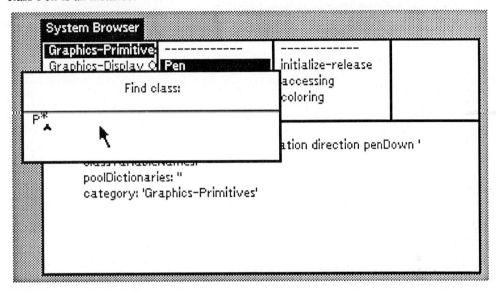

Figure 4.5 Searching for class names matching the pattern 'P*'.

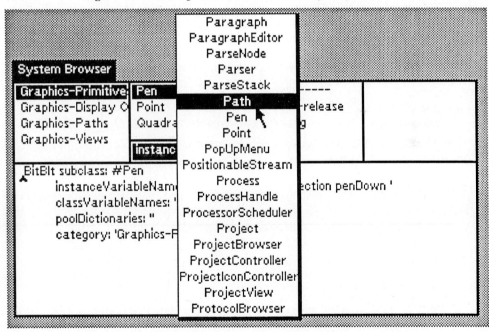

Figure 4.6 Menu of class names matching the pattern string 'P*'.

---

[1]The role of metaclasses is described in detail in Chapter 6 – classes are objects and therefore must be instances of some class. A class is the only instance of its own metaclass.

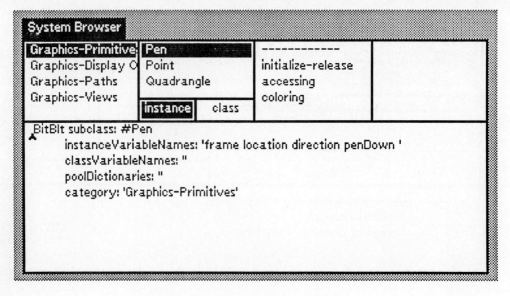

Figure 4.7 Definition of class Pen.

Display the definitions of each of the following classes: Date, Integer, Spline, Quadrangle, Bag, and Character.

4.3.3 Viewing the Class Hierarchy

To determine the inheritance hierarchy for a class, proceed with the following four steps:

- Select the class category from the category pane.
- Select the class from the class names pane.
- Set the instance-class switches to **instance**.
- Select **hierarchy** from the yellow button menu of the class names pane.

The class hierarchy is displayed in the text pane and shows the superclass chain above and below the class. In addition, the instance variables for each class in the hierarchy are also displayed. Remember that instances of a class inherit the instance variables of all their superclasses. The set of instance variables for a class consists of all the instance variables in the class itself plus the instance variables of all the superclasses. Selecting **hierarchy** when **class** is selected from the **instance-class** menu displays the hierarchy for the metaclass[2] of class **Pen**.

Fig. 4.8 illustrates the inheritance hierarchy for class **Pen**. **Pen** is a subclass of class **BitBlt**, which is itself a subclass of class **Object**. In addition to its own instance variables, class Pen inherits the instance variables of class **BitBlt**. **Pen** has no subclasses.

---

[2]As you may discover by viewing the hierarchy when the class switch is selected, the metaclass hierarchy actually extends above the metaclass for Object. More details are provided in Chapter 6.

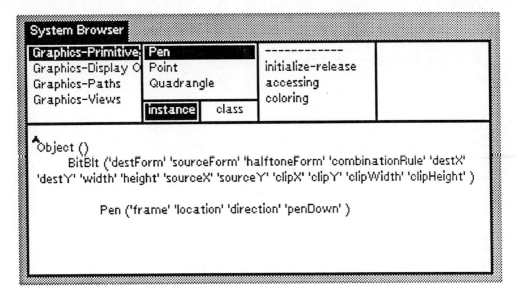

Figure 4.8 Class hierarchy for class Pen.

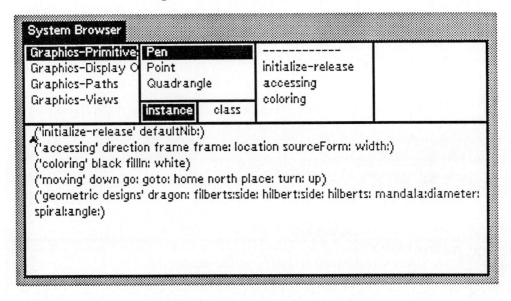

Figure 4.9 Instance protocol for class Pen.

4.3.4 Viewing the Protocol Supported by a Class

To determine the instance or class protocol of a class, proceed with the following four steps:

- Select the class category from the category pane.
- Select the class from the class names pane.

- Set the instance-class switches to **instance** to display the instance protocol or to **class** to display the class protocol.

- Select **protocols** from the yellow button menu of the class names pane.

The instance or class protocol is displayed in the text pane (see Fig. 4.9 for the instance protocol of Pen). Each entry in the text pane describes the protocol associated with a particular message category and has the form

('message category name' nameOfMethod1 nameOfMethod2 ...)

For each of the following classes, display the class hierarchy along with the instance and class protocols: Date, Integer, Spline, Quadrangle, Bag, and Character.

4.3.5 Viewing Methods

To display the source code for a method in the browser, proceed with the following five steps:

- Select the class category from the class categories pane.
- Select the class from the class names pane.
- Set the instance-class switches to either **instance** or **class**.
- Select the method category from the method categories pane.
- Select the message selector from the message selectors pane.

Fig. 4.10 shows the instance method with selector **spiral:angle:** in class **Pen**.

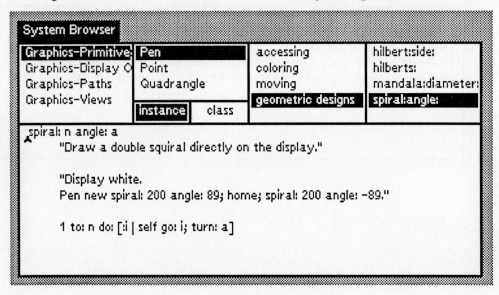

Figure 4.10 Displaying instance method spiral:angle: in class Pen.

4.3.6 Finding a Method

If you do not know the category of a method or are unsure of its spelling, the **find method**[3] entry in the yellow button menu of the class names pane may be used. Operation **find method** displays a menu of the messages implemented by the currently selected class. For example, in Fig. 4.11, the messages implemented by class Pen are displayed. To view a particular method definition, select the desired message selector from the menu.

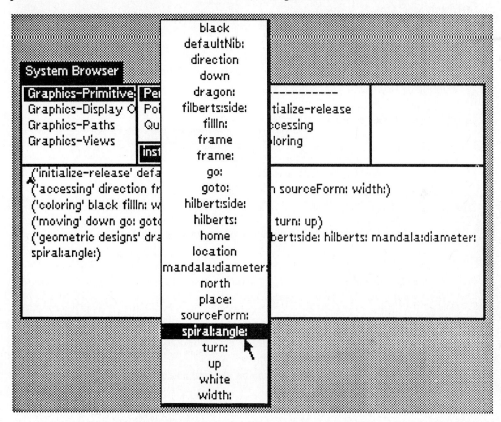

Figure 4.11 Message List Menu generated by using 'find method' for class Pen.

4.3.7 Obtaining Explanations

The **explain** entry in the yellow button menu of the text pane can be used to display limited explanations of the code in a method. To use the explanation facility, a token must first be selected, then menu entry **explain** causes a short explanation of the token selected to be displayed as a comment embedded in the code immediately following the token. For example, in Fig. 4.12, the token @ has been selected and the resulting explanation displayed. The explanation also indicates how to create a message-set browser on the selector

---

[3]Menu item **find method** is not available in all versions of Smalltalk.

(see Section 4.6.3). Tokens which can be explained include message selectors, variable names, and even symbols such as '↑'.

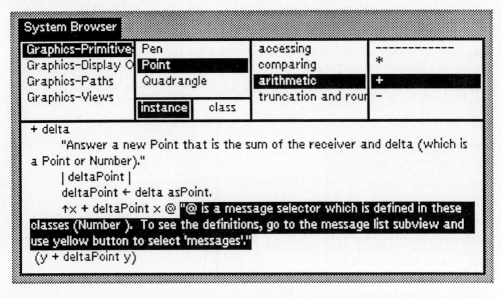

Figure 4.12 Explanation of the message selector @.

Browse through the methods in each of the following classes: Date, Integer, Spline, Quadrangle, Bag, and Character. Use the explanation facility to gain a better understanding of some code fragment.

4.4 EVALUATING CODE FROM WITHIN A BROWSER

Any code in the text pane of a browser may be selected and evaluated as follows:

- Select or type the text to be evaluated in the text pane.
- Choose **do it** or **print it** from the yellow button menu of the text pane.

When viewing classes and methods with a browser, it is convenient to be able to evaluate code at any time without leaving the context of the browser. For this reason, it is common practice among Smalltalk programmers to include code that illustrates the use of a class or method within the class or method itself. For classes, the common convention is to include explicit **example** methods under the class message category **examples**. For methods, this is most often done by embedding code within a comment at the beginning or end of the method. For example, in Fig. 4.13a, the method **spiral:angle:**, which draws a spiral on the display, contains the following code embedded within a comment.

```
Display white.
Pen new spiral: 200 angle: 89; home; spiral: 200 angle: 89
```

This is an example of how the **spiral:angle:** method might be used. The code within the comment can be selected and evaluated by choosing **do it** (or **print it**) from the yellow button **text pane menu**. A double spiral will be drawn on a white display screen (see Fig. 4.13b). We strongly suggest that you adopt the practice of including example methods whenever new classes are defined.

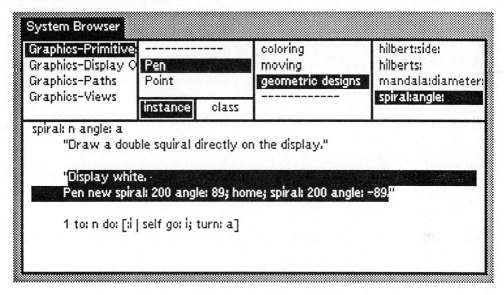

Figure 4.13a Evaluation of expression to draw a double spiral.

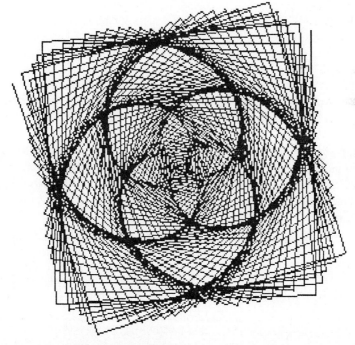

Figure 4.13b Double spiral resulting from evaluation of code in Fig. 4.13a.

Many of the example methods in the system are called example. Evaluate the example methods in the following classes: Pen, TextCollector, String, Arc, Curve, Spline, and FillInTheBlank. Make sure you read the comments stored with the examples before you evaluate them.

4.5 ADDING AND MODIFYING METHODS AND CLASSES

4.5.1 Modifying Existing Methods

Existing methods can be modified as follows:

- Display the existing method in the text pane.
- Edit the method as required using the **cut**, **copy**, **paste**, **again**, and **undo** operations available from the yellow button menu of the text pane.
- Select **accept** from the yellow button text pane menu to compile the new method.

For example, we could modify the **spiral:angle:** method in class **Pen** (see Fig. 4.13) and accept the change. Obvious cosmetic changes include changing the names of the arguments (from "n" to "turns" and "a" to "angle") and fixing the typographical error in the comment (the error is in the Smalltalk source).

Accepting Changes to Methods

Before a modified method can be used, it must be compiled by choosing **accept** in the text pane's **yellow button menu**. Alternatively, choosing **cancel** will undo any changes made since the last compilation. Compiling a class definition or a method permanently records the change in the system. Smalltalk keeps track of two versions of the code for every class: a compiled version and a source version. Accepting a modified class or method installs the compiled version of the code in the Smalltalk environment and also ensures that the modified source code is retrieved whenever the class or method is viewed through a browser — any browser.

When changes are made to text in a text pane, browsing some other part of the system (a new request) is not permitted. The user must first **accept** or **cancel** the changes. Otherwise, a **confirmer window** appears (see Fig. 4.14) to determine whether the changes made in the text pane are to be saved or discarded. It is answered by selecting the appropriate response ('yes' or 'no') from the confirmer menu.

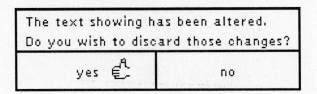

Figure 4.14 Confirmer Window.

Choosing 'yes' discards the change. Choosing 'no' cancels the new request and gives the programmer another opportunity to do something with the changed text; e.g., to **accept** it.

Note that it is possible to temporarily deactivate a browser window without accepting or cancelling a change. Simply click on some other window. When the browser is reactivated later on, the changes will still have to be accepted or cancelled before further browsing is possible or before the browser can be closed. Before accepting a change, it is often useful to be able to browse some other part of the class library. If it is not possible to do so in the current browser, the solution is to create a second browser and use it to query the class library. This is one of the reasons why Smalltalk programmers use multiple browsers.

Edit method 'spiral:angle:' in class Pen as described earlier. Accept the new method and test it by evaluating the comment

> *Display white.*
> *Pen new spiral: 200 angle: 89; home; spiral: 200 angle: 89*

*that is part of the method (remove the spiral from the display by choosing 'restore display' from the System Menu). Now edit (but **do not** accept or cancel) the comment to read*

> *Display white.*
> *Pen new defaultNib: 2; spiral: 200 angle: 89; home; spiral: 200 angle: -89*

The effect of this change is to draw the spiral using a Pen with a thicker nib or brush shape; i.e., with thicker lines. Evaluate the modified comment; i.e., draw the spiral with thick lines (see Fig. 4.15).

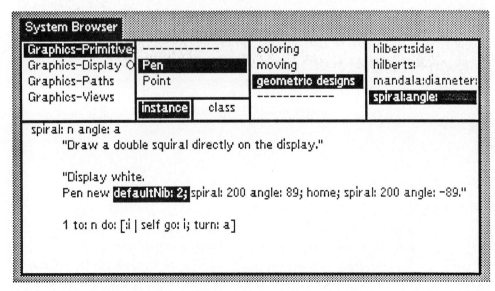

Figure 4.15 Evaluation of code to draw a thick double spiral.

Without accepting or cancelling the change, try to view the definition of another method in the class. A confirmer window will appear asking you to save or discard the changes. Choose 'no'.

4.5.2 Adding New Classes

In Chapter 2, we described the implementation of **Complex** — a class for manipulating complex numbers. We will use its definition to illustrate how new classes are added to the class library. To add a new class to the system, we must first decide whether the new class should be included under an existing class category or whether a new category should be added. In this situation, it is appropriate to add class **Complex** under the category **Numeric-Numbers**[4]. Select class category **Numeric-Numbers** in a browser. The class pane displays the classes in this category and the text pane displays a template for a class definition (see Fig. 4.16).

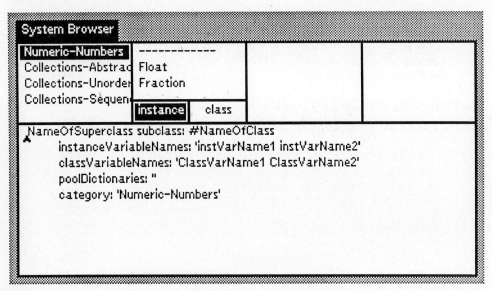

Figure 4.16 Class definition template.

To add a new class to an existing class category, proceed with the following three steps:

- Select the class category to which the new class is to be added.
- Edit the class template in the text pane to contain the name of the class, the name of the superclass of the class, any instance and class variable declarations, and any required pool dictionaries (the class category is already correct).
- Select **accept** from the text pane yellow button menu to compile the new class definition. The new class appears in the class names pane and is selected.

---

[4]The addition of new class categories is discussed later in the chapter.

114   Inside Smalltalk

For class **Complex**, in accordance with the definition of the class in Fig. 2.5, the template would be edited as shown in Fig. 4.17. It is important not to change any of the syntax of the class definition template. For instance, the list of instance variable names must be a string (**'realPart imaginaryPart'**) and the class name must be preceded by a hash mark or sharp (#). Also remember to remove the dummy variable names from the list of instance and class variables. To add the new class definition to the system, choose **accept** from the yellow button menu for the text pane. The new class **Complex** now appears in the list of classes in the class pane and is selected (see Fig. 4.17).

Alternatively, you could select and evaluate all of the code in the text pane and. Note that the class definition template is simply the message expression required to send the

subclass:instanceVariableNames:classVariableNames:poolDictionaries:category:

message to the superclass of the new class; i.e., tell the superclass to create a new subclass with the desired characteristics.

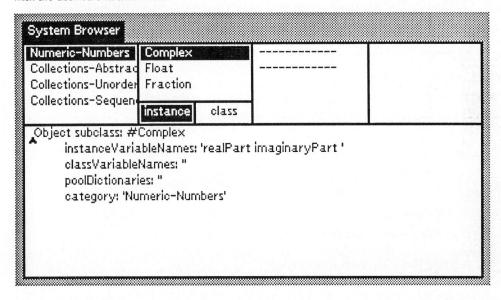

Figure 4.17 Addition of class definition for class Complex.

Add class Complex to the system under the class category Numeric-Numbers as described above.

Adding/Modifying Class Comments

It is a Smalltalk convention to associate a comment with each class describing the purpose of the class. To display and/or modify the comment for a class, perform the following:

- Select the class category and class.
- Select **comment** from the yellow button class pane menu to display the class comment in the text pane.

- If required, edit the comment in the text pane.

- Select **accept** from the yellow button text pane menu to compile the modified comment.

Fig. 4.18 shows the comment associated with class **Rectangle**. A default comment **"This class has no comment"** is automatically provided when a class is created.

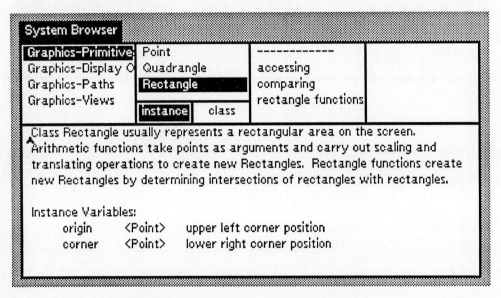

Figure 4.18 Class comment for class Rectangle.

Examine the comments associated with selected Smalltalk classes.
Add a suitable comment to the class Complex.

Adding New Method Categories

To add a new message category to a class, proceed with the following four steps:

- Select the class category and class.

- Select **instance** or **class** as appropriate in the instance-class switch panes.

- Select **add protocol** (see Fig. 4.19) from the yellow button menu of the message categories pane.

- Respond to the resulting prompter window by typing the new message category. By convention, the category should be a sequence of lowercase words separated by spaces.

To type a new category, type the successive lowercase words of the new category into the prompter window and **accept** (see Fig. 4.20). The new category will be added to the list of message categories. If no message category was selected when **add protocol** was invoked, the new category will be added at the end of the list of categories. If a message category was selected, the new category will be inserted before the selected category in the list.

In Fig. 4.21, the instance method category **accessing** has been added to class **Complex.** This category is selected, and the method definition template is displayed in the text pane.

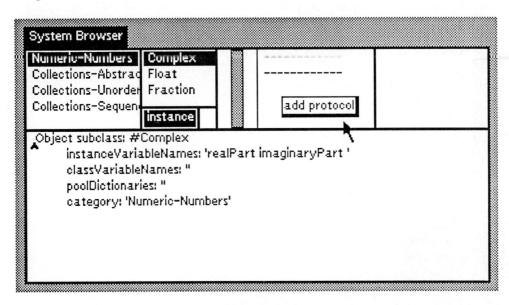

Figure 4.19 Select 'add protocol' to add a new method category.

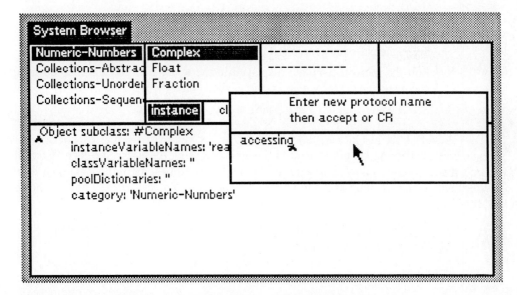

Figure 4.20 Adding a new method category to a class.

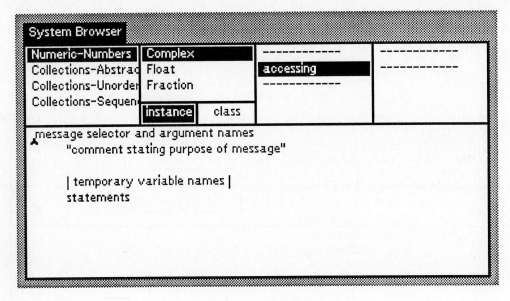

Figure 4.21 Method definition template.

Add the following method categories to class Complex:

class method categories: *initialization*
instance method categories: *accessing*   *arithmetic*

4.5.3 Adding New Methods

A new method can be added to an existing message category as follows:

- Select the class category, class, and message category.
- Edit the method template displayed in the text pane; i.e., the method header, comment, temporary variables, and method body.
- Select **accept** from the text pane's yellow button menu.

In Fig. 4.22, instance method **realPart** (which retrieves the real part of a complex number) has been added to the method category **accessing** for class **Complex**. Rather than edit the method definition template, it is common to edit the definition of some already existing method. As long as the modified method is given a new name, a new method will be added.

Add the following methods to the class Complex (see Fig. 2.5 for a listing of the source code for the methods).

class methods
     initialization
         newWithReal: realValue **andImaginary**: imaginaryValue

```
instance methods
    accessing
            realPart
            imaginaryPart
            realPart:
            imaginaryPart:
    arithmetic
            + aComplex
            * aComplex
```

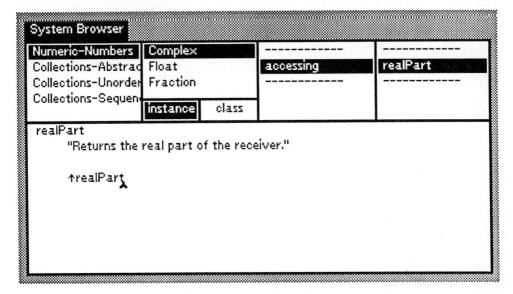

Figure 4.22 Addition of instance method realPart to class Complex.

4.5.4 Adding New Class Categories

A new class category can be added to the system as follows:

- Select **add category** from the yellow button menu of the class categories pane.
- Respond to the resulting prompter window by typing the new class category. By convention, class categories are uppercase words separated by dashes.
- Select **update** from the yellow button menu of the class categories pane to display the new class category in the class category list pane.

4.5.5 Modifying Existing Class Definitions

To modify the definition of an existing class, perform the following steps:

- Select the class category and class (if already selected, choose **definition** from the yellow button menu of the class names pane to display the class definition in the text pane).
- Edit the class definition displayed in the text pane.

- Select **accept** in the text pane's yellow button menu to compile the new class definition.

- Depending on the nature of the change, some modifications to other pieces of code may be required. See the discussion below for more details.

There is more to modifying a class definition than may be immediately apparent. Although some changes, such as editing the class category of a class, do not impact the system in any significant way, modifying the superclass or instance/class variables requires greater care. Remember that inheritance brings advantages in terms of shared code, but as a result, modifications to one class may impact others. We suggest that you do not change the names, superclasses, instance variables, or class variables of classes that were provided with your Smalltalk system. Reserve such changes, when necessary, to classes that you have added to your system.

Modifying a Class Name

Simply editing the name of a class in the class definition and accepting the change does not affect the name of the existing class but instead creates a copy of the old class definition with the new class name. Note that the methods from the old class are not copied to the new class — only the class definition is copied. To rename a class, select **rename** from the **yellow button menu** of the **class name pane** (see the next section).

Edit the class definition of class Complex to create a new class NewComplex. The old class Complex will be unaffected by this operation.

Modify class NewComplex so that it is in the new class category ComplexNumbers.

Modifying a Superclass

Changing the superclass of a class has implications for the methods and variables that can be inherited. Methods or variables that were previously inherited may no longer be part of the inheritance chain and therefore are no longer accessible to the class. If the superclass of a class is changed, all of the class's methods (and its subclasses) must be recompiled. This takes place automatically when the superclass change is accepted into the system. A report on the recompilation is displayed in the System Transcript window and any problems, such as methods referring to variables that are no longer accessible, are identified. The programmer must correct any reported problems.

Modifying Instance or Class Variables

Modifying the instance variables or class variables of a class can create similar problems to those encountered when changing the superclass of a class. For example, deleting an instance variable requires modifications to the methods, including inherited methods, that refer to that variable. When changes to variables are accepted, methods belonging to the class and its subclass are recompiled and the programmer notified of any problems through the System Transcript window.

When instance variables are added to or removed from a class, all existing instances of the class become obsolete. If accessed, they will be manipulated according to the definitions of the old obsolete class. The obsolete class will remain in the system until all references to it disappear. It is the responsibility of the programmer to recreate such instances under the new class definition. This will not likely be evident unless instances are stored globally. Global instances are typically initialized by a class method called **initialize** that is explicitly executed by the programmer making the change.

Remove the instance variable realPart from the class definition of class Complex. Watch the System Transcript window as the class is recompiled.

Avoiding Direct References to Inherited Variables

Some of the pitfalls of class modification can be avoided by following sound object-oriented programming practices. For example, although inherited variables may be referenced directly by a method, it is far safer to send a message to gain access to information from a superclass. Suppose a class A is the superclass of class B and supports an instance variable x. Instance methods for class B can gain access to x directly without message-passing. Alternatively, A could provide methods **x** and **x: aValue** and methods in class B could use these. Which is better? In terms of code maintenance, the latter is preferred. If we subsequently change class A so that x is no longer part of the representation, then as long as class A still supports the messages **x** and **x: aValue**, the code in the subclasses does not require modification. The important point here is that the class being changed can be modified so that the subclasses function without change; i.e., changes are localized to the class being modified. However, if methods in the subclasses make direct references to the inherited variables, they will no longer function correctly and will require modification.

4.5.6 Renaming Class Categories, Classes, Method Categories, and Methods

A class category, class name, message category, or method name can be renamed as follows:

- Select the class category, class, message category, or method name to be renamed.
- For class categories, class names, and message categories, select **rename** from the yellow button menu of the selected pane. Respond to the resulting prompter window by providing the new name.
- For methods, edit the name of the method in the text pane and accept it to create a new method with the new name. Remove the old method by selecting it and then choosing **remove** from the yellow button menu of the message selectors pane.

Renaming a system class is relatively easy. However, it is not enough just to change the name of the class, because the class may be referenced directly by any method in the system. These methods must be located and physically modified so that references to the old name are replaced by references to the new. This is not as difficult as it sounds, because Smalltalk will generate a message-set browser (see Section 4.6.3) containing those methods that reference the old name. The source code for each method can be manually edited one by one to replace the old name by the new and recompiled. It is the programmer's responsibility to ensure that every affected method is properly modified and recompiled. Fortunately, the system greatly simplifies the task by handing the programmer all the affected methods. Similar care must be used when renaming a method since there can be many users of that method. However, determining if a method is actually using the removed method or is just another one with the same name is a little more difficult to determine. The semantics of the method must be taken into account.

4.5.7 Removing Class Categories, Classes, Method Categories, and Methods

A class category, class, message category, or method can be removed as follows:

- Select the class category, class, message category, or method name to be removed.
- Select **remove** from the yellow button menu of the selected pane.
- Respond to the resulting confirmer window to confirm the deletion.

When initiating a remove operation, a **confirmer menu** (see Fig. 4.23) will appear asking the programmer to confirm whether or not the deletion should really be performed. Confirmation is useful because removing a class or whole category of classes is an irreversible operation. The confirmer is answered by selecting the appropriate response to the query. For example, Fig. 4.23 shows a typical **confirmer window** generated in response to a request to remove all the methods in a particular message category.

Remove is a potentially dangerous operation. Great care is needed when removing classes that are used by other classes in the system. For example, you may be attempting to remove a class that has subclasses or a class that is critical to the operation of Smalltalk itself. Before removing any class or method from the system, be sure you understand what the impact will be on other classes in the system.

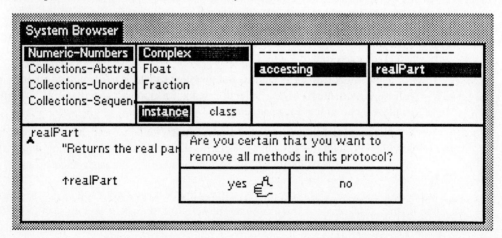

Figure 4.23 Removing all methods in a method category.

Rename class NewComplex (using rename) to OldComplex.

Remove class OldComplex.

4.6 SPECIALIZED BROWSERS

System browsers provide access to the entire Smalltalk system. It is often convenient to create browsers that provide more limited views of the system or views that are not organized along class or message category boundaries. Specialized browsers may be created for three reasons:

- To browse specific class categories, classes, message categories, or messages.
- To browse classes in a specific superclass or inheritance chain.
- To browse sets of related methods; e.g., those methods that send a particular message.

4.6.1 Browsing by Category, Class, Message Category, and Message

Category, **class**, **message category**, and **message browsers** are browsers that limit access to specified categories, classes, message categories, and messages respectively. They are simply limited access system browsers.

A **category browser** provides access only to the classes within a specified category. In all other respects, they provide the same functionality as system browsers. A category browser may be opened from a system browser as follows:

- Select the class category to be browsed.
- Select **spawn** (sometimes labelled **browse**) from the yellow button menu of the class categories pane.
- Frame the class category browser.

Fig. 4.24 illustrates a category browser on the class category **Graphics-Primitives**. Notice that a category browser has the same structure as a system browser except that the class categories pane is missing.

A **class browser** limits access only to a specified class. In all other respects, it provides the same functionality as a category browser. A class browser may be opened from a system browser or a category browser as follows:

- Select the class to be browsed.
- Select **spawn** (sometimes labelled **browse**) from the yellow button menu of the class names pane.
- Frame the class browser.

Fig. 4.25 shows a class browser on class **Pen**.

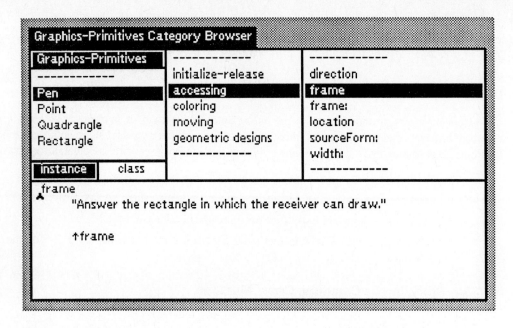

Figure 4.24 Category Browser on the category 'Graphics-Primitives'.

Pen Class Browser

Pen		instance	class

accessing
coloring
moving
geometric designs

----
down
go:
goto:
home

```
,down
▲   "Set the state of the receiver's pen to down (drawing)."

    penDown ← true
```

Figure 4.25 Class Browser.

Finally, there are two other seldom used types of browsers: **message category browsers**, which limit access to a specified message category within a class, and **message**

browsers, which allow only a single method to be viewed. A message category browser or message browser may be opened from a browser as follows:

- Select the message category or message to be browsed.
- Select **spawn** (sometimes labelled **browse**) from the yellow button menu of the message category or message selectors pane respectively.
- Frame the class browser.

Fig 4.26 shows a message category browser on the message category **moving** of class **Pen**. Fig. 4.27 shows a message browser for the instance message with selector **go:** in class **Pen**.

Open the following specialized browsers:

A Category Browser on class category Numeric-Numbers.

A Class Browser on class Fraction.

A Message Category Browser on category 'converting' in class Fraction.

A Message Browser on method 'asFloat' in category 'converting'.

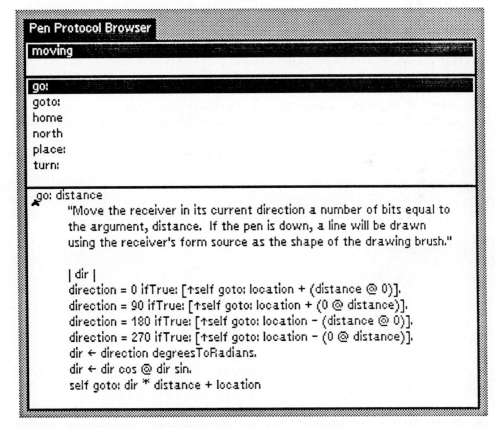

Figure 4.26 Message Category Browser.

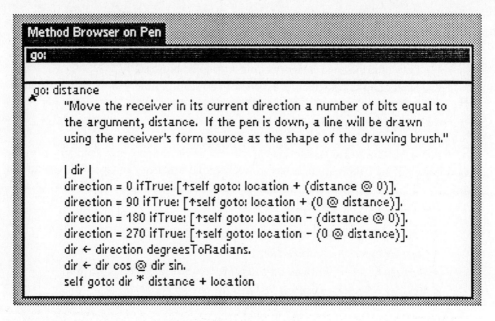

Figure 4.27 Message Browser.

4.6.2 Browsing the Superclass Chain

Class hierarchy browsers[5] are organized around the class hierarchy rather than around class categories. They are particularly useful when trying to view the full protocol supported by a class or when adding and debugging new subclasses. They expedite the viewing of classes in the superclass chain — remember that a class inherits both representation and methods (unless overridden) from its superclasses. The definition of a class, therefore, should not be viewed in isolation. To get the full picture, we must also consider its superclasses. A class hierarchy browser simplifies browsing the classes in the superclass chain of a specified class. In structure and functionality, class hierarchy browsers are similar to category browsers, except that the classes displayed include only the superclasses and subclasses of a specified class rather than the classes in the category of the class. A class hierarchy browser may be opened as follows:

- Select the class to be browsed.
- Select **spawn hierarchy** from the yellow button menu of the class names pane.
- Frame the class browser.

Fig. 4.28 shows a class hierarchy browser on class **Integer**. The class names pane contains class **Integer**, superclasses **Number**, **Magnitude**, and **Object**, along with subclasses **LargeNegativeInteger**, **LargePositiveInteger**, and **SmallInteger**.

---

[5]Note that hierarchy browsers are not supported by Version 1 Smalltalk.

Inside Smalltalk

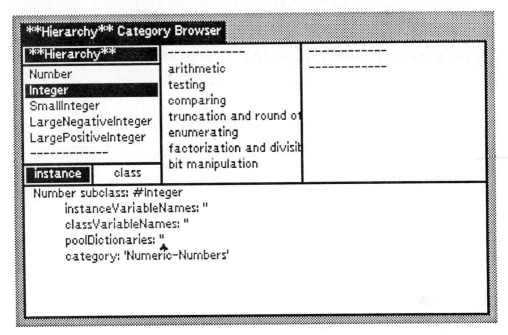

Figure 4.28 Class Hierarchy Browser.

Use a Class Category Browser to answer the following queries:

What is the exact representation of instances of class Quadrangle?
What methods are inherited by class Quadrangle from class Rectangle?

4.6.3 Browsing Selected Sets of Methods

Message-set browsers allow the programmer to browse a collection of methods that share some common characteristic; e.g., methods for the set of messages sent by a specific method. Since the messages selected cut across class boundaries, message selectors are uniquely identified by listing them together with their respective class names. Message-set browsers are important programming and debugging tools. We briefly describe some of their most important uses.

Browsing the Set of Methods that Send a Particular Message

An excellent way to understand how to use a message is to examine methods that already use it. A message-set browser on the set of methods that send a particular message can be created as follows:

- Select (in a browser) the method whose use is to be examined.
- Select **senders** from the yellow button menu of the message selectors pane.
- Frame the message-set browser.

Fig. 4.29 shows a message set browser created on the class method with selector **fromUser** in class **Rectangle**. Alternatively, the same message-set browser could have been created by evaluating the following expression (see the System Workspace for a template).

Smalltalk **browseAllCallsOn**: #fromUser

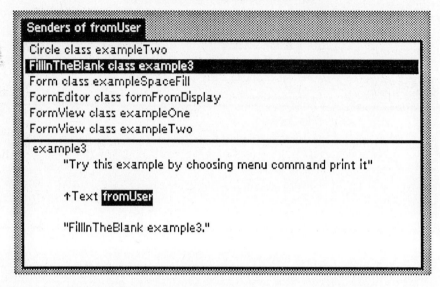

Figure 4.29 Message-set Browser on senders of **fromUser**.

Note that the message-set browser is created on the selector of the message. The browser will therefore contain references to the use of any method with that selector. Since the same selector may be used by any number of classes, some of the references in a message-set browser may not be to the method under scrutiny. For example, the message-set browser created in Fig. 4.29 contains references to the use of method **fromUser** in class **Form** as well as class **Rectangle**.

Use a Message-set browser to answer the following query: which methods send the message with selector 'go:'?

Browsing the Set of Methods that Implement a Particular Message

It is often useful to browse through the implementations of methods with a given selector. A message-set browser on the set of methods that implement a particular message can be created as follows:

- Select (in a browser) any method with the selector whose implementations you wish to examine.

- Select **implementors** from the yellow button menu of the message selectors pane.

- Frame the message-set browser.

Earlier in this chapter, we suggested browsing through the system to look for classes that had **example1** methods associated with them. The aim was to examine and evaluate the examples to learn about the capabilities of the classes in the system. A more convenient method of finding the **example1** methods would be to create a message-set browser on all implementors of **example1**. An alternative way to create a message-set browser on all classes that have **example1** methods (see Fig. 4.30) would be to evaluate the following expression (see the System Workspace for a template).

Smalltalk browseAllImplementorsOf: #example1

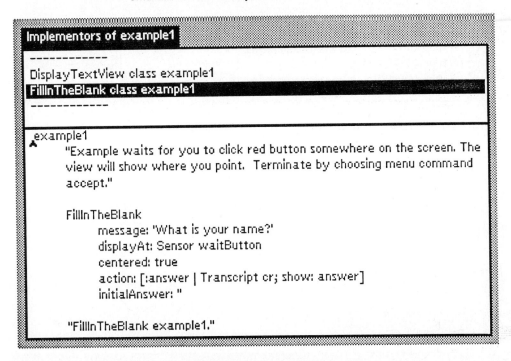

Figure 4.30 Message-set Browser on implementors of example1.

Use a Message-set browser to answer the following query: which classes implement the message with selector 'at:put:'?

Browsing the Set of Methods that Are Sent in a Particular Method

When trying to understand the implementation of a method, it is often useful to browse the methods for messages sent by the method under study. A message-set browser on the implementors of a particular message sent within a method definition can be created as follows:

- Select (in a browser) the method whose implementation is under study.
- Select **messages** from the yellow button menu of the message selectors pane.

- From the message selector menu, choose the selector to be investigated.
- Frame the resulting message-set browser on all implementors of the selector.

Suppose we were viewing method + in class Point. Selecting **messages** from the yellow button menu of the message selector pane displays a menu containing the selectors used by + (see Fig. 4.31). Selecting **asPoint** from the menu, for example, opens a message-set browser on all implementors of **asPoint** (see Fig. 4.32).

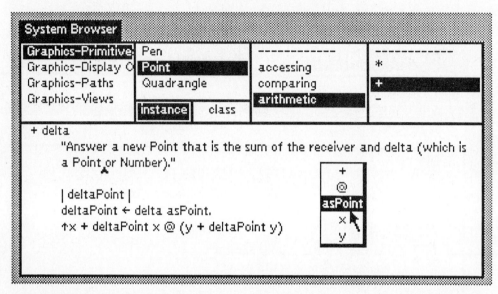

Figure 4.31 Message Selector Menu for messages sent in method +:in class Point.

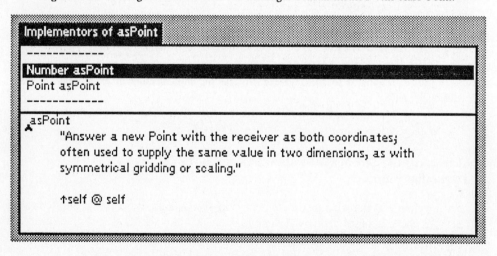

Figure 4.32 Message-set Browser on implementors of asPoint

Use a Message-set browser to investigate the messages sent by instance method 'intersects:' in class Rectangle.

Browsing the Set of Methods that Reference a
Particular Instance or Class Variable

Message-set browsers can also be created to browse methods that reference a particular variable or literal. The method used to open the browser is dependent on the type of variable or literal involved. If no methods are found that reference a particular variable or literal, the string 'Nobody' is displayed in the System Transcript window (if open). A browser can be opened on methods that reference a particular **instance** or **class variable** as follows:

- Select in a browser the class whose variables are to be studied.

- Select **inst var refs** or **class var refs** from the yellow button menu of the class names pane.

- From the menu of variables that appears, select the instance or class variable to be studied.

- Frame the resulting message-set browser on all methods of the class and subclasses that reference that variable.

Fig. 4.33 shows the menu of instance variables displayed when **inst var refs** is selected on class **Pen**. Fig. 4.34 shows the result of selecting **frame** from this menu — a message-set browser on methods that reference **frame** is created.

Investigate the instance variables and their users in class Path; investigate the class variables in classes Form and Date.

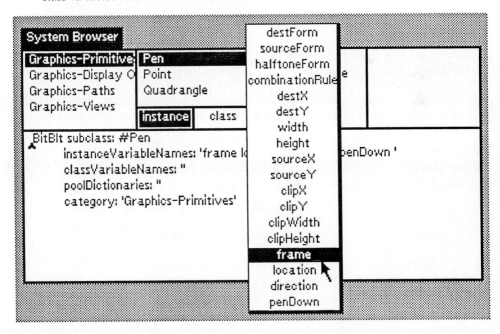

Figure 4.33 Instance Variable Menu for class Pen.

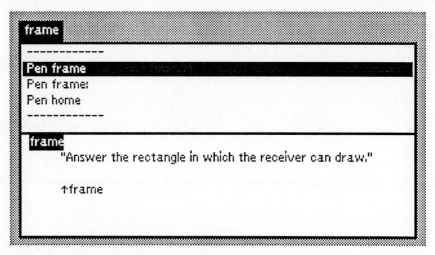

Figure 4.34 Message-set Browser on the instance variable 'frame'.

Browsing the Set of Methods that Reference a Particular Class

To open a browser on methods that reference a particular **class**, perform the following:

- In a browser, select the class whose references are to be studied.
- Select **class refs** from the yellow button menu of the class names pane.
- Frame the resulting message-set browser on all methods that reference that class.

Browsing the Set of Methods that Reference a Particular Global Variable

To open a browser on methods that reference a **global variable** or **pool dictionary variable**, evaluate an expression of the following form:

Smalltalk **browseAllCallsOn:** (aSystemDictionary **associationAt:** #aSymbol)

For example, to create a browser on methods that reference the global variable **Display**, evaluate the following:

Smalltalk **browseAllCallsOn:** (Smalltalk **associationAt:** #Display)

Use message-set browsers to answer the following queries:

Which methods reference the instance variable 'hours' in class Time?
Which methods reference the class variable 'Pi' in class Float?
Which methods reference the class Interval?
Which methods reference the class Random?
Which methods reference the global variable Transcript?
Which methods reference the variable 'Tab' in pool dictionary TextConstants?

4.7 SAVING YOUR WORK

In this section, we discuss ways in which modifications and additions to Smalltalk can be saved. We also provide a little more insight into the global organization of the Smalltalk system. The three fundamental techniques for saving changes made to a Smalltalk system include the following:

- Writing (or **filing out**) Smalltalk source code to external files in a form that can subsequently be read back (or **filed in**).
- Updating the Smalltalk image.
- Using the changes file maintained by the Smalltalk system.

4.7.1 Filing Out

The simplest way to save modifications to a Smalltalk system is to file or write out those parts that have been changed to an external file in a format that can be subsequently recompiled into Smalltalk. This is also a simple way of transferring Smalltalk source code to other Smalltalk users or to another machine. For example, if you wish to give a class definition to a colleague, the class can be filed out from one Smalltalk system and filed into the next.

Source code can be selected for filing out at four levels: class categories, classes, message categories, or individual methods. Each of the yellow button pane menus in a system browser has a **fileOut** entry corresponding to the four levels of output. Selecting the **fileOut** entry in a pane writes the corresponding selected item to an external file. File names are automatically generated according to the following convention.

Information Filed Out	File Name
category	categoryName.st
class	className.st
message category	className-messageCategoryName.st
method	className-messageSelectorName.st

Files are written out in a special standard format so that they can be read back into Smalltalk using **fileIn**, the inverse of **fileOut**. It is not necessary to understand this file format. Unless you are an experienced Smalltalk programmer, we suggest that you do not edit files in this format before filing them back in. The format is readable but uses the ! (exclamation) character as a special delimiter and writes the source code in a form that can be used to recreate the classes and methods when read using **fileIn**.

Format of Filed Out Code

Each isolated executable expression ends with one exclamation mark. However, an exclamation mark signals the beginning of a list of methods associated with a category; e.g., see '!ConstrainedPen methodsFor: 'moving'!' below — note that an exclamation mark also terminates this header. Each method in the category ends with one exclamation mark. The last one has two but there is exactly one space between them — this space is crucial. Two exclamation marks in a row (without intervening characters) denote an actual exclamation mark in the code.

Fig. 4.35 shows the file created by filing out class **ConstrainedPen**, the subclass of **Pen** described in Chapter 2.

```
'From Smalltalk-80 of March 1st, 1987 on 18 June 1985 at 3:33:01 pm'!
Pen subclass: #ConstrainedPen
    instanceVariableNames: ''
    classVariableNames: ''
    poolDictionaries: ''
    category: 'Graphics-Primitives'!

!ConstrainedPen methodsFor: 'moving'!
east
    "The direction of the receiver is set to face the right of the screen."
    direction ← 0!

go: distance
    "Move the pen in its current direction a number of bits equal to the argument,
    distance. If the pen is down, a line will be drawn using the receiver's source form as
    the shape of the drawing brush. If distance is zero, nothing happens."

    | angle newDirection |
    angle ← direction degreesToRadians.
    newDirection ← angle cos @ angle sin.
    super goto: newDirection * distance + location!

goto: aPoint
    "This message is not appropriate for this object."
    self shouldNotImplement!

south
    "The direction of the receiver is set to face the bottom of the screen."
    direction ← 90!

turn:degrees
    "The direction of the receiver is turned clockwise through an amount equal to the
    argument degrees. The argument is constrained to be a multiple of 90 degrees by
    rounding."
    super turn: (degrees roundedTo: 90).!

turnLeft
    "The direction of the receiver is turned to the left 90 degrees."
    super turn: -90.!

turnRight
    "The direction of the receiver is turned to the right 90 degrees."
    super turn: 90.!

west
    "The direction of the receiver is set to face the left of the screen."
    direction ← 180! !

"-- -- -- -- -- -- -- -- -- -- -- -- -- -- -- -- -- -- -- "!
```

```
ConstrainedPen class
    instanceVariableNames: ''!

!ConstrainedPen class methodsFor: 'examples'!
example
    "Illustrates the use of constrained pens."
    | quill |
    quill ← ConstrainedPen new.
    quill home; place: 300@300; down.
    4 timesRepeat: [quill go: 100; turnLeft]

    "ConstrainedPen example"! !
```

Figure 4.35 File created by filing out class ConstrainedPen.

4.7.2 Printing

The entry **printOut** also appears in each of the pane menus of a system browser. It is designed to write out class descriptions in a formatted or 'pretty printed' form suitable for reading by a human reader. By comparison, the form produced by **fileOut** is designed to be readable primarily by the system. Files generated using **printOut** cannot be subsequently evaluated back into Smalltalk using **fileIn**. The implementation of the **printOut** method is system dependent. Typically, implementations take advantage of special control character sequences to allow for different fonts and different emphasis, such as bold or italic, and may support PostScript™ formatted output to a laser printer. In implementations that do not support printing, **printOut** defaults to **fileOut**. Consult your system documentation for details of the specific implementation for your system.

4.7.3 Filing In

Files created using **fileOut** can be subsequently read back into Smalltalk with the **fileIn** operation using an expression of the following form (see the **System Workspace** for a template).

(FileStream oldFileNamed: 'fileName') fileIn

A log of the progress of the **fileIn** operation is displayed in the **System Transcript** window. Any errors encountered during the evaluation of the file will be reported in this log. To avoid errors of this nature, we suggest you do not edit files that have been filed out. Note also that when new class descriptions are added to the system during the filing in process, browsers that are already open will not automatically contain their description. Select **update** from the yellow button menu in the **class categories pane** to update the browser.

File out class Pen, exit from Smalltalk, examine but do not modify the file with your system editor, reenter Smalltalk and file in the file.

4.7.4 Using the File List Browser

The preferred method of obtaining code in an external file is through a **file list browser**. A file list browser is opened by selecting **file list** from the system menu. This browser consists of three vertically stacked panes (see Fig. 4.36): one to select a set of candidate files, one to provide feedback on which ones are available, and the final one to provide the actual file information.

The topmost pane is used to locate a disk, directory, or file name either via mouse interactions through pop-up menus or via keyboard interactions by typing the name. The former is more convenient but the latter is faster and more direct if you know the file name or if you can specify it with a pattern. A pattern can contain wild card characters '*' to represent any string and '#' to represent a single character. Given an accepted entry in the top pane, the middle pane displays the files or directory names matching the selection or pattern. For an exact match, both panes contain exactly the same name. The contents of a file or directory are displayed in the bottom pane. Typically, this information is either filed in (compiled and integrated with the existing library), edited and saved, or simply browsed.

File list browsers are necessarily somewhat dependent on the capabilities of the underlying operating system. Most Smalltalk systems support hierarchical file systems but the actual names or patterns used for files and directories will depend on the supporting operating system; e.g., Unix, Macintosh, or MS-DOS. They also provide a subset of the operations typically provided by the file system; e.g., operations for renaming files or deleting them.

File list browsers have slightly different menu entries from one system to another — a typical set of file list browser yellow button menus is shown in Fig. 4.37. In the sections that follow, we will describe how to access, edit, save, and file in files using file list browsers. For a brief description of the functionality of other menu selections not explicitly discussed below, see the glossary at the end of this chapter.

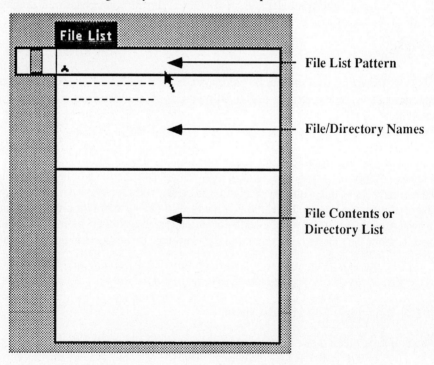

Figure 4.36 Structure of a File List Browser.

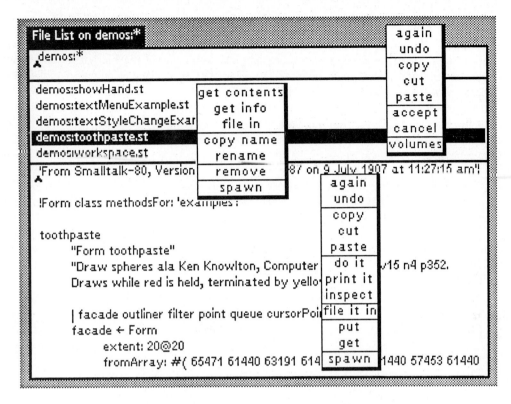

Figure 4.37 Typical File List Browser Menus.

Accessing a File

Most of the time, the exact location or name of a file is not known. In this case, a search for the file in a hierarchical file system might proceed as follows. First select **volumes** from the yellow button menu of the top pane. The names of the disk volumes accessible will be displayed in a menu. Select the desired volume. This feature allows you to select from any number of hard and floppy disk drives that may be connected to your system. The pattern

volume-name.*

will be displayed in the topmost pane. Additionally, the files and directories matching this pattern will be displayed in the middle pane. Entries in the middle pane are selectable. Selecting a file will display the contents of the file in the bottom pane. Selecting a directory will list the subfiles and subdirectories. Entries in the bottom pane are not selectable. To view entries in this list, the pattern in the topmost pane must be changed to select files in the chosen middle pane directory. This is most simply achieved by selecting the menu entry **new pattern** from the middle pane. This sequence of operations may be iterated as many times as necessary to locate a given file.

To repeat, choosing **volumes** (in the top pane) provides entries in the middle pane. Selecting one of these entries (say a directory) and choosing **new pattern** (in the middle pane) causes this entry to move to the top pane. The entries for the new top pane are then displayed in the middle pane. This can be repeated as long as there are subdirectories to "walk through." Ultimately, the middle pane will contain the file you wish to manipulate. If you are using a hierarchical file system, the complete path name of the file will be available; e.g., instead of 'toothpaste.st', a name like 'Hard Disk:ParcPlace Smalltalk:demos:toothpaste.st' will be provided in the middle pane. If the path name becomes too long, it will be truncated as shown in Fig. 4.37. If the file in the middle pane is now selected, the contents of the file can be brought into the bottom pane by selecting **get contents** from the middle pane's yellow button menu. This does not compile the file, it only provides access in the bottom pane so that you can view the contents and, for example, copy bits and pieces of it.

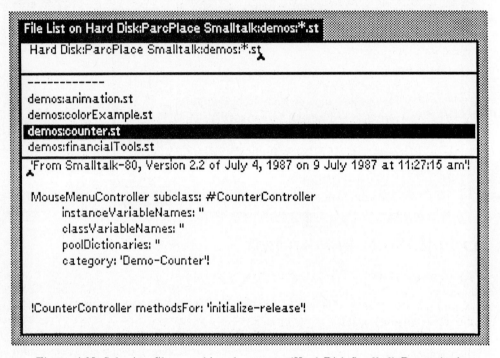

Figure 4.38 Selecting files matching the pattern 'Hard Disk:Smalltalk:Demos:*.st'.

When a file list browser is first opened, the file list pattern in the top pane is empty. It is possible to avoid the protocol discussed above by entering a pattern string directly into the top pane and choosing **accept** from the top pane's yellow button menu. For example, to view those files terminating in '.st' in directory 'ParcPlace Smalltalk:demos', pattern 'Hard Disk:ParcPlace Smalltalk:demos:*.st' might be provided in the top pane. The matching file names will appear in the middle pane as shown in Fig. 4.38. Selecting one of these entries and choosing **get contents** from the middle pane's yellow button menu will bring the file into into the bottom pane. The characters in the file are now available for viewing or editing.

Editing a File

The text within the file contents (bottom) pane may be edited using the standard **again**, **undo**, **copy**, **cut** and **paste** editing commands. It is important to realize that when you edit the text you are not changing the text in the file. Only the copy of the text in the browser is being changed. The two commands **put** and **get** are used to store the contents of the file contents pane back into the file and to read or reread the contents of the file into the file browser pane respectively.

Filing In From the File List Browser

To compile the complete contents of a file, select **file in** from the yellow button menu of the file/directory (middle) pane. Alternatively, if you wish to compile only a portion of the file, select the desired part with the mouse (to highlight it) and choose **file it in** from the yellow button menu of the file contents (bottom) pane. In this case, great care must be taken to include the exclamation marks that surround the code. See Section 4.7.1, *Filing In*, for a discussion of the external file format.

> *Experiment with File List Browsers:*
> *File out a particular class, read the contents of the file containing the class definition into a file list browser, make some cosmetic changes to the file, save the updated file, and file in the updated version of the file.*
>
> *Try traversing the file/directory structure of your system.*
> *What happens if you type a pattern for which no files match?*
> *How would you open a File List Browser by evaluating a piece of code?*
> *What happens if you try to access the contents of a non-text file?*

4.7.5 Updating the Smalltalk Image

When we enter Smalltalk, we are actually loading a snapshot of the Smalltalk environment known as a **Smalltalk image**. The image is a snapshot in the sense that it recorded the precise state of the system when it was created. The state of the system at any time includes the compiled version of the Smalltalk class library and the state of the desktop. The system remembers what windows are open, their location on the screen, and so on. When an image is loaded, the state of the Smalltalk system is restored to what it was at the point when the image was created.

If you have added new classes to the Smalltalk library, you may wish to incorporate those classes permanently into a new Smalltalk image. A few words of caution about making snapshots are necessary. The Smalltalk image is large — make sure you have enough room on your disk to create the new image. Always keep a backup copy of the original Smalltalk image that came with your system. If you share your Smalltalk system with other programmers, be aware that they will be forced to use your new image. This may or may not be desirable. Alternatively, each programmer can have his own image.

The Smalltalk image may be updated at any time during a session by selecting **save** (sometimes relabelled **snapshot**) from the **system menu**. Alternatively, when quitting from Smalltalk, select **Save, then quit** from the quit menu generated when **quit** is selected from the **system menu**. In both cases, a prompter window will appear requesting the name of the file in which to store the new image. The prompter initially displays the name of the current image file. If you do not want to overwrite the old image, edit the name in the prompter window. By convention, images have names like **fileName.im** or **filename.image** depending on the system you are using. Another file, a **changes** file (see the next section), with the name **fileName.changes** is also created whenever a new image is created. When an image file is used to reload Smalltalk, the corresponding changes file must also be available.

4.7.6 Using the Changes File

Three external files are required to run Smalltalk: a sources, image, and changes file.

Sources File	Contains the Smalltalk source code for the Smalltalk class library. This file is normally not changed by the programmer and thus represents the source code library as delivered with your Smalltalk system.
Image File	A file representing the state of the entire Smalltalk system at the time the image was created. Includes the compiled versions of the class library and the state of all objects that make up the Smalltalk environment.
Changes File	A log file (in fileOut format) containing the source code for all changes that have been made to the Smalltalk environment. Entries are automatically logged to this file whenever an expression is evaluated, whenever a method definition is changed, and so on.

The sources file represents the source for the current release of Smalltalk and is therefore shared by all programmers using the Smalltalk system. Changes made to the Smalltalk class library do not modify the sources file — rather they are logged in the changes file. This makes it possible to exit from Smalltalk at the end of a session without saving any of the changes that were made. These changes remain logged in the changes file and can subsequently be examined, edited, or filed in, if necessary. It is important to remember that image and changes files must be coordinated — you must use the changes files created when the image was created.

By maintaining their own personal copies of the image and changes file, many programmers can share the same sources file. If space does not permit multiple copies of the image file to be maintained, a single image file may also be shared. The changes file can be used as a way of exchanging Smalltalk source code and is a valuable aid in recovering from any kind of system crash.

The Smalltalk environment keeps an internal form of the contents of the changes file called the **change set**. Modifications made to the system are recorded in both the change set and the changes file. The change set differs from the changes file in that it only contains modifications to the class library, not expressions that were evaluated. A simple way of creating a changes file containing only the changes made during a single Smalltalk session is to evaluate the expression

Smalltalk **noChanges**

at the beginning of the session. This empties the change set but has no effect on the changes file. At the end of the session evaluate the expression

(FileStream **fileNamed:** 'changeFileName') **fileOutChanges**

If a Smalltalk system is shared by a number of users, each user can maintain a personal changes file by evaluating 'Smalltalk **noChanges**' after loading Smalltalk and then filing in the personal changes file. At the end of the session, file out the change set as shown above.

Over time, changes files can become quite large. Every evaluated expression and changed definition is included in the log. Moreover, the changes file contains redundant information. For example, if you have changed the definition of a method several times, each re-definition of the method is stored in the changes file. Of course, only the latest definition matches the compiled version of the method, and therefore all earlier versions of the method can be removed from the changes file. Consequently, it is worth removing these redundancies periodically by condensing the changes file. This can be done by evaluating the expression

Smalltalk condenseChanges

4.7.7 Surviving a System Crash

Since the changes file maintains a log of all the changes made to the class library, it can be used to recover from a system crash. It is best, of course, to avoid crashing the system in the first place. Smalltalk is a robust system but it is also an open system. The programmer has access to the most fundamental system classes. Modifying such classes can easily render Smalltalk inoperable! In this kind of situation it is advisable, if space permits, to save the image before making any changes that may have catastrophic effects.

If your system has crashed, the best way to recover is to load the latest image and file in the changes file. If the changes file is large, you can avoid filing in the complete file by creating a file containing only those changes that have taken place since the last snapshot was made. Each time a snapshot is made, a comment line **"----SNAPSHOT----"** is inserted into the changes file.

Smalltalk provides specialized browsers for manipulating the changes file and change set. For information on these, consult the Orange book or experiment with the expressions in the System Workspace for manipulating changes files.

4.8 SUMMARY

This chapter has described the central role played by browsers in the Smalltalk programming process. In particular, we have discussed the following:

- System browsers for viewing the entire Smalltalk class library.
- Adding, viewing, and modifying class and method definitions.
- Class hierarchy browsers for browsing hierarchically related classes.
- Message-set browsers for browsing collections of related methods.
- Filing out to and filing in from external files.
- File list browsers for browsing and editing external files.
- Saving the Smalltalk image.
- The role of the Smalltalk changes file.
- How to survive a system crash.

4.9 EXERCISES

The exercises that follow involve the evaluation of Smalltalk code. When a semantic error is discovered during the evaluation of Smalltalk code, execution halts and a notifier window is displayed. The notifier displays a message describing the cause of the error. If you are not familiar with the use of notifiers and debuggers to debug Smalltalk code, we suggest that, until these topics are fully covered in Chapter 5, you simply close the notifier window (select close from the window menu) and debug your code manually.

1. Complete paper exercises 3 through 8 from Chapter 2 in Smalltalk.

2. In this chapter, we asked the reader to attempt to find classes with **example** methods. Explicitly looking for a method called **example** will not be sufficient — many methods in the **examples** category are called **example1, example2**, and so on. Create a message browser on all methods in category **examples** for all classes by evaluating the following expression (see the System Workspace for a template).

   Smalltalk
       browseAllMethodsInCategory:
         #examples

   Select and evaluate the methods found in this browser.

3. There is no menu entry for renaming a method in the message selectors pane menu of a browser. What is the best method of renaming a method?

4. Suppose you wanted to move or copy all methods in a particular category of one class to a new category in a different class. Moving or copying the methods one by one is far too slow and tedious. Browse the system classes for a simple way of achieving this and other similar large-scale copy operations. Hint: see class category Kernel-Classes.

5. As previously mentioned, it is important to understand the impact of making changes such as removing or renaming classes on the class library. How would you use message-set browsers to identify the impact of a change? For example, imagine you are going to rename or remove one of the instance variables of a class.

6. A specialized **change-management browser** can be created to browse over the changes in a changes file by evaluating the expression

   ChangeListView **recover**

   For safety, you should keep a backup of the changes file before creating the change-management browser.

   To browse the change set, a message-set browser, known as a **change-set browser**, can be created by evaluating the expression

   Smalltalk **browseChangedMessages**

   Create change-management and change-set browsers and experiment with them to determine their capabilities. In particular, identify major differences between them.

7. Find all implementors of +.

8. Find all users of **display**.

9. Choose an arbitrary method and find all implementors of one of the message selectors it uses.

10. Create a hierarchy browser for class Array. Use this to find out how to make a copy of an array in which all zeroes are replaced by -1.

11. ParcPlace™ Smalltalk includes separate source code for protocol browsers. **Protocol browsers** view the entire protocol of a class; i.e., not only the protocol supported directly by the class but also protocol inherited from superclasses. If your system supports protocol browsers, file in the source code and explore their functionality.

4.10 GLOSSARY

Smalltalk browsers

System Browser A window supporting many programming activities; e.g., viewing the class library, modifying existing classes and methods, and adding new classes.

Class Category Browser A browser providing access only to information relating to a specific class category.

Class Browser A browser giving access only to information relating to a specific class.

Class Hierarchy Browser A browser organized on a class hierarchy rather than class categories. Provides access only to a class, its superclasses and subclasses.

Message Category Browser A browser providing access only to information relating to a specific message category within a class.

Message Browser A browser providing access only to a particular method within a class.

Message-Set Browser A browser providing access only to a related set of methods. The set of methods share some common characteristic; e.g., being the senders of a particular message.

File List Browser A browser providing access to and editing on the contents of external text files.

yellow button menu commands for the class categories pane

print out Creates a file in 'pretty print format' containing a description of the classes in the selected class category; the file name is system dependent; the file created cannot be filed back in. In some systems **printout** and **file out** are synonymous.

file out Creates a file in 'file out format' containing a description of the classes in the selected class category. This file has the name 'classCategoryName.st' and can be subsequently filed back into the system.

spawn Opens a class category browser on the selected class category.

add category Adds a new class category to the system either before the selected class category or at the end of the list if no category is currently selected. A prompter window requests the name of the new category. Typically, class category names are capitalized multi-word names separated by dashes.

rename Changes a class category name. Requests the new name from a prompter window.

remove Removes a selected class category and any classes in that category from the system. If any classes are to be deleted, a confirmer appears to request confirmation.

update Updates the information displayed in the browser. Changes to the class library made external to a browser (e.g., filing in a class definition) are not automatically visible to the browser.

edit all Displays the class categories together with the classes in each category in the text pane. The list may be edited to change the class categories or the order in which categories are displayed. Changes must be **accept**ed into the system.

find class Used to locate a class in a browser. A prompter window requests the name of the class. If a pattern string is provided, all classes matching the pattern string, if any, are displayed in a list menu.

yellow button menu commands for the class names pane

print out Creates a file in 'pretty print format' containing a description of the classes in the selected class category; the file name is system dependent; the file created cannot be filed back in. In some systems **printout** and **file out** are synonymous.

file out Creates a file in 'file out format' containing a description of the selected class. This file has the name 'className.st' and can be later filed back into the system.

spawn Opens a class browser on the selected class.

spawn hierarchy Opens a class hierarchy browser on the selected class.

hierarchy Displays the superclass/subclass hierarchy of the selected class in the text pane. Depending on the instance-class switch setting, displays either a class or a metaclass hierarchy.

definition Displays the definition of the selected class in the text pane. Depending on the instance-class switch setting, displays either the class or metaclass definition. The definition may be edited and **accept**ed into the system.

comment Displays the comment associated with the selected class in the text pane. Depending on the instance-class switch setting, displays either the class or metaclass comment. The comment may be edited and **accept**ed into the system.

protocols Displays the entire message protocol associated with the selected class in the text pane. Depending on the instance-class switch setting, displays either the instance or class protocol. It may be edited and **accept**ed into the system.

inst var refs Displays a menu of the instance variables of the selected class and its superclasses. Selecting from the menu opens a message-set browser on all methods in the system that refer to the selected instance variable.

class var refs Displays a menu of the class variables of the selected class and its superclasses. Selecting from the menu opens a message-set browser on all methods in the system that refer to the selected class variable.

class refs Opens a message-set browser on all methods in the system that refer to the selected class.

find method Used to locate a method in a class. A list menu of the messages implemented by the currently selected class is displayed, allowing the user to select the method to be viewed.

rename Renames a selected class. Generates a prompter window that requests the new class name. Opens a message-set browser on all methods that refer to the class, enabling all such references to be manually changed to the new name.

remove Removes a selected class from the system. A notifier window appears if the class to be removed has subclasses. Close the notifier window to abort the remove or select proceed from the yellow button menu to continue.

yellow button menu commands for the message categories pane

print out Creates a file in 'pretty print format' containing a description of the classes in the selected class category; the file name is system dependent; the file created cannot be filed back in. In some systems **printout** and **file out** are synonymous.

file out Creates a file in 'file out format' containing a description of the methods in the selected class category. The name 'className.messageCategoryName.st' is given to this file — it can subsequently be filed back into the system.

spawn Opens a message category browser on the selected message category.

add protocol Adds a new message category to the selected class. A prompter window requests the name of the new category. The category is inserted before the selected message category or at the end of the list if no category is currently selected. Typically, message category names consist of a series of lowercase words.

rename Changes a selected message category name. Generates a prompter window that requests the new name.

remove Removes a selected message category from the system. If any methods are to be deleted as a result, a confirmer appears to request confirmation.

yellow button menu commands for the message selectors pane

senders Opens a message-set browser on all methods in the system that send the selected message.

spawn Opens a message browser on the selected message.

file out Creates a file in 'file out format' containing a description of the selected method. This file has the name 'className.messageSelector.st' and can be subsequently filed back into the system.

print out Creates a file in 'pretty print format' containing a description of the classes in the selected class category; the file name is system dependent; the file created cannot be filed back in. In some systems **printout** and **file out** are synonymous.

implementors Opens a message-set browser on all methods in the system that implement the selected message.

messages Displays a menu of the message selectors used in the currently selected method. Selecting from the menu opens a message-set browser on all implementors of the selected message selector.

move Moves a selected message from one category to another. A prompter requests the new destination either in the form 'className>categoryName' or 'category-Name' if in the same class. A new category name is added if it does not already exist.

remove Removes a selected message from the system. A confirmer requests confirmation.

yellow button menu commands for the text pane

undo An editing operation reversing the effects of the last edit command; e.g., **undo** can be used after a **cut** to paste back the deleted text or after a **paste** to delete the pasted text and restore the original, if any.

again An editing operation that repeats the last **replace**, **copy**, or **cut** operation. Can be used after a **replace** to repeat the replace operation on the next occurrence of the text that was changed. Selecting **again** with the **shift** key depressed replaces **all** occurrences of the text with the replacement text; **again** can be used after a **cut** or **copy** operation to find and select the next occurrence of the text to be cut or copied.

paste Pastes a copy of the text from the most recent **cut** or **copy** operation so that it replaces the selected text in the active window. If there was no selected text, the copy is inserted after the current insertion point. Paste operations may be repeated to paste the same text into a document more than once.

cut Deletes the currently selected text.

copy Makes a copy of (or remembers) the currently selected text.

do it Evaluates the currently selected text.

print it Evaluates the currently selected text and displays the result.

accept Accepts the text in the text pane into the system. Used to compile method definitions and class definitions, to introduce class and message category reorganizations, and to modify class comments.

cancel Restores the text in the window to its original state or the state immediately after the last accept.

format Formats the code in the text pane to a standard Smalltalk style. The text must not have been edited since the last accept.

spawn Opens a message browser on the selected method.

explain Displays an explanation of any selected variable name or selector such as 'x', 'sum', '+', 'at:put:' or 'Smalltalk'.

file list browsers - file list pattern yellow button menu commands

again, undo, copy, cut, paste Standard text editing commands.

accept Saves the current file list pattern and displays any files matching the list pattern in the files/directories names pane.

cancel Restores the file list pattern to its state as of the last previous save.

volumes In systems with multiple disk volumes, displays a list menu of available volumes. Selecting a volume makes that volume the default volume for subsequent file selections.

file list browsers - file/directory yellow button menu commands

copy name Makes a copy of the text of the file or directory name so that it may be subsequently pasted.

file in Reads and evaluates the contents of the selected text file. The text must be in the standard format for filing in. Note that the contents of the external file is filed in rather than the contents of the file contents pane in the browser.

get contents Reads the contents of the selected external file into the file contents pane of the file list browser. No evaluation of the text takes place.

get info Lists information relating to the selected file in the file contents pane of the file list browser. Typical information listed includes the size of the file and when the file was created and last modified.

new pattern Copies the currently selected directory into the topmost pane so that all the files in the selected directory will be shown when the new pattern is accepted.

rename Changes the name of the selected file. Respond to the resulting prompter by typing in the new name of the file.

remove Deletes the selected file. This operation requires confirmation.

spawn Opens a new file browser on the currently selected file. If the file is a directory rather than a text file, a new file browser opens and displays the files in the directory in the file contents pane of the browser.

file list browsers - file contents or directory list yellow button menu commands

again, undo, copy, cut, paste Standard text editing commands.

do it, print it, inspect Standard evaluation and inspection commands.

file it in Files in (i.e., reads and evaluates) the selected text into the Smalltalk system.

put Replaces the contents of the external file with the current contents of the file contents pane.

get Replaces the contents of the file contents pane with the contents of the currently selected text file.

spawn Opens a new file list browser on the contents of the file contents pane. The new browser reflects any changes made to the original since it was opened. The original browser remains open but any changes that have been made are cancelled.

5

Debugging with Inspectors, Notifiers, and Debuggers

5.1 INTRODUCTION

In this chapter, we consider how the Smalltalk programmer can use the Smalltalk environment to detect and correct run-time errors. In general, there is no need to understand the intricate details of the Smalltalk run-time system to appreciate and effectively use its debugging and development tools. Nevertheless, we can better appreciate the tools if we understand that Smalltalk owes much of its power and integrated nature to the cohesiveness of its underlying object-oriented philosophy.

If something can be manipulated, Smalltalk endeavors to treat it as an object. Hence Smalltalk supports objects like collections and forms that can be potentially very large all the way down to very small objects like integers and characters. In keeping with this philosophy, compilers and debuggers too are objects. Indeed, even the run-time data structures can be manipulated as objects; i.e., the environmental data structures can be sent messages and manipulated in the normal Smalltalk fashion. This permits the compiler and debugger, for example, to be implemented directly in Smalltalk. Programmers and designers directly benefit from the features and facilities provided by the Smalltalk environment.

In this chapter, we discuss the intricate details associated with debugging. Six aspects are isolated and discussed.

- Viewing and modifying the internal state (instance variables) of an object.
- Identifying the point in a computation where an error occurred.
- Setting breakpoints to interrupt a computation at a user-selected point.
- Incrementally stepping through a computation.
- Viewing and modifying the state of an interrupted computation.
- Restarting an interrupted computation.

Inspectors, notifiers, and **debuggers** are the main software development tools for debugging in the Smalltalk environment.

Inspector	A window through which the internal state of an object can be viewed and modified.
Notifier	A window generated when a run-time error or user-generated interrupt occurs. The window displays the state of the computation at the point of interruption and indicates the cause of the interruption; e.g., a message not being understood by its receiver.
Debugger	A window in which detailed debugging of an interrupted computation takes place. Debuggers incorporate the functionality of both inspectors and notifiers and provide facilities for viewing the state of a computation: for single stepping through a computation, for modifying methods to correct errors, and for resuming a suspended computation.

It is important to note that the techniques described in this chapter are not only applicable to the debugging process but also can be used to determine how existing code actually works. This is particularly important in an environment where so much emphasis is placed on the reusability of code.

5.2 INSPECTING OBJECTS

An **inspector window** allows the internal state of an object to be viewed and modified. For example, **inspectors** allow a Smalltalk programmer to examine and modify the current values of the instance variables of an object. In addition, the object and its components may be interrogated by sending messages to them or evaluating expressions involving them.

An inspector window can be created on any object simply by sending it the message **inspect**. For example, suppose we evaluate the following code fragment in a workspace:

```
| location |
location ← (200 @ 300).
location inspect.
```

The response to an **inspect** message is a request to frame a window for the inspector. An inspector window (see Fig. 5.1) is then generated on the object **location**. Inspector windows are always labelled with the name of the class of the object being inspected, in this case class **Point**. Structurally, an inspector window is divided into two panes (see Fig. 5.2): a **variable** pane and a **value** pane. The variable pane contains a menu list of the instance variables of the object. The contents of the value pane are dependent on the selection made from the list of variables in the variable pane. Selecting a variable name from the variable pane causes the current value of that variable to be displayed in the value pane. The value pane is a text pane in which expressions may be entered, edited, and evaluated. The value pane may also be used to modify the values of instance variables of an inspected object. Inspectors take us inside the object in the sense that any expression we evaluate can reference the object and its instance variables directly; i.e., they allow the programmer to override the normal requirement that the representation of an object can only be accessed and/or modified using the message protocol supported by the object. Typical yellow button menus associated with the variable and value panes are shown in Fig. 5.2. Note that the inspect entry in the variable pane menu is only available if a variable is selected.

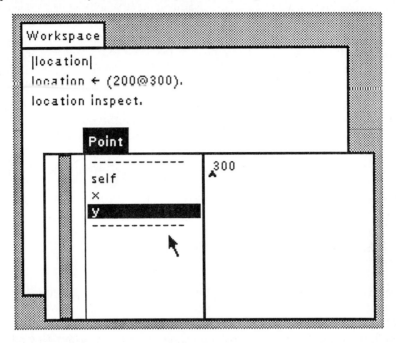

Figure 5.1 Inspector Window on 'location'.

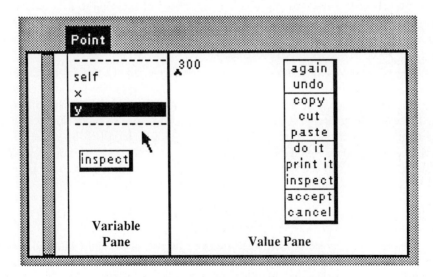

Figure 5.2 Structure of an Inspector Window.

5.2.1 Inspecting the Instance Variables of an Object

Instances of class **Point**, such as the point bound to **location**, have two instance variables, **x** and **y**, representing the x and y coordinates of the point. The variable pane therefore contains menu entries labelled **x** and **y**. In addition, the first entry in the variable pane of any inspector is **self**, an entry that allows reference to the object being inspected. In general, the variable pane will contain a complete list of the instance variables of the object, including those inherited from superclasses. In Fig. 5.1, the entry **y** is selected in the variable pane; the value of **y**, i.e., **300**, is displayed in the value pane. Selecting **x** would display **200**. Selecting **self** would display **200@300**, representing the point (200,300).

The string to be displayed as the value of a variable is computed internally by sending the message **printString** to the variable. By default, **printString** simply prints the name of the class to which the object bound to the variable belongs. Many classes provide more specialized printed representations. Integers print as a character string of their digits (e.g., 123), characters print as a dollar sign followed by the character (e.g., $a), strings print as their constituent characters surrounded by single quotes (e.g., 'a string'), and so on. Other classes, such as **Point** or **Dictionary**, have even more specialized printed representations (e.g., 200@300, Dictionary ('hi' => 'bye' 'white' => 'black')).

5.2.2 Modifying the Values of the Instance Variables of an Object

The value of any instance variable in an inspected object can be modified by selecting the variable to be changed in the variable pane and then typing an expression into the value pane. Selecting **accept** from the value pane's yellow button menu evaluates the expression and binds the result to the selected instance variable. The new value of the instance variable is displayed in the value pane.

Suppose we wished to change the x coordinate of **location** to **100**. Selecting **x** in the variable pane displays the current value of the x coordinate (200) in the value pane. Edit this to read **100** and **accept** the changed value. Selecting **self** in the value pane will confirm that the new value of **location** is **100@300**.

Expressions in the variable pane may directly reference any instance variable of an inspected object. In addition, they may also use pseudo-variables **self** and **super** to refer to the object being inspected. For example, an alternative method of modifying the x-coordinate to **100** would be to accept the expression, **self x - 100**, or even more simply, **x - 100**, as the new value for **x**. Note that the value for **self** cannot be modified by selecting **self** in the variable pane and accepting an expression in the variable pane — only instance variables may be modified; **self** and **super** are pseudo-variables. Pseudo-variables can never be targets of assignment statements.

5.2.3 Evaluating Expressions within an Inspector

Any expression may be typed into the value pane, selected, and evaluated using **do it** or **print it** from the value pane's yellow button menu. Evaluation of the expression is done in the context of the inspected object. The instance variables of the object, together with the pseudo-variables **self** and **super**, may be directly referenced within any expression.

Another method of modifying the point **location** from **200@300** to **100@300** would be to evaluate the expression

self **x**: (x - 100)

in the value pane. The selector **x: anArgument** defined on points changes the x coordinate of the receiver to **anArgument**. Select **self** in the variable pane to confirm that **location** has been modified correctly.

5.2.4 Inspecting the Instance Variables of an Inspected Object

Sometimes it is necessary to inspect the instance variables of an inspected object. In general, we wish to be able to inspect an object to any level of detail by creating additional inspectors. For example, when inspecting an array object, we might wish to create an inspector on some individual element of the array. An inspector can be created on any selected instance variable within an inspector by selecting **inspect** from the **variable pane's yellow button menu**.

For example, suppose we evaluate the following code in a workspace:

```
| triangle |
triangle ← Array new: 3.
triangle
    at: 1 put: 100@140;
    at: 2 put: 300@250;
    at: 3 put: 300@15;
    inspect
```

An inspector is created on the array of three points named **triangle** (see the leftmost inspector in Fig. 5.3). The array has three indexed instance variables that are referenced by indices **1**, **2**, and **3** in the variable pane of the inspector. Selecting **3** from the list in the variable pane displays the value stored at position 3 in the array, namely, the point **300@15**. If we now select **inspect** from the **variable pane's yellow button menu**, an inspector is created on the currently selected instance variable (see the rightmost inspector in Fig. 5.3). We can now examine the instance variables of the third point in the array. Selecting x from the **variable pane** displays the x coordinate of this point, **300**.

Note that if we modify the values of the instance variables of the point within the point inspector, the change in value will also be reflected in the inspector on the array.

Inspect the object created by evaluating each of the following expressions. For each, inspect and modify the instance variables of the object, evaluate expressions involving the inspected object, and open inspectors on the instance variables (if appropriate).

```
Pen new inspect
(7/2) inspect
Date today inspect
Rectangle fromUser inspect
(PopUpMenu labels: 'doit printit exit' lines: 2) inspect
```

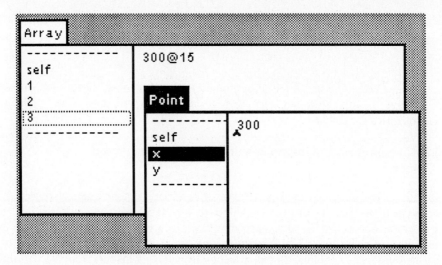

Figure 5.3 Nested Inspector Windows.

What happens if you try to activate the yellow button menu of the variable pane when no variable has yet been selected?

5.2.5 Inspecting Dictionaries

It is sometimes convenient to create special inspectors for browsing certain kinds of objects. Several specialized inspectors are already present in the Smalltalk environment. We will limit discussion to **dictionary inspectors**. Dictionaries in Smalltalk are sets of key-value associations. The user of an inspector on dictionaries should be able to browse through the key-value associations; i.e., select a key and see the corresponding value in the value pane. Dictionary inspectors provide this capability and, in addition, allow values to be modified and entries (key-value associations) to be added to and removed from the dictionary.

Suppose we create a simple telephone directory, add a few entries, and then inspect it.

```
| telephoneNumbers |
telephoneNumbers ← Dictionary new.
telephoneNumbers
    at: #John put: '564-7548';
    at: #Dave put: '564-7545';
    at: #Wilf put: '564-6301';
    inspect.
```

The resulting dictionary inspector is shown in Fig. 5.4. Dictionary inspectors are structurally identical to normal inspectors. However, rather than a list of instance variables, the variable pane contains the names of the keys for which there are entries in the dictionary. Selecting a key displays the value associated with that key in the value pane. In Fig. 5.4, key **Wilf** is selected and his telephone number, **564-6301**, is displayed.

The yellow button menu associated with the variable (or key list) pane of a dictionary inspector (see Fig. 5.5) has entries that are different from those provided by a regular inspector. In addition to menu entry **inspect**, new menu entries **references**, **add field**, and

remove are also provided. The full menu list appears only if a key is selected from the list of keys in the variable pane. If not, only **add field** appears in the menu. A selected key is an implicit argument required by **inspect**, **references**, and **remove**.

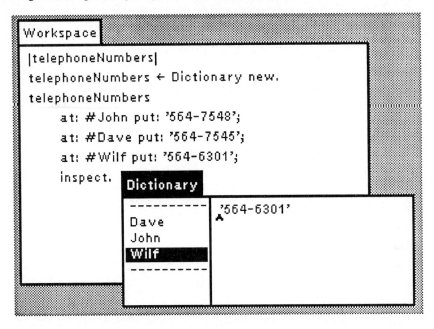

Figure 5.4 A Dictionary Inspector.

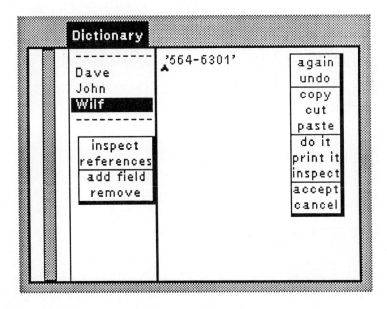

Figure 5.5 Organization of a Dictionary Inspector Window.

inspect	Opens an inspector on the object (value) associated with the selected key.
references	Creates a message-set browser on all references to the selected key.
add field	Adds a new entry to a dictionary. A prompter window will appear and request the name of the key to be added. An entry will then be added to the dictionary with associated value **nil**. If desired, another value can be associated with the key by entering the value in the value pane and selecting **accept**.
remove	Removes the key selected in the key list pane. A confirmer will appear to request confirmation that this undoable operation should be carried out.

Why is a specialized inspector for dictionaries desirable? What if we had simply created a normal inspector on the dictionary? To create a regular inspector on the dictionary **telephoneNumbers,** evaluate the expression **super inspect** in the variable pane of the inspector (see Fig. 5.6). Using **super** instead of **self** will cause the search for the **inspect** method to start in the superclass of **Dictionary** — recall that the class for **telephone-Numbers** is **Dictionary**. The effect of this will be to invoke the inspect method for normal inspectors defined in class **Object** rather than the inspect method in class **Dictionary**.

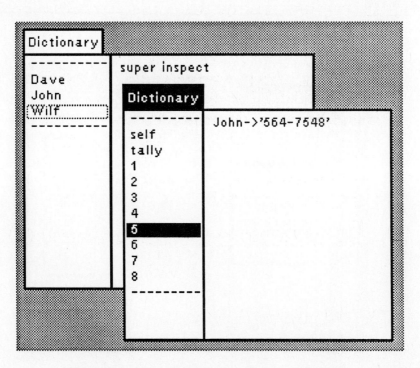

Figure 5.6 A normal Inspector opened on a dictionary.

The inspector on **telephoneNumbers** is shown in Fig. 5.6. Notice that the variable pane now contains the indices of the indexed instance variables rather than the keys. This view of the dictionary emphasizes the fact that a dictionary is an array of associations. Clearly, this is a physical view of the dictionary, appropriate for an implementor, but not the logical view required by the user. To a user, integer indices are meaningless in general. For example, the association with key **John** (see Fig. 5.6) is referenced through index **5**! The instance variable, **tally**, keeps track of the number of entries in the array that are in use; i.e., those entries consisting of key-value associations (as opposed to **nil**).

*Evaluate the expression: Dictionary **new inspect**. Within the resulting inspector, gain experience adding, setting the value of, and removing entries.*

What happens if you try to add a new field with a duplicate key?
What happens if you select accept when no key is selected?

*Inspect **Smalltalk** — a system dictionary.*

5.3 ERROR NOTIFICATION WITH NOTIFIERS

When an error is discovered during the evaluation of a Smalltalk expression, a **notifier window** is automatically displayed. The label of the notifier (see Fig. 5.7) displays a message indicating the cause of the interruption. The notifier window displays the sequence of messages that led up to the point of interruption; i.e., those messages that have been sent but for which no response has yet been generated.

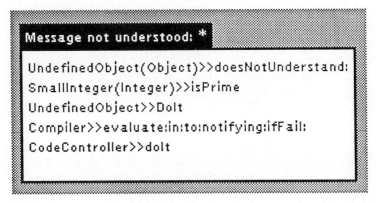

Figure 5.7 Notifier Window.

5.3.1 Interpreting Notifier Windows

The notifier in Fig. 5.7 was generated in response to evaluating the expression **53 isPrime** in a user workspace. Two errors have been deliberately inserted into the method. At the time of evaluation, the **isPrime** method on integers was defined as follows:

```
isPrime
    "Tests whether the receiver is prime or not."
    | divisor |
    self <= 0 ifTrue: [↑false].
    (self >= 1 & self <= 3) ifTrue: [↑true].
    self \\ 2 = 0 ifTrue: [↑false].
    divisor ← 3.
    [divisor * divisor < self] whileTrue: [
        self \\ divisor = 0
            ifTrue: [↑false]
            ifFalse: [divisor ← divisor + 2]].
    ↑true
```

The label of the notifier indicates that the interruption was caused by a message with selector ***** being sent and not understood by its receiver. Although many different errors may occur at run-time, by far the most common error is that of a message not being understood by its receiver.

The notifier window helps identify the point at which the error occurred by listing the last few messages that were sent but not completed prior to the error interrupt. The list of entries represents the activation stack of the interrupted computation. The first entry represents the last message that was sent before the interruption, the second entry is the previous message, and so on. Each entry is said to represent a single **message send** and has one of the following two forms:

ClassOfReceiver>>MessageSelector
ClassOfReceiver(ClassOfMethodSelected)>>MessageSelector

Each entry lists the selector of the message that was sent and the class of the receiver of the message. If a class is listed in parentheses after the class of the receiver, it indicates the class where the associated method was found; i.e., the result of looking for the method in the superclass chain. This class is not listed if the method is found in the class of the receiver. For example, if we examine the entries shown in the notifier window in Fig. 5.7, we see that the last three entries are concerned with the compilation and request for evaluation (**do it**) of the expression **53 isPrime**. These entries are of little interest. The second entry

SmallInteger(Integer)>>isPrime

describes the sending of the message **isPrime** to the receiver **53**, an object of class **SmallInteger** (a subclass of class **Integer**). The class **Integer** appears in parentheses because the **isPrime** method was found in class **Integer**.

Together with the error message, **Message not understood: ***, the first message-send entry

UndefinedObject(Object)>>doesNotUnderstand

indicates that a message with ***** as the selector was sent to a receiver of class **UndefinedObject**. No method with selector ***** was found in class **UndefinedObject** or in its superclass **Object**. Any message that is not understood by any class in the superclass chain of the receiver will eventually be sent to class **Object**. This class automatically sends a **doesNotUnderstand: aSelector** message to the original receiver. If the class of the receiver and its superclasses do not implement a **doesNotUnderstand** message themselves, then the **doesNotUnderstand** will again reach class **Object**. In this case, a notifier is generated with a label of the form **Message not understood: MessageSelector**. This scheme provides a simple default error handling mechanism, while still allowing the user to provide more specialized error handlers by implementing a **doesNotUnderstand** message to override the inheritance of the default handler.

In this example, the notifier has provided enough clues to discover the cause of the error. The only time a message with selector * is sent in the **isPrime** method is in the expression **divisor * divisor**. However, the notifier indicates that the message was sent to an object of class **UndefinedObject**. We would have expected the receiver, **divisor**, to refer to an object of class **Integer** (or some subclass such as **SmallInteger**). However, notice that no object was bound explicitly to **divisor**; i.e., the variable **divisor** is an uninitialized variable. All Smalltalk variables are initially bound to the object **nil**, an object of class **UndefinedObject**. To correct the error, an initialization statement such as **divisor ← 3** should be inserted into the method definition.

5.3.2 Continuing After an Error Notification

Fig. 5.8 shows the entries in the yellow button menu of a notifier window. The programmer can either select one of them or none.

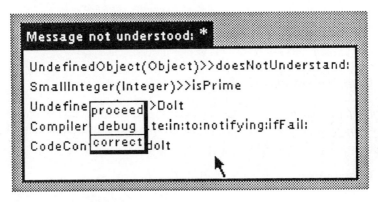

Figure 5.8 Notifier Yellow Button Menu.

After a notifier window has been generated, four separate scenarios are possible. We describe each of them in turn.

- **If the cause of the error was discovered:**

    close   Close the notifier by selecting **close** in the notifier's blue button menu. This has the effect of terminating the interrupted computation. The programmer may edit the method to correct the bug using a browser and try again.

- **If no problem was discovered, then execution can be continued:**

  proceed   Select **proceed** from the notifier's yellow button menu. The effect is to continue the evaluation from the point of suspension. This action is most useful after an interrupt explicitly caused by the programmer; i.e., a user-generated interrupt (see the next section).

- **If the probable cause is the misspelling of a message selector:**

  correct   Select **correct** from the notifier's yellow button menu. This invokes the spelling corrector that attempts to correct the misspelled selector. The system will try to find an alternative message selector with a spelling similar to the original.

- **If a bug exists and the cause was not discovered:**

  debug   This is the most common case. Select **debug** from the notifier's yellow button menu to generate a **debugger** — a window that allows more detailed debugging.

Evaluate each of the following expressions and attempt to identify the error that generates the notifier:

```
27 / (33 // 3)
Boolean new
1 to: 5 do: [:i :j | Transcript show: i; cr]
Collection new
(Pen new) dragoon: 10) "note the deliberate misspelling"
32 mod: 2 ifTrue: [Transcript show: 'divides by two'; cr]
```

5.3.3 User-Generated Notifiers

There are times when a programmer may wish to deliberately cause an error interrupt. Three situations are common: interrupting a nonterminating computation, setting a breakpoint, and handling exceptional conditions.

5.3.4 Interrupting a Nonterminating Computation

A Smalltalk computation may be interrupted at any time by depressing the **control** and **c** keys simultaneously. This generates a notifier window with the label **User Interrupt**. This is most useful when a programmer suspects that a computation will not terminate. For example, the code may contain an infinite loop or infinite recursion may be taking place.

Generate a user interrupt while a long running computation such as "1000 factorial" is taking place.

5.3.5 Setting a Breakpoint

When debugging a Smalltalk program, it is often useful to be able to halt a computation at a specific point, a **breakpoint**. The idea is to let the computation proceed normally until it reaches a point at which the programmer wishes to examine the progress of the computation more carefully. When the breakpoint is reached, the computation is interrupted and a notifier is generated that can then be used to open a debugger window to allow more detailed debugging.

To set a breakpoint, insert the expression **self halt** at the point in the code where the computation should be interrupted. A notifier with the label **Halt encountered** will appear when this expression is evaluated. Alternatively, the expression **self halt: 'messageString'** can be inserted. This has exactly the same effect as **self halt** except that the label of the notifier is the string **messageString**.

5.3.6 Handling Exceptional Conditions

It is good programming practice to notify the user of any unexpected or exceptional condition that occurs during evaluation of code. For example, if we were processing a list and we tried to return the first element of an empty list, the programmer should be notified in some way that this has happened. The simplest way of achieving this in Smalltalk is to include in the code an expression of the form **self error: 'error message'**. In the case of our list example, an expression of the form **self error: 'attempting to return the first element of an empty list'** would be appropriate. When an **error:** message is received, a notifier is opened with the error message as the label of the notifier. The computation is interrupted at the point at which the exceptional condition occurred, allowing the programmer to interrogate the cause of the condition by opening a debugger window. The **error:** protocol is inherited by most objects from class Object. Programmers may override the standard error handler to provide a more specialized handler if they wish.

Another method of warning the user of some exceptional condition is to use an expression of the form **self notify: 'warning message'**. This method is most often used to request confirmation that a computation can proceed. The notifier generated has the string 'Notifier' as its label and the warning message string in the message-send list pane. For example, the notifier in Fig. 5.9 was generated by evaluating the expression

4 notify: 'confirmation message'

The computation can be continued by selecting **proceed** from the yellow button menu, or a debugger can be opened by selecting **debug**.

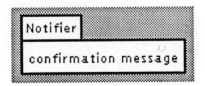

Figure 5.9 Notifier generated by the 'notify:' message.

Unless you want the option of opening a debugger, a confirmer is often better than a notifier as a method of requesting confirmation from the user. The confirmer in Fig. 5.10 was generated by evaluating the expression

4 confirm: 'warning message - continue evaluation?'

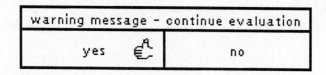

Figure 5.10 Confirmer generated by the 'confirm:' message.

Depending on the response to the confirmer window, true or false is returned as the result of sending the **confirm**: message.

> *Find out how pervasive the use of the standard error-handling mechanism is within the system. Open a message-set browser on senders of the **error:** message.*
>
> *How does Smalltalk implement the **shouldNotImplement** and **subclass-Responsibility** messages in class Object?*
>
> *Are there classes of objects that override the standard error-handling mechanism?*

5.4 DEBUGGERS

Debuggers are Smalltalk windows in which detailed debugging of an interrupted computation takes place. Debuggers incorporate the functionality of inspectors and notifiers and, in addition, provide facilities for viewing the state of a computation, single stepping, modifying methods to correct errors, and resuming a suspended computation.

5.4.1 Viewing an Interrupted Computation with a Debugger

Debugger windows are created from a notifier window by selecting **debug** from the notifier yellow button menu. A debugger window consists of six panes (see Figs. 5.11 and 5.12).

The top two panes resemble a message-set browser. The top pane (the **message-send list pane**) contains the activation stack of message-sends from the interrupted computation. These are the same message-sends from the notifier window except that a debugger shows more of the partially completed message-sends. Also, unlike in a notifier window, the message-sends in the top pane are selectable — selecting a particular message-send determines what can be viewed in the remaining five panes. When a message-send is selected, the source code for the method invoked by that message-send is displayed in the lower of the top two panes (the **method text pane**). Within the body of the source code, the message that caused the notifier to be generated is highlighted.

The bottom four panes are really two inspector windows. The leftmost two panes are the variable and value panes of an inspector (the **receiver inspector**) on the receiver of the message-send currently selected in the message-send list pane. The rightmost two panes are the variable and value panes of an inspector (the **method context inspector**) on the context or environment of the method invoked by the currently selected message-send. This inspector can be used to inspect the values of variables local to a method.

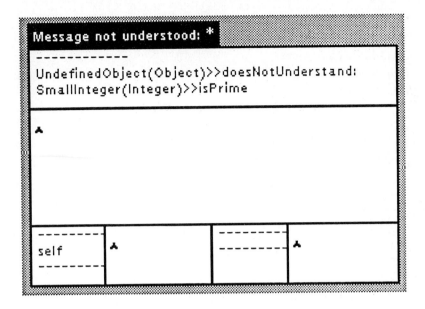

Figure 5.11 A Debugger Window.

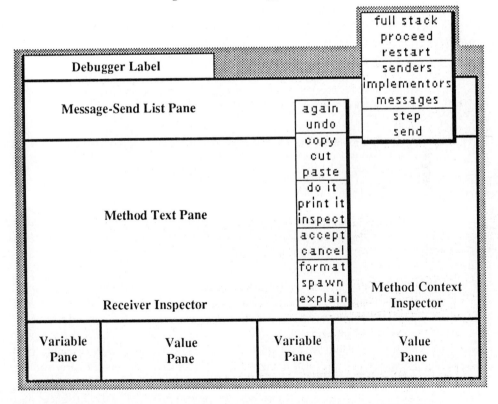

Figure 5.12 The structure of a Debugger Window and its Yellow Button Menus.

By selecting different entries from the message-send list pane, the programmer can follow the trail of interrupted message-sends and for each message-send can access the context in which the message was sent.

As an illustration of the use of debugger windows, consider the following definition of a method **isPrime** that is to be used to test whether an integer is prime or not. The method contains two deliberate errors.

```
isPrime
    "Tests whether the receiver is prime or not."
    | divisor |
    self <= 0 ifTrue: [↑false].
    (self >= 1 & self <= 3) ifTrue: [↑true].
    self \\ 2 = 0 ifTrue: [↑false].
    [divisor * divisor < self] whileTrue: [
        self \\ divisor = 0
            ifTrue: [↑false]
            ifFalse: [divisor ← divisor + 2]].
    ↑true
```

Evaluating the expression **53 isPrime** from a workspace generated the notifier window shown in Fig. 5.7. Selecting **debug** from the notifier menu generated the debug window shown in Fig. 5.11.

Initially, no message-send is selected from the **message-send list pane**. At this time the **message-send pane's yellow button menu** contains only two items, **full stack** and **proceed**.

full stack   Allows the complete set of partially completed message-sends to be viewed in the message-send list pane. Otherwise only the last nine message-sends may be displayed. In version 2.5, **full stack** has been replaced by **more stack**, which doubles the number of items in the viewable stack.

proceed   Allows computation to proceed from the point of interruption. Computation restarts as if the highlighted message in the method text pane had just been completed. The result of sending the highlighted message is taken to be the result of the last expression evaluated in the method text pane or **nil** if no expression has been evaluated. Proceeding with a computation closes the debugger.

Selecting the second message-send (see Fig. 5.13) brings method **isPrime** defined in class **Integer** into view in the **method text pane**. Moreover, the point in the code at which the interruption occurred is highlighted — in this case, the expression *** divisor**. Sending this message to receiver **divisor** gave rise to the **message not understood: *** notifier.

The **receiver inspector** allows receiver **53** of the selected message-send **isPrime** to be viewed. Selecting **self** in the variable pane displays **53** in the value pane. The **method context inspector** allows the context or temporary variables of the method **isPrime** to be viewed. The context of a method includes all arguments to the method and also temporary variables. In this case, the method **isPrime** has only one temporary variable **divisor**. Selecting it displays its value, **nil**, in the value pane. As discovered earlier, **divisor** was not explicitly initialized to an integer value and hence was bound to the object **nil**. The receiver of the message *** divisor** was therefore the object **nil** (the only instance of class **UndefinedObject**) — hence the error.

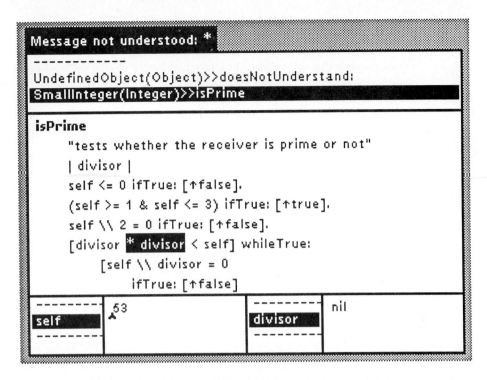

```
 Message not understood: *
 -------------
 UndefinedObject(Object)>>doesNotUnderstand:
 SmallInteger(Integer)>>isPrime

 isPrime
       "tests whether the receiver is prime or not"
       | divisor |
       self <= 0 ifTrue: [↑false].
       (self >= 1 & self <= 3) ifTrue: [↑true].
       self \\ 2 = 0 ifTrue: [↑false].
       [divisor * divisor < self] whileTrue:
             [self \\ divisor = 0
                    ifTrue: [↑false]
 -----------    ,53              --------    nil
               Å
 self                           divisor
 -----------                     --------
```

Figure 5.13 A Debugger Window illustrating the error point.

5.4.2 Error Correction within a Debugger

It is usually not necessary to leave the debugger to correct errors that have been discovered. In most cases, it is possible to make the error correction and restart or complete the computation within the debugger itself. Eliminating the need to switch to a browser just to fix up simple and obvious problems speeds up both debugging and development time. This is one reason the debugger provides the majority of the browser facilities.

In general, the debugger supports several kinds of activities each useful in its own way. These activities include the following:

- **Modifying the Receiver or the Context of a Method.**

  The inspectors on the receiver and method contexts can be used to modify the instance variables of the receiver or the local variables of an interrupted method.

- **Evaluating Expressions.**

  Expressions may be evaluated within a debugger in the context of the currently selected message-send. Such expressions may be evaluated in the method text pane or the value pane of either inspector. Expressions are evaluated in the current context. This context is defined by the current state of the receiver (i.e., values of the instance variables) and the current state of the method (i.e., value of temporaries and arguments).

- **Supplying a Result for an Interrupted Message-Send and Proceeding.**

  A result can be supplied for an interrupted message-send and the computation continued using that value. When proceed is selected from the message-send pane menu, computation restarts as if the highlighted message in the method text pane had just been completed. The result of sending the highlighted message is taken to be the result of the last expression evaluated in the method text pane or nil if no expression has been evaluated. Proceeding with a computation closes the debugger.

- **Accepting a Modified Method Definition.**

  The code for an interrupted method may be edited in the method text pane of a debugger and the modified method compiled using accept. Subsequent evaluations of the method will use the modified method. When a method is recompiled within a debugger, the method becomes the top of the message-send stack. Note also that the modifications to the method will not immediately show up in any open browsers on that method. Temporarily viewing some other method and then switching back will provide the latest version. Alternatively, select update in the browser to view the modified definition.

- **Restarting a Computation from a Selected Point.**

  After any of the above debugging operations, a computation can be restarted from some suitable point. Selecting restart from the message-send pane menu has the effect of resending the message currently selected in the message-send pane. Thus, a computation can be restarted by resending any of the messages in the message-send stack. Restarting a computation closes the debugger.

- **Creating Message-set Browsers.**

  When debugging a Smalltalk method, the capability to browse the methods used, to browse the implementation of a selected method, or to browse the implementation of messages sent in the currently selected method are important aids to both understanding how a method works and to discovering errors. To assist in the debugging process, message-set browsers can be created directly from within a debugger window using the senders, implementors, and messages entries in the message-send list pane menu. For a full discussion of the use of message-set browsers, refer to Section 4.6.3 in Chapter 4.

Consider the debugger of Fig. 5.12 generated by evaluating the expression **53 isPrime**. Recall the first problem discovered — temporary variable **divisor** was not initialized. One way of correcting the problem without leaving the debugger would be to modify the context of the method **isPrime** so that the value of the temporary variable **divisor** is **3** instead of **nil** and then restart the computation. To modify **divisor**, select it in the variable pane of the method context inspector. The current value **nil** is displayed in the value pane. Now, replace **nil** by **3** and choose **accept** from the **value pane's yellow button menu**. The interrupted computation can then be restarted by selecting **restart** from the **message-send pane yellow button menu**. Selecting **restart** closes the debugger and continues evaluation from the start of the currently selected method. In this case, method **isPrime** is re-evaluated in the modified context. Remember, however, that we have not modified the definition of the method **isPrime**. The same error will occur if we subsequently use **isPrime** again.

A more appropriate way of debugging the **isPrime** method is to correct the definition of the method within the debugger. Insert the missing initialization statement, **divisor ← 3**, into the method and **accept** the changed definition. Once the changed method is compiled, the currently selected message-send becomes the top of the message-send stack (see Fig. 5.14). In addition, the first message-send in the modified method is highlighted. This is the point at which evaluation should restart. Interrupted message-sends above the selected message-send are discarded since they are no longer relevant. When the computation is restarted with the modified method, new and different message-sends will result. To restart the computation, select **restart** from the **message-send menu**. Note that any changed method definition will not immediately appear in browsers that were open at the time the method was modified — select **update** in the browser to view the modified definition.

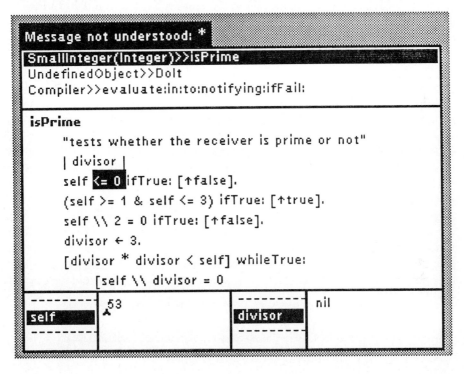

Figure 5.14 Single stepping through a computation.

Sometimes it is necessary to single step through a computation within a debugger window; i.e., to inspect the context of the receiver and the method as each message-send is evaluated. This is particularly useful in the case where evaluation of an expression yields erroneous results but does not generate an error notification. In this case, the usual debugging strategy is to choose some suitable breakpoint, insert a **self halt** expression at that point to generate an interrupt, and then to examine the evaluation on a step-by-step basis within a debugger window.

Single stepping through a computation is achieved through the **step** and **send** entries in the **message-send menu**.

step   Evaluates the next message-send. The effect of the message-send can then be determined using the inspectors on the receiver and the method context.

send   Allows the method involved in the next message-send to itself be viewed and single-stepped. It "opens up" the method associated with the next message-send. This message-send is placed at the top of the message-send stack and selected. The code for the method is displayed in the method text pane and the first message-send in the method is highlighted.

To illustrate the use of **step**, we will search for the remaining bug in the method **isPrime**. Evaluating the expression **25 isPrime** returns the erroneous result **true**. To determine the cause of the error, assume we insert the expression **self halt** after the assignment **divisor ← 3** in the method for **isPrime** and reevaluate the expression. A halt notifier will appear (see Fig. 5.15). Selecting **debug** to generate a debugger window and choosing the **isPrime** message-send result in the debugger window shown in Fig. 5.16. Evaluation of the expression is interrupted at the breakpoint. At this point, **self** is **25** and **divisor** is **3**.

Selecting **step** from the **message-pane menu** sends the highlighted message, in this case, the message **halt**, to its intended receiver. The next message (* **divisor**) is then highlighted (see Fig. 5.17). Selecting **step** performs the multiplication and then highlights **< self**. Selecting **step** again not only performs the comparison (**<**) but also sends the **whileTrue:** message to the result. The message \\ **divisor** within the block argument to the **whileTrue** is highlighted (see Fig. 5.18), indicating that the comparison must have returned **true**. As the last **step** operation indicated, some message-sends, notably sends to block receivers and assignments, are performed automatically when single stepping. If we continue single stepping, we will eventually reach the situation shown in Fig. 5.19, where the message **< self** is to be sent for the second time. Notice that, at this point, the temporary variable **divisor** has the value **5**. Single stepping once more highlights the expression ↑**true** (see Fig. 5.20). To reach this point the **whileTrue:** message must have been sent to the object **false**. The second error can now be seen — the method does not correctly handle the

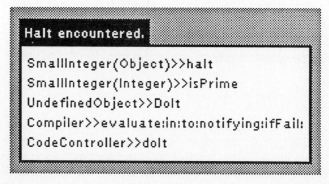

Figure 5.15 A Halt Notifier initiated explicitly by the **isPrime** method.

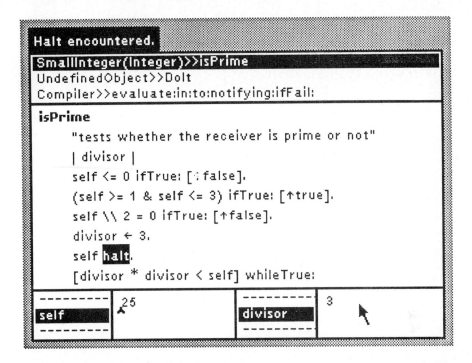

Figure 5.16 The Debugging Window showing the halt point in the **isPrime** method.

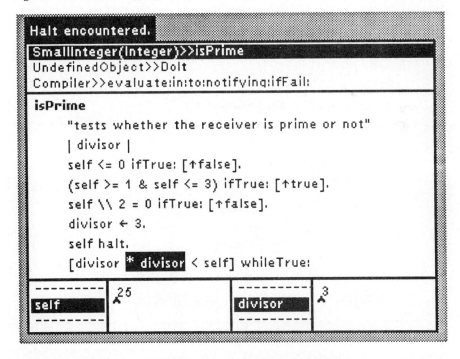

Figure 5.17 Step 1 in determining if 25 is prime.

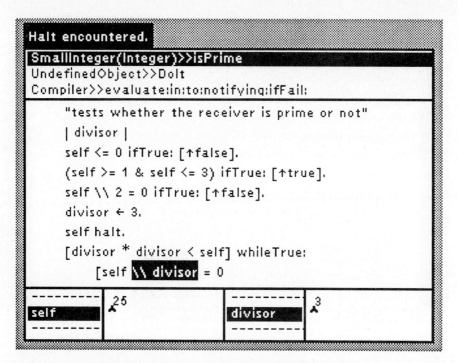

Figure 5.18 Step 2 in determining if 25 is prime.

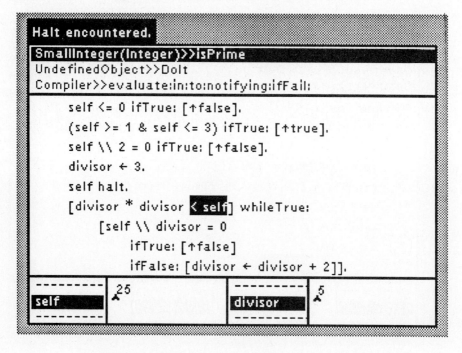

Figure 5.19 Step 3 in determining if 25 is prime.

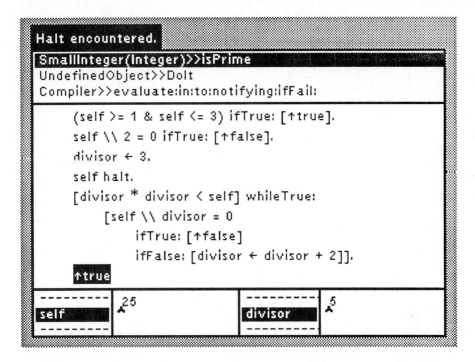

Figure 5.20 Step 4 in determining if 25 is prime.

situation where **divisor * divisor** is equal to **self**. In this case, we should evaluate the block argument to the **whileTrue:** message one more time; i.e., the comparison selector should be **<=** rather than **<**.

To illustrate the use of **send**, we will show how debugger windows can be used not only for debugging Smalltalk code but also for finding out how existing code in the Smalltalk library actually works. For example, suppose we wished to implement a specialized **printString** method for a new class of object that we had just defined. A good way of determining how this might be done is to examine how **printString** is implemented for an existing class of objects, for example, rectangles. Rectangles respond to **printString** with a string of the form **x1@y1 corner: x2@y2**. The points **x1@y1** and **x2@y2** represent the top left and bottom right corners of the rectangle respectively.

A convenient way of finding out how **printString** works for rectangles is to single step through a sample computation. For example, suppose we defined the following temporary class method **trace** in class **Rectangle**.

```
trace
    "Temporary method to determine how rectangles are printed."
    | aRectangle |
    aRectangle ← Rectangle fromUser.
    self halt.
    ↑aRectangle printString.

    "Rectangle trace"
```

Evaluating the expression **Rectangle trace** first generates a request to frame a rectangle and then generates a user-interrupt notifier when the **self halt** expression is evaluated. Opening a debugger window and selecting the message-send **Rectangle class>>trace** displays the source code for the method **trace** in the method text pane (see Fig. 5.21). Choosing **step** advances the computation to the point where the **printString** message is to be sent to the example instance (**aRectangle**) of class rectangle (see Fig. 5.22).

At this point, we want to see the code for method **printString**. Therefore, select **send** rather than **step**. The difference between step and send is that send evaluates the next message-send completely while step invokes the method associated with the next message-send. The code for this method is displayed in the method text pane and the first message-send in the method is highlighted. After the send, the code for the method **printString** is displayed in the method text pane (see Fig. 5.23) and the first message, **new: 100**, is highlighted. The message-send at the top of the stack is now **Rectangle(Object)>>printString** — the actual method invoked was therefore found in class **Object**. This suggests that **printString** is a message inherited by all objects.

We can find out if other classes implement **printString** by selecting **implementors** from the **message-send pane's yellow button menu**. This confirms that only class **Object** implements a **printString** method. Method **printString** creates a new write stream on a string and adds the printed representation of the object (by sending **printOn:** to the object) to

```
Halt encountered.
Rectangle class>>trace
UndefinedObject>>DoIt
Compiler>>evaluate:in:to:notifying:ifFail:
CodeController>>doIt

trace
    "method to determine how rectangles are printed"

    | aRectangle |
    aRectangle ← Rectangle fromUser.
    self halt.
    ↑aRectangle printString

    "Rectangle trace"

-----------    ^         -----------   69@81 corner:
self                      aRectangle   409@354
superclass               -----------
methodDict
```

Figure 5.21 At the halt statement in method **trace**.

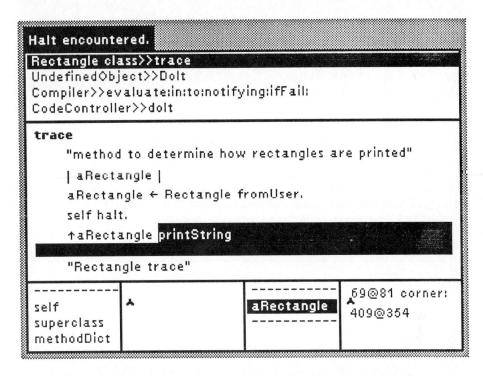

Figure 5.22 About to trace method printString.

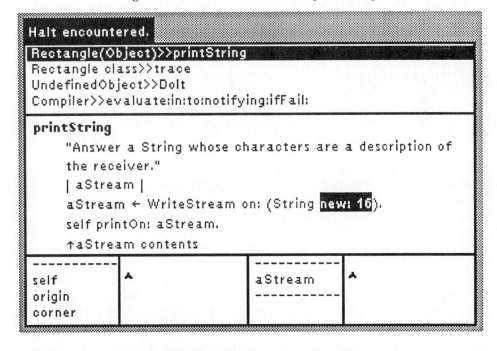

Figure 5.23 Having reached method printString.

the stream. The stream's content is then returned as the result. The stream is initially created on a string of size 16 (the character buffer) but this is automatically extended. We have discovered that solving the original problem of implementing a specialized **printString** method for a new class of object involves implementing a specialized form of **printOn: aStream** method for the new class. Of course, **printOn:** might also be inherited by all objects! To determine whether this is the case, **step** through the computation until the **printOn: aStream** message is the next message to be sent (see Fig. 5.24) and then select **send** to view the invoked method.

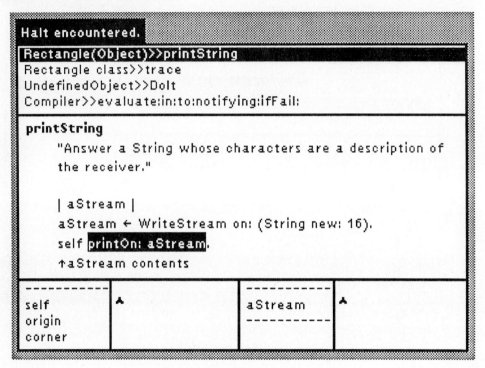

Figure 5.24 About to trace method **printOn:**.

The **printOn:** method in class **Rectangle** is invoked (see Fig. 5.25); i.e., class **Rectangle** has a specialized version of **printOn:**. The comment for the method refers us to the comment stored in the **printOn:** method of class **Object**. To view this method (without leaving the debugger), again select **implementors** from the **message-send pane's yellow button menu**. This displays a message-set browser on all **printOn:** methods (see Fig. 5.26). Notice that many classes implement this method, confirming the theory that a specialized **printOn:** method must be implemented for any new class we might define. Selecting entry **Object printOn:** from the top message list pane displays the source for the **printOn:** method in class **Object** (see Fig. 5.26). The default behavior for printing objects can now be seen. If a subclass does not provide a specialized method for printing instances, the default is to simply return a string identifying the class of the object. For example, if we send the message **printString** to an instance of class **Pen**, the result would be the string **'a Pen'**.

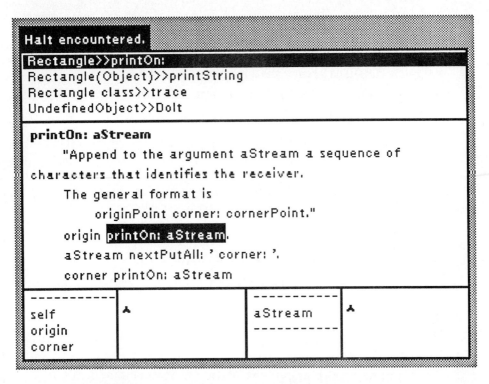

Figure 5.25 Having reached method **printOn**: in class Rectangle.

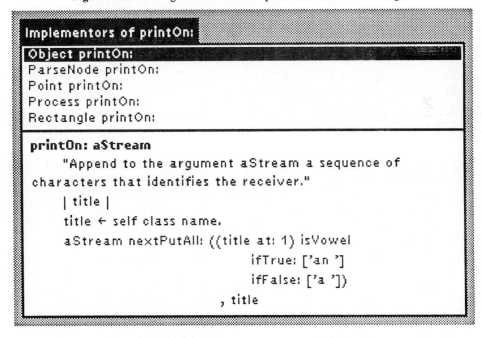

Figure 5.26 Potential implementors of method **printOn**:.

Closing the message-set browser and returning to the definition of **printOn:** for class **Rectangle** (see Fig. 5.25), we can see that **printOn:** for rectangles proceeds to

- send **printOn:** to instance variable **origin** (the top left corner of the rectangle),
- append string ' **corner:** ' to the print stream, and finally
- send **printOn:** to instance variable **corner** (the rectangle's bottom right corner).

Selecting **send** at this point invokes the **printOn:** message for instances of class **Point** (**origin** is a point), and the method for generating the specialized printed representation (**x@y**) for points can be viewed (Fig. 5.27). Single stepping through this method will eventually return us to the **printOn:** method for rectangles (Fig. 5.28). At this stage, selecting **proceed** allows the computation to run to completion and the printed representation of the rectangle to be printed.

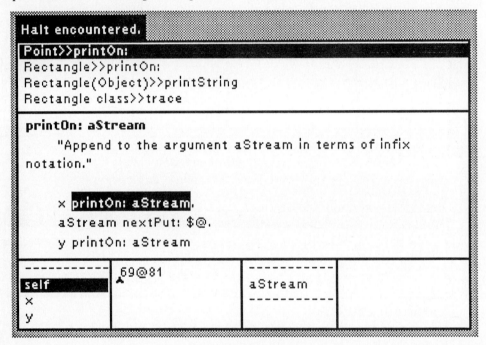

Figure 5.27 Having reached the Point **printOn:** method.

5.5 SUMMARY

In this chapter, we have described the use of **inspector, notifier,** and **debugger** windows as sophisticated aids for debugging Smalltalk programs. In particular, we have described:

- The use of inspectors to view and modify the internal state of an object.
- The use of specialized inspectors for viewing dictionaries.

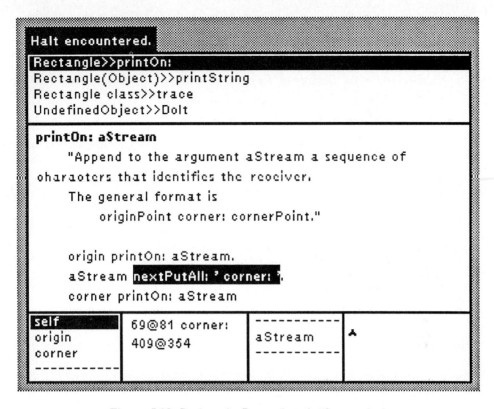

```
Halt encountered.
Rectangle>>printOn:
Rectangle(Object)>>printString
Rectangle class>>trace
UndefinedObject>>DoIt

printOn: aStream
      "Append to the argument aStream a sequence of
oharaoters that identifies the reoeiver,
      The general format is
            originPoint corner: cornerPoint."


      origin printOn: aStream,
      aStream nextPutAll: ' corner: '.
      corner printOn: aStream

┌─────────────┬─────────────────┬─────────────┬──────┐
│ self        │ 69@81 corner:   │ ─────────   │  ▲   │
│ origin      │ 409@354         │ aStream     │      │
│ corner      │                 │ ─────────   │      │
│ ─────────   │                 │             │      │
└─────────────┴─────────────────┴─────────────┴──────┘
```

Figure 5.28 Back to the Rectangle **printOn:** method.

- How to set breakpoints to interrupt a computation at a user-selected point.
- The use of notifiers for identifying the point and cause of a run-time error or user-generated interrupt.
- How debuggers incorporate the functionality of both notifiers and inspectors and may be used to view and modify the state of a suspended computation.
- How debuggers may be used to single step through a computation at any level of detail.
- How errors may be corrected within a debugger and a suspended computation resumed.

5.6 EXERCISES

The exercises that follow provide experience with the manipulation of inspectors, notifiers, and debuggers.

1. In this chapter, we saw that it is desirable to have specialized inspectors for dictionaries. What other kinds of objects might benefit from such specialized inspectors? Are there other inspectors present in your Smalltalk system? Hint: What about inspectors on Ordered Collections?

2. When a message reaches class Object because it was not understood by its intended receiver, why does class Object send a doesNotUnderstand message back to the receiver of the original message? Why doesn't class Object simply use its own doesNot-Understand method?

3. Each of the following expressions generates an error notifier when evaluated. Explain the reason for the notifier in each case.

    Character **new**
    Collection **new**
    3/0
    0 **ifTrue**: [↑'Zero']
    -10 **sqrt**

4. On occasion, we may have multiple occurrences of the same method in the message-send stack of a debugger; e.g., in a recursive method. Open a debugger on a computation such as 10 factorial and advance the computation until the message-send stack contains several factorial message-sends. Now modify the definition of factorial associated with one of the factorial message-sends. Are all the other definitions for factorial also modified? If not, try to understand why.

5. Why is evaluation of code within a debugger much slower than normal evaluation of the same code?

5.7 GLOSSARY

Smalltalk windows

inspector A window through which the internal state of an object can be viewed and modified.

notifier A window generated when a run-time error or user-generated interrupt occurs. The window displays the state of the computation at the point of interruption and indicates the cause of the interruption; e.g., a message not being understood by its receiver.

debugger A window in which detailed debugging of an interrupted computation takes place. Debuggers incorporate the functionality of inspectors and notifiers and, in addition, provide facilities for viewing the state of a computation, for single stepping through a computation, for modifying methods to correct errors, and for resuming a suspended computation.

yellow button menu commands for the inspector variable pane

inspect Opens an inspector on the instance variable selected in the variable pane of the inspector. Note that this menu item is only accessible if an item has been selected from the list in the variable pane.

yellow button menu commands for the inspector value pane

again, undo, cut, copy, paste Standard editing commands.

do it, print it, inspect Standard evaluation and inspection commands.

cancel Restores the text in the value pane to its original state or the state immediately after the last accept.

accept Evaluates the text in the value pane as a Smalltalk expression. Binds the result returned by evaluating the expression to the variable selected in the variable pane. Used to modify the value of an instance variable of an inspected object.

yellow button menu commands for the dictionary inspector variable pane

inspect Opens an inspector on the value associated with the selected key.

references Creates a message-set browser on all references to the selected key.

remove Removes the key selected in the key list pane. A confirmer menu will appear to request confirmation that this undoable operation should be carried out.

add field Adds a new entry with associated value **nil** to a dictionary. A prompter window will appear and request the name of the key to be added. Another value can be associated with the key by entering the value into the value pane and choosing **accept**.

yellow button menu commands for the notifier window

proceed Continues the evaluation of the computation from the point of suspension. May not be appropriate if error correction is required.

debug Opens a **debugger** window on the interrupted computation.

correct Used in the case of a misspelled message selector to invoke the spelling corrector. If the system's suggestion is confirmed by the user, the alternative replaces the misspelled selector.

yellow button menu commands for the debugger message-send pane

full stack Allows the complete set of incomplete message-sends to be viewed in the message-send list pane. Otherwise only the last nine message-sends may be displayed. In version 2.5, **full stack** has been replaced by **more stack**. Instead of showing the complete set of message-sends, **more stack** doubles the number of items in the viewable stack.

more stack See **full stack**.

proceed Allows computation to proceed from the point of interruption. Computation restarts as if the highlighted message in the method text pane had just been completed. The result of sending the highlighted message is taken to be the result of the last expression evaluated in the method text pane, or **nil** if no expression has been evaluated. Proceeding with a computation closes the debugger.

restart Resends the message currently selected in the message-send pane. A computation can be restarted by resending any of the messages in the message-send stack. Restarting a computation closes the debugger.

senders Opens a message-set browser on the senders of the method in the method text pane.

implementors Opens a message-set browser on the implementors of the method in the method text pane.

messages Displays a menu of all the messages sent by the method in the method text pane. Selecting from the menu opens a message-set browser on all methods that implement the selected message selector.

step Evaluates the next message-send and then halts. The effect of the message-send can then be determined using the inspectors on the receiver and method context.

send Allows the method involved in the next message-send to itself be viewed and single-stepped. It invokes the method associated with the next message-send. This message-send is placed at the top of the message-send stack and selected. The code for the invoked method is displayed in the method text pane and the first message-send in the method is highlighted.

yellow button menu commands for the debugger method text pane

again, undo, cut, copy, paste Standard editing commands.

do it, print it, inspect Standard evaluation and inspection commands.

accept Compiles the text in the method text pane. If successful, replaces the existing method definition in the system. Used to modify the definition of a method while debugging. When a method is recompiled within a debugger, that method is placed at the top of the message-send stack.

cancel Restores the text in the method text pane to its original state or the state immediately after the last accept.

format Formats the code in the text pane to a standard Smalltalk style. The text must not have been edited since the last accept.

spawn Opens a message browser for the selected message. Uses the method definition from the method text pane. If editing has taken place, this may or may not be the current saved version of the definition. A cancel operation is automatically carried out on the method text pane of the debugger.

explain Displays an explanation of any selected variable name or selector such as 'x', 'sum', '+', 'at:put:', or 'Smalltalk'.

6

Objects

6.1 INTRODUCTION

Understanding Smalltalk in detail requires a basic understanding of the protocol understood by **objects** in general (from class **Object**), along with an understanding of boolean objects **true** and **false**, undefined object **nil**, and **blocks** (short for **block contexts**).

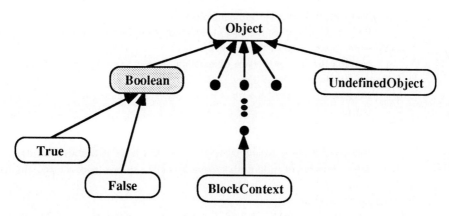

Figure 6.1 Object and other related classes.

Class **Object** (see Fig. 6.1) is the ultimate superclass of all classes. It provides the default behavior for such operations as copying, printing, and comparing. Class **UndefinedObject** provides the protocol for its one unique instance **nil**, the value provided to all uninitialized variables. Boolean objects **true** and **false** are the sole instances of classes **True** and **False** respectively; **True** and **False** are subclasses of **Boolean**. Class **Boolean** is an abstract class; i.e., a class with no instances, that serves as a repository for methods common to **True** and **False**. As a user, there is no need to know about classes **True** and **False**. However, one should be aware of their existence because they cannot be used as substitutes for instances **true** and **false**. The difference between uppercase and lowercase is important in Smalltalk. For example,

> True **ifTrue**: [Transcript **show**: 'it was true'] **ifFalse**: [Transcript **show**: 'it was false']

is not a legal if-statement because **True** is not a boolean instance. Class **BlockContext** provides the protocol for blocks. In the following example, [count ← count + 1. count < 10] is a block that is the receiver of the **whileTrue**: message. Parameter [Transcript **show**: count **printString**] is also a block.

> [count ← count + 1. count < 10] **whileTrue**: [Transcript **show**: count **printString**]

In the sections that follow, we will consider the protocol for classes **Object**, **UndefinedObject**, **BlockContext**, and **Boolean** (with its subclasses) in that order. To understand the **Object** protocol, a rudimentary knowledge of the other three classes is needed. In particular, the following undefined object and boolean object protocol should be sufficient for our purposes:

undefined object queries

- anObject **isNil**
  Returns true if the receiver is **nil** and false otherwise.

boolean operations

- aBooleanObject & anotherBooleanObject
  Returns the 'and' of the two objects; i.e., true if both are true.
- aBooleanObject | anotherBooleanObject
  Returns the 'or' of the two objects; i.e., true if one or both are true.
- aBooleanObject **not**
  Returns the 'not' of the object; i.e., true if the receiver is false and false if it is true.

- aBooleanObject **and**: aBlock
  Performs a short-circuit 'and'; i.e., returns false if the aBooleanObject is false; otherwise, additionally evaluates the block and returns the block result.
- aBooleanObject **or**: aBlock
  Performs a short-circuit 'or'; i.e., returns true if the aBooleanObject is true; otherwise, additionally evaluates the block and returns the block result.

In previous chapters, we provided a syntactic interpretation of blocks as special brackets that were required for control structures. This interpretation is neither object-oriented nor correct but it is sufficient for understanding the basic control structures like **whileTrue**: and **whileFalse**:. More detail, however, is needed to understand the implementation of the boolean objects. Hence, blocks are reviewed prior to considering the boolean objects in detail.

6.2 CLASS OBJECT

An **object** consists of a **representation** and **operations** (or **methods**) that it responds to. It is an **instance** whose class can be determined by sending it the message **class**; e.g., 1.2e3 **class** will reply with **Float**. The class is the repository for all the information about the instances; i.e., it stores both the representation information and the operations. However, the information in an individual class may not be complete; part of the information may reside in another class called the **superclass**.

In general, a class may have a superclass, which in turn may have its own superclass, which again has a superclass. This sequence culminates in a final class that has no superclass — this class is **Object**, the ultimate superclass of all classes. In general, many classes can have the same superclass — hence the relationship is a tree-structured hierarchy as shown in Fig. 6.1. Actually, Smalltalk permits classes to have several superclasses, leading to a concept called **multiple inheritance**. However, there are no examples in the system — we will not consider the concept further in this section.

The representation information and the operations associated with an instance are obtained by concatenating the partial information stored in each of the classes in the superclass chain that starts with the object's class and culminates in **Object**.

In the sections that follow, we first consider the detailed representation of an object. We investigate this representation ignoring the effects of the hierarchy. Then we consider Smalltalk's notion of bindings as it relates to parameter passing and assignments so that we can better appreciate the power of this representation. Next, we review this representation in the context of the hierarchy. We then investigate the operations provided by class **Object**, a protocol that is inherited by all classes in the system.

6.2.1 The Representation of an Object

Since an object consists of a representation and operations, it consists of anything that can be manipulated. In particular, any object can be **inspected**; e.g., 1957 **inspect**, #(1 2 3 4) **inspect**, 'hello' **inspect**, Integer **inspect**. Objects include such things as characters, integers, strings, arrays, ordered collections, sets, and classes themselves.

named instance variable 1
named instance variable 2
named instance variable 3
⋮
indexed instance variable 1
indexed instance variable 2
indexed instance variable 3
⋮

Figure 6.2 The representation of an object.

However, there are things that are not objects. For example, *a variable is not an object.* Variables cannot be manipulated as separate entities. They cannot be inspected nor can they be stored into arrays, for example. Of course, the value bound to a variable can be inspected and stored into an array. This is not the same thing. If variables were objects, one would be able to store one into an array and legitimately claim "this array contains a variable — independently, the variable also contains a value." Since variables cannot be manipulated, they are not objects.

In more detail, an object (see Fig. 6.2) consists of zero or more fields called **instance variables** partitioned into two groups: **named instance variables** and **indexed instance variables**. The named instance variables precede the indexed instance variables.

When a class is defined, the names of all named instance variables must be specified along with an indication as to whether or not indexed instance variables are permitted. If no indexed instance variables are permitted, all instances of the class will be the same size. Otherwise, distinct instances can be different sizes. Depending on the choices taken, several combinations are possible:

Classes with objects containing no instance variables.
Examples include Object, True, False, UndefinedObject, and InputSensor.

Classes with objects containing only named instance variables.
Most classes in the system and most user created classes will fall into this category.

Classes with objects containing only indexed instance variables.
Examples include classes like Array, String, Symbol, LargePositiveInteger, and LargeNegativeInteger.

Classes with objects containing both named and indexed instance variables.
Examples include OrderedCollection, Dictionary, Set, and SortedCollection.

Such classes are normally created with the browser. The easiest way is to find any class that already has the required structure and modify its definition. For example, the following definitions were obtained by investigating the class definitions for Fraction, Array, WordArray, String, and OrderedCollection:

Fraction (a class with only named instance variables)

    Number **subclass**: #Fraction
        instanceVariableNames: 'numerator denominator'
        classVariableNames: ''
        poolDictionaries: ''
        category: 'Numeric-Numbers'

Array (a class with only indexed instance variables that can contain arbitrary objects)

    ArrayedCollection **variableSubclass**: #Array
        instanceVariableNames: ''
        classVariableNames: ''
        poolDictionaries: ''
        category: 'Collections-Arrayed'

WordArray (another class with only indexed instance variables capable of containing only words)

> ArrayedCollection **variableWordSubclass**: #WordArray
> > **instanceVariableNames**: ''
> > **classVariableNames**: ''
> > **poolDictionaries**: ''
> > **category**: 'Graphics-Support'

String (another class with only indexed instance variables capable of containing only bytes)

> ArrayedCollection **variableByteSubclass**: #String
> > **instanceVariableNames**: ''
> > **classVariableNames**: ''
> > **poolDictionaries**: ''
> > **category**: 'Collections-Text'

OrderedCollection (a class with both kinds of instance variables)

> SequenceableCollection **variableSubclass**: #OrderedCollection
> > **instanceVariableNames**: 'firstIndex lastIndex'
> > **classVariableNames**: ''
> > **poolDictionaries**: ''
> > **category**: 'Collections-Sequenceable'

As you can see, classes without indexed instance variables are created with a method that begins **subclass:**...; the alternative uses methods **variableSubclass:**..., **variableWordSubclass:**..., or **variableByteSubclass:**... (indexed instance variables respectively contain arbitrary objects, word-sized integers, or byte-sized integers).

Named instance variables are normally accessed by referencing the variables by name. More specifically, when the receiver of a message is, say, an ordered collection, the corresponding method that executes can reference **firstIndex** or **lastIndex** by name. Indexed instance variables are accessed via the subscripting operations **basicAt:** and **basicAt:put:**. See the section on accessing and modification operations for more details.

- anObject **basicAt**: anInteger

    Returns the value of the indexed instance variable at index anInteger. Legal index values range between 1 and anObject **basicSize**. An error is reported if the index is not an integer or if it is out of range.

- anObject **basicAt**: anInteger **put**: anotherObject

    Changes the value of the indexed instance variable at index anInteger to anotherObject and returns anotherObject. Legal index values range between 1 and anObject **basicSize**. An error is reported if the index is not an integer or if it is out of range.

As a user, it is important to have this image of an object as a record with an arbitrary number of fields, some named and some indexed. On the other hand, the low-level operations that provide direct access to these fields should only be used for implementing higher level facilities.

6.2.2 Bindings: Assignments and Parameter Passing

In this section, we wish to consider the meaning of an assignment such as

$$a \leftarrow b$$

since it can lead to confusion if it is not properly understood. We can explain it from two perspectives: from the **logical** point of view, which concentrates on what it means, and from the **implementation** point of view, which concentrates on how it is done.

In a language like Pascal, C, or Ada, an assignment like $a \leftarrow b$ is interpreted as "*copy b into a*" and implemented by "*copying the contents of b into the space occupied by a.*" Thus, a and b must be the same type and, most importantly, the same size. This is a very restrictive requirement. For example, it makes it impossible for the arbitrary elements of a set data type to be manipulated unless the element types were previously specified by the user — it also makes it difficult to mix the element types.

In Smalltalk, $a \leftarrow b$ is interpreted as "*bind a to the same object that b is bound to.*" From the logical point of view, assignments do not copy — they simply rebind. From the implementation point of view, all variables contain pointers to objects; assignments physically copy pointers **but they do not copy the objects**. Fig. 6.3 illustrates this pictorially.

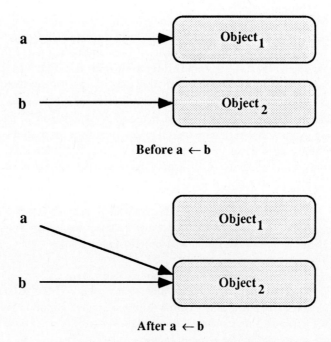

Before a ← b

After a ← b

Figure 6.3 The meaning of assignment.

To repeat, before the assignment, a is bound to $object_1$ and b is bound to $object_2$. After the assignment, a is also bound to $object_2$ — hence a and b are bound to the same object. We often shorten the expression "*x is bound to object o*" to "*x is o*." With this more concise terminology, the above can be rephrased as follows: "Before the assignment, a is object$_1$ and b is object$_2$; after the assignment, both a and b are object$_2$."

Smalltalk provides two operations for determining when two objects are the same: operation == (**identical**) and operation ~~ (**not identical**).

- anObject == anotherObject
    Returns true if anObject is the same as anotherObject and false otherwise.
- anObject ~~ anotherObject
    Returns true if anObject is **not** the same as anotherObject and false otherwise.

Before the assignment in Fig. 6.3, a == b is false; afterwards, a == b is true. Note that identity is not the same as equality. Two objects could be equal without being identical. Equality is considered in more detail after we discuss the copying operations. As implied, it is possible to obtain a copy of an object but this must be explicitly requested. For example, consider the following:

```
a ← Set new.
b ← a copy.
```

Here, a is first bound to a new set, then b is bound to a copy of this set. Clearly, a and b are equal; i.e., a = b is true. However, a and b are not identical; i.e., a == b is false because they are distinct objects.

Note that the notion of variables extends to method parameters and to fields of an object; i.e., instance variables. For example, suppose we execute the following:

```
a ← Set new.
b ← 'hello there'.
c ← Number.
result ← Array with: a with: b with: c
```

Class method **with:with:with:** in Array might be implemented as follows:

```
with: object1 with: object2 with: object3
    | newArray |
    newArray ← Array new: 3.
    newArray at: 1 put: object1.
    newArray at: 2 put: object2.
    newArray at: 3 put: object3.
    ↑newArray
```

Immediately before newArray is returned, it should be clear that variable a, variable **object1**, and the first indexed instance variable of **newArray** are the same set. Diagrammatically, this is illustrated in Fig. 6.4. The other cases are also shown for comparison purposes.

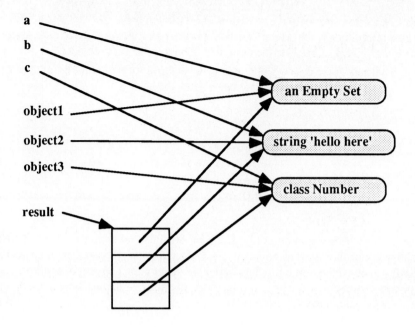

Figure 6.4 Object bindings.

Smalltalk has no 'call by reference' mechanism. In particular, there is no way that variable **a** can be modified by assignments to variables in the method. For example, if we changed **object1** in the method, this would rebind **object1** and only **object1** to some new object — it would not affect **a**. Actually, Smalltalk does not permit parameters like **object1** to be modified but that is beside the point. Later, we will consider an operation that has wider ranging effects, the **become:** operation.

6.2.3 The Inherited Representation of an Object

When a new class is defined, both a superclass and instance variables must be specified. For example, class Fraction is defined as follows:

```
Number subclass: #Fraction
    instanceVariableNames: 'numerator denominator'
    classVariableNames: ''
    poolDictionaries: ''
    category: 'Numeric-Numbers'
```

In this case, Number is the superclass of Fraction. All instances of fractions will have the instance variables numerator and denominator. Additionally, they will also have the instance variables of Number, Magnitude, and Object, since these are the classes in the superclass chain. As it turns out, these classes have no instance variables. Hence, no additional instance variables are included.

To provide a more relevant example, consider defining three classes Ball, PositionedBall, and MovingBall as follows:

```
Object subclass: #Ball
    instanceVariableNames: 'color radius'
    classVariableNames: ''
    poolDictionaries: ''
    category: 'Experimental'

Ball subclass: #PositionedBall
    instanceVariableNames: 'position'
    classVariableNames: ''
    poolDictionaries: ''
    category: 'Experimental'

PositionedBall subclass: #MovingBall
    instanceVariableNames: 'velocity'
    classVariableNames: ''
    poolDictionaries: ''
    category: 'Experimental'
```

Each new class describes the instance variables that are extra to the instance variables provided higher up in the hierarchy; i.e., instance variables in superclasses cannot be eliminated in subclasses. For example, the instance variables for instances of the above classes are the following:

the representation for all instances of Ball:
```
color
radius
```

the representation for all instances of PositionedBall:
```
color
radius
position
```

the representation for all instances of MovingBall:
```
color
radius
position
velocity
```

As you can see, instances of a class automatically **inherit** the representation of the instances described by the superclass. This **representation inheritance** is analogous to **method inheritance**; i.e., the notion that instances respond to messages that are either defined (as methods) in the instance's class or in some superclass higher up in the hierarchy (if at all).

This should explain why methods for balls also work for moving balls. More specifically, a method for balls can only access instance variables **color** and **radius**. Such a method also works for positioned balls and moving balls precisely because they have the **color** and **radius** instance variables in exactly the same locations.

Note that instance variables can only be added — it is not possible to create a subclass with fewer instance variables than in a superclass. Additional subclasses that introduce indexed instance variables can also be defined.

```
MovingBall variableSubclass: #IndexableMovingBall
    instanceVariableNames: ''
    classVariableNames: ''
    poolDictionaries: ''
    category: 'Experimental'

IndexableMovingBall subclass: #ProprietaryIndexableMovingBall
    instanceVariableNames: 'owner'
    classVariableNames: ''
    poolDictionaries: ''
    category: 'Experimental'
```

Instances of these classes appear as follows:

the representation for all instances of IndexableMovingBall:
```
    color
    radius
    position
    velocity
        1
        2
        3
        ...
```

the representation for all instances of ProprietaryIndexableMovingBall:
```
    color
    radius
    position
    velocity
    owner
        1
        2
        3
        ...
```

Note that individual instances can have a different number of indexed instance variables. All named instance variables precede the indexed instance variables even if they were added in a subclass whose superclass has indexable instances.

6.2.4 Querying Operations

General operations are provided for querying instances about class membership and legal selectors. Special querying operations for dealing with integers and undefined objects are also provided.

general queries

- anObject **class**
    Returns the receiver's class.
- anObject **isKindOf**: aClass
    Returns true if the receiver's class is aClass or inherits from aClass; false otherwise.

Inside Smalltalk

- anObject **isMemberOf**: aClass

  Returns true if the receiver's class is aClass; false otherwise.

- anObject **respondsTo**: aSymbol

  Returns true if aSymbol is a message selector for a method defined in anObject's class or a class it inherits from; false otherwise.

specific queries

- anObject **isInteger**

  Returns true if the receiver is an integer; false otherwise.

- anObject **isNil**

  Returns true if the object is undefined; false otherwise; **nil** is the undefined object.

- anObject **notNil**

  Returns true if the object is defined; false otherwise.

unusual queries

- anObject **yourself**

  Returns the receiver. Useful for cascading.

Normally, method **isKindOf:** is used rather than **isMemberOf:** because it applies to instances of all subclasses — 'anObject **isMemberOf:** aClass' is just short for 'anObject **class == aClass'. Note that a class may respond to a given selector without that operation being legal. For example, intervals such as '1 **to:** 6 **by:** 2' respond to **at:put:** messages, but such messages are not legal. There exists an **at:put:** method in class **Interval** but it is defined as follows:

```
at: index put: anObject
    self error: 'you can not store into an interval'
```

Messages **isNil** and **notNil** are implemented in two classes: **Object** and **UndefinedObject**. In **Object**, **isNil** always returns false (there is no if statement deciding what should be returned). In **UndefinedObject**, **isNil** always returns true. Clearly, this is an optimization that takes advantage of Smalltalk's polymorphic message sending capability.

Message **yourself** is useful for creating and initializing complex objects. For example, one way of creating an array with run-time computed values is to assign individual elements using **at:put:**.

```
anArray ← Array new: 6.
anArray at: 1 put: Form white.
anArray at: 2 put: Form veryLightGray.
anArray at: 3 put: Form lightGray.
anArray at: 4 put: Form gray.
anArray at: 5 put: Form darkGray.
anArray at: 6 put: Form black.
```

Using cascading, we can shorten this code. Semicolon is interpreted as follows: "The next message is to be sent to the same object that the previous message was sent to."

```
anArray ← Array new: 6.
anArray
    at: 1 put: Form white;
    at: 2 put: Form veryLightGray;
    at: 3 put: Form lightGray;
    at: 4 put: Form gray;
    at: 5 put: Form darkGray;
    at: 6 put: Form black.
```

A final simplification merges the two statements into one. However, message **yourself** is required. If it is omitted, the result returned (as expected) is the value returned by the last **at:put:**. But **at:put:** returns the value that was inserted; in this case, Form **black**. Since we want the array itself, sending a **yourself** message to the same object that the previous **at:put:** was sent to gives us the array we want.

```
anArray ← (Array new: 6)
    at: 1 put: Form white;
    at: 2 put: Form veryLightGray;
    at: 3 put: Form lightGray;
    at: 4 put: Form gray;
    at: 5 put: Form darkGray;
    at: 6 put: Form black;
    yourself.
```

6.2.5 Debugging, Inspecting, and Confirming

Class **Object** provides operations **notify:**, **halt**, and **halt:** for interfacing with the debugger; **basicInspect** and **inspect** for investigating the contents of objects; and **confirm:** for simple true/false request processing. Additionally, it provides the error messaging facility **error:**, the handler for messages not understood, and a few well-used error messages.

interfacing with the debugger

• anObject **notify:** aString

> Creates a notifier (see Fig. 6.5) that permits the user to either invoke the debugger or proceed as if nothing had happened. Used for inserting breakpoints during prototyping and testing.

• anObject **halt**
• anObject **halt:** aString

> As above but with a different style of notifier (see Fig. 6.6) that provides a short traceback of the methods called to that point. Parameter aString becomes the label for the notifier and debugger (if activated); when not supplied, default 'Halt encountered' is used.

interfacing with the inspector

- anObject **basicInspect**
- anObject **inspect**

   Creates an inspector (see Fig. 6.7) in which the user can examine all of the receiver's instance variables. Method **inspect** is redefined in subclasses to provide the contents of the object in a more convenient manner; **basicInspect** is never redefined.

interfacing with the user

- anObject **confirm**: aString

   Creates a menu (see Fig. 6.8) that requests the user to reply either yes or no to the question posed by aString. Returns the boolean result.

interfacing with the error handler

- anObject **error**: aString

   Creates a notifier via **halt**:. Can be redefined in subclasses.
- anObject **doesNotUnderstand**: aMessage

   The standard handler for messages not understood by the receiver.

often-used error messages

- anObject **primitiveFailed**

   Announces something like 'a primitive has failed'.
- anObject **shouldNotImplement**

   Announces something like 'this message is not appropriate for this object'.
- anObject **subclassResponsibility**

   Announces something like 'my subclass should have overridden one of my messages'.
- anObject **conflictingInheritanceError**

   Announces something like 'conflicting methods due to multiple inheritance'
- anObject **errorImproperStore**

   Announces something like 'improper store into indexable object'.
- anObject **errorNonIntegerIndex**

   Announces something like 'only integers should be used as indices'.
- anObject **errorSubscriptBounds**: index

   Announces something like 'subscript is out of bounds: index' where index is appropriately substituted for.

When a **notify**: message is executed, a notifier window is created. The string parameter is displayed as the contents of this notifier. A yellow button menu provides the user with two options: **proceed** or **debug**. The first causes the notifier to disappear and execution to continue from where it left off. The second causes a debugger to replace the notifier.

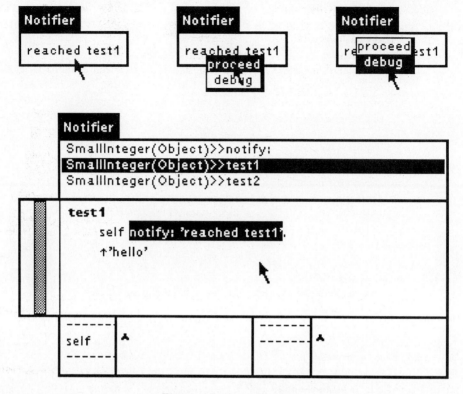

Figure 6.5 Using Notifiers.

Fig. 6.5 was constructed to show what happens if the following methods were temporarily added to class **Object**.

```
test1
    self notify: 'reached test1'.
    ↑'hello'

test2
    ↑self test1

test3
    ↑self test2

test4
    ↑self test3
    "2001 test4"
```

When 2001 **test4** is executed, the notifier in the upper left corner of Fig. 6.5 appears. If **proceed** is chosen, execution proceeds and 'hello' is eventually returned. Choosing **debug**, on the other hand, causes the debugger to appear.

The **halt:** message is similar to the **notify:** message. It differs in providing a short traceback of the messages that led to the **halt:**. Fig. 6.6 illustrates the traceback that results when **notify:** in **test1** above is replaced by **halt:**.

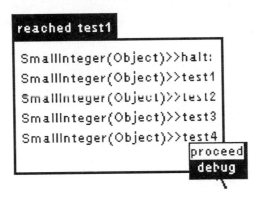

Figure 6.6 Using **halt:** instead of **notify:**.

The **inspect** (and **basicInspect**) messages create inspectors on the receivers of the messages. For example,

```
#(10 20 30) inspect
```

would create the inspector shown at the top of Fig. 6.7. Message **basicInspect** provides the default inspector for all objects. However, special classes redefine **inspect** for convenience. For example, the ordered collection

```
anOrderedCollection ← OrderedCollection new.
anOrderedCollection addAll: #(10 20 30).
```

could be inspected either with

```
anOrderedCollection basicInspect  or  anOrderedCollection inspect.
```

As can be seen in Fig. 6.7, the basic inspector provides details about the ordered collection that would be useful to the implementor. With this inspector, we can determine that the data occupies the central portion of the variable length object — firstIndex and lastIndex are used to keep track of the start and end points into this area. Presumably, this is done because data can be added to either end of the ordered collection. On the other hand, this particular ordered collection has only three items in it. The more specialized inspector provides us with a user's view of the data. It hides the implementation details that have to do with the actual position of the data. Indeed, this is the more relevant view to provide. To the user, the first element is at index 1 (independent of where it is actually stored); i.e., user subscripts are remapped and interpreted as offsets from firstIndex (plus or minus 1). This can be confirmed by the following queries:

anOrderedCollection **size** $\Rightarrow$ 3
anOrderedCollection **at**: 1 $\Rightarrow$ 10
anOrderedCollection **at**: 2 $\Rightarrow$ 20
anOrderedCollection **at**: 3 $\Rightarrow$ 30

So far, specialized inspectors are provided for classes OrderedCollection, Dictionary, and View. Specialized inspectors also provide special yellow button menu items. Inspectors for ordered collections, for example, additionally permit you to insert or remove items into the collection. Inspectors for dictionaries permit new keys to be added and existing keys to be removed. Finally, inspectors for views also display the associated model and controller and permit them to be manipulated with the same ease as the view.

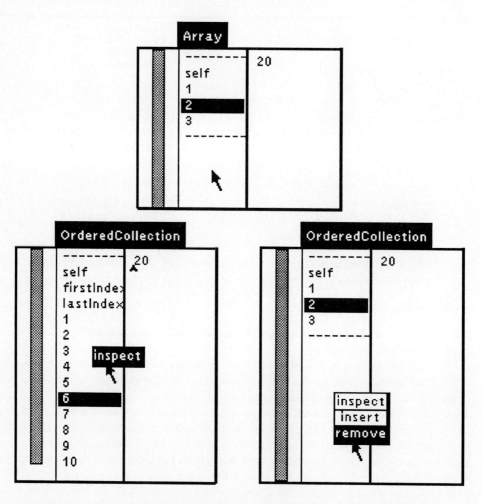

Figure 6.7   Using **inspect**: on an Array; also **basicInspect**: and **inspect**: respectively on an Ordered Collection.

Confirmers provide a very simple facility for interactive debugging and/or querying. Fig. 6.8 provides a simple illustration. When a confirmer appears, the user must choose either yes or no. The choice is returned as a boolean.

Figure 6.8 The result of executing "self **confirm**: 'Shall we meet Saturday?'".

6.2.6 Meta Operations for Accessing and Modifying Objects

Meta operations are operations that provide information about an object as opposed to information directly contained by the object. For example, an operation that determines the number of named instance variables in an instance is a meta operation. An operation that permits the value of a named instance variable to be extracted without knowing the name of the instance variable is another meta operation. Clearly, meta operations are nonstandard. They permit things to be done that are not normally possible — they are powerful and, consequently, dangerous.

In this section, we consider the meta operations that permit the instance variables, both named and indexed, to be accessed. The operations are intended for sophisticated users and sophisticated applications. The casual reader might read this section, not so much with the intention of using these operations, but rather with the goal of understanding them so that the subsequent section dealing with copying operations will be better understood.

Recall that an object consists of zero or more named instance variables and zero or more unnamed indexed instance variables. Operations are provided to determine the number of each category of variables and to access and change them.

size queries

- anObject **size**

    Returns the number of indexed instance variables. This is often redefined in subclasses to mean the number of items contained in an object; e.g., consider sets and ordered collections.

- anObject **basicSize**

    An alternative for **size** that is not redefined in subclasses.

- aClass **instSize**

    Returns the number of named instance variables. Note: must be sent to the instance's class.

classification queries

- anObject **isVariable**

    Returns true if and only if the instance is a member of a class that has indexed instance variables.

accessing and modifying named instance variables

- anObject **instVarAt**: anInteger

  Returns the value of the named instance variable at position anInteger. Legal positions range between 1 and the number of named instance variables, anObject **class instSize**. An error is reported if the position is not an integer or if it is out of range.

- anObject **instVarAt**: anInteger **put**: anotherObject

  Changes the value of the named instance variable at position anInteger to anotherObject and returns anotherObject. Legal positions range between 1 and anObject **class instSize**. An error is reported if the position is not an integer or if it is out of range.

accessing and modifying indexed instance variables

- anObject **at**: anInteger

  Returns the value of the indexed instance variable at index anInteger. Legal index values range between 1 and anObject **basicSize**. An error is reported if the index is not an integer or if it is out of range. This method is often redefined in subclasses.

- anObject **at**: anInteger **put**: anotherObject

  Changes the value of the indexed instance variable at index anInteger to anotherObject and returns anotherObject. Legal index values range between 1 and anObject **basicSize**. An error is reported if the index is not an integer or if it is out of range. This method is often redefined in subclasses.

- anObject **basicAt**: anInteger
- anObject **basicAt**: anInteger **put**: anotherObject

  Alternatives for **at**: and **at:put**: that are not redefined in subclasses.

As indicated, methods **size**, **at**:, and **at:put**: are often redefined in subclasses. The collection classes in particular provide these operations as standard operations. Hence, for collections, they are no longer meta operations. When the meta operations are desired, equivalents **basicSize**, **basicAt**:, and **basicAt:put**: should be used instead.

With these operations, it is possible to implement a general comparison operation that will work on arbitrary objects. The general = operation is defined to mean identity in Smalltalk — it can be found in class Object. A more conventional semantics is provided by redefining = in all subclasses. An attempt at implementing a more flexible and more accurate = is shown below.

Unfortunately, this method is inadequate because it gets into infinite loops with recursive structures. A revision that takes this into account is possible but it is more complex. One approach is to keep track of objects that are in the midst of being compared. If they are encountered a second time, they are assumed to be equal. If they are not, two corresponding fields will ultimately be found that are not equal.

= anObject
    "An example to show how equality could be implemented in Smalltalk. This method considers two objects to be equal if they are both instances of the same class, have the same number of instance variables, and corresponding instance variables are recursively equal."
    self == anObject **ifTrue**: [↑true].
    self **class** == anObject **class ifFalse**: [↑false].
    self **class instSize** = anObject **class instSize ifFalse**: [↑false]. "named fields"
    self **basicSize** = anObject **basicSize ifFalse**: [↑false]. "indexed fields"
    1 **to**: self **class instSize do**: [:index | "named fields"
        (self **instVarAt**: index) = (anObject **instVarAt**: index) **ifFalse**: [↑false]].
    1 **to**: self **basicSize do**: [:index | "indexed fields"
        (self **basicAt**: index) = (anObject **basicAt**: index) **ifFalse**: [↑false]].
    ↑true

We will use the notion of an **identity dictionary** and an **identity set** to keep track of the required information. These classes of objects are discussed in detail in the chapter on collections. Briefly, an identity dictionary is like an array except that the subscripts or keys are arbitrary objects. Each key has associated with it all other objects that are candidates as equal objects. These objects are kept in an identity set so that they can be distinguished.

= anObject
    "A better example to show how equality could be implemented in Smalltalk. This method considers two objects to be equal if they are both instances of the same class, have the same number of instance variables, and corresponding instance variables are recursively equal. It also takes circular structures into account."
    ↑self **privateCompare**: anObject **using**: IdentityDictionary **new**.

privateCompare: anObject **using**: comparisonInProgressDictionary
    "Private method supporting the implementation of = that handles circular structures."
    | candidatesInProgress |
    self == anObject **ifTrue**: [↑true].
    self **class** == anObject **class ifFalse**: [↑false].
    self **class instSize** = anObject **class instSize ifFalse**: [↑false]. "named fields"
    self **basicSize** = anObject **basicSize ifFalse**: [↑false]. "indexed fields"

    "Are we in the midst of comparing these two objects already?"
    candidatesInProgress ← comparisonInProgressDictionary
        at: self
        ifAbsent: [
            comparisonInProgressDictionary **at**: self **put**: Set **new** "returns the set"].
    (candidatesInProgress **includes**: anObject) **ifTrue**: [↑true "consider it equal so far"].
    candidatesInProgress **add**: anObject.

    "Continue testing corresponding fields of the objects."
    1 **to**: self **class instSize do**: [:index | "named fields"
        ((self **instVarAt**: index) **privateCompare**: (anObject **instVarAt**: index)
            using: comparisonInProgressDictionary) **ifFalse**: [↑false]].
    1 **to**: self **basicSize do**: [:index | "indexed fields"
        ((self **basicAt**: index) **privateCompare**: (anObject **basicAt**: index)
            using: comparisonInProgressDictionary) **ifFalse**: [↑false]].
    ↑true

It is important to note that the above is not the = method provided in class Object. Smalltalk takes a more conservative approach and dictates that the default = for all objects will be ==. Subclasses provide a more appropriate definition by redefining = when necessary. For example, it is redefined in class ArithmeticValue and Rectangle but not in other graphical classes like Form.

6.2.7 Copying Operations: Shallow versus Deep Copies

When an object is copied, a new instance with the same number of named and indexed instance variables is created. A **shallow copy** (see Fig. 6.9) is obtained if the fields of the new object are bound to the corresponding fields of the original; i.e., if the fields are not copied.

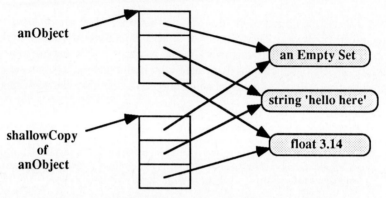

Figure 6.9 A shallow copy.

A **deep copy** (see Fig. 6.10) is obtained if the fields of the new object are bound to deep copies of the corresponding fields of the original — recursion stops for immutable objects like integers.

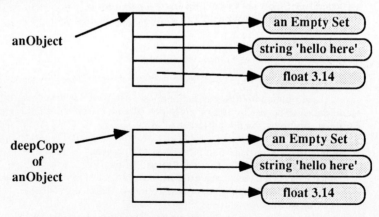

Figure 6.10 A deep copy.

As you might guess, deep copies are more expensive than shallow copies. Hence the standard copy defaults to shallow copying.

copying

- anObject **copy**

    Returns a shallow copy of anObject. Subclasses typically override this class when a shallow copy is not sufficient.

- anObject **deepCopy**

    Returns a deep copy of anObject. Gets into infinite loops for objects with circular structures. Fails to make a copy if the class of anObject is Object.

- anObject **shallowCopy**

    Returns a shallow copy of anObject. Fails to make a copy if the class of anObject is Object.

As you can see, there are two deficiencies. First, you cannot make a copy of an instance of class **Object**. This is likely to be historical since **Object** must have been an abstract class in the past; i.e., a class which did not permit instances. However, it is now perfectly legitimate to create instances of **Object**; e.g.,

```
object1 ← Object new.
object2 ← Object new.
object1 == object2 ⇒ false
```

is legal. We actually use this in the switch windows chapter for creating **connection** objects between one-on switches (see Volume 2, Section 5.2.4). The only requirement is that these connection objects be unique objects.

The second deficiency has to do with the deep copy operation — it does not handle circular structures and hence can get into an infinite loop. This is not a problem in practice because subclasses redefine this operation when problems occur.

It is instructive to examine one of these operations. We consider the **deepCopy** method; **shallowCopy** differs only by eliminating the recursive calls. New instances are created using **basicNew** or **basicNew:** depending on whether or not the instance is a member of a class with indexed instance variables.

deepCopy
    "Returns a copy of the receiver with its own copy of each instance variable."

```
| newObject class index |
class ← self class.
(class == Object) ifTrue: [↑self]. "Remove this line to make it work for Object
instances."

"First handle the indexed instance variables."
class isVariable
    ifTrue: ["has indexed variables"
        index ← self basicSize.
        newObject ← class basicNew: index.
        [index > 0] whileTrue: [
            newObject basicAt: index put: (self basicAt: index) deepCopy.
            index ← index - 1]]
    ifFalse: ["does not have indexed variables" newObject ← class basicNew].
```

```
"Second, handle the named instance variables."
index ← class instSize.
[index > 0] whileTrue: [
    newObject instVarAt: index put: (self instVarAt: index) deepCopy.
    index ← index - 1].
↑newObject
```

6.2.8 Comparison Operations: Identity versus Equality

This section summarizes the comparison operations previously mentioned above. **Identity** operations (== and ~~) permit the user to determine whether or not two objects are the same; **equality** operations (= and ~=) provide a comparison based on the contents of the objects. The identity operation is never redefined in subclasses. The default equality operation is defined to be identity in **Object**. Subclasses redefine it to provide a more appropriate version in special cases. For example, = is redefined in such classes as Character, Integer, Fraction, Float, Date, Time, Point, Rectangle, SequenceableCollection, and String.

When = is redefined in a new class, it is also customary to provide a definition for method **hash**, which is intended to return an integer unique to the object. This value is used to speed up lookup in container classes such as sets and dictionaries. An example is provided in the chapter on magnitudes in the context of class **Complex**.

Because the comparison operations are so simple, code implementing the methods is also shown. Note that only == and **hash** are primitive. All other operations are implemented in terms of these two.

identity comparisons

- anObject == anotherObject
    "Returns true if anObject and anotherObject are the same; otherwise false. Not redefined in any subclass."
        <primitive: 110>
        self **primitiveFailed** "a simple error message"
- anObject ~~ anotherObject
    "Returns true if anObject and anotherObject are **not** the same; otherwise false."
        ↑(self == anotherObject) **not**

equality comparisons

- anObject = anotherObject
    "Defined as ==. If = is redefined in a subclass, also consider redefining method hash."
        ↑self == anotherObject

- anObject ~= anotherObject
    "Returns the not of =."
        ↑(self = anotherObject) **not**

Inside Smalltalk

- anObject **hash**
    "Returns an integer unique to the object. Used to speed up searching."
        <primitive: 75>
        self **primitiveFailed** "a simple error message"

6.2.9 Read/Write Operations: PrintStrings and StoreStrings

When a new class of objects is defined, one of the first objectives is to provide operations that will enable the objects to be printed. A secondary objective might be to be able to store the objects into a file for later retrieval. Class **Object** provides the default protocol for both of these objectives.

Printing Objects Our Own Way: An Example

We can best illustrate the goals mentioned above with an example. Suppose we defined a class of objects called **Dog** with a simple protocol that permits dogs to be named.

Class Dog

```
class name              Dog
superclass              Object
instance variable names name

instance methods

name access and modification

name
    ↑name

name: aSymbol
    name ← aSymbol
```

It is now a simple matter to create two dogs as follows:

```
dog1 ← Dog new name: #Barfy.
dog2 ← Dog new name: #Woofy.
```

One of the first things we might do with such dogs is attempt to print one while in the browser or in a workspace. If we do, the answer will print as follows:

```
a Dog
```

A second goal might be to attempt to convert one into a string representation. We might have seen this done elsewhere in a previous chapter. So we might try to print the following:

```
dog1 ← Dog new name: #Barfy. ↑dog1 printString
```

Perhaps somewhat unexpectedly, the result is

```
'a Dog'
```

Clearly, there must be a connection between the print string of an object and the characters printed as a result of selecting **print it** in a browser or workspace. It is also possible to obtain another kind of string as follows:

dog1 ← Dog **new name**: #Barfy. ↑dog1 **storeString**

The result is

'(Dog **basicNew instVarAt**: 1 **put**: #Barfy; **yourself**)'

This string is interesting, not so much because it contains meta operations, but because it is executable code. If the contents were executed, the results would be an instance of **Dog** containing the same information as the original. We can now define the two kinds of strings.

A **print string** of an object is a string containing a textual representation of the object. It is often (but not always) sufficiently informative that alternative instances of the same class can be differentiated. A **store string** is a printable representation that can be used to re-create an equivalent instance. For some objects, like integers, the print and store strings are the same.

An obvious goal for our **Dog** class would be to provide methods that would enable better print and store strings to be created. The obvious solution is to redefine methods **printString** and **storeString** in class **Dog**. However, this turns out to be the wrong thing to do. If we ask for all implementors of **printString** (e.g., type **printString** in the browser and select **explain**), we find that there is exactly one — the same holds for **storeString**. It is worth looking at them because they reveal a better solution.

```
printString
    "Returns a string whose characters are a description of the receiver."
    | aStream |
    aStream ← WriteStream on: (String new: 16).
    self printOn: aStream.
    ↑aStream contents

storeString
    "Returns a string representation that can be used to reconstruct the receiver."
    | aStream |
    aStream ← WriteStream on: (String new: 16).
    self storeOn: aStream.
    ↑aStream contents
```

From these methods, it should be clear that the real work is being done by **printOn**: and **storeOn**:. Indeed, if we ask for all implementors of **printOn**:, we find a large number of distinct implementations. The same applies for **storeOn**:.

Each method constructs a write stream, an in-core file designed to store characters into a string that is initially sixteen characters long — the string is automatically extended if more space is required. The **printOn**: and **storeOn**: methods append characters to this stream. Afterwards, message **contents** extracts the stored characters and returns them as a string.

To design better print and store strings for instances of **Dog**, we must provide our own versions of **printOn:** and **storeOn:**. To do so, however, we need a basic understanding of the stream protocol. A summary is provided below (the complete protocol is discussed in depth in the chapter on collections).

- aStream **nextPut:** aCharacter
    Adds aCharacter to the end of the stream.

- aStream **nextPutAll:** aString
    Adds each character of aString to the end of the stream.

The next step is to decide on a suitable print and store string. A reasonable print string would be the dog's name. For the store string, we could generate the same code that was used to construct the dog in the first place. The result would be the following:

```
dog1 ← Dog new name: #Barfy. ↑dog1 printString ⇒ 'Barfy'
dog1 ← Dog new name: #Barfy. ↑dog1 storeString ⇒ '(Dog new name: #Barfy)'
```

Additionally, simply executing dog1 in a workspace would result in the print string being printed without the brackets; i.e.,

```
dog1 ← Dog new name: #Barfy. ↑dog1 ⇒ Barfy
```

Clearly, the workspace uses the print string to produce its result. We extend class **Dog** by adding the following instance methods:

printing and storing

printOn: aStream
    "Adds the receiver's name to the stream and returns the receiver."
    aStream **nextPutAll**: name

storeOn: aStream
    "Adds the code needed to re-create the receiver to the stream and returns the receiver."
    aStream **nextPutAll**: '(Dog new name: #'; **nextPutAll**: name; **nextPut**: $)

All of this can be summarized as follows:

To create a print string unique to a class:
    Redefine method **printOn:**.

To create a store string unique to a class:
    Redefine method **storeOn:**.

The Read/Write Protocol

Class **Object** contains the methods for operations **printString** and **storeString**, along with the default implementation of **printOn:** and **storeOn:** that are often redefined by subclasses.

In addition, it provides a default class method for converting a string to an object. The protocol is summarized as follows:

conversion from objects to strings (methods that need never be redefined)

- anObject **printString**

    Returns a string whose characters are a description of the receiver. Uses self **printOn**: aStream.

- anObject **storeString**

    Returns a string representation that can be used to reconstruct the receiver. Uses self **storeOn**: aStream.

writing into streams (methods normally redefined by users)

- anObject **printOn**: aStream

    Inserts a sequence of characters that identifies the receiver into aStream. Often redefined in subclasses. The default provided by this method is the class name preceded by 'a ' or 'an '.

- anObject **storeOn**: aStream

    Inserts a string representation that can be used to reconstruct the receiver into aStream. Often redefined in subclasses. The default provided by this method is code constructed via meta operations **basicNew** (or **basicNew**:), **instVarAt:put:**, and **basicAt:put:**; recursive structures are *not* handled.

reading from streams; i.e., converting from strings to objects

- Object **readFrom**: aStringOrAStreamContainingOneObject

    Compiles and evaluates the contents of the argument and returns the result. The inverse to **storeString**.

As can be seen, **storeString** and **readFrom**: are complementary operations; i.e.,

Object **readFrom**: anObject **storeString**

should re-create anObject. Note, however, that **storeString**, more specifically **storeOn:**, does not handle circular structures. When classes with inherently circular structures are defined, it is necessary to redefine **storeOn**: to ensure termination. To read multiple objects from a file, they must be separated by some distinguishable character. In some circumstances, a carriage return character is suitable; in others, a special character like $! might do. Special stream operations can be used to extract substrings bounded by the characters. The **readFrom**: method can be used on the individual substrings.

The **printOn**: and **storeOn**: methods for **Object** provide a useful default for new classes. They are defined as follows:

printOn: aStream
    "Inserts a sequence of characters that identifies the receiver into aStream. Often redefined in subclasses. The default provided by this method is to provide the class name preceded by 'a ' or 'an '."
    | title |
    title ← self **class name**.
    aStream **nextPutAll**: ((title **at**: 1) **isVowel ifTrue**: ['an '] **ifFalse**: ['a ']), title

storeOn: aStream
"Inserts a string representation that can be used to reconstruct the receiver into aStream. Often redefined in subclasses. The default provided by this method is to provide code constructed using meta operations **basicNew** (or **basicNew:**), **instVarAt:put:**, and **basicAt:put:**; recursive structures are **not** handled."
aStream **nextPut**: $(.
self **class isVariable**
    ifTrue: [
        aStream
            nextPutAll: '(', self **class name**, ' basicNew: ';
            store: self **basicSize**; **nextPutAll**: ') ']
    ifFalse: [aStream **nextPutAll**: self **class name**, ' basicNew'].
1 **to**: self **class instSize do**: [:i | "named instance variables"
    aStream
        nextPutAll: ' instVarAt: '; **store**: i;
        nextPutAll: ' put: '; **store**: (self **instVarAt**: i); **nextPut**: $;].
1 **to**: self **basicSize do**: [:i | "indexed instance variables"
    aStream
        nextPutAll: ' basicAt: '; **store**: i;
        nextPutAll: ' put: '; **store**: (self **basicAt**: i); **nextPut**: $;].
aStream **nextPutAll**: ' yourself)'

Note that 'aStream **store**: anObject' is equivalent to 'anObject **storeOn**: a stream' — for an object to be *stored*, so must the fields. The stream protocol relevant to the **storeOn**: method includes

writing characters and strings into streams

- aStream **nextPut**: aCharacter
  Adds aCharacter to the end of the stream.
- aStream **nextPutAll**: aString
  Adds each character of aString to the end of the stream.

writing other kinds of objects into streams

- aStream **print**: anObject
  Actually executes 'anObject **printOn**: aStream'.
- aStream **store**: anObject
  Actually executes 'anObject **storeOn**: aStream'.

Method **readFrom**: is much simpler. It is a class operation, not an instance operation.

readFrom: aStringOrAStreamContainingOneObject
"Compiles and evaluates the contents of aStringOrAStreamContainingOneObject and returns the result. The inverse to **storeString**."
| object |
object ← Compiler **evaluate**: aStringOrAStreamContainingOneObject.
(object **isKindOf**: self) **ifFalse**: [self **error**: self **name**, ' expected'].
↑object

Method **readFrom:** is redefined in classes **Date** and **Time** to permit a special syntax to be used as input. It is also redefined in classes such as **Number**, **Integer**, **Float**, and **String** for use by the compiler. A variation is also provided in class **Form**, which expects a file name instead of the usual string or stream as first parameter. Class **RunArray** also provides a variation for special run-arrays of small integers.

6.2.10 Meta Operations for Indirect Execution (perform:)

This section should be skipped on first reading. It is concerned with advanced Smalltalk facilities for manufacturing messages from data and subsequently executing the manufactured messages. We refer to the facility as **indirect message passing**. We document the methods first and then we consider examples that illustrate their use.

indirect message execution

- anObject **perform:** selectorSymbol
- anObject **perform:** selectorSymbol **with:** object1
- anObject **perform:** selectorSymbol **with:** object1 **with:** object2
- anObject **perform:** selectorSymbol **with:** object1 **with:** object2 **with:** object3
- anObject **perform:** selectorSymbol **withArguments:** anArrayOfObjects

Method **perform:withArguments:** causes the message indicated by selectorSymbol to be sent to anObject — the array contains the parameters for the message. The value computed is returned. The number of parameters provided must match the expected number; otherwise, error message **doesNotUnderstand:** is invoked. The first four operations are efficient variations of the last that don't require the parameters to be in an array.

Example

Trivial use of the facility is shown below to illustrate the correspondence between normal message passing and indirect message passing.

```
10 factorial
        ⇔ 10 perform: #factorial
        ⇔ 10 perform: #factorial withArguments: #()

1+2
        ⇔ 1 perform: #+ with: 2
        ⇔ 1 perform: #+ withArguments: #(2)

Array new: 3
        ⇔ Array perform: #new: with: 3
        ⇔ Array perform: #new: withArguments:#(3)

1 between: 0 and: 2
        ⇔ 1 perform: #between:and: with: 0 with: 2
        ⇔ 1 perform: #between:and: withArguments: #(0 2)
```

Using perform: to Simulate Case Statements

Once in a while, a method is designed with the following basic structure.

```
...                                          ...
character ← ...                              symbol ← ...
('0123456789' includes: character)           (symbol == #case1)
        ifTrue: [↑self numericCase].                 ifTrue: [↑self case1Process]
('([{' includes: character)                  (symbol == #case2)
        ifTrue: [↑self bracketCase].                 ifTrue: [↑self case2Process]
('+-*/' includes: character)                 (symbol == #case3)
        ifTrue: [↑self operatorCase].                ifTrue: [↑self case3Process]
...                                          ...
```

One way of avoiding long sequences of special tests is to construct an array containing the selector to be used for specific subscripts and invoke it using indirect message passing. For instance, in the character case above, we could construct an array as follows:

```
specialArray ← Array new: 256.
specialArray atAllPut: #errorCase.
'0123456789' do: [:aCharacter |
        specialArray at: (aCharacter asInteger) + 1 put: #numericCase].
'([{' do: [:aCharacter |
        specialArray at: (aCharacter asInteger) + 1 put: #bracketCase].
'+-*/' do: [:aCharacter |
        specialArray at: (aCharacter asInteger) + 1 put: #operatorCase].
```

Typically, this special array would be a class variable initialized in a class method such as **initialize**. This technique is used, for example, by the compiler. The original method is then modified to eliminate the series of tests as follows:

```
self perform: (specialArray at: character asInteger + 1)
```

A second approach is to actually manufacture the required selector when required. For the symbol case above, the method code could be replaced by the following:

```
self perform: (symbol, 'Process') asSymbol
```

Concatenating variable 'symbol' with 'Process' results in a string (rather than a symbol). It is converted back using **asSymbol**.

Recall a previous example concerned with explaining how **yourself** was intended to be used. The example was

```
anArray ← (Array new: 6)
        at: 1 put: Form white;
        at: 2 put: Form veryLightGray;
        at: 3 put: Form lightGray;
        at: 4 put: Form gray;
        at: 5 put: Form darkGray;
        at: 6 put: Form black;
        yourself.
```

An alternative using **perform**: and **collect**: can be written as follows. The **collect**: operation creates an array the same size as the receiver but with elements that are computed from the elements of the original.

```
anArray ← #(white veryLightGray lightGray gray darkGray black) collect: [:element |
    Form perform: element].
```

6.2.11 Advanced Meta Operations

In this section, we consider operations **become**: and **doesNotUnderstand**:. The former is a powerful object mutation operation. The latter is invoked when an inappropriate message is sent to an object. It is provided with an instance of class **Message** as parameter. The first section considers the **become**: operation in detail; the second reviews the protocol for **Message** and how it can be used to implement **doesNotUnderstand**:. The final section makes use of the two operations to implement a class of **indirection** objects that can be used for monitoring messages sent to specific objects.

The become: Operation

There are several classes of objects in Smalltalk that automatically grow to accommodate an arbitrary number of elements. For example, consider the following:

```
aSet ← Set new.
aBag ← Bag new.
aDictionary ← Dictionary new.
anOrderedCollection ← OrderedCollection new.

1 to: 1000 do: [:index |
    aSet add: index.
    aBag add: index.
    aDictionary at: index put: index+1.
    anOrderedCollection add: index]
```

Each of these instances is an object with a fixed number of indexed instance variables. When a new set is constructed, for example, it is created with room for a maximum number of elements. A reasonable initial size might be sufficient to hold, say, ten elements. What happens when we attempt to add the eleventh element?

From the user's point of view, the object simply grows bigger. At the implementation level, however, there is more to it. More specifically, a new larger object is created and initialized with the same elements as the original; i.e., a shallow copy is created. Next comes the more difficult task. All references to the original object are changed to refer to the new object. Such a powerful operation is provided as a user primitive.

object mutation

• anObject **become**: anotherObject
    All references to anObject are rerouted to anotherObject and vice versa.
    Does not work if anObject or anotherObject is a small integer.

Diagrammatically, the effects of the **become:** operation are shown in Fig. 6.11. All references to object1 and object2 are swapped.

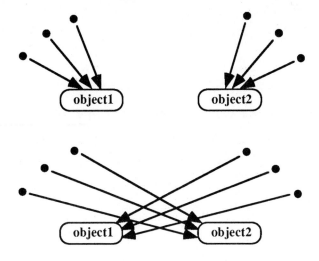

Figure 6.11 Operation **become:** swaps references.

Depending on the implementation, the **become:** operation can be either very *inexpensive* or very *expensive*. In particular, implementations that make use of an object table are very efficient. In these systems, all references are typically indices into an object table whose entries point at the actual objects. The **become:** operation is implemented by swapping two pointers in the object table. Because of the overhead incurred by continual indirection, more efficient implementations eliminate the notion of an object table in favor of direct pointers. In these systems, a naive implementation of **become:** requires a global search through all memory to change all references. More sophisticated implementations make use of special indirection objects that redirect messages to the intended recipient. In the worst case, both objects of the **become:** operation are copied into new objects and the originals are changed into these "invisible" indirection objects. The overhead that used to occur for all objects in implementations with object tables now occurs only for the special objects of **become:**. Over time, this slight increase in indirection overhead is permanently removed by the garbage collector — one of its tasks is to short-circuit indirection objects. To avoid slowing down the Smalltalk interpreter, special tricks are used to make sure that checking for indirection objects is not needed.

The **become:** operation is interesting because it permits virtually any object to be mutated into another. This could have application, for example, in the design of adaptive objects that monitor their access history. For a simpler example, suppose we intended to unify classes **Array** and **OrderedCollection**. The former is more efficient to access because there is no internal remapping of the subscripts. However, arrays do not automatically grow to accommodate more elements. Ordered collections are more flexible; for example, they can be extended by simply adding new elements. The **add:** operation could be added to **Array** as follows:

```
anArray add: anElement
    | arrayAlternate |
    arrayAlternate ← self asOrderedCollection.
    arrayAlternate add: anElement.
    self become: arrayAlternate.
    ↑anElement
```

Attempts to **add:** to an array automatically cause it to mutate into an ordered collection. Whether or not this is a good idea is a separate and independent issue.

Class Message and the *doesNotUnderstand:* Operation

When an inappropriate message is sent to an object, the message (both the selector and the arguments) is encoded in an instance of class **Message** and sent back to the same receiver as the parameter to **doesNotUnderstand:**.

the standard error handler

- anObject **doesNotUnderstand**: aMessage
    The standard handler for messages not understood by the receiver.

If we wish to introduce a variation of this method for a special class of objects (as we will in the next section), it is necessary to know the protocol for instances of **Message**.

instance creation

- Message **selector**: aSymbol
- Message **selector**: aSymbol **argument**: anObject
- Message **selector**: aSymbol **arguments**: anArray
    Returns a new instance of Message containing the selector and arguments.
    Variations are provided for situations with 0, 1, or many arguments.

accessing

- aMessage **selector**
- aMessage **arguments**
    Returns the selector symbol and the arguments array respectively.

printing

- aMessage **printOn**: aStream
    Adds a sequence of characters in the format 'a Message with selector: selector and arguments: arguments' to aStream.
- aMessage **storeOn**: aStream
    Adds a sequence of characters in the format '(Message selector: selector arguments: arguments)' to aStream.

With this protocol, a simple version of **doesNotUnderstand**: can easily be written as follows:

anObject **doesNotUnderstand**: aMessage
    "First, create a notifier that will permit a debugger to be scheduled."
    self **halt**: 'receiver does not understand ', aMessage **selector printString**.
    "Second, if the user proceeds, re-attempt the original message."
    "Another doesNotUnderstand: message will result if the problem was not fixed."
    self **perform**: aMessage **selector withArguments**: aMessage **arguments**

Indirection Objects — *become:* and *doesNotUnderstand:*

Sometimes it is useful to monitor specific messages sent to specific objects; e.g., to locate a design error. The usual approach is to modify the method to be monitored. Another less intrusive technique consists of creating a special indirection object for the task. To illustrate the approach, suppose we wish to monitor global variable **Smalltalk** to determine how often message **size** is sent to it.

We create a new class called **Indirection**, which can be later specialized for a specific application. The indirection object plays the role of a **gateway** for another object, the **intended receiver**, which it metaphorically surrounds. Using the **become**: operation, all references to the intended receiver are changed to the indirection object. The indirection object intercepts the messages meant for the intended receiver via method **doesNotUnderstand**: and reroutes them using **perform:withArguments:**.

To ensure that the **Indirection** class remains generic, we will subsequently specialize it to a subclass called **IndirectionForSmalltalk**.

Class Indirection

class name	Indirection
superclass	nil
instance variable names	intendedReceiver
comment	Create this class with superclass Object; afterwards, inspect Indirection and change the superclass to **nil**.

class methods

instance creation

on: anObject
    | anIndirection |
    anIndirection ← self **new initializePlease**.
    anObject **become**: anIndirection. "Indirections don't understand become:."
    "Now the two are switched: initialize the indirection object."
    anObject **intendedReceiverPlease**: anIndirection.
    ↑anObject

instance methods

instance initialization

initializePlease
    "No-op. Provided in case subclasses need to redefine it."

intended receiver access and modification

intendedReceiverPlease
    ↑intendedReceiver

intendedReceiverPlease: anObject
    intendedReceiver ← anObject

object redirection

doesNotUnderstand: aMessage
    ↑intendedReceiver
        perform: aMessage **selector withArguments**: aMessage **arguments**

deactivation

deactivate
    self **become**: intendedReceiver.
    ↑nil

To ensure that a maximal number of messages are rerouted through **doesNotUnderstand:**, it is essential that class **Indirection** not inherit from a class with a large number of operations. One solution is to use a superclass such as **UndefinedObject**. Unfortunately, it inherits a few too many operations from Object. Another solution is to use no superclass at all; i.e., like class **Object**, use **nil** as the superclass. Unfortunately, attempts to use **nil** as the superclass when defining **Indirection** will always result in error messages and an unsuccessful definition. The solution is to define **Indirection** with any legal superclass like **Object** and then change it using an inspector. The inspector will permit the superclass field of **Indirection** to be changed to **nil**. It is actually possible to file out this modified class although you cannot file it back in (unless it is restored to what it what before modification by the inspector).

Once the superclass of **Indirection** is set to **nil**, only four messages are directly understood by indirection objects: **initializePlease**, **intendedReceiverPlease**, **intended-ReceiverPlease:**, and **deactivate** — all others end up in **doesNotUnderstand:**, which reroutes them to the intended receiver.

To monitor messages sent to global variable **Smalltalk**, we create a special subclass of **Indirection** whose sole purpose is to record the number of times message **size** is sent to it. Of course, this message is also rerouted to the intended receiver. Any number of messages could be monitored this way (all of them if **doesNotUnderstand:** was suitably redefined).

An example method is provided to illustrate how **Smalltalk** can be monitored. Note that no attempt should be made to debug such a class unless you are prepared to restart the system because it is very easy to cause problems that result in infinite loops. For example, the first version of the system had the arguments to **become:** in method **on:** above switched. The indirection object of course did not understand **become:** since it is an operation associated with class **Object**. Hence, it was rerouted to the **doesNotUnderstand:** method, which sent it to the as yet uninitialized intended receiver, causing **nil** and **Smalltalk** to "become" each other. The sequence continued through other complications but the end result was an infinite loop that could not be stopped. The moral is simple: be prepared.

Class IndirectionForSmalltalk

class name	IndirectionForSmalltalk
superclass	Indirection
instance variable names	sizeReferences

class methods

examples

example1
    | anIndirection count |
    anIndirection ← IndirectionForSmalltalk **on:** Smalltalk.
    10 **timesRepeat:** [Smalltalk **size**].
    count ← anIndirection **sizeReferencesPlease**.
    anIndirection **deactivate**.
    ↑count
    "IndirectionForSmalltalk example1"

instance methods

special initialization

initializePlease
    super **initializePlease**.
    sizeReferences ← 0

special queries

sizeReferencesPlease
    ↑sizeReferences

monitored methods

size
    sizeReferences ← sizeReferences + 1.
    ↑intendedReceiver **size**

After successfully monitoring variable **Smalltalk**, temporary class **IndirectionFor-Smalltalk** can be removed from the system. A useful extension to class **Indirection** would be to add **become:** as one of the operations it understands. This would permit indirections to be created on arbitrary objects; i.e., either ordinary objects or other indirection objects.

6.3 CLASS UNDEFINEDOBJECT

UndefinedObject is the class for object **nil**, its sole instance. It is the value assigned to all uninitialized variables; i.e., both to local variables in methods and to named and indexed instance variables in objects created via messages such as **basicNew** and **basicNew:**.

    UndefinedObject is also a subclass of **Object** (see Fig. 6.12). Hence it inherits the general **Object** protocol. For instance, it responds to == and ~~ and equivalently to = and ~= since these default to == and ~~ in Object.

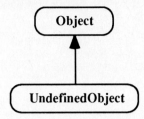

Figure 6.12 The UndefinedObject hierarchy.

In addition, **UndefinedObject** supports the following minimal protocol.

instance creation (disabled)

- UndefinedObject **new**
    Gives an error message; new instances not allowed.

dependency maintenance (disabled)

- nil **addDependent**: anObject
    Gives an error message; dependents not allowed.

no-ops for window management and copying

- nil **release**
    For window management, returns nil.
- nil **deepCopy**
- nil **shallowCopy**
    For copying, returns nil — the receiver.

printing

- nil **printOn**: aStream
- nil **storeOn**: aStream
    Stores and prints as 'nil'.

testing

- nil **isNil**
- nil **notNil**
    Returns true and false respectively. Equivalent methods in class Object
    return the converse.

6.4 CLASS BLOCKCONTEXT (BLOCKS FOR SHORT)

In languages like Pascal, C, or Ada, square brackets would be interpreted as syntax that
merely serves to bracket certain segments of the code; e.g.,

```
I sum index I
sum ← 0. index ← 1.
[index <= 10] whileTrue: [sum ← sum + index. index ← index + 1].
Transcript show: 'The sum from 1 to 10 is', sum printString
```

In Smalltalk, the bracketed constructs (square brackets included) are called **blocks** —
they are objects that can be manipulated like other objects. For example, it is perfectly legal
to execute the following:

```
| aSet  count aBlock |
"Add a block to a set."
aSet ← Set new. count ← 0.
aSet add: [count ← count + 1].

"Save a block in a local variable."
aBlock ← [count factorial]
aSet add:aBlock.
```

The block [count ← count + 1] is passed as a parameter to **add:** and inserted into the
set — the set now contains one element, a block. At first sight, this is confusing. Why
would you want to do this, or more to the point, what precisely is a block and what can you
do with one?

Technically, a **block** is an instance of class **BlockContext** (see Fig. 6.13).
Intervening classes are omitted because they are not essential to the discussion — they are
primarily of interest to compiler implementors.

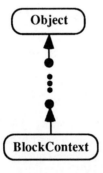

Figure 6.13 The partial Block hierarchy.

But functionally, a **block** is an **unnamed function**. It may have zero or more
parameters and it can be invoked with the following special protocol.

evaluating (invoking) a block

- aBlock **value**
- aBlock **value:** parameter
- aBlock **value:** parameter1 **value:** parameter2
- aBlock **value:** parameter1 **value:** parameter2 **value:** parameter3
- aBlock **valueWithArguments:** anArrayOfParameters

    Evaluates the block with the parameters provided. The number of
    parameters supplied must match the number expected. Returns the last
    expression computed unless an explicit ↑-statement is encountered; in that
    case, returns the ↑-statement value to the sender of the method in which
    the block was defined (not to the sender of the **value** message).

A block is **defined** by executing the square bracketed construct. For example, consider the following:

```
| block0 block1 block2 |

"Defining three blocks."
block0 ← [Transcript show: 'hello'].
block1 ← [:name | Transcript show: name].
block2 ← [:firstName :lastName |
     Transcript nextPutAll: firstName; space; show: lastName].

"Invoking the blocks."
block0 value. "Causes 'hello ' to output on the transcript."
block0 valueWithArguments: #(). "Also causes 'hello ' to output on the transcript."

block1 value: 'Wilf'. "Causes 'Wilf' to output on the transcript."
block1 valueWithArguments: #('Wilf'). "Same."

block2 value: 'Wilf' value: 'LaLonde'. "Causes 'Wilf LaLonde' to output on the transcript."
block2 valueWithArguments: #('Wilf' 'LaLonde'). "Same"
```

Blocks can consist of an arbitrary number of statements. When a block is invoked, the last expression computed is the value of the block. For example,

```
block ← [1+2. 10+20. 100+200].
block value ⇒ 300
```

Additionally, unless constructed in a workspace, blocks are defined through the normal course of events, while methods are executed. Where they are defined is important because they provide access to local variables at the definition point and also permit non-local returns. For example, suppose the following two methods were temporarily added to class **Object** and that message **hello** was sent to some arbitrary object. The value returned is 'smile'. More interesting is the execution sequence.

```
hello
     | count |
     count ← 20.
     self helloTest: [:title |
          Transcript nextPutAll: title; show: count printString.
          ↑'smile'.
          'frown'].
     ↑'cry'

helloTest: aBlock
     aBlock value: 'The counter is '.
     ↑'smirk'
```

When method **hello** is executed, we expect 'cry' to be returned unless something causes a premature return. The block with parameter **title** is defined in method **hello** but not invoked here. Instead, it is passed as a parameter to method **helloTest:**.

In method **helloTest:**, we expect 'smirk' to be returned unless a premature return occurs first. How could that happen? By sending message **value:** to aBlock, string parameter

'The counter is ' is bound to **title** and the block executes *in its defining context*. Thus, the transcript displays 'The counter is 20'. Note that the block accesses variable **count**. Normally, the statements in the block would execute one by one until the last one. If that were to happen, we would expect 'frown' to be returned to the **helloTest:** context. However, there is a return statement prior to string 'frown' in the block. So an immediate return with 'smile' as the answer results. But what do we return from — from **hello** or **helloTest:**? The answer is from the method *in which the block was defined* — not from the method that started the block executing. In this case, it is method **hello** and not **helloTest:**.

Since blocks are objects, they can be manipulated just like other objects. Assigning them to variables or passing them as parameters in messages is normal. However, we don't normally store blocks that contain imbedded return statements. The reason is clear — you can't return twice from the same method. After storing a block for use at some arbitrary point in the future, a return from the defining method is virtually guaranteed. Evaluating the block after that point causes an attempt to return a second time. This error situation is detected and signalled. The rule is simple: ***Blocks intended for long term storage should not have imbedded return statements***.

When blocks are not stored, imbedded return statements can be very useful. For example, a user could easily define a method such as the following:

```
getPermissionFor: aPerson password: aString ifFail: aBlock
    "Check the security clearances of the person. If it fails, execute the block."
    ... code to perform the checking ...
    checkingFailed ifTrue: [aBlock value].
    ... code to record the entrance of the person into the secure area ...
```

The method might then be used by an interactive system that first creates a person object for reference and performs the required checks.

```
checkIn
    "Prepare to track the person entering the secure area. Returns true if entry
    permission granted; false otherwise."
    | person password |
    ... code to obtain the person's name ...
    person ← Person named: aString.
    ... code to obtain the person's password ...
    password ← aString.
    "Verify clearances."
    self getPermissionFor: aPerson password: aString ifFail: [↑false].
    ... code to obtain entrance location ...
    ↑true
```

If the person fails to obtain permission, the **getPermissionFor:password:ifFail:** method returns control to the sender of **checkIn** — this occurs because executing 'aBlock **value**' causes '↑false' to be executed, which returns from **checkIn** (not from **getPermissionFor:password:ifFail:**). In other words, control never returns to execute '*code to obtain entrance location*'.

In general, return statements in blocks are essential for control structures. For example, code such as the following is pervasive.

```
testSatisfied
    ifTrue: [... ↑anObject]
    ifFalse: [... ↑anotherObject]
```

The particular semantics chosen for blocks and their response to the **value** messages is important because it permits users to define their own control structures. Even more important is the fact that these user defined control structures are indistinguishable from the built-in ones.

6.4.1 Blocks Provide Facilities to Design Control Structures

Blocks already respond to messages that are viewed as control structures. The following protocol is understood by blocks.

control structures

* aBlock **whileFalse**

    Repeatedly evaluates aBlock as long as it returns false.
* aBlock **whileFalse**: anotherBlock

    Repeatedly evaluates anotherBlock as long as aBlock evaluates to false.

* aBlock **whileTrue**

    Repeatedly evaluates aBlock as long as it returns true.
* aBlock **whileTrue**: anotherBlock

    Repeatedly evaluates anotherBlock as long as aBlock evaluates to true.

Each of these methods can be implemented using **value** messages and the boolean control structures. For example, the latter two can be implemented as follows:

```
whileTrue
    "Repeatedly evaluates aBlock as long as it returns true."
    ↑[self value] whileTrue: []

whileTrue: anotherBlock
    "Repeatedly evaluates anotherBlock as long as aBlock evaluates to true."
    ↑self value ifTrue: [anotherBlock value. self whileTrue: anotherBlock]
```

Some control structures, like **whileTrue**: and those associated with boolean receivers, are compiled inline for efficiency. But a great many are not. Examples include control structures such as the following:

```
1 to: 10 do: [:index | ...].
10 timesRepeat: [...].
aSet do: [:element | ...].
anOrderedCollection collect: [:element | ...].
'hello' collect: [:aCharacter | aCharacter asUppercase].
```

The collection classes, in particular, have a wide range of control structures defined explicitly in terms of blocks. We will subsequently investigate the control structures provided by class **Boolean**. An interesting series of control structures for sequencing over binary trees is included at the end of this chapter.

To illustrate the power of such extensions, it is easy but not worthwhile adding personalized variations of the basic control structures. For example, beginners often complain about the unnaturalness of the **ifTrue:ifFalse:** notation for if-statements. It is easily changed, for example, by adding the following to class **Boolean**.

```
then: aBlock else: anotherBlock
    ↑self ifTrue: [aBlock value] ifFalse: [anotherBlock value]
```

Better yet, we could add it as follows:

```
then: aBlock else: anotherBlock
    ↑self ifTrue: aBlock ifFalse: anotherBlock
```

It is subsequently legal to write

```
| n |
"For what minimum value of n does n factorial contain at least 100 digits."
n ← 10. "Some arbitrary starting point."
[true] whileTrue: [n factorial printString size < 100 then: [n ← n + 1] else: [↑n]]
```

Note that the else-part has an explicit return that gets it out of the infinite while loop — the then-part has no such return. Both parts work correctly because of the way **value** messages work.

6.4.2 Syntactic Details and Recursive Blocks

Syntactically, blocks satisfy the following syntax. Note that the syntax for version 2.4 and beyond is an upward compatible extension of the syntax provided in earlier versions. In version 2.4, there are two intervening bars "|" between the parameters and the local variables.

Before version 2.4	Version 2.4 and after

[:parameter$_1$:parameter$_2$ ... :parameter$_n$ |
    statement$_1$.
    statement$_2$.
    ...]
	[:parameter$_1$:parameter$_2$ ... parameter$_n$ |
	| local$_1$ local$_2$ ... local$_m$ |
	    statement$_1$.
	    statement$_2$.
	    ...]

Before version 2.4, local variables are not permitted. Note that locals are indicated with two '|' indicators — one after parameter$_n$ and one before local$_1$. A block is executed, as discussed previously, by sending it an appropriate **value** message with the required number of arguments.

All statements in a block can access block parameters in addition to variables declared outside the block; e.g., self, super, instance variables, method parameters, method locals, and parameters from containing blocks. Prior to version 2.4, block parameters could but need not have been declared as local variables in the method. In the new version, block parameters are strictly local to the block — a compiler warning will remind you. For example, the following variation from ParcPlace Systems™ generates a warning in version 2.4 but not in earlier versions.

```
example1
    | aClass |
    Object subclasses do: [:aClass |
        Transcript show: aClass name; cr].
    Transcript show: 'The last class was ', aClass name; cr.
        "aClass is nil in version 2.4"
```

Prior to version 2.4, method local 'aClass' and block parameter 'aClass' were the same. In the new version, they are distinct — standard lexical scoping rules apply. Additionally, blocks are not re-entrant prior to version 2.4; e.g., the following would not work.

```
example2
    | fibonacciBlock |
    fibonacciBlock ← [:n |
        n < 2
            ifTrue: [1]
            ifFalse: [(fibonacciBlock value: n-1) + (fibonacciBlock value: n-2)]].
    (fibonacciBlock value: 7) = 21
        ifTrue: [Transcript show: 'blocks are recursive']
        ifTrue: [Transcript show: 'blocks are not recursive']
```

Prior to version 2.4, the space for all block parameters resides in the containing method context. Invoking the same block a second time would overwrite the unique parameter n. Consequently, on return from sending the second **value:** message, the n would have its most recent value rather than the value it used to have before the invocation. After version 2.4, the space for block parameters is obtained each time a **value:** message is sent — the compiler optimizes those situations that don't require it. Hence, everything works as expected.

6.5 CLASS BOOLEAN

Class **Boolean** provides the general protocol for **true** and **false**. For efficiency reasons, the general protocol is specialized via subclasses **True** and **False** (see Fig. 6.14). Objects **true** and **false** are the sole instances of **True** and **False** respectively.

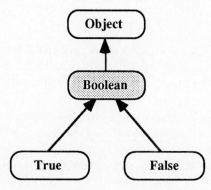

Figure 6.14 The Boolean hierarchy.

The protocol provided by **Boolean** provides a small number of generic methods that apply to both **true** and **false**. The protocol for **True**, on the other hand, applies only to instance **true**. Consequently, there is no need to determine the receiver in the code for the methods. The same holds in the protocol for **False**. Consequently, a method such as **not** is implemented differently in each subclass.

*instance creation (disabled, defined in **Boolean**)*

- Boolean **new**
  Gives an error message; new instances not allowed.

*logical operations (defined in **Boolean**)*

- aBoolean **eqv**: anotherBoolean
  Returns true if aBoolean and anotherBoolean are both true or both false; false otherwise.
- aBoolean **xor**: anotherBoolean
  Returns true if either aBoolean or anotherBoolean is true but not both; false otherwise.

*logical operations (defined in **True** and **False**)*

- aBoolean **not**
  Returns true if aBoolean is false and false otherwise.
- aBoolean & anotherBoolean
  The *and* operation. Returns true if aBoolean and anotherBoolean are both true; false otherwise.
- aBoolean | anotherBoolean
  The *or* operation. Returns true if either aBoolean, anotherBoolean, or both are true; false otherwise.

- aBoolean **and**: aBlock
  The short circuit *and* operation. If aBoolean is true, computes and returns the block result; otherwise, returns false without evaluating aBlock.
- aBoolean **or**: aBlock
  The short circuit *or* operation. If aBoolean is false, computes and returns the block result; otherwise, returns true without evaluating aBlock.

*copying (disabled, defined in **Boolean**)*

- aBoolean **deepCopy**
  New instances not allowed; returns self.
- aBoolean **shallowCopy**
  New instances not allowed; returns self.

*printing (defined in **Boolean**)*

- aBoolean **storeOn**: aStream
  Defaults to **printOn**:.

*printing (defined in **True** and **False**)*

- aBoolean **printOn**: aStream
    Adds either 'true' or 'false' to the stream depending on whether aBoolean is true or false respectively.

*control structures (defined in **True** and **False**)*

- aBoolean **ifTrue**: trueBlock
- aBoolean **ifFalse**: falseBlock
- aBoolean **ifTrue**: trueBlock **ifFalse**: falseBlock
- aBoolean **ifFalse**: falseBlock **ifTrue**: trueBlock
    If aBoolean is true, evaluates the true block if there is one and returns the result; otherwise, returns nil. Similarly, if aBoolean is false, evaluates the false block if there is one and returns the result; otherwise, returns nil.

For efficiency reasons, most of the control structures are compiled inline. Other operations like &, |, **not**, and **printOn**: are implemented differently in **True** and **False**. For example, consider the following summary.

In True	In False
not	**not**
↑false	↑true
& aBoolean	& aBoolean
↑aBoolean	↑false
| aBoolean	| aBoolean
↑true	↑aBoolean
and: aBlock	**and**: aBlock
↑aBlock **value**	↑false
or: aBlock	**or**: aBlock
↑true	↑aBlock **value**
printOn: aStream	**printOn**: aStream
aStream **nextPutAll**: 'true'	aStream **nextPutAll**: 'true'
ifTrue: trueBlock	**ifTrue**: trueBlock
↑trueBlock **value**	↑nil
ifFalse: falseBlock	**ifFalse**: falseBlock
↑nil	↑falseBlock **value**
ifTrue: trueBlock **ifFalse**: falseBlock	**ifTrue**: trueBlock **ifFalse**: falseBlock
↑trueBlock **value**	↑falseBlock **value**
ifFalse: falseBlock **ifTrue**: trueBlock	**ifFalse**: falseBlock **ifTrue**: trueBlock
↑trueBlock **value**	↑falseBlock **value**

In both cases, there is no need to interrogate the identity of the receiver. For example, the **not** for **true** simply returns **false** because the only way to have reached that method is for the receiver to have been **true**. On the other hand, if the receiver had been **false**, then the **not** method in class **False** would have been executed. This version of **not** simply needs to return **true**. The same idea applies to each of the operations defined in subclasses **True** and **False**.

Inside Smalltalk

Because **true** and **false** are instances of two different classes, there is no need to store data in the instances to differentiate them. Both **true** and **false** are objects *without instance variables*.

The few methods that are implemented in common superclass **Boolean** are very simple. For example, consider the following:

In Boolean

eqv: aBoolean
"Returns true if self and aBoolean are both true or both false; otherwise, returns false."
↑self == aBoolean

xor: aBoolean
"Returns true if either self or aBoolean is true but not both; otherwise, returns false."
↑(self == aBoolean) **not**

6.6 DESIGNING A NEW CLASS: BINARYTREE

In this section, we consider the design of a new class of objects, **binary trees**. Our main concern is to take into account all of the notions that we met in previous sections. Rather than evolve the design in stages, we present a final result, but we enumerate the questions and the answers we came up with in the process of developing the design. We will also consider two design extremes: a standard design using a single class and a non-standard design using several classes.

Typical Questions We Asked (With Answers)

- What kinds of operations are unique to binary trees?
  Operations like **depth**, **leftTree**, **rightTree**.

- Do we expect to be able to store data in binary trees?
  Yes, arbitrary objects. We'll call it the tree's **label** — we'll access it via **label** and change it via **label:**.

- Do we want to be able to tell the difference between an empty tree and a non-empty one?
  Yes, empty trees don't have subtrees nor can they be labelled (this last point is debatable).

- Should we use **nil** to denote an empty tree?
  Bad idea — **nil** does not respond to typical binary tree queries like **depth**. Moreover, we do not wish to modify **nil** so that it does.

- Do we need to be able to print trees?
  Yes, <'hi' -- <'there' <'you' -- --> --> is an example of the notation we settled on.

- What about store strings?
  How about (BinaryTree label: 'hi' leftTree: (BinaryTree empty) rightTree: etc.)?

- Do we care about the semantics for **copy**?

    Yes, it doesn't make much sense to provide a shallow copy (the default). So we'll redefine **copy** to provide a deep copy. There is no need to change **shallowCopy** or **deepCopy**.

- Should we design new control structures?

    Yes, preorder, inorder, and postorder traversals on binary trees are well known. These are control structures.

- Do we need to worry about comparison operations?

    Yes, equality for binary trees should take both the structure of the trees and their labels (the data) into account. The default inherited from object defines equality as identity.

- Do we need to define both = and ~=?

    No, just =. Operation ~= is defined in terms of = and **not**.

- Do we need to be able to modify existing trees?

    Yes, destructive operations like **leftTree:** and **rightTree:** would be useful.

- Is there ever a need to mutate an empty tree into a non-empty tree?

    Yes, once in a while, we could be referencing an empty tree that needs to change but we may not be aware of all other references to it. Rather than use **become:** to change it, we will extend the semantics of **label:**, **leftTree:**, and **rightTree:** so that attempts to add such information to an empty tree automatically causes it to mutate into a non-empty tree. Note: Our initial inclination had been to make this an error.

6.6.1 A Standard Design

These deliberations lead us to the following design. A **binary tree** is either an empty tree or a non-empty tree. Non-empty trees can have a **label**, a **left** subtree, and a **right** subtree. It is illegal to attempt to create a binary tree with invalid subtrees. Binary trees are created in one of two ways:

- BinaryTree **empty**

    Constructs a new empty binary tree and returns it.
- BinaryTree **label:** anObject **leftTree:** aBinaryTree **rightTree:** aBinaryTree

    Constructs a new non-empty binary tree with the information supplied and returns it.

Attempts to add a label, left tree, or right tree to an empty tree automatically cause the empty tree to mutate into a non-empty tree. This is an unusual feature that is not intended to be the normal way that binary trees are extended, but then, how are we to predict what users will do?

Note to implementors (please hide this fact from users): Since we don't permit non-empty trees to contain non-trees, both the left and right subtrees must be instances of class BinaryTree. Consequently, we will interpret a binary tree with a non-tree in one of the subtree fields as an empty tree; i.e., an empty tree is an ill-formed non-empty tree. For simplicity, we will assume that a binary tree is empty if the left subtree is **nil**. This is convenient because uninitialized trees are automatically empty.

Class BinaryTree

class name	BinaryTree
superclass	Object
instance variable names	label leftTree rightTree

class methods

instance creation

empty
    ↑super **new**

label: anObject **leftTree**: aBinaryTree **rightTree**: anotherBinaryTree
    ↑super **new**
        label: anObject; **leftTree**: aBinaryTree; **rightTree**: anotherBinaryTree;
        yourself

new
    ↑self **error**: 'empty trees are created with empty or label:leftTree:rightTree:'

examples

example1
    "Create a binary tree and see if it prints as <Hello <how -- --> <are <you -- --> -->>."
    ↑BinaryTree
        label: #Hello
        leftTree: (BinaryTree
            label: #how
            leftTree: BinaryTree **empty**
            rightTree: BinaryTree **empty**)
        rightTree: (BinaryTree
            label: #are
            leftTree: (BinaryTree
                label: #you
                leftTree: BinaryTree **empty**
                rightTree: BinaryTree **empty**)
            rightTree: BinaryTree **empty**)
    "BinaryTree example1"

example2
    "See if the store string is correct for example1."
    ↑self **example1 storeString**
    "BinaryTree example2"

example3
    "Construct an empty tree and see if it will mutate properly to a tree <testing -- -->."
    ↑self **empty label**: #testing
    "BinaryTree example3"

example4
    "Test depth which should be 3."
    ↑self **example1 depth**
    "BinaryTree example4"

example5
"Test size which should be 4."
↑self **example1 size**
"BinaryTree example5"

example6
| aTree |
"Test = and copy; should return true."
aTree ← self **example1**. ↑aTree = aTree **copy**
"BinaryTree example6"

example7
| aTree |
"Test = again; should return false."
aTree ← self **example1**.
↑aTree = (aTree **shallowCopy rightTree**: BinaryTree **empty**)
"BinaryTree example7"

example8
| aTree sum |
"Try out the control structures."

aTree ← self **example1**.

"First, modify the labels to contain numeric data."
aTree **label**: 1.
aTree **leftTree label**: 2.
aTree **rightTree label**: 3.
aTree **rightTree leftTree label**: 4.

"Next walk it, summing the information in the labels."
sum ← 0.
aTree **inorderDo**: [:label | sum ← sum + label].
↑sum
"BinaryTree example8"

instance methods

querying

depth
"The maximum distance between this tree and some subtree."
self **isEmpty**
    ifTrue: [↑0]
    ifFalse: [↑1 + (leftTree **depth max**: rightTree **depth**)]

size
"The number of non-empty subtrees in all."
self **isEmpty**
    ifTrue: [↑0]
    ifFalse: [↑1 + (leftTree **size** + rightTree **size**)]

isEmpty
"Special ill-structured binary trees with nil left subtrees are considered to be empty."
↑leftTree **isNil**

isNonEmpty
    ↑self **isEmpty not**

access and modification

label
    self **privatelyCheckForEmptyTreeAccessingError.**
    ↑label

label: anObject
    self **isEmpty**
        ifTrue: [self **privatelyMutateIntoNonEmptyTree label:** anObject]
        ifFalse: [label ← anObject]

leftTree
    self **privatelyCheckForEmptyTreeAccessingError.**
    ↑leftTree

leftTree: aBinaryTree
    self **privatelyCheckForABinaryTree:** aBinaryTree.
    self **isEmpty**
        ifTrue: [self **privatelyMutateIntoNonEmptyTree leftTree:** aBinaryTree]
        ifFalse: [leftTree ← aBinaryTree]

rightTree
    self **privatelyCheckForEmptyTreeAccessingError.**
    ↑rightTree

rightTree: aBinaryTree
    self **privatelyCheckForABinaryTree:** aBinaryTree.
    self **isEmpty**
        ifTrue: [self **privatelyMutateIntoNonEmptyTree rightTree:** aBinaryTree]
        ifFalse: [rightTree ← aBinaryTree]

comparing

= aBinaryTree
    "Two binary trees are equal if they have the same structure and their labels are
    equal."
    (aBinaryTree **isKindOf:** BinaryTree) **ifFalse:** [↑false].
    self **isEmpty ifTrue:** [↑aBinaryTree **isEmpty**].
    aBinaryTree **isEmpty ifTrue:** [↑false].
    label = aBinaryTree **label ifFalse:** [↑false].
    leftTree = aBinaryTree **leftTree ifFalse:** [↑false].
    ↑rightTree = aBinaryTree **rightTree**

copying

copy
    ↑self **deepCopy**

sequencing

do: aBlock
    "Sequences through all subtrees in inorder and executes the block with the labels."
    ↑self **inorderDo:** aBlock

inorderDo: aBlock
"Sequences through all subtrees in inorder and executes the block with the labels."
self **isEmpty**
    ifFalse: [
        leftTree **inorderDo**: aBlock.
        aBlock **value**: label.
        rightTree **inorderDo**: aBlock]

postorderDo: aBlock
"Sequences through all subtrees in postorder and executes the block with the labels."
self **isEmpty**
    ifFalse: [
        leftTree **postorderDo**: aBlock.
        rightTree **postorderDo**: aBlock.
        aBlock **value**: label]

preorderDo: aBlock
"Sequences through all subtrees in preorder and executes the block with the labels."
self **isEmpty**
    ifFalse: [
        aBlock **value**: label.
        leftTree **preorderDo**: aBlock.
        rightTree **preorderDo**: aBlock]

printing

printOn: aStream
"Empty trees print as '--'; non-empty tree print as '<label leftTree rightTree>'."
self **isEmpty**
    ifTrue: [aStream **nextPutAll**: '--']
    ifFalse: [
        aStream
            nextPut: $<; **print**: label;
            space; **print**: leftTree;
            space; **print**: rightTree; **nextPut**: $>]

storeOn: aStream
"We can do better than the default."
self **isEmpty**
    ifTrue: [aStream **nextPutAll**: '(BinaryTree empty)']
    ifFalse: [
        aStream
            nextPutAll: '(BinaryTree label: '; **store**: label;
            nextPutAll: ' leftTree: '; **store**: leftTree;
            nextPutAll: ' rightTree: '; **store**: rightTree; **nextPut**: $)]

private

privatelyCheckForABinaryTree: anObject
    (anObject **isKindOf**: BinaryTree)
        ifFalse: [self **error**: 'attempting to create an illegal subtree']

privatelyCheckForEmptyTreeAccessingError
self **isEmpty** **ifTrue**: [self **error**: 'illegal empty tree access attempted'].

privatelyMutateIntoNonEmptyTree
"For this implementation, empty trees have the same fields as non-empty trees. Hence there is no need to change one object into another object. Of course, the result must look like a non-empty tree."
leftTree ← BinaryTree **empty**. "Now it is non-empty."
rightTree ← BinaryTree **empty**. "Now it is non-empty and well-formed."

6.6.2 A Nonstandard Design

Most of the operations in the above design partition the code into two parts: what to do if the binary tree is empty and what to do if it is not. For example, the following code template is pervasive:

```
self isEmpty
    ifTrue: [...]
    ifFalse: [...]
```

This kind of testing can be eliminated if we adopt the approach taken by the designers of class **Boolean**. More specifically, we could create three classes of binary trees as shown in Fig. 6.15.

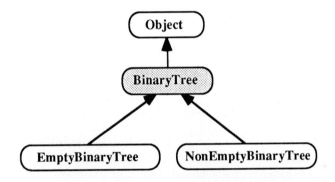

Figure 6.15 The nonstandard BinaryTree hierarchy.

BinaryTree is designed to play the role of an **abstract class**; i.e., a class without immediate instances. All empty binary trees are instances of **EmptyBinaryTree**; non-empty binary trees are instances of **NonEmptyBinaryTree**. Note that this new design is intended to work exactly the same way as the old. Logically, we want users of binary trees to think in terms of the simpler design. This design is purely an implementation technique to gain efficiency.

In this design, empty binary trees have no instance variables (fields). Only non-empty binary trees have the label, leftTree, and rightTree fields. As can be seen, almost all operations can be specialized for the two classes of trees. Only **isNonEmpty** and **do:** are in class **BinaryTree**. Of course, **BinaryTree** also contains all of the class methods for creating binary trees.

Class BinaryTree

class name	BinaryTree
superclass	Object
instance variable names	"none"

class methods

instance creation

empty
    ↑EmptyBinaryTree basicNew

label: anObject **leftTree**: aBinaryTree **rightTree**: anotherBinaryTree
    ↑NonEmptyBinaryTree **basicNew**
        label: anObject; **leftTree**: aBinaryTree; **rightTree**: anotherBinaryTree;
        yourself

new
    ↑self **error**: 'empty trees are created with empty or label:leftTree:rightTree:'

instance methods

querying

isNonEmpty
    ↑self **isEmpty not**

sequencing

do: aBlock
    "Sequences through all subtrees in inorder and executes the block with the labels."
    ↑self **inorderDo**: aBlock

The code in each of the methods for class **EmptyBinaryTree** was obtained from the corresponding code in the standard design by eliminating the **isEmpty** test along with the code for the non-empty case. Even the code for = was specialized.

Class EmptyBinaryTree

class name	EmptyBinaryTree
superclass	BinaryTree
instance variable names	"none"
comment	An empty binary tree is a binary tree with no label, left subtree, or right subtree.

instance methods

querying

depth
    "The maximum distance between this tree and some subtree."
    ↑0
size
    "The number of non-empty subtrees in all."
    ↑0
isEmpty
    ↑true

access and modification

label
    self **privatelySignalEmptyTreeAccessingError**
label: anObject
    ↑self **privatelyMutateIntoNonEmptyTree label**: anObject
leftTree
    self **privatelySignalEmptyTreeAccessingError**
leftTree: aBinaryTree
    ↑self **privatelyMutateIntoNonEmptyTree leftTree**: aBinaryTree
rightTree
    self **privatelySignalEmptyTreeAccessingError**
rightTree: aBinaryTree
    ↑self **privatelyMutateIntoNonEmptyTree rightTree**: aBinaryTree

comparing

= aBinaryTree
    "Two binary trees are equal if they have the same structure and their labels are
    equal."
    ↑aBinaryTree **isKindOf**: EmptyBinaryTree

sequencing

inorderDo: aBlock
    "Nothing to do in this case."
postorderDo: aBlock
    "Nothing to do in this case."
preorderDo: aBlock
    "Nothing to do in this case."

printing

printOn: aStream
    "Empty trees print as '--'."
    aStream **nextPutAll**: '--'
storeOn: aStream
    "We can do better than the default."
    aStream **nextPutAll**: '(BinaryTree empty)'

private

privatelyMutateIntoNonEmptyTree
    "For this implementation, empty trees are completely different from non-empty
    trees. Hence a become: operation must be used."
    self **become**: (BinaryTree
        label: nil **leftTree**: BinaryTree **empty rightTree**: BinaryTree **empty**)

privatelySignalEmptyTreeAccessingError
    self **error**: 'illegal empty tree access attempted'.

In the standard design, both empty and non-empty trees had the same representation. Mutating an empty tree into a non-empty tree was done easily with traditional code; i.e., it was as simple as changing the subtree fields to legal binary trees. With this newer design, it is no longer possible to use such a simple trick. The only solution is to use the **become:** operation.

Class NonEmptyBinaryTree

class name	NonEmptyBinaryTree
superclass	BinaryTree
instance variable names	label leftTree rightTree
comment	A non-empty binary tree is a binary tree with a label, left subtree, and right subtree.

instance methods

querying

depth
    "The maximum distance between this tree and some subtree."
    ↑1 + (leftTree **depth max:** rightTree **depth**)
size
    "The number of non-empty subtrees in all."
    ↑1 + (leftTree **size** + rightTree **size**)
isEmpty
    ↑false

access and modification

label
    ↑label
label: anObject
    label ← anObject
leftTree
    ↑leftTree
leftTree: aBinaryTree
    self **privatelyCheckForABinaryTree**: aBinaryTree.
    leftTree ← aBinaryTree
rightTree
    ↑rightTree
rightTree: aBinaryTree
    self **privatelyCheckForABinaryTree**: aBinaryTree.
    rightTree ← aBinaryTree

comparing

= aBinaryTree
    "Two binary trees are equal if they have the same structure and their labels are equal."
    (aBinaryTree **isKindOf:** NonEmptyBinaryTree) **ifFalse**: [↑false].
    label = aBinaryTree **label ifFalse:** [↑false].
    leftTree = aBinaryTree **leftTree ifFalse:** [↑false].
    ↑rightTree = aBinaryTree **rightTree**

copying

copy
    ↑self **deepCopy**

sequencing

inorderDo: aBlock
    "Sequences through all subtrees in inorder and executes the block with the labels."
    leftTree **inorderDo**: aBlock. aBlock **value**: label. rightTree **inorderDo**: aBlock
postorderDo: aBlock
    "Sequences through all subtrees in postorder and executes the block with the labels."
    leftTree **postorderDo**: aBlock.
    rightTree **postorderDo**: aBlock.
    aBlock **value**: label
preorderDo: aBlock
    "Sequences through all subtrees in preorder and executes the block with the labels."
    aBlock **value**: label. leftTree **preorderDo**: aBlock. rightTree **preorderDo**: aBlock

printing

printOn: aStream
    "Non-empty tree print as '<label leftTree rightTree>'."
    aStream
        nextPut: $<; **print**: label;
        space; **print**: leftTree;
        space; **print**: rightTree; **nextPut**: $>
storeOn: aStream
    "We can do better than the default."
    aStream
        nextPutAll: '(BinaryTree label: '; **store**: label;
        nextPutAll: ' leftTree: '; **store**: leftTree;
        nextPutAll: ' rightTree: '; **store**: rightTree; **nextPut**: $)

private

privatelyCheckForABinaryTree: anObject
    (anObject **isKindOf**: BinaryTree)
        ifFalse: [self **error**: 'attempting to create an illegal subtree']

6.7 CLASSES AND METACLASSES

A **class** is a repository for the information about instances. For example, the instance methods are stored in the class. For execution purposes, sending a message to an object results in a search process that begins by

- Extracting the class from the receiver.

- Looking in the class for a method with the same name.

- If one is found, a suitable context for execution is established and the method executed.

- If none is found, the superclass is found and the process repeated until either a method is found or no more superclasses exist, at which point **doesNotUnderstand**: is invoked.

Now what happens if a message is sent to a class instead of an instance? Exactly the same thing. But doesn't the search mechanism at least have to have a special case test like the following?

> **if looking for an instance method**
> **then**
> > **look in the spot reserved for instance methods**
> **else**
> > **look in the spot reserved for class methods**

The answer is that it could have been done that way but a better way was devised. Exactly the same mechanism can be used for both *without special case tests* if methods for classes are stored in some object other than the class itself. We call this object a **metaclass**. To repeat,

> **the methods for instances are stored in the instance's class**
>
> **the methods for classes are stored in the class's class**

We already know that classes are objects like instances — hence they too have a class. For example,

> 100 **class** ⇒ SmallInteger
> SmallInteger **class** ⇒ the metaclass for SmallInteger
> > (actually prints as 'SmallInteger class')

A **metaclass** is a repository for information about classes — it is a class for a class. Every class has a corresponding metaclass. For example, class Boolean, which inherits from class Object, has a corresponding Boolean metaclass that inherits from the Object metaclass, as shown in Fig. 6.16.

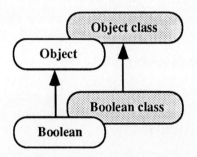

Figure 6.16 The Class and Metaclass hierarchies.

It is easiest to think of the class hierarchy as lying in the foreground; the metaclass hierarchy is a parallel hierarchy lying in the background.

As far as users are concerned, classes maintain instance methods and metaclasses maintain class methods. The system automatically manages the creation and removal of metaclasses when a user creates a new class or removes an existing one. Other than being aware of their existence, there is no need for users to do anything special about metaclasses.

Before we lay the topic to rest, we should be clear about what is **not in the system**. In particular, there is no third layer in the background constituting meta-metaclasses. There are only classes and metaclasses — the buck stops at metaclasses.

Although **class Object** has no superclass, it is easy to find out with the browser or with inspectors that **metaclass Object** does have a superclass. In fact, there is a small hierarchy above **metaclass Object**. We won't investigate this hierarchy here but it is important to realize that it contains all of the standard operations for creating, extending, modifying, deleting, and manipulating classes. We will present a very brief survey of these operations but we will not go into great detail. Too many are of use only to the system designers.

querying the structure of the instances

- aClass **instSize**

    Returns the number of named instance variables (as opposed to indexed variables) in instances of the class.

- aClass **isFixed**

    True if instances do not have indexed instance variables.
- aClass **isVariable**

    True if instances do have indexed instance variables.

- aClass **isPointers**

    True if indexed instance variables in instances contain objects (internally pointers); false otherwise.
- aClass **isBits**

    True if indexed instance variables in instances contain bytes or words; false otherwise.
- aClass **isBytes**

    True if indexed instance variables in instances contain bytes.
- aClass **isWords**

    True if indexed instance variables in instances contain words.

- aClass **kindOfSubclass**

    Returns one of the following strings: ' subclass: ', ' variableSubclass: ', ' variableByteSubclass: ', or ' variableWordSubclass: ' — note the leading and trailing space.

Each class normally has one **superclass** and zero or more **subclasses**. There are no examples of classes with multiple superclasses but the facility is available. We discuss it briefly below.

In descriptions that follow, information that must be accumulated by sequencing through a series of classes, either up or down the class hierarchy, is obtained via methods that begin with the prefix **all**.... For example, a method like **subclasses** would return only those subclasses that are **immediately** below the class being queried; **allSubclasses** would return the immediate subclasses in addition to their immediate subclasses, the subclasses of their immediate subclasses, and so on until no more are available. The latter method, for example, would be described as returning the **accumulated subclasses**.

accessing the class hierarchy

- aClass **superclass**

  Returns the receiver's immediate superclass; only the first one if there are several.
- aClass **superclasses**

  Returns a collection of the receiver's immediate superclasses.
- aClass **allSuperclasses**

  Returns a collection of the receiver's accumulated superclasses.
- aClass **withAllSuperclasses**

  Returns a collection containing the receiver in addition to all superclasses.
- aClass **hasMultipleSuperclasses**

  Returns true if the receiver has more than one immediate superclass; otherwise, false.

- aClass **subclasses**

  Returns a collection of the receiver's immediate subclasses.
- aClass **allSubclasses**

  Returns a collection of the receiver's accumulated subclasses.
- aClass **withAllSubclasses**

  Returns a collection containing the receiver in addition to all subclasses.

accessing class information

- aClass **name**

  Returns the name of the receiver.
- aClass **category**

  Returns the system organization category for the receiver.
- aClass **comment**

  Returns the receiver's comment.
- aClass **definition**

  Returns the receiver's definition.
- aClass **instVarNames**

  Returns a collection of immediate instance variable names.
- aClass **allInstVarNames**

  Returns a collection of accumulated instance variable names.
- aClass **classVarNames**

  Returns a collection of immediate class variable names.
- aClass **allClassVarNames**

  Returns a collection of accumulated class variable names.
- aClass **allSharedPools**

  Returns a collection of accumulated dictionaries used as shared pools.

- aClass **selectors**

    Returns a collection of message selectors (symbols) for all methods immediately understood by the receiver's instances; i.e., does not return selectors for methods higher up the hierarchy.

- aClass **sourceCodeAt**: messageSelectorSymbol

    Returns the source code as a string for the specified message selector. This selector must be immediately understood by the receiver.

accessing instances

- aClass **allInstances**

    Returns a collection of all instances of this class.

A large number of methods are concerned with extracting information accessible through the browser and debugger. Many of these methods (with sample usage) are listed in the system workspace.

6.7.1 Multiple Inheritance

Multiple inheritance is a generalization of standard inheritance that permits multiple superclasses. It is useful for creating new objects that share behavior common to several existing classes of objects. In Smalltalk, the facility is experimental since there are no examples using it. A standard example where it might have been used would be to define a class of objects called **ReadWriteStream** by combining the behaviors of **ReadStream** and **WriteStream**. For example, this could be done by executing the following code:

```
Class named: #ExperimentalReadWriteStream
    superclasses: 'ReadStream WriteStream'
    instanceVariableNames: ''
    classVariableNames: ''
    category: 'Experimental'
```

There is no facility for pool variables nor is it possible to use superclasses with indexed instance variables. From the implementation point of view, the first superclass plays the role of the standard superclass — its methods are inherited in the normal way. The methods of the other superclasses (those not shared by some class in the standard superclass chain) are recompiled in the new context. This is required because the instance variables introduced by secondary superclasses are no longer in the same relative positions. Compiled methods in Smalltalk normally reference the instance variables using a fixed offset.

To prevent ambiguity, the methods found by searching along distinct superclass chains must be the same. If they are not, a **conflict error** results. Conflict errors are determined when a class with multiple inheritance is defined. It is handled by creating a local method of the same name in the new class being created. The new method is placed in a special category called *conflicting inherited methods*. Its code body generates an error message when it is used. Such conflicting methods can be rewritten by the user to eliminate the error messages. For example, accepting the above definition causes the following class to be created.

Class ExperimentalReadWriteStream

class name	ExperimentalReadWriteStream
superclasses	WriteStream ReadStream
instance variable names	"none"

class methods

conflicting inherited methods

on: aCollection **from**: firstIndex **to**: lastIndex
    ↑self **conflictingInheritanceError**

instance methods

conflicting inherited methods

contents
    ↑self **conflictingInheritanceError**
next
    ↑self **conflictingInheritanceError**
nextPut: anObject
    ↑self **conflictingInheritanceError**
on: aCollection
    ↑self **conflictingInheritanceError**
on: aCollection **from**: firstIndex **to**: lastIndex
    ↑self **conflictingInheritanceError**
position: anInteger
    ↑self **conflictingInheritanceError**
reset
    ↑self **conflictingInheritanceError**
size
    ↑self **conflictingInheritanceError**

To work properly, each of the above methods must be rewritten. Often, it is sufficient to choose a specific variation of the method in a superclass. To enable specific methods in distinct superclasses to be referenced, a **dot notation** is provided. For example, it is legal to write

some test
    ifTrue: [↑self **ReadStream.size**]
    ifFalse: [↑self **WriteStream.size**]

It is also legal to use this dot notation on more complex selectors — binary or keyword operations; e.g.,

self **ReadStream.=** anotherStream
self **ReadStream.on**: aCollection **from**: firstIndex **to**: lastIndex

Generally, multiple inheritance is most useful when used to add standalone properties or attributes to new objects. For example, suppose we had defined three independent classes to manipulate three distinct attributes: a **name**, an **address**, and an **age** as follows:

Class Name

class name	Name
superclass	Object
instance variable names	name

instance methods

access and modification

name
    ↑name
name: aSymbol
    name ← aSymbol

Class Address

class name	Address
superclass	Object
instance variable names	address

instance methods

access and modification

address
    ↑address
address: aSymbol
    address ← aSymbol address

Class Age

class name	Age
superclass	Object
instance variable names	age

instance methods

access and modification

age
    ↑age
age: aSymbol
    age ← aSymbol

It is then a simple matter to construct a class that combines these attributes and adds additional behavior of its own.

Class Person

class name	Person
superclasses	Name Address Age
instance variable names	"none"

instance methods

= aPerson
    ↑(name = aPerson **name**) & (address = aPerson **address**) & (age = aPerson **age**)

6.8 SUMMARY

This chapter has described the important role played by the fundamental classes **Object**, **Boolean**, **Undefined Object**, and **BlockContext** in Smalltalk. In particular, we have described:

- How objects in Smalltalk are represented.
- The meaning of assignment, identity, equality, and copying in Smalltalk.
- The use of meta operations (**perform**) to access and modify objects and for indirect execution.
- How to read and write objects.
- Object mutation with the **become**: operation.
- Blocks as unnamed functions.
- The use of blocks to describe control structures.
- Class **Boolean** and its subclasses **True** and **False**, together with their special instances **true** and **false**.
- The use of abstract classes for supporting multiple representations.
- The **Class** and **Metaclass** hierarchies.
- The concept of multiple inheritance.

6.9 EXERCISES

The following exercises are intended to cause some of the material presented above to be reviewed and elaborated upon. Not all questions have the same degree of difficulty.

1. Determine whether or not shallow or deep copies are made for arrays and forms respectively. For example, investigate the results of #(hello there) **copy** and Form **black copy** respectively.

2. Create a more general version of **deepCopy** that works in the presence of circular structures. Hint: Use the same approach that was used for the general version of =.

3. Devise a general version of **storeOn**: that works for circular structures.

4. Change the implementation of **printOn**: for both characters and strings to make the operations uni-formly applicable. After the change, there should be no need for

   aStream **nextPut**: aCharacter
   aStream **nextPutAll**: aString

   Users would be able to use the following instead:

   aCharacter **printOn**: aStream
   aString **printOn**: aStream

   Currently, this does not work because print strings default to store strings for these classes of objects.

5. Investigate operations like **printOn:**, **storeOn:**, and = for a data type like **Fraction**. These could serve as useful templates when designing your own classes of objects.

6. Are equal small integers identical? What about equal large integers? For example, compare **3 factorial** with **3 factorial**; **100 factorial** with **100 factorial**.

7. Create a control structure called **do:** that permits sequencing over individual integer digits; e.g., the following adds 16 digits together.

    | sum |
    sum ← 0.
    1234567890123456 **do:** [:aDigit |
        sum ← sum + aDigit].
    ↑sum

8. Create a repeat-until control structure with the following form:

    aBlock
        repeatUntil: anotherBlock

9. Design and implement a recursive version of **factorial** using blocks.

10. Can blocks be used to provide a syntactically elegant case-statement construct? Ignore efficiency issues.

11. Extend binary trees so that it is possible to easily create non-empty trees that are automatically initialized with empty subtrees.

12. Create a subclass of **BinaryTree** called **BinarySearchTree** that has one additional operation

    aBinarySearchTree **add:** aLabel

    Is this extension more difficult if the nonstandard design is used instead?

13. Design and implement a **List** class in the Lisp tradition. Also, try a variation with three classes: **List**, **EmptyList**, and **NonEmptyList**. Use the **BinaryTree** example as the model.

6.10 GLOSSARY AND IMPORTANT FACTS

classes

BinaryTree An example class used to illustrate the basic ideas of this chapter. A **binary tree** is either an empty tree or a non-empty tree. Non-empty trees can have a **label**, a **left** subtree, and a **right** subtree.

BlockContext The class that provides the protocol for blocks. An example block is [count ← count + 1. count < 10].

Boolean An abstract class that provides the common protocol for **true** and **false**.

EmptyBinaryTree A subclass of **BinaryTree**; used to illustrate a nonstandard design that might gain in efficiency over more standard approaches.

Indirection An example class of objects that play the role of **gateways** for other objects, **intended receivers**.

Message A class of objects whose instances are manufactured by the system when a message is not understood by a receiver; instances are made parameters of **doesNotUnderstand:**; they respond to messages **selector** and **arguments**.

NonEmptyBinaryTree A subclass of **BinaryTree**; used to illustrate a nonstandard design.

Object The ultimate superclass of all classes; provides the default behavior for such operations as copying, printing, and comparing.

True, False Subclasses of **Boolean**; must not be confused with instances **true** and **false**.

UndefinedObject A subclass of **Object** that provides the protocol for its one unique instance **nil**, the value provided to all uninitialized variables.

instances

nil The sole instance of class **Undefined-Object**; the value assigned to all uninitialized variables; i.e., both to local variables in methods and to named and indexed instance variables in objects created via messages such as **basicNew** and **basicNew:**.

true, false The sole instances of classes **True** and **False** respectively; inherits protocol from class **Boolean**.

selected terminology

become: A powerful object mutation operation.

block An unnamed function; a bracketed construct (square brackets included) like [count ← count + 1. count < 10]; defined in the method that contains it when it is encountered at execution-time (not compile-time); can be invoked with messages like **value, value:, value:value:, value:value:value:,** and **valueWithArguments:**.

class A special kind of object that serves as a repository for information about the instances; i.e., it stores both the representation information and the operations. However, the information in an individual class may not be complete; part of the information may reside in another class called the **superclass**.

deep copy A copy whose fields are deep copies of the corresponding fields of the original; recursion stops for immutable objects like integers.

doesNotUnderstand: The default error handler; invoked when an inappropriate message is sent to an object.

equality operation An operation such as = and ~= that permits users to determine whether or not the contents of two objects are the same; can be redefined.

hash An operation that computes a unique integer from an object. Equal objects must have equal hashes, but the converse need not hold. Hashes are used in classes such as sets and dictionaries to speed up searches.

identity operation An operation such as == or ~~ that permits users to determine whether or not two objects are the same; cannot be redefined.

indexed instance variable A field of an object that is normally referenced by an index when the receiver is responding to a message; i.e., referenced via **at:** and **at:put:**.

indirect message passing A facility that permits manufactured messages to be executed via operations **perform:, perform:with:, perform:with:with:, perform:with:with:with:,** and finally **perform:withArguments:**.

instance variable A field of an object; there are two kinds: **named instance variables** and **indexed instance variables**.

meta operation A somewhat magical operation that permits nonstandard access and modification to objects. Examples include **instVarAt:, instVarAt:put:, basicAt:,** and **basicAt:put:**.

method inheritance The notion that an instance of a class responds to a specific message by executing the code associated with the first method of the same name that is found by traversing the class hierarchy bottom up.

multiple inheritance The mechanism that permits classes to have several superclasses.

named instance variable A field of an object that is normally referenced by name when the receiver is responding to a message.

notifier A special window created to inform the user of some specific fact. A yellow button menu provides the user with two options: **proceed** or **debug**. The first causes the notifier to disappear and execution to continue from where it left off. The second causes a debugger to replace the notifier.

object Anything that can be manipulated; consists of a **representation** and **operations** (or **methods**) that it responds to. It is an **instance** of some class that can be determined by sending it the message **class**; e.g., 1.2e3 **class** will reply with **Float**; consists of zero or more fields called **instance variables** partitioned into two groups: **named instance variables** and **indexed instance variables**. The named instance variables precede the indexed instance variables. Objects include such things as characters, integers, strings, arrays, ordered collections, sets, and classes themselves.

perform: An operation that permits execution of a manufactured message.

print string A string which is a textual representation of an object. It is often (but not always) sufficiently informative that alternative instances of the same class can be differentiated.

representation inheritance The notion that an instance of a class inherits the instance variables specified in classes higher up in the hierarchy.

shallow copy A copy whose fields are identical (not just equal) to the corresponding fields of the original; e.g., a shallow copy of an array shares the same elements as the original array.

store string A printable representation that can be used to re-create an equivalent instance. For some objects, like integers, the print and store strings are the same.

superclass The converse of subclass; e.g., **Object** is the superclass of **Boolean**.

variable Something (not an object) to which it is possible to bind a value (an object).

yourself A message used when cascading; useful for creating and initializing complex objects.

important facts

Variables are not objects They cannot be manipulated and stored.

Classes are objects They can be manipulated and stored; try inspecting **Object**, **UndefinedObject**, or **Boolean**.

a ← b This assignment is interpreted as "*bind a to the same object that b is bound to*." From the logical point of view, assignments do not copy; they simply rebind. From the implementation point of view, all variables contain pointers to objects; assignments physically copy pointers **but they do not copy objects**.

We can output as we wish To create a print string unique to a class, redefine method **printOn:**. To create a store string unique to a class, redefine **storeOn:**.

We can input arbitrary code Class method **readFrom:** in Object compiles and evaluates a string or stream; e.g.,

Object **readFrom:** '100 factorial'

become: is powerful Executing "anObject **become:** anotherObject" causes all references to anObject to be rerouted to anotherObject and vice versa. Does not work if either object is a small integer.

Blocks can be stored Blocks can be manipulated and stored; e.g., Junk ← [1+2]. Blocks are created at execution time when the square brackets are encountered. They are invoked with messages such as **value**; e.g., Junk **value**. A block executes *in its defining context*. In the absence of a return-statement, it returns the last computed value to the sender of the **value** message. If a return statement is encountered while executing a block, a return is made from the method *in which the block was defined* — not from the sender of the **value** message. *Blocks intended for long term storage should not have imbedded return statements*.

true and false are unusual They are objects *without instance variables.*

do not use True and False They are classes — not to be confused with corresponding instances **true** and **false**.

7

The Magnitude Classes

7.1 MAGNITUDES

Magnitude (see Fig. 7.1) is an abstract class for objects that can be compared using operations such as <, >, =, <=, >=, and ~= (although = and ~= are inherited from **Object**). Magnitudes include **numbers, characters, dates,** and **times.** Because of its close association with numeric classes, Fig. 7.1 also includes class **Random**, which provides a stream of randomized floats.

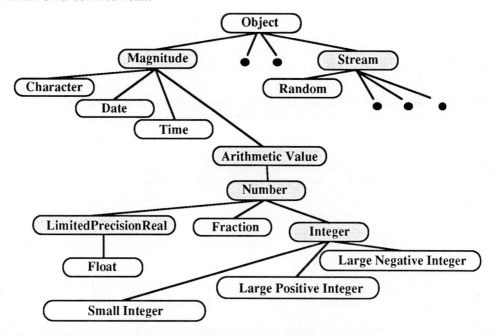

Figure 7.1 Magnitudes and other related classes.

Classes **ArithmeticValue** and **LimitedPrecisionReal** are both abstract classes with relatively little protocol. They are recent additions intended to anticipate future extensions.

In addition to providing the comparison operations, class Magnitude also provides the following operations:

- aMagnitude **between**: oneMagnitude **and**: anotherMagnitude (a range comparison)
- aMagnitude **max**: anotherMagnitude (the maximum of two magnitudes)
- aMagnitude **min**: anotherMagnitude (the minimum of two magnitudes)
- aMagnitude **hash** (a unique integer that can be used for faster searching)

Although 'a **between**: b **and**: c' is more convenient than 'a >= b **and**: [a <= c]', the operation is a bit more than a convenience because it prevents a from being evaluated twice. There is no corresponding operation such as 'a **exclusivelyBetween**: b **and**: c' that excludes the endpoints. Operations for finding the maximum and minimum are often used and should be memorized. The last operation **hash** is designed to compute a unique integer from a magnitude — equal magnitudes must have equal hashes but the converse does not hold. Hashes are used in classes such as sets and dictionaries for speeding up searches; e.g., by searching only those objects with equal hashes.

7.1.1 Class Magnitude Simplifies the Implementation of New Magnitudes

From the implementor's point of view, the existence of **Magnitude** simplifies the implementation of new classes that permit comparisons between their instances. When a new subclass of **Magnitude** is created, only methods for <, =, and **hash** must be provided — the other operations are implemented in terms of these two and are inherited from **Magnitude**. For example, 'a > b' is defined as 'b < a'; 'a <= b' is defined as '(a > b) **not**'.

To reintroduce an example partially discussed in a previous chapter, consider a revised definition of **Complex**. The original version was defined as a subclass of Object. We should now consider making it a subclass of Magnitude, and more specifically a subclass of Number. Since it is a magnitude, it should be sufficient to define methods <, =, and **hash** to satisfy the magnitude operations. To support the new methods, we also introduce an implementation of **abs** specifically for complex numbers. We will ignore issues dealing with automatic conversion until they are properly discussed in the numbers section.

```
abs
    "The absolute value of a complex number is its length."
    ↑(self realPart squared + self imaginaryPart squared) sqrt

< aComplex
    aComplex isKindOf: Complex
        ifTrue: [↑self abs < aComplex abs]
        ifFalse: [↑self error: 'complex operation requires a complex parameter']

= aComplex
    aComplex isKindOf: Complex
        ifTrue: [
            ↑self realPart = aComplex realPart and: [
                self imaginaryPart = aComplex imaginaryPart ]]
        ifFalse: [↑self error: 'complex operation requires a complex parameter']
```

hash
"Compute the absolute value of the complex number and return the integer's hash."
↑self **abs hash**

Although these operations are a minimum requirement for magnitudes, there is nothing preventing a designer from redundantly implementing <=, >, and >=, for example. Although it may not apply in this case, the usual reasons for overriding existing operations in some superclass are

* to correct an implementation that is not correct for the new class, or
* to obtain a more efficient version specialized for the particular subclass.

7.2 NUMBERS

Numbers include **integers**, **fractions**, and **floats**. Unlike traditional integers, Smalltalk integers are **unbounded**. Consequently, the notion of integer overflow does not exist. Of interest to implementors is the fact that integers are further partitioned into three classes: **small integers**, **large positive integers**, and **large negative integers**. As users of integers, however, there is no need to distinguish between the integer subclasses because interactions and conversions between them are transparent. Consequently, a computation such as

100 factorial

will compute an exact result that will end in 11 zeros (**1*2*...*10*...*20*...*30*... ...*90*...*100**). More dramatic is a computation like '1000 **factorial**' that can fill an entire screen with digits.

Floating point values can be written with the traditional notations such as 1.5 or 1.5e0. Fractions are new from the point of view of traditional languages. Fractions have both a numerator and a denominator each maintained as an integer (unbounded). Fractions represent Smalltalk's ultimate in high precision arithmetic. Consequently, computations such as the following are possible.

$$(1/2) + (1/3) \Rightarrow (5/6)$$
$$(1/4) + (1/4) \Rightarrow (1/2)$$
$$(1/3) + (2/3) \Rightarrow 1$$

7.2.1 The Notation for Number Constants

As is traditional, number constants are usually specified in radix 10. However, they may optionally be specified in any radix ranging from 2 to 36. For a radix greater than 10, alphabetic letters A through Z (lowercase or uppercase) serve as the corresponding digits. Radix 11 numbers can contain digits 0 through 9 along with A (but not B, C, ...); radix 12 numbers can contain 0-9,A,B; and so on. Only radix 36 can use all the alphabetic letters as digits. The facility provided is quite general. However, few users need a radix other than 2 (**binary**), 8 (**octal**), 10 (**decimal**), or 16 (**hexadecimal**). In formal detail, number constants satisfy the following syntax (the superscript $^?$ indicates that the preceding item is optional).

integers:	Radix$^{?}$-$^{?}$Digits
fractions:	anInteger / anInteger
floats:	Radix$^{?}$-$^{?}$Digits{.Digits}$^{?}$Exponent$^{?}$ (a decimal point or exponent is required)

The radix (if specified) is indicated by one of 2r, 3r, ..., 9r, ..., 16r, ..., 36r (the r must be lowercase). Although a minus sign is optional, a + sign is not allowed. Additionally, the minus sign is only allowed **after** the radix specification (if provided). If a decimal point is used, one or more digits are required both before and after the decimal point.

For scientific notation, an exponent of the form **e-?Digits** (the **e** must be a lowercase e) can be used — the exponent digits are always in decimal and the exponent raises the radix to the specified power. Logically, this implies the exponent has the effect of moving the decimal point left or right the specified amount. Finally, it is not possible to use the scientific notation with a radix greater than 14 because the exponent **e** is interpreted as a valid digit. Some examples include:

```
1999, -1999, 3.14159265358979, 1.0e0, -2.0e-10, 5e20    (2 integers and 4 floats)
2r1111, 8r17, 10r15, 16rF                                (equivalent integer values)
2r1111.0e0, 2r111.1e1, 2r11.11e2, 2r1.111e3, 2r0.1111e4  (equivalent float values in binary)
8r17.0e0, 8r1.7e1, 8r0.17e2, 8r0.017e3                   (equivalent float values in octal)
16.0e0, 1.6e1, 0.16e2                                    (equivalent float values in decimal)
2r11.11e2, 8r1.7e1, 10r1.5e1                             (equivalent float values)
1/2, 2r1/2, 1/10r2                                       (equivalent fractional values)
```

Note that it is not possible to show equivalent float values in hexadecimal; e.g. 16rF.0e0 **has no exponent specified** — the e is just another digit and does not signify an exponent.

7.2.2 Converting Numbers to Strings

Recall that two general methods are provided for converting objects to strings:

- anObject **printString**
  Produces a compact, though not necessarily complete, string representation of the object.
- anObject **storeString**
  Produces a string representation that re-creates an object equal to the original object when executed.

In the case of numbers, **printString** and **storeString** both return the same result. Some examples include:

```
-1999 printString ⇒ '-1999'
1.23456789e2 printString ⇒ '123.457' and 1.23456789e22 printString ⇒ '1.23457e22'
(the actual number of significant digits depends on the specific implementation)
(1 / 2) printString ⇒ '(1/2)'
```

Of course, the user may wish to store and/or print integers in a radix different from the standard decimal base. Two special methods are provided for this case (once again, these two are equivalent):

- anInteger **printStringRadix:** aRadix
  A string representation of the number in the specified radix — 2 to 36.
- anInteger **storeStringRadix:** aRadix
  (same as above)

Consequently, the following result is produced:

```
31 printStringRadix: 2 ⇒ '2r11111'
31 printStringRadix: 8 ⇒ '8r37'
31 printStringRadix: 10 ⇒ '10r31'
31 printStringRadix: 16 ⇒ '16r1F'
31 printStringRadix: 36 ⇒ '36rV'
```

Creating Specialized printString and storeString Methods

When designing a new class, it is natural to want to provide a specialized **printString** and **storeString**. However, if we browse through the class library, we will find that only one **printString** and one **storeString** exist in the entire system. These are defined as follows:

```
printString
    | aStream |
    aStream ← WriteStream on: (String new: 16).
    self printOn: aStream.
    ↑aStream contents

storeString
    | aStream |
    aStream ← WriteStream on: (String new: 16).
    self storeOn: aStream.
    ↑aStream contents
```

Instead of individual classes providing their own version of **printString** and **storeString**, we find them providing their own versions of **printOn:** and **storeOn:** instead. In the case of complex numbers, for example, we could define these methods as follows:

```
printOn: aStream
    realPart printOn: aStream.
    imaginaryPart negative ifFalse: [aStream nextPut: $+].
    imaginaryPart printOn: aStream.
    aStream nextPut: $i

storeOn: aStream
    aStream nextPutAll: '(Complex new realPart: '.
    realPart printOn: aStream.
    aStream nextPutAll: '; imaginaryPart: '.
    imaginaryPart printOn: aStream.
    aStream nextPutAll: '; yourself)'
```

You do need to understand the stream operations **nextPut:** (for output of an individual character) and **nextPutAll:** (for output of a string). With these methods added to class **Complex**, a complex number with real part 1.0 and imaginary part -2.0 will print and store (using **printString** and **storeString**) as '1.0-2.0i' and '(Complex new realPart: 1.0; imaginaryPart: -2.0; yourself)' respectively.

7.2.3 Converting Strings to Numbers

As in the previous section, conversions from strings to numbers require streams as an intermediary. The conversion is achieved via

* Number **readFrom:** (ReadStream **on:** aString)

In general, there is no facility to recover gracefully from errors of syntax. If the need arises, a more flexible version **readFrom:onError:** would have to be devised. Finally, if the remainder of the string (after the number) is desired, an alternative sequence of statements such as the following might be used.

```
aStream ← ReadStream on: aString.
aNumber ← Number readFrom: aStream.
aString ← aStream upTo: nil.
```

See the section on streams for a more detailed discussion of associated stream operations.

7.2.4 Type Conversion

Conversion between different classes of numbers is automatic and transparent to users. Conversion occurs in the direction (integer $\Rightarrow$ fraction $\Rightarrow$ float) in an attempt to maintain as much accuracy as possible. Explicit conversion operations can also be used; e.g.,

- aNumber **asInteger, asFraction, asFloat** (for integers, fractions, or floats).
- anInteger **asCharacter** (integers only).

From the point of view of implementors, this user view is insufficient. In order to design a new class of numbers, it is essential that the protocol used by the system for managing type conversions be used so as to integrate the new class as much as possible with the existing number classes.

Binary arithmetic operations in the system are designed to operate on operands of the same class; e.g., the float + operation requires both of its operands to be of class float. To ensure that this is the case, all binary operations check the class of the right operand. If the right operand class is different from the left operand class, one of the operands is converted to the class of the other and the same operation is retried. To determine which operand is to be converted, two approaches are used. The first technique is based on **generality numbers** and is used prior to version 2.5 of the system. The operand with the lowest generality number is converted to the class of the other. The second, more recent, technique is based on **double dispatching** — an efficient technique for determining the types of the two operands without having to explicitly interrogate the operand classes. Although double dispatching supersedes generality numbers, the latter is still used for default type conversion if the designer of a new number class did not provide the needed type conversion from existing classes to the new number class.

The Existing Generality Numbers

Each numeric class is provided with a **generality** number. Currently, the following generality numbers are being used:

- **float**: generality 80
- **fraction**: generality 60
- **large positive integer**: generality 40
- **large negative integer**: generality 40
- **small integer**: generality 20

Additionally, unless explicitly overridden, the generality number inherited by any new subclass of **number** is 40 (the method returning the generality number for both **large integers** was placed in **number** simply to avoid duplicating it).

The Existing Coercion Operations (Using Generality Numbers)

Once the system has determined that operand A, say, has a higher generality number than B, 'A **coerce**: B' is invoked to convert B to a number of the same class as A (the alternative would result in 'B **coerce**: A' being invoked). Method '**coerce**: Operand' for the respective classes is (or should be) defined as follows:

- Operand **asFloat** (for float)
- Operand **asFraction** (for fraction)
- Operand **asInteger** (for all three specializations of integer)

For the three integer specializations, method **asInteger** simply returns 'self truncated'. Unfortunately, the **coerce**: method for these return 'Operand **truncated**' instead of 'Operand **asInteger**', presumably as a speed optimization. As we will see, this will have to be repaired when we more fully integrate complex numbers into the number system — truncating a complex number is not the same as converting it to an integer.

Forcing Type Conversion on a Binary Operation (Via Generality Numbers)

If a binary operation is invoked with incompatible operands, there is no need for the method itself to go through the determination as to which operand to convert, to explicitly perform the conversion, and then to reinvoke the given operation. A general method has already been provided in Number[1] for this purpose:

- aLeftOperandNumber **retry**: anOperatorSymbol **coercing**: aRightOperandNumber

For an example of actual usage, method < for fractions (as it existed prior to version 2.5) is shown next:

```
< aFraction
    (aFraction isMemberOf: Fraction)
        ifTrue: [... detailed < code for fractions ...]
        ifFalse: [↑self retry: #< coercing: aFraction]
```

Note the manner in which the operator symbol is specified in the **retry:coercing:** message. Also, **isMemberOf:** is used instead of **isKindOf:** to ensure that specializations are converted to the more general type. For fractions, **isMemberOf:** and **isKindOf:** are equivalent because there are no specializations (yet).

---

[1] Actually, the method is in abstract class ArithmeticValue. Prior to version 2.5, this abstract class did not exist. It was introduced to document double dispatching.

Fully Integrating a New Number Class With Generality
Numbers (Automatic Type Conversion)

In order to fully integrate a new number class into the generality system, care must be taken to ensure that all the following details are attended to:

- The **generality** of the new number must be decided upon.

- Each binary operation must check that the right operand class is the same as the receiver's class; if not, an explicit **retry:coercing**: message must be sent.

- One **coerce**: method must be written that simply returns 'Operand **asNewNumber**' where NewNumber is the new class of numbers.

- One **asNewNumber** method must be added to each existing number class to effect the proper conversion.

- A conversion operation for each of the other classes; e.g., **asFloat, asFraction,** ... must be added to the **NewNumber** class.

To provide a flavor for the above steps, we will follow them in the context of our complex number example. The first step is to decide on the generality of complex numbers. An obvious choice is to make it the most general number, as follows:

```
generality
    ↑100.
```

The second step is to modify each binary operation to invoke **retry:coercing:**. Two examples are shown below:

```
< aComplex
    aComplex isKindOf: Complex
        ifTrue: [↑self abs < aComplex abs]
        ifFalse: [↑self retry: #< coercing: aComplex]

+ aComplex
    aComplex isKindOf: Complex
        ifTrue: [
            ↑ComplexNumber new
                realPart: (realPart + aComplex realPart);
                imaginaryPart: (imaginaryPart + aComplex imaginaryPart);
                yourself]
        ifFalse: [↑self retry: #< coercing: aComplex]
```

The next step is to define the **coerce**: method for Complex as follows:

```
coerce: aNumber
    ↑aNumber asComplex
```

The fourth step is to define conversion operator **asComplex** in each of the existing number classes. Currently, this means in float, fraction, and integer (there is no need to add one for each specialization of integer). Actually, we could make do with one method in Number and another in Float. However, the following organization is easier to extend when additional number classes are added.

In Class Float
asComplex
    ↑Complex **new realPart**: self; **imaginaryPart**: 0.0; **yourself**

In Class Fraction
asComplex
    "Keep the real part as a fraction; it will convert automatically if necessary."
    ↑Complex **new realPart**: self; **imaginaryPart**: 0; **yourself**

In Class Integer
asComplex
    "Keep the real part as an integer; it will convert automatically if necessary."
    ↑Complex **new realPart**: self; **imaginaryPart**: 0; **yourself**

The final step is to introduce all existing conversions into Complex.

asReal
    ↑self **abs**

asFraction
    ↑self **abs asFraction**

asInteger
    ↑self **abs asInteger**

Although complex numbers can be printed in a standard notation, they can't be specified (so far) in an equally convenient notation. The solution is to introduce a new operator **i** to numbers.

In Class Number
i
    ↑Complex **new realPart**: 0; **imaginaryPart**: self; **yourself**

It is now legal to write 1+3**i**, 5.0+7.0**i**, (1/3)-(1/4)**i**, and so on.

What the General retry:coercing: Method Looks Like

Having written code that uses the **retry:coercing:** method, it might be instructive to look at the actual method. The intuitive explanation that we gave about its functionality will thereby be made more concrete.

retry: aSymbol **coercing**: aNumber
    "Arithmetic represented by the symbol, aSymbol, could not be performed with the receiver and the argument, aNumber, because of the differences in representation. Coerce either the receiver or the argument, depending on which has the lower generality, and try again. If the symbol is the equals sign, answer false if the argument is not a Number. If the generalities are the same, create an error notification."

    (aSymbol == #= **and**: [(aNumber **isKindOf**: Number) == false])
        ifTrue: [↑false].
    self **generality** < aNumber **generality**
        ifTrue: [↑(aNumber **coerce**: self) **perform**: aSymbol **with**: aNumber].
    self **generality** > aNumber **generality**
        ifTrue: [↑self **perform**: aSymbol **with**: (self **coerce**: aNumber)].
    self **error**: 'coercion attempt failed'

Invoking '1 **perform**: #+ **with**: 2' is equivalent to '1 + 2'. The difference, of course, is that the operator can be a parameter.

Double Dispatching

Double dispatching is an efficient technique for discovering the types of both operands without having to explicitly query them. The easiest way to describe the technique is to show how complex numbers can be revised to incorporate double dispatching. We revise operation - as follows:

```
- aNumber
    ↑aNumber differenceFromComplex: self
```

Note that **differenceFromComplex**: is working with the operands in the reverse order; i.e., it will have to take into account that its receiver is the right operand while its argument is the left. Now add method **differenceFromComplex**: to each of the existing numeric classes as shown next. By the time one of these methods is invoked, the classes of both operands will be known. This additional knowledge can sometimes be used to advantage to generate more efficient code. For example, consider the version for class float — we know that the real part must ultimately convert to a float if it isn't already one. Is it faster to force the conversion (as we have done) or is the automatic conversion mechanism now faster (given that no conversion may be needed)? We'll leave that to the reader as an experiment.

```
In Class Complex
    differenceFromComplex: aComplex
        "aComplex - self (another complex)"
        ↑Complex new
            realPart: aComplex realPart - self realPart;
            imaginaryPart: aComplex imaginaryPart - self imaginaryPart;
            yourself

In Class Float
    differenceFromComplex: aComplex
        "aComplex - self (a float)"
        ↑Complex new
            realPart: aComplex realPart asFloat - self;
            imaginaryPart: aComplex imaginaryPart;
            yourself

In Class Fraction
    differenceFromComplex: aComplex
        "aComplex - self (a fraction)"
        ↑Complex new
            realPart: aComplex realPart - self;
            imaginaryPart: aComplex imaginaryPart;
            yourself

In Class Integer
        "aComplex - self (an integer)"
        ↑Complex new
            realPart: aComplex realPart - self;
            imaginaryPart: aComplex imaginaryPart;
            yourself
```

In general, five operations have been targeted for double dispatching: +, -, *, /, and <
with corresponding operations **sumFrom?:**, **differenceFrom?:**, **productFrom?:**, **quo-
tientFrom?:**, and **lessFrom?:**.

If the designer of a new class of numbers chooses not to handle automatic type
conversion (at least in the initial stages of development), it is still the case that some
automatic conversion may work because class **ArithmeticValue** contains a default for each
of these methods. For example, it contains the following method.

> *In Class Arithmetic Value*
> **differenceFromFloat**: aFloat
>   "aFloat - self (a number)"
>   ↑aFloat **retry**: #- **coercing**: self

Consequently, "5.3 + aComplex" will use the generality system to attempt to coerce 5.3
into a complex number. This may or may not work depending on the generality information
inherited by the new number class.

7.2.5 Division, Remainders, Truncation, and Rounding

Many programming languages provide a single operation for performing division and a
single operation for obtaining the remainder of the division. The semantics are usually very
precise for the positive case but are often imprecise or downright uncommitted for the
negative case. Not so with Smalltalk. In fact, because the semantics are precisely described
for both the positive and negative cases, the need arose to provide several alternatives to each
of these operations with slightly different semantics (or effects). This is advantageous for the
knowledgeable programmer but can be troublesome for those of us who use the operations
sparingly because it is easy to confuse them.

There are three division operations and two operations for finding the remainder after
division. The results of both of these operations can be either positive or negative. With N
and M denoting numbers, the operations can be summarized as follows:

Division operations.
- N / M (standard division, no rounding or truncation)
- N **quo**: M (integer division truncated toward zero)
- N // M (integer division truncated toward negative infinity)

Remainder operations.
- N **rem**: M (remainder after N **quo**: M)
- N \\ M (remainder after N // M)

Standard division is the more often used operation; **quo**: and **rem**: correspond to the
more usual notion of integer division; // and \\ are relatively unfamiliar. The names **quo**
and **rem** are clearly short for **quotient** and **remainder**.

Standard Division

Standard division follows the previously discussed conversion rule (integer $\Rightarrow$ fraction $\Rightarrow$
float) to maintain as much accuracy as possible. Consequently, $4 / 2 \Rightarrow 2, 3 / 2 \Rightarrow 3 / 2$,
and $3.0 / 2 \Rightarrow 1.5$. This explains why standard division is the constructor for fractions and
the usual division operation for floats.

Integer Division with Truncation Toward Zero

Division via **quo**: can be viewed as computing a float result and then truncating that result toward zero (this is not strictly true because the operations are not implemented with float arithmetic unless float operands are used). If the result of the "imagined" float division were one of the following, for example,

$$-5.7 \quad -4.2 \quad 3.4 \quad 7.8$$

the resulting integer answer would correspondingly be

$$-5 \quad -4 \quad 3 \quad 7$$

Thus "truncation toward zero" can be paraphrased as "locating the next integer nearest zero," assuming the number line extended from negative infinity on the left to positive infinity on the right. The same effect can be achieved more simply by dropping the fractional information.

Integer Division with Truncation Toward Negative Infinity

Division via // can be similarly viewed as computing a float result and then truncating that result toward negative infinity (once again, this is not strictly true because the operations are not implemented with float arithmetic unless float operands are used). If the result of the 'imagined' float division were one of the following, for example,

$$-5.7 \quad -4.2 \quad 3.4 \quad 7.8$$

the resulting integer answer would correspondingly be

$$-6 \quad -5 \quad 3 \quad 7$$

Thus "truncation toward negative infinity" can be paraphrased as "locating the nearest integer on the left."

The Remainder Operations

Method **rem**: is the corresponding remainder operation for **quo**:, whereas \\ is the corresponding remainder operation for //. It is relatively easy to remember the association between **rem**: and **quo** : and between // and \\. Unfortunately, it is also easy to mix up // with \\. Sporadic users of Smalltalk often find themselves performing experiments in order to recall which is which.

Fortunately, the effects of the remainder operations are easy to describe because their respective semantics can be provided in terms of their corresponding division operation. If we denote the integer division operation by D and the corresponding remainder operation by R, then R can be computed as follows:

$$R \Leftarrow \text{Numerator - (Denominator * (Numerator D Denominator))}$$

For example, to compute -11 **rem**: -5, simply subtract the denominator times the quotient (-5 * 2) from the original number (-11) to get (-11 - (-10)) or (-1). Clearly, the sign of the operands is important.

For those who have a pen or pencil and the patience, the above formula can be verified by examining the following short table of examples.

11 **quo**: 5 $\Rightarrow$ 2	-11 **quo**: 5 $\Rightarrow$ -2	11 **quo**: -5 $\Rightarrow$ -2	-11 **quo**: -5 $\Rightarrow$ 2
11 **rem**: 5 $\Rightarrow$ 1	-11 **rem**: 5 $\Rightarrow$ -1	11 **rem**: -5 $\Rightarrow$ 1	-11 **rem**: -5 $\Rightarrow$ -1
11 // 5 $\Rightarrow$ 2	-11 // 5 $\Rightarrow$ -3	11 // -5 $\Rightarrow$ -3	-11 // -5 $\Rightarrow$ 2
11 \\ 5 $\Rightarrow$ 1	-11 \\ 5 $\Rightarrow$ 4	11 \\ -5 $\Rightarrow$ -4	-11 \\ -5 $\Rightarrow$ -1

Table 7.1

Fortunately, applications that use any of the above four operations with negative numbers are rare. When (and mostly if) the need arises, the rule can be looked up.

Truncation and Rounding

Truncation is an operation that discards the fractional part (if there is one). Rounding of a number N can be defined as the truncation of N + (N **sign** * 0.5); i.e., if N is positive, N **rounded** is (N + 0.5) **truncated**; otherwise, (N - 0.5) **truncated**. Hence, both rounding and truncation return integers. Computationally, the rounding operation is implemented in such a manner that intermediate conversion to float is avoided (this prevents float overflows from occurring for large integers). If N denotes a number and I an integer, the two operations are summarized as follows:

- N **truncated** $\Rightarrow$ I (the integer nearest N in the direction toward zero)
- N **rounded** $\Rightarrow$ I (the nearest integer N + (N **sign** * 0.5) in the direction toward zero)

For instance, the result of truncating the following row of numbers (e.g., by writing -1.8 **truncated**)

$$-1.8 \quad -1.5 \quad -1.2 \quad 0.0 \quad 1.2 \quad 1.5 \quad 1.8$$

is

$$-1 \quad -1 \quad -1 \quad 0 \quad 1 \quad 1 \quad 1$$

respectively. Similarly, the result of rounding the following row of numbers (e.g., by writing -1.8 **rounded**)

$$-1.8 \quad -1.5 \quad -1.2 \quad 0.0 \quad 1.2 \quad 1.5 \quad 1.8$$

is

$$-2 \quad -2 \quad -1 \quad 0 \quad 1 \quad 2 \quad 2$$

respectively.

Another related pair of operations computes the truncation and rounding of a number N_1 as a multiple of another value N_2. Formally, they can be defined as follows:

- N_1 **truncateTo**: $N_2 \Rightarrow$ N (a multiple of N_2 nearest N_1
  — in the direction toward zero)
- N_1 **roundTo**: $N_2 \Rightarrow$ N (a multiple of N_2 nearest N_1 + (N_1 **sign** * (0.5 * N_2 **abs**))
  — in the direction toward zero)

Informally, the answer must differ from N_1 by no more than N_2 **abs** (for truncation) and $0.5 * N_2$ **abs** (for rounding). Some simple examples include

13 **truncateTo**: 5 $\Rightarrow$ 10	(first multiple of 5 computed by decreasing 13 toward zero)
13 **truncateTo**: -5 $\Rightarrow$ 10	(first multiple of -5 computed by decreasing 13 toward zero)
-13 **truncateTo**: 5 $\Rightarrow$ -10	(first multiple of 5 computed by decreasing -13 toward zero)
-13 **truncateTo**: -5 $\Rightarrow$ -10	(first multiple of -5 computed by decreasing -13 toward zero)
13 **roundTo**: 5 $\Rightarrow$ 15	(... 5 computed by decreasing 13+5/2 = 15.5 toward zero)
13 **roundTo**: -5 $\Rightarrow$ 15	(... -5 computed by decreasing 13+5/2 = 15.5 toward zero)
-13 **roundTo**: 5 $\Rightarrow$ -15	(... 5 computed by decreasing -13-5/2 = -15.5 toward zero)
-13 **roundTo**: -5 $\Rightarrow$ -15	(... -5 computed by decreasing -13-5/2 = -15.5 toward zero)

Finally, truncation toward negative and positive infinity is provided by **floor** and **ceiling** respectively:

- N **floor** (truncation toward negative infinity)
- N **ceiling** (truncation toward positive infinity)

Where possible, these operations should replace the rounding and truncation operations. Few people confuse their semantics even for negative numbers.

7.2.6 Mathematical Operations

Although Smalltalk does not provide a complete set of mathematical operations, it does provide a useful subset that includes the primary trigonometric functions. All operations are applicable to numbers although conversion (automatic) to float is performed. If N denotes a number, F a float, and I an integer, the operations can be summarized as follows (unless otherwise specified, assume they return float values):

- N **sin** (the sin of a N in radians)
- N **cos** (the cos of a N in radians)
- N **tan** (the tan of a N in radians)
- N **arcSin** (a value in radians whose sin is N)
- N **arcCos** (a value in radians whose cos is N)
- N **arcTan** (a value in radians whose tan is N)
- N **degreesToRadians**
- N **radiansToDegrees**
- N **exp** (the natural logarithm base e raised to the power of the receiver; i.e., e^N)
- N **ln** (the natural logarithm of N; i.e., $\log_e N$)
- N **log**: aNumber (the logarithm of N to base aNumber; i.e., $\log_{aNumber} N$)
- N **floorLog**: radix (a faster computation for (N **log**: aNumber) **floor**)
- N **sqrt** (the square root of N)

- N **raisedToInteger**: anInteger (returns the aNumber $N^{\text{anInteger}}$)
- N **raisedTo**: aNumber (returns an integer only when aNumber is an integer)

- N **squared** (an alternative to N * N)

- F **fractionPart** (e.g., the fraction part of 12.3456e2 is .56)
- F **integerPart** (e.g., the integer part of 12.3456e2 is 1234)

Some more specialized operations include

- I **gcd**: I (the greatest common divisor; always positive)
- I **lcm**: I (least common multiple; negative if either, but not both, operands are negative)

It isn't clear why **gcd**: should always give positive results while **lcm**: doesn't. One way to successfully predict the answer for **lcm**: is to include the factor -1 for negative numbers. The least common multiple can be obtained by factoring both operands and constructing a result using a minimum number of the factors, with the proviso that the factors of the original operands are all included in the factors for the answer. For example,

15 **gcd**: 20 $\Rightarrow$ 5 (largest value that divides both evenly)
15 **gcd**: -20 $\Rightarrow$ 5 (largest value that divides both evenly)

15 **lcm**: 20 $\Rightarrow$ 60 (15 = 1*3*5, 20 = 1*4*5, 1*3*4*5 = 60 is the answer)
15 **lcm**: -20 $\Rightarrow$ -60 (15 = 1*3*5, 20 = -1*4*5, 1*-1*3*4*5 = -60 is the answer)

Finally, class Float knows about the mathematical constant pi; e.g.,

Float **pi**

returns the value 3.14159.

7.2.7 Creating a New Subclass of Number

In order to integrate a new subclass of number with the existing system, several steps are required:

- Provide the operations required of **magnitudes**; i.e., <, =, and **hash** as a minimum.
- Provide the type conversion operations to permit automatic conversions between the new class and existing number classes (see the section on **type conversion**).
- Provide suitable print and store operations for input and output.
- Provide the standard arithmetic operations +, -, *, and /. Investigation is required to determine if other operations need to be revised.

In the case of complex numbers, the extensions provided so far appear to satisfy the above requirements. Indeed, that was our initial feeling. Testing, however, uncovers some problems. First, methods **truncated** and **quo**: are recursively defined in class Number as follows:

truncated
"Answer an integer nearest the receiver toward zero."
↑self **quo**: 1

quo: aNumber
"Integer quotient defined by division with truncation toward zero."
↑(self / aNumber) **truncated**

An infinite loop results if either method is used. The reason the loop doesn't exist for the existing specializations of Number is that each redefines **truncated** so that it doesn't use **quo**:. Similarly, for complex numbers, one or the other (or both) must be redefined. A simple (though perhaps incorrect approach) might be to define truncation for complex numbers as truncating the real and imaginary parts independently. With this approach, the method is revised as

truncated
"Answer aComplex with separately truncated real and imaginary parts."
↑Complex **new**
    realPart: self **realPart truncated**;
    imaginaryPart: self **imaginaryPart truncated**;
    yourself

The quotient operation above consequently performs a complex divide followed by a complex truncation. It would have to be revised if an integer result were expected.

We previously noted that explicitly coercing a complex number to an integer would not work correctly because of the optimization performed by the **coerce**: method. This integer method is revised as follows:

coerce: aNumber
    ↑aNumber **asInteger**

Querying operations like **odd**, **even**, **negative**, **positive**, **strictlyPositive**, and **sign** do not have an obvious intuitive meaning. Perhaps they should indicate an error; e.g.,

odd
    ↑self **error**: 'I do not know what an odd complex number is?'

7.2.8 Bit Manipulation on Integers

In Smalltalk, all integers (not just small integers) can be manipulated as a sequence of bits. The bits are numbered 1, 2, ... from right (the least significant bit) to left (the most significant bit). Non-negative integers are viewed as having an infinite number of 0 bits on the left; negative integers as having an infinite number of 1 bits on the left. The traditional bit operations like

* anIntegerAsABitSequence **bitAnd**: anotherBitSequence

* anIntegerAsABitSequence **bitOr**: anotherBitSequence

* anIntegerAsABitSequence **bitXor**: anotherBitSequence

- anIntegerAsABitSequence **bitInvert**

- anIntegerAsABitSequence **bitShift**: anAmountByWhichToShiftLeft

are available for bit manipulation. A negative amount for **bitShift** causes shifting to the right. In left shifts, zero bits are inserted on the right. Integers are maintained in two's-complement notation; hence

$$(X \text{ negated}) = (X \text{ bitInvert} + 1)$$

This relation is important for understanding the sequence of bits represented by negative integers. For example, consider the following positive and negative integers. The notation ...0 indicates that all bits to the left are 0; ...1 indicates they are all 1.

```
2r010 represents ...010
2r11111 represents ...011111
2r-1 represents ...11111        (see below for an explanation)
2r-1001 represents ...10111     (see below for an explanation)
```

Note that 2r-1 represents ...11111 because 2r-1 = ...01 negated = ...01 bitInvert + 1 = ...10 + 1 = ...11. Similarly, 2r-1001 represents ...10111 because 2r-1001 = ...01001 negated = ...01001 bitInvert + 1 = ...10110 + 1 = ...10111.

Integers are always printed so that the infinite number of implied digits is 0; i.e., if the infinite number of implied digits is 1, the integer is first negated and printed with a negative sign. Consequently, in binary notation

```
...01111 prints as 2r1111
...10011 prints as 2r-(...10011 negated) = 2r-(...10011 bitInvert + 1) = 2r-(...01100 + 1)
    = 2r-01101
...10000 prints as 2r-(...10000 negated) = 2r-(...10000 bitInvert + 1) = 2r-(...01111 + 1)
    = 2r-011111
```

Additional bit querying and extraction operations can be achieved with the following:

- anIntegerAsABitSequence **highBit** (returns the index of the highest order bit; 0 if all bits are 0; illegal if negative)
- anIntegerAsABitSequence **bitAt**: aBitIndex (returns the bit at the specified index)

Negative numbers do not have a highest order bit since an infinite number of bits at the extreme left are 1. Consequently, 2r-1 **highBit** is illegal; 2r01001 **highBit** is 4; 2r0 **highBit** is 0. There is no corresponding restriction on the bit extraction operations; e.g., 2r1000 **bitAt**: 4 is 1; 2r1000 **bitAt**: 3 is 0. In fact, 2r1 **bitAt**: 10000 is 0 (recall that there is an infinite number of zeros to the left of the 1). Similarly, 2r-1 **bitAt**: 10000 is 1 (recall that 2r-1 is ...11111).

There is no corresponding **bitAt:put:**, but it can be written easily in terms of **bitShift**, **bitOr:**, and **bitXor:** as follows:

```
bitAt: aBitIndex put: aZeroOrOne
    aZeroOrOne = 0 ifTrue: [↑self bitXor: (1 bitShift: aBitIndex)].
    aZeroOrOne = 1 ifTrue: [↑self bitOr: (1 bitShift: aBitIndex)].
    self error: 'bitAt:put: needs 0 or 1 value'
```

Note: method **bitAt:put:** does not modify an existing bit in the integer. Rather, it constructs a new integer suitably modified. Finally, the following **masking** operations are provided:

- anIntegerAsABitSequence **allMask**: aBitSequenceMask (all ones in the mask are also ones in the receiver)
- anIntegerAsABitSequence **anyMask**: aBitSequenceMask (one or more ones in the mask are also ones in the receiver)
- anIntegerAsABitSequence **noMask**: aBitSequenceMask (all ones in the mask are zeros in the receiver)

Method **allMask:** could be used to determine if one bit sequence is a subset of another. So far, these masking operations are rarely used in Smalltalk (under a dozen times). Most of the time, they are used in very simple tests; e.g., 'aValue **allMask:** 8' instead of '(aValue **bitAnd:** 8) = 8', or 'aValue **anyMask:** 8' as an alternative to '(aValue **bitAnd:** 8) ~= 0'.

Defining a BitString Class

Because of the flexibility of the integer bit manipulation operations, it is easy to define a class of arbitrarily long bit strings for use in specialized set applications. Using integers for the purpose may be inadequate if we wish to be able to modify the bit string in place. Additionally, we may wish to view the bit string as growing to the right and provide it with a specialized print representation that maintains this point of view. Finally, we might wish to use booleans as the bit elements instead of 1's and 0's. Portions of such a class definition are shown below:

Class BitString

class name	BitString
superclass	Number
instance variable names	string

class methods

instance creation

new
   "Returns a BitString instance initialized to zero bits."
   ↑super **new privateInitialize**

private

privateNewWith: anInteger
   "Returns a BitString instance initialized to anInteger interpreted as a bit sequence."
   ↑super **new privateInitialize**: anInteger

instance methods

access

at: aBitIndex
   ↑(string **bitAt**: aBitIndex) = 1

at: aBitIndex **put:** aBoolean
    aBitIndex <= 0 **ifTrue:** [self **error:** 'subscript out of bounds in bit string'].
    aBoolean = false
        ifTrue: [string ← string **bitAnd:** (1 **bitShift:** aBitIndex - 1) **bitInvert**. ↑self].
    aBoolean = true **ifTrue:** [string ← string **bitOr:** (1 **bitShift:** aBitIndex - 1). ↑self].
    self **error:** 'bitAt:put: needs a boolean value'.

printing

printOn: aStream
    "Examples are 0b1001... and 0b10010... (... indicates that all remaining bits are the same)."
    | theBits |
    aStream **nextPutAll:** '0b'.
    string **negative**
        ifTrue: [
            theBits ← string **bitInvert printStringRadix:** 2.
            "The above string conversion adds '2r' that must be removed"
            (theBits **copyFrom:** 3 **to:** theBits **size**) **reverseDo:** [:aCharacter |
                aStream **nextPut:** (aCharacter = $0 **ifTrue:** [$1] **ifFalse:** [$0])].
            aStream **nextPutAll:** '1...'.]
        ifFalse: [
            theBits ← string **printStringRadix:** 2. "This adds '2r' that must be removed"
            (theBits **copyFrom:** 3 **to:** theBits **size**) **reverseDo:** [:aCharacter |
                aStream **nextPut:** aCharacter].
            aStream **nextPutAll:** '0...']

storeOn: aStream
    "An example is (2046772 asBitString)."
    | theBits |
    aStream **nextPut:** $(. string **storeOn:** aStream. aStream **nextPutAll:** ' asBitString)'

comparisons

< aBitString
    (aBitString **isMemberOf:** BitString) **ifFalse:** [↑self **retry:** #< **coercing:** aBitString].
    ↑string < aBitString **asInteger**

= aBitString
    (aBitString **isMemberOf:** BitString) **ifFalse:** [↑self **retry:** #= **coercing:** aBitString].
    ↑string = aBitString **asInteger**

hash
    string **hash**

boolean arithmetic

or: aBitString
    "Returns a BitString instance equal to the or of the receiver and the argument."
    (aBitString **isMemberOf:** BitString) **ifFalse:** [↑self **retry:** #or: **coercing:** aBitString].
    ↑(string **bitOr:** aBitString **asInteger**) **asBitString**

and: aBitString
    "Returns a BitString instance equal to the and of the receiver and the argument."
    (aBitString **isMemberOf:** BitString) **ifFalse:** [↑self **retry:** #and: **coercing:** aBitString].
    ↑(string **bitAnd:** aBitString **asInteger**) **asBitString**

xor: aBitString
"Returns a BitString instance equal to the xor of the receiver and the argument."
(aBitString **isMemberOf**: BitString) **ifFalse**: [↑self **retry**: #xor: **coercing**: aBitString].
↑(string **bitXor**: aBitString **asInteger**) **asBitString**

not
"Returns an instance of class BitString equal to the complement of the receiver."
↑(string **bitInvert**) **asBitString**

shiftLeft: aShiftAmount
"Returns a BitString instance left shifted by the Shift Amount (true or false is discarded on the left)."
↑(string **bitShift**: aShiftAmount **negated**) **asBitString**

shiftRight: aShiftAmount
"Returns a BitString instance right shifted by the Shift Amount (false is added on the left)."
↑(string **bitShift**: aShiftAmount) **asBitString**

conversion

asInteger
↑string

private

privateInitialize
string ← 0

privateInitializeWith: anInteger
string ← anInteger

examples

example1
| aBitString |

"Zeros"
Transcript **cr**. aBitString ← 0 **asBitString**.
(1 **to**: 60) **do**: [:anAmount |
    Transcript **show**:
        aBitString printString, ' at: ', anAmount **printString**, ' => ',
        (aBitString at: anAmount) **printString**; **cr**].

"Ones"
Transcript **cr**. aBitString ← -1 **asBitString**.
(1 **to**: 60) **do**: [:anAmount |
    Transcript **show**:
        aBitString **printString**, ' at: ', anAmount **printString**, ' => ',
        (aBitString **at**: anAmount) **printString**; **cr**].

"Mixed"
Transcript **cr**.
aBitString ← 2r0101010101010101010101010101010101010101 **asBitString**.
(1 **to**: 60) **do**: [:anAmount |
    Transcript **show**:
        aBitString **printString**, ' at: ', anAmount **printString**, ' => ',
        (aBitString **at**: anAmount) **printString**; **cr**].

```
"Inserting into Ones (true)"
Transcript cr. aBitString ← 0 asBitString.
(1 to: 60) do: [:anAmount |
    Transcript show:
        aBitString printString, ' at: ', anAmount printString, ' put: true => ',
        (aBitString at: anAmount put: true) printString; cr].

"Inserting into Zeros (false)"
Transcript cr. aBitString ← -1 asBitString.
(1 to: 60) do: [:anAmount |
    Transcript show:
        aBitString printString, ' at: ', anAmount printString, ' put: false => ',
        (aBitString at: anAmount put: false) printString; cr]
```

Finally, numbers are extended by adding one type conversion operation for all specializations, as follows:

asBitString
 ↑BitString **privateNewWith:** self

7.3 DATE AND TIME

Date and **Time** provide a general protocol for manipulating date and time inquiries. Date was designed to include any year, month, and day since January 1, 1901, and time was designed to provide the hour, minute, and second after midnight.

For the most part, the protocol is quite useful but there are some idiosyncracies. In particular, not only do the classes construct the expected instances of **date** and **time**, but some methods return unusual instances like (1) an array containing both a date and a time with no special methods to manipulate the combination (**dateAndTimeNow**) and (2) a 4 byte array containing an unusable encoding of time (**timeWords**). Additionally, there are operations to convert dates to seconds (relative to January 1, 1901) but no corresponding operation to convert back. Some of the date operations are relative to January 1, 1901, while others simply view dates as extending infinitely far backward. Even dates such as January 1, 0 and January 1, -55 can be manipulated in some cases. In the same way, since time is relative to midnight, it can extend arbitrarily far forward (it is maintained as seconds since midnight) or backward (negative values). Not all methods are designed to handle such values. Nevertheless, if we stick to traditional usages; i.e., current dates and current time of day, no special care will be needed to ensure correct usage.

Date and **time** are independent in the sense that time is not dated; i.e., time is the number of seconds since midnight (no particular day is specified). Consequently, an absolute time can be manipulated only by keeping track of both a date and a time.

7.3.1 Class Operations for Dates and Times

In addition to providing a protocol for creating new dates and times, the classes also play a role in converting between the names of months (or days) and their corresponding integers. They are also the recipient of many useful inquiries. In general, the instance creation operations include:

* Date **today**
* Date **newDay:** aDayOfTheMonthInteger **month:** aMonthName **year:** aYearInteger

- Date **newDay**: aDayOfTheYearInteger **year**: aYearInteger
- Time **now**
- Time **fromSeconds**: aSecondCountSinceMidnight

An easy mistake to make is to mix up the two simplest methods; e.g., attempting to invoke Date **now** or Time **today**. They could be added easily. Although it is not particularly convenient for manipulation, it is also possible to obtain an array containing both the date and time as follows (either class returns the same result):

- Date **dateAndTimeNow**
- Time **dateAndTimeNow**

This is most useful for printing the current date and time. However, the user must specifically extract the components using the array operations **at:** (**at:** 1 for the date and **at:** 2 for the time).

Date operations for converting day and month names to integers are provided as follows:

- Date **dayOfWeek**: aDayName (returns 1, 2, ..., or 7)
- Date **indexOfMonth**: aMonthName (returns 1, 2, ..., or 12)
- Date **daysInMonth**: aMonthName **forYear**: aYearInteger (returns 1, 2, ..., or 31)

Day names must be exactly correct; e.g., **Monday** and not **Mon**, for method **dayOfWeek:**. Day numbers 1, 2, ..., 7 correspond to Sunday, Monday, ..., Saturday. By contrast, the month names can be specified by omitting trailing characters. Hence **January**, **Janu**, **Jan**, and **Ja** are all legal (**J** is interpreted as **January** even though **July** would match because it occurs first in the ordering). The last operation is the more useful of the three. Corresponding operations are provided for converting integers to names:

- Date **nameOfDay**: anIntegerFrom1To7
- Date **nameOfMonth**: anIntegerFrom1To12

Two other useful operations include:

- Date **daysInYear**: aYearInteger
- Date **leapYear**: aYearInteger (returns 1 for true and 0 for false)

7.3.2 Conversion Operations for Dates and Times

Date and time are easily converted to a string with the standard print and store operations **printString** and **storeString**. However, care must be taken when dealing with negative dates and times — anomalous values can be printed. Converting from a string to a date or a time is achieved via

- Date **readFrom**: (ReadStream **on**: aString)
- Time **readFrom**: (ReadStream **on**: aString)

As can be seen, the two **readFrom**: methods require a stream parameter. Date constants must adhere to the following formats:

- IntegerDay MonthName IntegerYear
  (with arbitrary non-alphanumeric separators)
- MonthName IntegerDay IntegerYear
  (with arbitrary non-alphanumeric separators)

A year XX that is less than 100 is assumed to be 19XX. Similarly, time constants must adhere to the following formats:

- IntegerHour:IntegerMinute:IntegerSeconds am (see below for options)
- IntegerHour:IntegerMinute:IntegerSeconds pm (see below for options)

The colons are required but ':IntegerMinute:IntegerSeconds' and ':IntegerSeconds' can be omitted. Additionally, am and pm can be uppercase or lowercase; if omitted, am is assumed. Some examples of correct constants are

> 25 December, 1986
> 5 Dec 86
> 5-Dec-1986
> December 5, 1986
> 5/12/86
>
> 5:30:00 am
> 2:40:50 pm
> 3am
> 5:44

Since dates like '5/12/86' are permitted, a date intended to be the year 0086 cannot be specified as a constant. A date such as January 1, 0 or even January 1, -55 can be constructed using

> Date **newDay**: 1 **year**: 0   or   Date **newDay**: 1 **year**: -55

Finally, it is possible to convert times to seconds and back via operations

- aTime **asSeconds**
- Time **fromSeconds**: anIntegerDenotingSeconds

It is permissible to construct a time via 'Time **fromSeconds**: -3600', for example. It is also possible to convert dates to seconds relative to January 1, 1901, but there is no direct conversion back. A reasonable substitute is shown.

- aDate **asSeconds**
- Date **fromDays**: anIntegerDenotingSeconds // 86400 "24*60*60"

7.3.3 Querying Operations for Dates and Times

Date and time querying operations on instances include the following:

- aDate **day** (an integer between 1 and 366 inclusive)
- aDate **dayOfMonth** (an integer between 1 and 31 inclusive)
- aDate **daysInMonth** (an integer between 28 and 31 inclusive; depends on leap years)
- aDate **daysInYear** (365 or 366; depends on leap years)
- aDate **daysLeftInYear** (an integer between 0 and 365 inclusive)

- aDate **firstDayOfMonth** (an integer between 1 and 366 inclusive)
- aDate **weekday** (Sunday, Monday, ..., or Saturday; the current day)
- aDate **weekdayIndex** (an integer between 1 and 7 inclusive; the current day)
- aDate **monthName** (January, February, ..., or December; the current month)
- aDate **monthIndex** (an integer between 1 and 12 inclusive; the current month)
- aDate **year** (an integer like 1986; the current year)
- aDate **leap** (integer 0 or 1; depends on leap years)

- aTime **hours** (an arbitrarily large positive or negative integer denoting the current hour)
- aTime **minutes** (an integer between 0 or 59 inclusive)
- aTime **seconds** (an integer between 0 or 59 inclusive)
- aDate **previous**: aDayName (the previous date with that day name)

7.3.4 Arithmetic Operations for Dates and Times

A few selected arithmetic operations are provided for constructing new dates and times:

- aDate **addDays**: anInteger (returns a Date)
- aTime **addTime**: aDateOrATime (returns a Time)

- aDate **subtractDays**: anInteger (returns a Date)
- aTime **subtractTime**: aDateOrATime (returns a Time)

- aDate **subtractDate**: aDate (returns the number of days as an integer)

Note that adding negative values is equivalent to subtracting a positive value. Hence, it is legal to compute 'Date **today addDays**: -10' or 'Time **now addTime**: (Time **fromSeconds**: -3600)'. Adding or subtracting a date to a time first causes the date to be converted to the number of seconds since January 1, 1901. There is no corresponding **addMonths**: or **addYears**: for dates.

7.3.5 Designing an Absolute Time Class

The easiest way to provide some examples using date and time is to design a new class that uses them. Since it wasn't provided by the system, we will consider an **absolute time** class; i.e., a class that maintains the current year, month, day, hour, minute, and second. The existing time class will be viewed as a **relative time** class. Absolute time is defined so that it can be extended indefinitely far back in time.

To simplify the implementation and inherit some of the existing operations, we should make this new class a subclass of either Date or Time. Since **Date** has the larger number of operations, we will choose it as the superclass. Because time is not inherited, a new instance variable called time is added to maintain the time.

Absolute time can be created by providing a specific year, month, day, hour, minute, and second. Correspondingly, each of these components will be referred to in the singular. Hence, extracting a month or changing it is achieved via 'anAbsoluteTime **month**' and 'anAbsoluteTime **month**: aNewMonth' respectively. For convenience, month can be specified either by name such as #January or by month index such as 1. All changes are normalized; e.g., changing the month to 25 actually increases the year by 2 and changes the month to 1; similarly, changing the month to -1 actually decreases the year by 1 and changes the month to 11 (changing it to 1 would have meant January, 0 December, -1 November). Arithmetic is provided with **add** methods that are specified by constrast in the plural; e.g., 'anAbsoluteTime **addMonths**: numberOfMonths' or 'anAbsoluteTime **addDays**: numberOfDays'.

The **readFrom**: method was obtained by combining the corresponding Date and Time **readFrom**: methods. A small bug was also removed. Can you find it? It expects an absolute time as a date, followed by a time with separators such as blanks, commas, and semicolons; e.g., '5 April 1982; 2:23:09 pm'.

Class AbsoluteTime

class name	AbsoluteTime
superclass	Date
instance variable names	time

class methods

instance creation

now
> "Returns an AbsoluteTime for today's date and time."
> ↑self **new privateInitializeNow**

today
> "Returns an AbsoluteTime for today's date and time."
> ↑self **new privateInitializeNow**

year: aYearInteger **month**: aMonthNameOrInteger **day**: aDayInteger
hour: anHourInteger **minute**: aMinuteInteger **second**: aSecondInteger
> "Returns an AbsoluteTime for the specified date and time."
> | aMonthInteger |
> aMonthInteger ←
>   (aMonthNameOrInteger **isKindOf**: Symbol)
>   **ifTrue**: [Date **indexOfMonth**: aMonthNameOrInteger]
>   **ifFalse**: [aMonthNameOrInteger].
> ↑self **new**
>   **privateInitializeYear**: aYearInteger **month**: aMonthInteger **day**: aDayInteger
>   **hour**: anHourInteger **minute**: aMinuteInteger **second**: aSecondInteger

readFrom: aStream
  "Note: assumes the reader has previously read the section on streams."
  "Reads a Date and time from the stream in the following form (non-alphanumeric
  separators are allowed to substitute for spaces, when shown, between the entries):
    <day> <monthName> <year> <hour>:<minute>:<second> <am/pm>
    <monthName> <day> <year> <hour>:<minute>:<second> <am/pm>
    <monthNumber> <day> <year> <hour>:<minute>:<second> <am/pm>
  where <hour>:<minute>:<second, :<minute>:<second>, :<second>, and <am/pm> may
  be omitted. Some examples include:
    5 April 1982 1:59:30 pm   5-APR-1982; 8AM
    April 5, 1982 18:53:00   4/5/8"

  | day month year hour minute second |
  aStream **skipSeparators**.
  aStream **peek isDigit ifTrue:** [day ← Integer **readFrom:** aStream].
  [aStream **peek isAlphaNumeric**] **whileFalse:** [aStream **skip:** 1].

  aStream **peek isLetter**
    ifTrue: ["number/name... or name..."
        month ← WriteStream **on:** (String new: 10).
        [aStream **peek isLetter**] **whileTrue:** [month **nextPut:** aStream **next**].
        month ← month **contents asSymbol**.
        day **isNil ifTrue:** ["name/number..."
            [aStream **peek isAlphaNumeric**] **whileFalse:** [aStream **skip:** 1].
            day ← Integer **readFrom:** aStream]]
    ifFalse: ["number/number..."
        month ← Date **nameOfMonth:** day.
        day ← Integer **readFrom:** aStream].
  [aStream **peek isAlphaNumeric**] **whileFalse:** [aStream **skip:** 1].
  year ← Integer **readFrom:** aStream.
  [aStream **atEnd not and:** [aStream **peek isAlphaNumeric not**]]
      whileTrue: [aStream **skip:** 1].

  "Now for reading the time portion"
  (aStream **atEnd not and:** [aStream **peek isDigit**])
    ifTrue: [
        hour ← Integer **readFrom:** aStream. minute ← 0. second ← 0.
        (aStream **peekFor:** $:)
            ifTrue: [
                minute ← Integer **readFrom:** aStream.
                (aStream **peekFor:** $:)
                    ifTrue: [second ← Integer **readFrom:** aStream]]]
    ifFalse: [hour ← 0. minute ← 0. second ← 0].

  aStream **skipSeparators**.
  (aStream **atEnd not and:**
  [aStream **peek asLowercase** = $p **or:** [aStream **peek asLowercase** = $a]])
    ifTrue: [
        aStream **next asLowercase** = $p **ifTrue:** [hour ← hour + 12].
        (aStream **peekFor:** $m) **ifFalse:** [aStream **peekFor:** $M]].

  ↑AbsoluteTime
      year: year **month:** month **day:** day **hour:** hour **minute:** minute **second:** second

  "AbsoluteTime **readFrom:** (ReadStream **on:** '5APR1982;2:23:09 pm')"

querying

firstDayOfMonth: aMonthInteger **forYear**: aYearInteger
 "FirstDayOfMonth is a class variable in Date."
 ↑(FirstDayOfMonth **at**: aMonthInteger) +
  ((aMonthInteger > 2) **ifTrue**: [Date **leapYear**: aYearInteger] **ifFalse**: [0])

instance methods

accessing

year
 "This method could be removed (it is here for completeness)."
 ↑super **year**

month
 "Returns the current month."
 ↑self **monthIndex**

day
 "Returns the current day."
 ↑super **day** - self **firstDayOfMonth** + 1

hour
 "Returns the current hour."
 ↑time **hours**

minute
 "Returns the current minute."
 ↑time **minutes**

second
 "Returns the current second."
 ↑time **seconds**

modification

year: aYearInteger
 "Updates the current year."
 year ← aYearInteger

month: aMonthNameOrInteger
 "Updates the current month taking normalization into account."
 | aMonthInteger oldDay newMonth newYear newDate |
 aMonthInteger ← (aMonthNameOrInteger **isKindOf**: Symbol)
  ifTrue: [Date **indexOfMonth**: aMonthNameOrInteger]
  ifFalse: [aMonthNameOrInteger].
 oldDay ← self **day**.
 newMonth ← (aMonthInteger - 1 \\ 12) + 1.
 newYear ← self **year** + (aMonthInteger // 12).
 oldDay <= (Date **daysInMonth**: (Date **nameOfMonth**: newMonth) **forYear**: newYear)
  ifFalse: [
    self **error**: (Date **nameOfMonth**: newMonth) **printString**,
     ' does not have ', oldDay **printString**, ' days'].
 "Avoid Date newDay:month:year: because it converts 0085 for example to 1985."
 day ← (AbsoluteTime **firstDayOfMonth**: newMonth **forYear**: newYear) + oldDay - 1.
 year ← newYear

day: aDayInteger
"Updates the current day taking normalization into account."
| newDate |
newDate ← Date **newDay**: self **firstDayOfMonth** + aDayInteger - 1 **year**: self **year**.
year ← newDate **year**. day ← newDate **day**

minute: aMinuteInteger
"Updates the current minute taking normalization into account (uses some inherited private methods)."
time **hours**: (time **hours**) **minutes**: aMinuteInteger **seconds**: (time **seconds**).
↑self **privateNormalize**

hour: anHourInteger
"Updates the current hour taking normalization into account (uses some inherited private methods)."
time **hours**: anHourInteger. ↑self **privateNormalize**

second: aSecondInteger
"Updates the current second taking normalization into account (uses some inherited private methods)."
time **hours**: (time **hours**) **minutes**: (time **minutes**) **seconds**: aSecondInteger.
↑self **privateNormalize**

arithmetic

addYears: aYearsInteger
"Constructs a new AbsoluteTime updated by the specified years and taking normalization into account."
↑self **copy year**: self **year** + aYearsInteger

addMonths: aMonthsInteger
"Constructs a new AbsoluteTime updated by the specified months and taking normalization into account."
↑self **copy month**: self **month** + aMonthsInteger

addDays: aDaysInteger
"Constructs a new AbsoluteTime updated by the specified days and taking normalization into account."
↑self **copy day**: self **day** + aDaysInteger

addHours: anHoursInteger
"Constructs a new AbsoluteTime updated by the specified hours and taking normalization into account."
↑self **copy hour**: self **hour** + anHoursInteger

addMinutes: aMinutesInteger
"Constructs a new AbsoluteTime updated by the specified minutes and taking normalization into account."
↑self **copy minute**: self **minute** + aMinutesInteger

addSeconds: aSecondsInteger
"Constructs a new AbsoluteTime updated by the specified seconds and taking normalization into account."
↑self **copy second**: self **second** + aSecondsInteger

comparing

= anAbsoluteTime
"Answer whether anAbsoluteTime precedes the absolute time of the receiver."
↑super = anAbsoluteTime **and**: [time = anAbsoluteTime **privateTime**]

< anAbsoluteTime
"Answer whether anAbsoluteTime precedes the absolute time of the receiver."
"aDate day (days since January 1) ~= anAbsoluteTime day (Days since beginning of month."
super = anAbsoluteTime "actually comparing only date portion"
ifTrue: [↑time < anAbsoluteTime **privateTime**]
ifFalse: [↑super < anAbsoluteTime "actually comparing only date portion"]

converting

asSeconds
"Answer the seconds between a time 24 hours before January 1 0000 and the receiver's time."
↑SecondsInDay * (self **subtractDate**: (Date **newDay**: 0 **year**: 0)) + time **asSeconds**

copying

copy
↑self **deepCopy**

printing

printOn: aStream
super **printOn**: aStream. aStream **nextPut**: $. time **printOn**: aStream

private

privateInitializeNow
"Initializes all components."
| aDate |
aDate ← Date **today**. day ← aDate **day**. year ← aDate **year**. time ← Time **now**

privateInitializeYear: aYearInteger month: aMonthInteger **day**: aDayInteger
hour: anHourInteger **minute**: aMinuteInteger **second**: aSecondInteger
"Initializes all components."
"Avoid Date newDay:month:year: because it converts 0085 for example to 1985."
day ← (AbsoluteTime **firstDayOfMonth**: aMonthInteger **forYear**: aYearInteger) +
aDayInteger - 1.
year ← aYearInteger.
time ← Time **fromSeconds**: (anHourInteger*60*60) + (aMinuteInteger*60) +
aSecondInteger.
↑self **privateNormalize**

privateNormalize
"Ensure that the month, day, hour, minute, and seconds are adjusted to proper units."
| remainingSeconds convertedDate |
remainingSeconds ← time **asSeconds**.
convertedDate ← super **addDays**: (remainingSeconds // ("24*60*60" 86400)).
"Now effect the changes."
day ← convertedDate **day**. year ← convertedDate **year**.
time ← Time **fromSeconds**: (remainingSeconds \\ ("24*60*60" 86400))

privateTime
↑time

7.4 CHARACTERS

There are 256 unique characters corresponding to integers 0, 1, ..., 255. Character constants begin with $ and are followed by the character to be specified; e.g.,

$1, $a, $A, $+, $$, and even $ (where the blank is difficult to see)

Since the characters are unique, not only is $a = $a **true** but also $a == $a. Conversion between characters and integers is achieved with methods

- aCharacter **asInteger**
- anInteger **asCharacter**

When converting an integer to a character, the integer must be in the range 0 to 255. Additional conversion operations include:

- aCharacter **asCharacter** (no effect)
- aCharacter **asLowercase**
- aCharacter **asUppercase**
- aCharacter **asSymbol**

Consequently, $A **asLowercase** is $a, $+ **asLowercase** is still +, $z **asUppercase** is $Z, $Z **asUppercase** is still $Z, and $a **asSymbol** is #a. Non-printable characters can be obtained by sending special messages to the class:

- Character **space**
- Character **cr**
- Character **tab**
- Character **backspace**
- Character **esc**
- Character **newPage**

Additional missing protocol could be added to the class as follows:

formFeed
   ↑self **newPage**

lineFeed
   ↑10 **asCharacter**

Special querying operations include:

•	aCharacter **isAlphaNumeric**	(**true** if $a..$z, $A..$Z, or $0..$9)
•	aCharacter **isDigit**	(**true** if $0..$9)
•	aCharacter **isLetter**	(**true** if $a..$z or $A..$Z)
•	aCharacter **isLowercase**	(**true** if $a..$z)
•	aCharacter **isUppercase**	(**true** if $A..$Z)

Inside Smalltalk

- aCharacter **isSeparator**   (**true** if space, cr, tab, line feed, or form feed)
- aCharacter **isVowel**   (**true** if $a, $e, $i, $o, $u, or $A, $E, $I, $O, $U)

For parsing purposes, the following complementary methods are provided to manipulate **extended radix digits** '0123456789abcdefghijklmnopqrstuvwxyz' in both uppercase and lowercase:

- Character **digitValue**: anIntegerBetween0and35 (returns an extended radix digit)
- aCharacter **digitValue** (returns an integer between 0 and 35 if it is an extended radix digit and -1 otherwise)

For example, if aRadix contains an integer between 0 and 36, then aCharacter is a valid digit if

aCharacter **digitValue between**: 0 **and**: aRadix-1

Alternatively, if aLetterPosition is an integer between 1 and 26 representing one of the letters, the letter can be obtained from

Character **digitValue**: (aLetterPosition + 10)

Finally, it is worth detailing the two lower level conversion operations that are actually used for implementing **asCharacter** (uses **value:**) and **asInteger** (uses **asciiValue**). These operations are sometimes a source of errors; e.g., **asciiValue** is often confused with **digitValue**. It is better to avoid them unless they are needed for performance reasons.

- Character **value**: anIntegerBetween0And255 (convert to character)
- aCharacter **asciiValue** (convert to integer)

7.5 RANDOM STREAMS

Class **Random** provides random number generators over the interval 0.0 and 1.0 exclusive (the endpoints are never provided). The generator is actually an infinite stream; i.e., a stream that cannot be exhausted. The protocol to use for obtaining such a stream is

- Random **new** (to obtain a new random number generator)
- aRandom **next** (obtains a random number from the random number generator)

The random numbers provided by each generator are generally different. A class of random streams, say called **RangedRandom**, that returns values between a and b exclusive could be defined as follows. The value returned is converted to the class of a (the lowerbound).

As defined, a generator for values between 1.0 and 100.0 exclusive would be obtained with

RangedRandom **from**: 1.0 **to**: 100.0

A generator for values between 1 and 100 exclusive would be obtained with

RangedRandom **from**: 1 **to**: 100

Class RangedRandom

class name	RangedRandom
superclass	Random
instance variable names	baseValue expansionAmount

class methods

instance creation

from: lowerValue **to**: upperValue
    "Returns a RangedRandom for the specified bounds."
    ↑super **new privateInitializeWith**: lowerValue **and**: upperValue

new
    "Not allowed."
    ↑self **error**: 'Use RangedRandom **from**: lowerValue **to**: upperValue.'

instance methods

accessing

next
    ↑baseValue **coerce**: baseValue+ (super **next** * expansionAmount)

private

privateInitializeWith: lowerValue **and**: upperValue
    baseValue ← lowerValue. expansionAmount ← upperValue - lowerValue.
    (baseValue **isKindOf**: Integer)
        "This prevents the lowerbound from being returned (conversion truncates)."
        ifTrue: [baseValue ← baseValue + 1. expansionAmount ← expansionAmount - 1].

7.6 SUMMARY

In this chapter, we have described the Smalltalk **Magnitude** classes. In particular, we have discussed the following:

- **Magnitude** as an abstract class with operations like <, >, =, <=, >=, and ~=.
- The steps to be followed when adding new subclasses of **Magnitude**.
- The literal representation for constants of class **Number**.
- Type conversion between numbers and the concept of generality.
- The division, remainder, truncate, and round operations.
- Mathematical operations.
- The steps to be followed when adding new subclasses of **Number**.
- The protocol supported by classes **Date** and **Time**.
- **AbsoluteTime** — a new subclass of **Date**.
- The protocol supported by class **Character**.
- The class **Random**.
- **RangedRandom** — a Random subclass providing fixed range random numbers.

7.7 EXERCISES

The following exercises may require some original thought, rereading some of the material, and/or browsing through the system.

1. As defined, the < operation for complex numbers is less than ideal. For instance, can you think of two complex numbers a and b such that a = b, a < b, and a > b are all false? How would you revise the operation?

2. Generalize methods **printString-Radix:** and **storeStringRadix:** so as to apply to fractions and/or floats.

3. Investigate the library to find out how many classes (if any) provide operation < and yet do not inherit from **Magnitude**. Is there a good reason in each case?

4. With infinite length bit strings, it is not possible to provide operations that take **substrings** and perform **concatenations** (how would you concatenate two infinitely long strings?). Devise a specialization called, say FiniteBitString, that would permit you to do this.

5. The complex number methods currently use a cumbersome notation for creating new complex numbers, namely "Complex **new realPart:** X; **imaginaryPart:** Y; **yourself**". This could be rewritten in the form "X + Yi" but it would be much less efficient because of the type conversion that results in +. A more efficient solution could make use of the comma as an operator, enabling you to write "X, Y"; no type conversion would be required. Where should this operator be placed in the number hierarchy and what should the code be? Would you change **printOn:** and **storeOn:** to take advantage of the more convenient notation?

6. Some classes like strings have comparison operations <, >, and = defined on them and yet they are not subclasses of Magnitude. Why?

7.8 GLOSSARY AND IMPORTANT FACTS

classes

ArithmeticValue An abstract class for documenting double dispatching.

Date A class that provides a date accurate to a specific day in a specific month of a specific year.

Float A class that provides manipulation for approximated values such as 1.0e-5 and 1.234.

Fraction A class providing manipulation for fractional values such as (1/3) and (1/2).

Integer An abstract class that includes large positive integers, large negative integers, and small integers. Integers provide unbounded precision arithmetic.

LimitedPrecisionReal An abstract class for anticipated extensions to floats; e.g., single versus double precision.

Magnitude An abstract class for objects that can be compared using operations such as <, >, =, <=, >=, and ~=.

Number An abstract class that includes integers, fractions, and floats.

Random A class that returns a random number generator for numbers between 0.0 and 1.0 exclusive.

Time A class that provides a time accurate to a specific second relative to midnight.

selected terminology

bit manipulation The process of manipulating integers as if they were a sequence of bits (zeros and ones). Typical operations include **bitAnd:**, **bitOr:**, **bitXor:**, **bitInvert:**, and **bitShift:**.

conversion The process of explicitly converting an instance of one class into an instance of another.; e.g., from an integer into a string.

coercion The process of converting a number from one class to another as required by the context; e.g., converting an integer operand to a float when the other operand is float.

double dispatching An efficient technique for discovering the types of both operands without having to explicitly query them and for performing fast automatic conversion.

generality number A conversion priority associated with each number class. An operation converts the operand with the lowest generality number (if they are different) to the class of the other. Existing generality numbers are 80 (float), 60 (fraction), 40 (large integers), and 20 (small integers).

hash An operation computing a unique integer from an object. Equal objects must have equal hashes but the converse need not hold. Hashes are used in classes such as sets and dictionaries to speed up searches.

radix An upper bound on the digits allowed for use in a number. For a radix between 2 and 36, the digits must have values between 0 and radix-1. Allowed digits are 0123456789abcd...xyz (both uppercase and lowercase letters are allowed). Digit a represents 10, b represents 11, and so on.

important facts

No operator priority Hence, A + B * C $\Rightarrow$ (A + B) * C (brackets are needed to change the order). Additionally, A = B & C = D (is not what you want).

No integer overflow Hence, large number + large number $\Rightarrow$ an even larger number.

Automatic type conversion Conversion order is Integer $\Rightarrow$ Fraction $\Rightarrow$ Float — A/B converts integers A and B to a fraction; A **coerce:** B converts B to number A's class.

Some operations renamed A **quo:** B $\Rightarrow$ quotient (called **mod** in other languages). A **rem:** B $\Rightarrow$ remainder after dividing A by B. A **raisedTo:** B and A **raisedToInteger:** B $\Rightarrow$ a number or integer power respectively.

Unary operations extensive No unary plus; **negated** is unary minus; others include **exp**, **ln**, **sqrt**, **odd**, **even**, **positive**, **negative**, **floor**, **ceiling**, **truncated**, **rounded**, **abs**, **reciprocal**, **factorial**, **asCharacter** (Integer only); **fractionPart**, and **integerPart** (Float only).

Sequencing over numbers

A **to:** B **do:** aBlock; e.g.,
  5.1 **to:** 10.1 **do:** [:index |
    sum ← sum + index]
A **to:** B **by:** C **do:** aBlock; e.g.,
  10.1 **to:** 5.1 **by:** -0.2 **do:** [:index |
    sum ← sum + index]
It is also legal to write
  (A **to:** B) **do:** aBlock
  (A **to:** B **by:** C) **do:** aBlock
  anInterval ← (A **to:** B **by:** C).
  anInterval **do:** aBlock.
  (intervals are a special class of collections)
Note: 1 **to:** 10.0 **by:** (1/3) **do:** aBlock works (range is 1, (4/3), (5/3), ...; note type conversion)

Range comparisons

(A <= B) & (B <= C),
(A <= B) | (B <= C)
  (everything evaluated)
(A <= B) **and:** [B <= C],
(A <= B) **or:** [B <= C]
  (short circuit evaluation)
B **between:** A **and:** C
  (everything evaluated)

Random (a subclass of Stream)

    Random values from 0.0 to 1.0 exclusive.

    seed ← Random **new**
        ⇒ (an instance)

    (seed **next** * 10) **truncated** + 1
        ⇒ random integer between 1 and 10

Class Float knows about pi

    sum ← 0.
    1 **to:** 10 **by:** Float **pi do:** [:element |
        sum ← sum + element]

8

The Collection Classes

8.1 INTRODUCTION

Collectively, collections comprise one of Smalltalk's **major** work-horse data types.
Collection (see Fig. 8.1) is an abstract class for objects that are **containers** for other
objects. The specializations include such familiar classes as **sets, strings**, and **arrays**. Also
included are lesser known classes such as **bags, dictionaries, ordered collections**, and
sorted collections. There is a subtle distinction between being ordered and being sorted.
The elements of a linked list, for example containing successive elements 2, 3, 1, are ordered
but not sorted. Consequently, ordered collections are ordered but not usually sorted. Sorted
collections are always sorted according to some user-specifiable sorting criteria.

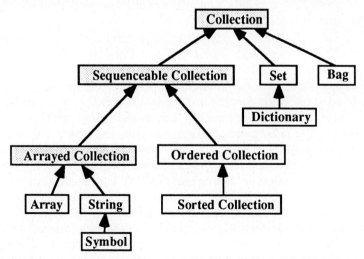

Figure 8.1 The most popular Collection classes — a physical view.

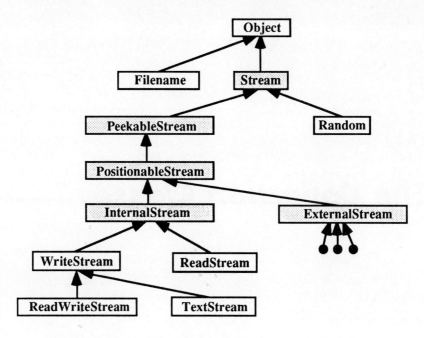

Figure 8.2 The most popular Stream classes — a physical view.

Logically, **streams** are also collections although they are implemented separately in their own special hierarchy (see Fig. 8.2). The stream hierarchy contains several abstract classes, notably **Stream**, **PeekableStream**, **PositionableStream**, **InternalStream**, and **ExternalStream** and several specializations of which **WriteStream**, **ReadStream**, and some version of external streams are the most used. Intuitively, streams are files that have been generalized to permit reading and writing over collections. Corresponding external streams are created automatically from instances of **Filename** when a specific kind of stream for that file name is requested.

From an implementation viewpoint, the physical collection hierarchy is quite large (see Fig. 8.3) containing four abstract classes: **Collection**, **SequenceableCollection**, **ArrayedCollection**, and **IntegerArray**. It is important to distinguish them (and the abstract classes for streams mentioned above) since one of the more common errors is to attempt to construct corresponding instances — remember, there can be no instances of abstract classes. Arrayed collections; e.g., **arrays** and **strings**, are fixed-size while **ordered collections** (similar in behavior to arrays) can grow and shrink automatically. This latter feature is also a property of **sets**, **bags**, and **dictionaries**. **Dictionaries** generalize arrays by providing keys that are arbitrary objects. Two varieties exist, **(equality) dictionaries** and **identity dictionaries**; the former uses **equality** to compare keys while the latter uses **identity**. Sets are also distinguished in the same way as **(equality) sets** and **identity sets**. **Symbols** are special kinds of strings that are immutable; i.e., do not permit changes, and consequently can ensure that only one copy exists for each instance with a unique set of characters. Hence, they can be compared for equality without considering the individual characters. **Texts** are strings with emphasis information; e.g., whether or not it is in **boldface** or **italic**.

Several anomalies can be observed. For example, even though users consider sets and bags to be related from an implementation point of view, there is no apparent relationship between them in the existing hierarchy. Although there are identity sets, there are no identity bags. Some classes like **Semaphore** don't seem to be containers and probably shouldn't be viewed as special cases of collections at all. Many of the classes are also private in the sense that they are used primarily by the system and are of little concern to typical users; e.g.; **SystemDictionary**, **LiteralDictionary**, **ByteArray**, **WordArray**, and **TextLine-Interval**. Many others have not been shown in Fig. 8.3. For example, there exists several other private dictionary classes such as **DependentsDictionary**, **HandleDictionary**, an identity set subclass called **SignalCollection**, a subclass of ordered collection called **HandlerCollection**, subclasses of arrays called **DependentsCollection** and **Scanner-Table**, and various string and symbol subclasses such as **ByteString**, **ByteSymbol**, **twoByteString**, and **twoByteSymbol**.

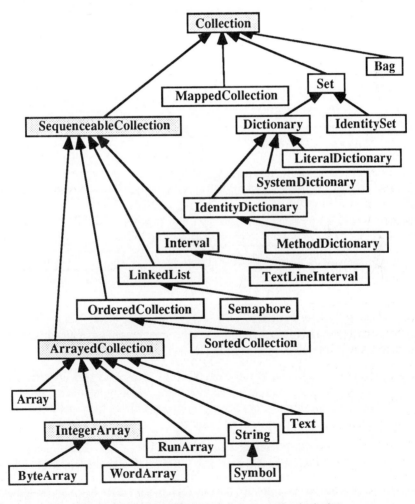

Figure 8.3 The Collection classes — a physical view.

8.1.1 A Logical Organization

We can obtain a better understanding of collections (streams included) if we consider the relationships from a logical perspective. From the point of view of usage, the collection classes can be partitioned into four major logical groups: keyed classes, streamable classes, ordered classes, and unordered classes (see Fig. 8.4). As we will see, the classes belonging to each of these groups are not mutually exclusive. In more detail,

- **Keyed Classes** associate elements with keys; e.g., arrays.
- **Streamable Classes** provide access to the elements using a specialized file-like protocol; e.g., read streams.
- **Ordered Classes** provide an ordering on the elements; e.g., strings.
- **Unordered Classes** provide no ordering on the elements; e.g., sets.

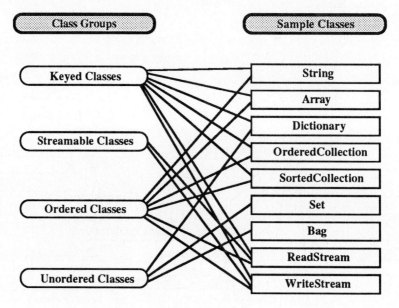

Figure 8.4 The Collection (Stream) classes — a logical partitioning with representative members.

These groups are best understood by analyzing representative members and considering how they are typically used. For instance,

- **Arrays** typify the keyed classes. Keys (or subscripts) are used to access and modify the elements contained by the array. The more general representative is an **identity dictionary** that permits arbitrary objects to be used both as keys and as elements. Typical operations include:

  - aKeyedCollection **at:** aKey   (subscripting operation)
  - aKeyedCollection **at:** aKey **put:** aValue   (element modification)

Ordered collections are part of this group since they can be manipulated just like arrays; i.e., they contain an extensive array-like protocol. **Read** and **write**

streams can also be considered keyed classes because random access to the stream is possible as shown below.

- aStream **position** (subscripting operation)
- aStream **position:** anIntegerKey (element modification)

The keyed classes (exclusive of the stream classes) include: **IdentityDictionary, Dictionary, SystemDictionary, LiteralDictionary, Array, RunArray, ByteArray, WordArray, Interval, TextLineInterval, String, Text, Symbol, MappedCollection, OrderedCollection, SortedCollection, ReadStream,** and **WriteStream.**

- **ReadStreams** typify the streamable classes. The elements in streams are accessed via specialized file-like operations. The more general representative is **Read-WriteStream,** which permits both element access and modification. Specialized variations include **Random** and **external variants** for file accessing. **Filename** provides an interface with external streams. Typical operations include:

  - aReadStream **atEnd** (an interrogation)
  - aReadStream **next** (accessing an element; move right)
  - aReadStream **peek** (accessing an element without moving)
  - aWriteStream **nextPut:** anElement (modifying or appending)
  - aReadOrWriteStream **close** (when completed)

The streamable classes include: **Stream, PeekableStream, Positionable-Stream, InternalStream, ReadWriteStream, ReadStream, WriteStream,** external variants of the previous three, **ExternalStream,** and **Random.**

- **Ordered collections** typify the ordered classes. The elements in the collection are assumed to be in a specific order; access and/or modifications based on this order is permitted. Generally, ordered collections behave like arrays but can additionally grow or shrink at either end. Typical operations include:

  - anOrderedCollection **first** (accessing an element)
  - anOrderedCollection **last**
  - anOrderedCollection **at:** aKey (subscripting operation)
  - anOrderedCollection **at:** aKey **put:** aValue (element modification)
  - anOrderedCollection **do:** [anElement I someCode] (accessing all elements)
  - anOrderedCollection **add:** anElement (adding an element)
  - anOrderedCollection **addFirst:** anElement
  - anOrderedCollection **addLast:** anElement
  - anOrderedCollection **removeFirst** (removing an element)
  - anOrderedCollection **removeLast**

Generally, the ordered classes include any of the keyed classes that require integer keys; e.g., arrays, strings, symbols and the streamable collections since their elements are sequentially accessible. The ordered classes (exclusive of the stream classes) include: **OrderedCollection, SortedCollection, LinkedList, Array, RunArray, ByteArray, WordArray, Interval, String, Text, Symbol,** and **MappedCollection.**

- **Sets** typify the unordered classes. After a set is constructed, access to the contained elements is provided in some arbitrary order, one that is independent of the order used to insert the elements into the set. The more general representative is a **bag** that permits any number of occurrences of the same object. Typical operations include:

  - aSetLikeCollection **do**: [anElement | someCode]   (accessing all elements)
  - aSetLikeCollection **add**: anElement   (adding an element)
  - aSetLikeCollection **remove**: anElement   (removing an element)

  The unordered classes include: **Bag**, **IdentitySet**, and **Set**.

8.1.2 Creating Collections

Even though we have not yet discussed the individual collection classes in detail, it is still possible to provide a summary of the different methods for constructing collections. These include

- constants,
- copying,
- conversion from existing collections, and
- explicit construction.

Constant Collections

Only three classes of collections provide a special syntactic notation for constants: symbols, strings, and arrays. Examples include:

- #Wilf   (a symbol)
- 'Hello John'   (a string)
- #('hi' Dave () 25.5)   (an array)

Empty strings and empty arrays are allowed; e.g. '' (two single quotes) and #() respectively. However, empty symbol constants are not permitted (it is possible to create one by executing '' **asSymbol**, however). Strings containing single quotes can be constructed by doubling the imbedded quotes as follows:

'you''re his best friend''s pal' ⇒ you're his best friend's pal

Although symbols were intended to be names (possibly imbedded with colons), it is possible to obtain symbols such as #~, #!, #@, #$, #%, #), #[, #}, #|. However, some combinations like ##, #", #', #(are illegal. If names with unusual characters are really desired, they should be constructed by converting a string to a symbol (using aString **asSymbol**). Array constants permit nested arrays where internal sharps may be omitted. Thus

#(the #(internal name) is deliberate) is equivalent to #(the (internal name) is deliberate)

There is an anomaly with symbols, however. For instance,

| #(try :hello:there) | is really the 3-element array | #(try : hello:there) |
| #(try #:hello:there) | is really the 2-element array | #(try :hello:there) |

Thus, #:hi:there is considered a single symbol although #(:hi:there) is an array with two symbols, #: and #hi:there.

Copying Collections

Instances of collections can be copied in the usual way (see Chapter 6 for more details about copying — both deep and shallow copies). Additionally, there are a few more specialized copy operations.

- aCollection **shallowCopy**
- aCollection **deepCopy**
- aCollection **copy**
    Returns a similar collection with elements that are either the same as the originals (shallow copy) or copies of the originals (deep copy). Operation copy defaults to shallowCopy.
- anOrderedCollection **copyEmpty**
- aCollection **copyEmpty: anIntegerSize**
    Returns a similar collection of the specified size. The elements are not initialized. Note that the first operation does not apply to arbitrary collections.

Assuming, for example, that an array is already available, constructing another uninitialized array that is larger by one can be done in two ways:

    newArray ← Array **new**: oldArray **size** + 1.
    newArray ← oldArray **copyEmpty**: oldArray **size** + 1.

Clearly, there is not much advantage in using **copyEmpty**: for this task. The advantage comes when you have to construct another collection of the same class as some arbitrary collection (of unknown class).

Converting Between Collections

Generally speaking, conversion operations result in new classes of collections being constructed; i.e., the receivers of conversion operations are never modified. Additionally, the result of the conversion generally contains the same elements as the original collection; i.e., the elements in the result are identical to the elements in the original. In other words, conversion operations provide the equivalent of shallow copies but in a new class of collection. Although many conversion operations are available, they are incomplete.

Most (but not all) instances of collections (streams excluded) can be converted to **ordered collections, sorted collections, sets,** and **bags.** Only integer-keyed collections can be converted to **streams** — either read streams or write streams. Additionally, integer-keyed collections can be converted to **arrays** but not conversely; e.g., a **string** can be converted to an **array** but an **array** cannot be converted to a **string.** In general, conversion operations are not supplied if element compatibility must be checked. In the latter example, conversion from an array to a string would be legal only if all the elements happened to be characters. There are operations for converting between **strings, text,** and **symbols.** Finally, special operations are provided for converting integer-keyed collections to streams and vice versa — actually, they are really operations for constructing streams rather than actual type conversion operations.

The following summarizes the conversion operations applicable to the non-streamable classes. Restrictions are supplied via the exceptions table that follows the list.

- aCollection **asOrderedCollection**$^{\$\$\$}$

    Returns a collection of elements; e.g., for keyed collections, the keys are discarded.

- aCollection **asSet**$^{\$\$\$}$

    Returns a collection of elements; e.g., for keyed collections, the keys are discarded.

- aCollection **asBag**$^{\$\$\$}$

    Returns a collection of elements; e.g., for keyed collections, the keys are discarded.

- aCollection **asSortedCollection**$^{\$\$}$

    For dictionaries and identity dictionaries, returns a collection of associations; otherwise, a collection of elements; e.g., for integer-keyed collections, the keys are discarded.

- aCollection **asSortedCollection:** aSortBlock$^{\$\$}$

    For dictionaries and identity dictionaries, returns a collection of associations; otherwise, a collection of elements; e.g., for integer-keyed collections, the keys are discarded.

- aCollection **asArray**$^{\$}$

    Returns a collection of elements.

- aCollection **readStream**$^{\$}$
- aCollection **writeStream**$^{\$}$

    Returns a corresponding stream for sequencing over the collection of elements.

- aCollection **asString**[***]
- aCollection **asText**[**]
- aCollection **asSymbol**[*]

Exceptions

$$$:	Applicable to all collections except streams.
$$:	Applicable to all collections except streams and linked lists.
$:	Applicable only to integer-keyed collections.
***:	Applicable only to byte arrays, strings, texts, and symbols.
**:	Applicable only to strings, texts, and symbols.
*:	Applicable only to strings and symbols.

When **dictionaries** are converted to **sorted collections**, the result is a collection of **associations** (key-value pairs); for all other conversions of dictionaries, only the values (not the keys) are kept. When linked lists are converted; e.g., using **asSet**, the result is a collection of **links** (not a collection of values supplied by the links; see linked lists in the ordered classes section).

Strings, **texts**, and **symbols** all have slightly different restrictions on the applicable conversions. Nevertheless, you won't go too far wrong by assuming any one of the three can be converted to the other.

Conspicuously absent are such plausible operations as the following:

- aCollection **asDictionary**   (note: none of these operations exist)
- aCollection **asIdentityDictionary**
- aCollection **asIdentitySet**
- aCollection **asMappedCollection**
- aCollection **asMappedCollectionMappedBy**: aMapArray
- aCollection **asLinkedList**
- aCollection **asRunArray**
- aCollection **asByteArray**

Although we might have expected the string-like conversion operations to apply to arbitrary collections with appropriate element checking, this is not the case. This lack of generality and completeness is understandable in a new system and will likely change as users extend it.

Examples

```
#(the never ending story) asOrderedCollection
      ⇒ OrderedCollection (the never ending story)
#(once upon a time) asSortedCollection ⇒ SortedCollection (a once time upon)
#(when every one was happy) asSortedCollection: [:x :y | x >= y]
      ⇒ SortedCollection (upon time once a)
#(there was an interesting) asArray ⇒ (there was an interesting)
#(never ending story) asSet ⇒ Set (ending never story)
#(which begins as the first line above) asBag
      ⇒ Bag (line which first above begins as the)
(Interval from: 1 to: 10 by: 3) asSet ⇒ Set (1 4 7 10)
'Will this work?' asArray ⇒ Array ($W $i $l $l $    $t $h $i $s $    $w $o $r $k $?)
'try' asText ⇒ Text for 'try'
'also try' asSymbol ⇒ also try
'' asSymbol ⇒ (nothing printed)
#hello asString ⇒ 'hello'
#there asText ⇒ Text for there
```

Additional conversions between integer-keyed collections and streams are possible using the following operations:

- anInternalStreamClass[1] **on**: anIntegerKeyedCollection
- anInternalStreamClass **on**: anIntegerKeyedCollection **from**: startKey **to**: endKey
- anInternalWriteStreamClass[2] **with**: anIntegerKeyedCollection
- anInternalWriteStreamClass **with**: anIntegerKeyedCollection **from**: start **to**: end

- anInternalStream **contents**

The **on** protocol creates streams positioned at the beginning of the collection, whereas the **with** protocol creates them positioned at the end, making it convenient to append

---

[1]An internal stream class is either ReadStream, WriteStream, or ReadWriteStream.
[2]We mean either WriteStream or ReadWriteStream.

additional elements. Operation **contents** converts the streams back to the original class of collections from which the streams were originally constructed. See the special section on streams for a more detailed discussion.

Typical Methods for Creating Collections

It would be much easier to remember how to create collections if a single standard protocol were used. On the other hand, since distinct collections were introduced for specific purposes, it is only reasonable that differences will arise. Prior to detailing all of the individual techniques in their respective sections, we list a sample of typical ways in which new collections are constructed.

The Keyed Collections
- IdentityDictionary **new**
- Dictionary **new**
- Array **new**: 100
- RunArray **runs**: anArrayOfCounts **values**: anArrayOfPairwiseDistinctElements
- ByteArray **new**: 100
- aNumber **to**: aNumber **by**: aNumber "an interval"
- String **new**: 100
- Text **string**: aString **emphasis**: 1 "for bold, 2 for italic, 4 for underlined"
- aString **asSymbol**
- MappedCollection **collection**: collectionOfElements **map**: aMappingCollection

The Streamable Collections
- ReadStream **on**: anIntegerKeyedCollection
- WriteStream **on**: anIntegerKeyedCollection
- ReadWriteStream **on**: anIntegerKeyedCollection
- (Filename **named**: aString) **readString**
- (Filename **named**: aString) **writeString**

Other Ordered Collections
- OrderedCollection **new**
- SortedCollection **sortBlock**: [:x :y | x <= y]
- LinkedList **new**

The Unordered Collections
- Bag **new**
- IdentitySet **new**
- Set **new**

8.1.3 Comparing Collections

For comparison purposes, it is too restrictive to insist that two comparands be instances of the same class. A less restrictive requirement is that they belong to the same collection **species**. The species notion is also important when creating copies of existing collections.

Collection Species

When collection operations like the sequencing operations (to be discussed later) construct new collections, the result is usually but not always the same class as the receiver. More specifically, the returned collection is of the same **species** as the original. Except for the following, the species of collections associated with a given instance (of a collection) is an instance of the same class.

```
for anInterval  ⇒  Array.
for aMappedCollection  ⇒  same species as the collection being mapped (not the map).
for aSymbol  ⇒  String.
```

The implication is that sequencing operations do not return intervals, mapped collections, or symbols. Instead, they return arrays, collections of the same class as the collection being mapped, and strings respectively.

The Comparison Operations

Collections can be compared using the four comparison operations ==, ~~, =, and ~=. Since **equality** comparisons (= and ~=) default to **identity** comparisons (== and ~~) in class **Object**, all collections that do not explicitly provide special equality comparison operations will default to identity comparisons. Examples where this happens include sets, dictionaries, and streams. When implemented, equality comparison operations for collections are quite **slow** by comparison with the corresponding identity comparison operations since they must consider, in the worst case, all elements of the collection.

- aCollection == anotherCollection
- aCollection ~~ anotherCollection
- aCollection = anotherCollection
- aCollection ~= anotherCollection

    For sets, bags, dictionaries, mapped collections, and streams, equality comparisons default to identity comparisons. For other classes, an equality comparison returns true if both the receiver and parameter are (1) collections of the same species, (2) the same size, and (3) the corresponding elements of the collections are equal; otherwise, it returns false. For sorted collections, the operation also requires the sort blocks to be identical.

Examples

Equality Comparisons that Default to Identity Comparisons

```
aTest ← Dictionary new at: #hello put: #there; yourself.
aTest = aTest copy  ⇒  false
anotherTest ← MappedCollection collection: #(1 2) map: #(1 2).
anotherTest = anotherTest copy  ⇒  false
(ReadStream on: #(a short stream)) = (ReadStream on: #(a short stream))  ⇒  false
(Filename named: 'aTest') readStream = (Filename named: 'aTest') readStream  ⇒  false
#(a big bad boy) asSet = #(a big bad boy) asSet  ⇒  false
#(one one two) asBag = #(one one two) asBag  ⇒  false
```

Specialized Equality Comparison Operations

```
#(a short array) = #(a short array)  ⇒  true
```

Examples (continued)

RunArray **runs:** #(10 20) **values:** #(0 -1) = RunArray **runs:** #(10 20) **values:** #(0 -1) $\Rightarrow$ **true**
(1 **to:** 10) = (1 **to:** 10) $\Rightarrow$ **true**
'Will this work?' = 'Will this work?' $\Rightarrow$ **true**
'try' **asText** = 'try' **asText** $\Rightarrow$ **true**
#hello = #hello $\Rightarrow$ **true**
#(this too) **asOrderedCollection** = #(this too) **asOrderedCollection** $\Rightarrow$ **true**
#(and this) **asSortedCollection** = #(and this) **asSortedCollection** $\Rightarrow$ **true**
LinkedList **new** = LinkedList **new** $\Rightarrow$ **true**

8.1.4 Sequencing Over Collections

Because there are so many distinct collection classes, each with specialized operations and representations, it is essential to provide a common set of operations for accessing the elements. The following sequencing operations were designed to hide the details of the representation and to provide a uniform facility for sequencing through the elements in a controlled manner. The common factor with all of these operations is that a block is provided to operate on the individual elements. Usually, this block requires one parameter for the collection element, although some variations require zero or two.

The Sequencing Protocol

In the following, exceptionBlock requires no parameters, aBlock requires one parameter, and aBinaryBlock requires two. The superscripted $ and * specify exceptions that are summarized below. Although it it not a sequencing operation, **reverse** is included because of its relationship to **reverseDo:**.

- aCollection **do:** aBlock [$$$]
  Evaluates aBlock with the successive elements of the collection. Returns the receiver.
- aCollection **reverseDo:** aBlock [****]
  Same as **do:** but in reverse order.
- aCollection **collect:** aBlock [$]
  Evaluates aBlock with the successive elements of the collection. Returns the successive results in a collection of the same species as the receiver. For dictionaries and identity dictionaries, the result is anomalous (a bag of values; i.e, keys are discarded).
- aCollection **select:** aBlock [$]
  Returns only the elements for which aBlock was true. The elements are returned in a collection of the same species as the receiver. For dictionaries and identity dictionaries, the operation is anomalous — although values are sent to the select block as the elements, the result is a dictionary of associations (key/value pairs).
- aCollection **reject:** aBlock [$]
  Same as above but returns the elements for which aBlock was false. The same anomaly applies for dictionaries and identity dictionaries as above.
- aCollection **detect:** aBlock {**ifNone:** exceptionBlock} [$$]
  Returns the first element for which aBlock is true. If there are none, the exception block (no parameters) is executed; if no exception block was provided, an error is generated.

- aCollection **inject:** initialValue **into:** binaryBlock $$

  Evaluate binaryBlock with initialValue and the first element, then again with its result and the second element, then its result with the third, and so on. Returns the final result.

- aCollection **with:** aCollection **do:** binaryBlock ****

  The receiver collection and aCollection must be the same size. Evaluates the binaryBlock with successive elements from each of the two collections as the parameters. Returns the receiver.

- aCollection **findFirst:** aBlock ***

  Returns the key of the first element which aBlock evaluates to true; returns 0 if none exists. Applies only to the integer-keyed collections.

- aCollection **findLast:** aBlock ***

  Returns the key of the last element which aBlock evaluates to true; returns 0 if none exists. Applies only to the integer-keyed collections.

- aCollection **associationsDo:** aBlock **

  Applies only to dictionaries and identity dictionaries. Evaluates aBlock with the successive associations of the dictionary or identity dictionary. **Association** is a special class with instances that contain both the key and the value; 'anAssociation **key**' provides the key while 'anAssociation **value**' provides the value. Returns the receiver.

- aCollection **keysDo:** aBlock **

  Applies only to dictionaries and identity dictionaries. Evaluates aBlock with the successive keys of the dictionary or identity dictionary. The corresponding value can be obtained via 'aDictionary **at**: aKey'. Returns the receiver.

- aCollection **reverse** ***

  Returns a collection of the same species but with the same elements and in the opposite order; i.e., the elements are not copied.

Exceptions

$$$:   Applicable to all collections including streams.

$$:   Applicable to all collections except streams.

$:   Applicable to all collections except streams, linked lists, and run arrays.

****:   Applicable to all collections except streams, linked lists, mapped collections, sets, bags, dictionaries, and identity dictionaries.

***:   As above but also excludes run arrays.

**:   Applicable to all integer-keyed collections.

*:   Applicable only to dictionaries and identity dictionaries.

Operation **do:** is the most used; **reverseDo:**, **collect:**, and **inject:into:** are occasionally used; the others are used only in special situations. Non-sequencing operation **reverse** is used mainly for string processing. Operations **select:**, **reject:**, and **detect:** are difficult to remember and properly distinguish without experience. For the occasional situation where they might be useful, it is best to look them up. Operation **inject:into:** provides a general loop summation facility, but most Smalltalk programmers (experts excepted, of course) tend to revert to using **do:** for that purpose. Operations **findFirst:** and **findLast:** are more limited since they apply only to integer-keyed collections. Moreover, there exists no corresponding operations like '**findNext:** aBlock **after:** aKey' and '**findPrevious:** aBlock **before:** aKey' for carrying out further searches.

Dictionaries and identity dictionaries enable users to obtain either keys, values, or associations (key/value pairs). Keys and values can be extracted from associations via 'anAssociation **key**' and 'anAssociation **value**' respectively. Operation **associationsDo:** sequences through associations, **keysDo:** through keys, and **do:** through values. Except for **associationsDo:** and **keysDo:**, all of the standard sequencing operations sequence through values for dictionaries. Consequently, we might expect the result to be a collection of values. This is not the case. Following the usual species rule implies the result must be a dictionary (a dictionary is a species of Dictionary). Consequently, even though the sequencing operation provides the associated block with only the value, a dictionary is constructed with both the correct key and value. This rule makes sense but there is an exception. Operation **collect:** returns a bag of values (not associations) instead of the expected dictionary.

Sequencing operations applied to streams have side effects on the stream. For example, performing a **do:** operation sequences through the 'unread' stream elements leaving the stream positioned at the end. A second **do:** would find no elements to sequence through.

Examples of Sequencing Operations

We consider an example of each of the above operations to provide a feel for the operations and then we consider a few isolated examples dealing with dictionaries.

```
aSack ← OrderedCollection new.
#(Marble Quartz Gold) do: [:word | aSack add: word].
#(Stick Frog Rock) reverseDo: [:word | aSack add: word].
aSack  ⇒  OrderedCollection (Marble Quartz Gold Rock Frog Stick)

#(1 2 3 4 5 6) collect: [:value | value squared]  ⇒  (1 4 9 16 25 36)

#(1 2 3 4 5 6) select: [:value | value even]  ⇒  (2 4 6)
#(1 2 3 4 5 6) reject: [:value | value <= 2]  ⇒  (3 4 5 6)
#(1 2 3 4 5 6) detect: [:value | value > 2] ifNone: [0]  ⇒  3

#(1 2 3 4 5 6) inject: 0 into: [:sum :element | sum + element]  ⇒  21

result ← OrderedCollection new.
#(1 2 3 4 5 6 7) with: #(1 2 3 4 5 6 7) do: [:v1 :v2 | result add: v1 + v2].
result  ⇒  OrderedCollection (2 4 6 8 10 12 14)

#(1 2 3 4 5 6) findFirst: [:element | element even]  ⇒  2
#(1 2 3 4 5 6) findLast: [:element | element even]  ⇒  6

#(a short memo) reverse ⇒ (memo short a)
(1 to: 5) reverse ⇒ (5 4 3 2 1)
#(one two three) asOrderedCollection reverse ⇒ OrderedCollection (three two one)
'a string' reverse ⇒ 'gnirts a'

aDictionary ← Dictionary new
    at: #Key1 put: #Value1;
    at: #Key2 put: #Value2;
    yourself. "This dictionary will be used several times below."
```

Note: when sequencing through aDictionary below, it is a coincidence that Key1 is encountered before Key2 since there is no ordering for the keys."

```
aSack ← OrderedCollection new.
aDictionary associationsDo: [:something | aSack add: something].
aDictionary keysDo: [:something | aSack add: something].
aDictionary do: [:something | aSack add: something].
aSack ⇒ OrderedCollection (Key1->Value1 Key2->Value2 Key1 Key2 Value1 Value)

aDictionary collect: [:value | value] ⇒ Bag (Value1 Value2)

aDictionary select: [:value | value <= #Value1] ⇒ Dictionary (Key1->Value1)
aDictionary select: [:value | value <= #Value2] ⇒ Dictionary (Key1->Value1 Key2->Value2)

aDictionary reject: [:value | value <= #Value1] ⇒ Dictionary (Key2->Value2)
aDictionary reject: [:value | value <= #Value2] ⇒ Dictionary ()

aDictionary detect: [:value | value <= #Value1] ifNone: [0] ⇒ Value1

aDictionary inject: '' into: [:string :value | string, value] ⇒ 'Value1Value2'
     "Note: the comma is a concatenation operation."
```

We mentioned above that experts would use the **inject:into:** method for adding, multiplying, or generally operating on successive elements. For some additional examples, consider the following. Note that the comma message; i.e., "," is a string (and more generally a collection) concatenation operator. We first present the novice approach (using **do:**) and then the expert approach (using **inject:into:**). Note that the expert approach eliminates the need to define a temporary variable.

The novice approach

```
| product |
product ← 1.
(1 to: 6) do: [element | product ← product * element].
product ⇒ 720 (note: this is equivalent to 6 factorial)

| string |
string ← ''.
(Collection subclasses) do: [element |
     string ← string = '' ifTrue: [element name] ifFalse: [string, ' ', element name]].
string ⇒ 'Set Bag Dictionary OrderedCollection ...'

| count |
count ← 0.
aCollection do: [element |
     (element isKindOf: Collection) ifTrue: [count ← count + 1]].
count ⇒ 7 "The number of elements that are themselves collections."
```

The expert approach

```
(1 to: 6) inject: 1 into: [:product :element | product * element]
     ⇒ 720 (note: this is equivalent to 6 factorial)

(Collection subclasses) inject: '' into: [:string :element |
     string = '' ifTrue: [element name] ifFalse: [string, ' ', element name]]
     ⇒ 'Set Bag Dictionary OrderedCollection ...'

aCollection inject: 0 into: [:count :element:
     (element isKindOf: Collection) ifTrue: count + 1] ifFalse: count
     ⇒ 7 "The number of elements that are themselves collections."
```

Designing Your Own Sequencing Operations

In order to provide corresponding sequencing operations, it is sufficient to understand how to invoke blocks; namely,

- aBlock **value**
- aBlock **value**: aParameter
- aBlock **value**: aParameter **value**: anotherParameter

The sequencing operation is implemented by considering the individual elements and then invoking the block with each element in turn. When implementing new sequencing operations, care must be taken to ensure that the elements are passed to the block in the proper order.

As a simple example, consider extending integers by adding **do:** and **reverseDo:** operations that sequence through the individual digits:

```
do: aBlock
    "Evaluate aBlock with each of the receiver's digits as parameter; process the digits
    from left to right. The sign is ignored. The receiver is returned."
    | value rightmostDigit |
    self < 0 ifTrue: [↑self negated do: aBlock].
    self < 10 ifTrue: [aBlock value: self].
    rightmostDigit ← self \\ 10. "The remainder"
    (self // 10) do: aBlock. "Do the leftmost digits first"
    aBlock value: rightmostDigit "Do the rightmost digit last"

reverseDo: aBlock
    "Evaluate aBlock with each of the receiver's digits as parameter; process the digits
    from right to left. The sign is ignored. The receiver is returned."
    | value rightmostDigit |
    self < 0 ifTrue: [↑self negated do: aBlock].
    self < 10 ifTrue: [aBlock value: self].
    rightmostDigit ← self \\ 10. "The remainder"
    aBlock value: rightmostDigit. "Do the rightmost digit first"
    (self // 10) reverseDo: aBlock "Do the leftmost digits last"
```

On a grander scale, it is easy to define new sequencing operations. For instance, consider defining a more specific operation **collect:when:** with two blocks, a block for constructing new values and a block for determining whether or not to construct new values. We will define it as an operation in class Array. Had we decided to add it to class Integer instead, we would have additionally had to define the method **species** for Integer to return the class Array.

```
collect: aValueConstructingBlock when: aTestingBlock
    "Evaluates aTestingBlock with each of the receiver's elements as the argument. If
    the result is true, it computes a new value using aValueConstructingBlock. The new
    values are collected together and returned as an array."
    | newCollection |
    newCollection ← OrderedCollection new.
    self do: [:element |
        (aTestingBlock value: element)
            ifTrue: [newCollection add: (aValueConstructingBlock value: element)]].
    ↑newCollection asArray
```

In order to generalize **collect:when:** for all collections, we need a technique for converting 'newCollection' to the receiver's species. This is difficult with the existing techniques for type conversion. What would be needed is the ability to write

> self **species convert:** newCollection

The alternative is to provide this method everywhere that **collect:** is now provided. In abstract class **ArrayedCollection**, the last line of the above method is replaced by

> convertedCollection ← self **species new:** newCollection **size**
> Additional code to copy the elements from newCollection into convertedCollection.

In **OrderedCollection**, it is replaced by

> convertedCollection ← self **species new**
> Additional code to copy the elements from newCollection into convertedCollection.

One of the reasons Smalltalk is so powerful is that it permits (and generally encourages) users to generalize. This flexibility often provides alternative (and usually simpler) techniques for reimplementing existing methods.

For instance, having provided **collect:when:** to all classes that already provide **do:**, it is tempting to look for a small subset of the sequencing operations that can be used to implement the others. If we refer to the subset as **primitives** and to the others as **nonprimitives**, we could implement the nonprimitives once, say in Object — with the understanding that they are valid only if the primitives are valid. When defining new classes that require sequencing operations, designers would only need to provide the primitive sequencing operations (assuming they were not already inherited). The only reason for providing alternative definitions for the nonprimitives would be efficiency considerations.

For example, we could postulate that **do:**, **reverseDo:**, and **collect:when:** are suitable primitives and attempt to define the others in terms of these three. Actually, a more careful analysis would likely also provide a **reverseCollect:when:**, **keysDo:**, and perhaps even **reverseKeysDo:** as primitives.

As an exercise in implementing sequencing operations, consider the following selected operations, implemented solely in terms of **do:**, **reverseDo:**, and **collect:when:**.

collect: aBlock
> "Evaluates aBlock with each of the receiver's elements as the argument. Collects the resulting values into a collection like the receiver. Returns the new collection."
> ↑self **collect:** aBlock **when:** [:value | true]. "All elements are collected."

select: aBlock
> "Evaluates aBlock with each of the receiver's elements as the argument. Collects into a new collection like the receiver only those elements for which aBlock evaluates to true. Returns the new collection."
> ↑self **collect** : [:element | element] **when:** aBlock "Only the true subset is collected."

reject: aBlock
> "Evaluates aBlock with each of the receiver's elements as the argument. Collects into a new collection like the receiver only those elements for which aBlock evaluates to false. Returns the new collection."
> ↑self **select:** [:element | (aBlock **value:** element) == false] "The false subset ."

detect: aBlock
> "Evaluates aBlock with each of the receiver's elements as the argument. Returns the first element for which aBlock evaluates to true."
> ↑self **detect:** aBlock **ifNone:** [self **error:** 'no elements detected']

detect: aBlock **ifNone**: exceptionBlock
> "Evaluates aBlock with each of the receiver's elements as the argument. Returns the first element for which aBlock evaluates to true. If none evaluate to true, then evaluates the argument, exceptionBlock."
> self
>> **collect**: [:unused |]
>> **when**: [:value | (aBlock **value**: value) **ifTrue**: [↑value] **ifFalse**: [false]].
>
> "The collect block is never invoked since the when block either returns from this method with a value or returns false indicating the element is not to be collected."
> ↑exceptionBlock **value**

inject: thisValue **into**: binaryBlock
> "Accumulates a running value associated with evaluating the argument, binaryBlock, with the current value of the argument, thisValue, and the receiver as block arguments. For instance, to sum the numeric elements of a collection, use
>> aCollection **inject**: 0 **into**: [:subTotal :next | subTotal + next]."
>
> | nextValue |
> nextValue ← thisValue.
> self **do**: [:each | nextValue ← binaryBlock **value**: nextValue **value**: each].
> ↑nextValue

with: aCollection **do**: aBlock
> "Evaluates aBlock with each of the receiver's elements along with the corresponding element from aCollection."
> | aStreamOnACollection |
> self **size** ~= aCollection **size** **ifTrue**: [↑self **error**: 'unequal-sized collections'].
> aStreamOnACollection ← ReadStream **on**: aCollection.
> self **do**: [:receiverElement |
>> aBlock **value**: receiverElement **value**: aStreamOnACollection **next**]

8.2 THE KEYED COLLECTIONS (NON-STREAMS)

The **keyed** collections (excluding streams) are characterized by the array-like operations for accessing and modifying elements associated with individual keys; e.g.,

- aKeyedCollection **at**: aKey   (subscripting operation)
- aKeyedCollection **at**: aKey **put**: aValue   (element modification)

Streams are logically also keyed collections since they provide direct access to the elements via corresponding methods; e.g.,

- aStream **position**: anIntegerKey   (subscript specification)
- aStream **next**   (subscripting)
- aKeyedCollection **nextPut**: aValue   (element modification)

Streams are considered in detail in a separate section. The keyed classes (exclusive of streams) are members of collection classes — they can be partitioned into two groups: the **arbitrary-keyed** classes and the **integer-keyed** classes. Those classes that permit arbitrary objects to be keys are **dictionaries** and those that permit only integer keys include **arrays**, **ordered collections**, and **strings** (and their variations). All keyed collections associate exactly one element with each key. However, not all keyed collections use the same operation for comparing keys — the **key matching** operation. Two distinct key matching operations are used: **equality** and **identity**. All integer-keyed classes use equality for matching keys. However, dictionaries use equality while identity dictionaries use identity. Thus instances of **Dictionary** are actually **equality dictionaries** (although the class name does not make this explicit). Instances of **IdentityDictionary** are clearly **identity dictionaries**.

An equality dictionary permits a new value to be associated with an old key if the new key is equal to the old; an identity dictionary permits it only if the keys are identical. In either case, associating a value with a key that does not already exist causes that key and value to be inserted. Integer keyed collection, on the other hand, will associate a new value with the key only if that key already exists. If it doesn't exist, a subscript out of bounds error will result. Thus neither arrays, strings, or even ordered collections can subscript out of bounds — the latter in particular can be made to grow with special operations like **addFirst:** and **addLast:** but not with the **at:put:** operation.

Additionally, there exists a specialization of **Dictionary** called **LiteralDictionary**, which uses both **value equality** and **class identity** for the key matching operation; e.g., even though they are equal, keys 1 and 1.0 would be distinct keys since they are not of the same class. For examples that distinguish between dictionaries and identity dictionaries, consider the following:

string1 ← 'a string with these characters'. string2 ← string1 **copy**.
string1 = string2 ⇒ **true**   string1 == string2 ⇒ **false**
anEqualityDictionary ← Dictionary **new**   anIdentityDictionary ← IdentityDictionary **new**
anEqualityDictionary **at:** string1 **put:** 1   anIdentityDictionary **at:** string1 **put:** 1
anEqualityDictionary **at:** string2 **put:** 2   anIdentityDictionary **at:** string2 **put:** 2
anEqualityDictionary **at:** string1 ⇒ 2   anIdentityDictionary **at:** string1 ⇒ 1
anEqualityDictionary **at:** string2 ⇒ 2   anIdentityDictionary **at:** string2 ⇒ 2

For the equality dictionary, both string1 and string2 represent the same key since they are equal. Hence, the second **at:put:** actually changes the value associated with string2 (and therefore string1) to 2 — the old value 1 is modified. For the identity dictionary, string1 and string2 represent distinct keys since they are not identical — hence, two values are maintained. A similar distinction can be made between dictionaries and literal dictionaries. We leave it to the reader to come up with the corresponding example.

Dictionaries tend to be accessed via the sequencing operations since the keys are so general and typically unknown. With integer-keyed collections like arrays and ordered collections, on the other hand, accessing is more key-based. Subscripts for all integer-keyed collections start at 1 and are bounded by the size of the collection; i.e., the number of elements they actually contain. Recall that arrays are fixed-size while ordered collections can grow and shrink automatically.

8.2.1 Individual Characterizations

The keyed collections are distinguishable along several dimensions (see Fig. 8.5). **Identity dictionaries** are more general than **dictionaries** (actually equality dictionaries) — logically, every dictionary can be converted to an identity dictionary but not the other way around (physically, the hierarchy is actually reversed). **Literal dictionaries** are a specialization of **dictionaries. Mapped collections** maintain two collections, one that maps an input set of keys to an intermediate set (the mapping collection) and the other that maps the intermediate keys to their associated values. **Dictionaries** grow automatically to accommodate new entries. **Arrays** and **run arrays** do not, although a special grow operation is provided for explicitly growing the collections. **Strings**, **text**, and **symbols** are specialized character arrays. **Intervals** are special integer arrays specifying an arithmetic sequence. They are primarily used for looping control.

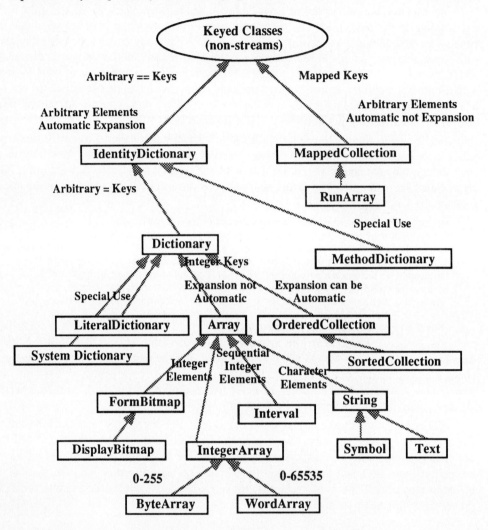

Figure 8.5 The keyed classes — a logical view.

8.2.2 Constructing New Keyed Collections

We consider increasingly sophisticated techniques for constructing keyed collections (other than streams): those that construct empty collections (where allowed), those that construct small collections (one message send is sufficient), and, finally, those that construct large collections (multiple message sends are required). The conversion operations discussed previously are omitted.

The keyed collections are constructed differently depending on whether or not the keys are integers. A summary follows:

General keys (all Dictionary Classes)

- aDictionaryClass **new**
- aDictionaryClass **new**: anInitialSize   (power of 2 for **IdentityDictionary**)
- (*anyCodeForCreatingANewDictionary*)

  > **at**: aKey$_1$ **put**: aValue$_1$;
  > **at**: aKey$_2$ **put**: aValue$_2$;
  > ...
  > **at**: aKey$_n$ **put**: aValue$_n$;
  > **yourself**

Integer keys (all Array classes except those shown below)

- anIntegerKeyedClass **new**
- anIntegerKeyedClass **new**: aMaximumSize
- anIntegerKeyedClass **new**: aMaximumSize **withAll**: anObject
- anIntegerKeyedClass **with**: object$_1$
- anIntegerKeyedClass **with**: object$_1$ **with**: object$_2$
- anIntegerKeyedClass **with**: object$_1$ **with**: object$_2$ **with**: object$_3$
- anIntegerKeyedClass **with**: object$_1$ **with**: object$_2$ **with**: object$_3$ **with**: object$_4$
- (*anyCodeForCreatingALargeEnoughIntegerKeyedCollection*)

  > **at**: aKey$_1$ **put**: aValue$_1$;
  > **at**: aKey$_2$ **put**: aValue$_2$;
  > ...
  > **at**: aKey$_n$ **put**: aValue$_n$;
  > **yourself**

Integer keys (ordered collection classes — see ordered classes for more details)

- anOrderedCollectionClass **new**
- anOrderedCollectionClass **with**: object$_1$
- anOrderedCollectionClass **with**: object$_1$ **with**: object$_2$
- anOrderedCollectionClass **with**: object$_1$ **with**: object$_2$ **with**: object$_3$
- anOrderedCollectionClass **with**: object$_1$ **with**: ...$_2$ **with**: ...$_3$ **with**: object$_4$
- (*anyCodeForCreatingALargeEnoughOrderedCollection*)

  > **add**: aValue$_1$;
  > **add**: aValue$_2$;
  > ...
  > **add**: aValue$_n$;
  > **yourself**

Interval

- Interval **from**: aNumber **to**: aNumber
- Interval **from**: aNumber **to**: aNumber **by**: aNumber
- aNumber **to**: aNumber
- aNumber **to**: aNumber **by**: aNumber

Symbol and Text

- aString **asSymbol** (symbols are almost always created this way)
- Text **string**: aString **emphasis**: 1 "for bold, 2 for italic, 4 for underlined"
- Text
    > **string**: aString
    >
    > **runs**: (RunArray **runs**: anArrayOfCounts **values**: anArrayOfEmphasis)

RunArray and MappedCollection

- RunArray **runs**: anArrayOfCounts **values**: anArrayOfPairwiseDistinctElements
- MappedCollection **collection**: collectionOfElements **map**: aMappingCollection
- anArray **mappedBy**: aMappingCollection

We mentioned above that dictionaries grow automatically as needed when space in the collection is exhausted. However, integer-keyed collections do not. Consequently, inserting elements outside the bounds of an integer-keyed collection will result in a **subscript out of bounds error**. This can only be guarded against by explicit testing in the usual way; e.g., as follows:

> aKey **between**: 1 **and**: anIntegerKeyedCollection **size**

If the collection is too small, it can be grown by executing the following:

> anIntegerKeyedCollection **grow**
> anIntegerKeyedCollection **growToAtLeast**: anInteger

In the first case, the collection usually grows by a percentage of the existing size. Hence there is no way of ensuring that the collection has grown large enough to accommodate the new key. The first method makes sense only if you need to grow by 1 element; e.g., if you were using an array as a stack and you could tolerate or take advantage of the fact that it might grow by more than one element.

On the other hand, if integer-keyed collections need to be grown explicitly, you are probably using the wrong kind of collection. Perhaps you should be using an ordered collection which can grow or shrink automatically when new elements are added or old elements removed. But beware — as we mentioned previously, for ordered collections, using a subscript out of bounds is not interpreted as a request to grow the collection. It is an error — just as it is for arrays. The ordered collection will only grow if new elements are added using messages like **add:**, **addFirst:**, and **addLast:**.

An easy mistake to make when creating integer-keyed collections is to make one too small. In fact, the more common mistake is to create an empty one; e.g., by executing "Array **new**" and then proceeding to add elements to the array. An immediate subscript out of bounds error occurs. Note that such arrays must not be forbidden since they are useful. For example, selecting all elements of an array which are strings beginning with a capital letter will result in an array containing the results (assuming sequence operation **select:** was used). If there are no such strings, then the array will be empty.

When fixed-size integer-keyed collections are created, all elements from 1 to the maximum size are specially initialized with a default element. For arrays, this default element is **nil**, for byte arrays it is 0, and for strings it is the character blank. For varying-sized integer-keyed collections like ordered collections, the collection itself keeps track of the actual number of elements used since it grows itself automatically when new elements are added. Hence there are no default uninitialized elements. The ordered collection contains only what has been explicitly added.

Although it is not specifically mentioned above, it is also possible to create initialized dictionaries using the integer-keyed methods **with:**, **with:with:**, **with:with:with:**, and **with:with:with:with:** as long as the elements are associations. See the section on dictionaries for a more complete discussion of associations. An example is

```
Dictionary
    with: (Association key: #One value: #A)
    with: (Association key: #Two value: #An)
```

Text strings are usually obtained by converting standard strings. For special applications, however, it is necessary to emphasize parts of the string; e.g., to bold face or italicize some of the characters. Text string emphasis is currently specified with an integer: 1 for **bold**, 2 for *italic*, 4 for underlined, and so on. This can also be mixed; e.g., 1 **bitAnd:** 2 (producing 3) gives ***bold italic***.

Some examples involving the creation of keyed collections include:

General keys
- anEmptyDictionary ← Dictionary **new**.
- anEmptyIdentityDictionaryWithAnInitialSize ← IdentityDictionary **new:** 128.
- aSmallDictionary ← Dictionary **new**
    at: #Jack **put:** #Jill; **at:** 'John' **put:** 'Wilf'; **at:** 1 **put:** #Dave; **yourself**.

Integer keys
- notAVeryUsefulArray ← Array **new**.
- anArrayOf100Nils ← Array **new:** 100.
- anArrayOf100Zeros ← Array **new:** 100 **withAll:** 0.
- anArrayWithOneElement ← Array **with:** #OneElement.
- anArrayWithTwoElements ← Array **with:** 1 **with:** 2.
- anArrayWithThreeElementsOneOfWhichIsItselfAnArray ←
    Array **with:** #Apple **with:** 'pear' **with:** (Array **with:** 'Internal potato').
- anArrayWithFourElements ← Array **with:** 1 **with:** 1.2 **with:** (1/3) **with:** 'four' **size**.
- anArrayWithFiveElements ← (Array **new:** 5)
    at: 1 **put:** 'one hot dog';   **at:** 2 **put:** 'two hamburgers';
    at: 3 **put:** 'three soft drinks'; **at:** 4 **put:** 'four candies';
    at: 5 **put:** 'five gum sticks';   **yourself**.
- anOrderedCollectionWithOneElement ← OrderedCollection **with:** #soup.
- anOrderedCollectionWithTwoElements ← OrderedCollection **with:** 1 **with:** 2.
- anEmptyCollection ← OrderedCollection **new:** 10. "10 is only an initial guess"
- aUsefulOrderedCollection ← OrderedCollection **new**.
- aUsefulOrderedCollection **add:** 1; **add:** 2; **add:** 3.
- anotherUsefulOrderedCollection ← OrderedCollection **new**
    add: 'one hot dog';
    add 'two hamburgers';
    yourself.

Exceptional keyed collections

- 'Santa' **asSymbol**
- aBoldKing ← Text **string**: 'king' **emphasis**: 1. "for bold"
- twoBoldKings ← Text
  - **string**: 'the first king said hello to the second king'
  - **runs**: (RunArray **runs**: #(10 4 26 4) **values**: #(0 1 0 1)). "0 normal, 1 bold"
- oneHundredXsFollowedByThreeYs ← RunArray **runs**: (100 3) **values**: #(X Y).
- aMappedCollection ← MappedCollection
  - **collection**: aSmallDictionary "See General Keys above"
  - **map**: (Array **with**: #Jack **with**: 'John' **with**: 1).
  - aMappedCollection **at**: 1 ⇒ Jill.   (1 maps to #Jack with associated value #Jill)
  - aMappedCollection **at**: 2 ⇒ 'Wilf'.   (2 maps to 'John' with associated value 'Wilf')
  - aMappedCollection **at**: 3 ⇒ Dave.   (3 maps to 1 with associated value #Dave)
- aMappingCollection ← #(2 3 1).   (maps 1 to 2, 2 to 3, and 3 to 1; i.e., rotates)
  - anotherView ← #(left middle right) **mappedBy**: aMappingCollection
  - anotherView **at**: 1 ⇒ middle.   (1 maps to 2 with associated value #middle)
  - anotherView **at**: 2 ⇒ right.   (2 maps to 3 with associated value #right)
  - anotherView **at**: 3 ⇒ left.   (3 maps to 1 with associated value #left)
- interval1 ← (Interval **from**: 1 **to**: 2). interval1 **do**: ["nothing"].
  - interval2 ← Interval **from**: 1 **to**: 10 **by**: 3.   interval3 ← 1 **to**: 10 **by**: 3.

Ordered collections and sorted collections have many of the same instance creation operations as the keyed collections.

8.2.3 The Dictionary Protocol

IdentityDictionaries and **Dictionaries** are array-like containers for objects that are associated with arbitrary keys. Only one object is associated with each key. Two different rules are used for deciding when two keys match. For **identity dictionaries**, two keys **match** if they are **identical**; for **dictionaries**, they **match** if they are **equal**. Hence, a more descriptive term for **dictionary** would have been **equality dictionary**. Alternatively, identity dictionaries and dictionaries can be viewed as unordered collections of **associations**. **Associations** are key/value pairs with a very simple creation and accessing protocol. Corresponding to this unordered collection view, there exists some (but not many) operations for accessing the associations. These operations are provided indirectly as a side effect of the chosen implementation strategy. Identity dictionaries and dictionaries are not provided with the string-like protocol that their integer-keyed variations, arrays, strings, and ordered collections are provided with. To summarize:

- Dictionaries and identity dictionaries can be viewed as arrays with subscripts of arbitrary type or unordered collections of associations.
- When viewed as arrays, dictionaries and identity dictionaries are provided with the usual array-like protocol, but they are also provided with some extensions for dealing with associations directly.
- Although integer-keyed collections have string-like operations for operations like concatenations and taking subcollections, the dictionary classes do not.

- When viewed as unordered collections, dictionaries and identity dictionaries are provided with a limited set-like protocol. However, this protocol is more appropriately viewed as private and is provided primarily as a side effect of this particular implementation.
- IdentityDictionary uses == for key comparisons whereas Dictionary uses =. We refer to == and = for the respective dictionaries as the **key matching** operation.

The Association Protocol

Associations are key/value pairs — they are a specialization of magnitudes whereby **comparisons are based only on keys**. Consequently, they are provided with all the usual comparison operations in addition to the following specialized operations for accessing and changing both the key and value parts.

- Association **key**: key **value**: aValue   (to obtain a new association)

- anAssociation **key**   (to extract the association
- anAssociation **value**   components)

- anAssociation **key**: anObject   (to modify the association
- anAssociation **value**: anObject   components)
- anAssociation **key**: anObject **value**: anObject

Although dictionaries and identity dictionaries can be viewed as collections of associations, this viewpoint need not be reflected in the implementation. In particular, it is not necessary to actually store associations as long as they can be materialized when required. Whether or not this is done, however, can result in small but noticeable differences in the semantics of the operations. For example, if associations are physically stored, operations like **associationAt:** and **associationsDo:** can be designed to provide either the actual association contained or a copy. If they are not physically stored, the same operations must provide newly manufactured associations — they appear to users as copies. The same semantics can be maintained for two implementations of dictionaries (one for dictionary and another for identity dictionary) if either (a) both classes physically store the associations, (b) both avoid physically storing the associations, or (c) both use copy semantics.

In Smalltalk, dictionaries physically store associations and provide them without copying, but identity dictionaries store keys and values separately and consequently materialize associations when required (copying semantics). The semantic differences are subtle and usually (but not always) inconsequential. For example, the following sequencing operations provide the receiver's associations in the case of dictionaries but only copies of the receiver's associations in the case of identity dictionaries.

```
aDictionary associationsDo: [:anAssociation | ...]
    provides the dictionary's associations.
anIdentityDictionary associationsDo: [:anAssociation | ...]
    provides copies of the dictionary's associations.
```

The semantic differences above are obvious. However, the implications may not be so clear cut. When problems arise, it may be necessary to understand the subtle differences in order to isolate the cause of the difficulty. For an example of a more subtle problem, consider the following. An observant user rightfully observes that anOldDictionary is being unexpectedly modified by the last modification to aNewDictionary.

```
anOldDictionary ← Dictionary new at: #Test put: #Value; yourself.
aNewDictionary ← anOldDictionary select: [:aValue | true]. "Select all the associations"
aNewDictionary at: #Test put: #SomethingElse.
anOldDictionary printString ⇒ 'Dictionary (Test->SomethingElse)'
```

Somehow, modifying aNewDictionary is affecting anOldDictionary! Why? The **select:** operation is provided with those associations in anOldDictionary that satisfy the select block — the same associations (not copies) are used to construct the new dictionary. The new dictionary actually **shares** the same associations as the old. Changing an **existing** association in the new dictionary actually results in modification to the association (only the value part is modified). Hence, both dictionaries are changed. Asking for a copy of the **select:** result doesn't help because the new dictionary constructed also shares the same associations. One solution is to ask for a **deepCopy** of the dictionary. Of course, this is unsatisfactory if we don't want copies of the values. A better alternative is to explicitly create a new dictionary with copies of the associations but without copies of the keys or values. Equivalently, we could add a special copy operation for Dictionary as follows:

```
copy
    | aDictionary |
    aDictionary ← Dictionary new.
    self associationsDo: [:anAssociation |
        aDictionary at: anAssociation key put: anAssociation value].
    ↑aDictionary
```

The fact that the existing copy operation does not work this way may be just an oversight (the existing copy operation simply produces a shallow copy — a new dictionary with identical associations). Another alternative might be to revise the **select:** operation.

On the other hand, the above problems are not encountered very often because most dictionaries are explicitly created by users for their specific application.

The Array-like Protocol

Viewed as arrays, identity dictionaries and dictionaries have the standard operations for accessing and changing the values associated with the keys. Because the keys can be arbitrary objects, special operations must also be provided for determining whether or not values are associated with specific keys and for obtaining all the keys. Additionally, operations are provided for accessing both keys and values simultaneously as associations. Accessing successive elements of a dictionary is usually done via the sequencing operations (repeated later for completeness).

size determination

- aDictionary **size**
    Returns the number of associations in the dictionary.
- aDictionary **isEmpty**
    Returns whether or not the size is zero.

- aDictionary **at**: key {**ifAbsent**: aBlock}

  The value associated with a key that **matches**. If no match is found, returns the result of evaluating aBlock (if there is one); otherwise, an error is reported.

- aDictionary **at**: key **put**: anObject

  Associates anObject with the key that **matches**. If no previous value was associated, creates a new association; otherwise, modifies the existing association. Returns anObject.

additional key-value operations

- aDictionary **includesKey**: key

  Returns whether or not the receiver has a key that **matches** the specified key.

- aDictionary **includesAssociation**: anAssociation

  Returns whether or not the receiver has a key that **matches** the specified association's key.

- aDictionary **removeKey**: key {**ifAbsent**: aBlock}

  If the receiver has an association with a **matching** key, removes it and returns the value associated with the key. If the receiver has no corresponding association, returns the result of evaluating aBlock (if there is one); otherwise, an error is reported.

- aDictionary **removeAssociation**: association {**ifAbsent**: aBlock}

  Same as above except that an association is provided instead of a key and the association is returned.

- aDictionary **associationAt**: key {**ifAbsent**: aBlock}

  An association whose key **matches** the specified key. If no match is found, returns the result of evaluating aBlock (if there is one); otherwise, an error is reported. More specifically, dictionaries return a unique contained association whereas identity dictionaries return a copy.

- aDictionary **keyAtValue**: aValue {**ifAbsent**: exceptionBlock}

  Returns any key whose value is **identical** to aValue. If there is none, the result of evaluating exceptionBlock is returned (if there is one); otherwise, an error is reported.

- aDictionary **keys**

  Returns a set containing the receiver's keys.

- aDictionary **values**

  Returns a Bag containing the receiver's values.

- aDictionary **associations**

  Returns an ordered collection containing the receiver's associations. More specifically, dictionaries return the unique contained associations whereas identity dictionaries return copies.

The **keyAtValue:** methods are designed for obtaining the key associated with a given value. Unfortunately, it is of limited utility since the same value could be associated with different keys. The method could be used to implement a more sophisticated query method.

For example, we could introduce

includesValue: value
      ↑self **keyAtValue**: value **ifAbsent**: [↑false]. ↑true

which returns whether or not the receiver has an association whose value is **identical** to the specified value.

More general methods that return all keys and that use equality instead of identity could be designed; e.g.,

keysAtValue: aValue **ifAbsent**: exceptionBlock
    "Returns a set containing the keys whose associated values are equal to aValue."
    | aSet |
    aSet ← Set new.
    self **associationsDo**: [:anAssociation |
        anAssociation **value** = aValue **ifTrue**: [aSet **add**: anAssociation **key**]].
    ↑aSet

Examples

dictionary1 ← Dictionary **new**.
dictionary2 ← Dictionary **new** at: #One **put**: #Red; **at**: #Two **put**: #Blue; **yourself**.

dictionary1 **printString** ⇒ 'Dictionary ()'
dictionary2 **printString** ⇒ 'Dictionary (One->Red Two->Blue)'

dictionary1 **size** ⇒ 0
dictionary2 **size** ⇒ 2
dictionary1 **isEmpty** ⇒ **true**
dictionary2 **isEmpty** ⇒ **false**

dictionary1 **includesKey**: #One ⇒ **false**
dictionary2 **includesKey**: #One ⇒ **true**
dictionary1 **includesAssociation**: (Association **key**: #One **value**: #Yellow) ⇒ **false**
dictionary2 **includesAssociation**: (Association **key**: #One **value**: #Yellow) ⇒ **true**
dictionary1 **at**: #One ⇒ (error)
dictionary1 **at**: #One **ifAbsent**: [#NotFound] ⇒ NotFound
dictionary2 **at**: #One ⇒ Red
dictionary2 **associationAt**: #One ⇒ One->Red
dictionary2 **associationAt**: #Two ⇒ Two->Blue

dictionary1 **at**: #One **put**: #Green
dictionary2 **at**: #One **put**: #Green
dictionary1 **printString** ⇒ 'Dictionary (One->Green)'
dictionary2 **printString** ⇒ 'Dictionary (One->Green Two->Blue)'

dictionary1 **removeKey**: #One ⇒ Green
dictionary2 **removeKey**: #One ⇒ Green
dictionary1 **printString** ⇒ 'Dictionary ()'
dictionary2 **printString** ⇒ 'Dictionary (Two->Blue)'

dictionary1 **at**: #One **put**: #Blue
dictionary2 **at**: #One **put**: #Blue
dictionary1 **printString** ⇒ 'Dictionary (One->Blue)'
dictionary2 **printString** ⇒ 'Dictionary (Two->Blue One->Blue)'
dictionary1 **keyAtValue**: #Blue ⇒ One
dictionary2 **keyAtValue**: #Blue ⇒ Two (which key you get is arbitrary)

Examples (continued)

dictionary1 **keys** ⇒ Set (One)
dictionary2 **keys** ⇒ Set (Two One)
dictionary1 **values** ⇒ Bag (Blue)
dictionary2 **values** ⇒ Bag (Blue Blue)
dictionary1 **associations** ⇒ OrderedCollection (One->Blue)
dictionary2 **associations** ⇒ OrderedCollection (Two->Blue One->Blue)

dictionary2 **printString** ⇒ 'Dictionary (Two->Blue One->Blue)'
dictionary2 **removeAssociation:** (Association **key:** #One **value:** #Red)
      ⇒ One->Blue Note: only the key was used for comparison purposes.
dictionary2 **printString** ⇒ 'Dictionary (Two->Blue)'

The Set-like Protocol

Since dictionaries can be viewed as collections of associations, they have a corresponding protocol that is set-like in nature. On the other hand, the "collections of associations" viewpoint is not meant so much for the user as it is for the implementor of the dictionary class — they might have been better categorized as **private**. Consequently, the protocol provided is rather minimal. Additionally, some of the inherited operations may not even be intended.

construction operations

- aDictionaryClass **with:** association$_1$
- aDictionaryClass **with:** association$_1$ **with:** association$_2$
- aDictionaryClass **with:** association$_1$ **with:** association$_2$ **with:** association$_3$
- aDictionaryClass **with:** association$_1$ **with:** ...$_2$ **with:** ...$_3$ **with:** association$_4$
     Returns a new dictionary with 1 through 4 associations respectively (assuming none have keys that **match**).
- aDictionary **add:** anAssociation
     Either adds the new association if no other association with **matching** key was there or modifies the existing one by changing its value to the new value. Returns anAssociation — this is not necessarily the same association contained by the dictionary.
- aDictionary **addAll:** anIntegerKeyedOrUnorderedCollectionOfAssociations
     Adds each element of the collection to the receiver. Returns the collection.

testing operations

- aDictionary **includes:** anAssociation
     Returns true if it contains an association with a **matching** key.
- aDictionary **occurrencesOf:** anAssociation
     Returns the number of associations with **matching** keys.

Examples

dictionary1 ← IdentityDictionary **new.**
dictionary2 ← IdentityDictionary
     with: (Association **key:** #One **value:** #Red)
     with: (Association **key:** #Two **value:** #Blue).

dictionary1 **printString** ⇒ 'IdentityDictionary ()'
dictionary2 **printString** ⇒ 'IdentityDictionary (One->Red Two->Blue)'

Examples (continued)

dictionary1 **includes**: (Association **key**: #One **value**: #Green) ⇒ **false**   (only keys
dictionary2 **includes**: (Association **key**: #One **value**: #Green) ⇒ **true**   are matched)

dictionary1 **add**: (Association **key**: #One **value**: #Green)
dictionary2 **add**: (Association **key**: #One **value**: #Green)
dictionary1 **printString** ⇒ 'IdentityDictionary (One->Green)'
dictionary2 **printString** ⇒ 'IdentityDictionary (One->Green Two->Blue)'

dictionary1 **addAll**: (dictionary2 **associations**)
dictionary1 **printString** ⇒ 'IdentityDictionary (One->Green Two->Blue)'
dictionary2 **printString** ⇒ 'IdentityDictionary (One->Green Two->Blue)'

The Sequencing Protocol

The sequencing protocol for dictionaries is repeated in this section both for completeness and because it does not follow the same conventions as other classes of collections. Examples can be looked up in the general section on sequencing operations.

In the following, exceptionBlock requires no parameters, aBlock requires one parameter, and aBinaryBlock requires two.

sequencing operations

- aDictionary **do**: aBlock

    Evaluates aBlock with the successive **values** in the dictionary. Returns the receiver.

- aDictionary **collect**: aBlock

    Evaluates aBlock with the successive **values** in the dictionary. Returns the successive results in a **bag**.

- aDictionary **select**: aBlock

    Returns a new dictionary (of the same class as the receiver) containing copies of all associations for which aBlock returns true when sent only the association's **value**.

- aDictionary **reject**: aBlock

    Same as above but the resulting dictionary contains only those associations for which aBlock returns false.

- aDictionary **detect**: aBlock {**ifNone**: exceptionBlock}

    Returns the first **value** for which aBlock is true. If there are none, the exception block (no parameters) is executed; if no exception block was provided, an error is generated.

- aDictionary **inject**: initialValue **into**: binaryBlock

    Evaluates binaryBlock with initialValue and the first **value**, then again with its result and the second **value**, then its result with the third, and so on. Returns the final result.

- aDictionary **associationsDo**: aBlock

    Evaluates aBlock with the successive associations of the dictionary or identity dictionary. Returns the receiver.

- aDictionary **keysDo**: aBlock

    Evaluates aBlock with the successive keys of the dictionary or identity dictionary. The corresponding value can be obtained via 'aDictionary **at**: aKey'. Returns the receiver.

8.2.4 The Array and OrderedCollection Integer-Keyed Protocol

Arrays and their specializations along with ordered collections are integer-keyed collections with the usual operations for accessing and changing values associated with the integer keys. Additionally, they provide a string-like protocol that permits users to concatenate integer-keyed collections, extract and modify subcollections, and search for special information.

The Array-like Protocol

This protocol provides the usual operations for accessing and modifying elements of arrays and ordered collections. Additionally, special methods are provided for determining the size of an integer-keyed collection, for accessing the first and last elements, and for initializing multiple elements. When initializing an entire integer-keyed collection (or a subcollection) with an initial value, the targetted elements are bound to the same initial value; i.e., distinct elements will be identical (not just equal) since no copy is made of the initial value.

size determination

- anIntegerKeyedCollection **size**
  Returns the number of elements in the collection; i.e., the maximum subscript if fixed-size like an array. The minimum subscript is 1.
- anIntegerKeyedCollection **isEmpty**
  Returns whether or not the size is zero.

traditional subscripting operations

- anIntegerKeyedCollection **at**: key
  Returns the value associated with the integer key. An error is reported if the key is outside the bounds 1 through the collection size.
- anIntegerKeyedCollection **at**: key **put**: anObject
  Associates anObject with the integer key. Returns anObject.

specialized operations

- anIntegerKeyedCollection **first**
  Returns the first element of the receiver; i.e., '**at**: 1'. An error is reported if the receiver contains no elements.
- anIntegerKeyedCollection **last**
  Returns the last element of the receiver; i.e., '**at**: (self **size**)'. An error is reported if the receiver contains no elements.
- anIntegerKeyedCollection **atAll**: anInterval **put**: anObject
  Associates anObject with every key specified by the integer elements of anInterval. Note: does not make a copy of anObject.
- anIntegerKeyedCollection **atAllPut**: anObject
  Associates anObject with every one of the receiver's integer keys. Note: does not make a copy of anObject.

Examples

```
array1 ← Array new. "Something that is not usually intended"
array2 ← Array new: 100.
array3 ← #(Red Blue)
```

Examples (continued)

```
array1 size ⇒ 0
array2 size ⇒ 100
array3 size ⇒ 2

array1 isEmpty ⇒ true
array2 isEmpty ⇒ false
array3 isEmpty ⇒ false

array1 at: 1 ⇒ (error)              "Subscript out of bounds"
array2 at: 1 ⇒ nil                  "All array elements are initialized to nil"
array3 at: 1 ⇒ Red

array3 first ⇒ Red
array3 last ⇒ Blue

array1 at: 1 put: #Green ⇒ (error)   "Subscript out of bounds"
array2 at: 1 put: #Green ⇒ Green
array3 at: 1 put: #Green ⇒ Green

array2 at All: (1 to: 3) put: #Black ⇒ Black
array2 ⇒ (Black Black Black nil nil ... nil)

array3 atAllPut: #Yellow ⇒ Yellow
array3 ⇒ (Yellow Yellow)

orderedCollection1 ← OrderedCollection new.
orderedCollection2 ← OrderedCollection new: 100.
     "Ensures room for 100 elements before growing; 100 is just a hint to help minimize
     automatic growing. It's not a limit nor an initial size."
orderedCollection3 ← #(Red Blue) asOrderedCollection.

orderedCollection1 size ⇒ 0
orderedCollection2 size ⇒ 0           "Note: same size as orderedCollection1."
orderedCollection3 size ⇒ 2

orderedCollection1 isEmpty ⇒ true
orderedCollection2 isEmpty ⇒ true
orderedCollection3 isEmpty ⇒ false

orderedCollection1 at: 1 ⇒ (error)     "Subscript out of bounds"
orderedCollection2 at: 1 ⇒ (error)     "Here too."
orderedCollection3 at: 1 ⇒ Red

orderedCollection3 first ⇒ Red
orderedCollection3 last ⇒ Blue

orderedCollection3 at: 1 put: #Green ⇒ Green
orderedCollection3 ⇒ (Green Blue)

orderedCollection3 add: #Red.
orderedCollection3 at All: (1 to: 2) put: #Black ⇒ Black
orderedCollection2 ⇒ (Black Black #Red)

orderedCollection3 atAllPut: #Yellow ⇒ Yellow
orderedCollection3 ⇒ (Yellow Yellow Yellow)
```

The String-like Protocol

This protocol provides the operations for searching, extracting, and modifying subcollections (subarrays), and for concatenating subcollections. The **destructive** replacement operations begin with **replace...** whereas the **nondestructive** versions begin with **copyReplace....**

searching operations

- anIntegerKeyedCollection **indexOf:** anElement {**ifAbsent:** exceptionBlock}

    Returns the key (index) of the first element in the receiver **equal** to anElement. If there isn't any, returns the result of evaluating the exceptionBlock (if one is provided), otherwise, returns 0.

- anIntegerKeyedCollection **nextIndexOf:** anElement **from:** start **to:** stop

    Returns the key (index) of the first element in the receiver between the specified bounds that is **equal** to anElement. If there isn't any, returns **nil**

- anIntegerKeyedCollection **prevIndexOf:** anElement **from:** start**to:** stop

    As above but processes in the reverse direction.

- anIntegerKeyedCollection **identityIndexOf:** anElement {**ifAbsent:** exceptionBlock}

    Returns the key (index) of the first element in the receiver **identical** to anElement. If there isn't any, returns the result of evaluating the exceptionBlock (if one is provided); otherwise, returns 0.

- anIntegerKeyedCollection **indexOfSubCollection:** aCollection **startingAt:** startIndex {**ifAbsent:** exceptionBlock}

    Returns the key (index) of the first element in the receiver such that a portion of the remaining elements is **equal** to aCollection. The search actually starts at position startIndex. If no equal subcollection is found, returns the result of evaluating the exceptionBlock (if one is provided); otherwise, returns 0. Parameter aCollection must be a collection with integer keys (even dictionaries are allowed if the keys are all consecutive integers starting at 1). Always fails to find an empty collection.

- anIntegerKeyedCollection **includes:** anElement

    Returns true if it contains an element **equal** to anElement; otherwise false.

- anIntegerKeyedCollection **occurrencesOf:** anElement

    Returns the number of elements **equal** to anElement.

destructive replacement operations

- anIntegerKeyedCollection **replaceElement:** oldElement **withElement:** newElement

    Destructively replaces all elements **identical** to oldElement by newElement. Returns the receiver.

- anIntegerKeyedCollection **replaceFrom:** start **to:** stop **with:** aReplacementCollection {**startingAt:** startIndex}

    Destructively replaces all elements in the receiver between start and stop **inclusively** by an equal length prefix of that portion of aReplacement-Collection starting at startIndex. An error results if the replacement is too short; it is truncated if too long. The replacement collection must be a collection with integer keys (even dictionaries are allowed if the keys are all consecutive integers starting at 1). Returns the receiver.

non-destructive replacement operations

- anIntegerKeyedCollection **copyFrom**: start **to**: stop

  Returns a copy of a portion of the receiver starting from key start to key stop **inclusively**. If start is greater than stop by exactly 1, an empty collection is returned.

- anIntegerKeyedCollection **copyReplaceAll**: oldCollection **with**: newCollection

  Returns a copy of the receiver in which all occurrences of oldCollection have been replaced by newCollection. Does not scan the replacement. The two collections must be a collection with integer keys (even dictionaries are allowed if the keys are all consecutive integers starting at 1).

- anIntegerKeyedCollection **copyReplaceFrom**: start **to**: stop **with**: newCollection

  Returns a copy of the receiver in which the portion from key start to key stop **inclusively** is replaced by newCollection. After the replacement, the elements of the new collection begin at key start. The new collection need not be the same size as the portion being replaced. If stop = start -1, i.e., to the left of start, an empty portion is being replaced by the new collection, i.e., an insertion. Interesting special cases occur when start = 1 and stop = 0 (inserts before first element) and when start = self size + 1 and stop = self size (inserts after last element). The same restrictions as above apply to the classes of allowable collections.

- anIntegerKeyedCollection **copyWith**: newElement

  Returns a copy of the receiver that is grown by one element and that has newElement as the last element.

- anIntegerKeyedCollection **copyWithout**: oldElement

  Returns a copy of the receiver in which all elements **equal** to oldElement have been left out.

specialized operations

- anIntegerKeyedCollection , aCollection

  Returns a new collection that is the concatenation of the receiver and aCollection. The elements of the new collection are identical to the elements in the receiver and aCollection; i.e., there are no copies of the elements made. Parameter aCollection must be a collection with integer keys (even dictionaries are allowed if the keys are all consecutive integers starting at 1).

The searching operations could be better organized. For instance, there is no method called **indexOfSubCollection:** or **indexOfSubCollection:ifAbsent:**. Most of them return 0 when a searched for element is not found — exceptions are the methods **nextIndexOf:-from:to:** and **prevIndexOf:from:to:** which return **nil**.

On the other hand, the operations are quite general; e.g., the subcollection being searched for need not be of the same class as the receiver. As long as its elements are equal (or identical — depending on the operation) to corresponding receiver elements, the search will succeed. Intuitively, one would therefore expect that an empty collection would satisfy this description for **any starting point**; i.e., an empty collection should always match. However, in the current design, the empty collection fails to match any subcollection.

There are three operations that perform **destructive** changes to the receiver: **replaceElement:withElement:**, **replaceFrom:to:with:**, and **replaceFrom:to:with:startingAt:**. The last two are not as general as the corresponding **non-destructive** operations that construct new collections. For instance, the destructive variety only permits individual elements to be replaced. It **does not permit** elements to be inserted or removed. Hence, care must be exercised to ensure that replacements are exactly the same size as the portion to be replaced. The nondestructive operations such as **copyReplaceAll:with:** and **copyReplaceFrom:to:with:** permit the replacement to have a size totally different from the portion being replaced. The reason for the difference is that the destructive operations are much more heavily used than the nondestructive variety — the restrictions ensure a much more efficient implementation. In hindsight, an alternative solution can be easily devised:

- Rename **replaceFrom:to:with:** to **inPlaceReplaceFrom:to:with:** (or some better choice of name) so that the functionality is still provided. The same applies to **replaceFrom:to:with:startingAt:**.

- Change the implementation of **replaceFrom:to:with:** to something like:

> **replaceFrom:** start **to:** end **with:** aNewCollection
> ↑self **become:**
>   (self **copyReplaceFrom:** start **to:** end **with:** aNewCollection)

Intuitively, 'X **become:** Y' means "for all objects in the system, change all X references to Y references (and vice versa)". This solution assumes that the **become:** operation is efficient. This is not true of every implementation.

The concatenation operator (comma) is very general and convenient. Moreover, it is a nondestructive operation. Consequently, long series of concatenations can be expensive. For example, 'A, B, C, D' constructs three successive collections with only the last returned — it is $O(n^2)$ for collections of size n. In general, any operation that results in the creation of objects of different sizes are expensive in Smalltalk.

As users of both destructive and nondestructive operations, the important point to remember is the difference in generality between the two varieties. The nondestructive versions are easily distinguishable from the destructive variety because they all start with **copy....**

Examples

```
anArray ← #(The little red fox has a little red foot)
anArray indexOf: #The  ⇒ 1
anArray indexOf: #the  ⇒ 0
anArray indexOf: #little  ⇒ 2
anArray indexOf: #foot  ⇒ 9
anArray indexOf: #rabbit ifAbsent: [anArray size + 1]  ⇒ 10

anArray nextIndexOf: #little from: 3 to: 9  ⇒ 7
anArray prevIndexOf: #little from: 1 to: 5  ⇒ 2
anArray nextIndexOf: #hot from: 3 to: 9  ⇒ nil

aString ← 'hello'.
anArray ← Array with: aString copy with: aString.
anArray identityIndexOf: aString  ⇒ 2
```

anArray ← #(The little red fox has a little red foot)
anArray **indexOfSubCollection:** #() **startingAt:** 1 ⇒ 0 "Not found"
anArray **indexOfSubCollection:** #(The) **startingAt:** 1 ⇒ 1
anArray **indexOfSubCollection:** #(little red) **startingAt:** 1 ⇒ 2
anArray **indexOfSubCollection:** #(little red) **startingAt:** 3 ⇒ 7
anArray **indexOfSubCollection:** #(little red) **startingAt:** 8 **ifAbsent:** [anArray **size** + 1] ⇒ 10

anArray ← #(The little red fox has a little red foot)
anArray **indexOfSubCollection:** (OrderedCollection **with:** #red) **startingAt:** 1 ⇒ 3
anArray **indexOfSubCollection:** (Dictionary **new at:** 1 **put:** #red; **yourself**) **startingAt:** 1 ⇒ 3
anArray **indexOfSubCollection:** (Array **with:** #red) **startingAt:** 1 ⇒ 3

anArray ← #(The little red fox has a little red foot)
anArray **includes:** #the ⇒ **false**
anArray **includes:** #The ⇒ **true**
anArray **includes:** #little ⇒ **true**
anArray **occurrencesOf:** #the ⇒ 0
anArray **occurrencesOf:** #The ⇒ 1
anArray **occurrencesOf:** #little ⇒ 2

aString ← 'hello'.
anArray ← Array **with:** aString **with:** aString **with:** aString **copy with:** 'there'.
anArray ⇒ ('hello' 'hello' 'hello' 'there')

anArray **replaceElement:** aString **withElement:** 'hi'.
anArray ⇒ ('hi' 'hi' 'hello' 'there')

anArray ← Array **with:** 1 **with:** 2 **with:** 3 **with:** 4.
anArray ⇒ (1 2 3 4)
(1 **to:** 3) **collect:** [:position |
    (anArray
        replaceFrom: 2 **to:** 3
        with: (Array **with:** 10 **with:** 20 **with:** 30 **with:** 40)
        startingAt: position) **printString**].
    ⇒ ('(1 10 20 4)' '(1 20 30 4)' '(1 30 40 4)')

anArray ← Array **with:** 1 **with:** 2 **with:** 3 **with:** 4.
anArray ⇒ (1 2 3 4)
(1 **to:** 3) **collect:** [:position |
    (anArray
        replaceFrom: 2 **to:** 3
        with: (OrderedCollection **with:** 10 **with:** 20 **with:** 30 **with:** 40)
        startingAt: position) **printString**].
    ⇒ ('(1 10 20 4)' '(1 20 30 4)' '(1 30 40 4)')

anArray ← Array **with:** 1 **with:** 2 **with:** 3 **with:** 4.
anArray ⇒ (1 2 3 4)
(1 **to:** 4) **collect:** [:position | (anArray **copyFrom:** position **to:** 3) **printString**].
    ⇒ ('(1 2 3)' '(2 3)' '(3)' '()')

aString ← 'abccabc'.
aString **copyReplaceAll:** 'abc' **with:** 'ab'. ⇒ 'abcab'

aString ← 'awo seasaws'.
aString **copyReplaceAll:** 'aw' **with:** 'hell' **asArray**. ⇒ 'hello seashells'

Examples (continued)

```
anArray ← #(Once upon a long long time).
aDictionary ← Dictionary new at: 1 put: #in; at: 2 put: #long; at: 3 put: #ago; yourself.
anArray copyReplaceFrom: 2 to: 5 with: aDictionary.  ⇒ (Once in long ago time)
anArray copyReplaceFrom: 1 to: 0 with: #(NOT).  ⇒ (NOT Once upon a long long time)
anArray copyReplaceFrom: 4 to: 3 with: #(very).  ⇒ (Once upon a very long long time)
anArray copyReplaceFrom: 7 to: 6 with: #(ago).  ⇒ (Once upon a long long time ago)

#(I am here) copyWith: #now.  ⇒ (I am here now)
#(I see I can be I) copyWithout: #I.  ⇒ (see can be)

#(Try again), #(for fun).  ⇒ (Try again for fun)
#(), #().  ⇒ ()
#(), #(Is this OK).  ⇒ (Is this OK)
#(Is this OK), #().  ⇒ (Is this OK)

#(Mix this), (OrderedCollection with: #up with: #now).  ⇒ (Mix this up now)
#(or), (Dictionary new at: 1 put: 'this'; yourself).  ⇒ (or 'this')
#(and), 'this'.  ⇒ (and $t $h $i $s)
#(or), #.this.  ⇒ (or $t $h $i $s)
'or ', 'this'.  ⇒ 'or this'
```

8.2.5 The String, Symbol, and Text Protocol

Strings, symbols, and texts are a family of related classes that manipulate collections of characters. Symbols are variations of strings that have been made unique; texts are variations that have attached font information. Since each is a specialization of array, they are provided with all of the array-like and string-like operations that arrays have; e.g., **copyFrom:to:**, **size**, and "," (the concatenation operator).

Since string constants are surrounded by single quotes, quotes are themselves represented by doubling the quotes. Consequently,

```
'he"s' asArray ⇒ ($h $e $' $s)
'''''' asArray ⇒ ($' $')
String with: $' ⇒ ''''
'a''b' at: 2 ⇒ $'
```

As a general rule, symbols cannot be modified. Consequently, destructive modifications like **at:put:** and **replaceFrom:to:with:startingAt:** are not allowed. Additionally, all string-like operations on symbols return strings rather than the expected new symbol. For one example, both string and symbol concatenation return strings (the comma is the concatenation operator); i.e.,

```
'string1', 'string2'  ⇒ 'string1string2'
#symbol1, #symbol2  ⇒ 'symbol1symbol2'
'string1', #symbol2  ⇒ 'string1symbol2'
```

Collections that serve as parameters to messages sent to strings and symbols need not be as specialized as strings and symbols themselves. In general, such collections are reasonably general. First of all, the elements must be characters. Second, the collections themselves must be integer-keyed collections — even dictionaries are allowed if the keys are all consecutive integers starting at 1.

Collection parameters to text receivers are not as general. In fact, only text is permitted (not even strings or symbols). This is not usually of any consequence since few users actually make use of text in new applications. Its primary use is restricted to the existing text browsers.

The Magnitude Protocol

As implemented, strings and symbols are magnitudes[3] but texts are not. Consequently, strings and symbols are provided with the usual comparison operations: ==, ~~, <, <=, >, >=, =, and ~=. Texts are only provided with ==, ~~, =, and ~=. String and symbol operations <, <=, >, >= treat corresponding uppercase and lowercase characters as equivalent. Operations = and ~= distinguish all characters. Strings and symbols provide an additional operation **sameAs:** that ignores case differences.

Comparisons between instances of different classes are allowed but not consistently across the three classes. However, comparisons are consistent between strings and symbols. Comparison between unequal length strings or symbols uses **null-padding semantics**; i.e., the shorter string is assumed to be padded with '0 **asCharacter**'. In other words, a proper prefix of a string is less than the string itself.

- aStringOrSymbolOrText == aStringOrSymbolOrText
- aStringOrSymbolOrText ~~ aStringOrSymbolOrText
  Identity versus non-identity.

- aStringOrSymbolOrText = aStringOrSymbolOrText
- aStringOrSymbolOrText ~= aStringOrSymbolOrText
  All characters distinguished; cross-class compares inconsistent.

- aStringOrSymbol **sameAs:** aStringOrSymbol
  Like = but case differences ignored.

- aStringOrSymbol < aStringOrSymbol
- aStringOrSymbol <= aStringOrSymbol
- aStringOrSymbol > aStringOrSymbol
- aStringOrSymbol >= aStringOrSymbol
  Uses ascii collating sequence with case differences ignored.

The fact that case differences are ignored for < and > but not ignored for = results in anomalous behavior in some cases. As can be seen from the example below, 'a' < 'A', 'a' > 'A', and 'a' = 'A' are all false.

Examples

```
'hello' = 'Hello' ⇒ false
'hello' sameAs: 'Hello' ⇒ true

'hello' = 'hello' asText ⇒ false
'hello' = #hello ⇒ true
```

---

[3]Logically, they are magnitudes even though they do not inherit from class Magnitude.

Examples (continued)

```
#hello = 'hello'  ⇒ false
#hello = 'hello' asText  ⇒ false

'hello' asText = 'hello'  ⇒ true "Opposite of the above"
'hello' asText = #hello  ⇒ true

'a' < 'A'  ⇒ false
'a' > 'A'  ⇒ false
'a' = 'A'  ⇒ false

'hell' < 'hello'  ⇒ true
'hell' > 'hello'  ⇒ false
'hell' = 'hello'  ⇒ false
'aMan' < 'aWoman'  ⇒ true
'aMan' < 'aBoy'  ⇒ false
```

Note that comparisons between texts and strings give different results depending on the choice of receivers. Text receivers explicitly extract the string parts and compare them. Hence, texts compared with strings work as expected. Strings inherit the = operation — this inherited version insists that both operands be of the same species. Hence, strings compared with texts are never equal (they are different species). The solution is either to not cross-compare or to extend the system.

The String-like Protocol

Because this family of classes inherits from Array, all of its string-like protocol is inherited. For completeness, we list them all without comment. However, new protocol special to this family is described in more detail.

> **Parameter Restrictions**: Unless otherwise noted, collections that serve as parameters to the following methods must contain characters and be integer-keyed collections (dictionaries are allowed if the keys are all consecutive integers starting at 1).

searching operations

- aStringOrSymbolOrText **includes**: anElement
- aStringOrSymbolOrText **occurrencesOf**: anElement
- aStringOrSymbolOrText **indexOf**: anElement {**ifAbsent**: exceptionBlock}
- aStringOrSymbolOrText **indexOfSubCollection**: aCollection **startingAt**: aStart
  {**ifAbsent**: exceptionBlock}
- aStringOrSymbolOrText **findString**: aCollection **startingAt**: aStart
    A better name for the previous method.
- aStringOrSymbol **match**: aStringOrSymbolOrText *
    Compares aStringOrSymbolOrText with the receiver ignoring case differences and returns true or false. Additionally, * in the receiver denotes 0 or more characters; # denotes 1 character. Hence, the following all return true: '(*)' **match**: '(hello)', '*: #' **match**: 'try: 1', and 'why *?' **match**: 'WHY TRY?'.

- aStringOrSymbol **match**: aStringOrSymbolOrText **ignoreCase**: aBoolean[*]

  As above but can additionally prevent case differences from being ignored.
- aStringOrSymbol **spellAgainst**: aStringOrSymbolOrText [*]

  Returns an integer between 0 and 100 indicating how similar aStringOrSymbolOrText is to the receiver. Does not perform case conversions.

destructive replacement operations

- aStringOrSymbol **replaceElement**: oldElement **withElement**: newElement [*]
- aStringOrSymbol **replaceFrom**: start **to**: stop **with**: aReplacementCollection {**startingAt**: aStart} [*]
- aStringOrSymbol **replaceFrom**: start **to**: stop **withByteArray**: aByteArray **startingAt**: aStart [*]

  A specialized version that works for byte arrays. The standard version only works for collections of characters (a byte array is a collection of very small integers).

non-destructive replacement operations

- aStringOrSymbolOrText **copyFrom**: start **to**: stop [**]
- aStringOrSymbolOrText **copyUpTo**: aCharacter

  Returns a copy of a portion of the receiver starting from key 1 up to but excluding the specified character.
- aStringOrSymbolOrText **copyReplaceAll**: oldCollection **with**: newCollection
- aStringOrSymbolOrText **copyReplaceFrom**: start **to**: stop **with**: newCollection
- aStringOrSymbolOrText **copyWith**: newElement [**]
- aStringOrSymbolOrText **copyWithout**: oldElement [**]

specialized operations

- aStringOrSymbolOrText, aCollection [**]

  Comma is the concatenation operator.

Exceptions

[**]: Applicable to strings, symbols, and text with the following restrictions:

    a.   Returns strings for both string and symbol receivers.

    b.   Returns text for text receivers but requires the collection parameters to be text.

[*]: Although these operations are inherited for text, they are applicable only to strings and symbols.

First we consider examples of operations that are not inherited. Inherited operations are considered last.

Examples

'thethethe' **findString**: 'the' **startingAt**: 1 ⇒ 1
'thethethe' **findString**: 'the' **startingAt**: 2 ⇒ 4
'thethethe' **findString**: 'the' **startingAt**: 8 ⇒ 0 "Not found"
'if*then*endif#' **match**: 'if a > b then run. play. eat endif?' ⇒ **true**

Examples (continued)

'*;*' **match**: 'OrderedCollection new add: #test; add #anotherTest' ⇒ **true**
'#+#' **match**: 'a+b' ⇒ **true**
'#+#' **match**: '10+5' ⇒ **false**

'help* **match**: 'help me' ⇒ **true**
'help* **match**: 'Help me' ⇒ **true**
'help* **match**: 'Help me' **ignoreCase**: false ⇒ **false**

'interesting' **copyFrom**: 5 **to**: 'interesting' **size** ⇒ 'resting'

'Smalltalk' **spellAgainst**: 'Smalltalk' ⇒ 100
'Smalltalk' **spellAgainst**: 'smalltalk' ⇒ 88
'Smalltalk' **spellAgainst**: 'Stalk' ⇒ 33
'Smalltalk' **spellAgainst**: 'Bigtalk' ⇒ 11

'hello. goodbye' **copyUpTo**: '.' ⇒ 'hello'
'hello. goodbye' **copyUpTo**: ';' ⇒ 'hello. goodbye'

The **match:**, **match:ignoreCase:**, and **copyUpTo:** methods provide a poor man's approach to parsing. The **match:** method is used to verify the form, and **copyUpTo:** is used to extract the components. For instance, if a user is prompted with a string of the form 'Name/Age', the answer could be verified and components extracted as follows:

```
'*/*' match: result
    ifTrue: [
        name ← result copyUpTo: $/.
        age ← result copyFrom: result size + 2 to: result size]
    ifFalse: [... error ...]
```

Examples

'once upon a time' **indexOf**: $o ⇒ 1
'once upon a time' **indexOf**: (Character **space**) ⇒ 5
'once upon a time' **indexOf**: $u ⇒ 6
'once upon a time' **indexOf**: $U ⇒ 0
'once upon a time' **indexOf**: $x **ifAbsent**: [-1] ⇒ -1

'the happening' **indexOfSubCollection**: '' **startingAt**: 1 ⇒ 0 "Not found"
'the happening' **indexOfSubCollection**: 'the' **startingAt**: 1 ⇒ 1
'the happening' **indexOfSubCollection**: 'pen' **startingAt**: 1 ⇒ 8
'the happening' **indexOfSubCollection**: 'pen' **startingAt**: 9 ⇒ 0
'the happening' **indexOfSubCollection**: 'penny' **startingAt**: 8 **ifAbsent**: [-1] ⇒ -1

redInOrderedCollection ← OrderedCollection **new add**: $r; **add**: $e; **add**: $d; **yourself**.
redInDictionary ← Dictionary **new at**: 1 **put**: $r; **at**: 2 **put**: $e; **at**: 3 **put**: $d; **yourself**.
redInArray ← Array **with**: $r **with**: $e **with**: $d.
'Freddy' **indexOfSubCollection**: 'red' **startingAt**: 1 ⇒ 2
'Freddy' **indexOfSubCollection**: redInOrderedCollection **startingAt**: 1 ⇒ 2
'Freddy' **indexOfSubCollection**: redInDictionary **startingAt**: 1 ⇒ 2
'Freddy' **indexOfSubCollection**: redInArray **startingAt**: 1 ⇒ 2

'Saturday' **includes**: $b ⇒ **false**
'Saturday' **includes**: $A ⇒ **false**
'Saturday' **includes**: $a ⇒ **true**
'Saturday' **occurrencesOf**: $b ⇒ 0
'Saturday' **occurrencesOf**: $S ⇒ 1
'Saturday' **occurrencesOf**: $a ⇒ 2

Examples (continued)

'sing song' **replaceElement:** $s **withElement:** $p ⇒ 'ping pong'

(1 **to:** 3) **collect:** [:position | 'test' **replaceFrom:** 2 to: 3 **with:** 'ooar' **startingAt:** position].
 ⇒ ('tart' 'tart' 'tart') "successively changes 'ar' to 'oo', 'oa', 'ar' but since the same
  string is changed, only the last change is visible."

(1 **to:** 3) **collect:** [:place | ('test' **replaceFrom:** 2 to: 3 **with:** 'ooar' **startingAt:** place) **copy**].
 ⇒ ('toot' 'toat' 'tart') "as above but collects copies, so all changes are visible."

(1 **to:** 'hi you' **size**+1) **collect:** [:position | 'hi you' **copyFrom:** position **to:** 'hi you' **size**].
 ⇒ ('hi you' 'i you' ' you' 'you' 'ou' 'u' '')

'the yum yum tree' **copyReplaceAll:** 'yum' **with:** 'happy' ⇒ 'the happy happy tree'
'ratattattatman' **copyReplaceAll:** 'tat' **with:** '' ⇒ 'raman'
'abccabc' **copyReplaceAll:** 'abc' **with:** 'ab' ⇒ 'abcab'

'awo seasaws' **copyReplaceAll:** 'aw' **with:** 'hell' **asArray**. ⇒ 'hello seashells'

'method' **copyReplaceFrom:** 4 to: 6 **with:** 'aphor' asArray ⇒ 'metaphor'
'method' **copyReplaceFrom:** 1 to: 4 **with:** 'r' ⇒ 'rod'
'method' **copyReplaceFrom:** 2 to:4 **with:** '' ⇒ 'mod'
'method' **copyReplaceFrom:** 7 to: 6 **with:** 'ological' ⇒ 'methodological'
'method' **copyReplaceFrom:** 1 **to:** 0 **with:** 'another ' ⇒ 'another method'

'brow' **copyWith:** $n ⇒ 'brown'
'mississippi' **copyWithout:** $i ⇒ 'msssspp'

'Try a', 'gain f', 'or fun'. ⇒ 'Try again for fun'
'', '' ⇒ ''
'', 'Is this OK' ⇒ 'Is this OK'
'Is this OK', '' ⇒ 'Is this OK'

'Mix', (OrderedCollection **with:** $u **with:** $p) ⇒ 'Mixup'
'bat', (Dictionary **new at:** 1 **put:** $s; **yourself**) ⇒ 'bats'

Type Conversion

The following list summarizes the conversion operations applicable to the string, symbol,
and text classes. The general conversions discussed previously are shown first. Specialized
operations follow.

- aStringOrSymbolOrText **asSortedCollection**
- aStringOrSymbolOrText **asSortedCollection:** aSortBlock
- aStringOrSymbolOrText **asOrderedCollection**
- aStringOrSymbolOrText **asSet**
- aStringOrSymbolOrText **asBag**
- aStringOrSymbolOrText **asArray**
- aStringOrSymbolOrText **asString**
- aStringOrSymbolOrText **asText**
- aStringOrSymbol **asSymbol**[*]

- aStringOrSymbolOrText **asUppercase**[**]
- aStringOrSymbolOrText **asLowercase**[**]
- aStringOrSymbolOrText **asNumber**

Exceptions

**: Returns strings for both string and symbol receivers. Returns text for text receivers.

*: Although these operations are inherited for text, they are applicable only to strings and symbols.

In keeping with the earlier general remarks, **asUppercase** and **asLowercase** return strings for both string and symbol receivers. They return text for text receivers. Operation **asNumber** converts a prefix (that portion which is a correct number) of the receiver to a number. In the simplest case, when no prefix is a number, 0 is returned.

There is no operation for converting individual characters to strings. This would be useful for the special unprintable characters

- Character **newPage**
- Character **backspace**
- Character **cr**
- Character **esc**
- Character **space**
- Character **tab**

It would be simple to add the following character to string conversion method to class Character:

asString
    ↑(String **with**: self

Examples

```
'singing' asUppercase ⇒ 'SINGING'
'SINGing' asLowercase ⇒ 'singing'
#Columbus asUppercase ⇒ 'COLUMBUS'
#CRUSOE asLowercase ⇒ 'crusoe'
'Cream' asText asUppercase ⇒ Text for 'CREAM'
'Powder' asText asLowercase ⇒ Text for 'powder'

'2000' asNumber ⇒ 2000
'2000' asSymbol asNumber ⇒ 2000
'2000' asText asNumber ⇒ 2000
'100+200' asNumber ⇒ 100
'junk' asNumber ⇒ 0
'1.5e10' asNumber ⇒ 1.5e10
'-40' asNumber ⇒ -40
'1/3' asNumber ⇒ 1 "There is no such thing as a fraction constant"
```

Special Purpose Operations

There are few specialized operations. Special text operations deal with text emphasis. Emphasis codes include the following:

- basal ⇒ 0 (the standard emphasis)
- bold ⇒ 1
- italic ⇒ 2

- boldItalic $\Rightarrow$ 3
- underlined $\Rightarrow$ 4
- overStruck $\Rightarrow$ 8
- subscripted $\Rightarrow$ 16
- superscripted $\Rightarrow$ 32
- subscriptedUnderlined $\Rightarrow$ 20
- superscriptedUnderlined $\Rightarrow$ 36

Operation **withCRs** is used for constructing menu items; e.g., 'red\blue\yellow' withCRs is equivalent to 'red
blue
yellow' where we have deliberately started a new line after red and blue. Operation **contractTo**: is used in displays.

- aText **allBold**
  - Returns text in boldface.
- aText **emphasisAt**: characterIndex
  - Returns the integer code for the emphasis at the specified index.
- aText **emphasizeFrom**: start **to**: stop **with**: anEmphasisCode
  - Changes the emphasis of the indicated portion of the receiver.
- aStringOrSymbol **withCRs**
  - Returns a new string with backslashes replaced by carriage returns.
- aStringOrSymbol **contractTo**: aMaximumSize
  - Shortens strings longer than the specified maximum by replacing the middle portion by '...'.

Examples

'hello' **asText allBold** $\Rightarrow$ (only displays in bold)
'test' **asText allBold emphasisAt**: 2 $\Rightarrow$ 1
'a hot potatoe **asText emphasizeFrom**: 3 **to**: 5 **with**: 1 $\Rightarrow$ (displays as 'a **hot** potato')
'longwinded' **contractTo**: 9 $\Rightarrow$ 'lon...ded'

8.2.6 The Mapped Collection and Run Array Protocol

Mapped collections (arbitrary keys) and run arrays (integer keys) provide access to their elements indirectly through a subscript **map**; i.e., a mapping that converts a user's subscript into a more appropriate internal subscript. For mapped collections, the map is an arbitrary keyed collection; for run arrays, it is a specially designed integer-keyed collection that maps sequences of consecutive values into the same internal subscript. Mapped collections are intended for general mapping purposes, while run arrays are intended for use as space-efficient sparse arrays. Neither can be automatically grown or explicitly grown with the built-in grow command, but special methods are provided for explicitly growing run arrays.

To be more specific, a mapped collection or a run array A has both a **map** M and an internal array B associated with it (the **mappee**). Access to A results in an indirect access to B through M; i.e.,

$$A_i \text{ means } B_{M(i)}$$

where M(i) maps i to some intermediate subscript actually used by B as follows:

M(i) is M **at:** i
    (for mapped collections)
M(i) is the smallest j such that the sum of the first j elements of M is >= i
    (for run arrays)

The run array situation is much easier to explain with an example that efficiently represents a 170-element array A using two 3-element arrays M and B where

M is #(100 20 50) and B is #(-1 -2 -3)

In this case, the first 100 subscripts (1, 2, ..., 100) map to -1, the next 20 subscripts (101, 102, ..., 120) map to -2, and the remaining 50 subscripts (121, 122, ..., 170) map to -3. Thus

A **at:** 20 maps to B **at:** 1
A **at:** 80 maps to B **at:** 1
A **at:** 110 maps to B **at:** 2
A **at:** 150 maps to B **at:** 3

An equivalent mapped collection could also be constructed to have the same effect, but the space efficiency would be lost. The map would have to be an array with one hundred 1's, followed by twenty 2's, in turn followed by fifty 3's.

It is clear that run arrays are a special case of mapped collections optimized for space. However, the two notions were developed independently. Consequently, the terminology imbedded in the methods for constructing them is not compatible. Fortunately, there are few special purpose methods and therefore they are easily differentiated.

The term **run array** itself comes from the observation that each entry in the map describes a series of consecutive subscripts with the same property (in this case, the same mapping — the entry position). Such a sequence is often called a **run**.

mapped collection operations

- MappedCollection **collection**: collectionOfElements **map**: aMappingCollection
  Returns a new mapped collection with the specified mappee and map.
- aMappedCollection **contents**
  Returns a collection like the map (the same species) that collapses the map and mappee. The result is not a mapped collection.
- anArray **mappedBy**: aMappingCollection
  Returns a collection like the map (the same species) that collapses the map and mappee (the receiver). The result is not a mapped collection.

run array operations

- RunArray **runs**: anArrayOfCounts **values**: anArrayOfSuccessivelyDistinctElements
  Returns a new run array with the specified elements conceptually repeated the number of times indicated by the corresponding entry in anArrayOf-Counts. The information is kept in a sparse space-efficient manner.
- aRunArray **runLengthAt**: index
  Returns the length remaining in the run beginning at the specified index.

- aRunArray **addFirst:** anElement

   Grows the run array by adding a new element at the front. Returns the element. Does not work if the map is a dictionary.

- aRunArray **addLast:** anElement

   Grows the run array by adding a new element at the rear. Returns the element. Does not work if the map is a dictionary.

text operations

- Text **string:** aString **runs:** aRunArrayOfEmphasisCodes

   This is the only method in the system associated with a class other than RunArray that explicitly requires a run array. This array could of course be constructed using

   (RunArray **runs:** anArrayOfCounts **values:** anArrayOfEmphasis).

Although the **contents** of a mapped collection is the same species as the map, sequencing operations like **select:** return collections that are the same species as the mappee. For example, consider

```
aDictionary ← Dictionary new at: 1 put: 1; at: 2 put: 1; at: 3 put: 1; yourself.
aMappedCollection ← MappedCollection collection: #(-1) map: aDictionary.

aMappedCollection contents ⇒ Dictionary (1->-1 2->-1 3->-1)
aMappedCollection collect: [:element | element] ⇒ (-1 -1 -1)      "an array"
```

In specific cases, either the map or the mappee could itself be a mapped collection. In general, the species represented by a mapped collection is the species of the mappee (recursively applicable to arbitrary depth). Thus it is operation **contents** above that is not conforming to the usual standard.

The problem does not arise with run arrays because sequencing operations like **collect:** are not permitted (yet). It also does not have an operation like **contents**. The contents of a run array can be obtained by executing the conversion operation **asArray**.

Examples

```
aClothingHeatMap ← (Dictionary new at: #black put: #hot; at: #white put: #cool; yourself).
aClothingHeatMapInFrench ←
     MappedCollection
         collection: aClothingHeatMap
         map: (Dictionary new at: #noire put: #black; at: #blanc put: #white; yourself).
aClothingHeatMapInFrench at: #noire ⇒ hot. (#noire maps to #black with value #hot)
aClothingHeatMapInFrench at: #blanc ⇒ cool. (#blanc maps to #white with value #cool)

aMappingFromIntegersToHeatInEnglish ←
     MappedCollection
         collection: aClothingHeatMapInFrench
         map: (Array with: #noire with: #blanc with: #noire).
aMappingFromIntegersToHeatInEnglish at: 1 ⇒ hot. (1 maps to #noire with value #hot)
aMappingFromIntegersToHeatInEnglish at: 2 ⇒ cool. (2 maps to #blanc with value #cool)
aMappingFromIntegersToHeatInEnglish at: 3 ⇒ hot. (3 maps to #noire with value #hot)

aClothingHeatMapInFrench contents ⇒ Dictionary (noire->hot blanc->cool)
aMappingFromIntegersToHeatInEnglish contents ⇒ (hot cool hot)
```

Examples (continued)

aMappingCollection ← #(2 3 1). (maps 1 to 2, 2 to 3, and 3 to 1; i.e., rotates left)
aDifferentViewOfArray ← #(left middle right) **mappedBy**: aMappingCollection
aDifferentViewOfArray **at**: 1 ⇒ middle. (1 maps to 2 with associated value #middle)
aDifferentViewOfArray **at**: 2 ⇒ right. (2 maps to 3 with associated value #right)
aDifferentViewOfArray **at**: 3 ⇒ left. (3 maps to 1 with associated value #left)
aDifferentViewOfArray ⇒ #(middle right left).

#(left middle right) **mappedBy**: #(2 3 1) ⇒ (middle right left). (left rotation, see above)
#(left middle right) **mappedBy**: #(3 1 2) ⇒ (right left middle). (right rotation)
#(left middle right) **mappedBy**. #(3 2 1) → (right middle left). (switch ends)

aFullHouse ← RunArray **runs**: (3 2) **values**: #(King Ten).

aFullHouse **runlengthAt**: 1 ⇒ 3.
aFullHouse **runlengthAt**: 2 ⇒ 2.
aFullHouse **runlengthAt**: 3 ⇒ 1.
aFullHouse **runlengthAt**: 4 ⇒ 2.
aFullHouse **runlengthAt**: 5 ⇒ 1.

aFullHouse **addFirst**: #Ace ⇒ Ace.
aFullHouse **addFirst**: #Ace ⇒ Ace.
aFullHouse **addLast**: #Two ⇒ Two.
aFullHouse ⇒ a run array like RunArray **runs**: (2 3 2 1) **values**: #(Ace King Ten Two).

aDictionary ← Dictionary **new at**: 1 **put**: #big; **at**: 2 **put**: #small; **yourself**.
tenBigsAndTwentySmalls ← RunArray **runs**: (10 20) **values**: aDictionary.

aVeryShortStory ←
    Text
            string: '"What a bold statement" said the bold boy.'
            runs: (RunArray **runs**: #(8 4 21 4 5) **values**: #(0 1 0 1 0)). "0 normal, 1 bold"

8.2.7 The Interval Protocol

Interval is a special kind of collection that describes an arithmetic sequence. The sequence is specified at creation time and may not be changed or grown. Thus, it is logically a special class of array with a particularly efficient representation for the elements. Hence the usual **at:** method (but not the **at:put:** method) is available. Typically, intervals are used for looping control. However, they can be manipulated as independent objects. In addition to providing the usual comparison operations, the following specialized methods are provided:

array-like operations

- anInterval **size**
- anInterval **isEmpty**
- anInterval **first**
    Returns the first element in the interval if it is non-empty; otherwise, returns the starting value.
- anInterval **last**
    Returns the last element in the interval if it is non-empty; otherwise, returns an undefined value.
- anInterval **increment**
    Returns the interval step-size.

- anInterval **at:** anIndex

  Returns the element at the specified position in the interval. If there is no such element; e.g., when the interval is empty, an error is reported.

searching operations

- anInterval **includes:** aValue

  Returns true if it contains an element **equal** to aValue; otherwise false.
- anInterval **occurrencesOf:** aValue

  Returns the number of elements **equal** to aValue.

construction operations

- Interval **from:** aStartNumber **to:** anEndNumber

  Returns a nondecreasing interval; i.e., the interval is empty if anEndNumber is less than aStartNumber.
- Interval **from:** aStartNumber **to:** anEndNumber **by:** aStepSizeNumber

  Returns a nonincreasing or nondecreasing interval depending on whether or not the step size is negative or positive respectively. A zero step-size leads to infinite loops.
- aStartNumber **to:** anEndNumber
- aStartNumber **to:** anEndNumber **by:** aStepSizeNumber

  Same as corresponding class methods in Interval (see above).

In general, intervals are created by specifying start and end points along with an optional step-size. Without the step-size, the interval must be nondecreasing as in (1 **to:** 1) or (1 **to:** 10). Otherwise, it denotes an **empty interval**; i.e., an interval without elements; e.g., (1 **to:** -10).

Intervals are more general than corresponding facilities in other programming languages because they can be constructed with arbitrary numbers. Consequently, it is legal to have intervals such as

```
1 to: 10
(1/3) to: (8/3) by: (1/3)
(1.5 to: 9.5 by: 0.5
1 to: 5.0 by: (1/3)
```

When accessed sequentially via the sequencing operations **do:, collect:,** ..., the elements obtained are not always of the same class. For instance, for the last example above, the elements accessed include 1 (an integer), (4/3) (a fraction), (5/3), 2, (7/3), ..., (14/3), 5.

Since an interval is logically an array with an efficient representation for the elements, it is possible to access (but not modify) the elements using the standard **at:** method. In this case, the elements obtained are not necessarily the same as the elements obtained via the sequencing operations, since each and every single element is computed on demand from the same algorithm. By contrast, the sequencing operations begin with the start point and continually add the step-size until all elements are exhausted. The difference is small but noticeable. For example, consider

```
anInterval ← (1 to: 5.0 by: 0.5)
```

The sequencing operations provide 1 (an integer) as the first element followed by 1.5, while anInterval **at:** 1 returns 1.0 (a real) and anInterval **at:** 2 returns 1.5.

Examples

    (1 **to:** 10 **by:** 3) **asArray** ⇒ (1 4 7 10)
    (1 **to:** 10 **by:** 3) **at:** 1 ⇒ 1, (1 **to:** 10 **by:** 3) **at:** 2 ⇒ 4, (1 **to:** 10 **by:** 3) **at:** 3 ⇒ 7
    (1 **to:** 10 **by:** 3) **size** ⇒ 4
    (1 **to:** 10 **by:** 3) **isEmpty** ⇒ **false**
    (1 **to:** 10 **by:** 3) **first** ⇒ 1
    (1 **to:** 10 **by:** 3) **last** ⇒ 10
    (1 **to:** 10 **by:** 3) **increment** ⇒ 3

    (1 **to:** -10 **by:** -3) **asArray** ⇒ (1 -2 -5 -8)
    (1 **to:** 10 **by:** -3) **at:** 1 ⇒ 1, (1 **to:** 10 **by:** -3) **at:** 2 ⇒ -2, (1 **to:** 10 **by:** -3) **at:** 3 ⇒ -5
    (1 **to:** -10 **by:** -3) **size** ⇒ 4
    (1 **to:** -10 **by:** -3) **isEmpty** ⇒ **false**
    (1 **to:** -10 **by:** -3) **first** ⇒ 1
    (1 **to:** -10 **by:** -3) **last** ⇒ -8

    (1 **to:** -1) **asArray** ⇒ ()
    (1 **to:** -1) **at:** 1 ⇒ (error)
    (1 **to:** -1) **size** ⇒ 0
    (1 **to:** -1) **isEmpty** ⇒ **true**
    (1 **to:** -10 **by:** 2) **first** ⇒ 1 "Even though the interval is empty"
    (1 **to:** -10 **by:** 2) **last** ⇒ - 11 "Even though the interval is empty"

    (1 **to:** 3 **by:** 0.5) **asArray** ⇒ (1.0 1.5 2.0 2.5 3.0)
    (1 **to:** 3 **by:** 0.5) **collect:** [:aValue | aValue] ⇒ (1 1.5 2.0 2.5 3.0) "Note first element"
    (1 **to:** 3 **by:** 0.5) **at:** 1 ⇒ 1.0, (1 **to:** 10 **by:** 3) **at:** 2 ⇒ 1.5, (1 **to:** 10 **by:** 3) **at:** 3 ⇒ 2.0
    (1 **to:** 3 **by:** 0.5) **first** ⇒ 1 "Note: an integer"
    (1 **to:** 3 **by:** 0.5) **last** ⇒ 3.0 "Note: a real"

    (1 **to:** 3 **by:** 0.5) **includes:** 2.0 ⇒ **true**
    (1 **to:** 3 **by:** 0.5) **includes:** 2.1 ⇒ **false**
    (1 **to:** 3 **by:** 0.5) **occurrencesOf:** 2.5 ⇒ 1
    (1 **to:** 3 **by:** 0.5) **occurrencesOf:** 2.6 ⇒ 0

    (1 **to:** 10) **do:** [:aValue | ... *code accessing 1, 2, 3, 4, 5, 6, 7, 8, 9, 10* ...].
    (1 **to:** 10) **reverseDo:** [:aValue | ... *code accessing 10, 9, 8, 7, 6, 5, 4, 3, 2, 1* ...].

8.3 THE STREAMABLE COLLECTIONS (STREAMS)

The **streamable collections (streams)** provide a mechanism for viewing and modifying a secondary collection — an integer-keyed collection or an external stream (a file). Unlike the traditional sequencing operations provided for collections, the stream operations permit interruptible sequencing; i.e., not only can successive elements be obtained on demand but repositioning is possible. It is even possible to have shared access (multiple positioning) to the same collection. External streams (files) are provided as a special case; they are created automatically from instances of **FileName** when an associated stream is requested.

    ReadStreams and **WriteStreams** typify the streamable classes. The elements in the stream (arbitrary objects) are accessed via specialized file-like operations. The more general representative is a **ReadWriteStream** that permits both element access and modification. The above stream classes are subclasses of **InternalStream**. As implied above, corresponding subclasses of **ExternalStream** also exist. Because streams provide direct positioning, they can be viewed as integer-keyed collections since subsequent **next** or **nextPut:** operations behave like the corresponding keyed operations **at:** and **at:put:**.

Consequently, they are also one of the many members of the ordered classes. Typical operations include:

- aReadStream **atEnd**   (an interrogation)
- aReadStream **next**   (accessing an element; move right)
- aReadStream **peek**   (accessing an element without moving)
- aWriteStream **nextPut**: anElement   (modifying or appending)
- aReadOrWriteStream **close**   (when completed)

- aReadStream **position**   (getting position)
- aReadStream **position**: anInteger   (setting position)

From the implementation point of view, a large number of stream classes are abstract; e.g., **Stream**, **PeekableStream**, **PositionableStream**, **InternalStream**, and **External-Stream** (see Fig. 8.2). Hence, users should not attempt to create corresponding instances. There are also a large number of external streams (not shown in Fig. 8.2) including **BufferedExternalStream**, **ExternalReadStream**, **ExternalReadAppendStream**, **ExternalReadWriteStream**, and **ExternalWriteStream**. There is no need to remember these streams explicitly since they are created automatically when the stream requesting protocol for **FileName** is used. See the section on file names for more details.

8.3.1 Individual Characterizations

The **stream classes** (Fig. 8.6) are distinguished primarily by their intended usage; i.e. by whether or not the elements are to be **read** (accessed) or **written** (changed or added). Internal streams providing read access include **ReadStream**, **WriteStream**, **ReadWriteStream** and **Random** — only **WriteStream** and **ReadWriteStream** provide write access.

A second dimension that can be used to distinguish streams is whether or not they are **finite** or **infinite**. **Random** is the only example so far of an infinite stream. It is infinite in the sense that there is no limit to the number of elements in the stream; e.g., it is not even legal to ask what the stream size is for random streams. All other streams are finite streams.

At the moment, only character file streams are supported. More general file streams like object file streams are the subject of future extensions.

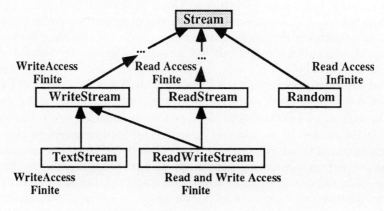

Figure 8.6 The Stream classes — a logical view.

8.3.2 Constructing New Streamable Collections

Streams **cannot** be constructed with the usual messages like **new** and **new:**. A more specialized protocol is required. The protocol for external (file) streams requires an instance of **FileName**. **Random** streams also have a unique protocol.

The ReadStream, WriteStream, ReadWriteStream protocol

- aReadOrWriteStreamClass **on:** anIntegerKeyedCollection
  Returns a stream capable of streaming over anIntegerKeyedCollection and initially positioned at the **beginning**.

- aReadOrWriteStreamClass **on:** anIntegerKeyedCollection **from:** firstIndex **to:** lastIndex
  Returns a stream capable of streaming over a portion of anIntegerKeyed-Collection starting at firstIndex and ending at lastIndex. The stream is initially positioned at the **beginning** (firstIndex). Additionally, ReadStreams will stream over the **original** collection, whereas WriteStreams stream over a **copy** of the subcollection.

- aWriteStreamClass **with:** anIntegerKeyedCollection
  Returns a stream capable of streaming over anIntegerKeyedCollection and initially positioned at the **end**. Applies only to WriteStreams.

- aWriteStreamClass **with:** anIntegerKeyedCollection **from:** firstIndex **to:** lastIndex
  Returns a stream capable of streaming over a **copy** of a portion of anIntegerKeyedCollection starting at firstIndex and ending at lastIndex. The stream is initially positioned at the **end**. Consequently, this method applies only to WriteStreams.

The FileName protocol

- FileName **named:** aString
- aString **asFileName**
  Returns a file name with characters specified by aString.

The Random protocol

- Random **new**
  Returns a new random number generator (a stream).

- aRandom **next**
  Returns a new random number from the random number generator. See the magnitudes chapter for an additional example.

The **on** protocol creates streams positioned at the beginning of the collection, whereas the **with** protocol creates them positioned at the end, making it convenient to append additional elements. The distinction is easily forgotten because there is no convenient way to remember that **on:** means **atBeginningOf:** and **with:** means **atEndOf:**.

The **on:from:to:** and **with:from:to:** variations should be interpreted as a request for a **copy** of a subcollection to stream over. Since read streams do not modify their collections, the copy request is optimized out.

A file name is specially created by indicating the external name of the file as a string or by using the special string conversion operation.

Examples

ReadStream **on:** #(Give me a break)   "A stream of symbols at the beginning"
WriteStream **on:** (String **new:** 10)   "A stream of characters at the beginning"
WriteStream **with:** 'Append to this'   "A stream of characters at the end"
ReadWriteStream **on:** (Array new: 100)   "A stream of objects at the beginning"

Filename **named:** 'Sample.st'   "A file name"
'aTest.st' **asFileName**   "Another file name"

8.3.3 How Read and Write Streams Are Typically Used

Before considering the operations in detail, it is best to have an informal working knowledge of streams. The paradigm that it supports is that of a one-element window on a collection with access provided only to the element in the window. If the beginning of the collection is on the left and the end of the collection is on the right, the window is viewed as moving sequentially from left to right providing access to the successive elements. In the extreme case, the window can ultimately be moved beyond the rightmost element, at which point no element is accessible. At this point, it is at the end of the stream.

Typical operations permit **reading** (extracting the object from the window and moving right), **writing** (modifying the object in the window, even if at the end, and moving right), and **peeking** (extracting the object from the window without moving it). Thus it makes sense to speak of the objects previously read and those yet to be read.

Operations for determining whether or not a stream is at the end, for repositioning the window more dramatically, e.g., to the extreme left end, and for terminating access to the stream, are also provided.

The typical operations (shown below) will be used to illustrate the manner in which streams are normally used. Operation **close** is usually used only for file streams; i.e., when internal streams are used, they are typically discarded after they are no longer needed — closing them is superfluous.

* aReadOrWriteStream **atEnd**   (an interrogation)
* aReadOrWriteStream **next**   (accessing an element; move right)
* aReadOrWriteStream **peek**   (accessing an element without moving)
* aWriteStream **nextPut:** anElement   (modifying or appending)
* aWriteStream **nextPutAll:** aCollection   (provides **nextPut:** for each element)
* aReadOrWriteStream **contents**   (includes both read and unread portions)
* aReadOrWriteStream **reset**   (repositions at the beginning)
* aReadOrWriteStream **setToEnd**   (repositions at the end)
* aReadOrWriteStream **close**   (when completed)

For the first example, consider methods **printString** and **storeString** provided in object, along with one of the many **printOn:** methods, in particular, one for collections.

Example

printString
        | aStream |
        aStream ← WriteStream **on:** (String **new:** 16).
        self **printOn:** aStream.
        ↑aStream **contents**

Example (continued)

```
storeString
    | aStream |
    aStream ← WriteStream on: (String new: 16).
    self storeOn: aStream.
    ↑aStream contents
```

"Generic printOn: for all collections ⇒ 'CollectionName (...)'"
```
printOn: aStream
    aStream nextPutAll: self class name.
    aStream nextPutAll: ' ('. "blank and left bracket."
    self do: [:element | element printOn: aStream. aStream space].
    self nextPut: $)
```

Both **printString** and **storeString** create new character streams; i.e., streams positioned (via **on:**) at the left end of a string of initial size 16. The stream operations will ensure that the string will grow if more space is needed. Alternatively, if not all characters are overwritten (because the result takes fewer than 16 characters), only the part actually written will be returned by **contents**. The methods invoke **printOn:** and **storeOn:** respectively to get a printable representation of the receiver. Finally, the entire contents of the stream is returned.

The **printOn:** method shown prints collections as 'CollectionName (...)'. Notice that all elements are followed by a blank. Consequently, even though an empty ordered collection would print as

OrderedCollection ()

one containing a sequence of numbers would print as

OrderedCollection (6 3 4)

with a blank preceding the right bracket. For another example, consider adding an operation for comparing streams.

Example

```
= aStream
    ((aStream isKindOf: Stream) and: [(aStream isKindOf: Random) not])
        ifFalse: [↑self error: 'Streams must be compared with streams'].
    self reset. aStream reset.
    [self atEnd | aStream atEnd] whileFalse:
        [[self next ~= aStream next] ifTrue: [↑false]].
    ↑self atEnd & aStream atEnd
```

After checking that the right operand of = is legal (this implementation will not work for **random** streams since they are infinite), both streams are repositioned at the beginning and then compared element by element. If the elements are not equal or if one stream is shorter than the other, **false** is returned; otherwise, **true**. A better implementation might record the initial stream positions and later reposition them to what they were.

Since comparing streams for equality is a rare task, it is understandable that no such method exists in class Stream. Indeed, if you needed to compare two streams (assuming they were not large external files), it is as simple as comparing their contents; e.g.,

aStream1 **contents** = aStream2 **contents**

We now consider streams in more detail.

8.3.4 Read, Write, and ReadWrite Streams

ReadStreams, **WriteStreams**, and **ReadWriteStreams** provide the ability to *stream over* finite collections of arbitrary objects. They are the Smalltalk equivalent to memory resident files. A useful special case is a corresponding stream of characters. Operations could be partitioned into two major groups: interrogation and positioning operations along with accessing and modification operations.

Interrogating and Positioning Streams

The interrogation and positioning operations include

interrogation operations

- aStream **size**
    Returns the number of elements in the stream.
- aStream **isEmpty**
    Returns true if the stream is at the beginning; should be called **atBeginning**.
- aStream **atEnd**
    Returns true if no more elements can be read; false otherwise.

positioning operations

- aStream **reset**
    Repositions the stream to indicate that no objects have been read or written.
- aStream **setToEnd**
    Repositions the stream to indicate that all objects have been read (or written).

- aStream **position**
    Returns the current position of the stream. Position is the index of the last object read or written by the stream (0 indicates none).
- aStream **position**: anInteger
    Sets position to anInteger as long as it is within the bounds of the stream; i.e., between 0 and the size of the collection being streamed over. It is an error to position the stream outside the bounds. Position is the index of the last object read or written by the stream (0 indicates none). Returns the receiver.

termination operations

- aStream **close**
    Indicates that the stream is no longer required. Provides compatibility with files that require the operation.

As noted above, **isEmpty** is misnamed. It should have been called **atBeginning**. For example,

(ReadStream **on:** 'This stream is not empty') **isEmpty** ⇒ **true**

As an example that should help to clarify the direct positioning operations, consider the task of adding methods **at:** and **at:put:** to stream. We are not suggesting that streams ought to be made to look like keyed collections although this would be a reasonable goal. In keeping with the existing operations, a check for subscripts out of bounds is performed.

at: anIndex
   (anIndex **between:** 1 **and:** self **size**) **ifFalse:** [↑self **error:** 'out of bounds'].
   self **position:** anIndex-1.
   ↑self **next**

at: anIndex **put:** anObject
   (anIndex **between:** 1 **and:** self **size**) **ifFalse:** [↑self **error:** 'out of bounds'].
   self **position:** anIndex-1.
   ↑self **nextPut:** anObject

Notice, in particular, that the stream must be positioned at the element prior to the position of the intended element; i.e., at position anIndex-1. Additional examples follow below.

Examples

```
seeTheCatRack ← ReadWriteStream on: #(see the cat rack).
seeTheCatRack size ⇒ 4
seeTheCatRack isEmpty "atBeginning" ⇒ true
seeTheCatRack atEnd ⇒ false
seeTheCatRack next ⇒ see

seeTheCatRack reset
seeTheCatRack size ⇒ 4
seeTheCatRack isEmpty "atBeginning" ⇒ true
seeTheCatRack atEnd ⇒ false
seeTheCatRack next ⇒ see

seeTheCatRack setToEnd
seeTheCatRack size ⇒ 4
seeTheCatRack isEmpty "atBeginning" ⇒ false
seeTheCatRack atEnd ⇒ true
seeTheCatRack next ⇒ (error)

seeTheCatRack position: 0
seeTheCatRack next ⇒ see
seeTheCatRack position: 2
seeTheCatRack next ⇒ rack

seeTheCatRack position: 1
seeTheCatRack nextPut: #hat ⇒ hat
seeTheCatRack contents ⇒ (see the hat rack)
seeTheCatRack next ⇒ rack

seeTheCatRack position: 4
seeTheCatRack nextPut: #now ⇒ now
seeTheCatRack contents ⇒ (see the hat rack now)
seeTheCatRack size ⇒ 5
```

Accessing and Modifying Streams

Although modification operations have been included with the accessing operations, it should be clear that instances of **ReadStream** cannot be modified.

extraction operations

- aStream **next**

    Returns the next object in the stream and positions the stream to the right of the object; i.e., reads the next object. It is an error to request an object if none exists.

- aStream **next**: aCount

    Returns the specified number of successive elements in the stream as a species-correct collection and positions the stream to the right of the elements; i.e., reads aCount elements. It is an error to request more elements than actually exist.

- aStream **nextAvailable**: anInteger

    Returns as many remaining elements as possible (up to the maximum specified by anInteger) in a species-correct collection.

- aStream **nextMatchFor**: anObject

    Reads and discards the next object in the stream. Returns whether or not the object was equal to anObject.

- aStream **through**: anObject

    Returns a species-correct collection containing all remaining elements *up to and including* the first element equal to anObject. The stream is left positioned after the equal element. If no such element is found, returns the remaining elements and the stream is positioned at the end.

- aStream **upTo**: anObject

    Similar to above but *excludes (yet erroneously reads past)* the first element equal to anObject.

- aStream **upToEnd**

    Returns all remaining elements in a species-correct collection.

- aStream **throughAll**: aCollection

    Returns a species-correct collection containing all remaining elements *up to and including* the first subcollection equal to aCollection. The stream is left positioned after the equal subcollection. If no such subcollection is found, returns the remaining elements and the stream is positioned at the end.

- aStream **upToAll**: aCollection

    Similar to above but *excludes (and does not read past)* the start of the first subcollection equal to aCollection.

- aStream **peek**

    Returns the next object without reading it; i.e., without changing the stream position. If the stream is at the end, returns **nil**.

- aStream **peekFor**: anObject

    Either reads and returns the next element if it is equal to anObject; or, returns false without affecting the stream.

- aStream **contents**

    Returns a copy of the entire contents of the stream independent of the number of objects read or written.

modification operations

- aWriteStream **nextPut**: anObject

    Inserts anObject at the current position in the stream and positions the stream to the right of the inserted object; i.e., writes anObject into the stream. Returns anObject.

- aWriteStream **next**: aCount **put**: anObject

    Writes anObject into the stream as many times as specified by aCount. Returns anObject.

- aWriteStream **nextPutAll**: aCollection

    Writes the successive elements of aCollection into the stream. Returns aCollection.

repositioning operations

- aStream **skip**: anInteger

    Repositions the stream by either going right, not moving, or going left the specified amount depending on whether anInteger is positive, zero, or negative respectively; i.e., positive indicates reading, negative unreading. Returns the receiver.

- aStream **skipUpTo**: anObject

    Repositions the stream *to the left* of the next element equal to anObject. If none is found, repositions at the end of the stream and returns nil; otherwise, returns self.

- aStream **skipThrough**: anObject

    Repositions the stream *to the right* of the next element equal to anObject. If none is found, repositions at the end of the stream and returns nil; otherwise, returns self.

- aStream **skipToAll**: aCollection

    Repositions the stream *to the left* of the subcollection equal to aCollection. If none is found, repositions at the end of the stream and returns nil; otherwise, returns self.

sequencing operations

- aStream **do**: aBlock

    Evaluates aBlock for each of the **remaining** elements of the stream.

In general, the operations are quite flexible. The major operations are **next**, **peek**, **nextPut:**, **nextPutAll**, and **contents**. Operations such as **nextMatchFor:**, **through:**, **upTo:**, **peekFor:**, **next:**, **skip:**, and **skipTo:** are useful for simple search and parsing applications. Methods **throughAll:**, **upToAll:** and **skipToAll:** permit searching for entire subcollections rather than individual objects. However, there is one discrepancy: "aStream **upTo:** $?" and "aStream **upToAll:** '?'" both return the same string but they have different side-effects. The former reads past the "?" but the latter doesn't. Also notice that there is only one sequencing operation; i.e., **do:**. Moreover, it **does not** sequence through all elements in the stream. Instead, it only sequences through the **remaining** elements.

A large example that exercises many of the above operations can be found in the chapter on magnitudes. In particular, refer to method **readFrom:** in class **AbsoluteTime**. Other less comprehensive examples follow:

Examples

```
sentenceFirstPart ← ReadWriteStream on: #(the whale began to blow). "At beginning"
sentenceSecondPart ← ReadWriteStream with: #(over). "At end"
sentenceFirstPart nextPut: #the; nextPut: #dust; nextPut: #started.
sentenceSecondPart nextPut: #the; nextPut: #land.
sentenceFirstPart contents ⇒ (the dust started to blow)
sentenceSecondPart contents ⇒ (over the land).

humptyDumpty ← ReadStream on: #(Humpty Dumpty sat on the wall) "At beginning"
humptyDumpty next ⇒ Humpty
humptyDumpty next: 3 ⇒ (Dumpty sat on)
humptyDumpty nextMatchFor: #wall ⇒ false "The next object was #the; moved right"
humptyDumpty nextMatchFor: #wall ⇒ true "The next object was #wall; moved right"
humptyDumpty atEnd ⇒ true

aStream ← ReadStream on: 'Yodelling: little old lady who?' "At beginning"
aStream through: $: ⇒ 'Yodeling:' "Now, the next character is a space"
aStream upTo: (Character space) ⇒ '' "We were already there; moved right, though"
aStream upTo: (Character space) ⇒ 'little' "To next space; moved right past it"
aStream upTo: $! ⇒ 'old lady who?' "Returns the rest since no '!'"

theBrackets ← ReadStream on: 'Let us pick out <the bracketed stuff>, OK?'.
theBrackets skipThrough: $< ⇒ aStream "Yes, '<' exists; now past it"
theBrackets upTo: $> ⇒ 'the bracketed stuff' "also moved right past it"
theBrackets peek ⇒ $,

theBrackets ← ReadStream on: 'Let us pick out <the bracketed stuff>, OK?'.
"Try it again but this time assume the brackets might not be there."
((theBrackets skipUpTo: $<) notNil and: [(theBrackets skipUpTo: $>) notNil ])
    ifTrue: [
            theBrackets reset.
            theBrackets skipUpTo: $<.
            result ← theBrackets skipUpTo: $>].

help ← ReadWriteStream on: 'help'.
help peekFor: $h ⇒ $h
help peekFor: $e ⇒ $e
help peekFor: $l ⇒ $l
help peekFor: $x ⇒ false
help nextPutAll: 'lo there, hey' ⇒ 'lo there, hey'
help contents ⇒ 'hello there, hey' "The first character overwrote the p"
help next: 5 put: $! ⇒ $!
help contents ⇒ 'hello there, hey!!!!!'
help skip: -8; nextPutAll: 'you'; contents ⇒ 'hello there, you!!!!!'

aStream ← ReadStream on: 'I live at 531 Yellow Road Street.'
aStream throughAll: 'live at ' ⇒ 'I live at ' "We wish to pick up the address"
address ← aStream upToAll: '.' ⇒ '531 Yellow Road Street' "Could have used upTo:"

remainder ← WriteStream on: (String new).
help do: [:aCharacter | remainder nextPut: aCharacter].
remainder contents ⇒ '!!!!!' "Notice that do: did not reset the stream"

remainder ← WriteStream on: (String new).
help do: [:aCharacter | remainder nextPut: aCharacter].
remainder contents ⇒ '' "There was nothing left to read"
```

Character Streams

Although the following operations apply to arbitrary write streams, they are generally most useful for streams on strings (character collections). It is noteworthy that all of the following operations return the stream (the receiver).

special print and store operations

- aWriteStream **print**: anObject
    Equivalent to 'anObject **printOn**: aWriteStream' but returns the stream.
- aWriteStream **store**: anObject
    Equivalent to 'anObject **storeOn**: aWriteStream' but returns the stream.

special repositioning operations

- aStream **skipSeparators**
    Reads and discards any separators that are next in the stream. Separators include space, cr, tab, line feed, and form feed. Returns the stream.

special character writing

- aWriteStream **cr**
    Writes a return character into the stream and returns the stream.
- aWriteStream **crtab**
    Writes both a return character and a tab character into the stream and returns the stream.
- aWriteStream **crtab**: aCount
    Writes a return character, followed by aCount tab characters, into the stream and returns the stream.
- aWriteStream **space**
    Writes a space character into the stream and returns the stream.
- aWriteStream **tab**
    Writes a tab character into the stream and returns the stream.

Operations **print**: and **store**: are useful because they permit more cascading (see below) but they are not often used by novices. The **skipSeparators** operation is used in read methods that perform some degree of parsing; e.g., the date and time **readFrom**: operations. The remaining operations are used for special formatting requirements. Tabs, in particular, are used extensively in browsers; e.g., to layout comments in a tabular manner. However, they are little used internally. Print strings, for example, genrally do not use tabs or carriage returns at all.

aStream **nextPutAll**: 'The answer is '. anObject **printOn**: aStream.

versus

aStream **nextPutAll**: 'The answer is '; **print**: anObject.

Although it is hardly worth mentioning, the fact that each operation returns the receiver enables some cascaded expressions to be avoided. For example, the following statements are equivalent:

aStream **crtab**; **print**: anObject.
aStream **crtab print**: anObject.

Text Streams

Text streams are write streams on strings with additional emphasis codes provided during the process of writing characters into the stream. The actual codes include (0) **basal**, (1) **bold**, (2) *italic*, (3) **boldItalic**, (4) **underlined**, (8) **overStruck**, (16) **subscripted**, (32) **super-scripted**, (20) **subscriptedUnderlined**, and (36) **superscriptedUnderlined**. When the contents of a text stream is requested, text as opposed to a string is returned.

special emphasis operations

• aTextStream **emphasis**

>   Returns the current emphasis code (as an integer)

• aTextStream **emphasis**: anInteger

>   Sets the current emphasis code so that all subsequent characters written (until the next change of emphasis) will be provided with this emphasis code.

Examples

aStream ← TextStream **on**: '' "Any string would do"
aStream **emphasis**: 0 "basal"; **nextPutAll**: 'The author''s name is '.
aStream **emphasis**: 1 "bold"; **nextPutAll**: 'Frank Fiala'.
aStream **emphasis**: 0 "basal"; **nextPutAll**: ', OK?'.

aStream **contents** ⇒ Text that prints like 'The author''s name is **Frank Fiala**, OK?'

8.3.5 File Names

Filename is an an interface class for interpreting strings as file names. Files can either contain byte information — typically characters, or other files in which case they are called **directories**. A string is typically a **path name**; i.e., a sequence of directories each containing the next followed by a specific character file in the last directory. Depending on the operating system supporting Smalltalk-80, directories may be omitted to default them to the currently active directory. Whether or not a string is a legal file name is system specific. Some examples are 'directory1\directory2\sample.st', or 'Hard Disk:ParcPlace:sample.st', or just simply 'sample.st'.

Instances of **Filename** provide operations (among many others) that will construct an appropriate external stream for reading or writing a file.

file name creation

• aString **asFilename**
• Filename **named**: aString

>   Returns a file name for the specified string.

file name interrogation

• aFilename = anotherFileName

>   Compares the corresponding strings for equality.

conversion

• aFilename **asString**

>   Returns the corresponding string.

file querying and setting

- aFilename **exists**
- aFilename **fileSize**
- aFilename **isReadable**
- aFilename **isWritable**
- aFilename **isDirectory**
- aFilename **makeWritable**
- aFilename **makeUnwritable**
- aFilename **makeDirectory**

      Test or set the attributes of the corresponding file.

directory query and manipulation

- aFilename **directory**

      Returns the directory portion of the path name for the file as another file name.

- aFilename **directoryContents**

      Returns an array of strings each the name of a file in the directory. The file name must already exist and be a directory.

- aFilename **filesMatching**: aPatternString

      Searches the file (which must be a directory) for files with names matching the pattern string — recall "#" denotes any character and "*" denotes any sequence of characters. Returns an ordered collection of strings (not instances of Filename).

external stream creation

aFilename **readStream**	"creation not allowed"
aFilename **readAppendStream**	"creation allowed"
aFilename **readWriteStream**	"creation allowed"
aFilename **writetream**	"truncate or create"
aFilename **newReadAppendStream**	"truncate or create"
aFilename **newReadWriteStream**	"truncate or create"
aFilename **appendStream**	"creation allowed"

      Creates and returns corresponding external streams. An error is reported if an illegal activity is attempted; e.g., attempting to get a write stream on a read-only file. The append variety positions the stream at the end of the file if it exists; otherwise, an empty file is created (and positions the stream at the end too).

utilities

- aFilename **edit**
- aFilename **fileIn**
- aFilename **delete**
- aFilename **copyTo**: anotherFilename

- aFilename **moveTo**: anotherFilename
- aFilename **renameTo**: anotherFilename
- aFilename **contentsOfEntireFile**

Operation **edit** creates and schedules an editing window on the file, **fileIn** causes the contents of the file to be compiled, **delete** permanently removes the file, **copyTo**: makes a copy, **moveTo**: makes a copy and then deletes the original, and **contentsOfEntireFile** is equivalent to asking for the contents of an associated read stream.

Examples

(Filename **named**: 'MyNewGame.Smalltalk') **fileIn**
(Filename **named**: 'Job.Application') **edit**

aFilename ← Filename **named**: 'NormalFile'.
aFilename **isDirectory**
    ifFalse: [
        aStream ← aFilename **readWriteStream**.
        data ← aStream **contents**.
        aStream **close**]

8.4 THE ORDERED CLASSES (NON-STREAMS AND NON-KEYED PROTOCOL)

The **ordered classes** are characterized by element sequences that are ordered in some user-controllable manner. Consequently it makes sense to refer to the ith or n^{th} element. Arrays, for example, provide that capability and so do random-access streams. The more general representative is an **ordered collection** that permits arbitrary objects as elements and flexible operations for changing and manipulating the sequence. Typical operations include

- anOrderedCollection **first**   (accessing an element)
- anOrderedCollection **last**
- anOrderedCollection **do**: [anElement | someCode]   (accessing all elements)
- anOrderedCollection **add**: anElement   (adding an element)
- anOrderedCollection **addFirst**: anElement
- anOrderedCollection **addLast**: anElement
- anOrderedCollection **removeFirst**   (removing an element)
- anOrderedCollection **removeLast**

The ordered classes include **OrderedCollection**, **SortedCollection**, and **Linked-List** along with the other integer-keyed collections like **Array** and **String** and the stream classes like **ReadStream** and **WriteStream**. We have already considered the detailed integer-keyed protocol in Sect. 8.2 and the detailed stream protocol in Sect. 8.3. In this section, we only consider the detailed protocol for the first three classes.

OrderedCollection, the most general class, is capable of containing arbitrary objects and has operations for adding and removing elements anywhere in the sequence. It is a generalization of Array that permits automatic (transparent) growing and shrinking when additions and removals are performed. **SortedCollection** is a specialization that maintains a

sorted order for the elements. In general, being **ordered** is not as restrictive as **sorted**; e.g., the consecutive elements in array #(1 5 2 3 1) are ordered but not sorted. **LinkedList** is a special kind of ordered collection primarily designed for use in process management by the system. Its elements must be instances of class Link.

8.4.1 Individual Characterizations

The **OrderedCollection, SortedCollection**, and **LinkedList classes** are distinguishable along three dimensions (see Fig. 8.7). With respect to generality of the elements, **ordered** and **sorted collections** are the most general permitting arbitrary objects. **Linked lists** permit only elements of type **Link**. With respect to restrictions on adding and removing elements, **ordered** and **sorted collections** have the least restrictions permitting elements to be added or removed anywhere in the sequence. **Linked lists** permit elements to be added and removed at the ends with one operation although multi-operation splicing is also possible. Finally, the collections can be categorized by the manner in which the elements are ordered. The ordering for **ordered collections** and **linked lists** is dictated externally by users; e.g., by suitably choosing the insertion and modification operations. The ordering for **sorted collections** is dictated internally by the sorted collection itself; i.e., the sorted order is independent of the order in which users insert the elements. A more detailed description of the individual classes follows.

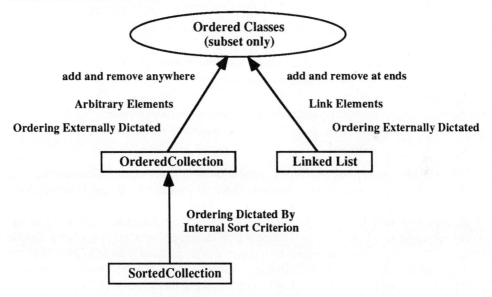

Figure 8.7 The ordered classes — a logical view (subset only).

8.4.2 Constructing New Ordered, Sorted, and LinkedList Collections

We consider increasingly sophisticated techniques for constructing ordered collections, sorted collections, and linked lists: those that construct empty collections (where allowed), those that construct small collections (one message-send is sufficient), and, finally, those that construct large collections (multiple message-sends are required). The conversion operations discussed in Sect. 8.1.2 are omitted. A summary follows:

OrderedCollections and SortedCollections

- anOrderedOrSortedCollectionClass **new**
- anOrderedOrSortedCollectionClass **new:** anInitialSize
- SortedCollection **sortBlock:** aTwoParameterBlock
- anOrderedOrSortedCollectionClass **with:** $object_1$
- anOrderedOrSortedCollectionClass **with:** $object_1$ **with:** $object_2$
- anOrderedOrSortedCollectionClass **with:** $object_1$ **with:** $object_2$ **with:** $object_3$
- anOrderedOrSortedCollectionClass **with:** $object_1$ **with:** $..._2$ **with:** $..._3$ **with:** $..._4$
- (*anyCodeForCreatingAnOrderedOrSortedCollection*)

    add: $aValue_1$;
    add: $aValue_2$;
    ...
    add: $aValue_n$;
    yourself

Linked Lists

- LinkedList **new**   (an empty linked list)
- LinkedList **nextLink:** aLink   (a one element linked list)
- (LinkedList **new**)

    add: (aSubclassOfLink **new** *yourInitialization*; **yourself**);
    add: (aSubclassOfLink **new** *yourInitialization*; **yourself**);

    ...

    add: (aSubclassOfLink **new** *yourInitialization*; **yourself**);
    add: (aSubclassOfLink **new** *yourInitialization*; **nextLink:** nil; **yourself**);
    yourself

Ordered collections and sorted collections have many of the same instance creation operations as the typical keyed collections. Since they are not fixed-size, however, operation **new:** does not have the typical array semantics. In particular, it does not mean "construct a collection pre-initialized with the specified number of **nil** elements." Rather, the initial size is interpreted as a hint about how large the collection is expected to get some time in the future. The system can then obtain an instance that is sufficiently large to ultimately contain this number of elements. If this estimate is totally wrong, it doesn't matter. The collection reorganizes itself transparently to handle any number of elements.

Linked lists are quite different from ordered collections or from any other kind of collection for that matter. They have their own special protocol. In particular, **LinkedList** differs from the other classes by requiring instances of class **Link**. Moreover, class **Link** must be viewed as an abstract class from the user's perspective because it only contains storage facilities and operations for linking with other links but neither linked lists nor links have any facilities for storing data. Users must explicitly construct a new class of links as follows, for example, in order to be able to store information with the linked list. Currently, there are very few subclasses — only one called **Process**.

Class ValueLink

class name	ValueLink
superclass	Link
instance variable names	dataValue

instance methods

access

value
　↑dataValue

modification

value: aNewValue
　　dataValue ← aNewValue

Examples

OrderedCollections and SortedCollections

anEmptyOrderedCollection ← OrderedCollection **new**.
anEmptySortedCollectionWithTheDefaultSortBlock ← SortedCollection **new**.
anEmptySortedCollectionWithTheDefaultSortBlockExplicitlyGiven ←
　　SortedCollection **sortBlock**: [:x :y | x <= y].

anEmptyOrderedCollectionWithAnInitialSize ← OrderedCollection **new**: 100.
anEmptySortedCollectionWithTheDefaultSortBlockAndAnInitialSize ←
　　SortedCollection **new**: 100.

aCollectionWithOneElement ← OrderedCollection **with**: #Gold.
aCollectionWithTwoElements ← OrderedCollection **with**: #Meat **with**: #Potatoes.
aCollectionWithThreeElements ← OrderedCollection **with**: 1 **with**: 2 **with**: 10.
aCollectionWithFourElements ← OrderedCollection **with**: 1 **with**: 1.0 **with**: (3/2) **with**: $1.
aCollectionWithFiveElements ←
　　OrderedCollection **new**
　　　　add: #Once;
　　　　add: 'upon';
　　　　add: $a;
　　　　add: 'midnight' **asText**;
　　　　add: 'clear' **asArray**;
　　　　yourself.

Linked Lists

anEmptyLinkedList ← LinkedList **new**.
aLinkedListWithOneElement ←
　　LinkedList **nextLink**: (ValueLink **new value**: #Hi; **yourself**).
aLinkedListWithThreeElements ←
　　LinkedList **new**
　　　　add: (ValueLink **new value**: #How; **yourself**);
　　　　add: (ValueLink **new value**: #Are; **yourself**);
　　　　add: (ValueLink **new value**: #You; **yourself**);
　　　　yourself.
aLinkedListWithFourElements ←
　　LinkedList
　　　　with: (ValueLink **new value**: #I; **yourself**)
　　　　with: (ValueLink **new value**: #Am; **yourself**)
　　　　with: (ValueLink **new value**: #Fine; **yourself**)
　　　　with: (ValueLink **new value**: #Thanks; **yourself**).

8.4.3 The Ordered Collection Protocol

OrderedCollection provides protocol for inserting, removing, and accessing elements of an ordered sequence. Elements are arbitrary objects. The ordered collections can be viewed in two ways: as arrays generalized to grow and shrink transparently or as a generalization of stacks, queues, and deques. Correspondingly, there are two entirely different protocols for manipulating ordered collections: a sequence-like protocol that is representation independent and an array-like protocol that acknowledges the underlying keyed implementation.

The Sequence-like Protocol

As sequences, the primary capability provided by ordered collections is controlled growing and shrinking. Related operations include

querying and search operations

- anOrderedCollection **isEmpty**
- anOrderedCollection **size**
    Queries about the number of elements actually contained.
- anOrderedCollection **first**
- anOrderedCollection **last**
    Returns the first (correspondingly last) element in the sequence. If the sequence is empty, an errror is reported.
- anOrderedCollection **includes**: anElement
    Returns true if it contains an element **equal** to anElement; otherwise false.
- anOrderedCollection **occurrencesOf**: anElement
    Returns the number of elements **equal** to anElement.
- anOrderedCollection **before**: oldObject
    Returns the element before oldObject; i.e., locates an element equal to oldObject and returns the object immediately preceding it in the sequence. If the sequence does not contain an element equal to oldObject, or if the sequence contains no elements after oldObject, an error is reported.
- anOrderedCollection **after**: oldObject
    Returns the element after oldObject; i.e., locates an element equal to oldObject and returns the object immediately following it in the sequence. If the sequence does not contain an element equal to oldObject, or if the sequence contains no elements after oldObject, an error is reported.

operations for adding

- anOrderedCollection **add**: newObject
    Adds newObject to the end of the sequence. Returns newObject.
- anOrderedCollection **addFirst**: newObject
    Adds newObject to the beginning of the sequence. Returns newObject.
- anOrderedCollection **addLast**: newObject
    Adds newObject to the end of the sequence. Returns newObject.
- anOrderedCollection **add**: newObject **after**: oldObject
    Adds newObject after oldObject; i.e., locates an element equal to newObject and inserts newObject immediately after it in the sequence. If the sequence does not contain an element equal to oldObject, an error is reported. Returns newObject.

- anOrderedCollection **add**: newObject **beforeIndex**: anInteger

    Adds newObject before the specified index which must be between 1 and the size of the receiver + 1. If the index is exactly one more than the size of the receiver, newObject is inserted at the end. It is an error to attempt to insert outside those bounds. Returns the modified receiver.

- anOrderedCollection **add**: newObject **before**: oldObject

    Adds newObject before oldObject; i.e., locates an element equal to newObject and inserts newObject immediately before it in the sequence. If the sequence does not contain an element equal to oldObject, an error is reported. Returns newObject.

- anOrderedCollection **addAll**: aCollection

    Adds each element of aCollection at the end of the sequence. Returns aCollection.

- anOrderedCollection **addAllFirst**: aCollection

    Adds each element of aCollection at the beginning of the sequence. Returns aCollection.

- anOrderedCollection **addAllLast**: aCollection

    Adds each element of aCollection at the end of the sequence. Returns aCollection.

operations for removing

- anOrderedCollection **removeFirst**

    Removes the first element of the sequence and returns it. If the sequence is empty, an error is reported.

- anOrderedCollection **removeFirst**: anInteger

    As above but anInteger specifies how many elements to remove. The removed elements are returned in an array. If the sequence contains fewer elements than requested, an error is reported.

- anOrderedCollection **removeLast**

    Removes the last element of the sequence and returns it. If the sequence is empty, an error is reported.

- anOrderedCollection **removeLast**: anInteger

    As above but anInteger specifies how many elements to remove. The removed elements are returned in an array. If the sequence contains fewer elements than requested, an error is reported.

- anOrderedCollection **removeAtIndex**: anInteger

    Removes the element at the specified index and returns it. If the index is out of bounds, an error is reported.

- anOrderedCollection **remove**: oldObject {**ifAbsent**: absentBlock}

    Removes oldObject; i.e., locates an element equal to oldObject and removes it from the sequence. If the sequence does not contain an element equal to oldObject, either absentBlock is executed (if provided) and its result returned or an error is reported. Otherwise, it returns oldObject.

- anOrderedCollection **removeAll**: aCollection

    Removes each element of aCollection from the sequence. If any element fails to be located, an error is reported. Otherwise, it returns aCollection.

- anOrderedCollection **replaceElement**: oldElement **withElement**: newElement

    Destructively replaces all elements **identical** to oldElement by newElement. Returns the receiver.

- anOrderedCollection **removeAllSuchThat**: aBooleanBlock

   Evaluates aBooleanBlock for each element of the sequence. Removes each element for which aBooleanBlock evaluates to true. Returns an ordered collection of the same species containing all elements that were removed.

Generally, the operations for adding and removing elements in a content independent way are well designed and complete. Users, however, must be careful with those operations that search, insert, and remove based on content (as opposed to key); e.g., **before:**, **after:**, **add:before:**, **add:after:**, and **remove:ifAbsent:**. The reason is that ordered collections can contain multiple entries. It is impossible, for example, to add an element after the second occurrence of an element with these operations alone. On the rare occasion where this is desirable, operations **removeAtIndex:** and **add:beforeIndex:** must be used.

Users should not be attempting to explicitly modify collections while in the process of sequencing through their elements — the results can be unpredictable because the bounds of the loop are generally computed at the start of the loop — not every time through.

Operations **addAll:**, **addAllFirst:**, and **addAllLast:** are more general than might be expected. In particular, **addAll:** and **addAllLast:** can accommodate any class of parameters that has a corresponding **do:** operation. Similarly, **addAllFirst:** can handle any parameter with a **reverseDo:** operation. Thus, it is perfectly reasonable to execute

   anOrderedCollection **addAll:** aSet

On the other hand, **addAll:** above could not be substituted by **addFirst:** since sets do not have a **reverseDo:** operation — a quirk of the implementation.

Examples

```
anEmptyCollection ← OrderedCollection new: 100.
redAndBlue ← #(Red Blue) asOrderedCollection.

anEmptyCollection size ⇒ 0
redAndBlue size ⇒ 2
anEmptyCollection isEmpty ⇒ true
redAndBlue isEmpty ⇒ false

anEmptyCollection first ⇒ (error)
redAndBlue first ⇒ Red
redAndBlue last ⇒ Blue
redAndBlue includes: #Red ⇒ true
redAndBlue includes: #Yellow ⇒ false
redAndBlue occurrencesOf: #Yellow ⇒ 0

redAndBlue before: #Blue ⇒ Red
redAndBlue after: #Red ⇒ Blue
redAndBlue add: #Yellow ⇒ Yellow.
redAndBlue ⇒ OrderedCollection (Red Blue Yellow)

aTongueTwister ← OrderedCollection new.
aTongueTwister addFirst: #rubber. "Now contains (rubber)"
aTongueTwister addLast: #bumpers. "Now contains (rubber bumpers)"
aTongueTwister add: #baby after: #rubber. "Now contains (rubber baby bumpers)"
aTongueTwister add: #buggy before: #bumpers.
aTongueTwister ⇒ OrderedCollection (rubber baby buggy bumpers)
```

Examples (continued)

aTongueTwister **add:** #phew **beforeIndex:** 5
aTongueTwister ⇒ OrderedCollection (rubber baby buggy bumpers phew)
aTongueTwister **add:** #two **beforeIndex:** 1
aTongueTwister ⇒ OrderedCollection (two rubber baby buggy bumpers phew)

counts ← OrderedCollection **new**.
counts **addAll:** Set **new**. "Nothing actually added"
counts **addAllFirst:** #(one) "Now contains (one)"
counts **addAllLast:** #(two two) "Now contains (one two two)"
counts **addAll:** '333' "Now contains (one two two $3 $3 $3)"
counts **removeFirst:** 3 ⇒ (one two two) "Now contains ($3 $3 $3)"
counts **removeLast:** 3 ⇒ ($3 $3 $3) "Now contains ()"

aSong ← #(Now go away Johnny fly very quickly away) **asOrderedCollection**.
aSong **removeFirst** "Now contains (go away Johnny fly very quickly away)"
aSong **removeLast** "Now contains (go away Johnny fly very quickly)"
aSong **remove:** #away **ifAbsent:** [] "Now contains (go Johnny fly very quickly)"
aSong **removeAll:** #(quickly very) "Now contains (go Johnny fly)"
aSong **replaceElement:** #fly **withElement:** #go "Now contains (go Johnny go)"
aSong **removeAtIndex:** 2 "Now contains (go go)"

anotherSong ← #($? Rock $a a bye $# $$ baby $*) **asOrderedCollection**.
whatDidIGet ← anotherSong **removeAllSuchThat:** [:element |
        element **isKindOf:** Character].
whatDidIGet ⇒ OrderedCollection ($? $a $# $$ $*)
anotherSong ← OrderedCollection (Rock a bye baby)

story ← OrderedCollection **with:** #once **with:** #upon.
story, #(a time) ⇒ OrderedCollection (Once upon a time)

Operations for copying and concatenation include the following:

copying and concatenation operations

- anOrderedCollection **copyEmpty**

    Returns a copy of the sequence without elements.

- anOrderedCollection **copyWith:** newElement

    Returns a copy differing from the original by containing newElement at the
    end.

- anOrderedCollection **copyWithout:** oldElement

    Returns a copy that does not contain any elements equal to oldElement.

- anOrderedCollection **copyReplaceAll:** oldCollection **with:** newCollection

    Returns a copy of the receiver in which all occurrences of oldCollection have
    been replaced by newCollection. Does not scan the replacement. The two
    collection parameters must be either keyed collections with integers keys
    (dictionaries are allowed if the keys are all consecutive integers starting
    at 1) or ordered collections.

- anOrderedCollection, aCollection

    Returns a new collection that is the concatenation of the receiver and
    aCollection. Parameter aCollection must be a collection with integer keys
    (even dictionaries are allowed if the keys are all consecutive integers
    starting at 1).

Examples

```
canYouBelieveIt ← #(can you believe it) asOrderedCollection.
canYouBelieveIt copyEmpty ⇒ OrderedCollection ()
canYouBelieveIt copyWith: #now ⇒ OrderedCollection (can you believe it now)
canYouBelieveIt copyWithout: #it ⇒ OrderedCollection (can you believe)
canYouBelieveIt copyReplaceAll: #it with: #(the man)
        ⇒ OrderedCollection (can you believe the man)
story ← #(Once upon) asOrderedCollection
story, #(a time) ⇒ OrderedCollection (Once upon a time)
```

The Array-like and String-like Protocol

Ordered collections can also be manipulated as arrays. Consequently, the traditional array operations **at:** and **at:put:** are available along with all of the string-like operations for searching, replacing, and destructively modifying the ordered collection. See Sect. 8.2.4 for details.

Ordered collections are implemented using the notion of a 'floating' array. Adding elements in front of a sequence can cause the entire sequence of elements to be shifted right to accommodate the insertion. In anticipation of further insertions, a reasonably large gap of unused space is left at the beginning (and the end). These end-gaps are totally invisible to users of ordered collections — even inspectors hide them (unless a basic inspector is used).

Ordered collections always maintain the illusion that the first and last elements are at subscript positions 1 and s where s is the size of the collection. If a new element is added to the left, for example, the subscripts are shifted over so that the new element is at subscript position 1. This is achieved efficiently, not by moving the elements, but by keeping track of the first and last element positions. The fact that implementation details for growing, shrinking, and shifting are totally hidden is what makes ordered collections so useful.

8.4.4 The Sorted Collection Protocol

SortedCollection is a subclass of ordered collection in which the elements are sorted. The sorting criterion is provided by means of a **sort block**, a two-parameter boolean-returning block for comparing successive pairs of elements in a partially sorted sequence. The sort block can be specified explicitly at creation time or the following default sort block used. If the sort block is changed, the entire collection is re-sorted according to the new sort block.

```
defaultBlock ← [:x :y | x <= y]
```

This default block indirectly requests that the elements be sorted in nondecreasing order. Note also that this default sort block is not applicable to arbitrary elements. For example, you cannot create a sorted collection of classes with the default sort block because classes cannot be compared using <=. Of course, a specially devised sort block can be created for this task.

Sect. 8.4.2 discusses the creation of sorted collections in detail; examples are provided below. Once a collection is created, the following methods (in addition to all of those already available for ordered collections) are available for use:

- **sortBlock**
    Returns the sort block used for sorting the elements of the sorted collection.
- **sortBlock**: aBlock
    Changes the sort block used for sorting the elements of the sorted collection and re-sorts the collection. Returns the new sort block.

Examples

theDigits ← #(3 7 9 0 2 1 6 4 8 5).
theDigits **asSortedCollection** ⇒ SortedCollection (0 1 2 3 4 5 6 7 8 9)
theDigits **asSortedCollection**: [:x :y | x <= y] ⇒ SortedCollection (0 1 2 3 4 5 6 7 8 9)
theDigits **asSortedCollection**: [:x :y | x >= y] ⇒ SortedCollection (9 8 7 6 5 4 3 2 1 0)

aWordList ← SortedCollection **sortBlock**: [:x :y |
    (x **size** < y **size**) | (x **size** = y **size and**: x <= y)].
aWordList **addAll**: #(its the one that is small itself).
aWordList ⇒ SortedCollection (is its the one that small itself)
aWordList **sortBlock**: [:x :y | x <= y]
aWordList ⇒ SortedCollection (is its itself one small that the)

8.4.5 The Linked List Protocol

LinkedList is a special sequence in which the elements are subclasses of **Link**. Currently, linked lists are used only for process management. In particular, the only existing specialization of **Link** is class **Process**. Since **LinkedList** cannot be used without a specialization of **Link**, we will assume that class **ValueLink** has been added (see the section on constructing new ordered, sorted, and LinkedList collections for a definition of class **ValueLink**). All linked lists are terminated by **nil**. The linked list protocol is a subset of the ordered collection protocol.

querying and search operations

- aLinkedList **size**
- aLinkedList **isEmpty**
- aLinkedList **first**

  Returns the first **link** in the sequence. If the sequence is empty, an error is reported.
- aLinkedList **last**

  Returns the last **link** in the sequence. If the sequence is empty, an error is reported.

- aLinkedList **includes**: aLink

  Returns true if it contains a link **equal** to aLink; otherwise false.
- aLinkedList **occurrencesOf**: aLink

  Returns the number of links **equal** to aLink.

operations for adding

- aLinkedList **add**: aLink

  Adds aLink to the end of the sequence. Returns aLink.
- aLinkedList **addFirst**: aLink

  Adds aLink to the beginning of the sequence. Returns aLink.
- aLinkedList **addLast**: aLink

  Adds aLink to the end of the sequence. Returns aLink.
- aLinkedList **addAll**: aCollectionOfLinks

  Adds the successive links in aCollectionOfLinks to the end of the sequence. Returns aCollectionOfLinks.

operations for removing

- aLinkedList **removeFirst**

  Removes the first link in the sequence and returns it. If the sequence is empty, an error is reported.

- aLinkedList **removeLast**

  Removes the last link in the sequence and returns it. If the sequence is empty, an error is reported.

- aLinkedList **remove:** aLink {**ifAbsent:** absentBlock}

  Removes aLink; i.e., locates an element **identical** to aLink and removes it from the sequence. If the sequence does not contain an element identical to aLink, absentBlock (if provided) is executed and its result returned or an error is reported. Otherwise, it returns aLink.

- aLinkedList **removeAll:** aCollectionOfLinks

  Removes the successive links in aCollectionOfLinks from the sequence. If it fails to locate any link (using **identical**), an error is reported. Otherwise, it returns aCollectionOfLinks.

In addition to the above, the usual sequencing operations like **do:**, **collect:**, ... are available (see the section on sequencing over collections for a more complete discussion). However, the above protocol is not complete without the **Link** protocol.

Link manipulation operations

- aLink **nextLink**

  Returns the link that comes after the current link.

- aLink **nextLink:** anotherLink

  Modifies aLink so that anotherLink comes after aLink. Returns anotherLink.

- aLinkClass **nextLink:** anotherLink

  Constructs a new uninitialized link and modifies it so that anotherLink comes after it. Returns anotherLink.

Examples

```
anEmptyLinkedList ← LinkedList new.
aLinkedListWithOneElement ←
    LinkedList nextLink: (ValueLink new value: #Hi; yourself).

aLinkedListWithThreeElements ←
    (LinkedList new)
        add: (ValueLink new value: #How; yourself);
        add: (ValueLink new value: #Are; yourself);
        add: (ValueLink new value: #You; yourself);
        yourself.

aLinkedListWithFourElements ←
    LinkedList
        with: (ValueLink new value: #I; yourself)
        with: (ValueLink new value: #Am; yourself)
        with: (ValueLink new value: #Fine; yourself)
        with: (ValueLink new value: #Thanks; yourself).
```

"Constructing a value list with integers 1 2 3 4 from right to left."
aLink ← ValueLink **new value**: 4; **yourself**. aLink **nextLink**: nil. "Note: nil is default."
aLink ← ValueLink **new value**: 3; **nextLink**: aLink; **yourself**.
aLink ← ValueLink **new value**: 2; **nextLink**: aLink; **yourself**.
aLink ← ValueLink **new value**: 1; **nextLink**: aLink; **yourself**.
aLinkedList ← LinkedList **new add**: aLink; **yourself**.

8.5 THE UNORDERED COLLECTIONS

By far the simplest protocol is associated with collections of unordered elements: **sets,
identity sets,** and **bags.** The **unordered collections** are characterized by the specialized
behavior of their element insertion operation **add:** (although other operations are provided)
and by the fact that no specific order is maintained for the elements. Consequently, the
standard sequencing operations are the normal operations for accessing the elements. Typical
operations include the following:

- anUnorderedcCollection **add:** anObject   (adding an element)
- anUnorderedcCollection **includes:** anObject   (testing for an element)
- anUnorderedcCollection **remove:** anObject   (removing an element)
- anUnorderedcCollection **do:** [:anElement | *someCode*]   (element accessing)

The **unordered collections** consist of **bags, sets,** and **identity sets. Bags** permit
arbitrary elements to be inserted independent of the previous contents of the bag. However,
equal elements are not maintained individually. Rather, they are counted and only one
representative element (the first) is kept. **Sets** and **identity sets,** on the other hand, do not
permit duplicates to be added. The duplicates are simply ignored; i.e., it is not considered to
be an error to attempt to add a duplicate. For **sets,** a candidate for insertion is considered to
be a duplicate if the set already contains an element **equal** to it. For **identity sets,** the
candidate is a duplicate if the identity set already contains an element **identical** to it.

The **unordered collections** do not provide the protocol expected by most users. In
general, users might expect more traditional operations like **union:, intersection:,** and
subtraction: (set subtraction)[4]. As indicated above, what distinguishes these classes from
the other collection classes is the insertion behavior and the fact that the elements are
maintained in some arbitrary order.

8.5.1 Individual Characterizations

The **unordered collections** are distinguishable by three characteristics: (1) by the
matching operation used to compare elements (either operation **equal** or **identical**), (2) by
their willingness to admit **duplicates** (new elements that match existing elements), and (3)
by their treatment of the duplicates so admitted (see Fig. 8.8).

Bags should more properly be called **equality bags** since they use **equal** as the
matching operation, admit all duplicates, and maintain only one member of the duplicates
(the first inserted) with a count. The corresponding class of bags that uses **identity** as the

---

[4]Actually, version 2.5 now includes set subtraction as the operation "-".

matching operation, **identity bags**, is not provided in Smalltalk. **Sets** and **identity sets** respectively use **equal** and **identical** as the matching operation and **do not** admit duplicates. Thus, **sets** should more properly be called **equality sets**.

None of these classes are interchangeable — reflecting the fact that an (equality) set is not an identity set, for example, or vice versa. Of course, an (equality) set is like an identity set — it differs only in the matching operation used.

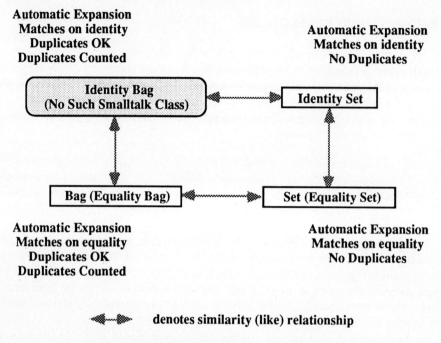

Automatic Expansion
Matches on identity
Duplicates OK
Duplicates Counted

Automatic Expansion
Matches on identity
No Duplicates

Automatic Expansion
Matches on equality
Duplicates OK
Duplicates Counted

Automatic Expansion
Matches on equality
No Duplicates

◄◆► denotes similarity (like) relationship

Figure 8.8 The unordered collections — a logical view.

The unordered collections do have a few restrictions associated with their use. In particular, object **nil** is not allowed as an element of an unordered collection. Attempts to insert or remove **nil** do not result in an error report — insertions simply result in the value disappearing while retrievals always fail to find it.

Although bags permit equality duplicates, the fact that only the first instance is kept is quite apparent. For example, a bag newly constructed by adding 2 and 2.0 (in that order) prints as Bag (2 2). Note that 2.0 is equal to 2. Conversely, if the elements are added in the order 2.0 and 2 instead, the bag would print as Bag (2.0 2.0).

Additionally, unordered collections are implemented using a hashing technique. A consequence of the implementation is an anomaly that is sometimes disturbing. In particular, equal elements with different hashes are sometimes not distinguished. This is not really a fault of the ordered collections implementation. Rather it is a problem with the design of the hash method for certain classes of values. For example, '2 **hash** $\Rightarrow$ 2' while '2.0 **hash** $\Rightarrow$ 0' — the hash method is supposed to be designed in such a way that equality implies equal hashes (but not necessarily vice versa). The consequence is that adding 2 and 2.0 to a set actually adds both (not an expected result).

8.5.2 Constructing New Unordered Collections

There is only one way to construct empty unordered collections; i.e., via **new** (**new:** *initialSize* also works for sets but not for bags). Non-empty unordered collections can be constructed in two ways: using the standard **add:** protocol and using the **with:** protocol.

Bag, Set, or IdentitySet

- anUnorderedCollectionClass **new**
- aSetClass **new:** anInitialSize
- anUnorderedCollectionClass **new add:** anObject; **add:** anObject; ... ; **yourself**
- anUnorderedCollectionClass **with:** $object_1$
- anUnorderedCollectionClass **with:** $object_1$ **with:** $object_2$
- anUnorderedCollectionClass **with:** $object_1$ **with:** $object_2$ **with:** $object_3$
- anUnorderedCollectionClass **with:** $object_1$ **with:** $object_2$ **with:** $object_3$ **with:** $object_4$

Examples

```
Bag new ⇒ Bag ()
Bag with: 1 with: 2 with: 2 ⇒ Bag (1 2 2)
Bag new add: 1; add: 2; add: 2.0; add: 2; add: 1.0; yourself ⇒ Bag (1 1 2 2 2)

IdentitySet new ⇒ IdentitySet ()
IdentitySet new: 10⇒ IdentitySet ()

me ← 'Me'. meCopy ← me copy.
IdentitySet with: me with: 'You' with: me ⇒ IdentitySet ('Me' 'You')
IdentitySet with: me with: 'You' with: meCopy ⇒ IdentitySet ('Me' 'Me' 'You')
IdentitySet new add: 1; add: 2; add: 2.0; add: 2; add: 1.0; yourself
        ⇒ IdentitySet (1 2 2.0 1.0)

Set new ⇒ Set ()
Set new: 10⇒ Set ()

me ← 'Me'. meCopy ← me copy.
Set with: me with: 'You' with: me ⇒ Set ('Me' 'You')
Set with: me with: 'You' with: meCopy ⇒ Set ('Me' 'You')
Set new add: 1; add: 2; add: 2.0; add: 2; add: 1.0; add: 1; yourself
        ⇒ Set (1 2 2.0) "2 hash ~= 2.0 hash (see discussion in previous section)"
```

8.5.3 The Unordered Collection Protocol

Unordered collections provide one of the simplest protocols for inserting, removing, and accessing elements of an unordered sequence. The **matching** operation for **bags** and **sets** is **equal**; for **identity sets**, it is **identical**.

querying operations

- anUnorderedCollection **isEmpty**
- anUnorderedCollection **size**
- anUnorderedCollection **includes:** anElement
    Returns true if it contains an element **matching** anElement ; otherwise false.
- anUnorderedCollection **occurrencesOf:** anElement
    Returns the number of elements **matching** anElement.

insertion operations

- anUnorderedCollection **add**: newObject
  Adds newObject to the unordered collection. Returns newObject.
- anUnorderedCollection **addAll**: aCollection
  Adds each element of aCollection to the unordered collection. Returns aCollection.

removal operations

- anUnorderedCollection **remove**: oldObject {**ifAbsent**: absentBlock}
  Removes oldObject; i.e., locates an element **matching** oldObject and removes it from the unordered collection. If no matching object is found, either absentBlock is executed (if provided) and its result returned, or an error is reported. Otherwise, oldObject is returned.
- anUnorderedCollection **removeAll**: aCollection
  Removes each element of aCollection from the sequence. If any element fails to be located, an error is reported. Otherwise, aCollection is returned.

special operations

- aSet - anotherSet
  Returns a new set containing those elements in aSet that are not in anotherSet.
- aBag **sortedCounts**
  Returns a sorted collection of associations (count of matching elements with associated matching elements) sorted by decreasing counts.
- aBag **sortedElements**
  Returns a sorted collection of associations (matching element with associated count) sorted by decreasing elements.

In addition to these, the standard sequencing operations like **do:**, **collect:**, ... are provided (see the section on sequencing operations for a more detailed discussion).

Examples

anEmptySet ← Set **new**. aNonEmptySet ← Set **with**: 'the' **with**: 'short' **with**: 'statement'.
anEmptySet **isEmpty** ⇒ **true**. aNonEmptySet **isEmpty** ⇒ **false**.
anEmptySet **size** ⇒ 0. aNonEmptySet **size** ⇒ 3.
anEmptySet **includes**: 'short' ⇒ **false**. aNonEmptySet **includes**: 'short' ⇒ **true**.
anEmptySet **occurrencesOf**: 'short' ⇒ 0. aNonEmptySet **occurrencesOf**: 'short' ⇒ 1.

aNonEmptySet ← Set **with**: 'the' **with**: 'short' **with**: 'short' **with**: 'story'.
aNonEmptyBag ← Bag **with**: 'the' **with**: 'short' **with**: 'short' **with**: 'story'.
aNonEmptySet ⇒ Set ('the' 'short' 'story')
aNonEmptyBag ⇒ Bag ('the' 'short' 'short' 'story')
aNonEmptySet **size** ⇒ 3. aNonEmptyBag **size** ⇒ 4.
aNonEmptySet **includes**: 'short' ⇒ **true**. aNonEmptyBag **includes**: 'short' ⇒ **true**.
aNonEmptySet **occurrencesOf**: 'short' ⇒ 1. aNonEmptyBag **occurrencesOf**: 'short' ⇒ 2.

Bag **new**
    addAll: #(the boy and the man went to the railroad station);
    occurrencesOf: #the ⇒ 3
Bag **new addAll**: 'mississippi'; **occurrencesOf**: $s ⇒ 4

Inside Smalltalk

Examples (continued)

'aeiou' **asSet remove:** $u; **yourself** ⇒ Set ($e $i $o $a) "Order is not predictable (ever)"
'aeiou' **asSet remove:** $x **ifAbsent:** [#what] ⇒ what
'hippopotamus' **asSet removeAll:** 'aeiou'; **yourself** ⇒ **(error)** "$e is not in the set"
'hippopotamus' **asSet removeAll:** 'aiou'; **yourself** ⇒ Set ($h $m $p $s $t)
'hippopotamus' **asBag removeAll:** 'aiou'; **yourself** ⇒ Set ($h $m $o $p $p $p $s $t)

aNonEmptyBag ← Set **with:** 'the' **with:** 'short' **with:** 'short' **with:** 'story'.
aNonEmptyBag **sortedCounts** ⇒ SortedCollection (2->'short' 1->'story' 1->'the')
aNonEmptyBag **sortedElements** ⇒ SortedCollection ('short'->2 'story'->1 'the'->1)

#(1 2 3) **asSet** - #(2 3 4) **asSet** ⇒ Set (1)

So as not to leave the impression that set-like operations cannot be added, consider the following extensions added to Bag and Set. Operation **subtract:** is a substitute for "-"; alternatively, we might have used "+" for **union:** and "&" for **intersect:**.

union: aCollection
    ↑self **copy addAll:** aCollection; **yourself**

intersect: aCollection
    | selfCopy finalResult |
    selfCopy ← self **copy.** finalResult ← self **species new.**
    aCollection**do:** [:anElement |
        (selfCopy **includes:** anElement)
                ifTrue: [selfCopy **remove:** anElement. finalResult **add:** anElement]].
    ↑finalResult

subtract: aCollection
    ↑self - aCollection

Example

bag1 ← Bag **with:** #little **with:** #little **with:** #old **with:** #lady.
bag2 ← Bag **with:** #little **with:** #young **with:** #lady.
bag1 **union:** bag2 ⇒ Bag (#lady #lady #little #little #little #young #old)
bag1 **intersect:** bag2 ⇒ Bag (#lady #little)
bag1 **subtract:** bag2 ⇒ Bag (#little #old)

8.6 CREATING NEW COLLECTION CLASSES

Creating new collection classes can be difficult if the new class is designed to inherit from an existing collection class. Part of the difficulty has to do with deciding which methods should be inherited and which should be overridden. A specific method might not apply in the new context or it might have to be modified slightly. This generally requires careful study of the superclass to be resolved. Another problem has to do with the difficulty of ensuring that the specialization will work properly. This is much more difficult, as we will see. To underscore the difficulty, we will consider the design of two new collection classes; UselessStack (a pedagogic exercise only) and **List**. The former will be designed so as to inherit from an existing collection class. The latter, on the other hand, will be totally new — inheriting from Object and thereby avoiding some of the problems that will be encountered by the former.

8.6.1 Creating Specializations of Existing Collection Classes

Creating new specializations of existing collection classes is not an easy matter because there are many small issues that conspire to break the implementation. The more important issue, however, has to do with the problems that arise as a consequence of creating a subclass with additional instance variables.

Before we consider some of the details, suppose we wish to create a class called **UselessStack**. We could easily create a specialization of **OrderedCollection** for the purpose without introducing additional instance variables. To ensure that complications do arise (for didactic purposes only), suppose further that the instances are designed to

1. monitor the number of pushes and pops; i.e., we introduce an instance variable such as **pushesDone**. The number of pops done or the total number of operations executed can be computed from **pushesDone**.

2. be colored; e.g., such stacks might be associated with region growing algorithms that start off with different colors but which adopt a single unique color when they merge. The color, for our purposes, can be any arbitrary user-specific information.

Creating the specialization is usually done through the browser by choosing a class that has the desired relationship (or a similar one). The class creation method displayed by the browser is then modified and executed by having the modification accepted through a menu command. The only reason for mentioning this is to highlight the fact that the class creation code can be different for different collections and to emphasize that this aspect is not shown in the description of class **UselessStack** below.

The first issue is the need to initialize **pushesDone** at the time the stack is created. In fact, arbitrary collections will also have such initialization requirements themselves. Hence it is essential that we do not bypass this initialization code. With the browser, we can find many class methods designed for initializing the class and a few isolated instance methods for initializing instances. Sometimes (especially for class initialization), these methods are called **initialize**. At other times, they are give more private names but there is no consistency between the names.

We might have expected all creation operations like **new** or **new**: to automatically invoke **initialize**. This would work well if the default **initialize** method for Object were to do nothing. Adding a new class with special initialization requirements would simply require an instance method such as the following:

```
initialize
    super initialize.
    special initialization code for this instance
```

This strategy was not pursued in Smalltalk. Consequently, the instance creation operations must be rewritten to perform the initialization themselves. For our stack example, it is not sufficient to include **new**. We also must provide **new**: independently. If we were considering a specialization of stream, for example, we would instead have to provide new versions of **on**: and **with**:. As implementors, we have to be careful to get all the primitive constructors. A preliminary implementation such as the following would be easily devised. Although it seems unnecessary to parameterize initialization, we will use it later when we can take advantage of it. We have chosen to inherit from **OrderedCollection** since this class already can be used in a stack-like fashion; it should therefore be easy to extend.

Class UselessStack

class name	UselessStack
superclass	OrderedCollection
instance variable names	pushesDone color

class methods

creation

new
    ↑super **new privateStackInitialize:** 0
new: anInitialSize
    ↑(super **new:** anInitialSize) **privateStackInitialize:** 0

instance methods

accessing

push: anObject
    pushesDone ← pushesDone + 1
    ↑self **addLast:** anObject
pop
    ↑self **removeLast**
top
    ↑self **last**

monitoring tests

pushesDone
    ↑pushesDone
popsDone
    ↑pushesDone - self **size**
pushesAndPopsDone
    ↑2 * pushesDone - self **size**

color manipulation

color
    ↑color
color: aNewColor
    ↑color ← aNewColor

private

privateStackInitialize: anInitialValue
    pushesDone ← anInitialValue

The above seems sufficient but experimentation will confirm that it is not adequate. For example, suppose we create a stack and associate color #red with it. After pushing and popping for a while, inspecting the stack will show that **pushesDone** has an incorrect value and that **color** has been reset to **nil**. Debugging can be used to locate the culprit, in this case the **grow** operation. Once the stack grows in size beyond its initial space requirements, the **addLast:** operation automatically grows it. However, the **grow** method appears as follows:

```
grow
    | newSelf |
    newSelf ← self species new: self size + self growSize.
    self do: [:each | newSelf addLast: each].
    self become: newSelf
```

The problem is that newSelf above is a new stack. Because we specifically designed **new:** for stacks to initialize **pushesDone**, it is reset to zero and left at that value (**addLast:** does not modify **pushesDone**). In this new stack, **color** is untouched and therefore contains the default value **nil**. A solution is to provide our own grow as follows:

```
grow
    | savedPushesDone savedColor |
    savedPushesDone ← pushesDone. savedColor ← color.
    super grow.
    pushesDone ← savedPushesDone. color ← savedColor
```

By now you should have guessed the general problem. Any operation that creates a new version of an existing stack instance will fail to properly initialize the additional fields. It is not that easy to find all such methods. Some that immediately come to mind include **reverse**, **collect:**, **select:**, **reject:**, and **copy**. Also, inherited operations like **copyEmpty**, **copyWith:**, **copyWithout:**, **copyReplaceAll:**, concatenation (operation ','), and **removeAllSuchThat:** can also be a problem.

There are generally two solutions open to Smalltalk programmers: redefinition or generalization. We will consider both independently.

- **The redefinition approach**: Redefine the methods that are incorrect by inheriting the incorrect behavior and initializing the new instance variables (usually, this just means copying them).

- **The generalization approach**: Generalize the methods to avoid the problem in the future. Only Smalltalk is powerful enough to permit users the generalization luxury.

For the redefinition approach, each misbehaving method must be locally redefined as we have done for **grow**. Two additional examples include

```
collect: aBlock
    | result |
    result ← super collect: aBlock.
    result privateStackInitialize: self size. "It is a new stack"
    result color: self color.
    ↑result

select: aBlock
    | result |
    result ← super select: aBlock.
    result privateStackInitialize: self size. "It is a new stack"
    result color: self color.
    ↑result
```

For the generalization approach, we need to find a technique that can make the introduction of new collection subclasses relatively easy; e.g., by requiring the user to provide a pre-specified number of special methods. A simple technique is suggested by an instance method already provided for **OrderedCollection** and **SortedCollection**; i.e., **copyEmpty**, which can be interpreted as "create me a copy with the same fields as the receiver but without elements" (for subsequent addition). For simplicity, we can actually permit this operation on arbitrary objects. We add instance methods **copyEmpty** and **copyEmpty**: corresponding to class methods **new** and **new**: respectively to class **Object**.

copyEmpty
    ↑self **class new**

copyEmpty: anInitialSize
    ↑self **class new**: anInitialSize

All methods explicitly creating new collections for the purposes of transferring elements (possibly modified) from an old collection are modified to use **copyEmpty** and **copyEmpty**: instead. For example, method **collect**: in **Collection** is modified as follows:

Old version

collect: aBlock
    "Evaluates aBlock with each of the receiver's elements as the argument. Collects the resulting values into a collection that is like the receiver. Returns the new collection."
    | newCollection |
    newCollection ← self **species new**.
    self **do**: [:each | newCollection **add**: (aBlock **value**: each)].
    ↑newCollection

New version

collect: aBlock
    "Evaluates aBlock with each of the receiver's elements as the argument. Collects the resulting values into a collection that is like the receiver. Returns the new collection."
    | newCollection |
    newCollection ← self **copyEmpty**.
    self **do**: [:each | newCollection **add**: (aBlock **value**: each)].
    ↑newCollection

Although finding such methods is difficult in general, the problem is not so difficult in this situation — the majority of the methods can be found using the browser by locating all users of **species**. Note that the modification actually eliminates the need for the **species** concept discussed in Sect. 8.1.4. For instance, there are currently four **species** methods implemented in Smalltalk. Consider the **species** instance method in class Inverval, for example — it simply returns the **Array** class. We can remove the **species** method and replace it by

copyEmpty: anInitialSize
    ↑Array **new**: anInitialSize

For our **UselessStack**, we need to provide **initialize, copyEmpty,** and **copyEmpty:**. However, the addition of a history dependent variable **pushesDone** complicates the issue. Normally, **copyEmpty** and **copyEmpty:** would be designed to simply copy all new fields. At the very least, when a new stack is constructed, we would like **pushesDone** to correspond to the number of pushes required to construct the stack manually (independent of the number actually used in the source stack). The easiest solution is to modify **addLast:** rather than **push:** to perform the counting and to reimplement **grow** to preserve the value in **pushesDone** as follows:

Class UselessStack

class name	UselessStack
superclass	OrderedCollection
instance variable names	pushesDone color

class methods

creation

new
    ↑super **new initialize**
new: anInitialSize
    ↑(super **new**: anInitialSize) **initialize**

instance methods

accessing

addLast: anObject
    pushesDone ← pushesDone + 1
    ↑super **addLast**: anObject
addFirst: anObject
    ↑self **error**: 'cannot add elements to bottom of a stack'
push: anObject
    ↑self **addLast**: anObject
pop
    ↑self **removeLast**
top
    ↑self **last**

monitoring tests

pushesDone
    ↑pushesDone
popsDone
    ↑pushesDone - self **size**
pushesAndPopsDone
    ↑2 * pushesDone - self **size**

color manipulation

color
    ↑color
color: aNewColor
    ↑color ← aNewColor

initialize
> super **initialize** "To initialize fields inherited from the hierarchy"
> pushesDone ← 0
> color ← #grey "or any other default color"

copyEmpty
> | aCopy |
> aCopy ← self **class new**. "Now pushesDone is 0 but color is grey"
> aCopy **color**: self **color**.
> ↑aCopy

copyEmpty: anInitialSize
> | aCopy |
> aCopy ← self **class new**: anInitialSize. "Now pushesDone is 0 but color is grey"
> aCopy **color**: self **color**.
> ↑aCopy

grow
> | savedPushesDone savedColor |
> savedPushesDone ← pushesDone. savedColor ← color.
> super **grow**.
> pushesDone ← savedPushesDone. color ← savedColor

We can also further generalize **new** (and **new**:) to initialize by default by providing a **nonInitializingNew** (and **nonInitializingNew**:). New subclasses would no longer have to provide their own special version of new since the task would be subsumed by **initialize**. See exercise 16 for a short discussion.

To summarize, creating a subclass of collection with its own instance variables will usually require attention to the following considerations:

1. Determining which methods in the superclass can be inherited unchanged, which need to be modified to report an error, and which need to be modified to behave slightly differently.

2. Determining if the object constructors (usually **new** and **new**:) need to be written locally to provide for special initialization requirements.

3. Determining which operations create new versions of existing collections and redefining them locally so as to copy the instance variables from the old versions to the new. Operations like **grow**, **copy**, **select** are typical methods needing special treatment.

In general, problems (if any) will begin to surface only after extensive use of the new class. It is even more crucial than usual to extensively test the new implementation.

8.6.2 Creating a Totally New Sharable Collection Class

One way to avoid the problems associated with the inheritance of methods that fail to work for specializations is to avoid them by creating a totally new subclass of **Object**. The challenge in this case is to provide enough of the traditional collection operations so that the new class is still viewed logically as a member of **Collection**. We will consider doing this for a class of collections that is well known to the Lisp and Prolog community; i.e., **Lists**. By comparison with the existing collection classes, **Lists** provide a property that is lacking:

sharability. A **sharable** data type is a class of objects satisfying the property that part of an instance is itself a separate instance of the same class as the original and independently manipulated as such by design. In Fig. 8.9, for example, lists L_1 and L_3 share the common suffix L_2; $L_1, L_2,$ and L_3 are all independent lists.

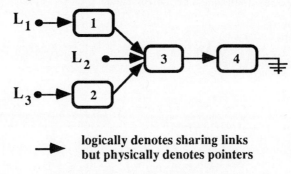

logically denotes sharing links
but physically denotes pointers

Figure 8.9 The Lisp sharing model.

List instances can be partitioned into two classes: empty lists and non-empty lists. We would like to be able to differentiate them without introducing a special instance variable for the purpose. We also would like to provide multiple empty lists (by contrast with Lisp, which provides only one empty list) to avoid special-cased semantics; e.g., copy will always provide a new list independent of whether or not it is empty. Additionally, we would like to provide a design that avoids the pervasive use of code that matches the following template:

```
receiver is empty
    ifTrue: [Do the empty list case]
    ifFalse: [Do the non-empty list case]
```

One solution is to adopt a design based on **prototypes** or **exemplars**; i.e., create two specializations of lists, one for handling empty lists and another for handling non-empty lists. Intuitively, we design as if we were implementing two sample lists: an empty sample and a non-empty sample. This is exactly the same approach taken to implement class **Boolean** with its two specializations **True** and **False**, each designed for its one instance **true** and **false** respectively. Instead of having boolean operations that perform the distinguishing test of the previous template, they are instead implemented differently for each sample boolean or examplar as follows:

```
"for true"                          "for false"
and: anotherBoolean                 and: anotherBoolean
    ↑anotherBoolean                     ↑false
```

In our case, we design specializations EmptyList and NonEmptyList as shown in Fig. 8.10. Non-empty lists are constructed via operation **precede:** (the object-oriented equivalent to the Lisp **cons** operation), which simply encapsulates its two parameters. This information can be subsequently retrieved using **first** and **rest**.

Because of the examplar-based design, **first** for empty lists reports an error whereas, **first** for non-empty lists simply returns the first element of the list. Similarly, **rest** for empty lists reports error, while **rest** for non-empty lists returns the remaining elements

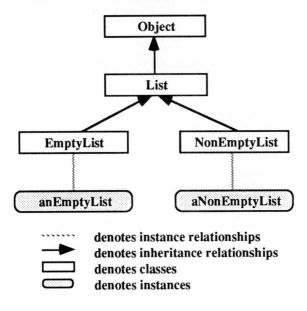

denotes instance relationships
denotes inheritance relationships
denotes classes
denotes instances

Figure 8.10 A design using exemplars.

(uncopied). Another example would be operation **size**, which returns 0 for empty lists and 1 more than the size of the rest of the list for non-empty lists. In all cases, the need to perform an explicit test to distinguish the two cases is avoided.

Rather than analyze the design in detail, we will simply present it and leave it for the reader to discover the design issues underlying the implementation.

Class List

```
class name              List
superclass              Object
instance variable names "none"

class methods

creation

from: aCollection
    | aList |
    aList ← self empty.
    aCollection reverseDo: [:anObject | aList ← aList precede: anObject].
    ↑aList.
empty list creation

empty
    ↑EmptyList new

non-empty list creation

nonEmpty
    ↑NonEmptyList new
```

of: aCollection
    | result |
    result ← self **empty**.
    aCollection **reverseDo**: [:element | result ← result **precede**: element].
    ↑result

with: element
    ↑self **empty precede**: element

with: element1 **with**: element2
    ↑(self **empty precede**: element2) **precede**: element1

with: element1 **with**: element2 **with**: element3
    ↑((self **empty precede**: element3) **precede**: element2) **precede**: element1

with: element1 **with**: element2 **with**: element3 **with**: element4
    ↑(((self **empty precede**: element4) **precede**: element3) **precede**: element2) **precede**: element

instance methods

converting

asArray
    | anArray nextElement |
    anArray ← Array **new**: self **size**. nextElement ← 1.
    self **do**: [:element | anArray **at**: nextElement **put**: element. nextElement ←
    nextElement + 1].
    ↑anArray

asOrderedCollection
    | collection |
    collection ← OrderedCollection **new**.
    self **do**: [:element | collection **add**: element].
    ↑collection

asList
    ↑self **copy**

constructing

precede: anObject
    "Works for both empty and non-empty lists."
    ↑(self **class nonEmpty replaceFirst**: anObject) **replaceRest**: self

---

Class EmptyList

class name	EmptyList
superclass	List
instance variable names	"none"

instance methods

querying

isEmpty
    ↑true

```
length
    ↑0

size
    ↑0
```

comparing

```
= aList
    ↑aList isKindOf: EmptyList
```

accessing

```
allButLast
    ↑self error: 'allButLast is not legal on empty lists'

element: position
    ↑self error: 'position outside bounds of list'

first
    ↑self error: 'first is not legal on empty lists'

last
    ↑self error: 'last is not legal on empty lists'

prefix: newlength
    newlength = 0 ifFalse: [↑self error: 'illegal prefix length'].
    ↑self class empty "Must make a copy"

rest
    ↑self error: 'rest is not legal on empty lists'

rest: anInteger
    anInteger = 0
        ifTrue: [↑self]
        ifFalse: [
            ↑self error: 'rest: anInteger on an empty list is legal only if anInteger = 0']

sublist: start for: size
    size = 0 ifFalse: [↑self error: 'illegal sublist length'].
    ↑self class empty "Must make a copy"

sublist: start to: end
    (start >= (end + 1)) ifFalse: [↑self error: 'illegal sublist length'].
    ↑self class empty "Must make a copy"

suffix: newlength
    newlength = 0 ifFalse: [↑self error: 'illegal suffix length'].
    ↑self "Must not make a copy"
```

constructing

```
copy
    ↑self class empty
```

append: list
      (list **isKindOf:** List) **ifFalse:** [↑self **error:** 'cannot append a nonlist to a list'].
      ↑list

follow: element
      ↑(self **class empty**) **precede:** element

reverse
      ↑self **class empty** "Must make a copy"

destructive modifications

replaceFirst: element
      ↑self **error:** 'replaceFirst is not legal on empty lists'

replaceRest: list
      ↑self **error:** 'replaceRest is not legal on empty lists'

printing

printOn: aStream
      aStream **nextPutAll:** '()'

storeOn: aStream
      aStream **nextPutAll:** '(List **empty**)'

sequencing

collect: block
      ↑self **class empty**

collect: block **when:** testBlock
      ↑self **class empty**

do: block
      "Nothing to do; return self"

inject: value **into:** binaryBlock
      ↑self **error:** 'inject is not legal on empty lists'

reverseDo: block
      "Nothing to do; return self"

Class NonEmptyList

class name	NonEmptyList
superclass	List
instance variable names	firstPart restPart

instance methods

querying

isEmpty
    ↑false

length
    ↑1 + self **rest length**

size
    ↑1 + self **rest length**

comparing

= aList
    ↑(aList **isKindOf**: NonEmptyList) **and:**
        [self **first** = aList **first and:** [self **rest** = self **rest**]]

accessing

allButLast
    self **rest isEmpty**
        ifTrue: [↑self **class empty**]
        ifFalse: [↑(self **rest allButLast**) **precede:** (self **first**)]

element: position
    position = 1 **ifTrue:** [↑self **first**].
    position < 1
        ifTrue: [↑self **error:** 'illegal element position']
        ifFalse: [↑self **rest element:** position - 1]

first
    ↑firstPart

last
    self **rest isEmpty ifTrue:** [↑self **first**] **ifFalse:** [↑self **rest last**]

prefix: newlength
    newlength <= 0 **ifTrue:** [↑self **class empty**].
    ↑(self **rest prefix:** newlength - 1) **precede:** (self **first**)

rest
    ↑restPart

rest: anInteger
    anInteger < 0 **ifTrue:** [
        ↑self **error:** 'rest: anInteger is legal only if anInteger >= 0 and <= list length'].
    anInteger = 0 **ifTrue:** [↑self].
    anInteger = 1 **ifTrue:** [↑restPart] **ifFalse:** [↑restPart **rest:** anInteger - 1]

sublist: start **for:** size
    ↑(self **suffix:** self **length** - start + 1) **prefix:** size

sublist: start **to:** end
    ↑(self **suffix:** self **length** - start + 1) **prefix:** end - start + 1

suffix: newlength
    | result size |
    result ← self. size ← self **length**.
    (newlength < 0) | (newlength > size) **ifTrue:** [↑self **error:** 'illegal suffix length'].
    1 **to:** (size - newlength) **do:** [:i | result ← result **rest**].
    ↑result

constructing

copy
    ↑self **rest copy precede:** self **first**

append: list
    (list **isKindOf:** List) **ifFalse:** [↑self **error:** 'cannot append a non-list to a list'].
    ↑(self **rest append:** list) **precede:** (self **first**)

follow: element
    ↑(self **rest follow:** element) **precede:** (self **first**)

reverse
    ↑self **inject:** self **class empty into:** [:result :element | result **precede:** element]

destructive modifications

replaceFirst: element
    firstPart ← element

replaceRest: list
    (list **isKindOf:** List) **ifFalse:** [↑self **error:** 'cannot replace the rest of a list by a non-list'].
    restPart ← list

printing

printOn: aStream
    aStream **nextPut:** $(. self **first printOn:** aStream.
    self **rest do:** [:element | aStream **nextPut:** $. element **printOn:** aStream].
    aStream **nextPut:** $)

storeOn: aStream
    aStream **nextPutAll:** '(List empty precede: '. self **first printOn:** aStream.
    self **rest do:** [:element |
        aStream **nextPutAll:** '; precede: '. element **printOn:** aStream].
    aStream **nextPut:** $)

sequencing

collect: block
    ↑(self **rest collect:** block) **precede:** (block **value:** self **first**)

collect: block **when:** testBlock
    (testBlock **value:** self **first**)
        ifTrue: [
            ↑(self **rest collect:** block **when:** testBlock) **precede:** (block **value:** self **first**)]
        ifFalse: [↑(self **rest collect:** block **when:** testBlock)]

do: block
    block **value:** self **first**. self **rest do:** block

inject: value **into:** binaryBlock
    | lastValue |
    lastValue ← value.
    self **do:** [:element | lastValue ← binaryBlock **value:** lastValue **value:** element].
    ↑lastValue

reverseDo: block
    self **rest reverseDo:** block. block **value:** self **first**

8.7 SUMMARY

In this chapter, we have described the **Collection** classes — Smalltalk's workhorse data types. In particular, we have discussed the following notions:

- The physical and logical organization of the **Collection** and **Stream** classes.
- Approaches for creating, comparing, and sequencing over collections.
- The protocol supported by the keyed collection classes.
- Dictionaries as array-like containers for objects associated with arbitrary keys.
- The association, array, and set protocol supported by dictionaries.
- The array and string protocol supported by arrays, ordered collections, strings and their subclasses.
- The magnitude, string, and conversion protocol supported by classes **String**, **Text**, and **Symbol**.
- The protocol supported by classes **MappedCollection**, **RunArray**, and **Interval**.
- Streams as mechanisms for accessing and modifying collections through inter-ruptible sequencing.
- Read, write, read-write, and character streams.
- **Filename** as the interface with external streams (files).
- Classes **OrderedCollection**, **SortedCollection**, and **LinkedList** as members of the ordered classes and their detailed protocol.
- **Set**, **IdentitySet**, and **Bag** as unordered collections.
- Defining a new stack class — a pedagogic example illustrating possible pitfalls.
- An exemplar-based approach to the implementation of a shared **List** type.

8.8 EXERCISES

The following exercises may require some original thought, rereading some of the material, and/or browsing through the system.

1. Define some of the missing conversion operations; e.g., **asDictionary**.

2. Where should the methods **bold**, *italic*, and **underlined** be added to facilitate users? Define one of these methods.

3. Some classes, like strings, have comparison operations <, >, and = defined on them, and yet they are not subclasses of Magnitude. Why?

4. In the section on adding your own sequencing operations, we introduced a **do:** for sequencing through the digits of an integer. In this version, the sign was ignored. Show what changes are needed to associate the sign with the leftmost digit.

5. Operations **findFirst:** and **findLast:** are defined either in abstract class **SequenceableCollection** or **ArrayedCollection**. First, decide

which class is logically correct for the operation and then find out whether or not this is the choice used in the current system.

6. Devise an alternate strategy for type conversion based on the notion that all collections have a **do:** operation. As a suggestion, consider adding class methods like the following to abstract classes Collection and Stream (or to Object):

```
convert: aCollection
    | newCollection |
    newCollection ← self new:
        aCollection size.
    aCollection do: [:element |
        newCollection
            add: element].
    ↑newCollection
```

Note that users would now make conversion requests to the class; e.g., Dictionary **convert:** #(1 2 3) or Set **convert:** #(1 2 2 3 3 3). How many variations need to be added to permit conversions between all classes?

7. Transform the existing **findFirst:** method into 'findNext: aBlock after: aKey'. Similarly, transform the **findLast:** method into 'find-Previous: aBlock before: aKey'.

8. Generalize **associationsDo:** and **keysDo:** so that they also work for **arrayed** collections.

9. Perform an experiment to determine whether or not methods **includes:**, **includesAssociation:**, and **oc-currencesOf:** work correctly for IdentityDictionaries. Performing such experiments is a useful technique for determining undocumented semantics or verifying documented semantics.

10. Design additional operations for **OrderedCollection** that eliminate the *first-occurrence bias* of the basic operations.

11. Provide alternative stream construction operations **atBeginningOf:** and **atEndOf:** for **on:** and **with:** respectively. Additionally, design a variation **positionedAt:** that permits more general initial position-

ing. None of these should make a copy of the collection being streamed over. Investigate the feasibility of removing **on:** and **with:** from the system.

12. Investigate the idea of changing the semantics of the stream operation **contents** so that it returns the original collection rather than a copy. One requirement, for instance, would be the need to truncate the as yet unwritten parts of the collection; e.g., consider the **printString** method.

13. Locate and modify stream methods **through:** and **upTo:** so that the elements returned for 'aStream **through:** anObject' include anObject whereas those returned for 'aStream **upTo:** anObject' exclude anObject. Additionally, change the operations so that they return all **remaining** elements in the situation where no element equal to anObject is found.

14. Design and implement a stream operation 'upToAll: aCollection' that searches for the next occurrence of aCollection and returns a collection of the elements up to that point. The stream is repositioned at the beginning of the portion that matches aCollection. If no such matching collection is found, return the **remaining** elements.

15. Redesign (and complete) the sequencing operations for streams so that they have no side effects; i.e., once complete they reposition the stream to its original position.

16. Perform an experiment on the = method for **intervals** by executing the following:

```
| anInterval |
anInterval ← 1 to: 10.
anInterval = anInterval copy
```

If there is a problem, decide on a solution and fix it.

17. Design method = for selected collections that lack it. In particular, design an = for streams that has no side effects.

18. Since most objects need to be initialized to work properly, it is reasonable to extend (or modify) the system so that both class methods **uninitializedNew** (the old new) and an initializing version (the new version) be provided along with a default instance method **initialize** as follows:

aClass **new**
    ↑self **uninitializedNew initialize**

anObject **initialize**
    ↑self "default is to do nothing"

When designing a new specialization, implementors would have to provide their own version of **initialize** (when necessary) as follows:

anObject **initialize**
    super **initialize**
    specialization specific
    initializations
    ↑self

There should be no need to provide a special version of **new**. However, if a version such as the following were inadvertently provided, would its use lead to infinite loops or simply be inefficient?

aClass **new**
    ↑super **new initialize**

19. Design and implement additional **set** and **bag** operations.

20. Design a variation of Interval that can handle a geometric progression (intervals currently handle an arithmetic progression).

21. Investigate the correctness and feasibility of providing the following **copyEmpty** instance method in **Object**.

copyEmpty
    | aCopy |
    aCopy ← self **class new**.
    1 **to:** self **class instSize**
    do: [:component |
        aCopy
            instVarAt: component
            put: (self **instVarAt:**
                component)].
  ↑aCopy

8.9 GLOSSARY AND IMPORTANT FACTS

The Abstract Collections

ArrayedCollection An abstract class for the integer-keyed collections. Does not include ordered collections.

Collection The most general abstract class. It does not include streams as a subclass.

ExternalStream The most general abstract class for streams that permit access to files.

IntegerArray An abstract class for ByteArray and WordArray.

InternalStream An abstract class for finite streams on integer-keyed collections.

PositionableStream An abstract class for all finite read and write streams that can provide random access to arbitrary locations in the stream.

PeekableStream An abstract class for all finite read and write streams that can peek at least one object ahead.

SequenceableCollection An abstract class for the ordered classes (excluding streamable classes and mapped collections).

Stream An abstract class for all streamable collections.

Array A class that maintains a set of associations between integer keys and elements. The keys must be integers in the range 1, 2, ..., anUpperBound where the upper bound is determined at creation time. The elements can be arbitrary objects. Arrays do not expand automatically (hence, subscripting out of bounds is a possible error). However, Arrays may be specifically grown if desired.

ByteArray A special kind of array in which the elements are integers restricted to the range 0 to 255.

Dictionary An array-like class that maintains a set of associations between keys and elements. Both keys and elements can be arbitrary objects. It differs from Identity-Dictionary in that two keys match iff they are equal; i.e., if $key_1 = key_2$. Dictionaries expand automatically as required. Specializations include **System-Dictionary**, which has only one instance named *Smalltalk* containing all global variables, and **LiteralDictionary**, which permits constants as keys without allowing type conversion (thus, keys 1 and 1.0 would be distinct — this is not the case for **Dictionary**).

IdentityDictionary An array-like class that maintains a set of associations between keys and elements. Both keys and elements can be arbitrary objects. Two keys match iff they are identical; i.e., if $key_1 == key_2$. Identity dictionaries expand automatically as required. A specialization is **MethodDictionary**, used by Smalltalk to maintain compiled code.

Interval A special kind of integer array that specifies an arithmetic sequence. The sequence is determined at the time the instance is created and may not be changed or grown. It is usually used for looping control. Specialization **TextLineInterval** is used for managing paragraphs of text and is not intended for public use.

MappedCollection A special kind of array that provides access to another array via a subscript map. For example, if map_1 maps subscript i to subscript j (say) and $array_1$ contains elements accessible by subscript i, then a mapped collection $test_1$ can be constructed from map_1 and $array_1$ such that accessing $test_1$ with i is equivalent to accessing $array_1$ with map_1 of i. For example, in a Pascal-like syntax, $test_1$ [i] == $array_1$ [map_1 [i]]. MappedCollections may not be grown.

OrderedCollection A container for arbitrary objects. The sequence used for entering the elements determines the order — typical operations are provided for adding at the beginning or the end of the collection. Ordered collections are automatically expanded when more room is needed.

RunArray A special kind of array that is space efficient if it contains long runs of equal values. RunArrays may not be grown.

SortedCollection A special kind of ordered collection that sorts its elements according to a predefined sort block. The default sort block bases the sort on comparison operation <=.

String A special kind of array in which the elements are characters. It is also logically a Magnitude; i.e., it permits comparisons using <, >, =, <=, >=, and ~=. Strings may be grown if explicitly requested.

Symbol A special kind of string that denotes a name. All symbols with the same characters are identical; i.e., if $symbol_1 = symbol_2$, then $symbol_1 == symbol_2$. Symbols cannot be grown.

Text A special kind of string with associated font information. Texts may be grown if explicitly requested.

WordArray A special kind of array in which the elements are integers restricted to the range 0 to 65,535.

The Streamable Collections

Filename A special interface class for keeping track of a file via a name provided as a string; provides access to external streams for manipulating the file contents.

Random An infinite stream of reals in the range 0.0 to 1.0 exclusive of the end points.

ReadStream A finite stream that permits elements of an arbitrary collection to be read (accessed). Repositioning within the stream is also possible.

ReadWriteStream A finite stream that permits both access and modification to the elements (including addition) in a sequential fashion and additionally provides repositioning capabilities.

WriteStream A finite stream that permits elements to be overwritten (or added) to an arbitrary collection. Repositioning within the stream is also possible.

Remaining Ordered Collections

LinkedList A special kind of ordered collection in which the elements must be of type Link. It is currently used only by the system for process management.

The Unordered Collections

Bag (logically an equality bag) An arbitrary collection of objects with equality duplicates allowed; an element is an equality duplicate if it is equal (operation =) to another element. The elements in a bag are normally accessible in some arbitrary order. Duplicates are maintained by keeping only one representative element along with a count. Bags are automatically expanded when more room is needed.

IdentitySet An arbitrary collection of objects in which identity duplicates are discarded; an element is an identity duplicate if it is identical (operation ==) to another element. The elements in an identity set are normally accessible in some arbitrary order. Identity sets are automatically expanded when more room is needed.

Set (logically an equality set) A variation of an identity set (or bag) in which equality duplicates are discarded. Sets are also automatically expanded when more room is needed.

selected terminology

becoming An operation that transforms one object A into another object B by redirecting all A-references to B (and vice versa).

container An object that can contain many other objects.

destructive Having side-effects on (modifying) the receiver.

emphasis Additional text information such as **bold**, **underlined**, and **italic**. The actual codes include (0) basal, (1) bold, (2) italic, (3) boldItalic, (4) underlined, (8) overStruck, (16) subscripted, (32) superscripted, (20) subscriptedUnderlined, and (36) superscriptedUnderlined.

growing The act of extending a collection so that it can accommodate additional elements.

map A keyed collection that is used to transform a user subscript into a more appropriate internal subscript.

mappee The collection accessed indirectly via the map.

matching A term used to describe the operation used to compare elements — the matching operation for identity sets is identity, and for sets it is equality. Also a specific string operation **matchFor:**.

ordered Position dependent values; e.g., #(4 7 2 4 1).

sequencing operation An operation like **do:**, **collect:**, and **inject:into:** that provides access to all elements in a collection.

sorted An ordered sequence in which adjacent elements satisfy a sort criterion; e.g., #(1 2 4 4 7) with sort criterion **nondecreasing**.

species The class to be used when creating a modified copy of a collection.

important facts

Experts use inject:into: Novices tend to overuse sequencing operation **do:** even when more appropriate operations like **inject:into:** are available.

Most applicable conversions X asOrderedCollection, X asSet, X asArray.

No abstract class instances One of the more common errors is to attempt to create an instance of an abstract class; e.g., Collection **new**.

Stream on: versus with: Executing 'aStreamClass **on:** aCollection' creates a stream positioned at the beginning whereas 'aStreamClass **with:** aCollection' creates a stream positioned at the end.

Most common mistake Getting an empty array (or string) using Array **new** or String **new** and then attempting to insert an element into it (a subscript out of bounds error).

Another common mistake Attempting to get an instance of an abstract class; e.g., via Collection **new**.

9

The Graphics Classes

9.1 INTRODUCTION

When the Macintosh computer was introduced in 1983 by Apple Computer, it was loudly praised as the "personal computer for the rest of us." The implication was that now there was a computer that was so friendly and easy to use that it could be used by non-programmers. How was this achieved? Applications no longer required users to type complicated command line sequences from the keyboard. Instead, most user interaction became graphics-based and used a simulation metaphor that was familiar to users. For example, the Macintosh adopted the desktop metaphor as its primary interface to the user. Iconic representations of applications and documents sit on a virtual desktop (the display screen). Tasks are carried out interactively and intuitively. For example, a document is deleted simply by dragging its iconic representation to the icon that looks like a garbage can. User interfaces built on the use of icons, overlapping windows, pull-down menus, dialog boxes, and so on have now become the standard for personal computers and are often referred to as WIMP (Window-Icon-Menu-Pointer) interfaces.

What is not so well known is that much of the research work that led to the development of systems like the Macintosh was done as part of the Smalltalk research effort at Xerox PARC (Palo Alto Research Center). Alan Kay, Adele Goldberg, and Dan Ingalls and others foresaw that inexpensive personal computers would soon be able to support high resolution bit-mapped displays and that, together with interactive devices such as mice, a new style of programming and user interface was required. The key realization was that graphics and graphical interaction would form the core of all future computer systems. In this chapter, we discuss the Smalltalk classes that support the interactive creation and manipulation of graphical images. We devote all of the second volume to a discussion of the model-view-controller metaphor and the user-interface classes used to support the development of interactive graphical applications in Smalltalk.

9.1.1 The Smalltalk Graphical Model

Smalltalk is implemented on workstations that support a high resolution bit-mapped display. The term **bit-mapped** originates from the fact that display images are (at least logically) thought of as two-dimensional arrays of bits, where the value of each bit (e.g., 1 for black, 0 for white) indicates the color of the corresponding pixel in the image. Smalltalk adopts this model for describing graphical images; e.g., the normal Smalltalk cursor is shown in Fig. 9.1 both in an expanded form to show the individual bits that make up the image and in standard size.

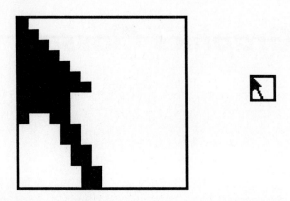

Figure 9.1 An expanded view of the bits in a cursor.

9.1.2 Graphic Capabilities of Smalltalk

The Smalltalk system provides support for a wide range of graphic functions. We can isolate five distinct applications.

Painting pictures   Graphical images may be constructed and edited by electronically "painting" pictures on the display — the display screen becomes an artist's canvas and the mouse becomes a paintbrush. Images may be constructed freehand using brushes of different textures, shapes, and sizes. In particular, Smalltalk provides two tools, a **form editor** and a **bit editor**, for creating pictures. The form editor is the predecessor of the paint programs now commonly found on personal computers (e.g., MacPaint on the Macintosh). Editing of an image at the individual bit level is performed using the bit editor (the equivalent of Fat Bits in MacPaint).

Simple animation   Simple animation sequences can be constructed by cycling through a sequence of predetermined frames, by dynamically modifying a single frame, or by displaying one frame while constructing the next (double buffering).[1]

---

[1]Chapter 10 discusses the implementation of film loops – a primitive animation facility.

     Inside Smalltalk

Turtle graphics   Images may also be created algorithmically. **Pens** are the Smalltalk equivalent of the turtles found in the programming language LOGO. Pens are objects whose heading and position can be manipulated using simple "robot-like" commands such as **turn through 90 degrees** or **go forward 100 units**. When a pen is moved with its nib in the down position, a trail follows its path. The notions of turtle graphics, turtle geometry, and of using the computer as a medium for mathematical discovery, originate from the work of Seymour Papert et al.[2] at MIT.

Displaying text   Text in Smalltalk may be displayed in a variety of different fonts (e.g., serif, sans serif, ...), sizes (e.g., 10 point, 12 point, ...), and styles (e.g., italic, bold, underlined, ...). Fig. 9.2 illustrates some of the available text styles.

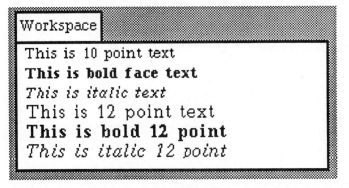

Figure 9.2 Smalltalk text styles.

Constructing paths   Geometric objects such as arcs, circles, lines, curves, and splines may be displayed also. These objects are displayed by storing or computing the points that lie on the path or trajectory of the object. Fig. 9.3 shows a cubic spline curve drawn through five control points.

Figure 9.3 Cubic spline.

---

[2]Papert, S., Mindstorms: Children, Computers, and Powerful Ideas (New York; Basic Books, 1980).

Before we can describe the Smalltalk graphical classes in detail, we must describe the spatial classes **Point** and **Rectangle**, which are heavily used by the graphical classes, and also discuss classes **Form** and **BitBlt**, which are the key to understanding how all images are represented and displayed in Smalltalk.

9.2 POSITIONS AND AREAS: CLASSES POINT AND RECTANGLE

The classes **Point** and **Rectangle** are used to represent spatial information. Individual pixels within a graphic image or on the display screen can be located by instances of class Point. Similarly, rectangular areas of pixels within a graphic image or on the display screen can be located by instances of class Rectangle.

As illustrated in Fig. 9.4, Smalltalk adopts a coordinate system for images (and the display screen) that has the origin in the top left-hand corner with the x-axis increasing to the right and the y-axis increasing downwards. A point is a single x-y integer pair in this system, while a rectangle is a rectangular region specified by two points representing the top left and bottom right corners of the region.

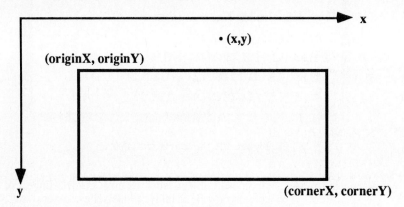

Figure 9.4   Smalltalk coordinate system.

Note that points and rectangles are not displayable objects — they represent spatial quantities only. There are no operations provided by Smalltalk to display a point or a rectangle.

9.2.1 Creating Points and Rectangles

Creating Points

Points may be created in two different ways: using the binary operator @ defined on integers or by using the class method x:y:.

* anInteger **@** anotherInteger
    Returns a point with x and y coordinates set to anInteger and anotherInteger respectively.

- Point **x**: xCoordinate **y**: yCoordinate
    Returns a point with x and y coordinates set to xCoordinate and yCoordinate respectively.

For example, the expressions

100 @ 150
Point **x**: 100 **y**: 150

both return the point with x coordinate 100 and y coordinate 150. Note that points are really pairs since any two objects can be supplied for x and y — no run-time checks are implemented. Programmers should be aware that this may cause difficulties; e.g., the expression Point **x**: -5.6 **y**: 100@100 returns a 'point' whose y coordinate is another point.

Creating Rectangles

Rectangles can be created in a variety of ways. The most common method is by sending an **extent**: aPoint or **corner**: aPoint message to a point. For example, both of the following expressions return a rectangle with origin (top left corner) at 100@100 and bottom right corner at 300@300.

100@100 **corner**: 300@300
100@100 **extent**: 200@200

In general, the protocol is the following:

- aPoint **corner**: cornerPoint
    Returns a rectangle whose origin is aPoint and whose corner is cornerPoint.
- aPoint **extent**: extentPoint
    Returns a rectangle whose origin is aPoint and whose width and height are provided by extentPoint.

As with points, rectangles are really simply pairs, and any two objects can be supplied for the origin and corner. In the case of rectangles, it is also important to ensure that the bottom right corner really is below and to the right of the top left corner; e.g., Rectangle **origin**: 100@100 **corner**: 50@50 is not a valid rectangle.

Alternatively, rectangles may be created by sending the following messages to class Rectangle:

- Rectangle **origin**: originPoint **corner**: cornerPoint
    Returns a rectangle whose top left and bottom right corners are originPoint and cornerPoint respectively.
- Rectangle **origin**: originPoint **extent**: extentPoint
    Returns a rectangle whose top left corner is originPoint and whose width and height are provided by extentPoint.
- Rectangle **left**: leftX **right**: rightX **top**: topY **bottom**: bottomY
    Returns a Rectangle with left, right, top, and bottom coordinates as given.

For example, the expressions

Rectangle **origin**: 100@100 **corner**: 300@300
Rectangle **origin**: 100@100 **extent**: 200@200
Rectangle **left**: 100 **right**: 300 **top**: 100 **bottom**: 300

all return the same rectangle.

Creating Rectangles Interactively

Alternatively, the user can create a rectangle by interactively selecting a rectangular area on the display.

- Rectangle **fromUser**

  Returns a rectangle whose top left and bottom right corners are designated interactively by the user. This is achieved in the same manner as framing a window.

- Rectangle **originFromUser**: extentPoint

  Returns a rectangle with the top left corner selected interactively by the user and width and height determined from extentPoint.

Creating Rectangles Using Grids and Aspect Ratios

In addition, class methods are provided that constrain a rectangle specified interactively to have either corner points that must lie on some user-specified grid or a width and height that must satisfy some given aspect ratio. Grids and aspect ratios are specified as points. For example, a grid specified as 5@10 constrains the x coordinates of the corners of the rectangle to be a multiple of 5 and the y coordinates of the corners to be a multiple of 10. Gridding is useful for accurate positioning of rectangles. An aspect ratio specified as 2@3 constrains the width and height of a rectangle to have the ratio 2 to 3. Note that any gridding and aspect ratios are to assist in the initial creation of rectangles only. They are not maintained by rectangles; i.e., subsequent modifications to any existing rectangle will not satisfy any originally specified constraints.

- Rectangle **fromUser**: gridPoint

  Returns a rectangle whose top left and bottom right corners are designated interactively by the user and where the x and y coordinates of the corners are constrained to be multiples of the x and y coordinates of gridPoint respectively.

- Rectangle **fromUserAspectRatio**: aspectPoint

  Returns a rectangle whose top left and bottom right corners are designated interactively by the user and where the rectangle is constrained so that the ratio of width to height is determined by aspectPoint.

- Rectangle **originFromUser**: extentPoint **grid**: scaleFactor

  Returns a rectangle whose top left corner is designated interactively by the user and where the width and height are determined by extentPoint. The gridding for user selection is scaleFactor. Assumes that the sender has determined an extent that is a proper multiple of scaleFactor; if not, the bottom right corner will not lie on the grid.

9.2.2 Printing and Storing Points and Rectangles

Classes Point and Rectangle both implement specialized methods for the printing and storing of points and rectangles. The standard **printString** and **storeString** protocol for all objects calls the **printOn:** aStream and **storeOn:** aStream methods associated with each class.

Points print in infix notation, for example, '100@100', and store using the form 'Point x: 100 y: 100'. Rectangles print in the form '100@100 corner: 300@300' and store in the form 'Rectangle origin: 100@100 corner: 300@300'.

- aPoint **printString**
- aPoint **storeString**
- aPoint **printOn:** aStream
- aPoint **storeOn:** aStream

- aRectangle **printString**
- aRectangle **storeString**
- aRectangle **printOn:** aStream
- aRectangle **storeOn:** aStream

9.2.3 Copying Points and Rectangles

Deep and shallow copy operations are reimplemented in class Point purely for efficiency reasons. Note that the default copy operation for rectangles is a deep rather than a shallow copy.

- aPoint **deepCopy**
- aPoint **shallowCopy**
- aRectangle **copy**
  Returns a deep copy rather than a shallow copy.

9.2.4 Accessing and Modifying Points and Rectangles

Accessing and Modifying Points

The x and y coordinates of a point may be accessed and modified using the **x, y, x:,** and **y:** instance methods.

- aPoint **x**
- aPoint **y**
- aPoint **x:** anInteger
- aPoint **y:** anInteger

It is very unusual to use the **x:** and **y:** methods to modify a point. Points are normally thought of as immutable.

Accessing and Modifying Rectangles

A wide variety of rectangle components may be accessed and modified. Fig. 9.5 describes the terminology used in describing the parts of a rectangle.

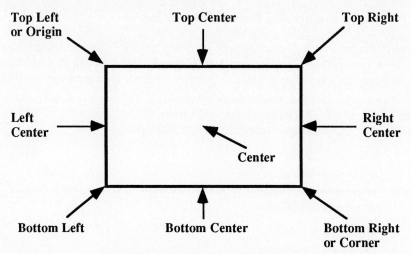

Figure 9.5 Rectangle class terminology.

Additionally, the terms **left** and **right** are used to refer to the x values of the left and right sides of the rectangle. Similarly, **top** and **bottom** are used to refer to the y values of the top and bottom of the rectangle.

- aRectangle **width**
- aRectangle **width**: widthInteger
- aRectangle **height**
- aRectangle **height**: heightInteger

- aRectangle **left**
- aRectangle **left**: anInteger
- aRectangle **right**
- aRectangle **right**: anInteger
- aRectangle **top**
- aRectangle **top**: anInteger
- aRectangle **bottom**
- aRectangle **bottom**: anInteger

- aRectangle **topLeft**
- aRectangle **topLeft**: topLeftPoint
- aRectangle **topRight**

- aRectangle **bottomLeft**
- aRectangle **bottomRight**
- aRectangle **bottomRight**: bottomRightPoint

- aRectangle **leftCenter**
- aRectangle **rightCenter**
- aRectangle **topCenter**
- aRectangle **bottomCenter**

Inside Smalltalk

- aRectangle **origin**
- aRectangle **origin**: originPoint **corner**: cornerPoint
- aRectangle **origin**: originPoint **extent**: extentPoint

- aRectangle **center**
- aRectangle **corner**
- aRectangle **corner**: cornerPoint
- aRectangle **extent**
- aRectangle **extent**: extentPoint

- aRectangle **area**

Note that, of the corners of a rectangle, only the top left and bottom right corners may be modified directly.

9.2.5 Conversion Operations

The method **asPoint** supported by integers converts an integer to a point. For example, the expression 150 **asPoint** returns the point 150@150.

- anInteger **asPoint**
  Returns a new point with both x and y values set to anInteger.

- aPoint **asPoint**
  Returns aPoint (self).

No conversion operations are supported by class Rectangle.

9.2.6 Arithmetic Operations

The standard arithmetic operators are supported on points. For each of the binary operators, +, -, *, /, and //, the argument may be a point or a number. Note that since the methods **coerce**: aNumber and **generality** are implemented for class Point, the argument for the binary arithmetic operators can be a point or any number. Indeed, binary arithmetic messages may be sent to the numeric classes with points as arguments; i.e., messages such as 3 * (50@50) are valid. Points have a generality of 90 — greater than any other number class. When coerced, numbers are converted to points with x and y values both equal to the number.

Arithmetic operations are carried out by independently applying the operation to the corresponding x and y coordinates; e.g.,

```
100@150 + (200@100)     ⇒ 300@250
3@2 * (100@100)         ⇒ 300@200
100@100) / (10@5)       ⇒ 10@20
```

More generally, the protocol is the following:

- aPoint * aPointOrNumber
  Returns a new point that is the product of aPoint and aPointOrNumber.

- aPoint + aPointOrNumber
  Returns a new point that is the sum of aPoint and aPointOrNumber.
- aPoint - aPointOrNumber
  Returns a new point that is the difference of aPoint and aPointOrNumber.
- aPoint / aPointOrNumber
  Returns a new point that is the quotient of aPoint and aPointOrNumber.
- aPoint // aPointOrNumber
  Returns a new point that is the result of applying integer division to aPoint
  and aPointOrNumber and truncating the result toward negative infinity.
- aPoint **abs**
  Returns a new point whose x and y coordinates are the absolute values of
  the x and y coordinates of aPoint.

No arithmetic operations are supported on rectangles.

9.2.7 Comparing Points and Rectangles

Comparing Points

The relational operators are defined on points as follows. A point is said to be less than
another if both its x and y values are less than the other. Alternatively, this can be expressed
spatially by stating that one point is less than another if it is above and to the left of the
other. Similar mathematical or spatial interpretations can be given to each of the relational
operators.

You might expect that, since arithmetic operators successfully coerce numbers to
points when one of the arguments is a number, the relational operators would behave in the
same way. Unfortunately, this is not the case. Binary operators on points must have a point
as argument. On the other hand, numbers will accept relational operators where a point is
given as the argument; e.g.,

```
100@100 < (50@50)      ⇒ false
100@100 < 50           ⇒ error
100 < (50@50)          ⇒ false
```

The relational operators include the following:

- aPoint < anotherPoint
  Returns true if aPoint is above and to the left of anotherPoint.
- aPoint > anotherPoint
  Returns true if aPoint is below and to the right of anotherPoint.
- aPoint <= anotherPoint
  Returns true if aPoint is neither above nor to the left of anotherPoint.
- aPoint >= anotherPoint
  Returns true if aPoint is neither below nor to the right of anotherPoint.
- aPoint = anotherPoint
  Returns true if the x and y coordinates of each point are equal.
- aPoint **hash**
  Implemented because = is reimplemented.

Additionally, the maximum and minimum of any pair of points can be found with respect to the relational operators defined earlier.

- aPoint **max**: anotherPoint
  Returns the lower right corner of the rectangle defined by aPoint and anotherPoint.
- aPoint **min**: anotherPoint
  Returns the upper left corner of the rectangle defined by aPoint and anotherPoint.

Comparing Rectangles

Rectangles may only be compared for equality.

- aRectangle = anotherRectangle
  Returns true if the origin and corner points of aRectangle and anotherRectangle are equal.
- aRectangle **hash**
  Implemented because = is reimplemented.

9.2.8 Truncating and Rounding Points and Rectangles

Protocol is supported for rounding and truncating points in two ways. The x and y coordinates can be rounded using **rounded**. In addition, points can be rounded or truncated to lie on some specified grid using **grid:**, **truncatedGrid:**, and **truncateTo:**.

- aPoint **rounded**
  Returns a new point with x and y values derived by independently rounding the x and y values of aPoint.

  (125.5@120.4) **rounded** $\Rightarrow$ 126@120

- aPoint **grid**: aGridPoint
  Returns a new Point that is the nearest rounded point to aPoint on the grid specified by aGridPoint.

  126@133 **grid**: 5@5 $\Rightarrow$ 125@135

- aPoint **truncatedGrid**: aGridPoint
  Returns a new Point that is the nearest truncated point to aPoint on the grid specified by aGridPoint.

  126@133 **truncatedGrid**: 5@5 $\Rightarrow$ 125@130

- aPoint **truncateTo**: integerGridValue
  Like truncatedGrid except that the argument must be a number rather than a point. The comment in the Smalltalk system suggests that the argument should be a point. Note that this method fails if given a point for the argument.

  126@133 **truncateTo**: 5 $\Rightarrow$ 125@130

In the case of rectangles, protocol is supported to round a rectangle by rounding the origin and corner points.

- aRectangle **rounded**

    Returns a new rectangle with origin and corner derived by rounding the origin and corner points of aRectangle.

    (125.5@120.4 **corner:** 45.8@32.1) **rounded** ⇒ 126@120 corner: 46@32

9.2.9 Points in Polar Coordinate Form

Information about a point can also be returned to the programmer in polar coordinates. In the polar coordinate system (see Fig. 9.6), a point is represented by the distance from the origin to the point (radius) and the angle a line joining the origin to the point makes with the positive x-axis. Angles are measured clockwise from the x-axis; right is 0, down is 90 degrees or $\pi/2$ radians. A point in the polar coordinate system is commonly referred to by its (r, θ) components; θ is measured in radians.

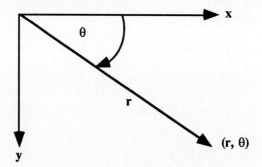

Figure 9.6 Polar coordinate system.

- aPoint **r**

    Returns the radius (the distance from the origin) of the receiver.
- aPoint **theta**

    Returns the θ component (the angle a line joining the x-axis makes with the positive x-axis) of the receiver.

9.2.10 Miscellaneous Point Operations

Methods are provided to compute the distance between two points and the distance between a point and a line.

- aPoint **dist:** anotherPoint

    Returns the distance between aPoint and anotherPoint.
- aPoint **pointNearestLine:** point1 **to:** point2

    Returns a new Point nearest to aPoint that is on a line from point1 to point2.

The normal and unit vector of a point and the dot product of two points can also be computed.

- aPoint **dotProduct**: anotherPoint

  Returns the dot product of aPoint and anotherPoint.

- aPoint **normal**

  Returns a new point representing the unit vector rotated 90 degrees toward the y-axis.

- aPoint **unitVector**

  Returns aPoint scaled to unit length.

9.2.11 Miscellaneous Rectangle Operations

Three methods deal with testing for spatial relationships between points and rectangles. They answer the following queries: Is a rectangle contained within another? Is a point within a rectangle? Do two rectangles intersect? These operations are particularly important since some of the later methods work successfully only in prescribed situations. These testing methods can be used to test the applicability of a message before it is sent.

- aRectangle **contains**: anotherRectangle

  Returns true if anotherRectangle is equal to or is contained within aRectangle.

- aRectangle **containsPoint**: aPoint

  Returns true if aPoint is within aRectangle.

- aRectangle **intersects**: anotherRectangle

  Returns true if aRectangle and anotherRectangle intersect.

The methods **expandBy:**, **insetBy:**, and **insetOriginBy:cornerBy:** are concerned with expanding and contracting rectangles by given amounts. Each method can take scalars, points, or rectangles as arguments except for **insetOriginBy:cornerBy:** which allows only scalars and points as arguments. The method **amountToTranslateWithin:** calculates the amount by which one rectangle must be moved to lie within another. The method **areaOutside:** returns a collection of rectangles that lie inside one rectangle but not within its intersection with a second rectangle. The intersection of two rectangles is found through **intersect:**, while the smallest rectangle that contains two rectangles is found using **merge:**.

Note that any message sent must be appropriate for the rectangles involved. For example, **intersect:** only returns a valid result if the two rectangles do intersect. In the examples that follow, assume the following:

```
rectangle1 ← 100@100 corner: 200@200
rectangle2 ← 150@150 corner: 250@250
```

- aRectangle **expandBy**: delta

  Returns a new rectangle that expands aRectangle by delta — delta is a rectangle, point, or number.

  ```
  rectangle1 expandBy: 10 ⇒ 90@90 corner: 210@210
  rectangle1 expandBy: 10@10 ⇒ 90@90 corner: 210@210
  rectangle1 expandBy: (10@10 corner: 20@20) ⇒ 90@90 corner: 220@220
  ```

- aRectangle **insetBy**: delta

  Returns a new rectangle that contracts aRectangle by delta — delta is a rectangle, point, or number.

  rectangle1 **insetBy**: 10 ⇒ 110@110 corner: 190@190
  rectangle1 **insetBy**: 10@10 ⇒ 110@110 corner: 190@190
  rectangle1 **insetBy**: (10@10 **corner**: 20@20) ⇒ 110@110 corner: 180@180

- aRectangle **insetOriginBy**: originDelta **cornerBy**: cornerDelta

  Returns a new rectangle that contracts aRectangle by independently contracting the origin and corner by specified amounts. Arguments can be points or scalars.

  rectangle1 **insetOriginBy**: 10 **cornerBy**: 10 ⇒ 110@110 corner: 190@190
  rectangle1 **insetOriginBy**: 10@10 ⇒ 110@110 corner: 190@190

- aRectangle **amountToTranslateWithin**: anotherRectangle

  Returns a point, delta, such that aRectangle + delta is forced to be inside anotherRectangle.

- aRectangle **areasOutside**: anotherRectangle

  Returns an ordered collection of rectangles made up of the parts of aRectangle that lie outside anotherRectangle. If the rectangles do not intersect, aRectangle is returned as the result.

  rectangle1 **areasOutside**: rectangle2 ⇒
      OrderedCollection (100@100 corner: 200@150   100@150 corner: 150@200)

- aRectangle **intersect**: anotherRectangle

  Returns a rectangle equal to the intersection of aRectangle and anotherRectangle. The rectangles must intersect for a valid response.

  rectangle1 **intersect**: rectangle2 ⇒ 150@150 corner: 200@200

- aRectangle **merge**: anotherRectangle

  Returns the smallest rectangle that contains both aRectangle and anotherRectangle.

  rectangle1 **merge**: rectangle2 ⇒ 100@100 corner: 250@250

9.2.12 Transforming Points and Rectangles

Transforming Points

Points may be translated, scaled, and transposed to produce a new point. Note that **scaleBy**: must have a point as argument, while **translateBy**: accepts either a point or a number.

- aPoint **scaleBy**: scalePoint

  Returns a new point whose x and y values are derived by scaling the x and y values of aPoint by scalePoint.

  100@100 **scaleBy**: 3 ⇒ error
  100@100 **scaleBy**: 2@3 ⇒ 200@300

- aPoint **translateBy**: deltaAmount

    Returns a new point whose x and y values are derived by translating the x and y values of aPoint by deltaAmount (a point or a number).

    100@100 **translateBy**: 50 $\Rightarrow$ 150@150
    100@100 **translateBy**: 50@-50 $\Rightarrow$ 150@50

- aPoint **transpose**

    Returns a new point whose x and y coordinates are those of aPoint but interchanged.

    200@100 **transpose** $\Rightarrow$ 100@200

Transforming Rectangles

Rectangles support scaling and a number of ways of moving and translating. It is important to note which methods return new points and which return the modified receiver. Note also that some methods will accept numbers as arguments where a point is normally accepted while others do not. In the examples that follow, assume the following:

rectangle1 $\leftarrow$ Rectangle **origin**: 100@100 **corner**: 200@200

- aRectangle **scaleBy**: scaleFactor

    Returns a new rectangle formed by scaling aRectangle by scaleFactor (a point or a number).

    rectangle1 **scaleBy**: 3 $\Rightarrow$ 300@300 corner: 600@600
    rectangle1 **scaleBy**: 2@3 $\Rightarrow$ 200@200 corner: 400@600

- aRectangle **translateBy**: deltaAmount

    Returns a new rectangle formed by translating aRectangle by deltaAmount (a point or a number).

    rectangle1 **translateBy**: 50 $\Rightarrow$ 150@150 corner: 250@250
    rectangle1 **translateBy**: 50@100 $\Rightarrow$ 150@200 corner: 250@300

- aRectangle **align**: aPoint **with**: anotherPoint

    Returns a new rectangle formed by translating aRectangle by an amount equal to 'anotherPoint - aPoint' — as a result, aPoint in the rectangle is displaced so as to be at anotherPoint after the alignment.

    rectangle1 **align**: 150@150 **with**: 200@200 $\Rightarrow$ 150@150 corner: 250@250

- aRectangle **moveBy**: aPointOrNumber

    Modifies aRectangle so that it is translated by aPointOrNumber.

    rectangle1 **moveBy**: 50 $\Rightarrow$ 150@150 corner: 250@250
    rectangle1 **moveBy**: 50@50 $\Rightarrow$ 150@150 corner: 250@250

- aRectangle **moveTo:** aPoint

     Modifies aRectangle so that its top left corner is aPoint. The argument must
     be a point.

     rectangle1 **moveTo:** 50 ⇒ error
     rectangle1 **moveTo:** 50@50 ⇒ 50@50 corner: 150@150

9.3 CREATING AND MANIPULATING GRAPHIC IMAGES

The two fundamental classes for creating and manipulating graphical images in Smalltalk are classes **Form** and **BitBlt**. Forms are used to represent images, while instances of class **BitBlt** represent operations on forms. At this point it may seem contradictory to say that instances of BitBlt represent operations. We will explain the rationale behind this design decision in a moment. The name BitBlt is derived from a powerful bit-boundary block transfer instruction of that name found on one of the first machines to support Smalltalk, the Xerox Alto. RasterOp is a synonym for BitBlt in many graphics systems. All text and graphical operations in Smalltalk can be described in terms of copying some source form to a destination form. For example, displaying a path involves copying a form onto the display at each point on the path. Similarly, displaying a text string involves copying the form representing each character in the string onto the display in sequence. In both of these examples, the destination form is the display. It is important to note that BitBlt makes no distinction between internal (memory-based) forms and external (display-based) forms.

9.3.1 Creating Images with Forms

Forms consist of a height, a width, an offset, and a bitmap that stores the image. For example, suppose we wished to construct an iconic form resembling a bug (see Fig. 9.7).

The following expression creates a form with width and height 16, an array of bits to display the required iconic shape, and an offset -7@-7. For further details on the creation of forms see Sec. 9.6.2.

```
bug ← Form
      extent: 16@16
      fromArray: #(
           2r0000000000000000
           2r0000000000000000
           2r0001000000001000
           2r0001000110001000
           2r0001100110011000
           2r0000111111110000
           2r0001111111111000
           2r0001111111111000
           2r0001111111111000
           2r0001111111111000
           2r0000111111110000
           2r0001100000011000
           2r0001000000001000
           2r0000000000000000
           2r0000000000000000)
      offset: -7@-7.
```

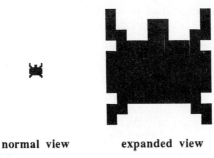

normal view   expanded view

Figure 9.7 A bug form.

The offset of a form is the amount by which the form should be offset when it is displayed or when its position is tested. Every form has an assumed origin at the top left-hand corner of the image. When a form is sent a message to display itself, for example,

bug **displayAt**: 150@150

the form is displayed with its origin at the specified point plus the offset; i.e., 143@143. The bug is therefore displayed so that its center is located at the point 150@150. The ability to specify an offset is particularly useful when defining cursors that have logical origins or "hot spots." For example, the logical origin of the crosshairs cursor is at the center of the crosshairs.

9.3.2 Manipulating Images with BitBlts

Instances of class BitBlt describe a single graphical operation. As we mentioned earlier, it may seem contradictory to say that graphical images are manipulated by instances of class BitBlt. Operations on objects are normally described as methods, not by instances of a class. Fundamentally, an instance of BitBlt specifies a modification to some destination form based on some source form. In the simplest case, the source form may simply be copied to the destination form. However, many other useful operations are special cases of the copy operation. For example, clearing the display screen, inverting a rectangular area of the display to provide feedback to a user operation, or moving a graphics cursor on the display while retaining the original contents of the display can all be described in terms of copy operations. For a very general copy operation, the number of parameters that must be specified to fully describe the operation is large. However, very often, large numbers of copy operations are carried out in a context where most of these parameters remain the same. As a result, it was decided to use instances of a class (BitBlt) rather than a method to represent copy operations. The protocol for BitBlt supports modification of individual parameters to the copy operation. The copy operation is carried out when a **copyBits** message is sent to an initialized instance of class BitBlt. Method **copyBits** is a primitive operation that can be optimized to take advantage of any special bit copying hardware that may be available on the host computer. Operation **copyBits** is so fundamental that small increases in its performance have dramatic effects on the responsiveness of the Smalltalk user interface as a whole.

The parameters involved in specifying a BitBlt operation are

source form   The source form — all or part of which is to be copied.

destination form	The destination form — all or part of which is to be modified by the copy operation.
halftone form	A 16 by 16 mask or halftone form used to fill areas with textures or patterns.
combination rule	A rule (an integer) that dictates how pixels in the modified destination form are to be produced from the source form and the original contents of the destination form. There are sixteen possible combination rules.
source origin	Together with the extent, the source origin specifies the part of the source form to be copied.
extent	See above.
destination origin	Together with the extent, the destination origin specifies the part of the destination form to be modified.
clipping rectangle	Notwithstanding the specification for the destination form, the clipping rectangle specifies a rectangular region outside of which no modification of the destination form can take place.

Fig. 9.8 illustrates the use of these parameters to carry out a simple copy operation from a source form to a destination form. No halftone form is required for a simple copy. The area of the source form to be copied is specified by the **source form**, the **source origin** (a point), and **extent** (a point) parameters. A **combination rule** (an integer) is chosen to specify that pixels in the source are to replace (or be copied over) corresponding pixels in the destination. The area of the destination form to be modified is the same size as the source to be copied and is described by providing the **destination origin** (a point). As well as performing a copy operation, BitBlt also performs clipping. The area of the destination form modified by a copy operation is the intersection of the **clipping rectangle** (a rectangle) and the area specified by the destination origin.

A primitive copy is carried out in Smalltalk by creating an instance of class BitBlt and sending it a **copyBits** message. For example, an alternative method of displaying the form **bug** on the display at location 150@150 would be

```
(BitBlt
    destForm: Display
    sourceForm: bug
    halftoneForm: nil
    combinationRule: Form over
    destOrigin: 150@150
    sourceOrigin: 0@0
    extent: bug extent
    clipRect: Display boundingBox
) copyBits
```

The message Form **over** selects combination rule 3, the replace or "copy over" mode of copying. The message **extent** to a form returns the size (a point) of the form. The message **boundingBox**, sent to **Display**, returns a rectangle specifying the size of the display. The resulting copy operation is therefore clipped (if necessary) to the display screen. Note that there is a subtle difference between using **copyBits** to display the bug and using the form message **displayAt:**. The display message for forms handles the form offset while the **copyBits** operation for class BitBlt does not.

Source Form

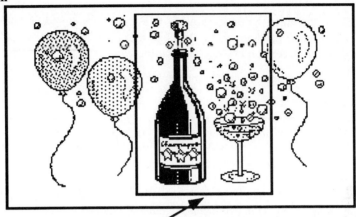

**Portion of Source Form to be copied specified
by Source Origin and Extent**

Destination Form

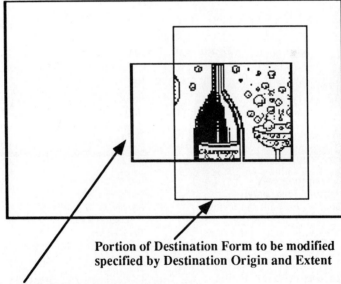

**Portion of Destination Form to be modified
specified by Destination Origin and Extent**

**Modifications to the Destination Form are only
performed within the Clipping Rectangle**

Figure 9.8 Copying from a source form to a destination form.

Using Halftone Forms

Halftone forms are most commonly used to fill forms with textures or patterns. They are 16 by 16 forms that, when used in place of the source form for a BitBlt, replicate themselves to fill the destination form with the halftone pattern. For example, the standard Smalltalk display background could be formed by replicating a gray halftone pattern with Display as the destination form.

The 7 common halftone forms (see Fig. 9.9) are stored as class variables of class Form and may be accessed using the class messages **black**, **veryDarkGray**, **darkGray**, **gray**, **lightGray**, **veryLightGray**, and **white**.

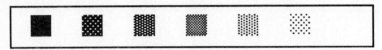

Figure 9.9 Halftone forms.

Combining Source and Halftone Forms

Normally, either a source form or a halftone form is used in a BitBlt operation. However, if both are supplied then the two forms are 'anded' together to form the composite source form for the BitBlt operation. For example, if we supply a bug as the source form and a gray halftone as the halftone form, the composite form will be a halftone bug, as illustrated in Fig. 9.10.

Figure 9.10 Adding texture to the bug.

Halftones used in this way are often known as masks, since only those pixels in the source that correspond to black pixels in the halftone appear in the composite source form; i.e., the halftone acts as if it were a mask placed on top of the source form. The effects of the four possible combinations of source and halftone forms are shown below.

Parameters Supplied	Composite Source Supplied to BitBlt
Source form only	Source Form
Halftone form only	Halftone Form
Source and halftone forms	Source AND Halftone (source bits masked by halftone pattern)
NO source or halftone form	Black Form (a black halftone form is used as the source)

Using Combination Rules

Most BitBlt operations are simple copies where the source pixels (sometimes masked) replace the corresponding pixels in the destination form. This kind of copy operation makes use of only the pixels in the source to determine the modified destination pixels. Other useful graphical operations are obtained if we allow the original contents of the destination form to be included in determining how the destination form is to be modified; i.e., in the general case the copy operation is a function of the corresponding pixels in the source form and the original destination form. Several useful combinations and their uses are described below. In each case, we show the results of applying the combination using a double size bug as the source form and a very light gray background form as the destination form.

Mode	Description
and	A copy operation where corresponding pixels in the source and destination forms are 'anded' together to produce the modified destination form.

Figure 9.11 And mode.

erase	A copy operation where black pixels in the source erase (or set to white) corresponding pixels in the destination form.

Figure 9.12 Erase mode.

over	The standard and most used copy operation where source form pixels replace or copy over the corresponding destination form pixels.

Figure 9.13 Over mode.

under	Under mode is so called because it allows a source form to be painted "underneath" a destination form. Black pixels in the source form are painted into the corresponding pixels in the source form; i.e., it is an or operation applied to the source and the destination forms to produce the modified destination form. This is useful when painting a character onto a display background where any white pixels surrounding the character in the source form are not to be copied.

Figure 9.14 Under mode.

reverse	Reverse mode is so called because it allows reversible changes. It is most often used to display temporary images such as cursors over an already

existing image. In this mode, the modified destination is formed by taking the exclusive-or of the source (the temporary image) and the destination. The effect is to superimpose the temporary image on top of the existing image. Pixels in the temporary image appear black or white in the modified destination depending on the underlying pixel in the original destination form. If the operation is repeated, the temporary image is removed leaving the original destination form unaltered. This mode provides an efficient way of moving a cursor across a display screen, although it has the disadvantage that the underlying screen image distorts the image of the cursor.

Figure 9.15 Reverse mode.

There are sixteen possible combination rules or different ways of stating how each pixel in a source form is to be combined with each pixel in the destination form to produce a new destination pixel. Each of the diagrams in Fig. 9.17 illustrates a different combination rule. For each rule, the integer representing that rule is given together with the common name (if any) for the rule. To avoid having to remember rule numbers, numbers for common combination rules can be obtained by sending messages **and**, **erase**, **over**, **reverse**, and **under** to class Form. As an illustration of how to interpret each diagram, consider the example of mode reverse shown below. The top two rectangles depict the source and destination forms before the BitBlt operation is carried out. The bottom rectangle depicts the destination form after the operation has been carried out. Notice that the bottom rectangle is formed by taking the exclusive-or of the source form and the original destination form. Fig. 9.17 was created by modifying class method **exampleOne** in **Form** to ignore halftone forms.

Inverting a Form

It is often useful to be able to invert or complement a form as shown in Fig. 9.16. For example, this is often a convenient way of providing feedback to the user. Smalltalk uses this technique for highlighting selected text, selected menu items, the label of the active window, and so on. The invert operation may be efficiently achieved by using a black halftone mask, no source and reverse mode. In the example below, a black halftone mask is used with a bug as the destination form.

Figure 9.16 Inverting a form.

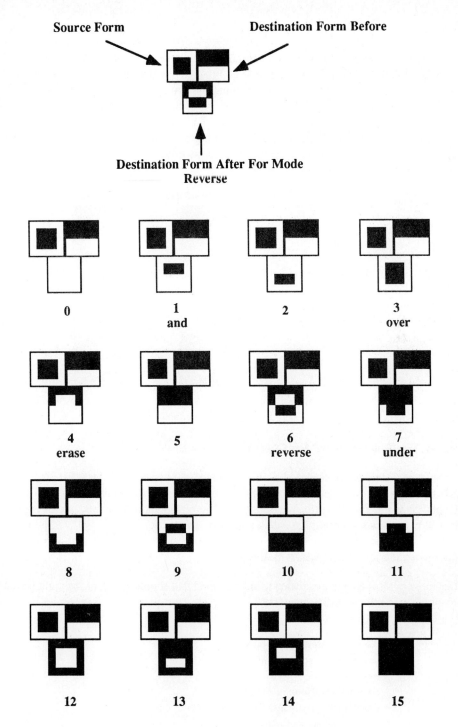

Figure 9.17 BitBlt combination rules.

Painting

Paint mode (or mode **16**) is an additional mode used for painting on the display with brushes of different shapes, sizes, and textures. The brush shape and size is supplied through the source form, with the halftone form supplying the brush texture. In the general case, this mode requires two BitBlt operations. The first cuts (or erases) a hole in the destination in the shape and size of the brush and the second fills the hole with the desired texture pattern. In Fig. 9.18, a round brush shape is selected with a gray texture pattern. The brush is painted onto a black destination form. The first stage cuts a circular hole in the result while the second stage fills the hole with the brush texture.

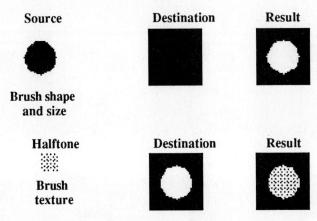

Figure 9.18 The paint mode.

9.3.3 The Full Protocol for Class BitBlt

In this section, we describe the full protocol supported by class BitBlt. Smalltalk programmers do not often have to consider operations at the individual BitBlt operation level. All graphical classes provide high level implementations of fundamental operations that indirectly call the primitive BitBlt **copyBits** operation.

Creating Instances of Class BitBlt

Instances of class BitBlt are created using a method that supplies each of the eight parameters required to describe a BitBlt operation.

- BitBlt
    - **destForm:** destinationForm
    - **sourceForm:** sourceForm
    - **halftoneForm:** aHalfToneForm
    - **combinationRule:** ruleInteger
    - **destOrigin:** destinationOrigin
    - **sourceOrigin:** sourceOrigin
    - **extent:** extent
    - **clipRect:** aClippingRectangle

Copying and Line Drawing

The copyBits operation was described at length in Section 9.3.2. It is important to realize that many graphic entities are displayed as repeated calls to the basic copyBits operation on a BitBlt. Many of these entities, for example graphics paths and text, are described in higher level graphical classes. BitBlt also provides the basic protocol for drawing lines on the display. Lines are drawn by repeatedly sending the copyBits message to a BitBlt. The destination origin of the BitBlt is modified before each copyBits message is sent, so that the destination takes on the values of points lying on the line between the specified start and endpoints. The points at which the copyBits operation is to take place are calculated using the line drawing algorithm of Bresenham (IBM Systems Journal, Vol. 4, No. 1, 1965). By modifying the parameters of the BitBlt instance, lines of different thicknesses and textures may be generated easily.

- aBitBlt **copyBits**
  For a full description of this operation, see Section 9.3.2.
- aBitBlt **drawFrom**: startPoint **to**: endPoint
  Draws a line from startPoint to endPoint by repeatedly sending the copyBits message to aBitBlt. Bresenham's algorithm is used to determine points along the line at which the copyBits operation should be applied. The style of line is governed by the parameters of aBitBlt.

Accessing and Modifying

Class BitBlt allows modification of all the variables that make up the specification for a BitBlt operation. For each of the source and destination forms, the form along with its origin and the x and y coordinates of the origin may be individually set. The clipping rectangle may also be modified. The operations **sourceRect**: aRectangle and **destRect**: aRectangle provide a shorthand way of setting the height and width of the extent parameter and the source or destination origins respectively.

Note that the only parameters of a BitBlt that can be directly accessed are the destination and clipping rectangles.

- aBitBlt **destForm**: aForm
- aBitBlt **destOrigin**: aPoint
- aBitBlt **destRect**
- aBitBlt **destRect**: aRectangle
- aBitBlt **destX**: anInteger
- aBitBlt **destY**: anInteger

- aBitBlt **sourceForm**: aForm
- aBitBlt **sourceOrigin**: aPoint
- aBitBlt **sourceRect**: aRectangle
- aBitBlt **sourceX**: anInteger
- aBitBlt **sourceY**: anInteger

- aBitBlt **clipHeight**: anInteger
- aBitBlt **clipWidth**: anInteger

- aBitBlt **clipRect**
- aBitBlt **clipRect**: aRectangle
- aBitBlt **clipX**: anInteger
- aBitBlt **clipY**: anInteger

- aBitBlt **combinationRule**: anInteger
- aBitBlt **mask**: aForm
- aBitBlt **height**: anIntegerHeightForExtent
- aBitBlt **width**: anIntegerWidthForExtent

9.4 DISPLAYABLE OBJECTS

9.4.1 An Overview of the Graphics Classes

The abstract class **DisplayObject** describes the protocol supported by objects that can display themselves. Fig. 9.19 displays the major Smalltalk graphical classes and their inheritance relationships.

The five immediate subclasses of class **DisplayObject** are

DisplayMedium
Supports protocol for objects that can both act as a canvas on which images can be painted and that can also paint themselves onto a medium. In addition, DisplayMedium supports protocol for coloring (or texturing) images and for bordering images with textures. Class **Form**, the most used class for graphic images, is a subclass of DisplayMedium and inherits its protocol for coloring and bordering. Form has two subclasses, Cursor and DisplayScreen.

DisplayText
Used in two different ways by the system: as a container for textual characters managed by a ParagraphEditor and as a container for cached forms that can be used to display the characters efficiently. The use of display text in the context of text windows is discussed in Volume Two.

Path
The basic superclass for the classes that generate trajectories or paths like lines and circles. The instance variable 'form' is the "brush" used for displaying the Path. The image is displayed by copying the form at each point in the path. Path has subclasses Arc, Curve, Line, LinearFit, and Spline. Circle is defined as a subclass of Arc.

InfiniteForm
A form obtained by replicating a pattern indefinitely in all directions.

OpaqueForm
A form that includes a shape form as well as a figure form. The shape form indicates what part of the background should get occluded during display so that patterns other than black in the figure form will still appear opaque.

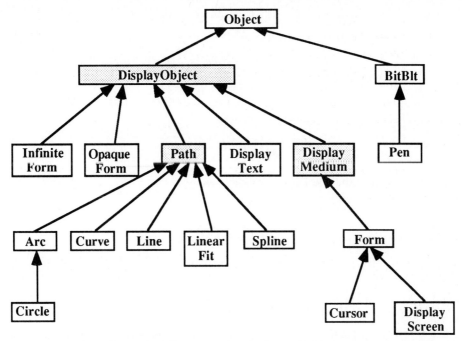

Figure 9.19 The major Smalltalk graphical classes.

9.4.2 Standard Protocol for Displayable Objects

The abstract class DisplayObject describes displayable objects that are able to:

- display themselves on a display medium with and without transformations
- compute a containing bounding box
- display themselves on a display medium with and without transformations
- support scaling and translation operations, and support an offset.

Subclasses of DisplayObject actually divide themselves into two groups: those that when asked to transform themselves create a new object (e.g., class Path and its subclasses) and those that modify themselves by maintaining an explicit offset (e.g., class Form) Because of this dichotomy, the default implementations of some methods in DisplayObject are overridden by some subclasses.

The Generic Display Operation

Every subclass of **DisplayObject** must support the generic display message:

- aDisplayObject **displayOn**: aDisplayMedium **at**: aDisplayPoint
  clippingRectangle: clipRectangle **rule**: ruleInteger **mask**: aForm
    Displays aDisplayObject at aDisplayPoint on aDisplayMedium using
    combination rule ruleInteger, halftone mask aForm, and clipping rectangle
    clipRectangle.

The link to the underlying BitBlt copyBits operation is clear. Earlier, we used the copyBits operation directly to display the form **bug** on the display at location **150@150** using the expression

bug **displayAt**: 150@150

An alternative expression using the generic display operation implemented in class Form (a subclass of DisplayObject) would be

bug
    displayOn: Display
    at: 150@150
    clippingRectangle: Display **boundingBox**
    rule: Form **over**
    mask: Form **black**

Display Protocol with Default Specifications

The standard copy operation is so common that alternative protocol is supported to provide default values for selected arguments. When arguments are omitted, defaults are 0@0 for the point at which the object should be displayed, the entire display screen for the clipping rectangle, over for the combination rule, and a nil or black mask for the halftone mask.

The display protocol supported requires the programmer to override only those arguments that are different from the default values.

- aDisplayObject **displayOn**: aDisplayMedium
  Displays aDisplayObject at the top left corner of aDisplayMedium.
- aDisplayObject **displayOn**: aDisplayMedium **at**: aDisplayPoint
  Displays aDisplayObject at aDisplayPoint on aDisplayMedium.
- aDisplayObject **displayOn**: aDisplayMedium **at**: aDisplayPoint
  clippingRectangle: clipRectangle
  Displays aDisplayObject at aDisplayPoint on aDisplayMedium with clipping rectangle clipRectangle.
- aDisplayObject **displayOn**: aDisplayMedium **at**: aDisplayPoint **rule**: ruleInteger
  Displays aDisplayObject at aDisplayPoint on aDisplayMedium with rule ruleInteger.

The following commonly used protocol assumes that the display medium is the global variable **Display**.

- aDisplayObject **display**
  Displays aDisplayObject at the top left corner of the display screen.
- aDisplayObject **displayAt**: aDisplayPoint
  Displays aDisplayObject at aDisplayPoint on the display screen.

Display Protocol with Transformations

Class DisplayObject also supports protocol for displaying objects where a transformation is to be applied as part of the display process. Display transformations consist of a scale and a translation and are instances of class **WindowingTransformation** (see Volume 2).

The most general display message which involves a display transformation is shown below:

- aDisplayObject **displayOn**: aDisplayMedium **transformation**: displayTransformation
  clippingRectangle: clipRectangle **align**: alignmentPoint **with**: relativePoint
  rule: ruleInteger **mask**: aForm

    Displays aDisplayObject on aDisplayMedium using combination rule
    ruleInteger, halftone mask aForm, and clipping rectangle clipRectangle.
    What is displayed is determined by the scale and translation of the
    displayTransformation and the alignment and relative points.

The actual implementation of the method depends on the particular subclass of **DisplayObject** involved. As an example of a display operation involving a transformation, consider the following. Suppose we have a 100 by 100 form, aForm, that is to be doubled in size and translated by the amount 100@100. Suppose also that the alignment point is 150@150 and the relative point is 200@200.

```
aForm
    displayOn: Display
    transformation: (WindowingTransformation scale: 2@2 translation: 100@100)
    clippingRectangle: Display computeBoundingBox
    align: 150@150
    with: 50@50
    rule: Form over
    mask: Form black
```

A display transformation effects a transformation from one coordinate system (the source coordinate system) to another (the destination coordination system). Fig. 9.20(a) shows the coordinate system of the source form. Note that the relativePoint, 50@50, is specified in the source coordinate system. Fig. 9.20(b) shows the transformed form in the destination coordinate system. The form has been scaled by a factor of two and translated by 100 in both x and y. The final display position of the transformed form is determined by translating by an amount equal to the difference between the alignment point 150@150 and the transformed relative point 200@200. Note that the alignment point is specified in the destination coordinate system. Fig. 9.20(c) shows the final displayed form.

We have described the display with transformation operation supported by class Form. The default implementation for this method provided in class **DisplayObject** assumes that the object involved cannot be scaled. Otherwise, the implementation is identical. This method could well have been made the responsibility of subclasses.

Alternative methods are available that support default values for particular arguments. They are listed below.

- aDisplayObject **displayOn**: aDisplayMedium **transformation**: displayTransformation
  clippingRectangle: clipRectangle

- aDisplayObject **displayOn**: aDisplayMedium **transformation**: displayTransformation
  clippingRectangle: clipRectangle **align**: alignmentPoint **with**: relativePoint

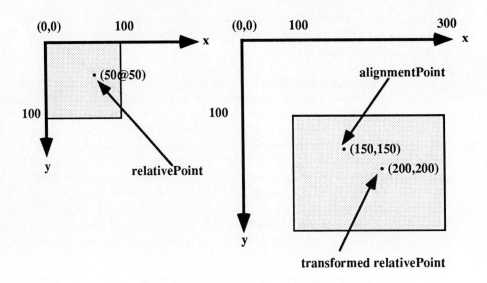

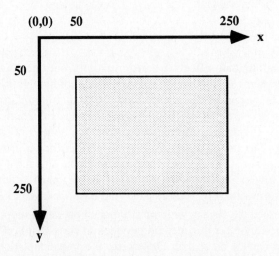

Figure 9.20 Display transformations.

- aDisplayObject **displayOn**: aDisplayMedium **transformation**: displayTransformation **clippingRectangle**: clipRectangle **fixedPoint**: aPoint
  No translation is involved with this method.

- aDisplayObject **displayOn**: aDisplayMedium **transformation**: displayTransformation **clippingRectangle**: clipRectangle **rule**: ruleInteger **mask**: aForm
  No translation is involved with this method.

Offsets, Bounding Boxes, and Transformations on Display Objects

As mentioned earlier, class DisplayObject assumes that instances of any subclass will support an offset, be able to compute a bounding box, and scale and translate themselves. All existing subclasses support the following protocol relating to the bounding box of a displayable object. A **bounding box** is a rectangle that completely encompasses the object. Bounding boxes can be used to make fast decisions concerning the intersection of objects; e.g., for clipping purposes. Each subclass must provide an implementation for the method **computeBoundingBox**. The complete protocol for manipulating bounding boxes is

- aDisplayObject **computeBoundingBox**
  Must be implemented by all subclasses.
- aDisplayObject **boundingBox**
  Returns the bounding box of the object.
- aDisplayObject **extent**
  Returns the extent (a point) of the bounding box of the object.
- aDisplayObject **height**
  Returns the height of the bounding box of the object.
- aDisplayObject **width**
  Returns the width of the bounding box of the object.

Class **DisplayObject** supports the notion of storing an offset with the object. The offset represents the amount by which the object should be moved when it is displayed or when its position is tested. Display objects that maintain offsets, for example forms and cursors, add the offset to any specified display position before displaying themselves. The following protocol is supported.

- aDisplayObject **offset**
  The amount by which aDisplayObject should be offset when it is displayed or its position tested. This method must be supplied by all subclasses.
- aDisplayObject **offset**: aPoint
  Sets the offset associated with aDisplayObject to aPoint.
- aDisplayObject **rounded**
  Modifies the offset of aDisplayObject to consist of integer coordinates only.
- aDisplayObject **relativeRectangle**
  Returns a rectangle with origin equal to the offset of aDisplayObject and extent equal to the extent of the bounding box of aDisplayObject.

In addition, operations are supported to scale and translate the offset of a display object.

- aDisplayObject **scaleBy**: aPoint
  Scales the offset of aDisplayObject by aPoint.
- aDisplayObject **translateBy**: aPoint
  Translates the offset of aDisplayObject by aPoint.
- aDisplayObject **align**: alignmentPoint **with**: relativePoint
  Translates the offset of aDisplayObject by an amount equal to relativePoint - alignmentPoint.

Simple Path Animation

Class DisplayObject also supports protocol for creating very simple animation sequences. The basic capability provided is to be able to move an image around on the display while continuously restoring the background. See class method **example** in OpaqueForm for an example. The method **follow:** locationBlock **while:** durationBlock continuously displays an image at locations supplied by evaluating locationBlock as long as durationBlock evaluates true. For example, the code below attaches the object named anImage to the position of the cursor. As the cursor moves (the cursor itself is not displayed since its image has been made blank), anImage is displayed at the cursor point. Whenever the image is displayed at a new position, the previous background is restored. The process continues until a mouse button is depressed (details of classes Cursor and InputSensor are provided later in this chapter).

```
Cursor blank showWhile: [
    anImage follow: [Sensor cursorPoint] while: [Sensor noButtonPressed]]
```

- aDisplayObject **follow:** locationBlock **while:** durationBlock
  See above.
- aDisplayObject **backgroundAt:** location
  Returns a form containing the background if aDisplayObject were to be displayed at location (a point). The form remembers location in its offset.
- aDisplayObject **moveTo:** newLocation **restoring:** backgroundForm
  Moves aDisplayObject from its current location on the display to a new location (a point) restoring the original background when the object is moved; backgroundForm must contain the background to be restored and have the current location stored as its offset.

9.4.3 Summary

In summary, any subclass of class DisplayObject must implement the generic display operations, a method to compute the bounding box, and a method to return the offset of the object.

9.5 DISPLAY MEDIUMS

9.5.1 Display Mediums as Canvas and Brush

As we have seen earlier, objects of class **DisplayMedium** are display objects that act as a canvas for painting images. The display primitives of display objects have a display medium as their canvas. However, objects of class DisplayMedium can also paint themselves onto a medium; i.e., they support the display object display protocol themselves.

9.5.2 Coloring and Adding Borders to Images

Class DisplayMedium distinguishes itself from class DisplayObject by providing support for coloring (or texturing) images and for bordering images with textures. Class Form, the most used class for graphic images, is a subclass of DisplayMedium and inherits its protocol for coloring and bordering.

Coloring Images

Class DisplayMedium allows an image to be filled with a textured pattern. Methods for six standard textures are directly provided. For example, if we have a 100 by 100 form named testForm, sending the message darkGray will propagate a dark gray texture pattern across the whole form (see Fig. 9.21(a)). Cases (b) and (c) are discussed below.

testForm **darkGray**

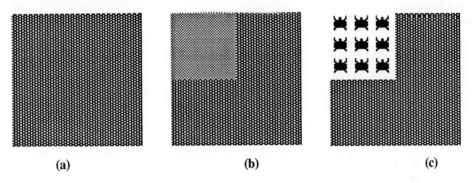

       (a)   (b)   (c)

Figure 9.21 Coloring images.

- aDisplayMedium **black**
- aDisplayMedium **veryDarkGray**
- aDisplayMedium **darkGray**
- aDisplayMedium **gray**
- aDisplayMedium **lightGray**
- aDisplayMedium **veryLightGray**
- aDisplayMedium **white**

Coloring Part of an Image

Alternatively, a specified rectangular area of a form can be filled with the following protocol. For example, to fill only the top quarter of the form with a dark gray texture (see Fig. 9.21(b)), use the expression

testForm **darkGray**: (0@0 **corner**: 50@50)

- aDisplayMedium **black**: aRectangle
- aDisplayMedium **veryDarkGray**: aRectangle
- aDisplayMedium **darkGray**: aRectangle
- aDisplayMedium **gray**: aRectangle
- aDisplayMedium **lightGray**: aRectangle
- aDisplayMedium **veryLightGray**: aRectangle
- aDisplayMedium **white**: aRectangle

The primitive method for coloring an image is **fill:** aRectangle **rule:** anInteger **mask:** aHalfToneForm. This allows an image to be filled with any halftone mask and any BitBlt combination rule. This method must be provided by all subclasses of DisplayMedium. The methods **fill:** aRectangle and **fill:** aRectangle **mask:** aHalfToneForm are also provided. For example, to fill the top left quarter of testForm with the form bug (see Fig. 9.21(c)), use the expressions

testForm **darkGray**.
testForm **fill:** (0@0 **extent:** 50@50) **mask:** bug

The fill protocol consists of the following:

- aDisplayMedium **fill:** aRectangle
  Fills the rectangular region of aDisplayMedium specified by aRectangle with the default background, gray.
- aDisplayMedium **fill:** aRectangle **mask:** aHalfToneForm
  Fills the rectangular region of aDisplayMedium specified by aRectangle with the halftone pattern given by aHalfToneForm.
- aDisplayMedium **fill:** aRectangle **rule:** ruleInteger **mask:** aHalfToneForm
  Fills the rectangular region of aDisplayMedium specified by aRectangle with the halftone pattern given by aHalfToneForm according to the combination rule ruleInteger. This method must be provided by all subclasses.

Inverting All or Part of an Image

Methods are also supported to invert or complement bits in an image. For example, to fill testForm with the form bug and then reverse only the bottom right quarter of the form (see Fig. 9.22), use the expression

testForm **fill:** (0@0) **extent:** (100@100) **mask:** bug.
testForm **reverse:** (50@50 **extent:** 50@50)

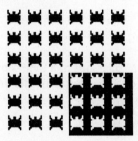

Figure 9.22 Reversing images

The reverse protocol consists of the following.

- aDisplayMedium **reverse**
  Inverts or complements all bits in aDisplayMedium.
- aDisplayMedium **reverse:** aRectangle
  Inverts or complements all bits in the rectangular area of aDisplayMedium specified by aRectangle.

- aDisplayMedium **reverse**: aRectangle **mask**: aHalfToneForm

    Inverts or complements all bits in the rectangular area of aDisplayMedium specified by aRectangle with mask aHalfToneForm.

Adding Borders to Images

The second major contribution of class DisplayMedium is to support protocol for placing a rectangular patterned border into an image. The border is specified by a rectangle that describes the external boundary of the border and a width for each of the four sides of the border. For borders with equal width on all sides, use **border**: aRectangle **width**: borderWidth and **border**: aRectangle **width**: borderWidth **mask**: aHalfToneMask. For example, the following expression places a black border of width 16 into testForm, where the external boundary of the border is given by the rectangle with origin 20@20 and extent 60@60 (see Fig. 9.23(a)).

    testForm **veryLightGray**; **border**: (20@20 **extent**: 60@60) **width**: 16 **mask**: Form **black**

For unequal border widths, use **border**: aRectangle **widthRectangle**: insets **mask**: aHalfToneMask. In this case, the left border width is given by the x coordinate of the origin of the rectangle insets, the top border width by the y coordinate. The right border width and bottom border width are given by the x and y coordinates of the corner point of the rectangle insets. The following example specifies a left width of 20, a top width of 10, a right width of 10, and a bottom border width of 20 (see Fig. 9.23 (b)).

```
testForm veryLightGray
testForm
    border: (20@20 extent: 60@60)
    widthRectangle: (20@10 corner: 10@20)
    mask: Form black
```

The bordering protocol consists of the following:

- aDisplayMedium **border**: aRectangle **width**: borderWidth

    Modifies aDisplayMedium to have a black border where the external boundary of the border is given by aRectangle and the width of the border is borderWidth.

- aDisplayMedium **border**: aRectangle **width**: borderWidth **mask**: aHalfToneForm

    Modifies aDisplayMedium to have a border where the external boundary of the border is given by aRectangle and the width of the border is borderWidth. The color of the border is given by aHalfToneForm.

- aDisplayMedium **border**: aRectangle **widthRectangle**: insets **mask**: aHalfToneForm

    Modifies aDisplayMedium to have a border where the external boundary of the border is given by aRectangle and the color of the border is given by aHalfToneForm. The left, top, right, and bottom widths of the border are given by the left, top, right, and bottom of widthRectangle.

- aDisplayMedium **border**: aRectangle **widthRectangle**: insets

    mask: aHalfToneForm **clippingBox**: clipRectangle

    Modifies aDisplayMedium to have a border where the external boundary of the border is given by aRectangle and the color of the border is given by aHalfToneForm. The left, top, right, and bottom widths of the border are given by the left, top, right, and bottom of widthRectangle. Modifications occur only within the clipping rectangle clipRectangle.

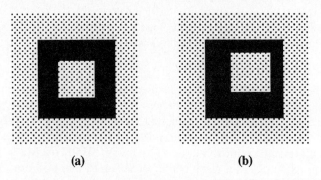

(a)   (b)

Figure 9.23 Bordering images.

9.5.3 Bit Copying and Drawing Lines

All subclasses of DisplayMedium must implement the following two fundamental operations: the bit copying operation **copyBits:from:at:clippingBox:rule:mask:** and the line drawing operation **drawLine:to:clippingBox:rule:mask:**.

- aDisplayMedium **copyBits:** sourceRectangle **from:** sourceForm **at:** destOrigin
  clippingBox: clipRectangle **rule:** ruleInteger **mask:** aHalfToneForm
    Must be implemented by all subclasses.

- aDisplayMedium **drawLine:** beginPoint **to:** endPoint **clippingBox:** clipRectangle
  rule: ruleInteger **mask:** aHalfToneForm
    Must be implemented by all subclasses.

9.6 FORMS

As described in Section 9.3.1, instances of class Form represent basic graphical images in Smalltalk. Forms extend abstract classes DisplayObject and DisplayMedium by providing a concrete representation for a graphic image. As shown in Fig. 9.24, forms inherit the ability to display themselves from class DisplayObject and to color and border themselves from class DisplayMedium. Forms themselves add protocol for creating, editing, and transforming images. Every form has an assumed origin at the top left-hand corner of the image.

The instance variables associated with a form are

height	The height (in pixels) of the form.
width	The width (in pixels) of the form.
offset	The amount (a point) by which a form should be offset when it is displayed or when its position is tested.
bits	Representation for the graphic image. In implementations prior to version 2.5, bits was an instance of class WordArray. In version 2.5, bits is an instance of class FormBitmap.

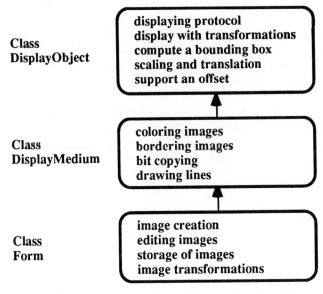

Class
DisplayObject

> displaying protocol
> display with transformations
> compute a bounding box
> scaling and translation
> support an offset

Class
DisplayMedium

> coloring images
> bordering images
> bit copying
> drawing lines

Class
Form

> image creation
> editing images
> storage of images
> image transformations

Figure 9.24 Method inheritance hierarchy for class Form.

9.6.1 Bitmaps

In implementations prior to version 2.5, the representation (bits) of a graphical image was visible; bits was an instance of class WordArray[3], a subclass of ArrayedCollection. The bitmap associated with a form was represented as a WordArray with **height** rows, where each row consists of the smallest integral number of 16 bit words required to represent the **width** pixels in each row. Thus, the physical bitmap was often larger than the logical size of the bitmap. For example, suppose we create a form with width 187 and height 69. The physical bitmap will be an instance of WordArray of length 828. To store each row of 187 bits requires 12 16-bit words (192 bits); with 69 rows this gives 828 (12 * 69) words. Bitmaps are stored row by row (or, in graphics terminology, scan line by scan line) with a set bit (1) indicating a black pixel and an off bit (0) representing a white pixel. The most significant bit of each word represents the pixel at the least x-coordinate.

In version 2.5, bits are represented as an instance of class FormBitmap. The actual representation of a FormBitmap is implementation dependent and differs from platform to platform. It is not necessary for a user to understand the internal representation. If a user accesses the bitmap of a form by sending the **bits** message, the bitmap will be returned as an instance of class WordArray as was the case with versions prior to 2.5. Additional protocol (**bitsWordat:**, **bitsWordAt:put:** and **bitsWordSize**) has been added to class Form to allow manipulation of FormBitmap instances in the same manner as was previously possible with instances of class WordArray. The bitmap for the form displayed on the screen (an instance of DisplayScreen) is an instance of class DisplayBitmap (a subclass of FormBitmap).

---

[3]Class WordArray was originally called Bitmap in both version 1 of Smalltalk and in the Orange and Blue Books.

Instances of class WordArray provide an implementation independent representation for bitmaps and are used for creating bitmaps from a user supplied array and also for saving and restoring bitmaps where the restoration may be performed on a different platform.

9.6.2 Creating Forms

Forms may be created in two basic ways. By specifying the width, height, and bitmap explicitly or by capturing a form from a rectangular area of the display.

- Form **extent**: extentPoint

  Returns a blank (or white) form with width and height specified by extentPoint. The offset is 0@0.

- Form **extent**: extentPoint **fromArray**: anArray **offset**: offsetPoint

  Returns a form with width and height specified by extentPoint, offset specified by offsetPoint, and bitmap initialized from anArray (a WordArray).

It is now possible to elaborate on the creation of the 'bug' form — an example given earlier in the chapter (see Fig. 9.7). The following expression creates a form with width 16 and height 16, an array of bits to display the required iconic shape, and an offset -7@-7. In this case, the bitmap is specified using an array of 16 16-bit words with the first word specifying the bits of the first row or scan line of the bug. Each word is specified as a 16-bit integer of radix 2. The offset (-7@-7) ensures that when the bug is displayed at a specific point the bit the eighth bit of the eighth word will be aligned with the display point.

```
bug ← Form
    extent: 16@16
    fromArray: #(
        2r0000000000000000
        2r0000000000000000
        2r0001000000001000
        2r0001000110001000
        2r0001100110011000
        2r0000111111110000
        2r0001111111111000
        2r0001111111111000
        2r0001111111111000
        2r0001111111111000
        2r0000111111110000
        2r0001100000011000
        2r0001000000001000
        2r0000000000000000
        2r0000000000000000)
    offset: -7@-7.
```

Alternatively, a Form may be created from the display screen by explicitly specifying the rectangle from which to generate the form or by interactively using the mouse to frame the desired rectangular area (with or without a gridding constraint).

- Form **fromDisplay**: aRectangle

  Returns a form with width, height, and bitmap obtained from the area of the display screen specified by aRectangle. The offset is 0@0.

- Form **fromUser**

    Returns a form with width, height,and bitmap specified by the size and contents of the area of the display screen designated by the user. The offset is 0@0.

- Form **fromUser**: aGridPoint

    Returns a form with width, height, and bitmap specified by the size and contents of the area of the display screen designated by the user. The grid for selecting an area is specified by aGridPoint. The offset is 0@0.

Finally, a method is provided to create forms consisting of circular black dots of any diameter. The offset is calculated so that when a dot is displayed at a particular point, its center will lie at that point. For example, for a dot of diameter 8, the offset would be -4@-4.

- Form **dotOfSize**: diameter

    Returns a form that contains a round black dot with the given diameter. The offset is such that the form displays with the center of the dot at the specified display position.

9.6.3 Querying Forms

The offset, bitmap, and the size of the bitmap associated with a form can all be accessed. Methods for querying the extent (**extent**), width (**width**), and height (**height**) of a form are inherited from class DisplayObject. The implementation of these methods in DisplayObject returns the extent, width, and height of the bounding box of the object. In the case of forms, the extent of the bounding box is identical to the extent of the form allowing the methods to be inherited. Additionally, the color of a bit in the bitmap can be queried (**valueAt:**).

- aForm **offset**

    Returns the point representing the offset of aForm.

- aForm **bits**

    Returns the word array corresponding to the bitmap of aForm.

- aForm **bitsWordAt**: index

    Returns the 16-bit word with the given index from the bitmap of aForm when viewed as an array of 16-bit words.

- aForm **bitsWordAt**: index **put**: value

    Modifies the 16-bit word with the given index in the bitmap of aForm (when viewed as an array of 16-bit words) to be aValue (a 16-bit word).

- aForm **bitsWordSize**

    Returns the size of the bitmap of aForm viewed as an array of 16-bit words.

- aForm **size**

    Same as bitsWordSize

- aForm **computeBoundingBox**

    Returns a rectangle representing the bounding box of the form. In the case of a form, this rectangle has origin 0@0 and an extent equal to the extent of the form.

- aForm **valueAt**: aPoint

    Returns the color (0 = white, 1 = black) of the bit at aPoint in the form aForm. The bit at the origin is at 0@0; i.e., 0-based indexing is used.

9.6.4 Modifying Forms

High-level Modification of Forms

Forms may be modified using a protocol similar to that used to create them; i.e., by specifying the modified width, height, offset, and bit pattern (as a WordArray) or by specifying a rectangular area on the display from which to extract the modified data for the form.

- aForm **extent**: extentPoint
  Changes aForm to a blank (or white) form with width and height specified by extentPoint and offset 0@0.
- aForm **offset**: offsetPoint
  Changes the offset of aForm to offsetPoint.
- aForm **bits**: aWordArray
  Changes the bitmap of aForm to aWordArray. The size of aWordArray must be compatible with the size of the bitmap of aForm
- aForm **extent**: extentPoint **offset**: offsetPoint
  Changes aForm to a blank (or white) form with width and height specified by extentPoint and with offset offsetPoint.
- aForm **extent**: extentPoint **offset**: offsetPoint **bits**: aBitmap
  Changes aForm to a width and height specified by extentPoint, an offset specified by offsetPoint, and a bitmap initialized from aBitmap.
- aForm **fromDisplay**: aRectangle
  Changes aForm to a have a width, height and bitmap initialized from the area of the display screen specified by aRectangle. The offset is 0@0.

Modifying Forms at the Bit Level

Additionally, individual bits in the bitmap of a form may be modified.

- aForm **valueAt**: aPoint **put**: zeroOrOne
  Modifies the bit in the bitmap of aForm specified by aPoint to either zero or one as specified by zeroOrOne. The bit at the origin is at 0@0; i.e., 0-based (rather than 1-based) indexing is used.

9.6.5 Displaying Forms

Class Form inherits the family of protocol for displaying images (see Section 9.4.2) from class DisplayObject. Form provides an implementation for the basic display message.

- aForm **displayOn**: aDisplayMedium **at**: aDisplayPoint **clippingRectangle**: clipRectangle **rule**: ruleInteger **mask**: aForm
  Displays aDisplayObject at aDisplayPoint on aDisplayMedium using combination rule ruleInteger, halftone mask aForm, and clipping rectangle clipRectangle.

Since forms have offsets, the form is actually displayed with its origin at a point given by the sum of aDisplayPoint and the offset of the form. The protocol for displaying images with transformations is also inherited from DisplayObject. For details see Section 9.4.2.

Class Form Supports Methods for Common Combination Rules

Methods that return the integers representing commonly used combination rules for BitBlt and displaying operations are provided as class methods in class Form.

- Form **and**
- Form **erase**
- Form **over**
- Form **paint**
- Form **reverse**
- Form **under**

Class Form Supports Common Halftone Masks

Methods that return the 16 * 16 forms representing commonly used halftone masks for BitBlt and displaying operations are provided as class methods in class Form. These masks are stored as class variables (constants) of the class.

- Form **black**
- Form **veryDarkGray**
- Form **darkGray**
- Form **gray**
- Form **lightGray**
- Form **veryLightGray**
- Form **white**

9.6.6 Bit Copying and Line Drawing

In addition to implementing the protocol for the basic bit copy and line drawing operations (see Section 9.5.3), forms support the convenient message **copy:from:in:rule:**, which is a useful shorthand method for modifying a rectangular region of a form by copying a similar sized region from some source form. For example, the following expression copies one region of the display screen to another.

> Display **copy:** (100@100 **extent:** 200@200) **from:** 200@200 **in:** Display **rule:** Form **over**.

Notice that in this case the source and destination forms are identical and that the source and destination regions overlap.

- aForm **copy:** destinationRectangle **from:** sourcePoint **in:** sourceForm **rule:** rule
  Modifies aForm (the destination form) by copying a region of the source form with extent given by destinationRectangle and origin sourcePoint to a region of aForm specified by destinationRectangle, using the specified combination rule and default clipping rectangle given by aForm's boundary.

9.6.7 Coloring and Bordering Forms

Class Form inherits the protocol for coloring and bordering images from class DisplayMedium (see Section 9.5.2). Form supplies an implementation for the primitive coloring method **fill:rule:mask:** and provides the following additional protocol for placing a border around the perimeter of a form.

- aForm **borderWidth:** anInteger

  Modifies aForm to have a black border where the external boundary of the border is the perimeter of aForm and the width of the border is anInteger.
- aForm **borderWidth:** anInteger **mask:** aForm

  Modifies aForm to have a border with color specified by aForm and where the external boundary of the border is the perimeter of aForm and the width of the border is anInteger.

9.6.8 Storing Images

Forms can be filed out to an external file and subsequently filed back in again in the same fashion as Smalltalk code is filed in and out. This permits the external storage of forms and the exchange of forms between users. A standard file format is used.

- aForm **writeOn:** aFile

  Saves aForm on the file aFile in the format: fileCode, extent, offset, bits.
- Form **readFrom:** aFile

  Returns the form stored on the file aFile in the format: fileCode, extent, offset bits.

9.6.9 Converting Forms to Strings

No specialized print string representation for forms is provided; forms respond to **print-String** messages by printing 'a Form'. Forms respond to **storeString** by creating a compact representation of a form that can subsequently be executed to recreate the original form.

9.6.10 Transforming Images

Forms support protocol for transforming images by scaling them up or down, obtaining reflections and rotations, and for filling enclosed regions within a form. We will not give

Figure 9.25 Magnifying and shrinking images.

detailed descriptions of the algorithms used to implement these methods but it is important to realize that fundamentally, they are all implemented as repeated calls to the primitive BitBlt operation.

Magnifying and Shrinking Images

Forms may be magnified and shrunk using the messages **magnifyBy:** and **shrinkBy:**. For example, Fig. 9.25 was produced by displaying the form elephant, magnifying the form by a factor of 2 in both x and y and displaying the result, and finally shrinking the original elephant (not the large one) by a factor of 2 in x and y and displaying the result.

The algorithms used to shrink and magnify are fairly primitive. Magnify blows up each bit in the original form by an amount equal to the scale. For example, if scale were 2@2, then each bit in the original is represented by four bits of the same color in the magnified form. As can be seen from the magnified elephant, this algorithm gives rise to increased "staircase" effects on the edges of images. Shrink works in exactly the opposite way. If we imagine a rectangular grid placed on the original form with the size of the grid specified by scale, then each bit in the shrunken form is produced by taking the upper left bit within each of the grid rectangles. If the scale is nonintegral, it will be rounded. This makes it difficult to magnify 'picture' forms in windows that can be resized arbitrarily by users.

- aForm **magnifyBy:** scale
  Returns a new form that is a scaled up version of aForm as specified by the argument scale.
- aForm **shrinkBy:** scale
  Returns a new form that is a scaled down version of aForm as specified by the argument scale.

Reflecting Images

Forms may be reflected horizontally or vertically using the message **reflect:**. For a vertical reflection, argument 0@1 should be provided; for a horizontal reflection, it should be 1@0. Fig. 9.26 shows the original elephant form, its vertical reflection, and its horizontal reflection.

Figure 9.26 Reflecting images.

- aForm **reflect:** specificationPoint
  Returns a new form that is a reflection of aForm as specified by the argument specificationPoint; vertical reflection is specified by 0@1, horizontal reflection by 1@0.

Rotating Images

Forms may be rotated clockwise in units of 90 degrees using the method **rotateBy:** angleSpecification. The argument angleSpecification is an integer where 0 is no rotation, 1 is rotate clockwise by 90 degrees, 2 is rotate clockwise by 180 degrees, and so on. Fig. 9.27 shows the original elephant form and the two forms obtained by rotating clockwise 90 and 180 degrees respectively.

• aForm **rotateBy:** angleSpecification

Returns a new form that is aForm rotated clockwise in units of 90 degrees by an amount specified by angleSpecification; angleSpecification specifies the integral number of 90 degree units to rotate by. Thus, 1 = 90 degrees, 2 = 180 degrees, and so on.

Figure 9.27 Rotating Images.

Scaling and Translating Images

Protocol for scaling (**scaleBy:**) and translating (**translateBy:**) forms are inherited from class DisplayObject. These operations simply scale or translate the offset of the form. In the case of scaling, this does not usually give the desired display effect — use the operations for magnifying and shrinking images described earlier.

Region Filling

An enclosed region within a form may be filled with any halftone mask using the message **shapeFill:interiorPoint:**. The arguments to the message are the required mask and a point that lies within the interior region. The example below shows a form before and after filling with a gray mask. An interior region is a region of white pixels that is surrounded by a boundary of black pixels. Algorithms that fill regions in this manner are often called flood fill algorithms because they "flood' a specified region with a texture or pattern. It is important to ensure that the desired region is completely enclosed, since the flood fill will escape through any gaps in the boundary and fill surrounding areas of the form. Similarly, the fill algorithm will not fill "islands" within a specified region that are themselves enclosed regions.

• aForm **shapeFill:** aMask **interiorPoint:** interiorPoint

Modifies the interior of some outlined region within aForm by filling it with a pattern specified by aMask. The argument interior point specifies a point within the interior region.

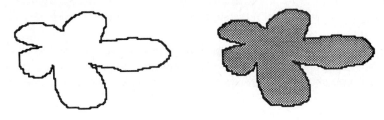

Figure 9.28 Region filling.

9.7 INFINITE AND OPAQUE FORMS

You might expect that classes with names such as InfiniteForm and OpaqueForm would be specializations of class Form. In fact, they are direct subclasses of DisplayObject. Therefore, they inherit the displaying protocol of all displayable objects, but since they are not display mediums they do not inherit protocol for bordering or coloring.

9.7.1 Infinite Forms

Infinite forms are patterned forms with an infinite extent. They have a single instance variable, patternForm, which is a 16 by 16 bit form that replicates itself to fill an infinite form when it is displayed. Within the existing Smalltalk system, infinite forms are used only once to represent the gray background that forms the backdrop to the windows on the Smalltalk display screen.

Creating an Infinite Form

Infinite forms are created using the protocol **with:** where the argument specifies the pattern form; e.g., **InfiniteForm with:** Form gray ⟹ an infinite form filled with gray

- InfiniteForm **with:** patternForm
    Creates an infinite form that when displayed is filled with patternForm.

Other Supported Protocol

Infinite forms do not add any additional instance protocol to class DisplayObject. They simply implement the methods required of all subclasses of DisplayObject. The primitive display method fills the display medium onto which the infinite form is to be displayed with the pattern form. The method **computeBoundingBox** returns a rectangle whose origin is 0@0 and whose corner is maximumSmallInteger@maximumSmallInteger. The offset of an infiniteForm is 0@0.

9.7.2 Opaque Forms

Unlike standard forms, **opaque forms** actually consist of two forms — a **shape form** and a **figure form**. The shape form can be thought of as providing coverage information for the figure form. The composite opaque form is obtained by combining the figure and shape forms. The composite form is equal to the figure form except that those bits in the figure that correspond to white bits in the shape form are considered transparent bits rather than black or white.

In Fig. 9.29, only the bits in the figure form that correspond to bits in the black square of the shape form are identical in the composite opaque form. Consequently, the circle and triangle are white, the surrounding square is black, and the surrounding bits are all transparent.

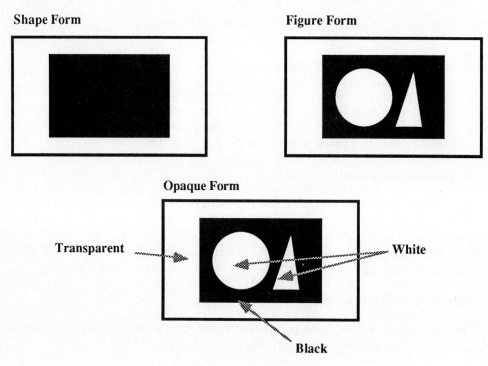

Figure 9.29 Opaque forms.

An alternative way of viewing an opaque form is as a two-bit map; i.e., we store two bits of information at each point (or pixel) in the image. This multiple bits per pixel view is the manner in which color bits might be stored in a red-green-blue color system. For each pixel in the two-bit map, there are four possible combinations. Fig. 9.30 shows the resulting pixel color in the opaque form for each combination. Note that the result of one of the possible states is undefined.

Shape	Figure	Meaning
0	0	Transparent
0	1	Undefined
1	0	White
1	1	Black

Figure 9.30 Viewing opaque forms as two-bit maps.

Figure 9.31 Opaque form displayed over a pattern background.

When an opaque form is displayed on a display medium, transparent bits in the opaque form leave the corresponding destination bits untouched. Otherwise bits from the opaque form will replace corresponding bits in the destination. For example, Fig. 9.31 shows the result of displaying the opaque form described earlier over a patterned background form.

The advantage of opaque forms is that they allow the user to work with black, white and transparent colors simultaneously. For example, opaque forms allow cursors to be defined where white bits can be made distinct from transparent bits and hence display as white bits. An example of this notion can be found by evaluating **OpaqueForm example**, which also illustrates the use of opaque forms in creating simple animation sequences.

Creating an Opaque Form

Two methods are supplied for creating opaque forms **figure:shape:** and **shape:**. In the latter case, both the figure and shape forms are the same.

- OpaqueForm **figure:** figureForm **shape:** shapeForm
  Creates an opaque form with figure and shape given by figureForm and shapeForm respectively. White in both forms denotes transparent.

- OpaqueForm **shape:** aSolidShapeForm
  Creates an opaque form with both figure and shape given by aSolidShapeForm; i.e., the opaque form is black where the aSolidShapeForm is black and transparent elsewhere.

Displaying an Opaque Form

The primitive display method for opaque forms requires two bitblt operations. First, the shape form is displayed on the display medium using the erase rule and then the figure form is displayed using mode under.

> **displayOn:** aDisplayMedium **at:** aDisplayPoint **clippingBox:** clipRectangle
> **rule:** ruleInteger **mask:** aForm.
>   "Displays an opaque form."
>
>   shape **displayOn:** aDisplayMedium **at:** aDisplayPoint **clippingBox:** clipRectangle
>   **rule:** Form **erase mask:** nil.
>   figure **displayOn:** aDisplayMedium **at:** aDisplayPoint **clippingBox:** clipRectangle
>   **rule:** Form **under mask:** aForm.

Other Protocol

Instances of class OpaqueForm support additional protocol to access the shape and figure forms and to access and modify individual pixels within an opaque form. In addition, specialized implementations of **storeOn:** and **bitEdit** are defined for opaque forms.

- anOpaqueForm **figure**
- anOpaqueForm **shape**
- anOpaqueForm **valueAt:** aPoint
    Returns the value at location aPoint within anOpaqueForm — 0 for white, 1 for black, and 2 for transparent.
- anOpaqueForm **valueAt:** aPoint **put:** aValue
    Modifies the value at location aPoint within anOpaqueForm — 0 for white, 1 for black, and 2 for transparent. The bit at the origin is at 0@0; i.e., 0-based (rather than 1-based) indexing is used.

9.8 CURSORS

Graphical cursors are represented in Smalltalk by instances of class Cursor. Cursors are used in Smalltalk to provide important graphical feedback to the user. The shape of the cursor is changed to reflect the activity that the system is carrying out. For example, a pair of reading glasses is displayed when Smalltalk is reading from an external file while a pen is displayed when writing to a file. Cursors are also used in conjunction with the mouse to indicate a location on the display screen. Movement of the mouse is coordinated with movement of the graphical cursor on the display. Confirmation of a particular location is achieved using the buttons on the mouse. Together with the mouse, cursors form the basis for the implementation of many interactive graphical operations; e.g., framing a window, selecting from a menu, changing the active window, selecting a section of text, or selecting the start and endpoints of a line.

Cursor is a subclass of **Form** that restricts the extent of a form to a 16 by 16 area, maintains class variables for most of the common cursors used by the system, and supports additional protocol to access and modify the currently active cursor. Most cursors used by Smalltalk are stored in class variables of class Form. These class variables include ReadCursor, WriteCursor, CrossHairCursor, and so on. Rather than accessing the names of the class variables directly, class methods are provided. Some of the more important predefined cursors accessible through class Cursor are shown in Fig. 9.32. Note that the first cursor is blank.

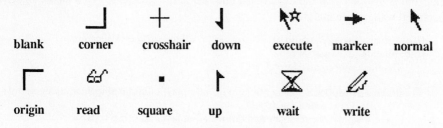

Figure 9.32 Smalltalk cursors.

Inside Smalltalk

The class methods used to access these cursors are shown below. Additional system cursors include the bulls-eye, caret, garbage and hand icons. See the class method category constants in class Cursor for a full list.

- Cursor **blank**

    No cursor shape — used to make cursor invisible.

- Cursor **corner**

    Bottom right corner shape — displayed when framing rectangular areas.

- Cursor **crossHair**

    Used in the Bit Editor.

- Cursor **down**

    Half down arrow shape — displayed when scrolling to view previous text.

- Cursor **execute**

    Displayed by the system when execution is taking place.

- Cursor **marker**

    Right arrow shape — displayed when jumping to a specific piece of a document.

- Cursor **normal**

    The regular Smalltalk cursor.

- Cursor **origin**

    Top left corner shape — displayed when framing rectangular areas.

- Cursor **read**

    Reading glasses shape — displayed when reading from a file.

- Cursor **square**

    A 4 x 4 square shape — not used by the Smalltalk system.

- Cursor **up**

    Half up arrow shape — displayed when scrolling to view subsequent text.

- Cursor **wait**

    Hour glass shape — displayed when a slow file operation is being performed.

- Cursor **write**

    Pen shape — displayed when writing to a file.

In early versions of Smalltalk, other cursors, such as the thumbs up and thumbs down cursors, were not accessible through class Cursor but rather were defined in the classes in which they were used. Thumbs up and down, for example, were defined in **BinaryChoiceView** — a class for constructing query windows that require a boolean answer to a 'yes' or 'no' question. In later versions of the system, all system cursors have been collected together in class Cursor.

- Cursor **thumbsUp**
- Cursor **thumbsDown**

Figure 9.33 Thumb cursors.

Note that the offset associated with a cursor is often very important. The offset ensures that the *hot spot* of the cursor is displayed at the correct position. For example, the *hot spot* of the normal Smalltalk cursor is the pixel representing the tip of the arrowhead; for the crosshairs it is the pixel where the hairs cross.

9.8.1 Installing a New Cursor

It is relatively simple to add a new cursor to the system. Suppose we want to define a new cursor in the shape of the bug used earlier in this chapter. First, install the name of the new cursor as a class variable in class Form. Next, define the required cursor shape and offset using the instance creation protocol inherited from class Form. The bitmap should be provided as an array of 16-bit words as described earlier. Although the protocol is inherited, the Cursor subclass ensures that the extent of the cursor is 16 by 16. Add a private class method **initializeBug** to initialize the class variable **bugCursor** as shown below.

```
initializeBug
    BugCursor ← Cursor
        extent: 16@16
        fromArray: #(
            2r0000000000000000
            2r0000000000000000
            2r0001000000001000
            2r0001000110001000
            2r0001100110011000
            2r0000111111110000
            2r0001111111111000
            2r0001111111111000
            2r0001111111111000
            2r0001111111111000
            2r0000111111110000
            2r0001100000011000
            2r0001000000001000
            2r0000000000000000
            2r0000000000000000)
        offset: -8@-9.
```

Now, include a call to this method, for example, self **initializeBug**, in the code for class method **initialize** and evaluate the expression **Cursor initialize** to install the new cursor. Finally, provide a convenient way of referring to the cursor by adding a **bug** class method to class Cursor.

```
bug
    ↑BugCursor.
```

Successful installation of the new cursor can be tested using an expression such as

```
Cursor bug showWhile: [(Delay forSeconds: 15) wait]
```

which replaces the current cursor with the bug and displays the bug while the block argument to **showWhile:** is evaluated. In this case, the new cursor will appear for fifteen seconds at which point the original cursor will be reinstalled.

9.8.2 Additional Protocol for Cursors

At any time, only one cursor is active. **Sensor**, a global variable of class **InputSensor**, keeps track of which cursor is currently being used and also its position on the display. In general, class InputSensor provides an interface to the user-input devices, the pointing device (mouse), and the keyboard. Protocol for class InputSensor as it relates to simple graphical interaction with the pointing device will be discussed in greater detail in the next section. Class Cursor also contains protocol that, through messages sent to Sensor, allows the current cursor to be manipulated.

- aCursor **show**
  - Makes aCursor the current cursor.
- aCursor **showGridded**: gridPoint
  - Makes aCursor be the current cursor and forces the location of the cursor to the nearest point on a grid specified by gridPoint.
- aCursor **showWhile**: aBlock
  - Makes aCursor the current cursor while aBlock is evaluated. The original cursor is restored after the block is evaluated.
- Cursor **currentCursor**
  - Returns the currently displayed cursor.
- Cursor **currentCursor**: aCursor
  - Makes aCursor the current cursor and displays it.
- Cursor **cursorLink**: aBoolean
  - If aBoolean is true, causes the cursor to track the pointing device location; otherwise, tracking is disabled.

9.9 CLASSES DISPLAYSCREEN AND DISPLAYBITMAP

Class **DisplayScreen** is a subclass of class Form. The Smalltalk system contains one distinguished global instance of class DisplayScreen named **Display**, which represents the image on the display screen. Instances of class DisplayScreen differ from normal forms in that their bitmap is represented by an instance of class **DisplayBitmap** rather than class **FormBitmap** (previously WordArray). This makes it possible to distinguish the particular bitmap that is being displayed. Various implementations can then treat this bitmap specially. Class DisplayBitmap is a subclass of class FormBitmap and supports no additional protocol. It is possible to have more than one instance of class DisplayScreen. For example, this might be useful in an animation context where screens are double buffered; i.e., where one screen is displayed while the next is being computed.

Class DisplayScreen provides additional protocol that allows manipulation of the whole display screen.

- DisplayScreen **currentDisplay**: aDisplayScreen
  - Makes aDisplayScreen be the current display image.
- DisplayScreen **displayExtent**: aPoint
  - Sets the extent (horizontal and vertical resolution) of the display image from aPoint. The logical screen size may differ from the physical screen size.

- DisplayScreen **displayHeight**: height

  Sets the height (vertical resolution) of the display image to height. The logical screen height can differ from the physical screen height.
- aDisplayScreen **flash**: aRectangle

  Flashes the area of the display screen defined by the rectangle aRectangle.

9.10 Graphical Interaction

When we think of graphics applications, we tend to think of the display process; i.e., graphical output. However, in the case of interactive graphics, graphical input is also vitally important. Smalltalk is one of the finest examples of an interactive graphical programming environment. Many operations require graphical interaction; e.g., framing a window, selecting from a menu, changing the active window, selecting a section of text, or selecting the start and endpoints of a line. In this section, we explore, describe, and illustrate with examples how Smalltalk code can be developed involving simple interactive graphics sequences. The chapter on windows deals with the issues of how to write complete interactive graphical applications.

For some graphical operations, such as choosing the endpoints of a line, the user wishes to indicate a physical point on the screen. In others, such as selecting from a menu, the user wishes to logically select some on-screen item. All of these higher-level interactive operations are built on two fundamental capabilities: selecting a position on the display and confirming such a selection to Smalltalk. When a mouse is used as the primary input device, the selection of a position on the display is achieved by moving a cursor on the display to coincide with physical movement of the mouse. Confirmation of a chosen position is achieved using the buttons on the mouse.

Class **InputSensor**, a subclass of class **Object**, provides an interface to the user input devices — Smalltalk assumes a keyboard and a three-buttoned mouse is available. Access to the input devices is provided through the global variable **Sensor**, a default instance of class **InputSensor**. For instance, we can detect whether a mouse button has been pressed using the message Sensor **anyButtonPressed**.

Protocol is supported to interrogate the state of the three mouse buttons (named red, yellow, and blue) and the location of the mouse as well as methods to wait for a certain kind of mouse activity before returning the location of the cursor.

- **redButtonPressed**

  Is the red mouse button being pressed?
- **blueButtonPressed**

  Is the blue mouse button being pressed?
- **yellowButtonPressed**

  Is the yellow mouse button being pressed?
- **anyButtonPressed**

  Is any mouse button being pressed?
- **noButtonPressed**

  Is no mouse button being pressed?
- **mousePoint**

  Returns a point indicating the coordinates of the current mouse location.

- **mousePointNext**

  Returns the mouse point if the red button is down; false otherwise.
- **waitButton**

  Waits for the user to press any mouse button and then answer with the current location of the cursor.
- **waitClickButton**

  Waits for the user to click (press and then release) any mouse button and then answers with the current location of the cursor.
- **waitNoButton**

  Waits for the user to release any mouse button and then returns the current location of the cursor.

Sensor also keeps track of which cursor is currently in use and the position of the cursor on the display. Both of these attributes may also be modified using the protocol shown below.

- **currentCursor**

  Returns the cursor currently in use.
- **currentCursor**: newCursor

  Sets newCursor to be the displayed cursor form.
- **cursorPoint**

  Returns a point indicating the location of the cursor 'hot spot'.
- **cursorPoint**: aPoint

  Sets aPoint to be the current location of the cursor 'hot spot'.

9.10.1 Examples of Graphical Interaction

The following examples of Smalltalk code illustrate the use of **Sensor** in constructing simple examples of graphical interaction.

Magnifying an Area on the Display

In the Form class method **exampleMagnify**, a form with origin at the cursor point and extent 50@50 is captured interactively from the display and redisplayed at the left corner of the display (0@0) magnified by a scale factor of 3@3. The position of the origin of the form to be magnified can be changed by moving the mouse.

```
exampleMagnify
    [Sensor redButtonPressed] whileFalse: [
        ((Form fromDisplay: (Sensor cursorPoint extent: 50@50))
            magnifyBy: 3@3)
                displayAt: 0@0]
```

Animating a Form by Attaching It to the Cursor

An example given earlier can now be fully understood. The following method below attaches the receiving form to the cursor position. As the cursor moves (the cursor itself is not displayed since its image is blank), aForm is displayed at the cursor point. Whenever the image is displayed at a new position, the previous background is restored. The process continues until a mouse button is depressed. The method **follow:** locationBlock **while:** durationBlock continuously displays an image at locations supplied by evaluating locationBlock as long as durationBlock evaluates to true.

```
animateForm
    Cursor blank showWhile: [
        self follow: [Sensor cursorPoint] while: [Sensor noButtonPressed]]
```

Drawing a Sequence of Connected Lines on the Display

The method **connectedLines** (implemented as a class method for class Form) shown below allows a user to interactively display a sequence of connected line segments.

```
connectedLines
    "Displays a sequence of connected line segments where the endpoint of each line is
    interactively selected by pressing the red (or selection) mouse button. To terminate
    the method press any other mouse button."

    | aForm endOfLineSegments startPoint endPoint oldCursor |
    aForm ← Form new extent: 5 @ 5; black.          "creates a black 5 by 5 form"
    oldCursor ← Sensor currentCursor.
    Display white.                                  "clear the display screen"
    Cursor crossHair showWhile: [
        startPoint ← Sensor waitButton.             "get start point for first line"
        endOfLineSegments ← false.
        [endOfLineSegments] whileFalse: [
            endPoint ← Sensor waitButton.
            Sensor redButtonPressed
                ifTrue: [
                    Display drawLine: aForm from: startPoint to: endPoint
                        clippingBox: Display boundingBox rule: Form over mask: nil.
                    startPoint ← endPoint. Sensor waitNoButton]
                ifFalse: [endOfLineSegments ← true]]].
```

The example illustrates how a different cursor may be used within a method by saving and restoring the existing cursor. Endpoints of the lines are specified using the red (or selection) button of the mouse. Pressing any other button terminates the method.

9.11 GENERATING GRAPHICS PATHS AND TRAJECTORIES

The graphical class **Path**, a subclass of **DisplayObject**, provides the basic functionality for classes that represent trajectories. Specializations of class **Path** include **Arc**, **Circle**, **Curve**, **Line**, **LinearFit**, and **Spline** (see Fig. 9.34).

The graphical representation of any path is generated by displaying some graphical form at a collection of points on the display. The collection of points is chosen to best approximate the selected path or trajectory. For example, for a line, the points are chosen to approximate a continuous line drawn between the two endpoints. Clearly, since the selected points must be restricted to pixel positions on the display, the displayed line may not be smooth.

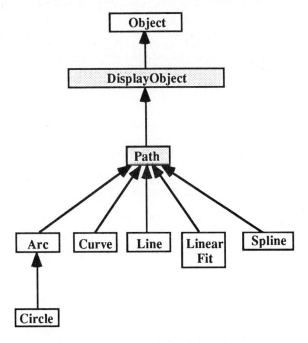

Figure 9.34 The graphics path classes.

Instances of class Path and its subclasses can be logically thought of as consisting of an ordered collection of points and a form. The ordered collection of points are those required to uniquely specify the selected path. In the case of class Path, this collection consists of all the points at which the form is to be copied onto the display to generate the path. For most subclasses, only a few points are needed to specify the path — all other points are computed when the path is displayed. For example, for a line, only the endpoints of the line need to be specified. The choice of form governs the actual displayed representation. For example, a thin line can be generated by selecting a form consisting of a single black pixel or a thick line by selecting a form that is a 4 by 4 black square.

The basic functionality of class Path and its subclasses is described below. Examples of each class are shown in Fig. 9.35 — a 10 by 10 black form is used in each case.

Path	A path is specified by an ordered collection of points. When displayed, the path is generated by copying a given form onto the display at each point in the collection. No forms are displayed between the points.
Line	A line is specified by two endpoints. A line is displayed as a collection of points that generate a path approximating the actual line between the endpoints.
LinearFit	A linear path is specified by an ordered collection of points. When displayed, it computes a piece-wise linear approximation by generating lines between successive points in the collection.

Curve	A curve is specified by three points: p1, p2, and p3. When displayed, a continuous hyperbola or conic section is fitted through the points that interpolate p1 and p3 and is tangent to the lines joining (a) p1 and p2 at p1, and (b) p2 and p3 at p3.
Spline	A spline is specified by an ordered collection of points. When displayed, a smooth continuous curve is fitted through the points.
Arc	A quadrant of a circle is specified by a center, a radius, and a quadrant number (1 through 4). When displayed, computes a collection of points that generate a continuous quarter circle approximating the specified quadrant.
Circle	A circle is specified by a center and a radius. Displayed by generating a continuous circular curve representing the four quadrants of the circle.

9.11.1 Generating Paths

Instance Creation

Paths support the class protocol **new** and **new**: anInteger for creating uninitialized instances of class Path. The latter message specifies the initial size of the path; i.e., how many points in the path. The default form is a 1 by 1 black form (a black dot). All subclasses except **Curve** and **Line** inherit these messages.

- Path **new**
- Path **new**: numberOfPoints

Path, LinearFit, and Spline drawn through same 5 points

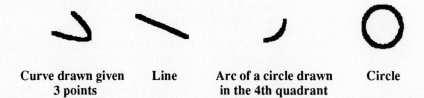

Curve drawn given 3 points	Line	Arc of a circle drawn in the 4th quadrant	Circle

Figure 9.35 Examples of graphics paths.

A subset of the protocol for ordered collections is supported for accessing, testing, adding to, removing from, transforming, and enumerating over the ordered collection of points associated with a path. Strangely, paths do not currently support **do**: although they do support **collect**: and **select**:. The **do**: method may easily be added by refining the **collect**: method.

Accessing and Modifying the Points on a Path

The protocol **at**: index and **at**: index **put**: aPoint allow points to be retrieved and modified by position. In addition, paths support protocol for directly accessing and/or modifying the first, second, third, and last elements of the collection of points.

- aPath **at**: index
- aPath **at**: index **put**: aPoint
- aPath **first**
- aPath **firstPoint**
- aPath **firstPoint**: aPoint
- aPath **secondPoint**
- aPath **secondPoint**: aPoint
- aPath **thirdPoint**
- aPath **thirdPoint**: aPoint
- aPath **last**
- aPath **last**: aPoint

Determining the Size of a Path

The size of a path may be tested using the protocol **size** and **isEmpty**.

- aPath **size**
- aPath **isEmpty**

Adding Points to or Removing Points from a Path

Points may be added to or removed from a Path using the protocol **add**: aPoint and **removeAllSuchThat**: aBlock.

- aPath **add**: aPoint
- aPath **removeAllSuchThat**: aBlock

Sequencing over the Points on a Path

A subset of the familiar enumeration protocol from collections, namely **collect**: aBlock and **select**: aBlock, is also supported by paths.

- aPath **collect**: aBlock
- aPath **select**: aBlock

Scaling and Transforming the Points on a Path

There are basically two kinds of display objects in the Smalltalk system — those that when asked to transform themselves and create a new object and those that modify themselves by maintaining a record of the transformation request (typically an offset). Paths, like rectangles and points, are display objects of the first kind. A scaled or translated version of some existing path may be created using **scaleBy**: aPoint and **translateBy**: aPoint.

- aPath **scaleBy**: aPoint
  Returns a new path with a collection of points equal to those of aPath scaled by aPoint.
- aPath **translateBy**: aPoint
  Returns a new path with a collection of points equal to those of aPath translated by aPoint.

Accessing and Modifying the Form Associated with a Path

The form associated with a path may be accessed and modified using the protocol **form** and **form**: aForm. If no form has been associated explicitly with a path, a default 1 by 1 black form (a black dot) is returned by **form**.

- aPath **form**
- aPath **form**: aForm

Displaying a Path

All subclasses of **DisplayObject** (the superclass of **Path**) must provide their own protocol for graphically displaying themselves and for computing a display bounding box (**computeBoundingBox**). Class Path and its subclasses each implement specialized methods for displaying. Class Path provides an implementation for computing the display bounding box based on computing the smallest rectangle that encloses all points on the given path. This method is inherited by all existing subclasses of class Path, although it is not appropriate for use with arcs and circles.

- aPath **displayOn**: aDisplayMedium **at**: aDisplayPoint **clippingBox**: clipRectangle
  rule: ruleInteger **mask**: aForm
- aPath **displayOn**: aDisplayMedium **transformation**: displayTransformation
  clippingBox: clipRectangle **rule**: ruleInteger **mask**: aForm
- aPath **computeBoundingBox**

Note that it is usually unnecessary to specify all the parameters to the display operations. In most cases the simplified displaying protocol, **displayOn**: aDisplayMedium, is sufficient.

To illustrate the use of paths, suppose we want to create and display a path with a given form where individual positions on the path are interactively specified using the mouse. The following example class method for class Path would accomplish this task.

pathDrawingExample

"Creates a path from points interactively selected with the mouse and displays the path on the display. A path is generated by pressing the red mouse button to indicate each point on the path; pressing any other mouse button terminates the example."

```
| aPath aForm endOfPath aPoint |
aForm ← (Form new extent: 3 @ 3) black.        "creates a 3 by 3 black form"
aPath ← self new form: aForm.                  "create a new path"
                                               "use the form for displaying the path"
Display white.                                 "clear the display screen"
[aPoint ← Sensor waitButton. Sensor redButtonPressed]
      whileTrue: [
            aPath add: aPoint.                 "add the new point to the path"
            Sensor waitNoButton].
aPath displayOn: Display                       "display the path"
↑aPath
```

"Path **pathDrawingExample**"

9.11.2 Generating Lines

Instance Creation

Lines can be thought of as paths with a path length of 2 where the two points indicate the beginning and end of the line respectively. Instances of class **Line** are best created using the protocol **from:** beginPoint **to:** endPoint **withForm:** aForm. **Line** overrides **new** to return a line with both endpoints initialized to be the point 0@0.

- • aLine **from:** beginPoint **to:** endPoint **withForm:** aForm
  Returns a new line with endpoints beginPoint and endPoint and form aForm.
- • aLine **new**
  Returns a new line with endpoints 0@0 and a single black pixel as the default form.

Accessing and Modifying a Line

In addition to the protocol inherited from class **Path**, class **Line** supports additional protocol for accessing and modifying the beginning and endpoints of the line.

- • aLine **beginPoint**
- • aLine **beginPoint:** aPoint
- • aLine **endPoint**
- • aLine **endPoint:** aPoint

Displaying a Line

Many algorithms have been devised for displaying an approximation to a straight line on a bit-mapped display. The **displayOn** family of messages for lines uses an efficient line drawing algorithm developed by Bresenham [IBM Systems Journal, Vol. 4, No. 1, 1965] that involves only integer arithmetic.

An Example: Rubber-Band Lines

Rubber-banding is a common technique for interactively positioning a line. One end point of the line is fixed while the other is "attached" to the position of the cursor. Whenever the cursor moves, a new line is drawn from the start point to the current cursor location and any previous line is erased. This process is repeated, providing the user with a view of the currently selected line at all times. The process terminates when the final end point is selected. Using a mouse, the initial start point can be selected by depressing a mouse button, intermediate lines will be displayed as long as the button remains depressed, and the final line will be selected when the button is released. Similar rubber-banding techniques can be used to interactively create other graphic objects, for example, rectangles and circles.

The class method **rubberBandLineFromUser** below returns a line created using a rubber banding technique. Note that intermediate lines drawn on the display should not modify the original contents of the display. This is achieved by displaying and erasing the lines using exclusive-or (**reverse**) mode.

class methods

instance creation

rubberBandLineFromUser
"Creates a line using rubber-banding techniques. Depress the red button to indicate the start point of the line. As long as the button is kept depressed, a line will be drawn between the start point and the current cursor position. As the cursor moves, so does the line. When the button is released, the final line is drawn and returned ."

```
| firstPoint endPoint aForm |
aForm ← (Form new extent: 1@1) black.
firstPoint ← Sensor waitButton.
endPoint ←
    self rubberBandFrom: firstPoint until: [Sensor noButtonPressed] with: aForm.
↑(Line from: firstPoint to: endPoint with: aForm)
```

private

rubberBandFrom: startPoint **until:** aBlock **with:** aForm
"While aBlock evaluates to true, displays a line in reverse mode from startPoint to the current cursor point. If the cursor point changes then remove the line and draw a new line from the startPoint to the new location of the cursor. When aBlock evaluates to false, erase the final line and return the final end point."

```
| line endPoint |
line ← Line from: startPoint to: startPoint withForm: aForm.
line displayOn: Display at: 0@0 clippingBox: Display boundingBox
    rule: Form reverse mask: nil.          "display first line"
[aBlock value] whileFalse: [
    (endPoint ← Sensor waitButton) = line endPoint ifFalse: [
        line displayOn: Display at: 0@0 clippingBox: Display boundingBox
            rule: Form reverse mask: nil.          "erase existing line"
        line endPoint: endPoint.                   "change the end point"
        line displayOn: Display at: 0@0 clippingBox: Display boundingBox
            rule: Form reverse mask: nil.          "display new line"]].
line displayOn: Display at: 0@0 clippingBox: Display boundingBox
    rule: Form reverse mask: nil.          "erase final line"
↑line endPoint
```

9.11.3 Generating Linear Fits

Instances of class **LinearFit** are paths that are displayed as piece-wise linear approximations on an ordered collection of points. They support no additional protocol — all protocol is either inherited from Path or is a redefinition of some part of the display protocol from class Path. A linear fit is displayed as a connected sequence of line segments drawn between each pair of adjacent points in the ordered collection of points. The line drawing algorithm from class Line is used to draw each line segment.

To test class LinearFit, use the example methods in class **Path** and send them to class **LinearFit** instead. The previous examples would also work if tested on class **LinearFit**.

9.11.4 Generating Curves

Instances of class **Curve** are paths specified by an ordered collection of three points. They support no additional instance protocol — all protocol except for specialized display protocol is inherited from class Path. A curve specified by three points p1, p2, and p3 is displayed as an approximation to a hyperbola that interpolates p1 and p3 and is tangent to the lines joining p1 and p2 at p1 and p2 and p3 at p3 (see Fig. 9.36).

Curve reimplements **new** so that the three points specifying the curve are all initialized to 0@0. Use **firstPoint:** aPoint, **secondPoint:** aPoint, and **thirdPoint:** aPoint to specify the points from which the curve is to be generated.

Example

An example class method for interactively creating and displaying instances of class Curve is shown below.

```
curveDrawingExample
    "Designate three points on the screen by clicking any mouse button. A 10 by 10
    black form will be displayed at each selected point. A hyperbolic curve based on the
    three selected points will be displayed using the same form."

    | aCurve aForm |
    aForm ← (Form new extent: 10 @ 1 black.    "create a 10 by 10 black form"
    Display white.                             "clear the display"
    aCurve ← Curve new form: aForm.            "use the black form for display"

    "Collect and display three points on which to base the curve."

    aCurve firstPoint: Sensor waitButton. Sensor waitNoButton.
    aForm displayOn: Display at: aCurve beginPoint.
    aCurve secondPoint: Sensor waitButton. Sensor waitNoButton.
    aForm displayOn: Display at: aCurve beginPoint.
    aCurve thirdPoint: Sensor waitButton. Sensor waitNoButton.
    aForm displayOn: Display at: aCurve beginPoint.

    aCurve displayOn: Display.                 "display the curve"

    "Curve curveDrawingExample"
```

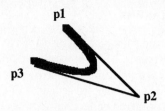

Figure 9.36 Curve specified by the points p1, p2, and p3.

9.11.5 Generating Splines

Splines are used extensively in graphics applications for generating approximations to smooth curves through a given collection of control points. Class **Spline** inherits protocol from class **Path** but reimplements its own display protocol. The cubic spline display method must compute first, second, and third derivatives. These derivatives may be accessed using the protocol **derivativePointsAt**.

- aSpline **derivativePointsAt**

If the first and last points in the collection are coincident, a closed spline curve will be generated.

- aSpline **isCyclic**

The following method interactively creates and displays instances of class **Spline**.

```
splineDrawingExample
    "Designate points on the Path by clicking the red button. Terminate by pressing any
    other button. A 10 by 10 black form will be displayed at each selected point. A cubic
    spline curve will then be displayed through the selected points, using the same
    form."

    | splineCurve aForm endOfPath |
    aForm ← (Form new extent: 10 @ 10) black.        "create a 10 by 10 black form"
    Display white.                                    "clear the display"
    splineCurve ← Spline new form: aForm.
    endOfPath ← false.
    [endOfPath] whileFalse: [
        Sensor waitButton.
        Sensor redButtonPressed
            ifTrue: [
                splineCurve add: Sensor waitButton. "add point to spline"
                Sensor waitNoButton.
                "display point on spline"
                aForm displayOn: Display at: splineCurve last]
            ifFalse: [endOfPath ← true]].
    splineCurve computeCurve.                          "compute derivatives"
    "display spline"
    splineCurve isEmpty ifFalse: [splineCurve displayOn: Display].
    ↑splineCurve

    "Spline splineDrawingExample"
```

You may have noticed that the pathDrawingExample method can be inherited by Spline. Instead of the above we could write 'Spline **pathDrawingExample**; **computeCurve; displayOn:** Display'.

9.11.6 Generating Arcs and Circles

Although class **Arc** inherits representation from **Path**, it also introduces additional instance variables to specifically maintain the quadrant, radius, and circle of an arc. Arcs should perhaps be renamed quadrants since only quadrants of a circle, rather than arcs, can be represented. Arcs require the quadrant of the circle to be specified as well as the radius and center. Quadrants are labelled 1 through 4, as shown in Fig. 9.37.

Figure 9.37 Quadrant labels for class Arc.

Instance Creation

Arcs (and circles) are best created by invoking the inherited method **new** from class Path and then explicitly initializing the radius, center, and quadrant of the arc.

Accessing and Modifying an Arc or Circle

Arcs (and circles) support additional protocol to access and modify the radius, center, and quadrant (arc only). Other arc protocol allows concurrent modification of the center, radius, and quadrant.

- anArcOrCircle **radius**
- anArcOrCircle **radius:** aPoint
- anArcOrCircle **center**
- anArcOrCircle **center:** aPoint
- anArc **quadrant**
- anArc **quadrant:** quadrantNumber
- anArcOrCircle **center:** aPoint **radius:** aPoint
- anArc **center:** aPoint **radius:** aPoint **quadrant:** quadrantNumber

It is important to note that although the protocol for the points on a path (e.g., **at:** index, **firstPoint**, and so on) is inherited by arcs and circles, it is clearly inappropriate to use it. Classes Arc and Circle do not override these methods. Similarly, it is inappropriate to use the protocol involving quadrants when sending messages to circles.

Bounding Boxes for Arcs and Circles

Arcs and circles inherit operation **computeBoundingBox** from class Path. However, the inherited method operates on the inherited representation not the additional instance variables introduced by arcs and circles. The operation must be reimplemented for both classes to work properly.

Example

The following example illustrates the creation of a **Moire** pattern (see Fig. 9.38) using concentric circles. Moire patterns are patterns generated by viewing similar patterns at different angles or distances. The pattern shown was generated by displaying a set of concentric circles, then displacing the center of the circle to the left, and displaying the same set of concentric circles again.

```
moirePatternExample
    "Click any button somewhere on the screen. This point will be the center of a set of
    closely spaced concentric circles. The center will be shifted to the left and a similar
    set of concentric circles drawn to construct a Moire pattern."

    | aCircle aForm maximumRadius leftShift |
    Display white.
    maximumRadius ← 75. leftShift ← 20.
    aForm ← (Form new extent: 1@1) black.
    aCircle ← Circle new form: aForm; radius: 4; center: Sensor waitButton.
    [aCircle radius < maximumRadius] whileTrue: [
        aCircle displayOn: Display; radius: aCircle radius + 2].
    aCircle center: aCircle center - (leftShift @ 0) radius: 4.
    [aCircle radius < maximumRadius] whileTrue: [
        aCircle displayOn: Display; radius: aCircle radius + 2]

    "Circle moirePatternExample"
```

Figure 9.38 Moire pattern.

9.11.7 Generating New Paths: Ellipses

What must be done to add new path classes to Smalltalk? For example, suppose we wished to add a new subclass of **Path** to represent ellipses. All subclasses of **DisplayObject** (the superclass of **Path**) must provide their own protocol for graphically displaying themselves and for computing a display bounding box. They must at least implement the two primitive displaying operations (**displayOn:** aDisplayMedium **at:** aPoint **clippingBox:** clipRectangle **rule:** anInteger **mask:** aForm, and **displayOn:** aDisplayMedium **transformation:** aTransformation **clippingBox:** clipRect **rule:** anInteger **mask:** aForm) and the operation **computeBoundingBox.**

As with classes **Arc** and **Circle**, we will adopt the approach of augmenting the representation inherited from class Path. Additional protocol will also be needed to access and modify this extension. To simplify discussion of the display algorithms, we will limit the implementation to ellipses whose axes are parallel to the x and y axes. Such ellipses can be specified in terms of the lengths of the semimajor and semiminor axes lengths and a center point (see Fig. 9.39).

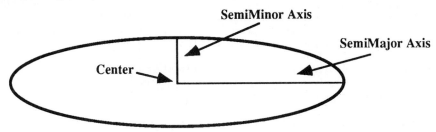

Figure 9.39 Specification of an Ellipse.

Accessing and Modifying an Ellipse

Ellipses support additional protocol to access and modify the center, semiMajorAxis and semiMinorAxis.

- anEllipse **center**
- anEllipse **center**: aPoint
- anEllipse **center**: aPoint **semiMajorAxis**: majorLength
  semiMinorAxis: minorLength
- anEllipse **semiMajorAxis**
- anEllipse **semiMajorAxis**: aLength
- anEllipse **semiMinorAxis**
- anEllipse **semiMinorAxis**: aLength

The following is an example method illustrating the use of the class **Ellipse**.

ellipseDrawingExample
　　"Click the button somewhere on the screen. The designated point will be the center of an ellipse with semimajor axis of length 60 and semiminor axis of length 30."

```
| aForm |
aForm ← (Form new extent: 5 @ 5) black.      "make a black Form for display"
Ellipse new
      form: aForm;                           "set the form for display"
      center: (Sensor waitButton) semiMajorAxis: 60 semiMinorAxis: 30;
      displayOn: Display.
```

"Ellipse **ellipseDrawingExample**"

How is the path followed by an ellipse to be generated in a form suitable for display? Since an ellipse is a conic section just like a circle, we might investigate how a circle is displayed. A circle is generated by displaying the four quadrants (arcs) of the circle. Each arc or quadrant is generated using the following method.

instance methods

displaying

displayOn: aDisplayMedium **at:** aPoint **clippingBox:** clipRect **rule:** anInteger **mask:** aForm

```
| nSegments line angle sin cos xn yn xn1 yn1 |
nSegments ← 12.0.
line ← Line new. line form: self form. angle ← 90.0 / nSegments.
sin ← (angle * (2 * Float pi / 360.0)) sin. cos ← (angle * (2 * Float pi / 360.0)) cos.
quadrant = 1 ifTrue: [xn ← radius asFloat. yn ← 0.0].
quadrant = 2 ifTrue: [xn ← 0.0. yn ← 0.0 - radius asFloat].
quadrant = 3 ifTrue: [xn ← 0.0 - radius asFloat. yn ← 0.0].
quadrant = 4 ifTrue: [xn ← 0.0. yn ← radius asFloat].
nSegments truncated timesRepeat: [
      xn1 ← xn * cos + (yn * sin). yn1 ← yn * cos - (xn * sin).
      line beginPoint: center + (xn truncated @ yn truncated).
      line endPoint: center + (xn1 truncated @ yn1 truncated).
      line displayOn: aDisplayMedium at: aPoint clippingBox: clipRect rule: anInteger
          mask: aForm.
      xn ← xn1. yn ← yn1]
```

The quadrant is generated using an algorithm based on the parametric form of a circle. In parametric form, each coordinate of a point on a circle centered at the origin is represented as a function of θ:

$$x = r \cos\theta$$
$$y = r \sin\theta$$

where r is the radius of the circle and θ is the angle in radians. Choosing equal increments of θ from 0 to 2π generates equally spaced points on the circle. An approximation to the circle can be displayed by drawing lines between adjacent points on the circumference. Only values of θ in the range 0 to $\pi/2$ need be considered since by symmetry each point in this range generates one point in each of the other three quadrants. Choosing a smaller amount by which to increment θ generates more points and hence more lines and a better approximation. However, for each point, two costly trigonometric functions must be evaluated.

Fortunately, the recalculation of the trigonometric functions can be avoided. If $d\theta$ is the amount by which to increment θ between the generation of adjacent points, then using the parametric form

$$x_n = r \cos\theta \text{ and } x_{n+1} = r \cos (\theta + d\theta)$$
$$y_n = r \sin\theta \text{ and } y_{n+1} = r \sin (\theta + d\theta)$$

and

$$\cos (\theta + d\theta) = \cos\theta \cos d\theta - \sin\theta \sin d\theta$$
$$\sin (\theta + d\theta) = \cos\theta \sin d\theta + \sin\theta \cos d\theta$$

it follows that

$$x_{n+1} = x_n \cos d\theta - y_n \sin d\theta$$
$$y_{n+1} = x_n \sin d\theta + y_n \cos d\theta$$

Since $d\theta$ is constant, the values of $\sin d\theta$ and $\cos d\theta$ need be computed only once. The points generated can be translated to allow the center of the circle to lie at points other than the origin. Note that in Smalltalk the y-axis is the inverse of a normal coordinate system; i.e., y is 0 at the top of the display. In the method for displaying an arc of a circle the parametric equations are modified to allow for this; i.e., y is scaled by a factor of -1.

A similar parametric form based approach can be adopted to generate ellipses. For an ellipse with semimajor axis **a** and semiminor axis **b** centered at the origin, the parametric form is

$$x = a \cos\theta$$
$$y = b \sin\theta$$

If $d\theta$ is again the amount by which to increment θ between the generation of adjacent points, using the parametric form

$$x_n = a \cos\theta \text{ and } x_{n+1} = a \cos(\theta + d\theta)$$
$$y_n = b \sin\theta \text{ and } y_{n+1} = b \sin(\theta + d\theta)$$

reduces the computation for each point on the ellipse to the following:

$$x_{n+1} = x_n \cos d\theta - (a/b) \, y_n \sin d\theta)$$
$$y_{n+1} = (b/a) \, x_n \sin d\theta + y_n \cos d\theta)$$

Class **Ellipse** is shown below. We leave it to the reader to modify the class to permit ellipses with axes that are not parallel to the x and y-axes.

Class Ellipse

class name	Ellipse
superclass	Path
instance variables	semiMajorAxisLength
	semiMinorAxisLength
	center

class methods

examples

ellipseDrawingExample
   "Click the button somewhere on the screen. The designated point will be the center of an Ellipse with semimajor axis of length 60 and semiminor axis of length 30."

```
| aForm |
aForm ← (Form new extent: 5 @ 5) black.      "make a Form for display"
Ellipse new
     form: aForm;                             "set the form for display"
     center: (Sensor waitButton) semiMajorAxis: 60 semiMinorAxis: 30;
     displayOn: Display
```

   "Ellipse **ellipseDrawingExample**"

instance methods

accessing

center
    ↑center
center: aPoint
    center ← aPoint

semiMajorAxis
    ↑semiMajorAxisLength
semiMajorAxis: aLength
    semiMajorAxisLength ← aLength
semiMinorAxis
    ↑semiMinorAxisLength
semiMinorAxis: aLength
    semiMinorAxisLength ← aLength

center: aPoint **semiMajorAxis**: majorLength **semiMinorAxis**: minorLength
    center ← aPoint. semiMajorAxisLength ← majorLength.
    semiMinorAxisLength ← minorLength

display box access

computeBoundingBox
    ↑center - (semiMajorAxisLength @ semiMinorAxisLength) + form **offset**
        extent: form **extent** + (2 * (semiMajorAxisLength @ semiMinorAxisLength))

displaying

displayOn: aDisplayMedium **at**: aPoint **clippingBox**: clipRectangle **rule**: anInteger
mask: aForm
    | nSegments line angle sin cos xn yn xn1 yn1 ratio inverseRatio quadrant |

    nSegments ← 48.0. line ← Line **new form**: self **form**. angle ← 360.0 / nSegments.
    sin ← (angle * (2 * Float **pi** / 360.0)) **sin**. cos ← (angle * (2 * Float **pi** / 360.0)) **cos**.
    ratio ← semiMajorAxisLength / semiMinorAxisLength.
    inverseRatio ← semiMinorAxisLength / semiMajorAxisLength.
    xn ← semiMajorAxisLength **asFloat**. yn ← 0.0.
    nSegments **truncated timesRepeat**: [
        xn1 ← xn * cos + (ratio * yn * sin). yn1 ← yn * cos - (inverseRatio * xn * sin).
        line **beginPoint**: center + (xn **truncated** @ yn **truncated**).
        line **endPoint**: center + (xn1 **truncated** @ yn1 **truncated**).
        line **displayOn**: aDisplayMedium **at**: aPoint **clippingBox**: clipRect **rule**: anInteger
            mask: aForm.
        xn ← xn1. yn ← yn1]

displayOn: aDisplayMedium **transformation**: aTransformation **clippingBox**: clipRectangle
rule: anInteger **mask**: aForm
    |newCenter |

    newCenter ← aTransformation **applyTo**: self **center**.
    Ellipse **new center**: newCenter **x truncated** @ newCenter **y truncated**;
        semiMajorAxis: (self **semiMajorAxis** * aTransformation **scale x**) **truncated**;
        semiMinorAxis: (self **semiMinorAxis** * aTransformation **scale y**) **truncated**;
        form: self **form**;
        displayOn: aDisplayMedium **at**: 0 @ 0 **clippingBox**: clipRect **rule**: anInteger
            mask: aForm

9.11.8 Revisions to Paths

Class Path and its subclasses Arc, Line, Circle, ... have a number of minor problems which should be identified and rectified.

Class Path and its specializations Arc, Circle, Line, Curve, LinearFit, and Spline each have method **displayOn:transformation:clippingBox:rule:mask:** specially implemented to properly handle the transformation. On the other hand, **displayOn:transformation:–clippingBox:align:with:** was not redefined and is therefore inherited from DisplayObject. This method does not work with paths because the scaling information is ignored; i.e., the method assumes the graphical object is fixed-size. For example, if a line from 0@0 to 10@10 were to be displayed using a transformation of the form 'scale: 10 translation: 5@5', the latter method simply offsets the display by 5@5 so that the line actually displayed begins at 5@5 and ends at 15@15. The correct version requires more than a simple offset; the entire line must be transformed and in this case magnified. It should display the line from 5@5 (0@0 transformed) to 105@105 (10@10 transformed).

A correct version of **displayOn:transformation:clippingBox:align:with:rule:mask:** can be created by adding the additional parameters 'align: destinationPoint1 with: destinationPoint2' to the existing **displayOn:transformation:clippingBox:rule:mask:** method in Path and each of its subclasses (7 classes in all).

For all classes except **Circle**, 'at: 0@0' in the code body is replaced by the difference of the alignment points. More specifically, if the method is of the following form, '0@0' is replaced by '(destinationPoint2 - destinationPoint1)'.

```
aPathOrArcOrCurveOrSplineOr...
    displayOn: aDisplayMedium transformation: displayTransformation
    clippingBox: clipRectangle align: destinationPoint1 with: destinationPoint2
    rule: ruleInteger mask: aForm
        ...
        aTransformedCopy
            displayOn: aDisplayMedium
            at: 0 @ 0
            clippingBox: aClippingRectangle
            rule: aRuleInteger
            mask: aMaskForm
    ...
```

For class **Circle**, 'super **displayOn:**...**transformation:**...**clippingBox:**...**rule:**... **mask:**...' in the code body is replaced by 'super **displayOn:**...**transformation:**... **clippingBox:**...**align:** destinationPoint1 **with:** destinationPoint2 **rule:**...**mask:**...'.

Note that method **displayOn:transformation:clippingBox:rule:mask:** can be removed from each of the subclasses since the version inherited from DisplayObject makes use of the new corrected methods.

The generic **displayOn:transformation:clippingBox:** method inherited from DisplayObject fails for **Path** and its subclasses. A copy of the DisplayObject version can be added to **Path** (all subclasses can inherit from this one) and modified as follows: "change the **align:?with:?** portion of the **displayOn:transformation:clippingBox:align:with:rule:–mask:** message to contain any point constants that are identical; e.g., **align:** 0@0 **with:** 0@0".

The **Spline displayOn:transformation:...** method constructs a new transformed spline prior to displaying it. However, it fails to compute the curve using **computeCurve**. Simply add 'newSpline **computeCurve**' after the code that constructs it.

Example

The following can serve as a test of the above modifications. The intent is to draw 6 special paths in 2 rows of 3 squares. The squares should be adjacent to each other without overlapping.

```
| aDot aLine aCircle aCurve aPath aLinearFit aSpline aTransformation aBox d t |

aDot ← (Form extent: 4@4) black.

"Create display objects intended for display on a 10 by 10 area."

aLine ← Line from: 2@2 to: 8@8 withForm: aDot.
aCircle ← Circle new
     form: aDot; radius: 4; center: 5@5; yourself.
aCurve ← Curve new
     form: aDot; firstPoint: 2@8; secondPoint: 5@2; thirdPoint: 8@8; yourself.
aPath ← Path new
     form: aDot; add: 2@8; add: 2@2; add: 5@8; add: 8@2; add: 8@8; yourself.
aLinearFit ← LinearFit new
     form: aDot; add: 2@8; add: 2@2; add: 5@8; add: 8@2; add: 8@8; yourself.
aSpline ← Spline new
     form: aDot; add: 2@8; add: 2@2; add: 5@8; add: 8@2; add: 8@8; yourself.
aSpline computeCurve. "Otherwise, the spline cannot be displayed"

"Display them in two rows of three squares each 113 by 113 units (just to pick an odd size)."

aTransformation ← WindowingTransformation
     window: (0@0 corner: 10@10) viewport: (0@0 corner: 113@113).
aBox ← Display boundingBox. "The rectangle for the entire display"

Display white. "Start with a nice display"

d ← Display. t ← aTransformation. "Just to fit subsequent statements into one line."
aLine displayOn: d transformation: t clippingBox: aBox align: 0@0 with: 100@100.
aCircle displayOn: d transformation: t clippingBox: aBox align: 0@0 with: 213@100.
aCurve displayOn: d transformation: t clippingBox: aBox align: 0@0 with: 326@100.
aPath displayOn: d transformation: t clippingBox: aBox align: 0@0 with: 100@213.
aLinearFit displayOn: d transformation: t clippingBox: aBox align: 0@0 with: 213@213.
aSpline displayOn: d transformation: t clippingBox: aBox align: 0@0 with: 326@213.

"By aligning  0@0 with 213@100, for example, we are causing the display to shift right
by 213 pixels. Clearly, 213 must be in destination coordinates. If it were in source
coordinates, the actual amount shifted would be "t applyTo: 213"; to get exactly 213, we
would have to actually supply "t applyInverseTo: 213" (the display method would then
transform it to cancel out the inverse operation; i.e., "t applyTo: (t applyInverseTo: 213)"
is 213."

ScheduledControllers restore. "To place the display into its previous state"
```

9.12 DRAWING WITH PENS

Class **Pen**, a subclass of class **BitBlt**, extends the line drawing capabilities of BitBlt in two directions. Pens may be used as tools for scribbling or doodling on the display and may also be used to emulate the notion of turtles and turtle graphics found in the programming language LOGO.

Pens inherit the representation and methods of class BitBlt. Recall that instances of class BitBlt represent the parameters required to carry out the fundamental bit copying operation (copyBits). Within the context of class Pen, several of the inherited BitBlt attributes play an important role.

source form	The tip or nib of a pen.
mask	The color of a pen.
destination form	The canvas on which a pen writes — usually but not necessarily the display.
clipping rectangle	The size of the canvas.

Additionally, pens support the following attributes:

drawing frame	A frame within which a pen can draw — equivalent to the clipping rectangle of the bitblt associated with the pen.
pen state	The state of a pen — up or down. The pen only writes on the display when its state is down.
location	The position of a pen on the display screen.
direction	The direction (in degrees) the pen would move if asked to do so; 0 degrees is equivalent to a heading of north or up the display screen. Positive directions are measured clockwise from this heading.

9.12.1 Creating Pens

The class method **new** returns an instance of class Pen with the following default attributes:

source form	1 by 1 black dot
halftone form	black
destination form	display screen
combination rule	paint
clipping rectangle	display bounding box
frame	display bounding box
pen state	down
location	display screen center
direction	north

Note that in early versions of the system, the default combination rule for a pen was **paint**. While this mode allows for additional functionality, in the general case it requires two BitBlt copy operations rather than the one required for other modes. For most applications of pens, such as drawing a geometric design like a spiral, a better combination rule and the one used in the current system is **under**; i.e., pixels from the source form are "or-ed" with pixels from the display to produce the modified display.

9.12.2 Scribbling and Doodling with Pens

Pens are often used for scribbling or doodling. BitBlt provides the method **drawFrom:to:** for drawing lines between two points, but pens provide a higher level and friendlier protocol. More specifically, a pen can be moved from its current location to any new location. If the pen is moved with the pen down, a line is drawn between the two points using the source form (or nib) associated with the pen.

- aPen **down**

    Sets the drawing state of aPen to down (the pen will draw when it is moved).

- aPen **up**

    Sets the drawing state of aPen to up (the pen will **not** draw when it is moved).

- aPen **goto**: aPoint

    The pen is moved from its current location to aPoint. If the pen is down a line will be drawn between the two points.

- aPen **place**: aPoint

    The pen aPen is moved to the point aPoint. No lines are drawn irrespective of the state of the pen.

Example: Pens as Sketching Tools

The following method illustrates how pens may be used as a sketching tool.

```
doodle
    "A simple method that facilitates interactive sketching using a pen. Use the mouse
    to move the cursor to a desired starting position. Depress the red button on the
    mouse to start drawing. Moving the mouse with the red button still depressed
    displays a trail on the display using a black pen. Releasing the red button causes
    drawing to cease. This procedure may be repeated as many times as desired. To
    exit the method, depress any other mouse button."

    | aPen |
    aPen ← Pen new combinationRule: Form under.

    [Sensor waitButton. true] whileTrue: [
        Sensor redButtonPressed
            ifTrue: [
                aPen place: Sensor cursorPoint.
                [Sensor redButtonPressed] whileTrue: [aPen goto: Sensor cursorPoint]]
            ifFalse: [↑self]]

    "Pen doodle"
```

9.12.3 Turtle Graphics with Pens

Smalltalk pens emulate the turtle graphics capabilities found in the programming language LOGO. Pens facilitate the construction of images algorithmically rather than by painting. In LOGO, turtles are robot-like creatures whose domain is the display screen. Turtles maintain a position and a heading and respond to simple commands such as move **forward** a certain amount, turn **left** through a certain number of degrees, and so on. Turtle graphics visualizes the notions of turtle geometry, a unique explorative approach to the teaching of geometry and mathematical concepts developed by Seymour Papert and his colleagues at the Massachusetts Institute of Technology.

In addition to the protocol introduced earlier, pens support the following turtle-oriented operations:

- aPen **home**

    Places aPen at the center of its frame.
- aPen **north**

    Sets the direction of aPen to be facing toward the top of the display screen.
- aPen **go**: distance

    Moves aPen in its current direction a number of bits equal to the argument, distance. If the pen is down, a line will be drawn using the source form of aPen as the shape of the drawing brush.
- aPen **turn**: degrees

    Changes the direction that aPen faces by an amount equal to the argument, degrees. Positive degree values result in clockwise changes in direction.

For example, the following code draws an equilateral triangle with sides of length 200 on the display.

```
| aPen |
aPen ← Pen new.
3 timesRepeat: [:count | aPen go: 200 turn: 120]
```

This code can be extended to produce any regular polygon by modifying the number of times the iteration is repeated and the angle through which the pen is turned. For example, to draw an octagon with sides of length 50, modify the change in direction to be 45 degrees (i.e. 360 divided by the number of sides).

```
| aPen |
aPen ← Pen new.
8 timesRepeat: [: count | aPen go: 50 turn: 45]
```

Extending the idea one step further, we can produce a primitive circle drawing algorithm by drawing a 360-gon. This is a very poor way to draw a circle — see class Circle for a better algorithm

```
| aPen |
aPen ← Pen new.
360 timesRepeat: [:count | aPen go: 1 turn: 1]
```

Constructing Geometric Designs Using Pens

Class Pen contains several instance methods that illustrate how pens may be used to construct interesting geometric designs. These include spirals, dragon curves, and hilbert curves.

- aPen **dragon**: order
  Draws a dragon curve of order 'order' in the center of the screen using aPen.
- aPen **hilbert**: index **side**: sideLength
  Uses aPen to draw a space-filling curve with the given index where the length of each side is given by sideLength.
- aPen **mandala**: numberOfPoints **diameter**: diameter
  On a circle of diameter 'diameter', places numberOfPoints points, and then draws all possible connecting lines using aPen.
- aPen **spiral**: n **angle**: angle
  Draws a double spiral using aPen.

Example: C-Curves

The following example illustrates how another attractive geometric figure, a c-curve, may be drawn. C-curves are described recursively as follows. A c-curve of level 0 is a straight line of a given length. A c-curve of level n consists of two c-curves of level n-1 that are drawn at right angles to each other, followed by a final 90 degree turn to restore the original heading. Fig. 9.40 shows a c-curve of level 10 where each line in the curve is of length 4.

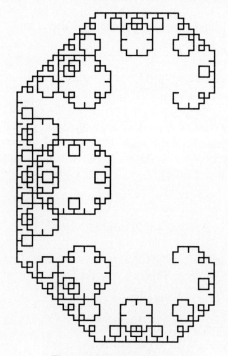

Figure 9.40 Level 10 C-curve.

cCurve: level **side**: sideLength
    "Draw a c-curve with the specified level and side length."

    level = 0 **ifTrue**: [↑self **go**: sideLength].
    self **cCurve**: level - 1 **side**: sideLength. self **turn**: 90.
    self **cCurve**: level - 1 **side**: sideLength. self **turn**: -90.

    "Pen **new** home; **turn**: -90; **cCurve**: 10 **side**: 4."

9.12.4 Additional Pen Operations

Pens have a number of useful attributes that can be interrogated and changed; e.g.,

- aPen **black**
  Sets the halftone or mask form of aPen to black.
- aPen **white**
  Sets the halftone or mask form of aPen to white.
- aPen **direction**
  Returns the current direction of aPen in degrees. 0 is toward the top of the screen, positive is clockwise, and negative is anticlockwise.
- aPen **frame**
  Returns the rectangle in which aPen can draw.
- aPen **frame**: aRectangle
  Sets the rectangle in which aPen can draw to be aRectangle.
- aPen **location**
  Returns a point that is the location of aPen.

9.13 SUMMARY

In this chapter, we have surveyed the classes that support the interactive creation and manipulation of graphical images. In particular, we have discussed the following:

- The underlying Smalltalk graphical model.
- The protocol supported by the classes **Point** and **Rectangle** that are used to represent spatial information.
- The use of forms and bitblts to create and manipulate images.
- The standard protocol supported by objects that can display themselves.
- The transformation of images through magnification, scaling, reflection, rotation, translation, and fill operations.
- The use of infinite and opaque forms.
- Graphical cursors.
- Simple interactive graphical interaction techniques using the mouse and keyboard.
- Graphical paths including arcs, circles, curves, lines, linear fits, and splines.
- The use of pens.

9.14 EXERCISES

The following exercises may require some original thought, rereading some of the material, and/or browsing through the system.

1. Implement an interactive, graphical solution to the 'eight-square puzzle' in Smalltalk. Eight square tiles numbered from 1 to 8 are located within a frame that will hold exactly nine tiles, as shown in Fig. 9.41. The objective of the game is to rearrange the tiles within the frame from some initial configuration (such as that shown on the left) to a target configuration where the numbered tiles are arranged in order around the edge of the frame (as shown on the right). Tiles can only be moved one at a time and can only move by sliding into the currently open tile position within the frame. Tiles cannot be lifted. For example, from the starting configuration shown on the left, only the tiles numbered 1, 8 and 7 may be moved.

   The user should indicate that a particular tile is to be moved by moving the cursor inside the tile and clicking the red button. Provided the tile movement is legal, the tile will be moved to occupy the vacant tile position within the frame. Think of a way of "sliding" a tile when it is moved; i.e., display the tile in intermediate positions between its original and final position. The game should be terminated by clicking on the yellow button.

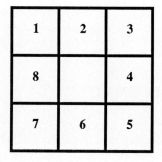

Figure 9.41 Eight square puzzle.

2. Create a Smalltalk animation system that emulates the turtle microworlds as described in [H. Abelson, and A. Di Sessa, "Turtle Geometry: The Computer as a Medium for Exploring Mathematics," MIT Press, 1980]. The basic idea is to give turtles "animal-like" characteristics and to study their movements and interactions in particular environments. For example, a simple microworld might simply allow turtles to roam randomly on the display screen. Interesting problems to consider here are how turtles should behave when they hit the edge of the display screen or when they collide with each other. A variation might introduce directed rather than random motion where the movement of the turtles is governed by some instinct or desire. For example, predatory animals such as foxes could be introduced into the simulation. The natural instinct of a fox is to chase the nearest turtle. The natural instinct of a turtle is to avoid being caught by a fox. An interesting problem to consider is how turtles and foxes should "see" each other; i.e., how is sight to be modelled?

Inside Smalltalk

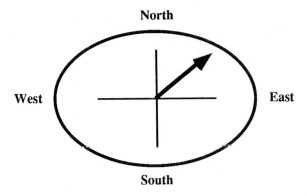

Figure 9.42 Direction indicator.

3. In interactive graphical applications, it is often convenient to input numeric values graphically rather than simply typing them in. For example, angular input could be achieved through a rotary dial (see Fig. 9.42) where the user drags the indicator of the dial to indicate the desired direction. Implement Smalltalk classes that emulate rotary dials as described above.

4. There are several other approximations to smooth curves that are useful in graphics applications. Implement new classes **Bezier** and **BSpline** to represent Bezier curves and B-splines (most graphics texts will have a section on curve generation).

5. Modify class **Ellipse** given in this chapter so that the major and minor axes of the ellipse do not have to be parallel to the x- and y-axes.

6. Potentiometers or scales are useful for obtaining values within some predetermined range. For example, a graphical potentiometer (see Fig. 9.43) allows the user to interactively select a real value between 0.0 and 1.0 by dragging the slider horizontally across the scale. As the slider moves, the number displayed beneath it changes to indicate the currently selected value. Implement Smalltalk classes that emulate gauges and scales as described above.

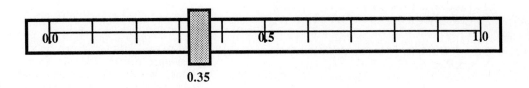

Figure 9.43 Graphical potentiometer.

7. Generalize the Smalltalk class **OpaqueForm** to provide a full set of operations on two-bitmaps (opaque forms). Refer to the paper "Two-Bit Graphics" by Saliesin and Barzel in the June 1986 issue of **IEEE Computer Graphics and Applications** for a full discussion of two-bit compositing, painting, and region filling operations.

8. Class **Arc** and **Circle** use a display algorithm that approximates the arc or circle by a sequence of connected straight line segments drawn between sample points on the arc. For arcs of large radii and/or a small selection of points on the arc, this approximation is poor. A better approximation can be achieved using the point plotting algorithm of Bresenham. [J. E.

Bresenham, "A Linear Algorithm for the Incremental Digital Display of Circular Arcs," Communications of the ACM, Vol. 20, No. 2, February 1977, pp. 100-106]. Implement classes **NewArc** and **NewCircle** based on Bresenham's algorithm. Class **NewArc** should represent arbitrary arcs rather than only quadrants, as in class **Arc**.

9.15 GLOSSARY AND IMPORTANT FACTS

classes

Arc A subclass of class **Path**. Arcs are specified by a center, a radius and a quadrant number (1 through 4). When displayed, they compute a collection of points that generate a path approximating a quadrant of a circle — it is not possible to generate an arbitrary arc.

BitBlt Instances of class BitBlt represent fundamental graphical operations described in terms of copying some source form to a destination form in a particular way.

Circle A subclass of class **Arc**. A circle is specified by a center and a radius. Displayed by generating paths representing the four quadrants of the circle.

Cursor A subclass of Form that restricts the extent to 16 by 16 and is used to represent small icons or cursors. Cursors are used in Smalltalk to indicate the activity that the system is carrying out; e.g., a pair of reading glasses is displayed when Smalltalk is reading from an external file, while a pen is displayed when writing to a file.

Curve A subclass of class **Path**. Curves are specified by three points p1, p2, and p3. When displayed, a hyperbola is fitted through the points that interpolate p1 and p3 and is tangent to the lines joining (a) p1 and p2 at p1, and (b) p2 and p3 at p3.

DisplayObject An abstract class describing the protocol supported by objects that can display themselves. Subclasses include **DisplayMedium, DisplayText, Path, Form, InfiniteForm,** and **Opaque-Form.**

DisplayMedium A class that supports protocol for objects that can act as a canvas on which images can be painted and that can also paint themselves onto a medium. DisplayMedium supports protocol for coloring images and for bordering images with textures. Class **Form** is a subclass of DisplayMedium and inherits its protocol for coloring and bordering.

Form Instances of class Form are used to represent graphical images. Forms may be internal (memory-based) or external (display-based). Forms inherit the ability to display themselves from class **DisplayObject** and to color and border themselves from class **DisplayMedium**. Forms themselves add protocol for creating, editing, and transforming images.

FormBitmap A subclass of Object (FormBitmap was originally called Word-Array in earlier versions of Smalltalk). Instances of class FormBitmap are used to store the bits making up a form.

InfiniteForm Forms that are obtained by replicating a pattern indefinitely in all directions. Within the existing Smalltalk system, infinite forms are used only once to represent the gray background that forms the backdrop to the windows on the Smalltalk display screen.

InputSensor A class providing an interface to the keyboard and the mouse. Access to the input devices is provided through the global variable **Sensor**, a default instance of class **InputSensor**.

Line A subclass of class **Path**. Lines are specified by two endpoints and are displayed as a continuous collection of points that generate a path approximating the actual line between the endpoints.

LinearFit A subclass of class **Path**. LinearFits are specified by an ordered collection of points and displayed as a piecewise linear approximation by generating lines between successive points in the collection.

OpaqueForm Forms that include a shape as well as a figure form. The shape form indicates what part of the background should get occluded while displaying — black is opaque, white is transparent.

Path The basic superclass of classes such as **Line** and **Circle** that generate trajectories. Paths are specified by an ordered collection of points. A path is displayed by copying a given form onto the display at each of the points in the collection. For most subclasses, only a few points are needed to specify the path; all other points are computed when the path is displayed.

Pen A subclass of class BitBlt. Pens are used as tools for scribbling or doodling on the display and to emulate the notion of turtles and turtle graphics as found in the programming language LOGO.

Point Class Point is used to represent positions in an x-y coordinate system. Most often used to specify pixel positions within a form or on the display.

Rectangle Class Rectangle is used to represent rectangular areas. Most often used to specify rectangular areas within a form or the display screen.

Spline A subclass of class **Path**. Splines are specified by an ordered collection of points. When displayed, a smooth continuous curve is fitted through the points.

WordArray A subclass of ArrayedCollection, WordArray provides an external representation for the manipulation and storage of the bitmap of a form. In earlier versions of the system, instances of WordArray were used to represent the bits of a form. In the current version, instances of class FormBitmap are used for this purpose.

selected terminology

and mode A combination rule used for a copy operation in which corresponding pixels in the source and destination forms are 'anded' together to produce the modified destination form.

bit editor The Smalltalk bit editor allows editing of forms at the bit or individual pixel level. The bit editor is normally used in conjunction with the form editor.

bounding box A bounding box is a rectangle that completely encompasses a displayable object. Bounding boxes can be used to make fast decisions concerning the intersection of displayable objects; e.g., for clipping purposes.

clipping rectangle A parameter to a BitBlt operation. Notwithstanding the specification for the destination form, the clipping rectangle specifies a rectangular region outside of which no modification of the destination form can take place.

combination rule A parameter to a BitBlt operation. A rule (an integer) that dictates how pixels in the modified destination form are to be produced from the source form and the original contents of the destination form. There are sixteen possible combination rules including **and, over, under,** and **erase**.

destination form A parameter to a BitBlt operation. Specifies the destination form; all or part of which is to be modified by the copy operation.

destination origin A parameter to a BitBlt operation. Together with the extent, the destination origin specifies the part of the destination form to be modified.

display transformation A transformation from one coordinate system to another that is to be applied as part of the display process.

erase mode A combination rule used for a copy operation in which black pixels in the source erase (or set to white) corresponding pixels in the destination form.

extent A parameter to a BitBlt operation. Together with the source and destination origins, the extent parameter specifies the part of the source form to be copied and the part of the destination form to be modified in a copy operation.

form editor The Smalltalk form editor provides 'MacPaint' style facilities for creating and editing forms— graphical pictures.

halftone form A parameter to a BitBlt operation. A 16 by 16 mask used to fill areas with textures or patterns. Combining a halftone and a source form is often used to place a texture or pattern on a form.

offset The amount by which a displayable object should be moved when displayed or when its position is tested. Forms and cursors maintain offsets and add the offset to any specified display position before displaying themselves.

over mode The most popular combination rule used with the copy operation — the source form pixels replace or copy over the corresponding destination form pixels.

paint mode A combination rule used for painting on the display with brushes of different shapes, sizes, and textures. The brush shape and size are supplied through the source form, with the halftone form supplying the brush texture.

reverse mode A combination rule that allows reversible changes. It is most often used to display temporary images such as cursors over an already existing image or for rubber-banding.

source form A parameter to a BitBlt operation. Specifies the source form; all or part of which is to be copied.

source origin A parameter to a BitBlt operation. Together with the extent, the source origin specifies the part of the source form to be copied.

under mode A combination rule that allows a source form to be painted "underneath" a destination form. This is useful when painting a character onto a display background where any white pixels surrounding the character in the source form are not to be copied.

important facts

bitblt The name bitblt is derived from a powerful bit-boundary block transfer instruction of the same name found on the Xerox Alto, an early machine supporting Smalltalk.

nondisplayable objects Points and rectangles are not displayable objects — they represent spatial quantities only. There are no operations to display points or rectangles.

hot spot When some graphical cursors are to be displayed at a certain location, it is the cursor's "hot spot" rather than its origin that should be displayed at that position. For example, the "hot spot" of the normal Smalltalk cursor is the pixel representing the tip of the arrowhead; for the crosshairs it is the pixel where the hairs cross.

10

Graphical Applications

10.1 INTRODUCTION

To illustrate the use of the Smalltalk graphical classes and how simple graphical applications are developed in Smalltalk, we present three graphics-oriented examples:[1] a film loop facility, a magnifying glass, and a simple video game. Film loops are never-ending movies and show how simple animation sequences can be developed. Techniques for obtaining flicker-free displays and for storage of graphical forms on disk are also introduced. The latter technique illustrates the use of object mutation — the ability of one object to mutate into another. The magnifying glass application allows a user to move a magnifier over the display magnifying the image under the glass of the magnifier. This application illustrates advanced graphical programming techniques and, in particular, describes how circular rather than rectangular forms may be manipulated. Finally, the simple video game illustrates the evolutionary approach that characterizes the design and development of Smalltalk applications. The design decisions that took place during the development of the game are described in detail along with the use of notions such as reusability, specialization, and generalization that differentiate object-oriented design from more traditional design methodologies.

10.2 FILM LOOPS: NEVER-ENDING MOVIES

A **film loop** is a never-ending movie in which the end is spliced with the beginning; i.e., a circular sequence of frames repeatedly displayed at a fast enough rate to provide the illusion

---

[1] Earlier versions of these examples appeared in issues of the *Journal of Object-Oriented Programming*. This material is republished by kind permission of SIGS Publications, Inc., New York, NY.

of motion. Film loops are used in VideoWorks II[2], for example, to provide rudimentary animated objects with a simple recurring behavior; e.g., a bird flapping its wings in flight or the flames in a fire. The speed at which the film loop is displayed is called the **frame rate**. For typical animation purposes, a frame rate of at least twenty-four frames per second is required to avoid flicker. Faster frame rates result in speeded up motion; e.g., a fast flying bird.

The basic idea is to create a collection of frames as shown in Fig. 10.1. Each frame is a form. In the ideal situation, the forms are constructed by a sophisticated animation system. More typically, they are hand-constructed from some kind of paint program. A base picture is first constructed and then modifications are obtained by perturbing it by small amounts. The forms are then read into Smalltalk using some suitable utility. The details will vary from system to system. In our case, we constructed MacPaint[3] images and read them into Smalltalk.

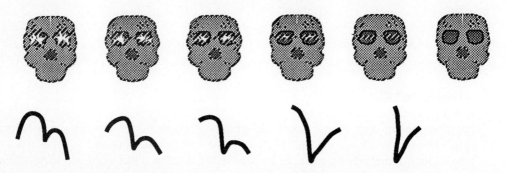

Figure 10.1 A sequence of frames in a simple animation.

On the other hand, forms can also be created from within Smalltalk, either by obtaining them directly from the screen (see class method **example1** below), by computing them (see **example2**), or by using the form and bit editors.

10.2.1 A Simple Film Loop Facility

To begin with, consider the **SimpleFilmLoop** class definition. Instances keep track of a name, the forms in a collection called frames, and how long each frame is to be displayed. The latter is needed because the processor is generally too fast for small forms. An extra delay is required to slow it down.

Each example has a comment that can be executed to test it. Method **example1** could be used, for example, to extract the sequence of skull or bird pictures shown in Fig. 10.1 (assuming the entire collection of pictures was first displayed on the screen). In addition to framing each picture, the user is also prompted for a **hot spot**; i.e., a point that is to be considered the center of the picture. In the case of the birds, the center would always be the middle of the body. This hot spot is recorded by providing an offset to the form. When the

---

[2]VideoWorks II is a trademark of MacroMind Inc.

[3]MacPaint is a trademark of Claris Inc.

form is later displayed at aPoint, it is offset by the stored amount, usually a negative amount, although there is no limitation on the actual value of the offset. Once a film loop is constructed, the film loop can be made to track the mouse by sending it a **followMouse** message.

Method **example2** starts with a white form and progressively darkens it by adding random black dots. To ensure that the film loop doesn't make an abrupt change when the switch from the last form to the first occurs, a copy of the original sequence (in reverse order) is appended to the film loop.

Method **example3** uses the film loop's **follow:while:** control structure, a generalization of the corresponding instance method in class Form.

Although the user provides the frame rate in frames per second, it is converted internally to the number of milliseconds per frame since the latter is more convenient for computing the required delay (see method **follow:while:**). For didactic purposes, we will consider methods **followMouse, follow:while:**, and **display:at:restoring:at:** in that order.

Method **followMouse** changes the current cursor to a crosshair. Note that **showWhile** is not a loop — it ensures that the new cursor is in effect while the code in the block executes and it restores the cursor to its previous state when the block code terminates.

Class SimpleFilmLoop

class name	SimpleFilmLoop
superclass	Object
instance variables	name frames millisecondsPerFrame
comment	A simple film loop provides the capability form displaying a sequencing of frames at the mouse point. Each frame is a form with a negative offset if the interior of the form is to be at the mouse point; i.e., a zero offset implies the top left corner of the form will display at the mouse point.

class methods

instance creation

new
   ↑super **new initialize**

examples

example1
   "Create a film loop using forms specified by the user. The first prompt is to specify a rectangle for an area of the screen to make up a frame. The second prompt, with a caret, waits for you to specify the frame's hot spot."
   "SimpleFilmLoop example1 followMouse"

   | aLoop answer size |
   aLoop ← self **new name:** 'Film'.
   answer ←
      FillInTheBlank **request:** 'How many forms in the loop?' **initialAnswer:** '5'.
   size ← Integer **readFrom:** (ReadStream **on:** answer).
   size **timesRepeat:** [aLoop **add:** self **formFromUser**].
   ↑aLoop

example2
"Create a film loop of increasing haze."
"SimpleFilmLoop example2 followMouse"

```
| aLoop aCollection aForm aRandom nextRandom |
aLoop ← self new name: 'Haze'.
aCollection ← OrderedCollection new.
aForm ← Form extent: 60@60. aRandom ← Random new.
nextRandom ← [aRandom next * 60 truncated + 1].
30 timesRepeat: [
    30 timesRepeat: [
        aForm
            valueAt: nextRandom value @ nextRandom value
            put: 1].
    aCollection add: (aForm deepCopy offset: -30@-30)].
aCollection do: [:form | aLoop add: form].
aCollection reverseDo: [:form | aLoop add: form deepCopy].
↑aLoop
```

example3
"Display a film loop in the center of the screen for a fixed period."
"FilmLoop example3"

```
| startTime endTime |
startTime ← Time millisecondClockValue.
(self example2)
    follow: [Display boundingBox center]
    while: [
        endTime ← Time millisecondClockValue
        (endTime - startTime) / 1000 < 30 "seconds"]
```

form creation

formFromUser
"Prompt the user for a rectangle from which the underlying form is copied and wait
for the user to indicate the hot spot; i.e., the spot which later becomes the center of
the form for display purposes. In other words, when the form is later displayed at
aPoint, the form's hotspot will be located at aPoint."

```
| aRectangle aForm |
aRectangle ← Rectangle fromUser.
aForm ← Form fromDisplay: aRectangle.
Cursor caret showWhile: [
    aForm offset: aRectangle origin - Sensor waitButton.
    Sensor waitNoButton].
↑aForm
```

instance methods

instance initialization

initialize
"Clear the film loop and set the default delay between frames."

```
frames ← OrderedCollection new.
self frameRate: 24 "frames per second"
```

access and modification

add: aForm
    "Add a form to the film loop."

    frames **add**: aForm

frameRate
    ↑(1000 "milliseconds per second" / millisecondsPerFrame) **rounded**

frameRate: framesPerSecond
    millisecondsPerFrame ←
        (1000 "milliseconds per second" / framesPerSecond) **rounded**.

name: aName
    "Set the name of the film loop."

    name ← aName

tracking

follow: positionBlock **while**: conditionBlock
    "While conditionBlock is true, animate the receiver at the position specified by positionBlock."

    | oldLocation background startTime frameIndex newLocation endTime |

    "Handle the special case that almost never happens."
    frames **isEmpty ifTrue**: [[conditionBlock **value**] **whileTrue**: []. ↑self].

    "The usual situation."
    oldLocation ← positionBlock **value**.
    background ← (Form **extent**: 0@0) **offset**: oldLocation.
    startTime ← Time **millisecondClockValue**.
    frameIndex ← 0.

    [conditionBlock **value**] **whileTrue**: [
        frameIndex ← (frameIndex \\ frames **size**) + 1.
        newLocation ← positionBlock **value**.
        background ← self **display**: (frames **at**: frameIndex)
            at: newLocation
            replacing: background
            at: oldLocation.
        oldLocation ← newLocation.
        endTime ← Time **millisecondClockValue**.
        self **delayToMatchFrameRate**: endTime - startTime.
        startTime ← endTime].
    background **displayAt**: oldLocation

followMouse
    "Continue showing the film loop until the mouse is released."

    Cursor **crossHair showWhile**: [
        Sensor **waitButton**.
        self **follow**: [Sensor **cursorPoint**] **while**: [Sensor **redButtonPressed**]]

private

delayToMatchFrameRate: millisecondsUsedSoFar
   | delayAmount |

   delayAmount ← millisecondsPerFrame - millisecondsUsedSoFar **max**: 0.
   delayAmount > 0 **ifTrue**: [(Delay **forMilliseconds**: delayAmount) **wait**]

display: frame **at**: location **replacing**: background **at**: oldLocation
   "Place the background back at oldLocation, copy the new background from location
   and place the frame on the screen. Note: both frame and background may have
   offsets."

   | newBackground newRectangle |
   background **displayAt**: oldLocation.
   newRectangle ← location + frame **offset extent**: frame **extent**.
   newBackground ← Form **fromDisplay**: newRectangle.
   newBackground **offset**: frame **offset**. "remember the offset"
   frame **displayAt**: location.
   ↑newBackground

Method **follow:while**: cycles through the frames as long as the condition block result is **true**. Variable frameIndex is used to keep track of the frame to be displayed. When it reaches value 'frame **size**', its next value is 1. The position block result indicates where the next frame should be displayed.

Before a frame can be displayed, the picture beneath the previously displayed frame (the **background**) must be restored. Hence the need for a method that (1) displays the old background, (2) saves the part of the screen that will become the new background, and (3) displays the new frame. To avoid special case code, we start off with an old background that is an empty frame; i.e., a frame with extent 0@0. At the end, we also have to restore the very last background that was saved. Fig. 10.2 illustrates the three step sequence used by method **display:at:restoring:at:**.

10.2.2 Extending Film Loops: Flicker-Free Display

There is a limitation to the display algorithm shown in Fig. 10.2 — flicker is observed whenever the old background and the new frame intersect. This can be solved with a slightly more complex display algorithm. When the frame to be displayed and the background to be restored overlap, the simple display algorithm results in flicker due to the two separate display operations. Because the first display gets undone by the second, the eye easily discerns the discrete steps. This is not apparent without the overlap because the eye simply perceives them as being done in parallel.

The solution is to ensure that only one display step is used rather than two. This can be achieved by constructing the final image offscreen. More specifically, a copy of that part of the screen that contains both the frame and background areas is updated and this updated form is displayed in one step (see the revised **display:at:restoring:at:** method).

One complication arises from an inadequacy in all Smalltalk systems. Although a form with an offset can be displayed on another form without an offset, the converse is not

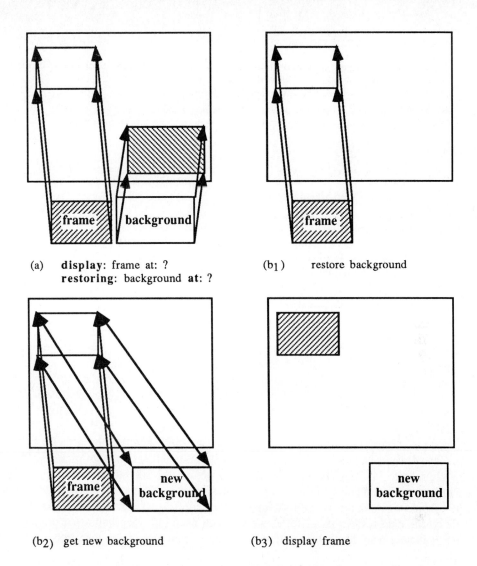

(a)   **display**: frame at: ?
      restoring: background at: ?

(b₁)   restore background

(b₂)   get new background

(b₃)   display frame

Figure 10.2 The three steps used by method '**display:at:restoring:at:**'.

properly handled; i.e., attempts to display an object on a form with an offset result in the offset being completely ignored. Were this not the case, the code in the **display:at:restoring:at:** method could be simplified by judiciously adding offsets to the forms used.

display: frame **at**: location **replacing**: background **at**: oldLocation
    "Place the background back at oldLocation, copy the new background from location
    and place the frame on the screen. To prevent flickering, only one bitblt operation
    to the screen is performed."

    | combinedRegion aForm newBackground |

"Make a copy of that part of the screen that contains both the background area and the frame area."
combinedRegion ← (oldLocation + background **offset extent**: background **extent**)
    merge: (location + frame **offset extent**: frame **extent**).
aForm ← Form **fromDisplay**: combinedRegion.

"Restore the combined region to its original state."
background **displayOn**: aForm **at**: oldLocation - combinedRegion **origin**.

"Save the area to become the new background."
newBackground ← Form **extent**: frame **extent**.
aForm **displayOn**: newBackground **at**: combinedRegion **origin** - (location + frame
offset).
newBackground **offset**: frame **offset**.

"Display the new frame in the combined region."
frame **displayOn**: aForm **at**: location - combinedRegion **origin**.

"Finally, perform the one display operation to the screen."
aForm **displayAt**: combinedRegion **origin**.
↑newBackground

10.2.3 Extending Film Loops: Disk Forms

A complication with the simple film loop facility is that associated forms take up considerable space if substantial use is made of them. We can envisage large libraries of these pictures being kept. Only a small part of this library, however, will be available in main memory; the majority will have to reside on disk. This will be all the more evident when high quality color is an integral part of our workstations. To provide an idea about the space requirements, consider one 24-bit color picture on a 1024 by 1024 screen. The space requirements are 3*1024*1024, or 3 megabytes. Lower quality 8-bit pictures still require 1 megabyte. Lower resolution screens might divide these numbers by a factor of 2, 3, or perhaps 4. Just displaying two seconds of high quality animation at 24 pictures per second would require 144 megabytes. It's easy to conjecture that 100 megabytes of main memory will be a minimum configuration for personal machines a decade from now. One solution to this problem is to make use of **disk forms**. Very briefly, disk forms are variants of forms in which the data resides in a file. However, they have one very important property. They automatically read themselves into main memory from disk and mutate into normal forms when they are used.

Currently, Smalltalk forms are black and white but extensions to color are currently being designed. So we can ignore the color aspects of the problem. With a large library of forms, some facility will be needed to manage and distinguish between those forms that are in main memory and those that are on disk. We also won't consider the complications of a **form manager**. Instead, we'll focus primarily on the **disk form** itself — a variant of a form in which the data resides in a file. Intuitively, we might expect a disk form to maintain a **file name**, an **offset** into the file, and a **size** — permitting many pictures to be stored in the same file.

Designing Disk Forms

Should a disk form have the same protocol as a normal form; i.e., should we be able to use it as if it were a normal form and have it take care of the discrepancy? It would be nice if that were the case, because all software that currently works with normal forms would then also work with disk forms. How do we achieve this goal?

The obvious approach would have us define DiskForm as a subclass of Form. But there are two problems: (1) the form's representation is no longer needed (since it is automatically inherited, the best we can do is **nil** each instance variable), and (2) we need to override every single form method to ensure that it pages the picture's bits from disk, as illustrated below for method **extent**.

```
extent
    self pageFromDiskIfNecessary.
    ↑super extent
```

A simpler solution is to forget about subclassing altogether; i.e., to design disk forms independently of forms but with a special property — the ability to change or mutate into a normal form as soon as a message is received.

The idea is simple: ensure that few form messages are understood by disk forms and provide a **doesNotUnderstand:** method for handling them. This method's task is to read in the required data from disk, construct a normal form containing it, and change the receiver into this form using the powerful **become:** operation.

Background for the Proposed Design

To understand how this works, we need a quick review of the **become:** operation, the **perform** operations, class Message, and the behavior of **doesNotUnderstand:**.

To begin with, when an attempt is made to execute an illegal message such as

$$123456 \text{ \textbf{copyFrom}: 3 \textbf{to}: 5}$$

the system manufactures an instance of **Message** containing the selector **copyFrom:to:** and an argument array containing 3 and 5 and then sends the message 'doesNotUnderstand: aMessage' to 123456.

The **doesNotUnderstand:** method inherited from **Object** displays an error message and prompts with a debugging window. However, we can write our own version that does something different. For the example above, we could resend the message to a print string of the receiver. To do this, the specialized variation could be

```
doesNotUnderstand: aMessage
    | selector arguments |
    selector ← aMessage selector.
    arguments ← aMessage arguments.
    ↑self printString perform: selector withArguments: arguments
```

For disk forms, we would like to do something a little more sophisticated. More specifically, we want to mutate it into some other object — a normal form. The **become:** operation can be used as follows for that purpose.

```
object1 become: object2
```

The proper way to read this is to say "object1 is changed into object2 and simultaneously object2 is changed into object1." This happens quite literally; any object that used to reference object1 in the system now references object2 and vice versa. For more details on the **become:** operation, refer to the meta-operations in Chapter 6.

Class DiskForm

class name   DiskForm
superclass   Object   "should be nil"
instance variables   filename offset size

class methods

class initialization

initialize
    "DiskForm initialize"
    self **confirm:** ('You must change the superclass of \',
       'DiskForm to nil using an inspector') **withCRs**.
    DiskForm **inspect**

instance methods

modification

name: aFileName
    "Set the name of the receiver."
    filename ← aFileName

offset: anInteger
    "Set the file offset of the receiver."
    offset ← anInteger

size: anInteger
    "Set the form size of the receiver."
    size ← anInteger

error handling

doesNotUnderstand: aMessage
    "Mutate the receiver into a normal form and try the message again."

    self **asForm become:** self.
    ↑self **perform:** aMessage **selector withArguments:** aMessage **arguments**

conversion

asForm
    "Answer the receiver as a normal form."

    | form file |
    Cursor **read showWhile:** [
        file ← FileStream **fileNamed:** filename.
        file **readOnly; position:** offset.
        form ← Object **readFrom:** (ReadStream **on:** (file **next:** size)).
        file **close**].
    ↑form

There are two interesting points about class **DiskForm**. First, it is not possible to directly create a class with no superclass. It is necessary to define it initially as inheriting, say, from **Object**. Then you can inspect class **DiskForm** and change the superclass to **nil**. Why do we want the superclass to be **nil**? So that any message we send to a disk form will cause it to mutate. This includes messages inherited by all objects, such as

```
aDiskForm printString
aDiskForm inspect
aDiskForm = anotherDiskForm
aDiskForm copy
```

There are at least two messages that slip through the net, however — message **class** and message '==' because they are hard-wired to bypass method lookup. Can you find any more?

The other important point is that the order of the parameters to message **become**: is crucially important; e.g., only the second case below works.

```
self become: self asForm    (1)
self asForm become: self    (2)
```

The reason is simple. Disk forms do not understand **become**: although normal forms do!

10.2.4 Integrating Disk Forms with Film Loops

One nice thing about object-oriented languages is that a more functional class can be created by inheriting from a less powerful version and extending it with the additional functionality. In our case, we don't even need to change the representation. It's sufficient to replace the collection of normal forms with disk forms since disk forms have the same behavior. The disk form facility is integrated with the film loop via three methods: **build**, **load**, and **unload**.

Method **unload** stores a complete film loop in a file in the format 'startOfFrameRate form-1 form-2 ... form-n frameRate offsets'. To get this information back later, method **build** constructs a film loop containing disk forms that reference the file information — the disk forms maintain only the file name, the offset into the file, and the size in bytes of the form information; i.e., there is no need to actually read in the information unless it is needed. Method **load** is used to force a film loop that was previously built to be totally in main memory; i.e., to mutate its disk forms to normal forms.

Method **build** needs access to the offset information to reconstruct the individual disk forms associated with a file name— actually an ordered collection of offsets, one offset per form. It would be ideal if the offsets could be first in the file. However, **unload** can't determine what the offsets will be until it actually outputs the forms into the file. Since the offset information is a collection and therefore arbitrarily long, it can't leave a fixed amount of space at the beginning (it could estimate an upper bound and waste a bit of space, however; e.g., it could assume a maximum of ten characters per offset multiplied by the number of entries — integers are converted to characters in the file). The alternative strategy we adopted was to store the offset information after the forms. However, enough room for the start of the offset information can be reserved at the beginning of the file. Since the frame rate is also needed, it might as well be stored at the end too. This should explain why *startOfFrameRate* was used — it permits us to locate the non-form information.

Method **examples** contains a series of comments that use the inherited examples. By constructing a film loop named 'Film' from **example1** and then unloading it, it is possible to later retrieve it by sending message '**new**: 'Film'' to FilmLoop. The film loop so obtained actually consists of disk forms. These get read in on demand when **followMouse** is executed. There is a noticeable delay as the disk forms get mutated to normal forms — this, of course, only happens on the first pass of the loop.

Class FilmLoop

class name	FilmLoop
superclass	SimpleFilmLoop
instance variables	"none"
comment	A more sophisticated class of film loops that avoids flickering and permits the loop to be stored on disk.

class methods

instance creation

new: aFileName
    "Create a new film loop from disk information."

    ↑(self **new name**: aFileName) **build**

examples

examples
    "FilmLoop1 ← FilmLoop example1"
    "FilmLoop1 unload"
    "FilmLoop1 followMouse"
    "(FilmLoop new: 'Film') followMouse"

    "FilmLoop2 ← FilmLoop example2"
    "FilmLoop2 unload"
    "FilmLoop2 followMouse"
    "(FilmLoop new: 'Haze') followMouse"

    "FilmLoop example3"

instance methods

caching

build
    "Re-create the film loop from disk."
    | file startOfFrameRate offsets sizes |

    Cursor **read showWhile**: [
        "startOfFrameRate form-1 form-2 ... form-n frameRate space offsets"
        file ← FileStream **fileNamed**: name.

        startOfFrameRate ← Integer **readFrom**: file.
        file **position**: startOfFrameRate.
        self **frameRate**: (Integer **readFrom**: file).

```
file next. "discard the space"

offsets ← Object readFrom: file.

sizes ← OrderedCollection new.
2 to: offsets size do: [:index | sizes add: (offsets at: index) - (offsets at: index-1)].
sizes add: startOfFrameRate - offsets last.

frames ← OrderedCollection new.
1 to: offsets size do: [:index |
    frames add: (DiskForm new
        name: name; offset: (offsets at: index); size: (sizes at: index))].
file close].
```

load
    "Force the film loop into main memory."

```
frames do: [:frame | frame extent "any query operation would do"]
```

unload
    "Save the film loop to disk."

```
| offsets file offset end |

Cursor write showWhile: [
    "Make sure all forms are in main memory since file is about to be rewritten."
    self load.

    "Leave room to store the position of the film loop information."
    "File format: startOfFrameRate form-1 form-2 ... form-n frameRate space offsets."
    (file ← FileStream fileNamed: name) writeShorten; nextPutAll: ' '; cr.
    "File out the film loop's frames."
    offsets ← OrderedCollection new.
    frames do: [:frame |
        offset ← file position. offsets add: offset. "save it"
        file store: frame; cr.
        frame
            become: (DiskForm new
                name: name; offset: offset; size: file position - offset)].

    "File out the header information."
    offset ← file position. "save it"
    file store: self frameRate; space; store: offsets.
    end ← file position.
    file reset; store: offset; position: end; cr; close]
```

10.3 GRAPHICS THROUGH THE LOOKING GLASS

In this section, we consider the implementation of a **magnifying glass** that can be attached to the mouse for close examination of a graphical image, as shown in Fig. 10.3. More specifically, we consider a magnifying glass in which it is possible to change the size of the viewing glass and also the amount of magnification (subject to limitation imposed by the implementation). Once a magnifying glass is created, it can be activated at any time. Activating a magnifying glass causes it to be attached to the mouse and to operate in the following manner: The area under the magnifying glass is magnified and displayed over the magnifier as long as the red mouse button is depressed. The magnified view stops being displayed when the red (normal) mouse button is released. The magnifying glass is deactivated when the yellow button is depressed. The magnifier can be moved whether or not it is magnifying. Of course, if it is moved while magnifying, the area viewed will change.

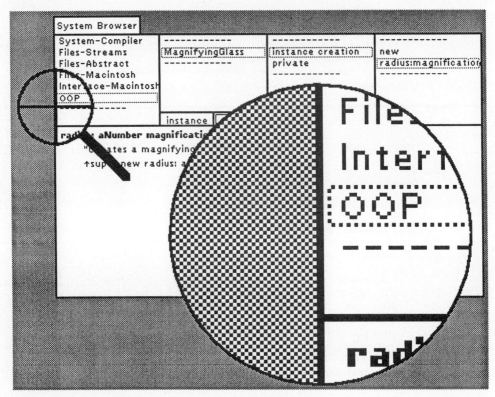

Figure 10.3 Using the magnifying glass for detailed study (magnified area displaced from actual position over the magnifier for comparison purposes).

To allow magnifying glasses with arbitrary radius and magnification, we can introduce instance variables and class protocol as shown in the following:

Class MagnifyingGlass

class	MagnifyingGlass
superclass	Object
instance variables	radius magnification

class methods

instance creation

new
   "Creates a default magnifying glass."
   ↑self **radius:** 20 **magnification:** 4

radius: anInteger **magnification**: anotherInteger
    "Creates a magnifying glass of a specified size and magnification."
    ↑super **new radius**: anInteger **magnification**: anotherInteger

instance methods

instance initialization

radius: anInteger **magnification**: anotherInteger
    "Initializes the magnifying glass instance."

    "Save the radius and magnification."
    radius ← anInteger. magnification ← anotherInteger.

What should the magnifying glass look like? Fig. 10.4 shows a possible design. Given that the glass itself is of radius **radius**, we define **magnifierForm** as a square form of size **3 * radius**. The handle is defined to be of thickness **radius // 4**. It will be too slow to construct the magnifier on the spot, so we precompute it, storing the result in the instance variable **magnifierForm**.

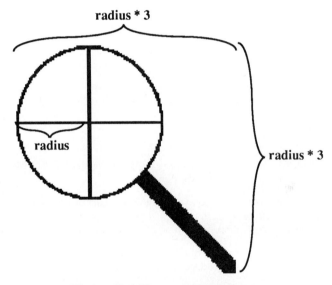

Figure 10.4 The magnifying glass.

The instance method **makeMagnifierForm** creates and initializes the form containing the magnifying glass and handle. First, a solid black handle is displayed on **magnifierForm** using an instance of class Line. Note that we initially draw the handle from the center of the glass to a point off the form. The bottom of the handle will automatically be clipped to the form. We must clip the top left part of the handle ourselves. This is achieved by drawing a solid white circle where the magnifying glass will eventually reside. To do this we create a solid black circle of the required size and then display it on the form using the erase mode to erase or set to white corresponding pixels in the magnifier form. Instances of class Circle and Line are then used to add the glass and crosshairs to the magnifier form.

Class MagnifyingGlass

class   MagnifyingGlass
superclass   Object
instance variables   radius magnification magnifierForm

instance methods

instance initialization

radius: anInteger **magnification:** anotherInteger
    "Initializes the magnifying glass instance."

    "Save the radius and magnification."
    radius ← anInteger.
    magnification ← anotherInteger.

    "Create the magnifier form."
    self **makeMagnifierForm**.

private form initialization

makeMagnifierForm
    "Creates and initializes the form containing the magnifying glass and handle."

    | diameter center dot |

    "Compute often used values."
    diameter ← 2*radius. center ← radius@radius.
    magnifierForm ← Form **new extent:** (radius@radius)*3.
    dot ← (Form **extent:** 3@3) **black**.

    "Draw a solid black handle."
    (Line **from:** center **to:** center*4 "off the form!!"
        withForm: (Form **new extent:** (radius // 4) @ (radius // 4); **black**))
            displayOn: magnifierForm.

    "Draw a solid white circle over the top left part of the handle."
    (Form **dotOfSize:** 2 * radius + 1)
        offset: 0@0; **displayOn:** magnifierForm **at:** 0@0 **rule:** Form **erase**.

    "Create the circle for the magnifying glass."
    (Circle **new form:** dot; **radius:** radius; **center:** center) **displayOn:** magnifierForm.

    "Create the horizontal line across the magnifying glass."
    (Line
        from: 0@radius **to:** diameter@radius **withForm:** dot) **displayOn:** magnifierForm.

    "Create the vertical line across the magnifying glass."
    (Line
        from: radius@0 **to:** radius@diameter **withForm:** dot) **displayOn:** magnifierForm.

10.3.1 Activating the Magnifier

Now that we have an image of the magnifying glass, we can look at how to activate the magnifier and the overall algorithm to track the movement of the mouse displaying either the magnifier or the magnified area, depending on the status of the red button. We want to be able to activate a magnifier using code of the form

    MagnifyingGlass **new activate**

Whenever the mouse moves, we must restore the original area occupied by the magnifying glass and redraw the magnifying glass at the new location. If the red button is depressed, the magnified image rather than the magnifier must be displayed. Depressing the yellow button deactivates the mouse and restores everything to its former state.

The basic strategy to be employed is described in pseudo code form in the following:

```
After hiding the cursor
      magnifying := false.
      while yellow button not pressed do
            if red button pressed then magnifying := true
            if red button released then magnifying := false
            if magnifying then
                  restoreBackgroundAndDisplayMagnifiedArea
            else    restoreBackgroundAndDisplayMagnifier
      endwhile
      restoreBackgroundAndDisplayNothing
restore the cursor
```

10.3.2 Restoring and Redisplaying

To be able to restore the background successfully (see Fig. 10.5) we must ensure that before displaying the magnifying glass at a new location we save the background area for future restoration. Remember that if the red button is depressed the magnified image is displayed instead of the magnifier. Note that this means that, in general, the old and the new area could either be the magnifier or the magnified area.

A further problem arises if the old and new forms overlap. If the background form were restored in one step, followed by a display of the new information (either the magnifier or a circular magnification area) in a second step, flickering would occur when the two areas overlap. We can avoid this by first displaying the information on a temporary form called the merged form and then displaying this merged form on the screen using one display message (see Fig. 10.6).

The merged form is a copy of the screen that contains both the background and display areas. However, if the background and/or display forms partially reside off the screen, we may need a larger merged form to avoid information loss by clipping (see Fig. 10.7).

Constantly creating new forms is slow, which suggests creating two forms, **backgroundForm** and **mergedForm**, at initialization time. Is the sized of **mergedForm** bounded by the size of the display? Unfortunately, the answer is no, as the scenario in Fig. 10.7 illustrates. The size of the background form is the maximum of the magnifier or the magnified image, while the size of the merged form is the rectangle that contains both the background form and the new display rectangle. We could compute a size that takes into account the situation shown in Fig. 10.7. However, this would have to be a function of the magnifier's radius. Even then, there are cases that would not be handled. For example, in Macintosh systems with multiple screens, it is possible to move the mouse outside the display area used by Smalltalk. In those cases, the merged form would have to be even larger

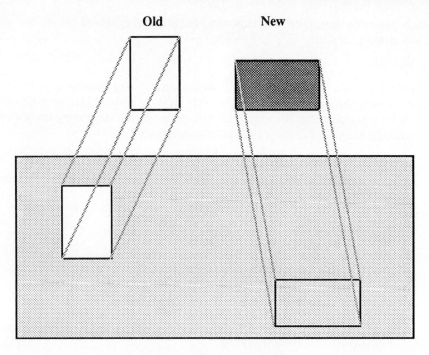

Figure 10.5 Restoring the old form and displaying the new form.

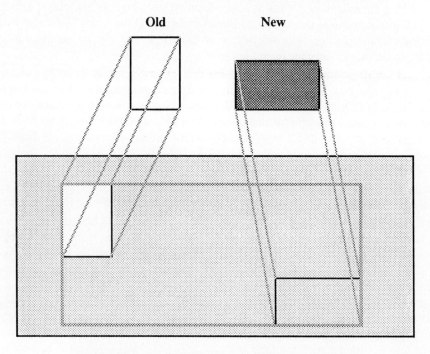

Figure 10.6 Avoiding flicker by using a merged form.

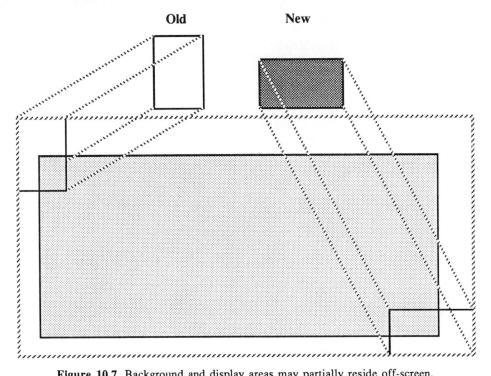

Old   **New**

Figure 10.7 Background and display areas may partially reside off-screen.

than computed in order to work properly. A simple strategy is to start with a reasonable size and extend it when (and only when) needed. Three instance variables, backgroundRectangle, mergedRectangle, and displayRectangle, are needed to keep track of the extents of their corresponding forms. Revisions to the class MagnifyingGlass so far are shown in the following:

Class MagnifyingGlass

class	MagnifyingGlass
superclass	Object
instance variables	radius magnification magnifierForm
	backgroundForm mergedForm backgroundRectangle
	displayRectangle mergedRectangle

instance methods

instance initialization

radius: anInteger **magnification**: anotherInteger
    "Initializes the magnifying glass instance."

    "Save the radius and magnification."
    radius ← anInteger. magnification ← anotherInteger.

    "Create the utility forms."
    self **makeMagnifierForm**. self **makeBackgroundAndMergedForms**

makeBackgroundAndMergedForms
"Creates forms for keeping track of the background and merged forms."

```
| size extent |
size ← radius * magnification * 2 max: radius * 3.
extent ← size@size.
backgroundForm ← Form new extent: extent.
mergedForm ← Form new extent: Display extent.
```

instance activation

activate
"Make the magnifier track the mouse and display a magnified version of the area underneath it if the mouse button is depressed; otherwise, display the magnifier itself. Depressing the yellow button (option + mouse down) deactivates the mouse and restores everything to its former state."

```
| magnifying newCenter |

"Initialize."
magnifying ← false. backgroundRectangle ← Sensor cursorPoint extent: 0@0.

"Hide the cursor."
Cursor blank showWhile:[

    "Quit when a yellow button is pressed."
    [Sensor yellowButtonPressed] whileFalse: [

        "Determine if magnification status has changed."
        magnifying ← Sensor redButtonPressed.

        "Display either the magnifier or the magnified area."
        newCenter ← Sensor cursorPoint.
        magnifying
            ifTrue: [
                displayRectangle ← newCenter - (radius@radius*magnification)
                    extent: radius * magnification * 2.
                self restoreBackgroundAndDisplayUsing:
                    #displayMagnifiedAreaOnMergedForm]
            ifFalse: [
                displayRectangle ← newCenter - (radius@radius)
                    extent: magnifierForm extent.
                self restoreBackgroundAndDisplayUsing:
                    #displayMagnifierOnMergedForm]].

    self restoreBackgroundAndDisplayUsing: #isNil]
```

There are several things to note about the **activate** method. The instance method 'showWhile: aBlock' is used to hide the cursor (to make it blank) while aBlock is evaluated. The original cursor is restored afterwards. In addition, note that one method **restoreBackgroundAndDisplayUsing:** handles the restore and redisplay process. We distinguish between the three cases by computing the new display rectangle and passing a different method as argument to **restoreBackgroundAndDisplayUsing:** in each case. For the case where the magnified image will be displayed, the code is:

```
displayRectangle ← newCenter - (radius@radius*magnification)
    extent: radius * magnification * 2.
self restoreBackgroundAndDisplayUsing: #displayMagnifiedAreaOnMergedForm
```

The method **displayMagnifiedAreaOnMergedForm** will deal with the computation specific to the magnified image. When the magnifier is to be displayed, the code is

```
displayRectangle ← newCenter - (radius@radius) extent: magnifierForm extent.
self restoreBackgroundAndDisplayUsing: #displayMagnifierOnMergedForm
```

For the final case, where the background must be restored but no redisplay is required, method **isNil** is passed — isNil is simply a nice way of specifying a null operation; it is understood by all objects and simply returns true or false depending on whether or not the receiver is nil.

```
self restoreBackgroundAndDisplayUsing: #isNil
```

10.3.3 Restoration and Redisplay Details

The restore and redisplay process can be decomposed into five basic steps.

1. **Obtain a screen copy containing both background and display areas.**

    The size of the merged rectangle is first computed taking into account the possibility that the rectangle may need to be extended if either the background or display rectangle lies partially off screen. The merged form is then extracted from the display using the copyBits:from:at:clippingBox:extent:rule:mask: message.

    ```
    mergedRectangle ← backgroundRectangle merge: displayRectangle.

    mergedRectangle extent x > mergedForm extent x |
    (mergedRectangle extent y > mergedForm extent y)
        ifTrue: [mergedForm ← Form new
            extent: (mergedRectangle extent max: mergedForm extent)].

    mergedForm copyBits: mergedRectangle from: Display at: 0 @ 0
        clippingBox: (0 @ 0 extent: mergedRectangle extent)
        rule: Form over mask: nil.
    ```

2. **Compute background and display rectangles relative to merged form origin.**

    The background and display rectangles will ultimately be extracted from or displayed on the merged form. Hence, it is convenient to translate the background rectangle in display coordinates into coordinates that are relative to the origin of the merged rectangle — the relative background rectangle. The same applies for the relative display rectangle.

    ```
    relativeBackgroundRectangle ←
        backgroundRectangle translateBy: 0 @ 0 - mergedRectangle origin.

    relativeDisplayRectangle ←
        displayRectangle translateBy: 0 @ 0 - mergedRectangle origin.
    ```

3. **Restore merged form and save the display area as the new background.**

The next step is to restore the merged form to what it used to be.

```
backgroundForm displayOn: mergedForm
    at: relativeBackgroundRectangle origin
    clippingBox: relativeBackgroundRectangle
    rule: Form over mask: nil.
```

Next, the display area is retrieved from the merged form and saved as the new background.

```
backgroundForm
    copyBits: relativeDisplayRectangle from: mergedForm
    at: 0@0 clippingBox: (0 @ 0 extent: relativeDisplayRectangle extent)
    rule: Form over mask: nil.

backgroundRectangle ← displayRectangle.
```

4. **Copy the display form onto the merged form (in-place modify).**

The next step copies the display form onto the merged form. If the red button is pressed (for magnification), method **displayMagnifiedAreaOnMergedForm** is invoked. If no magnification is taking place, method **displayMagnifierOn-MergedForm** is invoked. These methods are described in more detail in the next section.

```
Either
    self perform: #displayMagnifiedAreaOnMergedForm
Or
    self perform: #displayMagnifierOnMergedForm
```

5. **Display the merged form on the screen.**

Finally, we can display the merged form on the screen. Note that we have taken great care to ensure that at most one display operation is used to paint the screen.

```
mergedForm displayOn: Display
    at: mergedRectangle origin
    clippingBox: mergedRectangle
    rule: Form over mask: nil.
```

10.3.4 Displaying the Magnifier on the Merged Form

The method **displayMagnifierOnMergedForm** displays the magnifier form on the merged form. Note that the combination rule used is Form **under** so that we can see through the magnifier.

```
displayMagnifierOnMergedForm
    magnifierForm
        displayOn: mergedForm at: relativeDisplayRectangle origin
        clippingBox: relativeDisplayRectangle rule: Form under mask: nil
```

10.3.5 Displaying the Magnified Image on the Merged Form

If the magnified image were rectangular, it would be relatively easy to display the image on the merged form. However, the magnified image is circular, and this makes the problem considerably more interesting. Fig. 10.8 illustrates the steps necessary to display the circular magnified image. Five major stages may be identified and we will discuss each in detail. First, however, note that a black circular mask is used twice in the display process. The form **largeBlackHole** for the mask can be precomputed once and then used whenever required. We introduce a new method **makeLargeBlackHole** to create the black hole and save it in the instance variable **largeBlackHole**. Method **radius:magnification:** must be modified to invoke **makeLargeBlackHole** whenever the radius or magnification factor is modified.

> **makeLargeBlackHole**
> "Create a black hole (a large black dot) and save it in the instance."
> | magnifiedDiameter |
>
> magnifiedDiameter ← radius * magnification * 2.
> largeBlackHole ← (Form **dotOfSize**: magnifiedDiameter) **offset**: 0@0

Five steps are needed:

1. **Obtain a magnified square image.**

    The first step is to take the image under the magnifying glass and magnify it to the size it will appear in the magnified image. At this stage, we simply ignore the fact that the magnifying glass is round and extract and magnify a rectangular image from underneath the glass.

    > | imageRectangle imageForm magnifiedImage |
    >
    > "First, obtain a magnified square image of the area."
    > imageRectangle ← relativeDisplayRectangle **center** - (radius@radius)
    >   **extent**: (radius@radius)*2.
    > imageForm ← Form **new extent**: imageRectangle **extent**.
    > imageForm **copyBits**: imageRectangle **from**: mergedForm **at**: 0@0
    >   **clippingBox**: (0@0 **extent**: imageRectangle **extent**)
    >   **rule**: Form **over mask**: nil.
    > magnifiedImage ← imageForm **magnifyBy**: magnification@magnification.

2. **Obtain a circular image.**

    We can obtain the required magnified image in circular form by "anding" the magnified rectangular image with a large circular black mask of the required size. Note that "anding" is achieved using a display operation with the proper rule.

    > "Second, AND it with the black hole."
    > largeBlackHole **displayOn**: magnifiedImage **at**: 0@0
    >   **clippingBox**: magnifiedImage **boundingBox** rule: Form **and mask**: nil.

3. **Create a white circular hole in which to display the magnified image.**

    Next we create a white circular hole at the point where the circular magnified image is to be displayed. The large circular black mask can again be used but in this case we use combination rule erase to cut out the required white circular hole.

    > "Third, create a white hole in the magnified area (erase changes black to white)."
    > largeBlackHole **displayOn**: mergedForm **at**: relativeDisplayRectangle **origin**
    >   **clippingBox**: relativeDisplayRectangle **rule**: Form **erase mask**: nil.

Chapter 10 Graphical Applications   **479**

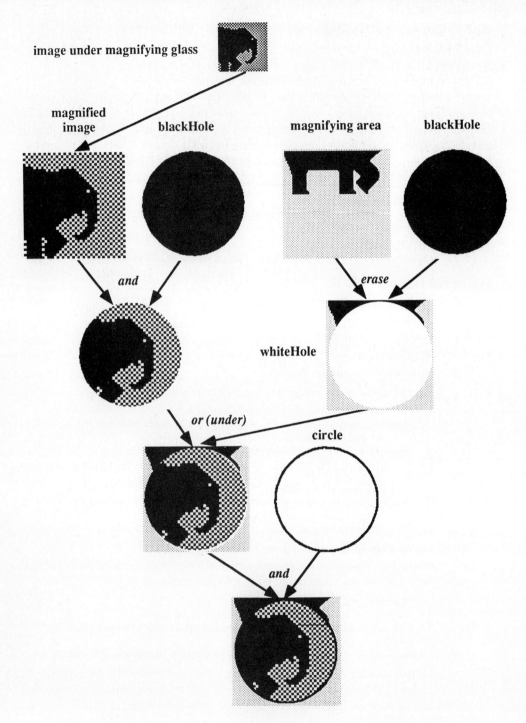

Figure 10.8 Displaying the magnified image on the merged form.

4. **Place the magnified image into the white circular hole.**

The magnified image can now be copied into the white hole using the "or" or under rule to ensure that only the circular portion of the magnified image form is copied.

```
"Fourth, OR the magnified image onto the magnification area with the white hole."
magnifiedImage displayOn: mergedForm at: relativeDisplayRectangle origin
    clippingBox: relativeDisplayRectangle rule: Form under mask: nil.
```

5. **Outline the circular hole.**

Finally, to make the magnified image stand out more clearly, we create a black circle around the display rectangle on the merged form.

```
"Fifth, draw a circle around the magnified section to make it stand out."
dot ← (Form extent: 3@3) black.
(Circle new form: dot; radius: radius * magnification - 1;
    center: relativeDisplayRectangle center - (1@1))
        displayOn: mergedForm at: 0@0
            clippingBox: relativeDisplayRectangle rule: Form over mask: nil.
```

10.3.6 Class MagnifyingGlass

For completeness, we include the final class definition for class MagnifyingGlass.

class	MagnifyingGlass
superclass	Object
instance variables	radius magnification magnifierForm backgroundForm largeBlackHole backgroundForm mergedForm backgroundRectangledisplayRectangle mergedRectangle relativeBackgroundRectangle relativeDisplayRectangle
comment	A magnifying glass (magnifier for short) of specified radius and magnification can be created and subsequently activated. When activated, the cursor is replaced by the magnifying glass. As long as the red (standard) mouse button is depressed, the area under the magnifying glass is magnified and displayed over it. Depressing the yellow (option+mouse) button deactivates the magnifying glass and restores the cursor to what it was. Note that the magnifier has a round (as opposed to square) glass.
	For speed, two forms are initialized at creation time: (1) magnifierForm which contains the magnifier icon and, (2) largeBlackHole, a circular mask to capture the portion of the magnified picture to be displayed.

class methods

instance creation

new
```
"Creates a default magnifying glass."
↑self radius: 20 magnification: 4
```

radius: anInteger **magnification:** anotherInteger
    "Creates a magnifying glass of a specified size and magnification."
    ↑super **new radius:** anInteger **magnification:** anotherInteger

examples

example1
    "MagnifyingGlass new activate"
    "(MagnifyingGlass radius: 40 magnification: 5) activate"

instance methods

instance initialization

radius: anInteger **magnification:** anotherInteger
    "Initializes the magnifying glass instance."

    "Save the radius and magnification."
    radius ← anInteger. magnification ← anotherInteger.

    "Create the utility forms."
    self **makeMagnifierForm**.
    self **makeLargeBlackHole**.
    self **makeBackgroundAndMergedForms**

instance activation

activate
    "Make the magnifier track the mouse and display a magnified version of the area
    underneath it if the mouse button is depressed; otherwise, display the magnifier
    itself. Depressing the yellow button (option + mouse down) deactivates the mouse
    and restores everything to its former state."
    | magnifying newCenter |

    "Initialize."
    magnifying ← false. backgroundRectangle ← Sensor **cursorPoint extent:** 0@0.

    "Hide the cursor."
    Cursor **blank showWhile:**[
        "Quit when a yellow button is pressed."
        [Sensor **yellowButtonPressed**] **whileFalse:** [
            "Determine if magnification status has changed."
            magnifying ← Sensor **redButtonPressed**.
            "Display either the magnifier or the magnified area."
            newCenter ← Sensor **cursorPoint**.
            magnifying
                ifTrue: [
                    displayRectangle ← newCenter - (radius@radius*magnification)
                        extent: largeBlackHole extent.
                    self **restoreBackgroundAndDisplayUsing:**
                        #displayMagnifiedAreaOnMergedForm]
                ifFalse: [
                    displayRectangle ← newCenter - (radius@radius)
                        extent: magnifierForm **extent**.
                    self **restoreBackgroundAndDisplayUsing:**
                        #displayMagnifierOnMergedForm]].

    self **restoreBackgroundAndDisplayUsing:** #isNil]

displaying

displayMagnifiedAreaOnMergedForm
    "In-place Magnifies a circular area centered at newCenter in aForm."
    | imageRectangle imageForm magnifiedImage dot |

    "First, obtain a magnified square image of the area."
    imageRectangle ←
        relativeDisplayRectangle **center** - (radius@radius) **extent**: (radius@radius)*2.
    imageForm ← Form **new extent**: imageRectangle **extent**.
    imageForm **copyBits**: imageRectangle **from**: mergedForm **at**: 0@0
        clippingBox: (0@0 **extent**: imageRectangle **extent**) **rule**: Form **over mask**: nil.

    magnifiedImage ← imageForm **magnifyBy**: magnification@magnification.

    "Second, AND it with the black hole."
    largeBlackHole **displayOn**: magnifiedImage **at**: 0@0
        clippingBox: magnifiedImage **boundingBox** rule: Form **and mask**: nil.

    "Third, create a white hole in the magnified area (erase changes black to white)."
    largeBlackHole **displayOn**: mergedForm **at**: relativeDisplayRectangle **origin**
        clippingBox: relativeDisplayRectangle **rule**: Form **erase mask**: nil.

    "Fourth, OR the magnified image onto the magnification area containing the white
    hole."
    magnifiedImage **displayOn**: mergedForm **at**: relativeDisplayRectangle **origin**
        clippingBox: relativeDisplayRectangle **rule**: Form **under mask**: nil.

    "Fifth, draw a circle around the magnified section to make it stand out."
    dot ← (Form **extent**: 3@3) **black**.
    (Circle **new form**: dot; **radius**: radius * magnification - 1;
        center: relativeDisplayRectangle center - (1@1))
            displayOn: mergedForm **at**: 0@0 **clippingBox**: relativeDisplayRectangle
                rule: Form **over mask**: nil

displayMagnifierOnMergedForm
    magnifierForm
        displayOn: mergedForm **at**: relativeDisplayRectangle **origin**
        clippingBox: relativeDisplayRectangle **rule**: Form **under mask**: nil

restoreBackgroundAndDisplayUsing: displayOnMergedFormSymbol
    "If the background form were restored in one step followed by a display of the new
    information (either the magnifier or a circular magnification area) in a second step,
    flickering would occur when the two areas overlap. We can avoid this by first
    displaying the information on a temporary form called the merged form and then
    displaying this merged form on the screen using one display message."

    "First, obtain a copy of the screen that contains both the background and display
    areas. Note: if the background and/or display forms partially reside off the screen,
    we may need a larger merged form to avoid information loss by clipping."

    mergedRectangle ← backgroundRectangle **merge**: displayRectangle.

    mergedRectangle **extent x** > mergedForm **extent x** |
    (mergedRectangle **extent y** > mergedForm **extent y**)
        ifTrue: [mergedForm ←
          Form **new**
              extent: (mergedRectangle **extent max**: mergedForm **extent**)].

```
mergedForm copyBits: mergedRectangle from: Display at: 0 @ 0
    clippingBox: (0 @ 0 extent: mergedRectangle extent)
    rule: Form over mask: nil.
```

"Second, compute background and display rectangles relative to the merged form
origin."
```
relativeBackgroundRectangle ←
    backgroundRectangle translateBy: 0 @ 0 - mergedRectangle origin.
relativeDisplayRectangle ←
    displayRectangle translateBy: 0 @ 0 - mergedRectangle origin.
```

"Third, restore the merged form to what it used to be and save the display area for
later use."
```
backgroundForm displayOn: mergedForm
    at: relativeBackgroundRectangle origin
    clippingBox: relativeBackgroundRectangle
    rule: Form over mask: nil.
backgroundForm
    copyBits: relativeDisplayRectangle from: mergedForm
    at: 0@0 clippingBox: (0 @ 0 extent: relativeDisplayRectangle extent)
    rule: Form over mask: nil.
backgroundRectangle ← displayRectangle.
```

"Fourth, display the display form onto the merged form (in-place modify)."
```
self perform: displayOnMergedFormSymbol.
```

"Finally, display the merged form onto the screen."
```
mergedForm displayOn: Display at: mergedRectangle origin
    clippingBox: mergedRectangle rule: Form over mask: nil
```

private form initialization

makeMagnifierForm
"Creates and initializes the form containing the magnifying glass and handle."
| diameter center dot |

"Compute often used values."
```
diameter ← 2*radius. center ← radius@radius.
magnifierForm ← Form new extent: (radius@radius)*3.
dot ← (Form extent: 3@3) black.
```

"Draw a solid black handle."
```
(Line from: center to: center*4 "off the form!!"
    withForm: (Form new extent: (radius // 4) @ (radius // 4); black))
        displayOn: magnifierForm.
```

"Draw a solid white circle over the top left part of the handle."
```
(Form dotOfSize: 2 * radius + 1)
    offset: 0@0; displayOn: magnifierForm at: 0@0 rule: Form erase.
```

"Create the circle for the magnifying glass."
```
(Circle new form: dot; radius: radius; center: center) displayOn: magnifierForm.
```

"Create the horizontal line across the magnifying glass."
```
(Line from: 0@radius to: diameter@radius withForm: dot) displayOn: magnifierForm.
```

"Create the vertical line across the magnifying glass."
```
(Line from: radius@0 to: radius@diameter withForm: dot) displayOn: magnifierForm
```

makeLargeBlackHole
> "Create a black hole (a large black dot) and save it in the instance."
> | magnifiedDiameter |
>
> magnifiedDiameter ← radius * magnification * 2.
> largeBlackHole ← (Form **dotOfSize**: magnifiedDiameter) **offset**: 0@0

makeBackgroundAndMergedForms
> "Creates forms for keeping track of the background and merged forms."
> | size extent |
>
> size ← radius * magnification * 2 **max**: radius * 3.
> extent ← size@size.
> backgroundForm ← Form **new extent**: extent.
> mergedForm ← Form **new extent**: Display **extent**

10.4 THE DESIGN AND IMPLEMENTATION OF A SIMPLE VIDEO GAME

Designing applications is not made easier by object-oriented languages — in fact, it's harder. The goal of writing down a good design on paper in one pass is rarely achieved — it is possible only with hindsight; i.e., if you've done it before. More likely, your design, if it's any good, will have undergone an extensive evolution. To do this properly, a desktop — even an electronic desktop with diagramming tools — is inadequate. An interactive design tool is needed. We claim that the Smalltalk environment (not the language) is in fact such a tool.

In this case study, we focus not so much on the tool but on the notion that design is an interactive process. We present a design history for a simplified version of the **Brickles**[4] game. Working code for the end product is provided, but the important issue is the ongoing evolution of the design. Because of space limitations, it will not be possible to detail everything that transpired during the evolution, much less show all the discarded code. Nevertheless, we will attempt to provide a condensed but reasonable idea.

At the very least, we hope to convey the notion that designing is hard. A secondary goal is to show that designing must include programming to be properly evaluated and that most of what we do in an environment like Smalltalk's is design.

A typical display for the game is shown in Fig. 10.9. The objective of the game is to remove all the bricks from the wall. When the ball strikes a brick, the brick disappears. The ball can be redirected using the paddle, which the player can move to the left or right using the mouse. The ball bounces off the sides, bricks, and paddle in a conventional fashion. The player has three balls with which to remove all the bricks. A ball is lost if it passes below the paddle; i.e., if the player misses it!

10.4.1 Designing Is Prototyping

We started off by **finding the objects**; i.e., attempting to determine the object classes and their representation — the object fields (see Fig. 10.10). Next we introduced an abstract

---

[4]Shareware distributed by Ken Winograd.

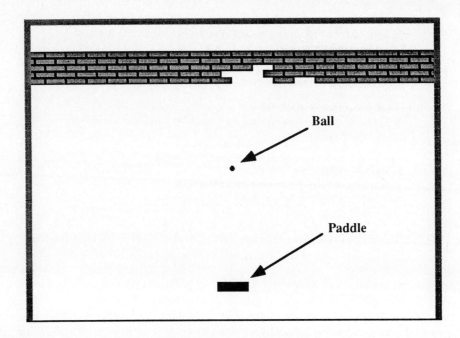

Figure 10.9 The video game.

class **VideoGameComponent** to tie together the game elements. This also led to an abstract class **MovingGameComponent** to tie together the **Ball** and **Paddle** classes. For the moment, it was to contain only a direction (actual contents undecided).

The **VideoGame** fields suggest the creation of a container class for the bricks called **Wall** (the notion brick wall comes to mind), and another one, called **Sides**, to contain the left, top, and right side of the game.

We considered creating an abstract superclass for **Wall** and **Sides**, because they are examples of components with parts, but put it on hold for later. We decided instead to temporarily add a field **parts** to **VideoGameComponent** with the understanding that only **Wall** and **Sides** would really use them.

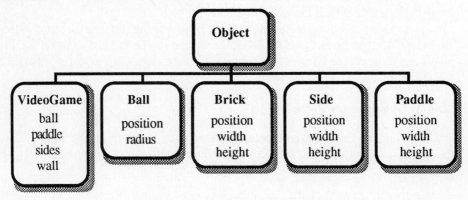

Figure 10.10 Initial class hierarchy.

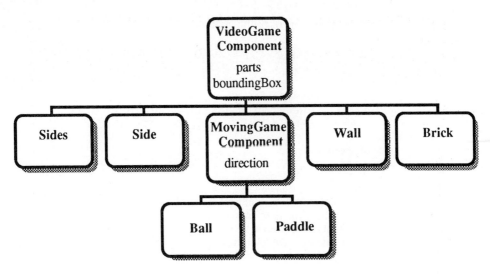

Figure 10.11 Next class hierarchy.

The resulting design so far (ignore field changes for the moment) is summarized in Fig. 10.11. It suggested that we might be able to move the **radius** and **width/height** fields into the superclass if a more general notion was used. We decided on the concept of a **boundingBox**.

With respect to operations, we introduced **new** at the top level for creating initialized instances, protocol for accessing and changing the fields, an **addPart:** at the top level, and both an **initialize** and **display** method unique to each class at the bottom of the hierarchy. Since the **display** methods for **Sides** and **Wall** were the same (they just displayed the parts), it was moved up to the superclass. The reader could glance ahead to the end of the chapter for a look at the ball, brick, paddle, and side initialization code — most of it came from this early stage.

We also introduced protocol for determining and changing the position of an object (**position** and **position:**) and changing the size of the bounding box without moving it (**extent:**). Soon afterward, we replaced the **position** concept by a **center** notion to eliminate confusion (the position of a rectangle is usually understood to be the top corner; for a circle, it's usually the center). Finally, we added **play** to VideoGame so that it could at least display the sides, wall, ball, and paddle. We now had a prototype without moving objects.

10.4.2 Getting into Details

We deliberated over whether direction should be an angle that would ultimately require the use of **sin** and **cos** or a quantized direction — we chose the latter because we suspected a potential future speed problem, but we were prepared to change our minds (see **directionIndex**). Anticipating bouncing objects, we added method **reverseDirection**.

We added **move** methods to classes **Ball** and **Paddle** — using a fixed step size of 5 pixels in x and/or y to begin with. **VideoGame** method **play** was extended so that the ball started in the center and moved upward in a loop (for testing).

The **move** methods give a flavor of the quantization and the distinction between a ball and a paddle.

Moving Methods

```
aMovingGameObject directionIndex
    ↑#(left right up down leftUp rightUp ...) indexOf: direction

aBall move
    | delta aPoint |
    delta ← #(
        (-5 0) "left" (5 0) "right"
        (0 -5) "up" (0 5) "down"
        (-5 -5) "leftUp" (5 -5) "rightUp"
        (-5 5) "leftDown" (5 5) "rightDown"
        ) at: self directionIndex.
    aPoint ← (delta at: 1)@(delta at: 2).
    self center: self center + aPoint

aPaddle move
    self center: Sensor cursorPoint x @ self center y
```

Now the ball could "climb up" the screen and the paddle could track the mouse but old images remained on the screen.

10.4.3 Taking Movement More Seriously

To prevent flicker, we modified the design to avoid displaying individual objects directly on the screen; i.e., we replaced the **display** methods by '**displayOn:** aForm' and displayed the form only after both the ball and paddle had been displayed on it.

When a moving object changes location, the old location must be restored to its former state — only then is the object displayed at the new location. To simplify the use of moving objects, we decided to have the moving object do this as part of the **displayOn:** protocol. We introduced fields **underneath** and **underneathOrigin** for this purpose. Note that after restoring the old background and before displaying the object, the new background is saved in the new fields.

To properly distribute the new functionality, we decided to have method **displayOn:** in **MovingGameComponent** restore the old and save the new. Existing methods **displayOn:** in **Ball** and **Paddle** were extended with an initial **super displayOn:**.

We introduced a naive collision handling method, '**bounceOff:** aGameObject', in **Ball**. It needs to do two things: detect a collision (required a top-level query method '**intersect:** aGameObject') and determine a rebound direction ('**pushOff:** aGameObject'). For composite objects, the **intersect:** method is relayed to the parts; for the others, a test for intersecting bounding boxes is used. For an explanation of the heuristic used in **pushOff:**, see class **ObstacleSet**.

Finally, we extended **play** to create a form the size of the display, repeat 'self **playOneBallOn:** aForm' three times, and finally display a "game over" message. Most of the work was done by method **playOneBallOn:**.

The Playing Algorithm

```
aVideoGame playOneBallOn: aForm
    ball center: Display center; direction: MovingGameComponent randomDirection.
    [self ballOutOfPlay] whileFalse: [
        ball
            bounceOff: sides;
            bounceOff: wall;
            bounceOff: paddle;
            move;
            displayOn: aForm.
        paddle move; displayOn: aForm.
        aForm display]
```

The next stage was to make the bricks vaporize. We extended **bounceOff:** to return the obstacles it intersected with (there could be more than one; e.g., two bricks at a time). Then if the obstacle was a brick, we removed it from the wall — we added a **removePart:** method to complement **addPart:**.

We also attempted to generalize the **intersects:** method at the top level so that we could eliminate the ones in the non-composite object subclasses. It ended up being too complex and we rejected it.

A Method That Was Too Complex

```
intersects: anObject
    self == anObject ifTrue: [↑false].
    (boundingBox intersects: anObject boundingBox) ifFalse: [↑false].
    self hasNoParts & anObject hasNoParts ifTrue: [↑true].
    self hasNoParts ifTrue: [↑anObject intersects: self].
    parts do: [:aPart | (aPart intersects: anObject)ifTrue: [↑true]].
    ↑false
```

We felt confident it was time to try out the game again. We found the rebound heuristic worked most of the time but it failed when hitting the side of a brick (as opposed to the bottom) — a new version worked better. On occasion, the ball escaped through the sides. The problem was the timing for the intersection test. It was performed when the ball was on one side of the barrier (before moving) and also when it was on the other side (after moving). It wasn't designed to consider the intermediate positions — the side was only 1 pixel wide and the ball jumped in increments of five.

10.4.4 Extending and Improving the Design

We next introduced an **interaction abstraction** to enable us to better understand how to control moving objects. More specifically, we defined **moveOn:** to mean the sequence 'hideOn:, move, showOn:', where **hideOn:** restores overwritten background and **showOn:** saves the new one about to be written and displays it. It's now possible to hide for long periods of time while other intervening displays are performed.

We also had to develop a more sophisticated collision detector that projected the receiver's bounding box from the start point to the end point.

Next, we replaced the notion of direction by a velocity vector of the form deltaX@deltaY, where each delta could be a floating point value. This also permitted directions at arbitrary angles to be specified. We introduced a corresponding protocol **direction**, **direction:**, **velocity**, **velocity:**. On a minor note, we tired of the name **GameComponent** and changed it to **GameObject**.

Finally, we decided to reorganize the hierarchy by (1) adding **CompositeGameObject** as a superclass of **Wall** and **Sides** and (2) **BasicGameObject** as a superclass of **Ball**, **Brick**, and **Paddle** (see Fig. 10.12). However, there were now two ways of classifying objects: composite/non-composite and moving/nonmoving — a multiple inheritance issue? No matter how we did it, we decided we didn't want to consider all combinations. The simple solution was to assume all objects could be moving — for our game, most would have velocity zero.

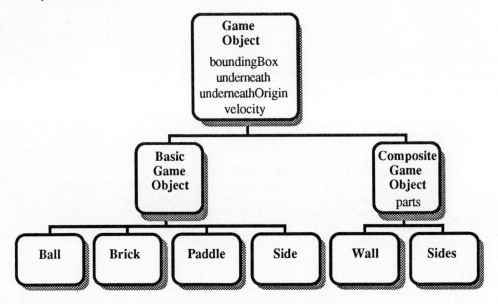

Figure 10.12 Final class hierarchy.

Finally, we had a working system (but see the conclusions). However, it was slow.

10.4.5 Designing for Speed

To speed up the game, we decided to precompute pictures of the basic objects and cache them into a new field **picture**. Since this would have to be recomputed if the size of the object changed, we introduced a method **reInitialize** to do this. We added this message at the end of methods that changed the receiver's bounding box size. We also decided that the bounding box for a composite object should automatically be recomputed if one of its parts was removed. Moreover, it was to be the union of the bounding boxes of its parts. Not unexpectedly, this slowed down the system.

Another possibility was to decompose the bricks into a hierarchy of composite objects, providing an O(log n) search path to the bricks rather than O(n). This helped a little, but removing a brick from the wall became slower because a more complex search was needed to find it.

To avoid drawing the complete form (the same size as the display) when little changed, we decided to maintain a rectangle that is the union of all the areas modified. When the form is written, only the area inside the rectangle is displayed and then the rectangle is reset to nil (unused). To isolate the changes, we created **GameForm**, a subclass of **Form**, which maintained this additional rectangle. All messages of the form '**displayOn**: aGameForm' ultimately result in a **copyBits:**... message to aGameForm. It simply merges the size of the form being copied with the existing rectangle it maintains and relays the message to the superclass. A **display** is also introduced to display only the portion specified by the rectangle. This extension was particularly interesting because it was a transparent change; i.e., no existing code had to be modified.

We finally decided to speed up the brick removal operation by ensuring that all contained objects kept track of their container; i.e., the addition of a **container** field to all game objects. We resisted this for a long time but it paid off — removing a brick was now O(1). With little additional overhead, we also provided a facility to recompute the bounding boxes covered by composite objects higher up (see **release** and **superRelease** in class **GameObject**). This sped up the system as the number of bricks decreased.

10.4.6 More Refinements and Further Polishing

Every now and then, bits and pieces of the code **failed to be object-oriented**; i.e., it considered the object types to determine what to do. Eliminating such code generally required high-level abstractions and usually caused the design to improve. A specific example is shown below— it led to the higher-level recoil abstraction. Now it was up to individual objects to decide what to do when they were hit; e.g., bricks hid and then released themselves from their containers; all other objects stayed put.

Obstacle Handling

```
"Old approach"

... determine all obstacles ...
obstacles do: [:obstacle |
        (obstacle isKindOf: Brick)
                ifTrue:[obstacle hideOn: aForm. wall removePart: obstacle]]
```

```
"New approach"

... determine all obstacles ...
obstacles do: [:obstacle | obstacle recoilOn: aForm]
```

The above statement suggested another abstraction to simplify the design — a complementary 'obstacle **pushOff**: approachingObject' operation. This made it simple to extend the paddle so that it imparts spin to the ball; all other objects push off by deflection.

Additionally, much of the collision detection code was designed to ask questions of a bounding box as opposed to a game object. Thus, some methods had the flavor of 'anyGameObject **queryAbout**: boundingBox **using**: additionalInformation'. We were able to remove about half of such methods by introducing a **virtual ball**, one that starts off as a copy of the original ball and then is successively modified as simulated movement is performed. We didn't want to use the original ball because alternative scenarios were successively tried.

Finally, we abandoned the field **underneathOrigin** since it occurred to us that we could store it in the **underneath** form's offset. In hindsight, we should have thought of this right at the beginning — did you? Various cosmetic name changes were also made.

And just when we thought we were finished, we tried it and 'the last bug' appeared. It was introduced by the **pushOff:** abstraction, which tried to distribute computation that was previously performed as a unit. More specifically, the heuristic used to determine the bounce direction could not be applied by having successive obstacles modify the approaching object's velocity. The solution required a new abstraction, **ObstacleSet**, which could perform this computation as a unit. It also enabled us to integrate at least one **Set** method that we placed in **GameObject** so as not to modify the system class.

Additional improvements to the collision detection algorithm then obviated the need or use for virtual balls and they were eliminated. The source code for the classes making up the video game application is listed at the end of this chapter.

10.4.7 The Video Game: Conclusions

We started this case study with the thesis that object-oriented software design is hard. We hope the case study has shown you some of the extra dimensionality that exists when designing in an OOP environment. In all, we produced eighteen variations of the game, each differing from the other in some major way. In many cases, the code size increases in one variation only to subsequently decrease in the next — something we couldn't explicitly show. The design process is clearly interactive and involves notions that don't exist using conventional methodologies; e.g., reusability, specialization, generalization, and so on. Designing with OOP cannot be done on paper. It requires an OOP environment with OOP tools that support exploratory programming, class reorganization, and protocol migration. The Smalltalk system is the best and perhaps the only system so far to support this process well.

But are we done? We don't believe so. There are still issues that haven't been properly abstracted, code that is too complex, and in fact bugs to eliminate. Perhaps some of you will wish to continue the design!

10.4.8 Source Code for Video Game

Class VideoGame

```
class                 VideoGame
superclass            Object
instance variables    ballObstacles sides wall paddle ball
class methods
```

instance creation

new
        "Create a new video game."
        ↑super **new initialize**

examples

example1
"VideoGame example1"
VideoGame **new play**

instance methods

instance initialization

initialize
"Obtain an instance of each game component."
ballObstacles ← CompositeGameObject **new**
    addPart: (sides ← Sides **new**);
    addPart: (wall ← BrickWall **with**: Brick **new**);
    addPart: (paddle ← Paddle **new**); **reInitialize**.
ball ← Ball **new radius**: 8

playing

play
"Play an entire game."
| aForm farewell magnifiedFarewell |
"Prepare to play."
ball **center**: Display **boundingBox center**.
aForm ← GameForm **extent**: Display **extent**.
self **showOn**: aForm.
aForm **display**.

"Hide the cursor and play."
Cursor **blank showWhile**: [3 **timesRepeat**: [self **playOneBallOn**: aForm]].

"Quit."
farewell ← ' Game Over ' **asDisplayText form**.
magnifiedFarewell ← farewell **magnifyBy**: 8@8.
magnifiedFarewell
    displayOn: Display
    at: Display **boundingBox center** - magnifiedFarewell **boundingBox center**.
(Delay **forSeconds**: 10) **wait**.
ScheduledControllers **restore**

playOneBallOn: aForm
"Play until the ball is lost."
| obstacles |
ball
    center: Display **boundingBox center**;
    velocity: GameObject **defaultVelocity**;
    direction: GameObject **randomUp**.
[self **ballOutOfPlay** | wall **parts isNil**] **whileFalse**: [
    ball **hideOn**: aForm.
    paddle **move**. "if the mouse moves after this, it will have velocity"
    obstacles ← ball **moveUpTo**: ballObstacles.
    obstacles **pushOff**: ball; **spin**: ball; **recoilOn**: aForm.
    paddle **moveOn**: aForm.
    ball **showOn**: aForm.
    aForm **display**].
aForm **display**. 4 **timesRepeat**: [Display **reverse**; **reverse**]

querying

ballOutOfPlay
  ↑ball **boundingBox corner y** > paddle **boundingBox corner y**

displaying

showOn: aForm
  "Show all components of the game."
  "We want the sides to be above the wall of bricks but when a brick is removed, we want it to appear as if were underneath the sides. We can achieve this by showing the sides twice (see below)."
  sides **showOn**: aForm.
  wall **showOn**: aForm.
  sides **showOn**: aForm.
  paddle **showOn**: aForm.
  ball **showOn**: aForm

Class GameObject

class   GameObject
superclass   Object
instance variables   container boundingBox underneath velocity

class methods

instance creation

new
  "Create a new video game component."
  ↑super **new initialize reInitialize**

querying

defaultVelocity
  ↑20@20

randomUp
  "Returns a random vertical direction as an angle. Vertical is 180 through 360 degrees exclusive (use 200 through 340)."
  ↑200 + (141 * (Random **new next**)) **rounded**

instance methods

instance initialization

initialize
  "Initialize so that there is nothing underneath and not moving."
  boundingBox ← 0@0 **corner**: -1@-1.
  underneath ← Form **extent**: 0@0.
  velocity ← 0@0
reInitialize
  "No-op unless redefined by a subclass."

query/modification

center
  ↑boundingBox **center**

center: aPoint
    boundingBox **moveTo:** aPoint - (boundingBox **extent** // 2)

boundingBox
    ↑boundingBox
boundingBox: aRectangle
    boundingBox ← aRectangle.
    self **reInitialize**

extent
    ↑boundingBox **extent**
extent: aPoint
    | oldCenter |
    oldCenter ← boundingBox **center**.
    boundingBox ← oldCenter - (aPoint // 2) **extent:** aPoint.
    self **reInitialize**

copying

copy
    ↑self **shallowCopy boundingBox:** self **boundingBox copy**

container

container
    ↑container
container: aGameObject
    container ← aGameObject

release
    "Makes the receiver no longer a part of some container and returns the container."
    | myContainer |
    (myContainer ← container) **isNil ifTrue:** [↑nil].
    container **removePart:** self.
    container ← nil.
    ↑myContainer

superRelease
    "Releases objects bottom-up as long as the containers have no parts (after the change). Also, causes the bounding boxes higher up to be adjusted. Returns self."
    | myContainer |
    (myContainer ← self **release**) **isNil ifTrue:** [↑nil].
    myContainer **parts isEmpty**
        ifTrue: [myContainer **superRelease**]
        ifFalse: [myContainer **superReInitialize**]

superReInitialize
    "ReInitialize bottom-up as long as changes occur."
    | save |
    save ← boundingBox.
    self **reinitialize**.
    save = boundingBox
        ifFalse: [container **isNil ifFalse:** [container **superReInitialize**]]

careless moving

direction
    ↑velocity **theta radiansToDegrees**

direction: angle
    | radians |
    radians ← angle **degreesToRadians**.
    velocity ← (radians **cos**@radians **sin**) * velocity **r**

reverseXDirection
    "Negate the x-component of the velocity."
    velocity ← velocity **x negated**@velocity **y**
reverseYDirection
    "Negate the y-component of the velocity."
    velocity ← velocity **x**@velocity **y negated**

velocity
    ↑velocity
velocity: aPoint
    velocity ← aPoint

move
    "Advance in the current direction."
    self **center:** self **center** + velocity **rounded**

moveOn: aForm
    self **hideOn:** aForm.
    self **move**.
    self **showOn:** aForm

recoilOn: aForm
    "React graphically to having been bumped (default is to do nothing)."
    ↑self

careful moving

projectedBoundingBox
    ↑boundingBox **translateBy:** velocity **rounded**

projectedBoundingBoxesDo: aBlock
    "Poor man's Bresenham's algorithm."
    | size offset previous current roundedCurrent repetitions increment |
    size ← boundingBox **extent**. offset ← size // 2.
    previous ← current ← roundedCurrent ← self **center**.
    repetitions ← velocity **x abs max:** velocity **y abs**.
    increment ← velocity / repetitions.
    repetitions **rounded** + 1 **timesRepeat:** [
        roundedCurrent = previous
            ifFalse: [aBlock **value:** (roundedCurrent - offset **extent:** size)].
        previous ← roundedCurrent.
        current ← current + increment. roundedCurrent ← current **rounded**]

moveUpTo: potentialObstacles
    "Performs a standard move if possible and returns an empty obstacle set.
    Otherwise, determines which potential obstacles (a composite object) are first hit,
    moves to the obstacles, and returns the non-empty obstacle set. Generally, more
    than one obstacle can be encountered; e.g. at a corner or between two objects."
    | roughObstacles |
    roughObstacles ← self **roughObstacles:** potentialObstacles.
    roughObstacles **isEmpty ifTrue:** [self **move**. ↑roughObstacles].
    ↑self **moveToExactObstacles:** roughObstacles.

roughObstacles: candidatesGameObject
"Determine which candidates are in the path from the start to the end point of the receiver's next movement using a simple but fast technique."
| roughObstacles box |
roughObstacles ← ObstacleSet **new**.
box ← boundingBox **merge**: self **projectedBoundingBox**.
(candidatesGameObject **intersects**: box) **ifFalse**: [↑roughObstacles].
candidatesGameObject **addTo**: roughObstacles **ifTouching**: box.
↑roughObstacles

moveToExactObstacles: candidates
"Determine which candidates are in the path from the start to the end point of the receiver's next movement using an exact but slower technique. We permit starting on an obstacle."
| onObstacles exactObstacles |
"Eliminate the obstacles we are currently on."
onObstacles ← ObstacleSet **new**.
candidates **addTo**: onObstacles **ifTouching**: boundingBox.
candidates **removeAll**: onObstacles.
candidates **isEmpty ifTrue**: [self **move**. ↑candidates].

exactObstacles ← ObstacleSet **new**.
self **projectedBoundingBoxesDo**: [:box |
    candidates **addTo**: exactObstacles **ifTouching**: box.
    exactObstacles **isEmpty ifFalse**: [self **center**: box **center**. ↑exactObstacles]].
self **move**. ↑exactObstacles "none after all"

colliding

containsPoint: aPoint
"The containsPoint: method in Rectangle considers points on the bottom to be outside."
↑boundingBox **origin** <= aPoint **and**: [aPoint <= boundingBox **corner**]

intersects: aRectangle
"The standard Rectangle intersects: uses < instead of <="
↑(boundingBox **origin max**: aRectangle **origin**)
    <= (boundingBox **corner min**: aRectangle **corner**)

spin: gameObject
"Add spin to the approaching object. Generally does nothing."
↑self

Class BasicGameObject

class	BasicGameObject
superclass	GameObject
instance variables	picture

instance methods

colliding

addTo: aSet **ifTouching**: aRectangle
    (self **intersects**: aRectangle) **ifTrue**: [aSet **add**: self]

displaying

displayOn: aForm
"Display the picture."
picture **displayOn**: aForm **at**: boundingBox **origin**

hideOn: aForm
"Restores the background of the receiver."
underneath **displayOn**: aForm.
underneath ← Form **extent**: 0@0

showOn: aForm
"Previously hidden, become visible."
"First, save the background of the object for later restoration."
underneath ← Form **extent**: boundingBox **extent**.
aForm **displayOn**: underneath **at**: 0@0 - boundingBox **origin**.
underneath **offset**: boundingBox **origin**.
"Second, display it."
self **displayOn**: aForm

Class Ball

class	Ball
superclass	BasicGameObject
instance variables	"none"

instance methods

instance initialization

initialize
super **initialize**.
boundingBox ← Display **extent** // 2 **extent**: 8@8
reInitialize
picture ← (Form **dotOfSize**: self **extent** x) **offset**: 0@0

query/modification

radius
↑self **extent** // 2

radius: anInteger
self **extent**: 2*anInteger

boundingBox: aRectangle
"Make sure it's square."
| diameter |
diameter ← aRectangle **width roundTo**: 2.
super **boundingBox**: (aRectangle **origin extent**: diameter@diameter)

Class Brick

class	Brick
superclass	BasicGameObject
instance variables	"none"

instance methods

instance initialization

initialize
  "Create a reasonably sized brick."
  | width |
  super **initialize**.
  width ← Display **extent x** // 20.
  boundingBox ← 0@0 **extent:** width@(width//3)

reInitialize
  "Create a black outline with a gray interior."
  picture ← (Form **extent:** boundingBox **extent**) **black**.
  (Form **extent:** boundingBox **extent** - (4@4)) **gray**
      displayOn: picture **at:** 2@2 **clippingBox:** picture **boundingBox**
      rule: Form **over mask:** nil

moving

recoilOn: aForm
  "React graphically to having been bumped (default is to do nothing)."
  self **hideOn:** aForm; **superRelease**

Class Paddle

class	Paddle
superclass	BasicGameObject
instance variables	"none"
instance methods	

instance initialization

initialize
  "Initialize the paddle."
  super **initialize**.
  boundingBox ← 0@0 **corner:** (Display **extent** // (10@30)).
  self **center:** (Display **extent x** // 2) @(Display **extent y** - 50)
reInitialize
  "Create a black rectangle."
  picture ← (Form **extent:** boundingBox **extent**) **black**

moving

velocity
  ↑(Sensor **cursorPoint x** - self **center x**) @ self **center y**
move
  "Move to the mouse location (horizontally only)."
  self **center:** Sensor **cursorPoint x** @ self **center y**

colliding

spin: gameObject
  "Add spin to the game object."
  | speed |
  (speed ← self **velocity x**) > 0
      ifTrue: [gameObject **direction:** gameObject **direction** + 10].
  (speed < 0) **ifTrue:** [gameObject **direction:** gameObject **direction** - 10]

Class Side

class	Side
superclass	BasicGameObject
instance variables	"none"

instance methods

instance initialization

reInitialize
> "Create a gray rectangle."
> picture ← (Form **extent:** boundingBox **extent**) **gray**

Class CompositeGameObject

class	CompositeGameObject
superclass	GameObject
instance variables	parts

class methods

instance creation

withAllParts: aCollection
> "Constructs a composite object with the given elements as parts."
> ↑self **new addAllParts:** aCollection; **reInitialize**

hierarchicallyWithAllParts: aCollection
> "Constructs a composite object with the given elements hierarchically decomposed
> into a binary tree of composite game objects parts."
> aCollection **size** <= 2 **ifTrue:** [↑self **withAllParts:** aCollection].
> ↑self **withAllParts:** (Array
>   **with:** (self **hierarchicallyWithAllParts:**
>   (aCollection **copyFrom:** 1 **to:** aCollection **size** // 2))
>   **with:** (self **hierarchicallyWithAllParts:**
>   (aCollection **copyFrom:** aCollection **size** // 2 + 1 **to:** aCollection **size**)))

instance methods

instance initialization

initialize
> "Initialize to no parts."
> super **initialize**.
> parts ← Set **new**.

reInitialize
> "Recompute the bounding box for the whole as the unions of those for the parts."
> boundingBox ← parts **isEmpty**
>   **ifTrue:** [0@0 **corner:** 0@0]
>   **ifFalse:** [parts
>   **inject:** (parts **detect:** [:part | true]) **boundingBox**
>   **into:** [:box :part | box **merge:** part **boundingBox**]]

part manipulation

parts
↑parts

addPart: part
"Adds the new part to the existing collection of parts."
parts **add**: part. part **container**: self

removePart: part
"Removes the old part from the existing collection of parts."
parts **remove**: part. part **container**: nil

addAllParts: aCollection
"Adds the new parts to the existing collection of parts."
parts **addAll**: aCollection.
parts **do**: [:anObject | anObject **container**: self]

colliding

addTo: aSet **ifTouching**: aRectangle
(self **intersects**: aRectangle) **ifTrue**: [
        parts **do**: [:part | part **addTo**: aSet **ifTouching**: aRectangle]]

displaying

displayOn: aForm
"Display all its parts."
parts **do**: [:part | part **displayOn**: aForm].

hideOn: aForm
"Hide all its parts."
parts **do**: [:part | part **hideOn**: aForm].

showOn: aForm
"Show all its parts."
parts **do**: [:part | part **showOn**: aForm].

Class BrickWall

class	BrickWall
superclass	CompositeGameObject
instance variables	"none"

class methods

instance creation

with: aSampleBrick
    | rowsOfBricks bricksPerRow |
    rowsOfBricks ← 5.
    bricksPerRow ← (Display **extent x** // aSampleBrick **extent x**) + 1. "to handle truncation"
    ↑self **new**
        reInitializeAt: 0@50 **extent**: bricksPerRow@rowsOfBricks **with**: aSampleBrick

instance methods

instance initialization

reInitializeAt: wallBase **extent**: aPoint "xBricks@yBricks" **with**: aSampleBrick
    "Initialize a wall."
    | brickSize bricksPerRow rowsOfBricks xOffset yOffset delta start |
    "Initialize the wall parameters."
    brickSize ← aSampleBrick **extent**.
    bricksPerRow ← aPoint **x**.
    rowsOfBricks ← aPoint **y**.

    "Create the wall out of properly positioned bricks."
    self **addAllParts**:
        ((0 **to**: rowsOfBricks-1) **collect**: [:brickRow |
            xOffset ← brickRow **odd ifTrue**: [(brickSize **x**//2) **negated**] **ifFalse**: [0].
            yOffset ← brickRow*brickSize **y**.
            delta ← brickSize **x**@0. start ← wallBase + (xOffset@yOffset) - delta.
            CompositeGameObject **hierarchicallyWithAllParts**:
                ((1 **to**: bricksPerRow+1) **collect**: [:brickIndex |
                    start ← start + delta.
                    Brick **new boundingBox**: (start **extent**: brickSize)])]).

    "Determine the overall wall boundaries."
    self **reInitialize**

Class Sides (a composite of side elements)

class	Sides
superclass	CompositeGameObject
instance variables	"none"

instance methods

instance initialization

initialize
    "Create three sides (no bottom)."
    | thickness |
    super **initialize**.
    thickness ← 10.
    self
        addPart: (Side **new** "left side"
            boundingBox: (0@0 **corner**: thickness@Display **extent y**));
        addPart: (Side **new** "top"
            boundingBox: (0@0 **corner**: Display **extent x**@thickness));
        addPart: (Side **new** "right side"
            boundingBox: (Display **extent x** - thickness@0 **corner**: Display **extent**));
        reInitialize.

Class ObstacleSet

class	ObstacleSet
superclass	Set
instance variables	"none"

instance methods

collision

addTo: anObstacleSet **ifTouching**: aRectangle
    self **do**: [:aGameObject |
        aGameObject **addTo**: anObstacleSet **ifTouching**: aRectangle]

pushOff: approachingObject
    "A simple test is used to determine the direction in which to push off an
    approaching object. Consider one of the possible four cases: that the bottom left
    corner of the object has met (is inside) the receiver; e.g., a wall. Then we will push
    it towards its center (more specifically, to the right and up; i.e., +1@-1). We do this
    for all corner points and then sum up the contributions. If it is opposite to the
    direction of the approaching object, we reverse its direction."
    | delta box |
    delta ← 0@0. box ← approachingObject **boundingBox**.
    self **do**: [:obstacle |
        (obstacle **containsPoint**: box **origin**) **ifTrue**: [delta ← delta + (1@1)].
        (obstacle **containsPoint**: box **bottomLeft**) **ifTrue**: [delta ← delta + (1@-1)].
        (obstacle **containsPoint**: box **topRight**) **ifTrue**: [delta ← delta + (-1@1)].
        (obstacle **containsPoint**: box **corner**) **ifTrue**: [delta ← delta + (-1@-1)]].
    (delta **x** * approachingObject **velocity** x) **negative**
        ifTrue: [approachingObject **reverseXDirection**].
    (delta **y** * approachingObject **velocity** y) **negative**
        ifTrue: [approachingObject **reverseYDirection**]

recoilOn: aForm
    self **do**: [:obstacle | obstacle **recoilOn**: aForm].
spin: gameObject
    "Add spin to the approaching object."
    self **do**: [:obstacle | obstacle **spin**: gameObject]

Class GameForm

class	GameForm
superclass	Form
instance variables	modifiedArea

instance methods

displaying

copyBits: aRectangle **from**: aDisplayObject **at**: aPoint **clippingBox**: clipRectangle
rule: ruleInteger **mask**: aForm
    | newArea |
    newArea ← aPoint **extent**: aRectangle **extent**
    modifiedArea ← modifiedArea **isNil**
        ifTrue: [newArea] **ifFalse**: [modifiedArea **merge**: newArea].
    super **copyBits**: aRectangle **from**: aDisplayObject **at**: aPoint
        clippingBox: clipRectangle **rule**: ruleInteger **mask**: aForm

display
    modifiedArea **isNil**
        ifTrue: [super **display**]
        ifFalse: [self **displayOn**: Display **at**: 0@0 **clippingBox**: modifiedArea].
    modifiedArea ← nil

10.5 SUMMARY

This chapter has focused on the use of graphics and graphics-oriented techniques. Examples focused on three major examples:

- A film loop facility that integrates simple animation, flicker-free displays, storage of graphical forms on disk, and object mutation.
- A magnifying glass that illustrates mouse control, bitblt rule selection, and techniques for displaying circular rather than rectangular forms.
- A simple video game that illustrates the evolutionary approach characterizing the design and development of Smalltalk applications.

10.6 EXERCISES

The following exercises are intended to cause some of the material presented in this chapter to be reviewed and elaborated upon. Not all questions have the same degree of difficulty.

1. Extend the film loop facility so that speed can be controlled with mouse buttons; e.g., speeding up with the red button and slowing down with the yellow button.

2. Extend the magnifying glass application so that magnification can be either increased or decreased while the magnifier is being used. More specifically, during magnification, if the user types the + key, magnification is to be increased by 1 unit; conversely, if the user types the - key, magnification is to be decreased by 1. Alternatively, use the technique suggested for Problem 1.

3. Create a class of forms called CircularForm that captures the functionality of the magnifying glass. Optionally, reimplement the magnifying glass with this more flexible form.

4. Generalize the CircularForm class to arbitrary shape. How does this generalization compare with opaque forms?

5. Extend the video game to allow any number of balls to be in play simultaneously. Alternatively, permit a grid of paddles to be used; i.e., what appears to be a larger paddle with rectangular holes.

10.7 GLOSSARY

selected terminology

disk form A form variant in which the data resides in a file.

film loop A never ending movie in which the end is spliced with the beginning; i.e., a circular sequence of frames repeatedly displayed at a fast enough rate to provide the illusion of motion.

frame rate The speed at which a film is displayed.

hot spot A point that is considered to be the center of a picture.

magnifying glass A facility that permits a circular area under the mouse to be magnified when the red button is down; illustrates processing required to draw circular forms.

object-oriented design A methodology for software development; much more powerful when integrated with a prototyping facility.

Class Index

SYSTEM CLASSES

DEMONSTRATION CLASSES

GLOBAL VARIABLES

Index

H

Hashing, 200-201, 246-247

I

Identity versus equality, 200-201
Image
    image file, 140
    updating the image, 139-141
Information hiding, 8, 23-24
Inheritance, 13, 51-62
    multiple, 237-239
Inspectors, 148-155, 193-195
    dictionary inspectors, 152-155
Instance, 10-11, 40
Instance variables, 10, 42-43, 46-47, 182
    indexed, 47, 182-183
    named, 47, 182-183

K

Keyed classes, 284, 298-329

L

Literal, 24-25
    collections, 286-287
    introduction, 24-25
    numbers, 247-248
Looping expressions, 35-37

M

Magnitudes
    bit manipulation, 260-265
    characterization (overview), 245-246
    comparing, 246-247
    converting, 248-255, 266-267, 274-275
    creating number subclasses, 259-260
    dividing, 255-258
    double dispatching, 254-255
    generality number, 250-254
    mathematical operations, 258-259
    truncating, 255-258
Mathematical operations, 258-259

Menus, 75
    blue button menu, 75
    quit menu, 93-94
    red button menu, 72-73, 78-79, 83, 85-87, 102
    system menu, 75
    yellow button menu, 75
Message-passing, 6, 25
Method, 6, 23, 43, 45
    categories, 41, 116-118
    method arguments, 48
    method lookup, 53
    method temporaries, 48
Messages, 7, 25-29
    binary, 26
    cascaded, 28-29
    keyword, 26-27
    priority, 28
    receiver, 7, 25
    selector, 7, 25
    unary, 25-26
Meta class, 233-237
Meta operations, 195-198
    perform:, 206-208
    become:, 208-210, 465-467
    doesNotUnderstand:, 210-211
Mouse, 73
    double clicking, 87, 95
    dragging, 86, 95
    selection, 70, 72
        extended selection, 70
    single clicking, 70, 95

N

Notifiers, 148, 155-160

O

Objects
    coercion (see converting)
    converting, 201-206, 248-255, 266-267,
        274-275, 287-290
    hashing, 200-201, 246-247
    identity versus equality, 200-201
    meta-operations, 195-198
        perform:, 206-208
        become:, 208-210, 465-467
        doesNotUnderstand:, 210-211